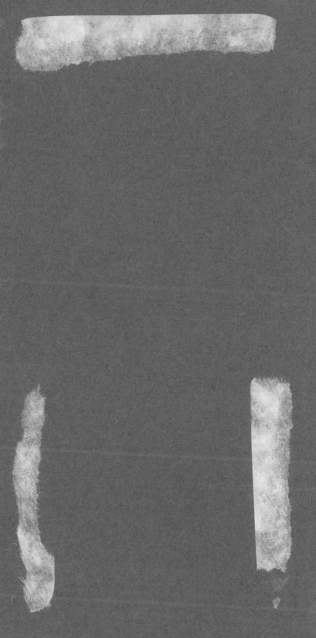

CHILD PSYCHOLOGY

CHILD PSYCHOLOGY

Dorothy Rogers

State University of New York,
College at Oswego

Brooks/Cole Publishing Company
Belmont, California
A Division of Wadsworth Publishing Company, Inc.

L. C. Cat. Card No.: 69–14580
Printed in the United States of America

To my nieces — Sylvia, Starr, and Dawn

PREFACE

This volume concerns child development from conception to adolescence. Its purpose is to portray behavior as the dynamic emergent of biological foundations, individual experience, and sociocultural milieu. Accomplishment of so broad a goal requires materials from areas of subject matter both inside and outside the field of psychology. Data are drawn from whatever research appears relevant: from experimental psychology, social psychology, differential psychology, learning and personality psychology, as well as other disciplines such as sociology, anthropology, behavioral genetics, and pediatrics.

Most of the data reported are recent, for research in the field of psychology generally, and of human development in particular, has grown vigorously, with increasingly sophisticated procedures. Correspondingly, the world itself has evolved at a pace unprecedented in history, so that the child's personal universe is completely different from that of his counterpart a few years ago. Obviously, any textbook in psychology, to be of practical value, must utilize the best of current research to develop whatever concepts seem of greatest potential value for helping the child deal with both today's world and tomorrow's. However, earlier research is freely introduced whenever it seems to be the most pertinent or valid evidence available. Also, students need to become acquainted with classic references in the field in order to attain a proper historical perspective.

Throughout the book, therefore, generalizations are heavily supported by data carefully chosen on the bases of recency, validity, and relevance. Concepts and data are presented largely in terms of those issues currently considered most controversial or vital, such as maternal deprivation, critical periods, and persistence of personality traits.

Running throughout such discussions, and gradually emerging from them, are certain underlying themes of behavior. Not all authors agree about which of these concepts are most important, and every writer necessarily discusses issues, selects evidence, and states conclusions according to his own convictions of what is most vital. Basic to my own philosophy of child development and implicit in what follows are the following assumptions:

That each period of life is important both for its own sake and for its impact on subsequent periods;

That each individual is a distinct personality at the same time that he is a social being;

That he follows a sequential, somewhat predictable pattern of growth, which nevertheless is distinctively his own;

That he develops as a whole, each aspect of development interacting with the rest and dependent upon the dynamic organization of the total personality pattern;

That understanding the individual depends on appreciating the way he experiences himself and perceives his environment;

That heredity furnishes the basic materials of human personality and sets certain limits, but that the realization of each individual's potentialities depends on the nature, sequence, and timing of events in life experience;

That normality is represented by a range rather than a point, and that it implies a standard of effective, relatively happy living rather than conformity to a pattern;

That the plasticity of human behavior during the periods of infancy and childhood affords a tremendous opportunity to parents and educators but at the same time constitutes a weighty responsibility. Every child is entitled to society's best efforts to help him become all he is capable of being.

However scholarly a book may be, it fails as a textbook unless it constitutes an effective tool of instruction. Certain features, therefore, have been incorporated to make this book teachable. In the first place, students want to feel they are "getting something" — they want "meat." At the same time, they want material presented in a stimulating fashion. Therefore, I have striven for a palatable presentation without sacrificing intellectual depth. The style is designed to be easily read, and concepts are fully explained and illuminated by authentic anecdotal illustrations. Where no source is given, the item is from my own files. Teaching aids include annotated reading lists and suggested activities.

I would like to acknowledge the helpful suggestions given at the manuscript stage by Professors Judith F. Rosenblith of Wheaton College and Thomas Spencer of San Francisco State College, as well as by my colleague, Professor Paul Hutko of the State University of New York, College at Oswego, all of whom offered reactions from the standpoint of the classroom instructor in child psychology. Mrs. Ann Crego, also of Oswego, provided helpful suggestions from the layman's point of view.

Special thanks go to several people at Brooks/Cole Publishing Company: to Bonnie Fitzwater and Charles Hendrix, for their helpful suggestions and encouragement in preparing the manuscript, to Joan Westcott for her editing of the manuscript, to Dale Smith for his work in providing many of the photographs and designing the book's format, and to Konrad Kerst for his highly talented assistance and supervision throughout the editing and production stages. I would also like to thank Cherie Blanchard, Ann Hoefer, and, particularly, Betty Moody for special assistance during various stages of writing and production.

Finally, for providing photographs I am indebted to Harley Clements, Paul Conklin, John and Regina Hicks, Earl Junghans, Larry A. Keenan, Jr., Manjit Mani, David Mitchell, Mt. Diablo Unified School District, Oakland Child Care Center, Louise Ostberg, Bryce and Patricia Pfanenstiel, Carl Purcell, Ann Rivera, N. Suzanne Robba, Stanford Nursery Center, Michael Sullivan, and Jack Thornton.

Dorothy Rogers

CONTENTS

1
AN INTRODUCTION TO THE CHILD

CHAPTER ONE What is the child, the "hero" of this volume? In this century the child has been described in scientific terms as:

> ... a complex physical-chemical system for converting food into energy; and ... a system of sense organs, nerves and muscles, which by responding to stimulation directs energy into the channels we know as behavior for action [Lawrence, 1960, p. 199].

It is highly doubtful that doting parents would approve of such a detached and impersonal description of their little cherubs. They would no doubt prefer this description, written in 1628:

> A child is a man in a small letter, yet the best copy of Adam before he tasted of Eve or the apple. . . . He is nature's fresh picture newly drawn in oil, which time and much handling dims and defaces. His soul is yet a white paper unscribbled with observations of the world, wherewith, at length, it becomes a blurred notebook [Earle, trans. by Aldington, 1928, pp. 191-192].

But how typical are these writers of their respective ages in history? Perhaps it is well to pause here for an encapsulized course on how our ancestors perceived children. For not always have youngsters been viewed in so benevolent a way as does the last writer quoted above. In ancient Sparta, for example, any deformed child was killed. In ancient Athens, parents were granted full authority to decide whether to rear such children or to destroy them at birth. **Infanticide*** was common among girl babies in the ancient Orient. Childhood may be said not to have existed in the Middle Ages, for the child was neglected and despised. As soon as he could live without the constant care of his mother, he was relegated to the adult world.

By contrast, present-day Americans

*Words appearing in boldface are defined in the Glossary (at the end of the book) either in the exact form shown in the text or in the standard singular noun form. Note that Glossary terms are in boldface only at their first important occurrence in the text.

2

value children highly. For instance, note the proliferation of popular articles on child care. However, Lawrence flavors this idyllic picture with a note of cynicism:

> Childhood in America is not only admired; it is looked upon as a national asset, somewhat on a par with the Declaration of Independence or the Mississippi River. We like to think of it as a good in itself and to lament its passing. We hang onto the images of youth that are thought to be traditional — the barefoot boy, the old swimming hole, the sandlot games — though in fact few of us may ever have known them in life. Tom Sawyer is a dominant picture of boyhood, just as Huckleberry Finn is almost a national epic; and the loss of innocence is a persistent theme in our literature.
> . . . [Children] are looked upon as important, however, largely in adult terms. . . . Toys are less often designed to please children than to please adults' ideas of what children should like; and the father who forces on the family the electric train he really wants for himself is a familiar figure in our folklore. . . [Lawrence, 1960, p. 199].

A recent and more scientific concept is to view the child as father of the man, the grandfather of the octogenerian, in the sense that older people spring from the children they once were. But the child differs from his successors — adolescent, adult, and old man — in significant ways. When college students were asked to write whatever words they connected with various age groups, these were some of the more common ones given:

> *Infant:* lovable; helpless; weak; dependent; cute; drooling; diapers; crib; crying; innocent; cuddly; hungry; messy; content.
> *Child:* active; playful; mischievous; sloppy; questioning; happy; noisy; imaginative; eager.
> *Adolescent:* confused; awkward; moody; silly; talkative; giddy; idealistic; restless; rebellious; questioning; experimental; vigorous; gregarious; impetuous.

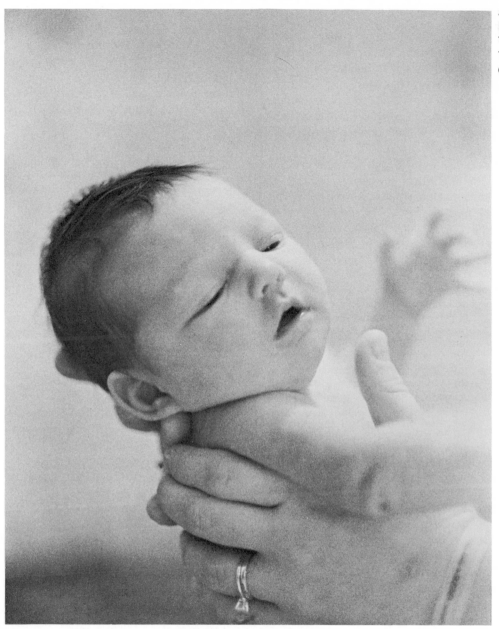

. . . the "hero" of this volume.

Adult: sensible; responsible; stodgy; bills; home; worries; sedate; competent; conservative.

Overall there was a considerable core of agreement, suggestive of the respective age roles in this society. Although we commonly recognize the infant's nuisance value, we nonetheless warmly regard him. We love the older child, too, but feel less sentimental and protective toward him. Society regards adolescents as somewhat unstable, and adults as stodgy and dull, except on the personal level. And so it has always been—that each period in history has had its way of feeling about infants and children and how they relate to people at other age-stages. Historically, the child has been a diversified enterprise to which society has attached fluctuating values, only lately regarding him as a blue-chip investment.

3

The recapitulation theory. Theories about children have varied quite as much as attitudes toward them. Until modern times they were one part whim, one part hunch, and no part scientific. One view, no longer supported today, was that children recapitulated in their own development the history of the race. Children's love for scrapping and climbing trees corresponded to the cave man era, while cowboy play related to frontier days. The infant's grasping reflex was his heritage from the branch-grasping days of his ancestors, the monkeys. As Philip Wylie expressed it:

The babe is the brainless, feeding beast that can cling to its mother's hair; the infant is the savage — unhouse-broken rage and hunger — a very ape; the tot with his sticks and mud pies and witless cruelty of investigation is a Stone Age person; after him comes the school barbarian — full of ritual and superstition, hero worship and familial prides; with the first tinge of adolescence the mysticisms of the Middle Ages appear; after that (not often, for we have been at this business but a few thousand years and in only a few categories) there occasionally emerges a rare figure, an adult — a human being whose acceptance of what has gone before and whose ever-expanding concern with the truths of what now is gives him insight into what is yet to be [Wylie, 1947, pp. 25–26].

The doctrine of innate sin. Another long-standing controversy, which has now subsided, was this: Is the child innately good, or sinful, or neither? In the eighteenth century, Rousseau argued that civilization, not the child's basic nature, was the source of moral pollution. Others, both before and after Rousseau — in fact, as recently as the 1920s — believed children to be endowed by nature with perverse tendencies that must be eradicated. Nowadays we believe that the child is born "amoral" — basically neither good nor bad — and that the best way to ensure proper behavior is to reinforce that which is good.

The child as a miniature adult. Another perennial bone of contention has been this: Should the child be treated as a child or simply as an adult-in-the-making? That is, should childhood be deemed important chiefly for its own sake or as a prelude to adulthood? Rousseau believed that boys should by all means be boys. A century later, however, children were considered miniature adults. Remnants of this notion are reflected in the parent's admonition to his son to be a "little man." Play was regarded merely as preparation for adulthood. Even children's stories were adult-centered and future-oriented. By contrast, today's children are usually permitted to adjust on their own level and are given time to grow up.

Recent theories. One of the most popular of recent theories has been **cultural determinism,** the theory that culture shapes the child's development. Mead and Benedict, with their anthropological studies of primitive cultures, gave strong impetus to this theory by showing that personality is plastic and hence permissive of infinite variation. Unfortunately, the doctrine of cultural determinism was carried to extremes. For example, Karen Horney (1937) suggested that societal pressures precipitate anal character traits. "A person does not have tight lips because of the tenseness of his sphincter," she wrote; "both are tight because his character tends toward one goal — to hold on to what he has and never give away anything."

Recent, though hardly new, is the concept that every child is an individual, with a unique blend of traits. Even in ancient Greece, Plato encouraged discovering and developing children's unique talents. But during the Middle Ages this belief lay dormant.

Today's personality theorists see the child as the complex product of heredity and environment. He is no longer merely passive clay, ready to be shaped by a capricious environment, as posited by Locke and his latter-day kin, the cultural anthropologists. He is now seen as possessing certain hereditary core-traits, which are shaped and added to by complex environmental forces. This theory is described in more detail later in the book.

• PEDIATRICS OF THE PAST

Theories about children have been paralleled by corresponding changes in child care. To appreciate how greatly recommendations about child care have changed, look at the following advice given to parents by a noted physician of the eighteenth century:

In comparison to the modern rest cure, the little consumptives of that day were subjected to the following strenuous regimen: I would recommend Bleeding 2 or 3 ounces every third Day, with a constant Riding on Horseback, and Change of Air. This will help Nature throw off the evil that threatens [the child], by calming the Blood, opening the Pores, and promoting insensible Perspiration. It may also enable [him] to make a vigorous Effort, by Means of a seasonable Boil . . . under the arms apply Poultices in order to draw the Mischief if possible that Way. And for inward Medicines, let him only chew Sassafras Root every Morning fasting. I would likewise entreat him before he goes to Bed, to take three Pills, made of Turpentine and Deer's Dung, in equal Quantities; and besides these let him take once a Week a Purge of Mallows and Syrup of Peach-Blossoms. Let his Diet be without Meat, and mixt with Abundance of Turnips, roasted Apples, Raisins, and Liquorice, and let his Drink be Bear brew'd with Ground-ivy; avoiding strong liquors of every sort, as he would poison. The way to prevent this wasting Disease, is never to suffer a Cough to dwell upon you; but bleed in time, and purge gently once a week. In the meantime eat not one morsel of Meat, nor drink anything stronger than a little sound Cyder; and to make the Game sure, ride every fair Day, and breathe as much as possible in the Open Air [Fisher, 1948, pp. 171–172].

In general, during the period 1550–1750, parents were somewhat permissive. Mothers nursed their infants for two years, weaned them gradually, and did not expect consistent "dryness" until age five. Masturbation, sex play, and nudity were permitted. On the other hand, infants were not encouraged to be independent. Parents rushed to brush flies off their noses, and rocked and sang to them in putting them to sleep. From 1750 to 1900 the kiddies' climate was somewhat less balmy. Toilet training was begun between three weeks and six months and completed by age three. Bitter substances were placed on the breast to hasten weaning, which was completed by nine months.

In both periods, 1550 to 1900 inclusive, strange ideas abounded. Before 1750, milk was believed to be white blood, and mothers' characteristics were supposedly transmitted via this medium. Teething was considered dangerous, and the child himself was believed born evil. After 1750, these ideas vanished, only to be replaced by others. Doctors warned mothers against nursing children when angry, lest the effect prove fatal for the infant. Children were held strictly responsible for their acts, perhaps a result of Wesley's Methodist Movement (McClelland, 1960). One mother, writing in the Mother's Magazine in 1834, told how a 16-months-old girl refused to say "Dear Mama," as Papa had ordered. She was led into a room alone, where she screamed wildly for ten minutes. She was again commanded, but again refused. She was then whipped and commanded again. For four hours the tug of war continued, until the child was subdued. Most parents reported permanent submission after one such struggle; however, not all parents resorted to beatings. One reported "constant though gentle drilling." Whatever the method, buck-private obedience was the order of the day.

The first of the twentieth century brought but small improvement. Playing with the baby was strictly warned against, for it ruined the baby's nerves.

5

Although parents enjoyed hearing their infants crow with delight, their techniques for eliciting such responses, such as tickling, punching, or tossing, were believed to make the baby irritable and restless. Children were deemed naturally sinful and endowed with dangerous impulses, a revival of an earlier view. Such feelings were believed to flare easily out of control, wrecking the child for life. To prevent thumbsucking, the child's sleeve might be sewed over the fingers of the offending hand, or a patent cuff used to hold the elbow stiff (Wolfenstein, 1951).

Meantime, activity and independence were also stressed — a commendable ideal but carried to silly extremes. Certainly, the methods recommended for achieving this goal would raise psychologists' eyebrows today (Escalona, 1949). For example, the mother was supposed to subordinate her own needs for recreation, sleep, or non-domestic interests in order not to thwart the child in any way.

The emphasis on making children active and self-sufficient continued; but the extreme concern for rigid routines died, only to gain fresh momentum following World War I. This resurgence of rigidity, scheduling, and rationing of manifest affection — the child-care recipes of the 1920s and '30s — Escalona relates to the cultural milieu, whose cohesiveness rested on a sense of technical mastery. Routines reigned supreme, and **John B. Watson** (1878–1958) was the Chief Priest of the Cult of Rules and Rigidity and most distinguished of the **behaviorists.** He was an exponent of objectivity and scoffed at the sentimental:

> Treat [children] as though they were young adults [he wrote]. Never hug or kiss them; never let them sit on your lap. If you must kiss them, kiss them once on the forehead when you say good night. Shake hands with them in the morning. . . . You will be utterly ashamed of the mawkish, sentimental way you have been handling [them] [Watson, 1928, pp. 81-82].

Parents took Watson's advice quite seriously, until the pendulum swung again. Perhaps Watson, by his very harshness, helped trigger a reaction. By the 1940s the erstwhile infant sinner had been rendered harmless. His dangerous inpulses had disappeared, and his erotic drives had become weak and incidental. If children had toys to play with, they would have no need to play with their bodies. Play was no longer viewed as unhealthily exciting and debilitating to the nerves. It was associated with muscular development, necessary exercise, and control. The new child-rearing practices reflected the generally permissive mood.

Now let us briefly recapitulate. For several decades, child life had been strictly scheduled. For instance, prescribed formulas, which could be carefully controlled, had been preferred to breast feeding. Children had been taught clear-cut boundaries between right and wrong. Standards of right and wrong had been precisely defined and rigidly taught.

But then came a new day, when the tone was permissiveness, ushered in by a gradual hybridization of seemingly incompatible factors, including Freud, Dewey, and later on the atom bomb and growing affluence. The gospel of **John Dewey** (1859–1952), that children's needs must be met, was widely accepted and falsely construed as a plea to let children do as they liked. Similarly, Freud's belief that adults' neuroses inevitably grew out of children's problems was translated to mean that the child must be sheltered from all stress, however slight. Succeeding and overlying these factors, the bomb convinced men of their own vulnerability and shook their faith in their capacity to blueprint their destiny. Science brought concepts of **probability,** while solid subjects like mathematics and science suddenly dissolved. Rules and, in consequence, the rigid blueprints of child-rearing forthwith evaporated.

Instead of commiserating about this state of things, people sought escape into a world of social-welfare schemes, fun, and frolic, abetted by the greatest affluence the world had ever known. Whereas this generation's grandparents would have suffered pangs of guilt at so escapist a solution, today's parents languished in the pallid afterglow of Puritanism. Parents might play, and so might Junior, without feeling wicked. Man's frailty was recognized and accepted. Spock's *Baby Care* became the Family Bible, and Spock himself Abraham, leading fathers and mothers out of the forbidding wilderness of self-discipline and child-discipline. "What mothers and fathers instinctively feel like doing for babies is usually best," Spock assured them soothingly.

Other factors, too, weakened the grip of rigid scheduling. Perhaps parents had begun to feel the wear and tear of too scheduled an existence. They must not feed the baby, they had been warned, until his face turned red with rage. Nor had they even enjoyed loving their child, when told that bouncing him on the knee would induce sex feelings.

The unconditional permissiveness that followed did not long prevail. Russia launched its Sputnik, and at about the same time came a new but still unclear trend in child training and education. The picture of child care grew hazy, a blend of conflicting theories that have failed to crystallize. Permissive influences remain strong, espoused by the neo-progressives and echoing the continuing though diminished influence of Dewey and the psychoanalysts. The seeds of neuroses are sown in the nursery, and the parent-child relation is crucial. Children must be happy if they will become happy adults.

However, Sputnik has left its mark, notably on education. In all aspects of his life but one, today's child leads a relatively carefree life. At least in middle and upper classes his parents generally treasure him, humor him, and shower him with toys and love. His only real ordeal is school, where he must meet exacting standards to ensure uninterrupted progression from nursery to graduate school.

Which trend will capture the child-training sweepstakes — ultra-permissiveness or responsibility — is unclear, though the former seems dominant now. Over the years, each emphasis tends alternately to sink or surface like a particularly viable whale. A better perspective on the present some future textbook must provide.

• THE SUBJECT MATTER OF CHILD PSYCHOLOGY

Only recently have the so-called experts had a respectable body of objective data, interpreted by highly trained persons, on which to base their advice. Perhaps one reason child study was slow to mature as a science was its broad-ranging subject matter, integrated mainly by its object of study, the child.

The unifying theme of **child psychology** is the pattern of **growth,** a process often divided for convenience into five stages of **childhood:** (1) the **prenatal period,** or the period from conception to birth, which is further subdivided into the *embryonic period* (from conception to eight weeks), the *middle fetal period* (nine weeks through six months), and the *late fetal period* (from then until birth); (2) **infancy,** or the period embracing the first two years, of which the first two to four weeks are termed the *neonatal period*; (3) *early childhood,* including ages two to six; (4) *middle childhood,* including ages six to nine; and (5) **preadolescence,** including the years from age nine to the onset of **adolescence.** Since individual children have somewhat different growth patterns, this **age-stage** outline should serve as a general frame of reference rather than as a hard-and-fast scale. Furthermore, age-stages are partially **psychosocial** in nature and thus determined partially by society. Today, for example, childhood is being shortened, in the **sociocultural** sense, as children are inducted precociously into adolescent behaviors such as wearing make-up and dating.

7

Some deny the need for a psychology of different age-stages. Don't the same laws apply to child, adult, and old person alike? Certain physiological laws do — for example, the laws governing intracellular oxidation and the formation of urine in the kidneys — but most behavioral phenomena undergo qualitative as well as quantitative changes over the years. It is for child psychologists to identify these phenomena, discover their status at each age-stage, and determine the significance of early development for later stages.

In a sense, child psychology is a hybrid, compounded of subject matter from many fields. Within the **psychology** family it draws on the fields of educational, abnormal, genetic, adolescent, social, industrial, clinical, differential, experimental, and comparative psychology. Sociology describes children's relationships with others; cultural anthropology reveals how child-rearing varies from culture to culture; physiology and biochemistry illuminate the roles of enzymes, **hormones,** and vitamins in child personality; and **pediatrics** contributes advice about child care.

Why, then, is a psychology of childhood necessary, if other sciences collectively provide so many answers? First, it pulls together data from other sciences and organizes them in usable form. Second, it shows how these data interrelate in the child, a unitary, growing organism.

A common argument, the trademark of the uninformed, is that child psychology is merely common sense. Psychoanalysts, despite their notable contributions to the field, are partly responsible for this attitude. In the first place, their theories are largely derived from the disturbed, hence atypical, subjects they treat. Second, many of their conclusions have been speculative and consequently not subject to rigid testing.

But scientific child psychology is fast destroying the underpinnings of the common-sense argument, thus belying many an old wives' tale. Take, for example, the popular saying "Spare the rod and spoil the child." Studies of the effects of corporal punishment have disproved this dictum over and over. Such punishment has been shown by psychologists to result more often in lying, stealing, cheating, and resentment toward people in authority than in the wish to be law-abiding.

Perhaps so, persist the uninformed, but we have more confidence in practitioners, such as pediatricians, who work with children all the time. Aren't they sufficient? The answer is that their aim is different. The practitioner's job is application; the child psychologist's is the discovery of principles governing children generally. In short, child psychologists provide professional workers in applied fields with the theoretical orientation and the crucial research data on which any sound treatment must be based. Presumably, having recourse to a body of scientific literature will foster in practitioners a critical attitude toward fads in child care and promote modification of treatment in the light of new findings. Of course the child psychologist might well argue that empirical evidence about human development is important in itself, quite apart from its relevance to practical problems.

Finally, child psychology provides a window on the child's world. It enables the adult to understand how children feel and in what ways they differ. Without such knowledge, the adult will probably interpret children's behaviors according to the way he himself felt as a child, remaining unaware of the range of children's feelings. Moreover, as an individual moves from one age-stage to another, he loses all too easily his appreciation for the problems and perceptions of former stages. An anecdote from *Pageant* magazine (January 1965, p. 113) illustrates how differently child and adult may see things. A minister was showing a Sunday school class a picture of early Christian martyrs in a den of lions. One little boy seemed about to cry. The minister asked him what was wrong.

"Gee," the little boy replied in quavering tones. "Look at the poor lion in the back. He's not getting any!"

• METHODS OF CHILD STUDY

Early Methods

In terms of sophistication and scope, present-day child research is something of a miracle when viewed against its humble, and historically recent, beginnings. For until the last century, interest in the child as such was practically nil. By contrast, today's child is a person in his own right; and childhood is no more considered merely the preface to adulthood than adulthood is considered the preparation for old-age, or old-age the threshold to death.

The earliest approaches to child study were completely subjective in nature. One such method, the **child biography,** was among the first systematic attempts to record child behavior. The observer, typically the baby's mother, set down chronologically whatever behaviors seemed significant, such as the baby's first word. The following excerpt from a recent baby diary is typical of such records:

22 months, 25 days, June 13
. . . When we took Ruth to the beach, she kept pointing to all the people in bathing suits, laughing and shouting, "Nude."

. . . Ruth has a doll she named Jimmy. One day I put a dress on Jimmy instead of his suit. This didn't bother Ruth; Jimmy was still a boy.

. . . Ruth saw a little boy sleeping with a rubber Mickey Mouse toy just like hers. She screamed "Mine!" and could not understand that he could have one just like hers until we showed her her own toy. Then she was perfectly happy to let the boy play with his Mickey Mouse.

23 months, 12 days, July 1
. . . Ruth pointed into her potty and asked, "What's this?" I answered, "Wee-wee." Ruth asked, "Where does it come from?"

23 months, 27 days, July 16
. . . When someone asked Ruth if she wanted a baby sister or a baby brother, she answered, "A baby mother" [Church, 1966, pp. 277–285].

The weaknesses of child biographies are readily apparent. Observations are made, characteristically, at irregular intervals, and the behaviors observed and recorded are more often unusual than typical. Also, doting parents are biased, and their recollections are filtered through the prisms of their own prejudices. Moreover, parent diarists tend to be highly selective and their children correspondingly exceptional. Therefore, the data obtained would hardly be applicable to the offspring of the masses.

Nevertheless, baby diaries have served a purpose. They proved the advantage of a systematic over a speculative approach, and they were the forerunners of the longitudinal study, which involves observation of the same subjects over the years. Two early longitudinal studies were especially important: Rousseau's *Émile* (1762), which eulogized the value of rearing the child naturally, unspoiled by civilization's taint, and Preyer's *The Mind of the Child* (1882), a careful record of several children's development over the years.

Even today the child biography, if used in conjunction with simple standardized tests and controlled experimentation, may yield important data. For one thing, it provides continuous, integrated observations by the only persons in a position to observe the child in all sorts of situations at any hour of the day or night. Biographical data are more useful, however, when observers are unbiased and specially trained for the task.

A related approach, the **autobiography,** gives insight into an individual's perceptions of self and others. However, autobiographies, like baby diaries, involve rather unusual subjects, and help little in the understanding of children in general.

The Early Twentieth Century

Precursors of more scientific approaches. The first investigations that

9

approached the scientific were carried out in the late nineteenth and early twentieth centuries. For example, G. Stanley Hall published a series of reports based on the results of questionnaires dealing with children's behavior. The best-known of his reports is *Content of Children's Minds on Entering School* (1883). The same methods have been used more recently by **Jean Piaget** (1896–) in conjunction with observation. The following excerpt represents an attempt made by Piaget to determine, through questioning, children's concepts of thought:

> Nic (a girl) supposes one could not see thought because, "I should have to speak to it." E. Kun and his sister M. Kun were questioned one after the other without being given time to compare. Both stated that thought is in the head and that it is "white" and "round." M. Kun said it was "as big as a large apple"; E. Kun that it was "little." This would seem to suggest traces of adult teaching on the brain. However, E. Kun at other times maintained that one thinks "with the mouth." Where is the thought? – In the middle of the mouth. – Can one see it? – Yes. – Touch it? – No. – Why not? – Because it is too far away. – Where? – In the neck. The combination of spontaneous convictions with instruction received is evident [Piaget, 1951, pp. 51–52].

The questionnaire is still widely used, despite its serious shortcomings. Even when respondents try to answer honestly, their answers are subject to forgetting and distortion, either unconscious or deliberate. Therefore, despite the ease of administration and compilation, psychologists take a skeptical view of this method. Let it be added, however, that some questionnaires are far better prepared than others.

Watson and Binet. Watson and the behaviorists, protesting against armchair theorizing, contended that only objectively observable behavior could be the subject matter of science. Precursor of this movement was the Russian physiologist **Ivan Pavlov** (1849–1936), who

found that animals learn by simple **conditioning** – that is, by forming new associations between stimuli and responses. Watson gave important impetus to scientific psychology, stressing as he did the need for objective appraisal. Unfortunately, however, he did not recognize the significance of subjective aspects of experience – that is, of feelings and views not objectively observable or measurable.

Also precipitating the child-study movement was **Alfred Binet** (1857–1911), who developed a method of testing intelligence. Working in conjunction with Simon, he published his first mental-test scale in 1905. In 1916 the test was restandardized by Lewis Terman and published in the United States as the Stanford-Binet Intelligence Scale.

Freud. More or less contemporary with Hall, Binet, and Watson was **Sigmund Freud** (1856–1939), a Viennese neurologist, whose psychoanalytic concepts permeate child psychology today, and who left an indelible, often undetectable stamp on current child-training practice. Psychologists may pick flaws in him all they will and may reject many of his conclusions as wholly or partially invalid, but all acknowledge his contributions, which Murphy summarizes as follows:

> . . . first, the specifications of drive; second, the conception that life tendencies are deeper, more primordial than the phenomenon of consciousness, which is at best an elaboration or screening technique which can in no way obliterate or weaken the basic drive modulations; third, as James Harvey Robinson said, the discovery that, "as children, we are at our most impressionable age"; fourth, the conception that the ego is a derivative rather than a primary expression of life; and fifth, most general of all propositions, that all psychological activity is motivated, driven, guided, directed by life tensions seeking resolution. It is in this latter sense that psychoanalysis is a consistently dynamic psychology. It begins with force and ends with the dissipation of force through a ten-

sion-reducing process always to be followed by fresh tension accumulations and further discharges. Every idle fancy, every quick calculation, every off remark, every whim and every great decision alike spring basically from the tensions of the tissues within us [Murphy, 1956, p. 664].

Freud arrived at a method, which he called **free association,** of asking his patients to say anything that came to their minds. They were to relate any thoughts that occurred to them, no matter how trivial or irrelevant or unpleasant they seemed to be.

Free association invariably brought the same result: the report of childhood experiences. The recollections proved to be predominantly sexual in nature, involving love and hate toward the parents, sexual incidents, and jealousies toward siblings. Nevertheless, Freud's patients often vigorously denied his interpretations of their motives, because they lived on one plane, the conscious, while their true feelings, as revealed in free association and in the relation of dreams, lay in their unconscious. To get at the unconscious, Freud gradually evolved the technique of **psychoanalysis,** a prolonged series of sessions involving free association and reports of dreams.

Freud can be said to have had several major influences on child psychology. Most important, by showing adults' neurotic symptoms to be the outcome of childhood experiences he focused attention on childhood as a critical period of development. Also, his free-association techniques for exploring unconscious feelings and motives have been modified for use with children. These play techniques allow children to display their real emotions in the world of toys.

Present-Day Methods

In the brief life of scientific psychology, many means have been devised for studying child behavior. Some methods have been adapted from other sciences; others have been devised by child researchers themselves. These methods are used both independently and in varying combinations. Each has its special uses, and each its particular advantages and disadvantages. The methods described in this section were designed for general use, but only their applications to child study will be treated here.

The normative approach. A major function of child research is to determine how specific behaviors develop and what behaviors may normally be expected at various age-stages. Such data are supplied by normative methods, notably the cross-sectional and longitudinal methods.

The cross-sectional approach. In the cross-sectional approach, groups of children at different levels of development are studied simultaneously. The purpose of these studies is to discover typical behaviors of children at various age-stages. The method is popular because, within a short period of time, large quantities of data can be obtained. For example, in one cross-sectional study, a nation-wide survey of adolescents showed that:

> . . . 14% of the nation's teen-age boys are easily excited; 32% of the girls. Among boys questioned, 27% have trouble keeping their temper, slightly fewer than the reported 38% of the girls. . . . Nervousness afflicts 21% of our male teen-agers and 32% of the girls. Girls also outnumber the boys in daydreaming, feeling lonesome, getting feelings hurt, having crushes, stage fright, etc. [Remmers and Radler, 1957, p. 59].

The longitudinal approach. More significant, and growing in favor, is the **longitudinal approach,** which involves observations of the same children over a period of years. The earliest longitudinal research worthy of the name was the Harvard Growth Study, begun in the 1920s, which studied the same group from the early elementary grades through high school. At present over 300 such studies are in progress, a dozen or so very widely known.

The procedures followed in longitudinal studies may be specialized, involving quite specific techniques or areas of child behavior, or they may be broad, making use of various techniques: experiments, testing, observations, ratings, interviews, and projective methods. Although longitudinal studies vary somewhat in technique, they all employ the same standard measures of intellectual function, and all accumulate extensive anthropometric data, which in time yield significant relations between growth variables. Results from various experiments are often pieced together, yielding many important if still tentative conclusions.

This form of research requires tremendous administrative skill and clerical assistance, as well as large sums of money. It also involves many problems. For example, a child's family may move, or the parents may remove their child from the experimental group before the project is completed. However, the potential payoff from longitudinal studies is great. Such studies make possible the analysis of interrelations among growth processes. They also help determine the relative permanence of traits, and they reveal long-term processes of interaction between the child and his environment. For example, one may note changing parental attitudes and the child's reaction to them as he grows.

Almost all available longitudinal data apply to children in this country. Recently, however, an international study has been launched through the Centre Internationale de l'Enfance in Paris. Eventually, therefore, long-term cross-cultural comparisons of child development can be made (Falkner, 1958).

The case history. The **case history** was originally devised for studying children in trouble. It is a useful method for studying the problems of children individually. All data about the child and his environment that may be relevant to a particular problem are collected.

Such data may be obtained from school records and from interviews with parents, teachers, and friends. Subjectively reported information may be supplemented by data obtained from standardized tests. After data have been gathered, the professional persons involved in helping the child — perhaps the school psychologist, the child's teachers, and the local guidance counselor — hold case conferences and examine the data to determine what may best be prescribed for the child.

In general, the same sort of problems arise in case studies as in child biographies. Persons interviewed give their own biased impressions, which are further distorted by errors of memory. The children involved commonly deviate from the norm and hence yield atypical data. Finally, the mere fact that certain problems appear concurrently with specific environmental situations does not necessarily prove causality. For example, if a child begins having nightmares at about the time his parents are divorced, one may assume a causal relationship that in fact does not exist.

Selected findings from a case study. Conclusions shown in the following case study were based largely on the subject's figure drawings, just one of numerous techniques that may be used:

Seymour, age 4 years 5 months, was referred primarily because of his attacks on his $1\frac{1}{2}$ year old sister. His mother could never allow the two children together, even in her presence, because he knocked the baby down, hit her on her head or threw things at her. Several times he wrapped a cord around the baby's neck; he also wrapped her head in a blanket and sat on it. He demanded his own way or screamed inordinately, sometimes for two hours at a stretch. His mother had to pour his milk first, or he refused to eat. Things had reached the stage, she said, that if she observed, "It's raining," Seymour would retort, "It's not!" and scream. The parents had tried spanking, ignoring, isolating, bribing, shaking, going to an extreme to give Seymour exactly what they gave to his two sisters — all without effect. The mother tried to show him more love by holding him on her lap, but he merely cried and struggled free or kicked and spat. Seymour was always a model child outside the home, so that outsiders could not imagine these problems. His father was strict and stronger than the mother; he was somewhat more successful in managing the child, as a consequence, but even he was thoroughly exasperated. In her attempts to avoid partiality, the mother had bought new shoes for Seymour when she got them for the girls, even though he did not need them. Seymour's bad tantrums occurred two or three times a day. He had had some before his younger sister's birth but his mother reported no signs of jealousy at the time of her birth. He tended to follow his $5\frac{1}{2}$ year old sister around, attempting to imitate her and her friends in all their activities. He wanted to sleep with his parents every night. This had begun six months prior to referral, when he had bad dreams (of snakes, alligators, being chased, being hurt), and because he was allowed in the parental bed then, he had insisted on it since. If he were ever persuaded to sleep alone, he would get up and wander around in the middle of the night. Not long before referral he had asked his mother if he had ever been a baby. He was very interested that everyone had, and in his own baby pictures. His mother thought this meant he wanted to be a baby, and so constantly pointed out to him the advantages of being grown up. His mother said Seymour had always been a difficult child. At 10 months he could flip out of his crib and go all over the house. He was a big eater and a large baby, bottle-fed from the beginning because the older child had lost weight when nursed. Toilet training was a struggle; he screamed and kicked when put on the pot, and had to be held by the mother because he soon broke the straps. It was begun at seven months and completed at $2\frac{1}{2}$ years. There was some smearing of faeces, which the mother was embarrassed to admit. When the younger baby was brought home from the hospital, the mother showed Seymour the diapers and told him he was too old for them; it was then that he was toilet trained. She considered him very different from both of his sisters and from other children. He was an unplanned baby; normal pregnancy and birth. The mother wanted a girl, because she enjoyed dressing them and fixing them up. Her father became ill with cancer when Seymour was three months old, and it was a hectic period, with mother leaving the children with strangers at times while she visited the hospital. Mother herself had been an only child, and a lonely, shy, retiring one who feared people. She was always an honor student in school. Her father was very conscientious, but lenient with her. Her mother was a strict disciplinarian and very efficient. Towards the end of her interview with the social worker, the mother "confessed" that she and her mother did not get along. The maternal grandmother helped pay for their home, and had an apartment upstairs which was entered through the house. She meddled in the children's discipline and made constant demands on them. She did not have friends of her own and so she tried to run the mother's life and competed with her for the children. The mother spoke resentfully of the extra time she had to play with the children because she had little housework to do. And she showed covert gratification in remarking that, although Seymour at one time seemed to prefer his grandmother to his mother, he lately had been kicking, hitting and swearing at her, too. This family had always lived with the maternal grandmother, and the mother felt doubtful that she could live apart from her mother. The father was the older of two boys. His parents quarrelled constantly. His father was selfish, concerned only with his own needs, refusing to work after getting a small inheritance during the father's boyhood. As a result, his sons had to assist him; at the time of referral the father spent three evenings a week at his father's home after a $10\frac{1}{2}$ hour working day, which was resented by his wife. The father hated quarrelling and got especially upset by Seymour, "seeing red" because of the dissension he caused. It was interesting that this man, a plant foreman, had obtained a promotion shortly before our contact, because "he could be firm with people" [Altman, 1960, pp. 341–342].

The personal interview. Since both longitudinal studies and case histories often make use of the personal interview, let us look at this technique. An advantage of the interview is that it permits the description of characteristic behaviors, whereas a child's reactions in an artificial laboratory situation may be atypical. Also, of course, interviews provide data on behaviors that the researchers have not been able to observe.

However, the method may be subject to various weaknesses, such as the subject's forgetting. In one study, retrospective accounts of child-rearing obtained from parents of three-year-olds were compared with reports previously given in the course of a longitudinal study begun with the birth of the child. The parents proved quite inaccurate in their memory of details (Robbins, 1963). Often, too, parents disagree between themselves on replies. In an investigation dealing with school relations and first-grade adjustment, Medinnus (1962) found little agreement between the parents.

As already pointed out, parents tend to distort their replies to make the picture of their family life conform to the cultural stereotype of the happy family. In one study, the picture obtained by interview was closer to the cultural stereotype than was the impression gained through direct observation (McCord and McCord, 1961).

Nevertheless, the method has been used with a considerable degree of sophistication. In an important study by Sears, Maccoby, and Levin (1957), personal interviews yielded highly valuable data about mothers' attitudes. Mothers were studied in one middle-class suburb and one working-class suburb of a large city in New England. Nearly 400 mothers were interviewed by 10 trained researchers employing standardized instruments. The results were then rated independently by 10 advanced graduate students, to test for reliability; final scores were made on the pooled judgments of the raters. Problems such as the following were posed: "Some people feel that it is very important for a child to learn not to fight with other children; and others feel that there are times when a child has to learn to fight. How do you feel about this?" Two mothers' replies are given below. The first was interpreted as a belief that a child need not be aggressive toward his peers; the second, that a child should stick up strongly for his rights:

[First mother:] I go out and ask other mothers what happened and when I find out, I say, "All right, come in the house now." Sooner than go to their mothers and fight with them, I bring her in the house and keep her in for a while and talk it all over with her and tell her where she's wrong or where the other child is wrong, and then after a while, I let her out again and tell her to go play with somebody else.

[Second mother:] Well, I believe that a child has a right to fight and to stick up for his own rights. I hate to see a kid that is always — well — I think if they don't they are whining babies and are always home with their mothers; and we have always taught Bill to hit them right back and to give them one better than what he got. And there are a few children, in this neighborhood, that Bill is afraid of and he will come home and tell me what they have done to him — but the only satisfaction that he has ever got was that, "We have told you if he hits you to hit him back, and until then don't tell me your stories" [Sears et al., 1957, pp. 246–247].

Observation. Certain current methods, although largely subjective like those of an earlier day, may be considerably refined. In one of these methods, an observer simply records children's behaviors in a natural situation, as on a playground. Depending on the purposes of the study, either general behaviors may be noted or specific details may be described. The observer's own feelings are carefully distinguished from purely objective details.

Recording may take several forms. One, the anecdotal record, consists of thumbnail sketches of behavioral episodes. For each item the date, place, and situation are noted, along with such details as children's words, gestures, and facial expressions. The teacher who recorded the following item believed such detail to be of special significance in this case:

> During the work period Larry (age 11) came to me, and as he whittled a propeller for a plane, asked, "Miss S. how can you have someone have confidence in you?" I told him various ways with concrete illustrations and then asked, "Are you thinking of a friend?" "Yes'm, a boy who doesn't like me but I like him." "Is he in this grade?" "No'm. He's in another room." We had quite a little talk about the matter and he asked me if I would lend the boy money in an effort to win his approval. I advised against this and told him that there were numerous better ways of winning friendship and suggested some . . . [*Childhood Education*, 1946, pp. 232–239].

Controlled observation. In **controlled observations,** researchers are concerned with only small segments of the child's behavior, and they record this behavior as it occurs naturally. Controlled observations are of two types: observations of natural situations and observations of specially devised situations. In natural situations, observers cannot record all that happens; they therefore use special devices to objectify results. One such device is the time-sampling technique, in which records are made at regular intervals for specified lengths of time. For example, each child in a group may be observed once a week for two minutes; or the observers may select only small segments of the child's behavior for systematic study— his questions, perhaps, or his outbursts of anger.

A second form of controlled observation involves specially arranged situations. For instance, in a study of individual differences in reaction to frustration, children may be placed one at a time in a room with several attractive toys, which are subsequently removed. The observer records each child's response to this unpleasant state of affairs.

A number of techniques have been devised for recording behavior contin-

uously without disturbing the child involved. For example, an infant may be placed in an experimental cabinet and observed through a conveniently placed window. Inside these experimental chambers, various instruments are employed. One is the **stabilimeter,** a device that, when attached to the platform on which the infant is placed, automatically records his movements. Another is the sound camera, which records simultaneously his vocalizations and activities. This **cinemanalysis** technique, developed by Arnold Gesell and his co-workers at Yale, permits the study of behavioral sequences frame by frame.

For observing older children, one-way screens are standard features in experimental schools. An entire class may sit, seeing but unseen, in a small chamber adjoining the classroom. A microphone pipes in what the children say.

The experimental method. A still more rigorous form of observation is the **experimental method.** This method is characterized by control and repetition.

Experiments are controlled by holding some conditions constant while others are changed in some designated way. The effects of such change can then be observed. For example, two similar classes of underprivileged children may be taught by the same teacher using the same methods. One class, however, is given a dietary supplement each day. If this class (the *experimental* group) makes better grades than the other (the *control* group), the observer might then conclude that the dietary supplement accounted for their superior performance.

To meet the second requirement of the experimental method, repetition, this experiment would have to be capable of repetition yielding the same results.

Animals are the most frequently chosen subjects for experimental research. Ethics that forbid exploiting

15

infants permit environmental manipulations with animals.

Such experiments have contributed considerably to the understanding of human behavior. For example, dogs reared in isolation, with little opportunity to experience pain, failed to show adaptive avoidance conditioning to a lighted match when they reached physical maturity (Melzack and Thompson, 1957). This result naturally raises the question: What sort of experiences in infancy may be crucial for behavioral adaptations in adulthood? While findings from animal research may not always be extrapolated directly to humans, they nevertheless suggest many fruitful hypotheses.

Standardized tests. Among the more exact instruments for studying children are **standardized psychological tests,** which come in many sizes and shapes. Norms are derived by determining how representative groups of children respond to specific test items; individuals are then evaluated against them. Standardized tests have been devised to measure all sorts of traits and patterns of behaviors. They may measure factors as specific as reaction time or as complex as personality.

Among the more highly refined and widely used of these instruments are the intelligence tests. Successful as they have proved, they nevertheless have weaknesses. First, there is disagreement about the very definition of what they purport to measure—that is, intelligence. What portion of an intelligence test should be devoted to reasoning, or to originality, or to rote memory? And how may atypical replies, not described in the test manual, be scored?

All standardized tests require carefully standardized scoring. For example, in the 1937 revision of the Stanford-Binet test—the most widely used test at the time for assessing the intelligence quotient of individual children —one of the tests on the seven-year level consisted of showing children pictures containing some incongruity. The child was shown each picture in turn and asked "Why is it funny (foolish)?" The examiner's manual indicated right and wrong answers. One of the pictures showed a cat with several mice, all apparently perfectly contented. The following statements illustrate the sort of replies scored as correct in the test manual:

> "A kitty has some little mouses instead of a mama mouse having little mouses."
> "The mouses are dumb. They don't know the cat will eat them and they're walking all around the cat instead of running away."

An example of a reply scored as incorrect is this one:

> "A mouse, a cat, a mouse, a mouse. The mouse is up on top of the cat and the mouse is talking to the cat and the cat is laying down and two little mouses are eating." (No credit, because the child merely describes the picture without answering the question) [Terman and Merrill, 1937, pp. 352–353].

Answers to be judged as correct or incorrect were established only after the test was standardized. That is, standards for administering and scoring were derived from trying out test items on a representative sampling of the population to be tested.

Projective techniques. **Projective techniques** consist of relatively unstructured or ambiguous test situations designed to elicit reactions indicating the subject's characteristic attitudes, motivations, or traits. The stimuli presented to the subject may consist of inkblots, cloud pictures, cartoons, incomplete sentences, play materials, or drawing tasks. Thus a child's response to an empty sheet of paper and colored crayons may reveal his emotional mood or sentiments. The child who portrays the boy in a picture as unhappy, and at odds with his mother, is presumably revealing aspects of his personal situation. Responses to these situations are standardized to ensure uniform interpretation.

The two best-known projective tests are the **Rorschach Inkblot Test** and the **Thematic Apperception Test,** better known as the T.A.T. In the

An example of a Thematic Apperception Test. Reproduced by permission.

Rorschach, the subject is shown a series of inkblots, one at a time, and asked to tell what he sees in them. A hostile child shown one of the blots might describe two forms as figures fighting, while a happy child might believe them embracing. In the T.A.T., 20 pictures are shown to the subject, who makes up a story about each. The examiner notes with whom the child identifies himself and what themes recur in his stories. While both tests are intended chiefly for use with adults, both have been adapted for children.

Other projective tests have been designed especially for children. The **Bellak Children's Apperception Test** consists of pictures of animals. Identification with animal characters is seen to reveal various things about the child's experience – conflicts with parents, sibling rivalries, sexual fears, and the like:

[In one picture is shown] a lion with pipe and cane, sitting in a chair. In the lower right corner a little mouse appears in a hole. The lion is usually seen as a father figure equipped with such masculine symbols as pipe and cane; or, on the other hand, the cane may turn this paternal figure into an old, helpless creature, of whom one need not be afraid. This is usually a defense process against the child's acute awareness of the father's strength. If the lion is viewed as a strong paternal figure, it will be important to note whether he is represented as benign or dangerous. The mouse is often taken as the identification figure. In such a case – by tricks and circumstances – the mouse may be turned into the more powerful animal. On the other hand, it may be totally at the lion's mercy. Some children identify with the lion, and there will be other subjects who will switch identification one or more times, suggesting conflicts between compliance and autonomy, etc. [Adelman, 1960, p. 84].

Similarly designed are the **Blacky Pictures,** composed of 12 cartoons depicting adventures of the dog Blacky.

The Blacky Pictures are designed especially for children. This is Cartoon VII (Identification Process) from the series. Reproduced by permission of Psychodynamic Instruments, Ann Arbor, Michigan.

The cartoons illustrate phases of psychosexual development and are designed to disclose such sex-related problems as oral sadism or eroticism, oedipal anxiety, masturbatory guilt, and penis envy.

One ingenious projective technique involves the use of pictures of unfamiliar women as well as the child's own mother, showing approving, angry, or neutral 17 facial expressions. (Purcell, 1962).

The **Bühler World Test** consists of miniature objects of the outdoor world — trees, cars, people, animals, and so on — which are constructed of wood and colorfully painted. Between 150 and 300 of these objects, called "elements," are available to the child, and assembled in standard distribution in an open box. The child is asked to "look at all these nice things" and "do something about them." The child may construct something, dramatize the objects, or simply tell a story about them. Ways of handling the materials may be symptomatic of distinctive personality patterns. These patterns, in turn, may indicate certain needs, such as a need for active aggression, or passive resistance, or rigidity.

Another projective test for children is the **Madeleine Thomas Test,** which includes 15 stories about the everyday activities and problems as well as fan-

This boy has a friend whom he likes very much. One day his friend tells him: "Listen, I am going to tell you something, but it is a secret, don't tell anybody." What is [his friend] going to tell him? [Wursten, 1960, p. 207.]

One type of semi-structured test is the Sentence Completion Test (SCT). The child is asked to write sentences beginning with given phrases. Here are some responses, all of which suggest emotional problems. The given portion of the sentence is in italics:

What I like is to take my knife and cut, cut, cut.
My father I wish he would die a horrible death.
I am under the control of a world-wide conspiring of hypnotical scientific agents that can lucidate anything whatandever into our recesses and crevasses.
I wish I was dead [Lindgren et al., 1966, p. 288].

Hand puppets are often used to provide a projective situation.

tasies and dreams of a purely fictional child of similar age and the same sex as the patient. One of these stories is this:

Doll play provides another rich projective situation. According to Erickson (1940), toys catch the child off guard; in the doll-play "microsphere" the child does what he does not dare do in reality. Irrespective of the particular child's family constellation, the dolls provided may be easily identified as father, mother, boy, girl, and baby. Also provided is realistically designed furniture, such as table, stove, and toilet. Instructions are usually general, amounting to nothing more than telling the child he may play with the toys.

Doll play, as a child-study technique, brings conflicting evaluations. Sears (1947) has asserted, however, that the child's doll-play reactions carry "an almost overwhelming aura of revelation to a sensitive observer." The following excerpt from a description of play therapy is a case in point:

> In the playroom Betsy Jo dropped her quiet and gentle ways. She took the nipple off the bottle and said in a blurred voice, "I'll take my whiskey straight!" She lifted the bottle to her lips and drank from it, wiped her mouth with the back of her hand and pushed the chair back from the table, knocking it over. She looked around, kicked it, swore at it and lurched across the playroom to the doll house. She swept the furniture out with her hands and grabbed up the mother doll and choked her. She screamed and yelled and then suddenly flung the doll away from her and lurched across the room toward the rag doll. She grabbed it up and began to tear its clothes off, swearing like a pirate all the time.
>
> This was Betsy Jo's perception of her father—for her father was an alcoholic—but no one thought Betsy Jo was "old enough yet" to be bothered by it [Axline, 1950, pp. 71–72].

Some years after Sears' comment and Axline's description were written, Levin and Wardwell (1962) reviewed 91 studies of doll play spanning 27 years. Unlike Sears, they concluded that "an over-all body of sensible interrelated findings is not apparent."

The laboratory approach. The foregoing techniques may be used either in the laboratory or out of it. The laboratory

approach simply connotes that study proceeds in a place designed especially for scientific research. For example, children might simply be left in a room alone, to determine their reaction to being left by themselves. Observers, meanwhile, would watch through a window and record what happens.

Research undertaken in a laboratory often lacks a certain authenticity. For example, the sort of emotions aroused in artificially designed emotion-arousing situations seem superficial when compared with feelings derived from real-life situations. Moreover, the stimuli designed to test the quality of child response in the laboratory are necessarily of relatively brief duration. The ethics of child research forbid that these stimuli be unusually intense. Therefore, the impact can hardly compare with the effects of persistent, or highly unusual, real-life situations. Finally, the behaviors investigated are often isolated and fragmentary, giving little idea of the total person involved.

Nevertheless, laboratory situations are not necessarily artificial. The main point of a laboratory study is to exercise more control over relevant variables than is possible in a naturalistic setting.

Studies of culture. A type of research that has proved especially fruitful is the sociocultural study. Sociocultural studies may be either intra-cultural or cross-cultural. Among **intra-cultural** studies, those of primitive peoples are most common, since primitive cultures pose somewhat less complex problems. In general, such cultural studies attempt to show the way of life of a relatively independent culture, sufficiently isolated to have maintained its distinctiveness. Although generalizations derived from studying such peoples may not apply directly to modern society, they nevertheless provide valuable insights into the various interrelationships between individuals and their environments. And just as human behavior often becomes more easily understood through studies of simpler forms of life, complex modern societies are sometimes illuminated by studies of primitive cultures. The following is a condensation from one of these studies (reported in Bateson and Mead, 1942):

> A study of the Balinese showed that infants are indulged and caressed the first year or two, then subjected to teasing. The mother ignores her child's demands and dramatizes her rejection by borrowing a child from a neighbor and caressing it within view of her own child. When her child screams with rage, she simply smiles, enraging him further. As a result of such experiences, the Balinese children withdraw, and find satisfaction within themselves rather than through warm interaction with others. As adults, they are characterized by withdrawn, passive detachment and dreaminess.

A related study is the **cross-cultural approach,** which attempts comparisons between two or more cultural groupings. One such study was conducted in New Haven, Connecticut, and Basle, Switzerland. Samples of mothers representing upper-lower and lower-middle classes were asked questions about their child-rearing practices, including their handling of stuttering, lying, masturbation, bed-wetting, and weaning. One finding was that the Swiss mothers placed pressure on their children to grow up, whereas the American mothers let their children be children (Jarecki, 1961).

Both intra-cultural and cross-cultural studies have been based largely on impressions rather than empirical data, and have thus lent themselves to loose interpretations. However, the data from such studies, intelligently used, have helped tease out those cultural factors that are most significant for personality development, and have added provocative hypotheses concerning sociocultural influences.

• PROBLEMS INHERENT IN CHILD RESEARCH

Pitfalls of Method

Every behavioral science, including child psychology, has its shortcomings.

Some problems have been pointed out already. One of these involves the choice of method. Take, for example, parents' retrospective reports, a common feature of many studies. Since present problems are rooted in the past, it becomes imperative to reconstruct the nature and sequence of early events. However, no matter how great the parents' integrity, their replies will hardly mirror the truth. They report the situation as *they* see it, as *they* remember it; and they are hardly unbiased observers. In one study, 25 mothers were interviewed three to six years later to determine whether they would give the same information in retrospect that they had reported originally. Forty per cent of their replies had changed drastically, in some areas more than others. They had changed least on such items as preferred sex of child and details of bottle-feeding and toilet-training, most on items like health in pregnancy, discipline, and relation of child to parents (Wenar and Coulter, 1962). Certainly parental recollections are no mere re-run of the original reel.

Such distortions are easy to explain. First of all, most parents either consciously or unconsciously try to put themselves in a favorable light. Almost all possess a strong need to believe they have been good parents, and they selectively seek proof from their memories. Furthermore, over the years parents may become confused about which of their children was involved in a specific incident or situation. They may also recall mostly the pleasant, having unconsciously blotted out the rest. McCandless (1961, p. 41) reports such a case. A friend with a new baby asked him, rather desperately, when his children had begun to sleep through the night. McCandless confidently replied, "At around two months," but later checked his children's baby books. His statement had been glaringly false; none of them had slept through the night consistently until he was about 14 weeks of age.

Pitfalls also lie in experimental methods of research. There is great concern lest children become not just the subjects but the victims of research. Laboratory experiments certainly permit greater precision than other research, and they have proved especially useful in studies of animal behavior, where variables can be altered at will; however, children cannot similarly be manipulated, for fear of resultant damage. This ostensible respect for child vulnerability can be taken to silly extremes. Largely to escape criticism by parents, colleagues, or administrators, researchers may dilute the worth of studies with unrealistic safeguards. For instance, one study involved a 60 second separation of mothers and their preschool children as a situational test, but the child was actually alone for only 15 seconds of that period—certainly an example of experimental timidity (Gardner and Pease, 1958). It is uncertain how much fear parents themselves possess on this score. Undoubtedly, many are willing to permit their children to be tested and studied, in return for the special benefits available in research centers.

Error in the experimental method also occurs through faulty assumptions. For instance, operational or experimental definitions are fallacious unless they indicate faithfully the concepts they purport to represent. By way of illustration, McCandless (1961, p. 43) cites the following case based on Otto Rank's hypothesis (1929) that personal maladjustments may be due in part to "birth trauma," the shock of the birth process. One investigator reasoned that this hypothesis could be tested by determining whether infants who had had a difficult birth showed greater-than-normal maladjustments. His criterion for difficult birth was the length of the mother's labor, as judged by the time from "in labor" admission to the hospital until delivery. His criterion for infant maladjustment was the length of time the infant spent crying (Ruja, 1948).

But are these criteria necessarily valid? It is possible that precipitate, hurried labor may produce more strain on the infant than a more gradual proc-

ess. It is also possible that the more deeply traumatized or damaged baby may lack the energy to cry. It is hardly surprising, concludes McCandless, that Ruja found no relationship between duration of labor and amount of crying. Unfortunately, much psychological research is based on such faulty assumptions.

Another problem is the experimenter himself, whose special biases inevitably color every aspect of his research, including hypothesis, research design, method, and interpretation. Each researcher is a unique individual himself, and thus a study of parent-child relations may easily metamorphose into a reflection of parent-child-expert relations.

Manifestation of bias is not the only way in which an experimenter may distort research. Whenever he observes or tests a child directly, his own personality complicates the latter's reactions. Experimenter effects have been clearly documented, for example, in doll play (Baldwin and Levin, 1964).

Finally, however sophisticated the method, the data may become invalidated by faulty interpretation. Even the most carefully derived data lend themselves to enough interpretations to support the biases of researchers possessing widely differing theoretical orientations.

A common error is oversimplification. One form of this error is overgeneralization—that is, the failure to show how, and to what extent, children differ. Certain generalizations indeed apply—for example, those relating to laws of developmental direction and sequential growth pattern. But even within the framework of that sequence, children's timetables differ. One child crawls or walks much sooner than another. Therefore, tables of averages are grossly misleading. In a group of children, not a single one may be average in height or weight. In fact, many distributions of human traits tend not to be normal.

However, one may not say that measures of central tendency have no

21

function. They serve as points of reference, indicating how far each child varies from some hypothetical norm. For example, exceptional deviance from the normal age for learning to walk may alert pediatricians to the need for making certain tests.

Obviously, deviations from the norm should be interpreted intelligently. All too often it is assumed that deviation signifies undesirable behavior, and that any violation of existing rules, psychological or physical, is an abnormal response.

Deviation on the physical level may simply represent a less typical, but normal, characteristic. Psychologically, deviation may be harmless, or even optimal. For example, a child who prefers being alone may simply be the sort of person who prefers a less crowded arena for skirmishes with creative ideas.

In short, the researcher should avoid losing sight of the individual in a mass of statistics. It is futile to attempt to distill the essence of a child into impersonal data. Research findings show children in black and white; they omit the color.

The concept of causality is also subject to oversimplification. Rarely, except under extreme conditions — for example, when an inadequately functioning thyroid leads to cretinism — does factor A always lead to effect B. It is a basic characteristic of human development that any specific behavior results from all of a child's past history and present stimulation. In the investigation of behaviors, then, many variables must be studied and weighed against each other. The notion of simple, single causes, says Ausubel (1958, p. 131), must be displaced by concepts of multiple causation, reciprocal relations, and the progressive cumulation of effect.

Needed Improvements in Methods

Certain precautions may help to reduce methodological defects. First, the method employed should be appropriate to the topic in question; no one technique is applicable to all age levels or behaviors. Special methods, for instance, must be devised to study children before they can talk.

Furthermore, new methods must be devised to keep pace with the greater funds, more highly trained staffs, and complex computers currently available. The trick is to devise and experiment with a variety of techniques, and to develop measurements that are imaginative, rigorous, and appropriate to the demand of an expanding universe (Bronfenbrenner, 1960).

Most important, researchers must learn to develop sound, imaginative, and sufficiently broad hypotheses to deal with human complexity.

Psychologists must also begin to explore new areas of subject matter. Many areas remain untapped, not so much from taboos as from lack of interest. For example, almost no studies exist of children's emotional experiences of wonder, repulsion, and joy. Furthermore, different aspects of behavior tend to be studied intermittently, instead of continuously. Few recent data are available about children's emotions; most references to the topic, even in recent textbooks, bear dates that are ancient by the standards of this fast-moving field.

Nor have children of various social classes and nationalities been studied extensively. Most studies represent Caucasian, middle-class homes. Also, aside from certain anthropological studies, we have few data to help understand the varied cultures of the earth. Overwhelmingly, research deals with the child of the Western world. Little note is taken of the fact that today's child is a child of the world.

Status of Research

Certainly the present picture of research is not all rosy. There is still much bad research, and many basic issues and theoretical dilemmas remained unresolved, as will become abundantly clear in succeeding chapters. We must evaluate research, however, in terms of its development. Early in the century psychologists dealt with the child in the manner of vivisectionists; they fragmentized him and analyzed isolated behavioral functions. Now the emphasis is on putting the child together again, on seeing how his many facets fit together and how the individual child evolves through the years. Recently, for example, more attention has been paid cognition, not as an isolated process but as a function of total personality. Development is the unifying theme; the child is now seen as a person instead of a collection of sensations and reflexes loosely held together by his skin.

Among researchers themselves cooperation has largely displaced competition; psychologists from widely varied disciplines and representing radically differing "schools" have pooled their resources. There are still significant differences, but the emphasis currently is on seeking answers rather than on proving one's point.

Meanwhile the computer promises to revolutionize the field of child psychology quite as much as it has the sphere of space. For the first time it has become feasible to study large samples of subjects and to employ sophisticated statistical procedures to unravel complex interrelationships between the child's personality and the manifold influences that impinge upon him. At the same time, grants for research have become available in quantities never dreamed of in earlier days, and many researchers possess sophistication of training and outlook that makes the so-called researchers of earlier days seem almost primitive by comparison.

• SUMMARY

Child study, which has only recently become a science, is a scientific hybrid of subject matter from many fields. **Child psychology** integrates research findings relating to child development and abstracts general principles. It is fast undermining speculative theories and providing a sound understanding of the child's world.

Early means of studying the child were somewhat crude. One of these was the **child biography,** which involved questionnaires and the systematic recording of child behavior. Early researchers of note included **Ivan Pavlov,** who helped launch the scientific study of behavior; **Alfred Binet,** who developed an important method of testing intelligence; and **John B. Watson,** who rejected subjective reports in favor of objective evidence. **Sigmund Freud's** contribution to child study included **psychoanalysis,** a prolonged series of sessions involving dream reports, and **free association,** or the report of whatever came into the patient's mind. The results of psychoanalysis focused attention on childhood as a critical period. Other giants were **Edward Thorndike** and **John Dewey,** who stressed children's individual differences in the context of education, and **Jean Piaget,** whose imaginative methods breathed new life into child study, and whose influence is very prominent today.

Across the years, concepts of children have varied greatly. The **recapitulation theory** viewed children as recapitulating the history of the race in their development. The infant's grasping reflex, for example, was proof of his descendence from monkeys. Other outdated theories now relegated to history's closet are the doctrines of **innate sin,** which portrayed the child as a born sinner, and the theory of the child as a miniature adult. Freud's theories have remained somewhat more viable, though often modified and interwoven with more recent theories. Another theory, **cultural determinism,** was popularized by anthropologists. This theory, that culture shapes what the child becomes, also remains alive with modifications. Nowadays most psychologists see the

23

child as the complex emergent of both genetic and environmental forces.

The years have also seen drastic changes in child care, with eras of permissiveness alternating with years of restriction. In this century, rigid control, as preached by the **behaviorists,** has been followed by the psychoanalysts' permissiveness, and lately by an ambivalent combination of permissiveness and responsibility.

Among the most fruitful methods of child study today is the **longitudinal approach,** which involves studying the same individuals over a period of months or years. This approach often embraces many techniques, including interviews, testing, and experiments of all kinds. In general, it demonstrates the relative permanence of traits and the multiple influences on the child, and shows how various strands of behavior interrelate; but it is very expensive and difficult to carry out. A related method is the **case history,** which consists of compiling all data about the child that may be relevant to his current problem. Both the longitudinal method and the case history may involve personal interviews of parents, especially the mother. But unless built around standardized procedures, such interviews may result in highly biased reports.

Another technique is observation, in which a trained observer records children's behaviors either in natural or in specially arranged situations. For the latter, special observation rooms and chambers have been designed. A related technique, the **experimental method,** involves repetition, to permit verification of results, and control, which suggests holding certain factors constant while allowing others to change, in order to determine their effect.

Other techniques are the **standardized test** and the **projective technique.** In standardized tests, individuals are evaluated against norms derived from pretesting representative groups of children. Projective techniques are also standardized; they are designed to get at an individual's characteristics by analyzing his responses to relatively unstructured, ambiguous situations. Among the better-known projective techniques for use with children are the **Bellak Apperception Test,** consisting of pictures of animal characters; the **Blacky Pictures,** which are cartoons depicting adventures of a dog, the **Madeleine Thomas Test,** involving stories or items representing samples of everyday activities and problems, and the **Bühler World Test,** consisting of miniature objects of the outdoor world. Doll play, too, provides projective miniature-life situations.

Any of the foregoing techniques may proceed either inside or outside the laboratory. **Laboratory approach** simply indicates that the study is carried out in a situation especially designed for scientific research. Its chief advantage is that greater control over relevant variables is possible than in the natural setting. A more naturalistic approach is illustrated in **sociocultural studies,** which may be either **intra-cultural** or **cross-cultural.** Among intra-cultural studies, those of primitive societies have been common. Cross-cultural studies make comparisons of two or more cultural groupings.

Among the common shortcomings in child-study research are the experimenter's bias, the hazard to the child, and the limitations on topics that may be studied. Actually, every type of method and technique employed in child study has its weaknesses, and so does every type of research report. Sometimes certain topics, such as emotions, are ignored, and the subjects used may be far from representative. There are also statistical problems — of **reliability, validity,** and appropriateness of technique. Other hurdles are the interpretation of data and the manner of reporting to be used. Fortunately, a combination of research grants, increasingly well-trained researchers, and the availability of computers is making possible giant strides in child study. Hopefully, gaps in research will be closed and plans for continuing study devised to keep every important phase of child study constantly updated.

• SUGGESTED QUESTIONS AND ACTIVITIES

1. Watch children in any situation and report whatever interests you about their behavior. What questions do their activities raise? Do these children behave any differently from the way children behaved when you were their age?
2. Make a case study, to be turned in near the end of the course, of some child you know well or, if you prefer, of yourself at a particular age of childhood. The individual chosen should be discussed in terms of each aspect of development treated in this and succeeding chapters. If the instructor distributes an outline of points to be included, he may choose to make it suggestive rather than prescriptive. Better still, the class can draw up a suggested outline under the guidance of the instructor.
3. Read current stories or books, or watch television programs, and analyze the portrayal of children. What seems to be the child's role in modern society?
4. Cut out advertisements and cartoons, and from them derive the differential characteristics currently ascribed to children, teen-agers, and adults.
5. Clip or copy, from both old and recent newspapers or periodicals, articles advising parents about child-rearing. Analyze the concepts involved and the changes that have taken place.
6. Invite someone to come to class who has conducted child research, and discuss with him the methods and problems involved.
7. Do you believe that research reports of what children are currently like have the effect of portraying whatever they do as "normal," thus retarding objective efforts to discover what children should or could be like? In other words, is there a tendency to confuse the currently typical with the ideal, thus obstructing constructive change?
8. Since a great deal of research about children has been poor, how can students know that the reports they read have any worth?
9. Should the United Nations pay teams of researchers to conduct studies of children in widely differing cultures? What special problems might be involved?
10. Much child study of the early 1900s seems naïve today. Will today's research seem equally naïve to future generations?
11. Is there a danger of making guinea pigs of children while conducting research on their behavior? What safeguards should be used?
12. What benefits or ills might result from federal subsidization of child research?

• SUGGESTED READINGS

Aries, P. (trans. by R. Baldick), *Centuries of Childhood.* New York: Alfred A. Knopf, Inc., 1962. This social history of the family shows how the idea of family and the idea of childhood developed and interrelate. The book provides an excellent background for current child study. For historical backgrounds of education, in terms of child life, see Part II, "Scholastic Life."

Baldwin, A. L., *Theories of Child Development.* New York: John Wiley & Sons, Inc., 1967. A survey of seven major theories of child development, a review of social-learning theory, and a chapter on common-sense psychology.

Frank, L. K., "The Beginnings of Child Development and Family-Life Education in the Twentieth Century," *Merrill-Palmer Quarterly,* Vol. 8, No. 4 (October 1962), pp. 207–227. An excellent historical overview indicating individuals and institutions that contributed significantly to the beginnings and progress of developmental psychology and outlining changes in major emphases across the years.

Kessen, W., *The Child.* New York: John Wiley & Sons, Inc., 1965. Papers written between 1942 and 1963 by such important persons as Rousseau, Darwin, Watson, Freud, and Piaget.

Maier, W. H., *Three Theories of Child Development.* New York: Harper & Row, Publishers, Inc., 1965. Describes the theories of Erik H. Erikson, Jean Piaget, and R. R. Sears.

Mussen, P. H., ed., *Handbook of Research Methods in Child Development.* New York: John Wiley & Sons, Inc., 1960. Includes papers that review research on various aspects of research method.

Palmer, C. D., "Child Development Articles in Popular Periodicals," *Merrill-Palmer Quarterly,* Vol. 6, No. 1 (Fall 1959), pp. 52–57. Compares 147 articles published in 10 popular monthly magazines with similar content on the same topics in seven "approved" child psychology books. While there was considerable agreement, the articles were prone to contain broad generalizations and vague statements.

CHAPTER ONE Smith, M. B., "Conflicting values affecting behavioral research with children," *Children,* Vol. 14, No. 5 (1967), pp. 377–382. The author discusses various ethical issues involved in conducting research on children's behavior; he quotes from the ethics code of the American Psychological Association and suggests certain additions. Instead of thinking in terms of what is permissible, he believes we should adopt the attitude of treating human subjects with genuine respect.

Solnit, A. J., and S. A. Provence, eds., *Modern Perspectives in Child Development.* New York: International Universities Press, 1963. The major portion of the book treats child development in various aspects—biological, psychological, psychosomatic, psychiatric, and educational—all being related to the practice and study of pediatrics today.

2
HUMAN BEGINNINGS

Throughout history, superstitions have existed about heredity and prenatal development. Deformities such as cleft palate, cleft lip, and idiocy were believed to be inherited, mostly from the maternal side of the family. Other abnormalities were attributed to the mother's bad blood flowing through the veins of the unborn child. Birthmarks were thought to result from some mystical relationship between mother and fetus. An incident related by Anatole France illustrates this sort of belief:

> Madame Morin informed the company that I had a red spot on the left hip due to a longing for cherries which had come upon my mother in Aunt Chausson's garden before I was born. Whereat old Dr. Fournier, who had a great contempt for all such popular superstitions, remarked that it was lucky Madame Noziere had kept her desires within such limits during the period of gestation, since, if she had allowed herself to hanker after feathers, trinkets, a cashmere shawl, a coach and four, a town house, a country mansion and a parakeet, there wouldn't have been skin enough on the whole of my poor body to hold the record of such inordinate ambitions [France, 1925, p. 12].

Such beliefs about birthmarks are clearly fallacious. First, similar markings are found in the lower animals, where it is improbable that maternal impressions exist. Second, there is no direct connection between mother and fetus; the mother's and child's blood do not mingle. Instead, oxygen, water, and nutrients are absorbed into the blood-

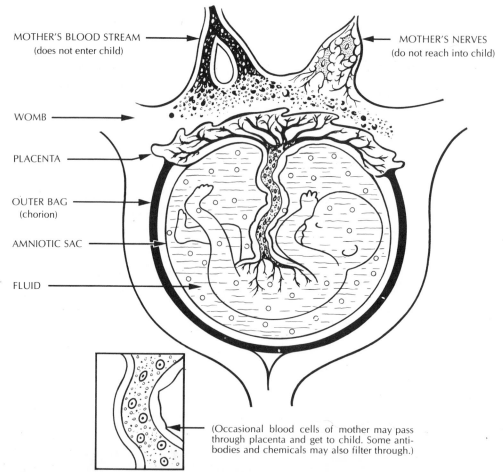

MOTHER'S BLOOD STREAM (does not enter child)

MOTHER'S NERVES (do not reach into child)

WOMB

PLACENTA

OUTER BAG (chorion)

AMNIOTIC SAC

FLUID

(Occasional blood cells of mother may pass through placenta and get to child. Some antibodies and chemicals may also filter through.)

28 The relationship of mother and child. From A. Scheinfeld, *Your heredity and environment*. Philadelphia: Lippincott, 1965. P. 34. Reproduced by permission.

stream through a sieve-like structure, the placenta, which is attached to the wall of the mother's uterus and connected to the baby's body by the umbilical cord. On the other hand, it is wrong to assume that there is no connection between the nervous systems of mother and fetus. Nervous changes in the mother affect the fetus through the neurohumoral system, which comprises the interrelated nervous and endocrine systems acting through the fluid medium of the blood. The endocrine systems of mother and child complement each other, and their common endocrine pool forms a neurohumoral bond. What are transmitted, however, are not maternal impressions, or psychological states as such, but gross chemical changes (Montagu, 1950, p. 152).

• THE PRENATAL PERIOD

To understand the development of the child, we must begin at the beginning, with a somewhat detailed discussion of fertilization, heredity, and the prenatal environment.

Fertilization

Fertilization occurs if one of some 20 million **sperm** released by the male during intercourse meets the **ovum** high in the **Fallopian tube.** Many sperm work their way through the zona pellucida, or slick membrane that surrounds the egg, but only one actually fertilizes the egg—apparently the one that reaches the nucleus of the ovum first. At this instant, much of a human's life is determined, for the chromosomes thus gained from father and mother dictate to some extent what kind of person he will become. Henceforth the pattern has been set for various traits, including eye color, facial configuration, complexion, and general body shape.

The influence of one's parents will be approximately equal, for a child inherits 23 **chromosomes** from his father and 23 from his mother, including one sex chromosome from each. Of course the new individual's parents obtained

half their chromosomes from each of their parents; therefore, the chances are one in four of duplicating any specific chromosome of a particular grandparent. Similarly, the chances are one in eight that one may inherit chromosomes from a particular great-grandparent, and so on.

Nature's Prenatal Timetable

The prenatal period is divided into three stages: the ovum stage, or the period from fertilization until the end of the second week; the embryo stage, or the period from the third week through the second month; and the fetal stage, or the period from then until birth.

The first month. Now let us follow the newcomer's timetable more precisely, beginning with the ovum stage. During this period, the fertilized egg remains practically unchanged in size because it lives off its own yolk, receiving little or no outside nourishment. About a week is required for the fertilized egg, now a hollow cluster of over a hundred cells, to traverse the Fallopian tube and become implanted in the uterine wall. Henceforth it is a parasite, obtaining nourishment from the mother.

By the end of the first month, three layers of cells have formed: the *ectoderm,* from which sense organs and nervous system will develop; the *mesoderm,* from which emerge circulatory, skeletal, and muscular systems; and the *endoderm,* which ultimately forms the digestive and glandular systems. Special cells in the uterus become the **placenta,** the sieve-like structure by means of which nutritive substances will be carried to the developing organism and wastes removed.

Meanwhile, a special layer of cells forms the *amnion,* or water sac, which will enclose the developing embryo except at the umbilical cord. Organs begin to take shape. By the end of the first month, the embryo is a quarter of an inch long and crescent-shaped, with small bumps on its sides indicating **29**

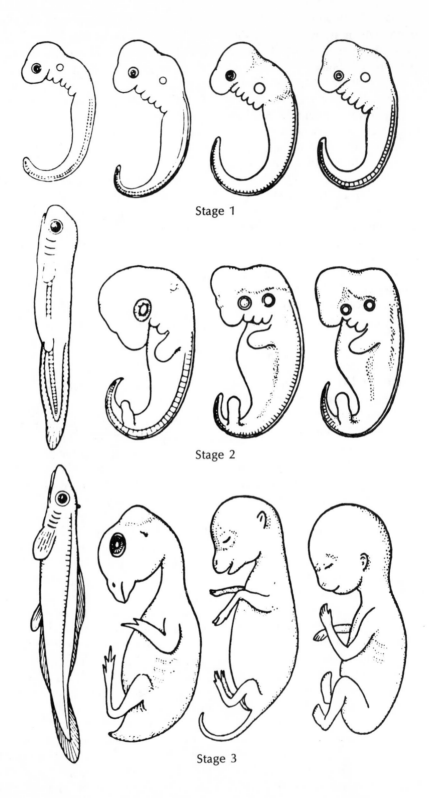

Stage 1

Stage 2

Stage 3

Fish   Chick   Calf   Man

30 Similarities in structure in various embryos at three comparable and progressive stages of development. From G. J. Romanes, *Darwin and after Darwin, I: The Darwinian theory*. Chicago: Open Court, 1896.

future arms and legs. The tiny creature also has a tail and tiny ridges along the neck resembling gills of the embryonic fish. For years Darwinians submitted this finding as proof of man's recapitulation, during gestation, of human evolution—from fish, to reptile, to mammal. Actually, the ridges are tissue folds that become thymus and thyroid glands, face and ears. The tail soon becomes encased in the rest of the body, forming the coccyx, or tip of the spine.

The second month. During this month, the embryo grows to about one and a half inches in length. Face, neck, fingers, and toes develop, giving the embryo a vaguely human appearance. Limb buds lengthen, muscles enlarge, and sex organs begin to form. The forehead is conspicuous, reflecting the early development of the brain.

The third month. This month introduces the fetal period, which extends from now until delivery. Sexual differentiation continues, with the male sex organs proceeding rapidly and the female organs remaining somewhat neutral. Buds for the teeth emerge; vocal cords appear; and stomach and kidneys begin to function.

The fourth month. About now the lower parts of the body accelerate in growth, and the fetus makes movements easily perceived by the mother.

The fifth month. Skin derivatives appear, including hair and nails. The fetus, which now weighs about a pound, becomes increasingly mobile. After this month, a sharp emotional shock to the mother may affect it in subtle ways.

The sixth month. Next, the eyelids, fused since the third month, reopen; taste buds appear; and eyes are completed. If born now, the fetus will live a few hours, or even longer if in an incubator.

The seventh month. Now the fetus resembles a very old person with red wrinkled skin. It is active at times, while resting at others. Reflex patterns involved in turning trunk and head are fully developed. The fetus may extend its arms when touched, or even grasp objects with the palm of its hand. If delivered at this stage, the baby cries when in discomfort or sucks when an object touches its mouth.

The eighth and ninth months. Finishing touches complete the fetus, which is outgrowing its home. Fat becomes evenly distributed over the body, and the red skin color fades, so that at birth pigmentation is usually very slight in all races. The fetus is very active, sometimes changing position, seeming to make clear its readiness to emerge (Gilbert, 1938).

The "Home" of the Embryo

Now let us retrogress, to obtain a better picture of the private world of the embryo and fetus. The fetus lives in a warm, dark chamber, immersed in fluid, and provided by the placenta with continuous room service. It is protected

The embryo lives in a private world.

from lights, blows, and sounds. Certain structures make up its small world, forming the accessory apparatus that provides nourishment and protection until the baby is born. Where the fertilized ovum embeds itself in the uterine wall, the placenta develops—a solid, somewhat pie-shaped mass. It may be likened to the trunks and roots of a tree, furnishing food to the fetus through blood vessels that extend through the umbilical cord. Through semipermeable membranes that form the walls of the fetal blood vessels, nourishment and oxygen pass from placenta to fetus, and waste returns to the mother's blood. The umbilical cord, which links embryo and placenta, is attached to the embryo's abdomen at one end and the placenta at the other. The cord grows to the thickness of a man's thumb, and measures 10 to 20 inches in length. Another structure, the amniotic sac, is a water jacket that protects the embryo from injury.

Maternal blood flows from arteries in the uterine wall into the placenta, while oxygen, water, and food reach the embryo through the umbilical cord. There is no direct connection between maternal and fetal bloodstreams. Instead, certain elements from the mother's blood pass from the placenta into the cord and thence to the embryo.

• BIRTH

In due time, however, this idyllic, sheltered existence is rudely terminated by birth, which in healthy babies is heralded by a loud wail, or cry. Kant believed that this outcry reflected the newborn's wrath at his inability to move. Adler interpreted the cry as the infant's feeling of helplessness at being so suddenly projected into a new and complex environment. A more prosaic explanation—but the only defensible one—is that this cry is the infant's response to air entering his lungs for the first time.

Otto Rank (1929) represented not only the birth cry but the whole birth process as a highly traumatic experience. The helpless infant, a squirming assortment of cells, must henceforth forage for his food, breathe to obtain oxygen, and adjust to changes in temperature. Rank's disciples theorized that grownups, buffeted by the world, often long to regress to the womb; the fetal position sometimes assumed in sleep is seen to represent the harassed adult's need to return. However, in view of the newborn's undeveloped brain, it is highly doubtful that he can experience any emotion clearly enough for it to have a lasting effect. Birth is indeed a physical shock, though, which may modify structures and thus possibly shift inherent developmental tendencies. In all the rest of the child's life, there will never be so sudden and complete a change in his locale; nor will any other journey ever start from so profound a seclusion. It is a brutal process, asserts Schwartz (1956), that endangers the life and health of the child.

A serious danger in the birth process is injury to the brain, resulting either from compression or from anoxia, an insufficiency of oxygen. Most infants are stunned for a day or two, because of compression of the brain in the birth canal, but sustain no permanent damage. However, when birth is long and difficult, the pressure on the brain is correspondingly increased, sometimes causing hemorrhages. Prematurely born infants, whose skulls are not well-formed, are especially susceptible. A more common cause of damage than pressure is anoxia, or deprivation of oxygen. Its causes may include delay in infant breathing after the umbilical cord is severed; breech birth, which may cut off oxygen until the head emerges; premature separation of the placenta, leaving the fetus without an oxygen supply; circulatory abnormalities, which rupture the fetal supply of nutrition and oxygen; and, in some cases, the use of anesthetics (Graham et al., 1962).

The effects of anoxia may be tragic. A total lack of oxygen will kill brain cells in 18 seconds and cause other damage in even less time. Children who survive a brief deprivation of oxygen may suffer intellectual deficiency, apathy, and motor retardation. In one study of 40,000 births, infants who had suffered anoxia manifested eight times the normal rate of feeble-mindedness (Benaron, 1960).

Each type of birth has its special hazard. According to data from longitudinal studies, instrument births are related to hyperactivity, poor coordination, and irritability, but not necessarily to intelligence. Even spontaneous births, if unduly prolonged, may involve asphyxia and consequent degeneration of brain cells. Fast labor, on the other hand, of less than two hours' duration, may introduce the infant to oxygen too suddenly.

Prematurely born infants, defined as weighing less than $5\frac{1}{2}$ pounds at birth, face even greater possibility of damage than full-term infants. At least 25% of those weighing under $3\frac{1}{2}$ pounds die, and those who live often suffer abnormalities. The biggest cause of "premie" fatalities is hyaline membrane disease (HMD). A tough protein membrane forms in the air sacs of the lung, preventing the passage of oxygen into the baby's blood or carbon dioxide from it. If the baby can be kept alive for about three days, the membranes disappear and the infant recovers. Presently, the only effective treatment is insertion of a breathing tube into the premie's windpipe to keep the lungs inflated.

By now you are probably wondering how you managed to survive your own birth. Actually, infants show a remarkable capacity for survival, even when born under trying circumstances. For example, healthy babies are born to lower-class Georgia women who eat clay to give their children lighter complexions. More often than not, babies manage to survive when delivered in taxicabs or hallways, or with a policeman acting as midwife.

A major reason for infant vitality is nature's rejection of faulty products long before they reach completion. For this reason, many authorities cast a jaundiced eye at elaborate efforts to retain fetuses that threaten to abort. Among these fetuses a high proportion, if permitted to live, would have malformations. Besides, the drugs used to prevent abortion, including certain steroid hormones, may masculinize girls or feminize boys in utero.

Perhaps science will in time reduce the threat of birth trauma. In his *Brave New World*, Huxley envisioned a process by which children would develop in demijohns instead of uteri; would have blood pumped mechanically through a synthetic lung; and, after being exposed to a sequence of carefully regulated conditions, would be projected into the world with a minimum of trauma.

In order to appreciate progress already made, however, note this advice written in the fifteenth century on the care of the newborn:

> When the infant, at the command of God, emerges from the womb, then the midwife with eager and gentle hand should wrap it up in a linen cloth which is not rough, but rather smooth and old, and place it on her lap, noting whether the infant be alive or not or spotted, i.e., whether black or white or of bluish color and whether it is breathing or not. If she finds it warm, not black, she should blow into its mouth, if it has no respiration, or into its anus; but if, as sometimes happens, the anus is closed by a little skin, she should cut it with a sharp knife or hot gold thread or some similar instrument [Paulus Bagellardus, in Rührah, p. 34].

• GENETIC BASES OF CHARACTERISTICS

The Determination of Traits

Genes may account for both the determination of specific human traits and for the infinite variation in traits. Note Sanford's lucid description:

> When one of 8,000,000 combinations of **chromosomes** in the sperm gets together with one of the 8,000,000 possible combinations in the ovum, the resulting event has a very great rarity about it. Theoretically, any two parents have a pool of about 150 trillion trait combinations, differing in some measure from each other in their inherited pattern of chromosomes. This figure becomes even greater when we recognize that the **genes,** the basic determiners of heredity, do not always stay put in the chromosomes that carry them. Chromosomes may exchange genes. If genes cross over from one chromosome to another in a sperm cell, or in an egg cell, the potential variation in heredity is even more enormously increased. This kind of computation underscores the individuality of the single human organism. When he is born, unless he has an identical twin,

33

there has probably never been another organism exactly like him. It can safely be said, for example, that the events transpiring when any student reads these paragraphs are unique in history; for not only has there never been an organism quite like him but, by the time he can read, he has lived through a unique pattern of life events [Sanford, 1965, p. 65].

To show how heredity operates to determine specific traits, Sanford explains the genetic bases of eye color:

Each pair of chromosomes contains parts, called *genes,* that are responsible for particular traits. It is believed that the pair of genes responsible for eye color lie in a specific pair of chromosomes; and each gene is located normally at a corresponding position in its respective chromosome. Each chromosome pair in any particular germ cell may possess similar genes (both bearing, for example, brown-eyed determiners or blue-eyed determiners); or the chromosome may carry opposing genes (the one bearing brown- and the other blue-eyed determiners). In the cell division involved in the maturation of the germ cell, the paired genes separate, so that only one of any pair of genes is retained in the mature germ cell, and passed on to the zygote.

Furthermore, these traits are classified as dominant or recessive; since brown eye color is dominant and blue eye color is recessive, an individual who receives a gene for brown eyes from one parent and a gene for blue eyes from the other parent will have brown eyes. If both parents have only brown-eye genes, the progeny will have only brown eyes; or if the parents have only genes for blue eyes, their offspring will all have blue eyes. But if each parent carries both brown-eye and blue-eye genes, the possible results are more varied. . . .

These statistical computations do not mean, however, that we can predict with any certainty just what will be the precise characteristics of the new individual. Theoretically, the 23 chromosomes coming from his father could occur in any one of 8,388,608 different combinations. Any father, then, has more than 8,000,000 different combinations of characteristics to pass along to his children. The same situation exists, of course, for the mother [Sanford, pp. 64–65].

Except for some rare exceptions, the new organism receives from each parent, at the instant of conception, 46 chromosomes—including 44 **autosomes,** and the sex chromosomes XX or XY. In turn, each chromosome contains about 10,000 pairs of genes.

The Genetics of Sex

Sex determination. Throughout time, couples have been interested in the sex of their unborn children and for centuries they believed the mother's thoughts related to its becoming a boy or girl. In the seventeenth century, the physician Claude Quillet advised mothers how they might determine the sex of the child:

Ye Pregnant Wives, whose Wish it is
  and Care,
To bring your Issue, and to breed it
  Fair,
On what you look, on what you think,
  beware.
A Boy your Wish, a beauteous Boy
  behold,
With Lips a Cherry red, and locks of
  Gold;
If Female Fruit you rather covet, view,
A Heav'nly Venus such as Titian
  drew.

A child's sex is now known to be determined as follows: Of the 23 pairs of human chromosomes, 22 are alike for both sexes—that is, any one pair could as readily be found in either sex. However, in the twenty-third pair, a woman has two X chromosomes, and the man an X chromosome and a much smaller Y chromosome, a "Mutt and Jeff" combination. We have already noted that the fertilized egg, or zygote, contains just half the respective parent's quota of chromosomes, or one from every chromosome pair. Therefore, the zygote automatically obtains an X chromosome from the mother, because her sex cells contain the XX combination. But when the male's unevenly matched pair of sex chromosomes separate, an X goes into one sperm, a Y into the other. Thus the ovum fertilized by an X-bearing sperm from the father now contains an XX combination and is a female. If a sperm

TWO HOMELY PARENTS MAY HAVE A BEAUTIFUL CHILD

Father: bald; murky-green eyes; lashes lost through disease; misshapen mouth due to bad teeth; bad nose due to accident.

Mother: dull, dark, straight hair; dull-brown eyes; drooping eyelids; bad skin (local disorder); protruding underlip.

But they may carry and pass on to their child hidden genes for blond, curly hair; blue eyes; long lashes; pretty nose; cupid's-bow mouth; lovely complexion. Result: a beauty contest winner.

TWO HANDSOME PARENTS MAY HAVE A HOMELY CHILD

Father: curly, black hair; large, dark eyes; long lashes; well-shaped mouth and chin.

Mother: wavy, blond hair; blue eyes; long lashes; regular teeth; pretty mouth.

But they may carry and pass on to their child hidden genes for dull-brown, straight hair; murky-green, small eyes; short lashes; protruding jaw and teeth; other irregularities, added to by environmental factors. Result: an ugly duckling.

Adapted from A. Scheinfeld, *Your heredity and environment.* Philadelphia: Lippincott, 1965. P. 129.

35

bears the Y-chromosome, the zygote now contains an XY combination, and becomes a male. It is sometimes theorized that more boy than girl babies are conceived because the Y-bearing sperms are smaller and lighter, therefore more mobile and likely to arrive at the ovum first (Scheinfeld, 1965).

Sex prediction. It is quite another matter to predict with certainty the sex of an unborn child, though attempts have been made throughout history to do so. Among primitives, a waning moon meant a girl would be born; a full moon, the more favorable sign, meant a boy. More recently, a coin tossed over the shoulder that fell heads-up foretold a boy, tails-up a girl. A heartbeat test revealing 125 fetal heartbeats or less predicted a boy; 144 or more foretold a girl. However, individual variations make such tests inaccurate.

A smear test, to determine the amount of estrogenic (female) or androgenic (male) hormones present, is more successful but also fallible. A certain chemical substance when found in the mother's saliva is somehow related to male sex hormone, but without high predictive value (Rapp and Richardson, 1952). Another method is the chromosomal count made possible by puncture of the amniotic sac.

The Number of Offspring

Whether a single pregnancy will involve one or more children is always of special interest. A child is referred to as a singleton if he is born alone, his birth typically separated by a period of about nine months from that of siblings. Multiple births include the arrival of two or more babies within minutes, hours, or days. According to estimates, twins occur once in 87 births; triplets, once in 7,000; quadruplets, once in 550,000; and quintuplets, once in 57 million (Stocks, 1952). Only six cases of sextuplets have been recorded, and none has long survived.

Twins are of two types: *fraternal* and *identical.* At the time of the first division of the cell, the new cell may split for some unknown reason. The twins thus formed are called *identical* and possess the same combination of genes. They possess the closest degree of kinship possible for distinct individuals, and they are always of the same sex. If the division of this cell is incomplete, Siamese twins may result. *Nonidentical* or *fraternal* twins result from the simultaneous fertilization of two ova. Each of the pair has its own set of chromosomes, no more alike than those found in ordinary siblings. Fraternal twins may be either of the same or of the opposite sex.

The Nature of Genes and Chromosomes

DNA and RNA: the essence of life. As noted already, the chromosomes of the father's sperm and the mother's egg combine during the first hour after fertilization to form a new cell, the core of a future destiny. Every one of these fertilized cells, or zygotes, consists of a combination of a sperm from the father and an ovum from the mother, which in turn are composed of chromosomes. Chromosomes, then—and their own components, the genes—are the building blocks of every living individual. The thread-like chromosomes are no more than 7 microns ($7/_{1000}$ millimeter) long, but they carry more than 30,000 genes, which are made of **DNA** (deoxyribonucleic acid) and **RNA** (ribonucleic acid), the two chemicals that are the very essence of life. These chemicals, or nucleic acids, constitute the basis of every living thing, from one-celled creatures to humans.

DNA determines whether the substance that makes eyes blue or brown will be produced. In various degrees, it also affects physique, voice timbre, and even language or mathematical facility. And it determines, to some extent, one's chances of suffering from chromosome diseases, which will be discussed later. DNA is believed to be the chemical blueprint for the cell;

locked within its molecular arrangement are patterns for all body parts, from toenails to lungs. DNA is at times portrayed as a grim judge pronouncing life sentence; at others, simply as a dispenser of potential.

The basic structure of DNA is a twisted ladder, perceived only vaguely under the most powerful electron microscope. Researchers believe the molecules forming this ladder are arranged in an intricate sequence that acts as a code for controlling protein production. The other basic nucleic acid, **RNA,** is believed to transport the protein blueprints from the DNA in the nucleus of the chromosome to points outside the nucleus where protein is made.

Cracking the genetic code. Scientists are now attempting to crack the genetic code—that is, to read the messages in DNA and RNA, and to determine which segment is a blueprint for each different protein. When the deciphering is complete, the possibilities of exploring the fundamental processes of life will be limitless.

Once scientists understand the genetic code, they may be able to duplicate protein-making in the laboratory. Partially synthetic forms of DNA and RNA have been made already. Therefore, one wonders if it will be possible someday to create living cells from nonliving chemicals. A more immediate goal may be disease-prevention, through the correction of errors in the DNA blueprint. It is believed that such errors are caused by viruses, which enter the cells and alter the DNA "program," thereby killing the cells. Perhaps, it is theorized, these errors may be corrected by chemicals, radiation, or the controlled use of viruses. Of course the ultimate goal is to prevent the hereditary defect itself.

Mutations. Generally, DNA ensures the replacement of each cell by a duplicate of itself; but sometimes an abrupt change occurs in the gene so that henceforth it is reproduced in a new form, or **mutation.** Every one of the thousands of genes an individual inherits possesses a tiny probability for change in his generation. For example, it is estimated that one sex cell in 50,000 produced by normal persons carries a new mutant gene that causes retinoblastoma, a cancer of the eye affecting children. Such mutations are termed spontaneous, since they occur in people not exposed to special **mutagens,** or agents that artificially induce mutation, such as X-ray or ionizing radiation. Since mutations account for changes in the gene itself, they play an important role in man's evolution (Dobzhansky, 1960).

Prenatal defects due to defective chromosomes. Defects involving genes and chromosomes account for almost one-fifth of birth defects. Each chromosome disease characteristically involves one of the 23 pairs of chromosomes. For example, the extra chromosome that causes mongolism is attached to pair number 21 or 22 (*Newsweek,* October 25, 1965, p. 68). In brief, the trouble arises like this: Most humans possess a normal complement of 46 chromosomes in each cell, half of them from each parent. But mongoloids have either 47 chromosomes or 46, the latter figure including one abnormally large chromosome. In either case, the excess genetic material harms rather than helps. Perhaps—though no one knows—overproduction of certain key chemical substances (enzymes) throws the body's carefully regulated growth process out of kilter (Bishop and Davis, 1966).

Chromosomal irregularities may result in both defective body structure and mental disorders. For example, Turner's syndrome is characterized by short stature, webbing of the neck, and sexual infantilism. Still other disorders, even cancer, possibly stem from chromosomal alterations caused by radiation exposure or by virus infections such as measles. Some researchers posit a chromosomal factor in the later development of schizophrenia, but so far they

What part does heredity play in a family of musicians?

have demonstrated no clear cause-effect relationship. About a dozen disorders, all told, have so far been diagnosed as due to enlarged, extra, or missing chromosomes.

Preventing chromosomal defects. Chromosomal disorders, it has been concluded, result from defects in particular genes. Each gene among the thousands within a chromosome is believed to direct the synthesis of a special enzyme, or chemical catalyst, required for normal growth. Researchers are just beginning to map the location of these genes on the chromosome, sometimes by tracing the occurrence of specific diseases in the general population. So far, progress in mapping genes has been painfully slow; once this mapping is accomplished, however, the chances of inheriting any specific disease will be predictable with considerable accuracy. Some scientists even suggest replacing defective genes with synthesized substitutes, but this prospect seems very distant (Bishop and Davis, 1966).

• HEREDITY'S ROLE IN DEVELOPMENT

Heredity versus Environment

Many persons, including some psychologists, have an abiding faith in the capacity of environment to compensate for genetic shortcomings. Others espouse the cause of genetics with a zeal worthy of a breeder of champion cattle. These polar views are implicit in certain old sayings. Some of them subtly stress the impact of heredity: "Blood will tell." "A leopard can't change his spots." "You can't make a silk purse out of a sow's ear." Others suggest the power of environmental factors: "He's a victim of circumstance." "One bad apple can spoil the barrel." "As the twig is bent, the tree's inclined."

The environmentalist position. Psychologists, especially in the second quarter of this century, hotly debated the relative significance of hereditary and environmental factors in development. Can environment turn any kind of human protoplasm into a prodigy? Or is one the puppet of his ancestral genes? The following statement, made by the famous behaviorist John B. Watson, is a classic in this controversy:

> Give me a dozen healthy infants, well-formed, and my own specified world to bring them up in, and I'll guarantee to take any one at random and train him to become any type of specialist I might select—doctor, lawyer, artist, merchant, chief, and yes, even beggarman and thief—regardless of his talents, penchants, tendencies, abilities, vocations, and race of his ancestors [Colley, 1902].

Environmentalists make much of the differences between man and the lower forms of life. Animals, they assert, are the victims of inborn instincts, but man can shape his own destiny. Let us note the difference. With no experience in nestbuilding, and never having seen another swallow in its life, a swallow builds a nest exactly like those that swallows have built since swallows existed. Similarly, the trapdoor spider builds his home in ways dictated by his nervous system. But humans have fewer of the hereditary trappings that would confine them to stereotyped responses. They are free to learn and to adopt infinitely varied ways of behaving. Any kind of human protoplasm, assert the extremists of this view, can be molded in infinite ways.

The hereditarian position. Other scientists, however, stress heredity's role in human behavior. Each organism, they assert, contains within itself its own patterns and the general outlines of its future. Every organism stubbornly insists on being itself.

Considerable research supports the hereditarian's position. In longitudinal studies, writes Jean Macfarlane (1952), we have seen many children with the cards stacked against them who should, by any ordinary prediction, have become delinquent or psychotic; however, they not only did not, but turned into "substantial, mature, and zestful adults." Apparently, she concluded, there is a

tough "essence" that resists environmental pressures. In effect, some children wag their fingers at fate and stubbornly determine their own destinies. In view of such evidence as the foregoing, Hirsch (1963) makes this decisive statement: "After two generations of 'excommunication,' the concept of heredity needs full restoration to respectability in the behavioral sciences." Nevertheless, few persons nowadays subscribe to a full-blown genetic determinism, which implies that heredity provides the script which the individual merely acts out.

Heredity's role in physical traits and conditions. To continue our study of the relative importance of heredity and environment, let us now consider the probable contribution of heredity to a variety of human traits and functions. In so doing, we shall often look at studies of identical twins, because, since gene patterns of identical twins are the same, any variations found in them may be considered the product of differences in their environments.

First, let us consider physical traits. The human zygote contains a rough blueprint for an individual's future physical traits, some of them modifiable to varying degrees. Some traits—eye color, hair color and texture, the number of fingers and toes, and hundreds of other physical and anatomical details—are firmly set by heredity. Other physical characteristics, such as height and aging effects, may be environmentally modified, but to a still unknown extent. In any case, by determining or even substantially modifying such traits, heredity inevitably plays a large though indirect role in one's life. The 6 foot tall boy may attain the popularity and success in high school forever denied the undersized youth.

Heredity also plays a part in certain physical disorders. Some cases of diabetes are caused by defective genes, and incidences of peptic ulcer and cancer of the stomach, colon, and rectum are related to blood groups that in turn are hereditary (Boyd, 1963). However, not all diseases that run in families have genetic bases—for example, the vitamin deficiency beri-beri. What appears to be "inherited" is actually a preference for vitamin-poor foods, which is learned from one's parents.

Heredity's role in major mental disorders. Heredity's role in mental disorders is more confusing. In one study, certain mental disorders were found to occur in one of each of five pairs of identical twins—an impossibility if the twins were actually identical and if mental illness were directly caused by germ plasm (Hobbs, 1941). Such findings raise doubts about whether most mental disorders follow a simple dominant or recessive genetic pattern. The only neuropsychiatric disorders that appear conclusively to be hereditary are **Huntington's chorea** (a chronic mental deterioration), certain other disorders of the central nervous system, and a few kinds of mental retardation.

Nevertheless, heredity's role in other mental disorders is not clear-cut. Kallman (1959) found that if one of a pair of identical twins developed schizophrenia, there was an 86% chance that the other would, too. On the other hand, if a fraternal twin developed schizophrenia, there was only a 14% chance that his twin would develop the disorder. Before concluding from this evidence that schizophrenia is inherited, one must remember the 14% who did not get the disorder, as well as the similar environment that most identicals share.

Heredity's role in neurosis. Heredity plays an even more subtle part in neurosis—mild functional personality disorder in which the patient does not ordinarily require hospitalization. Certainly an individual's constitutional energy level has a bearing on the way he discharges tension. Persons with high energy levels typically discharge tension through motor activity, whereas those with low energy levels are inclined toward ideomotor or fantasy discharge. Relevant here is the finding that

even in infants a mildly disturbing stimulus tends to produce either striped-muscle or visceral behavior, not both (Jones, 1930). Carrying this argument a step further, MacFarland and Huddleston (1936) point out that internalizing infants—those who react to stressful stimuli by developing circulatory, gastrointestinal, and other visceral symptoms—are often relatively free of overt behavior symptoms, while those inclined toward overt muscular discharge are often free of inner disturbance. Apparently, innate reaction tendencies predispose some to pathology but not others.

In one study of like-sex twins, the correlation of identical twins for "neuroticism" was .85, against .22 for like-sex fraternal twins (Eysenck and Press, 1951). Such data suggest the desirability of further inquiries in this area. Conclusions would be premature, however. As yet we have no clear-cut definitions of neuroticism and no methods of measuring it. Hence, conclusions about hereditary origins of neuroticism must be withheld until more extensive and definite evidence is acquired.

For the present, Coleman (1966) advises a retreat to the concept of inherited predisposition—the belief that inferior or mutant genes distort one of the body's biochemical systems, which in turn reduces one's resistance to various disorders. An individual thus "predisposed" is presumably more prone to mental illness than others, but his inherent weakness will remain undetected in more favorable life situations.

Heredity's role in mental ability. More evidence supports the role of heredity in mental ability than in neurosis. In one study of 20 pairs of infant twins, identicals were significantly more alike than fraternals in various mental and motor abilities (Freedman and Keller, 1963). Gamble (1952) believes that mental deficiency is caused by recessive genes. Heredity may operate somewhat differently in various types of retardation, however. Certain rare forms appear to be related directly to specific genetic combinations, but the more common types involve more general inheritance factors. Most cases apparently stem from an unfortunate combination of inferior genes rather than from specific dominant or recessive genes.

Heredity's role in personality. The picture of heredity's role grows still fuzzier where personality is involved. Jones (1955) declared that identical twins were little more alike than fraternals in personality traits. However, other research places Jones' conclusion in question. In one study of 68 pairs of like-sex twins, questions were asked involving demonstrated soberness versus enthusiasm, wishing to avoid people rather than desiring to be with others, and brooding about one's problems (Gottesman, 1960). A greater similarity was found between the answers of identical twins than between those of fraternal twins. These findings suggest the possibility of hereditary influence on personality traits.

In a study of rats, fearfulness, as measured by copious urination and defecation, was measured when rats were placed in an "open field" compartment, which usually elicits fear. Of the 145 original rats, the seven most emotional males were mated with the seven most emotional females. Similarly, the seven least emotional males were mated with the seven least emotional females. This type of inbreeding was continued for several generations; but the results were striking even in the first generation. The offspring of emotional animals were considerably more emotional than those of unemotional animals (Hall, 1938).

Among humans, a more limited but nevertheless substantial relationship has been demonstrated between heredity and the bodily states involved in emotion. Over a three-year period, the bodily states in emotion were measured in children aged six through 12. These states, known to be associated with emotion, included skin resistance, pulse and perspiration rates, and salivation. The correlations between identical twins proved consistently higher than those for siblings; these, in turn, were higher than those for unrelated individuals. It seemed clear that heredity plays a role in the bodily states concerned in emotion (Jost and Sontag, 1944, pp. 308–310).

Similarly, Eysenck (1956) found identical twins to be very much alike in autonomic reactivity and intelligence; in specific tests it looked almost as though the same person had been tested twice. Tests of other traits, such as introversion-extroversion, also seemed to show the influence of heredity, though to a lesser extent. Note that autonomic reactivity vitally affects an individual's "response style," dictating whether he will be energetic or sluggish, persistent or half-hearted.

Kallman (1952) goes so far as to suggest that genetic foundations of ego strength may be dominant over those for neuroticism and emotionality. However, Stagner notes that differences in both strength and motor coordination affect one's self-image. Furthermore, differences in glandular responsiveness lead some youngsters to perceive themselves as highly emotional and incapable of dealing with stress situations (Stagner, 1961). Thus the influence of heredity is often indirect.

Innate characteristics may also act on the environment in such a way as to modify the sort of stimulation received. For example, babies receive different kinds of information from the environment, depending on their activity levels. The active infant bumps, handles, chews, and tastes; the passive baby gets some of the same visual and auditory cues but not the tactual and proprioceptive inputs. Thus the active child develops percepts with strong kinesthetic components; these percepts will significantly affect his later perceptual style and even his self-image. Moreover, the active child will both stimulate and be stimulated by his parents, thus altering and being altered by his social milieu. The quiet child, on the other hand, will probably be predisposed to a dependency relationship and to the development of defense mechanisms such as withdrawal and fantasy.

Conclusions about heredity's role. To sum up, let us see what generalizations about the relation of heredity to human characteristics appear to be justified. First of all, heredity seems to make proportionately different contributions to various traits. It seems to play a greater role, for example, in physical traits, and a lesser (though still important) role in personality. Finally, it is not a constant, but varies with environmental conditions.

Another general conclusion is this: each species, including man, has characteristics that impose limits on what environmental influences may accomplish. Among the most dramatic ways to demonstrate this point is to raise chimpanzees like children. In one case, a nine-month-old boy, Donald, and a seven-month-old female chimpanzee, named Gua, were brought up as brother and sister. They were given similar demonstrations of affection, dressed alike, and accorded the same training for standing, walking, eating with a spoon, and using the toilet. Nevertheless, as might be expected, the chimpanzee proved superior to Donald in standing and walking. She also learned to eat from a spoon sooner and to respond earlier to verbal instructions. But after nine months, when the study was ended, Donald had caught up on almost everything except strength, and was beginning to develop capacities such as language facility, which Gua showed no signs of developing (Kellogg and Kellogg, 1933). In a similar situation, an ape, Vicki, was reared in a home and learned the same skills as Gua, besides two or three vocalizations (Hayes, 1951). However, both studies indicated conclusively that members of a given species maintain their distinctive characteristics, even under radically different conditions.

Let us close this section with two notes of caution. First, the fact that a trait is apparent at birth is no proof that it is genetically determined. For instance, newborn rats may appear emotional (as determined by defecation or other measures). However, emotionality in this case might have been produced during pregnancy by such environmental factors as irradiation, adrenalin, or tranquilizing drugs administered to the mother. One may assume certain characteristics to be hereditary simply because they are apparent at birth, when actually they derive from some prenatal influence.

Second, the foregoing pages should not be interpreted as supportive of genetic determinism—the belief that heredity writes the script that the individual simply enacts over a lifetime, in the manner of a puppet. From conception onward, countless unbelievably complex experiences will determine what becomes of the potential that heredity provides.

The Case for Eugenics

Causes of concern. At least in some quarters, authorities are raising questions that hold overwhelming significance for future children: Is the race declining? If so, what can or should be done about it? In some future Utopia, will instant geniuses be procreated with the ease of instant coffee? Will tomorrow's children be less capable of dealing with their world? Will more children arrive on earth handicapped by genetic defects, or less-than-normal potential? Is it not every child's birthright that he have the best heredity with which the human race can provide him? An illustration of this idea was an exchange between George Bernard Shaw and the dancer Isadora Duncan. Reputedly, Miss Duncan said to Shaw: "Just imagine what a child we two could have, one with my looks and your brains." To which Shaw is said to have replied, "Yes, but suppose the child had your brains and my looks!"

There are various factors suggesting that the race may indeed be declining. For one thing, medical technology is permitting many genetically defective persons to survive, marry, and pass along their hereditary taint. For example, persons with conditions related to excess secretion of sex hormones are treated with chemotherapy, after which they marry and produce children with the same sort of glands and resultant disorders. The inevitable result: The children of each generation must be medically treated if they are to lead productive lives. The race thus accumulates a great stock of these defective genes. It has been suggested that most people may ultimately have to carry with them an arsenal of hypodermic syringes, vials, and capsules, and remain within the radius of the laboratory that produces the synthetic chemicals on which they depend (Richter, 1959).

Reasons the problem is neglected. Laws in a number of states permit the sterilization of the unfit for several reasons, but the rate of such sterilization has dropped by 10 times over the last decade (*U.S. News and World Report,* 1965). Perhaps one reason is the lack of data concerning the effectiveness of such sterilization. For another, some authorities argue that the free mingling of human genes is needed and that artificially controlled selection might upset the natural balance of genetic factors. The so-called *sickle-cell trait* is an example. It comes from a genetic factor resulting in the production of hemoglobin S in the blood rather than hemoglobin A. Individuals who inherit a gene for hemoglobin S from one parent have an inborn resistance to malaria. But persons who inherit this gene from both parents usually die early in life of a blood disease called **sickle-cell anemia.** Therefore, **heterozygosity** becomes a defense against any similarly inherited conditions. Moreover, a race of persons homozygous for all ostensibly desirable traits might not prove to be a superior

population. In the words of Medawar (1960): "Human beings are committed to a genetic system which attaches a certain weight, perhaps great weight, to there being many different kinds of men." A great variety of individual differences, he asserts, is most favorable for producing a society capable of flourishing in many environments. In consequence, many join Medawar in recommending environmental improvement as more practical than human-genetics control. Assorted kinds of environment must be arranged, asserts Williams (1960), to permit the variation that different genotypes require.

In short, most authorities counsel caution. The phenomena involved are unbelievably complex, they argue, and no simple way exists for improving human hereditary quality. Among laymen, many object to eugenics programs for philosophical, religious, or emotional reasons. Some like to believe that all handicaps are remediable. Others denounce eugenics programs as contrary to divine law. Still others perceive efforts at upgrading the human species as a threat to individual liberty.

Advocates of action. On the other hand, a minority, including both laymen and scientists, dislike this reasoning, considering it defeatist and a concession to the status quo. As far back as 1927, Supreme Court Justice Oliver Wendell Holmes said, in affirming the right of states to impose sterilization: "Three generations of imbeciles are enough" (U.S. Supreme Court Report, 1927). Others suggest the desirability of discouraging parents with defective genes from having children. Take the case of Danny, age eight, who has never had normal hearing. Danny was born deaf, with an impressive history of deafness throughout his ancestry. When he grows up, says Davis, Danny should realize that a child fathered by him would very probably inherit his defect (Davis, 1958). On the other hand, much more study will be required to determine whether certain traits are genetically based. For instance, another child, Bobby, was born blind, and his disorder, retrolental fibroplasia, was at first believed to be hereditary. But research disclosed that it was actually caused by the oxygen given prematurely born infants to keep them alive (Davis, 1958).

Obviously, the whole question must be explored with open minds. Pending more definitive evidence, it is uncertain what, if any, short-term measures should be taken to upgrade or at least to prevent the further decline of homo sapiens.

Perhaps in this section the writer has emphasized eugenics control too much relative to euthenics measures. **Eugenics,** of course, refers to upgrading the species through heredity; **euthenics** deals with upgrading through better environment, both pre- and postnatally. However, almost all of this book in one way or another relates to environmental influences on the individual, while only this brief section applies specifically to heredity's effects. Moreover, eugenics has been largely ignored by society in general and by developmental psychologists in particular.

**• SIGNIFICANCE OF THE
PRENATAL PERIOD**

Ideas about the prenatal period, like those about heredity, have been shrouded by a haze of ignorance and superstition. Mothers have often been held responsible for irregularities such as birthmarks, blindness, and deafness. In consequence, they have suffered untold guilt, wondering whether some failure on their part has affected their offspring.

For whatever reason, a substantial number of pregnancies fail to yield completely healthy babies—in one study a full quarter of those surveyed. Fourteen per cent ended in fetal death, essentially miscarriage. Another $4\frac{1}{2}\%$ were prematurely born, and slightly

fewer than 1% died during the first 30 days of life (*U.S. News and World Report*, 1966).

We also underestimate the less obvious neurological consequences of prenatal and perinatal complications. A gradient of damage ranges from the fringe of the normal to the very abnormal. Lesser conditions would pass unnoticed in most research.

To see how closely prenatal factors link with later development, note how a single fetal factor, gross activity, relates to later behavior. In one study, 35 babies whose fetal movements had been recorded at 12, 24, and 36 weeks were tested postnatally in several areas of development. Total fetal activity at 12 weeks correlated significantly with postnatal motor and adaptive development; at 24 weeks, with motor, language, and total Gesell scores; and at 36 weeks, with all aspects of development studied (Walters, 1965).

Specific Prenatal Influences

The Rh factor. Fortunately, ever-increasing data are helping to differentiate specific influences on prenatal development. Among such influences, a relatively infrequent and not generally understood cause of trouble is the **Rh factor.** One in every 150 to 200 infants suffers from Rh, or an incompatibility between mother's and child's blood. If the mother is Rh negative (has no Rh blood factor) and has an Rh positive fetus, the mother's body, sensitized by the baby's blood, produces microscopic antibodies that attack the baby's red blood cells. The baby becomes anemic, and the oxygen-carrying capacity of its blood is reduced. As the baby's blood is progressively destroyed, its body becomes *dydropic*—that is, swollen with fluids. The result may be a spontaneous abortion, stillbirth, or, if the baby lives, low intelligence.

There are several ways of handling the Rh problem. One solution is to administer transfusions after birth or even before, via a long needle placed directly in the unborn child's abdomen. In either case, the aim is to flush out the mother's antibodies by several complete changes of blood. Other possibilities are still being explored. The most hopeful of these is the possibility that Rh can eventually be handled by innoculation of the mother. In any case, husbands and wives should be tested to discover their Rh blood type; if blood types are known in advance, preparations can be made and the negative effects of incompatibility significantly reduced.

Disease and endocrine disorders. Ordinarily, the fetus is protected against external hazards by the placenta, which acts as a liver and kidney by removing poisonous wastes and as a lung by providing oxygen from the mother's blood. It serves as a barrier between the two blood streams, allowing nutrients to reach the child, while keeping out noxious substances. It protects the child against most diseases, but not always against syphilis, gonorrhea, or German measles. Syphilis, when transmitted during pregnancy, may cause defects in the tooth buds, damage to ears and eyes, including deafness or blindness, or even miscarriage. Gonorrhea may also cause blindness, but the condition can easily be prevented through the administration of silver nitrate at birth.

German measles, if contracted by the mother during the first three or four months of pregnancy, may have serious effects on unborn children. It may cause stillbirths and neonatal deaths or such defects as cataracts, deafness, defective teeth, microcephaly, and heart abnormality. Since the effects of this disease during pregnancy are so serious, some authorities advocate that growing girls be exposed to measles, as well as other childhood infections, to increase the likelihood of their later immunity against them.

If the mother is diabetic, the fetus tends to be abnormally large, thus complicating the birth. The mortality rate, both pre- and postnatal, is high. How-ever, suitable medical care may vastly improve the diabetic mother's chances of having a healthy child.

Maternal endocrine disorders, especially thyroid deficiency, may also adversely affect the fetus. For example, a thyroid deficiency may result in cretinism, a condition characterized by rough, coarse skin, shaggy hair, a large, protruding abdomen, and fetal bone and cartilage that fail to develop properly. Intellectual impairment may range from slight to very serious, depending on the extent of the deficiency. In addition, endocrine imbalance may also result in microcephaly, a condition characterized by mental deficiency and a small pointed skull.

Other maternal disorders that may harm the fetus include rickets, tuberculosis, and the "salivary-gland" virus, which causes eye difficulties and malformed brains. No matter what the disease, the effects are potentially greater during the early months of the pregnancy period. The developing individual may become a casualty long before he reaches the firing line.

Maternal age. Another important factor in pregnancy is the mother's age. Early teen-age pregnancies are undesirable for various reasons—social, economic, psychological, and obstetric. In the first place, the girl is often unmarried and deeply worried, and hence suffers upsets in metabolic processes and physical function. Among a group of 500 mothers under 16 years of age, 20% experienced complications (Aznar and Bennett, 1961). Teen mothers are likely to produce a higher-than-average number of miscarriages, stillbirths, and fetal malformations. This data is of special significance because of the growing number of pregnancies at this age.

Complications become progressively more frequent from age 29 on, until menopause cuts short further hazard. Meantime, changes in the mother's endocrine balance increasingly retard maturation of the ovum and also of the fetus. After all, the aging ovum has been in the mother since birth and is only coming into use when the child is conceived. Small wonder that Eastman (1944) said the greatest asset a pregnant woman can possess is youth. On the other hand, older parents actually have more intelligent children than younger ones; but socioeconomic level, not parental age, is the probable reason.

The best age for having babies, according to present knowledge, is in the twenties, between ages 21 and 29. Not until that period are parents sufficiently mature emotionally; besides, sex hormones and reproductive apparatus continue to develop into the early twenties. Of course, the optimum time in specific cases is conditioned by other factors, including the mother's current health status and the number of children she has borne already.

Maternal nutrition. Like maternal age, the mother's diet during pregnancy affects the child. Even in the sixteenth century, Gaucher II, Sainte-Marthe wrote a verse describing the abnormal food cravings of pregnant women.

> But Teeming Women, when Desire
> grows strong,
> Are apt for ev'rything they see to
> Long.
> Sand, Chalk, and Dirt, their Appetite
> provoke,
> The Hearth's black Ashes, and the
> Chimney's Smoke.
> Nay, once I saw a Pregnant Wife
> devour
> A living Chick, and lick its reeking
> Gore;
> Cackling she seiz'd it, in the flut'ring
> Brood
> And tore its Flesh alive, and suck'd
> its Blood;
> Bones, Feathers, Garbidge in her
> Mouth were seen,
> And putrid Clotts defil'd her Breasts
> obscene [Rührah, 1925, p. 506].

While the modern woman's diet during pregnancy has undoubtedly improved, nutrition probably still constitutes the greatest potential hazard to uterine life. The maternal and fetal

blood are distinct, but nutritive elements diffuse through the semi-permeable membranes that separate the mother's blood from the child's.

Malnutrition. **Malnutrition** may stem from many causes. For example, certain foods, such as proteins, are expensive and hence often missing in lower-income diets. Lower-income groups also tend to be less educated, and therefore tend to know less about nutrition. Qualitative hunger is far more serious than quantitative hunger; beyond a certain minimum, *what* an individual eats is more important than *how much* he eats. In all social classes, women may unduly distort their diets in order to remain slender. Malnutrition may also arise from emotional problems; a woman may dislike food, or may eat too much, or may have unusual food cravings. At other times, whole geographical areas may experience malnutrition, due to such conditions as famine, poverty, economic disaster, and war.

Maternal malnutrition can have serious consequences. It can lead to miscarriages, stillbirths, premature births, and neonatal deaths. If the infant lives, he is prone to all sorts of disorders: rickets, cerebral palsy, epilepsy, anemia, and bronchitis. He is also more susceptible to colds, nervous tension, and neuropsychiatric disturbances (Stuart and Prugh, 1960).

Vitamin deficiencies. The lack of sufficient vitamins is especially damaging. When white rats were given a diet devoid of vitamin A, a high proportion of abortions followed, and many of the young that lived had malformations affecting the eyes (Bronsted, 1955). However, when the mothers were given high doses of vitamin A at certain stages of gestation, such malformations were reduced. In another study, mother rats that were fed a diet deficient in vitamin D produced offspring with skeletal deformities. Altogether about 600 kinds of congenital malformations have been produced in animals through experimental variation of vitamin deficiencies (Warkany, 1944).

Among humans, a vitamin B deficiency in the expectant mother's diet may affect the child's intelligence. The effects of other vitamins are well-known. It is also known that their effects are greatest during early gestation. "It is futile," says Peckos (1957), "to correct the maternal diet after the first trimester of a pregnancy in an attempt to prevent congenital abnormalities." Therefore, women should consult their doctors about such matters as soon as they plan to become pregnant.

On the other hand, too many vitamins may also be undesirable. Vitamin K, which assists blood-clotting, may, if taken to excess, damage the central nervous system and cause mental retardation. At one time, women were given ampules of vitamin K at the time of delivery; nowadays such dosages are not recommended. Likewise, too much vitamin D during pregnancy may cause excess calcium in the offspring. It is uncertain whether additions of vitamin D to milk afford greater risk or value. The important thing is that mothers have a reasonable amount of all the foods and vitamins that serve as building blocks for their babies' growth.

Toxic and chemical factors. The prenatal effects of various toxic and chemical agents on lower forms of life are well substantiated. Certain chemical stimuli will produce two-headed tadpoles, for example, and magnesium chloride will displace the eyes of minnows. Furthermore, the manipulation of environmental conditions may alter the balance of growth among different parts of the organism. By systematic reduction of oxygen at different periods of pregnancy, Ingalls (1959) induced specific defects in young mice. The nature of the deformity was determined by the intensity, duration, and timing of the oxygen deficiency. On the eighth day of pregnancy, deprivation of oxygen resulted in incompletely formed skulls, and on the twelfth, in harelip.

Among humans, drugs given pregnant women have sometimes resulted in deformities in their children. This fact has given rise to a serious ethical question: should abortions be legalized for

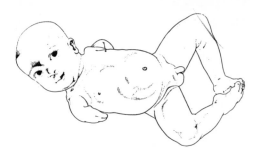

Victims of thalidomide syndrome typically have short, deformed arms and hands. Other abnormalities that may occur include deformed legs and feet and a wide variety of deformations of the ears, digestive tract, heart, and large blood vessels. Most afflicted children have normal intelligence. From H. B. Taussig, The thalidomide syndrome, *Scientific American,* 1962, **207(2)**, 29–35.

cases in which major abnormalities are suspected? The following is a case in point:

An American couple went to Sweden to have an abortion after they were told there was a 50–50 chance their child would be born deformed because the pregnant mother had taken **thalidomide.** American courts had refused to grant permission for the operation. The fetus was born with no arms or legs. The couple received letters commending them for their action ("I am a victim of Bulbar Polio . . . You are doing the right thing"); and letters violently condemning them (with salutations such as "You dirty murderess!" and "Dear Scum:" [Boroson, 1965, p. 29].

Smoking. Considerable interest has also been focused on the prenatal effects of the mother's use of alcohol, drugs, and cigarettes. Of these three, the effects of smoking are the least certain. Montagu (1959) points out that when nicotine, a narcotic poison, enters the embryonic and fetal circulation, it may adversely affect the circulatory system as well as various organs. In fact, the recent increase in cardiac and circulatory disorders has been linked, at least partially, with the smoking of pregnant mothers. The exact relationship between

47

maternal smoking and fetal well-being remains unclear. Mothers who smoke have twice the number of premature and small babies than those who do not. However, "smallness" in itself seems to impose no special risks (*U.S. News and World Report,* 1966).

Alcohol. The effects of alcohol on the fetus depend significantly on the amount used. Moderate drinking apparently does no harm, but heavy drinking by either parent may have an effect. The male germ cells may be weakened by alcohol even before fertilization occurs. If the mother is a heavy drinker, alcohol acts as a substitute for food, thus depriving the fetus of important nutritional needs. In this case, the harm derives not from alcohol but from the mother's failure to eat properly. Alcohol may also contribute to maternal accidents that result in damage to the fetus.

Drugs. The case against certain drugs is clear-cut. Quinine, often given for malaria, may cause fetal deafness if taken in excess. Barbiturates and other pain-killing drugs administered prior to delivery can affect the oxygen supply to the fetal brain, leaving brain damage. Thalidomide, as we have seen, may produce malformation of the glands, causing the long bones of the arms to fail to grow, and the hands to form close to the shoulder. Legs are also affected, though to a lesser extent (Taussig, 1962). In a few brief years, at least 5,000 youngsters affected by this seemingly innocuous tranquilizer once used for morning sickness were born with flipper-like arms and legs or with no limbs at all. Not until these tragedies were reported, in 1961, did the public begin to heed obstetricians' warnings about the hazards of drug-taking.

The constant introduction into the blood stream of any chemical substance may impose a burden of accommodation on the mother's physiological mechanism, which may, in turn, affect the fetus. When the limits of maternal accommodation are exceeded, danger signals such as wakefulness, nervousness, or irregular heart action should alert the mother to possible ill effects. Again, effects are more likely to be serious early in the pregnancy period.

Maternal emotion. The impact of the mother's emotional status on the unborn child has been the source of much speculation and controversy. Plentiful evidence indicates that the mother's emotional states may affect the developing organism, though exactly how is not clear. It is known that during emotional states, such as fear or rage, a mother liberates into the bloodstream various hormones and possibly other chemicals not presently understood, thereby producing chemical changes in her blood. These chemicals, which are absorbed through the placenta into the fetal bloodstream, act as irritants, with perhaps far-reaching effects (Hamilton, 1955).

The effect of maternal stress on human infants is striking. Harris and Harris (1946) reported increased violence of fetal movements when mothers experienced sudden anger or rage. Other researchers found that both prenatal movement and neonatal crying correlated positively with pregnant women's anxiety scores (Ottinger and Simmons, 1964). In another long-range study of several hundred children whose mothers had intense emotional experiences during pregnancy, pronounced increases in the rate of heartbeat and the amount of fetal activity were found, and relationships to postnatal schizophrenia suspected (Sontag, 1960).

Prenatal effects are especially great if the mother experiences stress early in pregnancy. Between the seventh and eighth weeks of prenatal life, hyperactivity of the maternal adrenal glands may stimulate excessive secretion of the hormone hydrocortisone, resulting in cleft palate. Early stress may also cause mental retardation, because it is during this period that the brain is developing.

The effects of prenatal maternal stress are clearly apparent in the newborn. Babies of mothers who were upset during this period tend to be irritable, to sleep poorly, to have frequent bowel movements, and to spit up often. To all intents and purposes, observes Sontag (1941), the infant is born neurotic; he has not had to wait for a bad home situation or other cause to make him one.

The effects of maternal stress do not stop with infancy. In one study, children whose mothers experienced unusual stress during pregnancy scored lower both in intelligence and adjustment than did children of nonanxious mothers (Davids et al., 1963). Of course, it is hard to distinguish between the effects of prenatal and postnatal stress, because mothers who are emotionally upset during pregnancy often continue to be disturbed afterwards. However, results such as those just cited occur even when children are separated from the mother at birth. The child's development seems to be affected, even prenatally, by unfavorable parental attitudes (Schaeffer and Bayley, 1960).

The overall effects of the mother's condition. The ways that the mother's condition, either physical or emotional, may affect the unborn child are as complex as the organism itself and the environmental stimuli that impinge upon it. The mother may suffer from a chronic fatigue that affects her overall condition. She may sustain mechanical trauma, such as falls and accidents, whose effects somehow penetrate the fetus's normally secure bomb shelter. Finally, the whole atmosphere of modern life, with its horde of drugs, food additives, air and water pollution, and noise and tension, may affect the pregnant mother and, indirectly, her unborn child.

The effect of each factor must be evaluated in the context of others. In one case, malnutrition may be the major factor in a child's condition; in another, it may be only a contributing factor. In any case, developmental irregularities apparently result from environmental disturbances in the uterus more often than they do from defective heredity, because nature tends to eliminate the genetically unfit either by miscarriage or stillbirth.

In conclusion, let us note a recent trend. Formerly the fetus was deemed a parasite, living a well-protected life and taking from the mother, at her expense, whatever was necessary. The relationship is now viewed as dynamic; the mother and the developing child are seen to interact with and significantly affect each other.

Multiple births. Certain other prenatal influences have to do with environment, both intrauterine and external to the mother. The importance of the intrauterine environment is clearly evident in the case of twins. Twins are of two types: one-egg or *identical* twins, which have the same placenta, and *fraternal* twins, from two distinct placentas, each with its own prenatal environment. In the truest sense, nonidenticals are not twins but the result of simultaneous pregnancies. Triplets may be of three types: identical, when all come from the same fertilized ovum; three siblings, each from a separate ovum; or two identicals and one sibling.

All children involved in multiple births suffer certain deficits. In the first place, they are crowded into the space meant only for one. Sometimes the uterus becomes incapable of further expansion, causing the infants to be ejected prematurely. Especially among identicals who share the same sac, one may occupy a more favorable position than the other. Less favored ones may be unable to obtain from the placenta the substance needed. In the case of the Dionne quintuplets, two were cramped prenatally and therefore smaller at birth. After birth, they often turned blue from respiratory problems, and lagged in motor and mental growth.

As a result of these and other handicaps, infants of multiple births are more likely than singletons to miscarry, to suffer birth injuries, or to be premature. They are also slower in sitting alone, walking, talking, and developing in other ways. On the average, those who survive are slightly inferior physically and mentally to singletons. Moreover, triplets suffer more defects than twins, quadruplets than triplets, and quintuplets than quadruplets.

The number of pregnancies a mother experiences also affects children's health and viability. First-born children are more commonly characterized by malformations and are less viable than later-borns. However, children born after several pregnancies are less healthy than those born in between. Consequently, in the very large family several of the children would be at some disadvantage in terms of prenatal environments.

The impact of environmental factors. Certain factors in the external environment, among them sounds, pressure, temperature, and X rays, all impinge on the unborn child. Unequal or abnormal pressures in the uterus may cause bodily deformities or asymmetrical skull development. Heavy doses of X ray cause chromosome fragments to break away from cell nuclei and produce genetic damage, especially during the first two months of pregnancy. In one study, over half the children of mothers undergoing X-ray therapy were imbeciles with abnormal-sized heads or other deformities (Montagu, 1950).

Radiation, such as that spread by atomic bombing, has proved highly damaging to prenatal growth. There is no so-called threshold dose of radiation below which there is no damage. The National Academy of Sciences, in discussing levels of radioactivity tolerable by the human organism, concluded that a minor shortening of life and an increase in tumors may be possible effects of radiation (*Saturday Review*, 1960). However, more definite conclusions about the long-term effects of radiation on heredity and prenatal or postnatal life will not be available for many years. Research has already indicated tragic outcomes from the Japanese bombings. The fetal mortality among mothers exposed to radiation at Naga-

saki was 23.3%, compared with 2.7% among controls; neonatal infant mortality was 26.1% compared with 3.6%; and cases of mental retardation were 25% compared with 3% (Yamazaki et al., 1954). Researchers at Hiroshima concluded that central-nervous-system defects can be produced in the fetus by atomic radiation if exposure occurs within 1200 meters of the explosion center. Seven of 11 children within this radius had microcephaly, with mental retardation, and nine of the 11 had much smaller head circumferences than normal (Neel, 1953).

The season of birth. More uncertain and certainly less direct in their influence on prenatal development than the foregoing are factors related to season of birth. According to the Bible, there is a time to be born and a time to die. The time to be born, said our progenitors, should be fixed by astrologers. Anyone born when the planet Jupiter was in a certain position would be jovial by disposition, but anyone born under Saturn was doomed to gloom and ill-fortune. Such superstitions are, of course, unfounded; but myths about the best season to be born may have some foundation. Children conceived in the springtime, when the mother's diet tends to be poorest, may suffer protein deficiency and, indirectly, developmental irregularities. Summer heat, by reducing protein intake, may result in fetal damage. Indeed, hot summers are associated with more mental defectives than cool summers, which show no rise in mental defect at all (Pasamanick and Knobloch, 1966). However, a British study (Orne, 1963) reported summer and autumn babies superior mentally to those born in winter and spring. After reviewing the evidence, Hurlock (1964) concludes that there is no best season of birth, since factors favorable at different seasons tend to balance each other.

The critical significance of timing. The effect of any specific prenatal influence will be largely a function of the developmental stage of the organism on which it impinges. Chronic disturbances of the mother, such as endocrine upsets and diseases of the uterus, may register their impact at selected vulnerable stages of growth rather than evenly through pregnancy. It is the timing, and not the agent itself, that determines the abnormality produced. That is, the limbs or parts being formed when the lethal agent is introduced are the ones affected. Furthermore, if an organ is not permitted to develop at its appointed time, it will not develop at all. However, since it is pretty well-known when various functions and parts develop, therapeutic measures may sometimes be taken.

In general, the younger the organism, the more serious the difficulty caused by whatever atypical condition exists. In fact, by the end of the second month, environmental circumstances have already determined some of the congenital characteristics that may help or hinder one throughout life. It is also during this period that malformations of the skeleton, a leading cause of crippling, typically occur. It is hardly surprising that Norris (1960) calls the first three months of gestation the most significant period of life.

While the developing organism is less vulnerable in later months, defects may still occur. As late as the last trimester, nutritional deficiencies may lead to unsound teeth, facial defects, and disturbances of behavior and personality. Prematurely born children, whose prenatal development excludes the last month, when mineralization of the skeleton is most active, may suffer from rickets. Fortunately, many of these malformations, including certain cardiac defects, can be corrected by surgery.

Perinatal Research

Some methods of studying the perinatal period, which lasts from conception until three months after birth, have long been used, and others are being devised. One method depends on mothers' reports, which, like all subjec-

tive reports, are subject to error. A second method involves the use of various technical aids, such as the stethoscope, cardiograph, electroencephalograph, and X ray, to study fetal heartbeat, activity, position, and the possibility of multiple birth. Microphones taped to the mother's abdomen have recorded decided reactions to loud noises, to the mother's voice, and even to the voices of others addressing the mother—a refutation of the popular picture of fetal bliss. A doctor in Scotland has used sonar equipment to photograph fetuses with sound waves; and a doctor in New York has used heat waves for the same purpose (Bishop and Davis, 1966, p. 105).

Information also comes from prematurely delivered fetuses, which for several reasons are of limited research value. In the first place, most of them are abnormal, delivered for therapeutic reasons. Besides, anesthetics used during and after delivery affect the behavior of the fetus. Furthermore, it dies in seconds unless means have been arranged to keep it alive. Nevertheless, the cumulative gains from such research make worthwhile all efforts to keep the fetus alive as long as possible.

The goals of such research involve nothing less than improving the quality of life itself. Many questions remain to be solved. Much has been learned, but much remains to be learned. So far, no method has been devised for observing the progress of the fertilized ovum down the Fallopian tube or the process by which it becomes imbedded in the uterine wall. Fortunately, important research on the perinatal period is currently underway. A collaborative project involving 14 medical institutions is accumulating detailed data on genetics, pregnancy, and delivery in 40,000 cases. Developmental and neurological examinations will continue until the offspring reach age seven (Collaborative Perinatal Research Project, 1963). Other groups involved in such research are the National Foundation (March of Dimes) and the National Institute of Child Health and Human Development.

• SUMMARY

Any particular individual's earth journey begins with fertilization, when a male germ cell, or **sperm,** unites with a female cell, or **ovum,** to form a **zygote.** After two weeks the rapidly developing organism is called the **embryo,** and after two months it is called the **fetus.** After about nine months — if all goes well — an infant is born, an unbeautiful creature to all but his doting parents. Sometimes birth injuries occur, perhaps due to compression of the brain, deprivation of oxygen (anoxia), or other trauma. The degree of shock sustained, even under benign circumstances, is in dispute.

At the instant of fertilization, except for rare exceptions, the fertilized cell, or zygote, receives from each parent cell 46 **chromosomes.** Each chromosome contains many thousand pairs of **genes.** Chromosomes and their components, the genes, represent the materials from which the individual is made. The genes are made of **DNA** (deoxyribonucleic acid) and **RNA** (ribonucleic acid), which determine the substances that decree particular types of voice timbre, eye color, and other characteristics. Scientists are now trying to unravel the secrets of DNA and RNA in order ultimately to modify future characteristics of the individual, especially errors that might otherwise occur. Ordinarily, DNA arranges that each cell will be displaced by a duplicate of itself; but occasionally a sudden change in the gene occurs so that it becomes reproduced in a new form, or **mutation.**

About a fifth of birth defects are caused by defective genes and chromosomes, perhaps — though no one knows — through overproduction of certain key chemical substances called *enzymes.* Chromosomal irregularities may produce defective body structures and, to an unknown extent, other disorders, possibly even schizophrenia. A beginning has been made toward mapping genes in the chromosomes, to permit tracing the occurrence of specific diseases and defects.

Psychologists differ over the relative significance they ascribe to heredity and environment. Extreme **environmentalists** believe in the almost limitless modification of genetic potential by environment. Extreme **hereditarians** emphasize the significance of maturation, or the gradual unfolding of heredity's plan across the years. They point out that the closer the blood relationship, the more nearly alike individuals are in a variety of ways, including both mental and other personality traits. What is most likely is this: that heredity and environment interact in controlling every aspect of one's growth and destiny, their respective roles varying in nature and degree with particular characteristics and functions. Heredity seems to play a dominant role in determining certain physical traits, such as eye color, and a significant but not controlling role in such traits as height, weight, and aging. The role of heredity in major mental disorders and neurosis is less certain. Genetics may even indirectly contribute to criminality — for instance, in influencing an individual's activity level and thus indirectly his tendency to attack rather than to withdraw.

The role of genetics in personality traits, such as degree of **introversion-extroversion,** is especially blurred. Identical twins are indeed more alike than fraternals in autonomic reactivity, neuroticism, and emotionality. Even at birth, infants' reactions differ greatly, suggesting an hereditary base.

In sum, heredity makes different contributions to different traits. Its effect varies with environmental conditions. Each species, including man, has hereditary characteristics that impose limits on what environmental influences may accomplish. However, from conception on, innumerable experiences operate in complex ways to determine what will become of hereditary potential. Questions concerning to what extent the species may or should be upgraded through improving heredity (**eugenics**) or environment (**euthenics**) are largely avoided.

In recent years, increasing attention has been paid to specific parental influences on the child's prenatal development. Recent developments include use of injections to help control the **Rh factor** (an incompatibility between the mother's and baby's blood). Thyroid deficiencies that result in physical and intellectual impairment may be ameliorated, or even avoided, if treated in time by thyroxin. Mothers generally may be encouraged to have their babies during their twenties, the period that normally provides the most favorable prenatal environment.

The developing individual may also be affected by maternal nutrition, toxic and chemical factors, drugs, alcohol, and tobacco. Beyond a certain minimum, what the mother eats during pregnancy is vastly more significant than how much she eats. Maternal malnutrition may increase the incidence of miscarriage, stillbirth, neonatal deaths, and so on. Vitamin deficiencies are especially damaging. A vitamin B deficiency in the maternal diet may affect the child's intelligence postnatally. Hence, a well-balanced diet, including a proper assortment of foods and vitamins, is essential. It is also well-substantiated that drugs of certain sorts or in improper amounts may result in deformities. The effects of alcohol depend largely on the amount used.

Maternal stress, especially during early pregnancy, is especially important. Hyperactivity of the maternal adrenal glands may result in excessive hormonal secretions, which in turn may help produce physical deformity or neurotic tendencies in the infant. In short, developmental irregularities apparently reflect environmental disturbances in the uterus more often than they do defective heredity. The fetus was formerly dubbed a parasite, living a well-protected life of bliss; now the relationship is viewed as dynamic, with the mother and child vitally affecting each other.

Other prenatal influences are environmental in nature, both intrauterine and external to the mother. All multiple-birth children suffer prenatally from being confined in space designed for one. Extrauterine factors that may impinge on the unborn child include sounds, pressure, temperature, and radiation. Even the season of birth may have an indirect effect because of foods available at particular times.

The effect of any particular influence during the prenatal period is largely a function of the time when it occurs. It is the timing, not the agency itself, that determines the sort of abnormality produced. In general, the younger the organism, the greater the impact. Sometimes certain congenital malformations can be corrected by surgery; sometimes they can be avoided altogether. In fact, research relating to genetics and the perinatal period is proceeding apace through the use of X ray and prematurely delivered fetuses, as well as new approaches. Especially significant will be the results of recently begun longitudinal studies that trace the history of individuals from conception onward.

• SUGGESTED QUESTIONS AND ACTIVITIES

1. Should pregnant women be required to attend clinics to discuss matters affecting the future welfare of their children?
2. Would it be a good idea to freeze the sperm of especially superior men, when such a plan becomes feasible on a long-term basis, in order to expand the number of outstanding persons produced?
3. Would you favor having women of lesser abilities serve as hosts prenatally for the fetuses of highly capable women, so that the latter might proceed uninterruptedly with their careers?
4. If a baby is entitled to sound heredity, should the right to have children be limited to adults with the best apparent genetic potential?
5. Since the lower classes have more children than higher classes and since the mortality of their infants has been greatly reduced, what will prevent a gradual deterioration of the human race? What, if anything, should be done about this matter?

53

6. Does modern society need people of lower capacities, or can machines do most of the work such people have traditionally done?
7. Would you have sufficient faith in the power of environment to adopt a child of any apparently normal parents, provided he had a sound body?
8. What practical problems might arise relative to child development if human life could be created in the laboratory?
9. Give your views on the following questions, posed by Scheinfeld (1965, pp. 710–711), relating to heredity:

The British Queen Victoria, as we know now, carried the gene for hemophilia, which was transmitted to a number of her descendants (but not to any members of the present British royal family). The disease in one of Victoria's great-grandsons, the Czarevitch, caused his parents to be victimized by the evil Rasputin, and thus helped bring on the Russian Revolution. If you had lived when Victoria was young and had known that she could transmit the hemophilia gene, would you have advocated that she either not marry or take steps not to have children? Or would you have held that her need to carry on the royal line made up for the danger?

Several thousand persons in the United States in the past three centuries have suffered the agonies of Huntington's chorea, most terrible of hereditary afflictions, as a result of receiving replicas of genes brought over and passed on by three English brothers in the 1700s. Many other descendants now face the same fate. If you had lived two centuries ago and could have looked into the future, would you have demanded sterilization of the three brothers? Would you today advocate sterilizing all identifiable carriers of Huntington's chorea genes before they reach maturity?

A delinquent girl in a New England state, where sterilization is authorized for mental defectives, was turned loose without an operation because she was just over the border of "legal feeblemindedness" (with an IQ of 72). In a few years she bore, illegitimately, three feebleminded children. What should have been done in such a case: Keep the girl in an institution throughout her reproductive period until she or her parents consented to her sterilization? Or release her without any operation, hoping she could be induced to abstain from sex relations or to use contraceptive measures?

Some years ago the daughter of a famous inventor (deceased) sued her mother for having had her sterilized on the grounds of feeblemindedness. The court upheld the mother. But there was this question: Might not the girl also have been carrying certain of her father's "superior" genes? And, lacking proof that the girl was *genetically* defective, should society have risked the passing on of some "feeblemindedness" genes in order to perpetuate the rare "superior" ones?*

• SUGGESTED READINGS

Beadle, G., and M. Beadle, *The Language of Life*. New York: Doubleday & Company, Inc., 1966. A fascinating introduction to genetics, written on an elementary level by a leading geneticist and his wife.

Bulletin of the Atomic Scientists, Vol. 20 (1964). This volume provides a background for discussing eugenics in a series of three articles: H. J. Muller, "Perspective for the Life Sciences," January, pp. 3–7; Hudson Hoagland, "Cybernetics of Population Control," February, pp. 2–6; and Theodosius Dobzhansky, "Evolution – Organic and Superorganic," May, pp. 4–8.

Hayes, C., *The Ape in Our House.* New York: Harper & Row, Publishers, Inc., 1951. A couple adopts a small chimpanzee and raises it like a child. This popularly written and entertaining book helps one appreciate the relative role of heredity and environment.

Melzack, R., and W. R. Thompson, "Early Environment," *Scientific American,* Vol. 3 (1956), pp. 38–42. A readable article that indicates how environmental influences at the beginning of life shape the future behavior of the animal. Evidence is derived from experiments in which Scottish terriers are raised in restricted surroundings.

Montagu, M. F. A., *Prenatal Influences.* Springfield, Ill.: Charles C. Thomas, 1962. Treats the topic of prenatal influences very broadly, and concludes by dealing with birth.

Neel, J. V., "The Genetic Potential," in E. M. Ginzberg, ed., *The Nation's Schools,* Vol. 1. New York: Columbia University Press, 1961, pp. 1–23. Shows some of the implications of our genetic heritage.

Rahner, K. (trans. by David T. LeFort),

*From *Your Heredity and Environment* by Amram Scheinfeld. Copyright 1939, 1950, © 1965 by Amram Scheinfeld. Published by J. B. Lippincott Company.

"Can Man Perfect Himself?" *Catholic World,* Vol. 203 (June 1966), pp. 138–144. The author discusses man's manipulation of his own nature for the sake of future generations.

Scheinfeld, A., *Your Heredity and Environment.* New York: J. B. Lippincott, 1965. This highly readable book treats genetics in many aspects and stresses the relationship between heredity and environment.

Smith, J. M., "Eugenics and Utopia," *Daedalus,* Vol. 94 (1965), pp. 487–505. The author attempts to discriminate between what we ought to do about genetics and what we can now do or shall be able to do.

Sonneborn, T. M., ed., *The Control of Human Heredity and Evolution.* New York: The Macmillan Company, 1965. Report of a symposium emphasizing the use of molecular and cell biology to influence heredity. See review of this book in *Science,* Vol. 148 (June 18, 1965), pp. 1579–1580.

Tyler, E. T. "The Control of Unborn Life," *Today's Health,* Vol. 44 (June 1966), pp. 58–62. The author considers how anti-fertility vaccines, artificial wombs, and sexless conception may change man and his world.

Wolstonholme, G., ed., *Man and His Future.* Boston: Little, Brown and Company, 1963. See especially the topic "Eugenics and Genetics."

3
PHYSICAL DEVELOPMENT

• DEFINITION OF TERMS

Like the proverbial penny, certain terms constantly turn up throughout child psychology, and certain concepts run like threads throughout. Primary among these are growth, development, and maturation—all concepts essential to perceiving the child as a constantly evolving individual. Some persons use the words "growth" and "development" interchangeably. Actually, they are different, though inseparable. **Growth** refers to quantitative change in size and structure; **development,** to qualitative change, involving orderly, directional sequences of behavior. While growth adds inches and pounds, development is the complex process of integrating functions.

Some people also use the terms "development" and "maturation" interchangeably. However, Olson (1959, pp. 3–4) uses "development" to designate the complex product of maturation (nature's design) and nurture (needs and requirements for growth), whereas he uses **maturation** to cover "the anatomic, physiologic and chemical changes of the body that occur with time and over which we have only slight control . . ." Maturation is a sort of master script writer outlining in detail the moves that growth will take.

Breckinridge and Vincent (1965, pp. 43–44) hold a similar concept of maturation, likening it to the "ripening" or **readiness** of capacity based primarily on the maturing of body organs or systems. For example, a certain maturing of the nervous system must occur before given capacities are ready for use. Until adequate development of the nerves leading from the bladder and the rectum occurs, the child cannot be aware of fullness of either organ, and he is not "ready" for toilet-training.

Despite the semantic confusion surrounding the term "growth" itself, authorities agree on the principles by which it proceeds. Primary among them is the constant process of change. This change is relatively uniform and pro-

ceeds in somewhat predictable fashion. Parents learn that babies sit before they walk, and that the majority walk before they talk. Meantime, whatever transpires—good, bad, trivial, or traumatic—all the child's experiences leave residues of change. That is, the effects of growth are cumulative, and the importance of experience rests more on residual effect than on immediate impact. Meanwhile, change varies in pace but is continuous and largely irreversible. Children grow rapidly from birth to age three, and from ages 11 to 15, and slowly during the years in between; but at no time does growth cease altogether.

• THE NORMAL SEQUENCE
OF PHYSICAL
DEVELOPMENT

Growth Patterns

Although growth overall is an integrated, unitary process, the various parts of the body have their own growth rates. For example, the head grows rapidly in fetal and infant life, and at a diminishing rate during the next 10 years, after which growth all but ceases. By contrast, the sex organs change very little during the first decade, after which they grow rapidly and continue to enlarge into late adolescence, even after the growth in height has ceased. The heart takes even longer to mature, completing its growth at about age 20.

While a basic pattern undergirds each individual's growth, the various glands affecting that pattern play relatively different roles during childhood and adolescence. Before puberty, the thyroid and pituitary glands are primarily responsible for bone growth and skeletal aging; after puberty, the gonads assume that function. The earlier of these two periods is more important in determining adult height and size. Hence, the longer puberty is delayed, the greater the potential for bone growth. Once the relatively brief period of puberty is over, skeletal growth all but ceases (Simmons and Greulich, 1943). In other words, preadolescent body build contributes more to adult build than does the growth spurt itself. After all, preadolescence lasts from 11 to 15 years, the growth spurt from 2 to 4 years (Broverman et al., 1964).

Other factors related to growth are body type and temperament. The ectomorph, with his tall, fragile body, grows for a longer period than does the stocky mesomorph, and placid children grow faster than tense ones — though tension has greater effect on weight than on height (Dupertuis and Mitchell, 1953).

The Catch-up Mechanism

In the process of development, each individual's growth is target-seeking. Children, like rockets, have their trajectories, which are governed by the control systems of their genetical constitutions. If the normal growth pattern is deflected from its trajectory by illness or other circumstances, a regulatory **catch-up mechanism** restores the pattern. For example, if growth has been slowed by acute malnutrition or by sudden lack of a hormone, the catch-up mechanism goes into operation as soon as the missing food or hormone is restored. However, if the arrest of growth has been prolonged, the catch-up may be incomplete.

The catch-up mechanism is not fully understood yet, but some general assumptions have been made. During the catch-up period, the whole organism grows rapidly and in proportionate manner; hence the control probably resides in a central mechanism — perhaps the hypothalamus at the base of the brain. Apparently, there is a time-tally mechanism that represents normal growth, so that the organism "knows" when to stop the rapid catch-up velocity.

This catch-up mechanism is significant for several reasons. For one thing, it allows genetically large children to develop in the uteri of small mothers. Since birth size is controlled almost entirely by uterine factors, genetically large children are born small. The catch-up mechanism usually enables them to reach their own growth curves within

six months after birth (Tanner, 1963).

• INDIVIDUAL PATTERNS OF PHYSICAL DEVELOPMENT

Each child has his distinctive body make-up and economy, so that among different infants, body organs such as stomach and heart differ markedly in size and shape. Body builds also differ, as well as the chemical compositions of body substances. For example, each child's saliva is probably as unique as his appearance, voice, or disposition (Williams, 1956, p. 59).

The child's functions are as distinctive as his body parts. Even among neonates, differences are clearly apparent — as, for instance, in the feeding cycle (nursing, retaining, or regurgitating food), in digestion and assimilation, and in elimination.

Individuals also differ in their rates of maturing. Because of this individuality, any child's present growth must be judged according to where he has been and where he is going. A child of five who compares favorably with others of his age at the moment may in fact be lagging in relation to his potential. Or a child of eight who is only as tall as the average seven-year-old may nevertheless have optimum height for him. In other words, he is and will continue to be short, because of genetic factors.

In most physiologic and endocrinologic functions, except perhaps those related to the pituitary gland, the sexes differ only slightly in the early years. However, small differences — for example, in skeletal development — are already apparent prenatally. Sex differences become more apparent at about age seven, when girls experience an increase in **estrogen** function. A subcutaneous layer of fat develops, producing a slight feminine rounding, and by age 10 a trace of breast growth appears. By age 13½, the average age of girls' puberty in the United States, menstruation begins. Boys, meanwhile, experience no comparable rhythmic variations or hormonal changes (Over-

59

street, 1963). Girls are on a faster timetable, both physically and mentally, until age 18 to 20, when the gap closes. Overall, girls' average growth is about one year ahead of boys', although the difference is less than that very early in life and greater during puberty.

In either sex, the pace at one age tends to affect the pace at another. Early maturers grow fast during infancy, early childhood, and childhood proper, but they end their adolescent growth spurt much earlier than do average or late maturers. In general, rapid growth before six years correlates with an early adolescent growth spurt and large mature size.

Another factor in pace of growth is the individual's own body economy, which depends on a unique blend of factors. Just as there are fast, moderate, or slow growers in height and weight, so there are fast, slow, or irregular schedules of skeletal maturation (Pyle et al., 1959). Among 133 children in one study, 35 were consistent in growth rate from birth to age 18; 35 changed to a faster pace; 30 changed twice; and 18 had irregular patterns. It may be concluded that individuals vary in their rates of progress: some progress consistently, a very few progress irregularly, and many make one or two substantial shifts in rate, usually between childhood and adolescence (Pyle et al., 1959).

Statistical Norms as Standards for Measuring Growth

Individual differences make it necessary to avoid rigid standards of growth. Statistical **norms** are indeed useful, but only if they are properly interpreted and their limitations recognized. Although "normal" is an evaluative term implying a desirable or wholesome state, statistical norms should be regarded merely as descriptive of the current status of some characteristic of the specific population being studied. By comparing individuals or groups, deviations readily become apparent, and trends recognized. Such figures, when related to various factors (such as nutrition, age, race, and sex) that contribute to development, make handy indices for comparing the effects of such variables.

When an individual's growth is measured against groups norms, several points should be kept clearly in mind. For one thing, each growth pattern is unique, and different parts develop at different rates within the same individual. Besides, what may be ideal for one child may not be for another. There are fat underweight children and lean overweight children. Without such additional measures as fat-folds, or radiographic measurements of outer fat, the information we desire is obscured by figures (Garn, 1960, p. 31).

In other words, we need to know more than that a child is large or small or growing slowly or rapidly. We are also interested in the quality of his tissues and the proportionate growth of bone, muscle, fat, and body segments (in other words, his physique). For instance, a large child is not necessarily healthier than a smaller one, who often has firmer muscles. Furthermore, a small child with straight bones that contain a good store of minerals may be healthier than a large child with flabby muscles and poorly mineralized bones. It is not weight, but what is weighed, that is important. An added pound may be composed of muscle, fat, or water.

In short, norms themselves explain nothing about growth. Moreover, norms obtained at a specific age level in children's growth do not determine whether a particular child is progressing satisfactorily over the years. Weight increases in early years have a completely different meaning from those in later years. For example, much of the weight increase in childhood is due to growth in brain and vital organs; in adolescence, weight increase is due to growth in bone and muscle.

Norms should also be related to the population on which they have been established. For some reason, such as nutritive deficiencies in the area, a group under study may possess some defects in common. Or the norms obtained from a particular population may be inappropriate as a standard for certain groups. Norms obtained on smaller Boston children would hardly do as a yardstick for middle-sized Iowa children, or even larger Los Angeles youngsters. Nor would norms derived from Minnesota's heavily Scandinavian stock be appropriate for measuring New York City's Puerto Ricans.

A final precaution is this: our present-day skill in amassing developmental data—the proliferation of published norms about growth is just one example—should not beguile us into overrating our present level of knowledge. The publication of norms would seem to suggest that they are to be taken as ideals—as the criteria of normality. However, many questions remain to be answered. For example, what is the practical importance of minor deviations? And why do some apparently normal children follow atypical growth patterns? Norms, both psychological and statistical, need recalibration in ways yet to be determined.

•FACTORS AFFECTING GROWTH

Hereditary versus environmental influences. Physical development hinges on a blend of genetic and environmental factors. Every individual is distinctive, requiring for his optimum development a unique blend of influences at every stage of growth. If certain needs are not met during the prenatal period, the organism dies or fails to develop normally. But if it can be determined just what requirements are lacking, and if they can be supplied, healthy development should proceed throughout life (Williams, 1956).

However, environmental influences may interfere with growth as well as facilitate it. The same plasticity often cited as a human asset, allowing con-

structive modifications of growth through a good environment, can under less favorable circumstances become a liability.

Body build. Among the various genetically derived factors, body build is related both directly and indirectly to physical development. More directly, it determines the general pattern of growth. For example, the ectomorphic body build is generally reported to correlate with later maturity and slower growth, though some authorities disagree. Indirectly, body build encourages or discourages activities conducive to growth. For example, the endomorphic or stout child is less well-equipped for vigorous play; hence he participates less often, and becomes still less adept.

Race. Racial differences in physical development are determined by both heredity and environment. While American children are typically taller and heavier than Japanese children, American-born Japanese are taller, heavier, and more advanced in skeletal growth than matched groups in Japan (Greulich, 1957). In short, race is indeed a factor in physical development; but environmental influences such as family surroundings, living standards, and emotional climate are also important (Meredith, 1951).

Intelligence. Sometimes environmental factors operate deviously—for example, in modifying the relationship between mental and physical development. Let us take an example. It has been reported that gifted children are also larger children, but Laycock and Caylor (1964) proved that such is not the case when the factor of home environment is held constant. While brighter children may indeed, on the average, be slightly bigger, one must remember that both bodies and brains are nurtured in the same families. Brighter parents will typically provide better foods for their children, whose physiques will grow correspondingly larger. Significantly, 61

Body build indirectly determines activities conducive to growth.

within the same home brighter children are no larger than less intelligent siblings.

The Relationship of Physical Factors to Personality and Adjustment

Body build. Body build is one of the major factors in personality and adjustment. Since the topic has aroused so much controversy, we shall examine it in some detail. For centuries people have believed that body build and personality are somehow related. We think of the big, muscular man as being aggressive, the fat man as easy-going and jolly, and the thin man as serious and tense. From Shakespeare's *Julius Caesar,* we recall Caesar's saying:

> Let me have men about me that are fat,
> Sleek-headed men, and such as sleep
>   o'nights.
> Yon Cassius has a lean and hungry
>   look.
> He thinks too much. Such men are
>   dangerous [I, ii].

The modern body–personality–type theory, as popularized by W. H. Sheldon et al. (1940), distinguishes three body types. The **endomorph** has a round body with small bones, smooth skin, and little hair; the **mesomorph** has large bones and well-developed muscles; and the **ectomorph** has a linear, fragile body build. Many investigators have claimed to find relationships between these body types and certain personality traits. Evidence of such relationships is less conclusive for women than for men, since the majority of these studies have involved men. For men, however, reports are reasonably consistent. Of the three body types, all studies indicate the male mesomorph to be the best adjusted and the endomorph least well-adjusted. College students asked to assign traits to silhouettes illustrating the three body types assigned to mesomorphs such descriptive phrases as "best athlete," "best soldier," "popular," and "self-sufficient." Extreme ectomorphs were judged "likely to have a nervous breakdown," "to be chain smokers," and "not to have many friends." The endomorph, who fared least well, was called "a glutton," "poor athlete," "heavy drinker," and "unpopular" (Brodsky, 1954).

Actual research with children yields a similar picture./ Sheldon (1949) described boys with an ectomorphic build as cautious, quiet, and hesitant to give offense. They were sensitive, lacked energy, and looked to adults rather than to peers for approval. For girls the composite picture was similar, although ectomorphic girls showed more soberness of outlook. They were unfriendly, tense, and irritable. Consistent with other studies, mesomorphs proved well-adjusted. Mesomorphic girls tended to channel their energies into social affairs; mesomorphic boys, into gross motor activities. Endomorphic children of both sexes showed a fondness for comfort and a need for affection and approval.

Walker (1962) had nursery school teachers rate children on 64 behavior traits, which were then reduced by cluster analysis to nine personality scales. Independent ratings of physique were made, using photographs of the naked child. A number of significant correlations were found, most of them in the expected directions. Mesomorphs of both sexes tended to show assertiveness, fearlessness, and a high amount of energy. Endomorphic boys tended to be aggressive, while endomorphic girls were docile and cooperative. Ectomorphic boys were cooperative, unaggressive daydreamers, while ectomorphic girls were unsocial, uncheerful, and tense, and generally showed a low-grade crankiness.

Although body type has proved a poor indicator of personality, in individual cases, one may easily see why some relationships have been found. For one thing, it is possible that the same genetic factors that modify body build also contribute to basic temperament (typical emotional pattern). Also, certain body builds may simply be conducive to the development of particular traits. For instance, the boy with a square, muscular body may find it easy to win fights, and he may therefore develop aggressiveness as a way of settling arguments. The thinner ectomorph, on the other hand, may be defeated easily and hence become tense and shy. Finally, if certain cultural expectations prevail, one may unconsciously conform to the cultural stereotype. For instance, the fat child who is expected to be jolly may respond at least overtly to this expectation.

Even the relationships that are found are generally slight. Besides, all available data depend on somewhat questionable classifications of body build as well as personality traits. While classification of adults by trained persons using standardized techniques is reasonably reliable, results with children are more variable. The same child will not always be assigned the same ratio of body components by different raters. Even more important, we lack the instruments for making valid judgments of such traits as tension, joviality, and the like, on which the theory depends.

Body maturity. Conclusions about body maturity—that is, overall body growth—rest on more secure empirical grounds. Regardless of a child's build, his body maturity correlates with his achievement in the first grade. Physical maturity, it would seem, is more than skin deep. It is reflected not only in superficial body features but also in the maturational status of the central nervous system, which underlies such behaviors as readiness to submit to restraints and to apply oneself to tasks (Simon, 1959).

Body Image. Body maturity is simply one of various factors that modify the child's perception of his physical self—his **body image.** A child's body is his equipment for living. Through it he receives impressions from the world and interacts with it. He uses his body to express his thoughts and feelings and to manipulate his environment. Others react to him in terms of his appearance. The lean, vigorous child is often invited to play; the weak, skinny one is ignored. Mary's body is small and chubby; others nickname her "Dumpy." By contrast, Sally is good-looking; other girls envy her, thus enhancing her self-image.

As a result of others' reactions, each child acquires a concept of how he looks. This concept is modified by his actual dimensions—fat, lean, large or small—and their relationship both to the cultural ideal and to his own goals. The very fat child is less disposed toward strenuous activity than his leaner brother; hence, he comes to perceive his fatness as undesirable. However, in some cultures he will suffer more than in others. In a country where food means affluence, he may actually possess prestige; but in a prosperous country, which places a premium on leanness, he will feel out of place. Again, suppose a girl's personal ideal is "the face and body beautiful." The burn that disfigures her face will shatter her morale.

The cultural ideal, by which children tend to measure their appearance, is portrayed on television and in reading matter. As Scheinfeld (1965, p. 471) points out:

> Fairy tales and children's stories, picturing the menacing, hateful characters as having warped bodies and ugly faces, continue to foster the prejudices of children regarding looks. Being nicknamed "baboon face," "eagle beak," "fish mouth," or "donkey ears" may leave a sharp imprint on a child's character.

Development of self-image. Self-image is no sudden acquisition. It is partially a function of age—or rather the maturation and experience that aging implies. The neonate shows no interest in how he looks; and when he first takes note of his mirror image, he reacts as to another infant. However, by six or seven months he vaguely relates the image to himself, and by one year he possesses true self-recognition (Dixon, 1957).

Again, consider the case of phantom limbs, the amputee's feeling that the missing limbs still exist. If the amputa-

tion is performed before age four, phantoms rarely occur; thereafter, their incidence increases with the years. After the age of eight, phantoms may reliably be predicted. As time passes on, the child comes to perceive all his parts as one of a piece (Simmel, 1962).

The child's body image also comes to symbolize his relation to self and others. For example, children correctly perceive themselves as smaller than their parents, and their fathers as larger than their mothers. However, certain factors lead to distortions. Girls more generally underestimate their heights than boys do (Shaffer, 1964). Understandably, girls react to the popular emphasis that girls be smaller than boys and that they themselves not grow very large. Their tendency also to overestimate men's sizes as compared with women's reflects their assimilation of society's higher evaluation of the male.

Upsets in homeostasis. Compared with problems related to body build, those involving upsets in bodily homeostasis have received little attention. Nevertheless, they are a matter of special concern. In the human body, perhaps a thousand bodily functions operate simultaneously and in equilibrium (Adolf, 1945). A continuous balance among these functions is necessary to ensure normal blood sugar, water balance, rate of oxygen utilization, and hundreds of other needs. This balance, called **homeostasis,** is achieved by the regulatory action of the **autonomic nervous system** (smooth muscles and **glands**). The glands of the **endocrine system** normally work together to produce chemical secretions, or hormones, to maintain a constant internal environment within the body. The most important of the glands, as far as homeostasis is concerned, are the **pituitary glands** at the base of the brain; the **thyroid,** in the throat; the **adrenals,** near the kidneys; and the **gonads,** attached to the sex organs.

Homeostasis may be upset in various ways—as, for instance, by excess of deficient secretion from one or more hormones. In one case, a three-year-old boy, brought to a hospital because of certain abnormalities, suddenly died. The boy had lost salt faster than he could replace it on the normal hospital diet. After his death, the parents mentioned that he had never eaten properly and hated anything sweet. He licked the salt off bacon and crackers, and although he would not eat them, he would always ask for more. He would scream for the salt shaker, and ate fairly well when given several times the normal amount of salt. On the basis of these reports, it was concluded that he had abnormal adrenal glands, and that the lack of extra salt in the hospital diet had produced death (Wilkins and Richter, 1940, pp. 866–868).

Homeostatic disturbances operate on both physical and psychological levels, since these interact with each other. For instance, a deficiency of growth hormones from the pituitary causes dwarfism. In this case, only the growth factor is affected, so the dwarf is normal except in size. However, such an individual leads an abnormal life because of society's reactions toward him.

Disturbances in homeostasis and their accompanying effects may be temporary or permanent. A common but temporary upset in body balance is produced by high fever, which causes children to become mentally and emotionally confused, with a tendency to resist suggestions from others. However, as the fever subsides, behavior reverts to normal (Stagner, 1951). More lasting, sometimes irreversible effects are produced by endocrine disorders.

The problems of overweight. The exact relationship between bodily homeostasis and overweight is unknown. In any case, the problem is largely the product of an affluent society. Calorie intake is at an all-time high; and an increasing number of the juvenile population are becoming fat. According to Garn (1960, p. 34):

The American child's diet, once characterized as one big milkshake, comes perilously close to a diet known to be atherogenic. If 35 per cent of his calories come from fats, is junior being prepared for starting in nursery school or for a coronary occlusion? . . . Frappés, fat-meat hamburgers, bacon-and-mayonnaise sandwiches, followed by ice cream, may be good for the farmer, good for the undertaker and bad for the populace.

Even within certain Western countries—the only ones wealthy enough to support chronic over-eating—eating patterns vary with the times and according to subgroups. Over the years children are gradually growing heavier. Between 1880 and 1950, the mean body weight for North American white boys age 6 years has risen between 11 and 15%. Whether this gain is good or not we simply do not know (Meredith, 1963).

Overweight in children constitutes a problem for several reasons. For one thing, the fat child is subject to all sorts of nonflattering allusions, such as "Fatty" or "Whale," which can have a devastating effect on his self-concept. Others refuse to take him seriously, making him the butt of their jokes; hence he can hardly maintain a position of status and dignity in either his own eyes or those of the group. Such cases as the following are not at all atypical:

I was so fat during my childhood that my schoolmates tagged such names on me as Fatty, tub-o'-lard, and 2 by 4. As a result, I had a crying spell almost every evening.*

A child's reaction to his own excess weight varies according to his accustomed ways of behaving under stress. A shy child may avoid other children and shrink within the security of his own home. As he grows older, he daydreams more and more, accomplishing in fantasy the things his bulk ordinarily forbids.

*Throughout this book, personal recollections such as this one are from the author's file of responses to questions asked of college students.

Another child may lash out at those who reject and taunt him. He misbehaves in school, harasses the neighbors, and becomes labeled a "pest." The first child internalizes his problem, rejecting himself; the second externalizes his, taking out his unhappiness on others.

Actually, we do not know all the effects of overnutrition in children. We do know that the overweight child grows faster, matures and reaches final stature earlier. The fat boy and girl, therefore, are not only less attractive sexually than the average, but mature sexually faster, making them physically ready for experiences they are not ready to handle.

Causes of overweight. The causes of overweight may be either constitutional or environmental, or both. Some children are undoubtedly predisposed, for various reasons, to the easy accumulation of fat. Since this basic factor cannot be changed, the child must learn to accommodate himself to it.

The problem is further complicated by psychological factors. If a mother pays little attention to a child except when feeding him, food may attain an exaggerated place in his scheme of things. In other cases, tension or boredom may cause a child to seek diversion in food. In a study of 500 obese patients, 365 said they ate more and more often when they were nervous and worried. Of the remaining 130, 95 consumed more when idle, bored, or tired (Freed, 1947).

Dealing with problems of overweight. Overweight, it has been said, is merely a case of too much exercise with the fork—but whatever the cause, the child should first see a physician. A diet can then be prescribed and the possible reasons for wrong eating patterns discussed. Sometimes hormonal treatment may be indicated. If no progress is made, a psychologist or psychiatrist should be consulted. Psychotherapy alone is better than either diet or drugs alone. Food should not be withheld unless the child is helped to solve the problems that precipitated over-

eating in the first place. Long-standing habits of overeating are hard to correct. Until change can be effected, the objectives should become those of avoiding further increases in weight and securing self-acceptance to the degree that overweight cannot immediately be corrected without undesirable consequences (Stuart, 1955). The use of thyroxin or a very stringent diet might indeed rapidly reduce the child's weight, but it could also have harmful effects on his health.

The problems of underweight. Less well recognized, and usually overlooked altogether, are the problems of underweight children. Such children often lack the stamina required for rough-and-tough children's games. And in late childhood, children may become sensitive about underweight, as these two cases, recalled from that period, show:

> I heard a boy whom I admired refer to me as "Canary Legs," which was a crushing blow to my self-image.

> I was so skinny as a child that I looked, and felt, more or less like a bag of bones, swaddled in generally ill-fitting clothes.

Like the overweight child, the underweight child should first be checked by a physician. Only such a check can determine what weight is best for him and to what extent the problem is a physiological one. In many cases, varying combinations of medical and psychological help may be needed.

Treatment should attack the causes of underweight. Among these are irregular or unappetizing meals, poor nutrition, excess fatigue, and tension. Another cause is anorexia—a rejecting attitude toward food, usually originating in early childhood. Refusal to eat is an easy way to get back at a rejecting parent. Or it may simply be a child's way of focusing attention on himself.

Obviously, basic to problems of atypical weight is sound training in nutrition. All too often there is little tie-up between health training in schools and practical weight problems. The best program is one in which pediatrician, psychiatrist, parent, teacher, and — to whatever extent his maturity warrants — the child himself work together to solve the problem.

Nutrition

Considerable evidence attests to the significance of nutrition for human development, among the best having been obtained in the Minnesota Study of Human Starvation (Schiele et al., 1948). The behaviors of healthy young men, observed when on a semi-starvation diet, were compared with those of the same men when adequately fed. During the starvation period, both physical and personality changes were striking. Food became the chief topic of their conversation, reading, and dreams. Some decided to go into agriculture; others decided to become cooks. Meanwhile, progressive biochemical changes made the men become tired, apathetic, irritable, and lacking in self-control. They lost ambition, humor, interest in appearance, and the capacity to stand stresses and strains. After an adequate diet was restored, many months passed before they recovered completely.

Malnutrition during childhood may prove even more devastating, and — because the body is still developing — irreversible in effect. Especially when experienced during the first year of life, and to a lesser extent from then on, gross malnutrition can limit the development of head circumference, thereby preventing brain growth and subsequent intellectual development (Stock and Smyth, 1963). Severe protein malnutrition may cause children to have a condition called kwashiorkor, which makes them dull, apathetic, and miserable. They sit without moving, indifferent to their surroundings; they rarely cry, just whimper (Brock and Autret, 1952).

Such evidence could be vastly expanded to show the gamut of mental and physical conditions that result from severe malnutrition. What is still lacking, however, is a definitive index of effects of lesser nutritional deficiencies. Just where is the critical point between adequate and inadequate nutrition? Even if the ill-effects of lesser deficiencies were proved, how might these border-line cases be identified? How might one determine the part that malnutrition, as one of multiple environmental influences, plays in a specific child's life? The welfare of a vast number of children hinges, at least partially, on these as yet unanswered questions. Meantime, many a person simply oozes through life, his energies deactivated by improper nutrition resulting from eating habits learned in childhood.

Principles of sound nutrition. Nutritionists, pediatricians, and psychologists have already established certain principles for children's nutrition. Parents should be flexible, allowing for children's individual needs and for normal variations in appetite. They should avoid, as far as possible, establishing negative associations with foods or the feeding situation. In a study of girls aged 12 to 14, negative attitudes toward food were related to parental criticism for eating the wrong foods, for eating too much or too often, and for eating too slowly (Hilton et al., 1962). Good eating habits depend on the parents' adaptability to growing children's changing needs.

Rest and Sleep

Fatigue. Improper nutrition is a major cause of fatigue, another common childhood problem. Among the many factors that may cause fatigue are inherited constitution, overstimulation, excess competition, insecurity, strained body positions or poor light while working, improper or inadequate food, and too strenuous activity. Of course, the effects of these stresses vary somewhat with the child.

Almost any acutely tired child is cranky and unreasonable, cries on slight provocation, and denies he is tired. On first becoming fatigued, he shows excess activity and excitability, but later he

67

grows listless and inactive. As the condition progresses, he may develop dark circles and puffiness under his eyes and, in some cases, twitches and tremors. If the condition becomes chronic, his initiative is reduced, his attention span shortened, and his appetite for social activity curtailed. The following item from a mother's diary illustrates one effect that fatigue may have on children:

> Usually Andy gets tired and cranky about five o'clock. He comes to the table and announces "I don't yike peas," or "I don't yike meat." Tonight he came in and saw the table still empty. He propped his fat arms up on the table and announced "I don't yike . . . I don't yike . . ." (nothing was there). Finally in a burst of unpleasantness . . . "I don't yike . . . sump'n!" [Piucci, unpublished].

To avoid fatigue, children need a balanced program of sleep, relaxation, and recreation geared to their individual needs. The chronically tired child needs a thorough physical examination, increased rest, a good diet, and a satisfactory emotional climate (Breckinridge and Vincent, 1965, p. 132). If this program fails, the problem may have deep-seated emotional causes, which create a chronic imbalance in the central and autonomic nervous system functions, producing feelings of exhaustion.

Sleep. Attention should be paid to children's sleep for several reasons. For one thing, rapidly growing children need correspondingly more sleep than children at ages of less rapid growth. Most young children require about 12 hours sleep, while older ones' needs are more variable. However, the amount of sleep is less important than the quality of sleep. A quiet, relaxing period before bedtime, a comfortable bed, and a bedroom free of noise are helpful. More basic still is an emotional climate that makes for happiness and relaxation (Breckinridge and Vincent, 1965, p. 131).

Illness and Disease

Every period of childhood has its health hazards. During babyhood, diseases are frequent and sometimes fatal. Between ages three and eight, children are often subject to such diseases as mumps, measles, and chickenpox. The next two years are normally as healthy as any other span in life. The extent of psychosomatic disorders during childhood is still unknown.

Causes of illness. Illness may be caused by bacteria or viruses — especially when a child's overall physical condition makes him vulnerable — or by psychosomatic factors. The conditions that precipitate a disease in one person may not affect another. Some individuals possess an innate susceptibility or resistance to diseases of a noninfective nature (Williams and Siegel, 1961).

Often a condition is a combination of mental and physical factors. For instance, asthma seems to be a product of certain respiratory structures coupled with tension and maternal overprotection (Long, 1958). At other times, disease may be purely imaginary, with no physical symptoms. How often or to what extent such illnesses occur in childhood is not known; however they unquestionably occur during adolescence.

Effects of illness. The effects of illness are varied, depending on the child concerned, the situation, and the nature of the illness itself. Ordinary illness produces no measurably permanent effects. The effects of serious illness depend on its nature and when it occurs. For instance, tuberculosis, if it occurs during a period of rapid growth, may reduce a child's final height. Rickets and polio may leave bone deformities, rheumatic encephalitis a damaged brain, and rheumatic fever a damaged heart.

The psychological effects of an illness depend on its length and on the parents' handling of the situation. If parents themselves become worried and irritable, the child grows tense, anxious, and sometimes prone to tantrums. If he is of school-age, he loses crucial academic instruction and valuable social experience. The effects are accentuated if the illness requires continued limitation of physical activity (Haggerty, 1959).

Here is a case illustrating certain of the unfortunate effects that illness and disease may have on children:

> When I was in the fifth grade, I got hepatitis, and before I realized how serious it was I felt sort of special. I wasn't allowed to play, ride my bike, go up or down stairs — in fact, all I could do was lie down, take pills, and eat starches and sugar. Briefly, I enjoyed being away from school, but then I began missing all the fun. I absolutely adore sports, but even after I got better I was unable to participate actively.

Good health is more than freedom from disease.

Illness may leave its scars on the child's personality, especially if he is very young and if the illness is prolonged. Since parents overprotect and cater to him, he comes to expect — but fails to receive — similar treatment from teachers and peers. Also, if lessened activity is required for some time, the child may come to look on himself as "ill." For whatever combination of reasons, childhood victims of certain diseases develop typical personality syndromes. For example, the asthmatic child is characterized by overanxiety, lack of self-confidence, dependency, psychoneurotic difficulties, and behavior problems. A similar syndrome is found for cardiac children. Children suffering from any chronic illness, whether physical or psychological, develop atypical emotional patterns (Neuhaus, 1958).

The need for a positive concept of sound health. Physicians and psychiatrists have long been concerned with illness but have all but ignored the special benefits of good health. Good health should be thought of not as freedom from disease but as the buoyant physical condition that provides the optimum physical basis for accomplishment and the good life. It encourages the healthy, zestful feeling that makes one a pleasant associate and energetic worker; it implies the sort of body tonus that makes one feel good and glad to be alive.

All too many children seem only half alive, suspended in a twilight zone between the absence of actual disease and the presence of buoyant health that makes full living possible. These children are victims of a hidden hunger as devastating as food hunger. Subclinical handicaps cripple confidence, initiative, and efficiency, impair daily achievement and satisfaction, shatter ambition, and cast a gray veil of uneasiness over what should be the joy of life (Todd, 1938).

Accidents

Although the problem of disease is serious, accidents are the number one cause of death in childhood. In addition, many children suffer either temporary or permanent ill effects from accidents. Two-thirds of the victims of these accidents are under age nine; and boys have far more accidents than girls. Home accidents are more common among younger children; outside accidents, usually on

69

An accident can handicap a child temporarily.

consciousness. For instance, *The Post Boy* contained rather grim lessons. In passages headed "The Post Boy's Bag Opened" were such packets as these:

Two little boys lost their lives in a pond! They went in to bathe and did not know how deep the water was. They asked to take a walk into the field, and as it was a hot day they went into the water. They were both put into one grave [Kiefer, 1948, p. 167].

Some children seem to be accident-prone; that is, they experience a disproportionately large number of accidents.

My mother always said I was more accident-prone than the rest of her children. I cut my knee, sat on a broken glass bottle, got run over by a car, stepped on a piece of broken glass in a lake, and smashed my fingers many times. Also, I broke an arm, later on burned the same arm, and still later put it through a glass door. I always had black and blue marks which I couldn't account for. And on one occasion, sister and I ate a box of aspirin and had to have our stomachs pumped out.

the playground or street, are more common among older ones. The most common childhood accidents are falls, burns, dog bites, fractures, cuts, bruises, poisonings, sprains, and dislocations. Deaths most often result from motor-vehicle accidents, firearms, explosives, suffocations, and drownings (Hurlock, 1964, pp. 154–155).

Accidents are most often caused by children's curiosity, impulsiveness, and immaturity, coupled with adults' lack of proper supervision. Curiosity leads children to explore their environment and to try out new situations. Boys, especially, are likely to do daring things to impress their peers or to enhance themselves in their own eyes. However, busy parents simply cannot watch children every minute; nor can boys be constantly supervised in their relatively free outside activities on vacant lots and streets.

Nowadays schools have integrated safety education into health and playground programs, while in our forefathers' day children's stories were deliberately designed to produce safety

Widely varying combinations of causes may underlie accident-proneness. Children who are very active, impulsive, hostile, or adventurous often disregard caution. Others who are high-strung and nervous are less precise in their actions and invite injury. Some children are so preoccupied with themselves and their problems that they fail to appraise all aspects of a situation intelligently. Still other children, especially boys, attempt to compensate for unpopularity or win social acceptance by daredevil acts.

The effects of accidents may be physical, psychological, or often a combination of both. A facial scar, for instance, may force an alteration in a child's body image, and affect his relations with his peers. Serious accidents may reduce, either temporarily or permanently, a child's experiences in sports and social activities. And for whatever time an accident requires confinement at home or in the hospital, the child loses valuable academic and social experience. Also, the accident may leave him with fears hard for him to overcome, especially if the adults concerned fail to handle the situation properly.

The adult's attitude is of great significance. As in the case of illness and disease, a parent or teacher may be so sympathetic that the child will feel sorry for himself. Afterward, the adult may unduly limit the child's activities, lest he hurt himself again. On the other hand, a father may scold his son for having been careless or clumsy and make the boy feel he is not quite masculine.

Other children's attitudes are important, too. Sometimes, the child may become something of a hero. Others may envy him the cast on his leg or the bandage on his arm. As a result, he may resist getting well and returning to his former quite ordinary status. On the other hand, if they do not like him, they may tease or make fun of him for his mishap. The child with the crutch may be called "Lame Duck," or the one who is accident-prone may be labeled "Clumsy."

Physical Handicaps

About one person in 18 suffers from a chronic disease or permanent physical impairment of some kind. As many more suffer from conditions that are chronic but less handicapping conditions (National Health Education Committee, 1961). Approximately half of the more severely handicapped persons are under age 50, and one-fifth under age 25.

The problems faced by handicapped children. The physically handicapped child experiences many disadvantages. For one thing, his developmental progress suffers, leaving him out of step with children his age. Blind children, for instance, are slower in learning to walk, eat, dress, and bathe (Lemkau, 1961).

In addition, the physically handi-

capped individual is often an underachiever. The child with poor vision may not see the blackboard well; the crippled child feels lonely and isolated and hence cannot relax and enjoy school activities. Teachers, although generally sympathetic with younger children, may be less tolerant of older ones. This attitude is most common in the case of milder defects—notably of speech, hearing, or sight—which reduce academic achievement and reflect on the teacher's effectiveness (Bernabeu, 1958).

Handicaps also impede social adjustment. If a child lacks motor skills, he rarely plays an important role in his group. Since his activities are restricted, he grows envious, resentful, and withdrawn—sustained only by the successes of fantasy. Or he may become anxious and angry, engaging in offensive aggression. Afterward he feels guilty, but his efforts to "make up" are rebuffed (Force, 1956).

Sometimes a child deliberately uses his handicap to gain selfish ends. In any case, his mood and attitude may make him such poor company that he becomes more rejected still—a vicious cycle. He may employ the handicap as an excuse to escape growing up or to take advantage of others. He may even feel a masochistic enjoyment in his defect, feeding on the sympathy of others.

The handicapped child also suffers simply because he is a child. Children are rarely sensitive to the feelings of less favored persons. They can be brutally frank, causing deep wounds. In one case, a lame child was called "Crip." In another instance, children mimicked a boy with a cleft palate, taking no pains to remove themselves from his hearing (Cruikshank and Johnson, 1958).

In short, contrary to Adler's theory that organic inferiority endows the child with a will to power and a strong drive to excel, the laws of compensation usually do not apply. As a matter of fact, severely handicapped children become neurotic more often than successful (Hughes, 1960). Some children simply give up, resigning themselves completely and accepting the role of recluse assigned them. Others demonstrate varying combinations of self-pity, fear, and hostility. In an intensive study of children severely crippled by poliomyelitis, core reactions of rage, anxiety, and frustration were typical (Bernabeu, 1958).

Some children do develop healthy compensatory behaviors; others develop exaggerated ones, such as boasting and fantasy; still others find alternative modes of expression. Most handicapped children deny or try to ignore the fact that they are different. However, figure drawings of children suffering from orthopedic disabilities following polio revealed that these children often omitted legs from their drawings, or showed a size discrepancy in the drawings of legs, or included some external support for the body in their drawings (Silverstein and Robinson, 1956).

The handicapped also suffer from societal attitudes toward them. While ostensibly heeding their welfare, people often feel pity or repulsion – or even an unconscious resentment that such people must somehow be provided for. The handicapped, in turn, come to expect society's negative attitudes toward them, and they often acquire deep-seated inferiority complexes. Despite intermittent struggles, the majority are unhappy and often doomed to social isolation (Elser, 1959).

A child's reactions depend somewhat on whether he attends regular or special schools. Especially in the case of blindness, deafness, or cerebral palsy, children have less favorable attitudes toward their defects and develop more disturbances when they associate primarily with normal children (Mussen and Newman, 1958).

Fortunately, some children whose conditions may not be correctable accept their lot and make the best of whatever talents they have. A few who have enough positive assets to offset the negative effects of the handicap may be quite

happy and successful. In effect, they defy the condition that has sought so relentlessly to shackle them.

Factors modifying the effects of crippling. Various factors limit the effects of crippling – for example, the extent to which a defect permits camouflage. A facial disfigurement is quite visible and plays a central role in the development of self-concept (McGregor, 1951). By contrast, a wooden leg covered by trousers is betrayed only by a limp; and a bad scar on the body may not be suspected at all. Sometimes, however, a child may be at a greater disadvantage merely because a handicap cannot be perceived. The child with a heart condition may be considered a poor sport or a sissy if he avoids vigorous play. The deaf child may be thought stupid or impolite because he does not answer questions.

The age of crippling is especially significant. In general, the earlier the child is crippled, the more easily he adapts his self-image and self-concept (Siller, 1960). Congenital defects, which are part of the child's original concept of self, seem to be easiest to accept. In the case of amputations, children under eight are less sensitive to social appraisal than older children. Psychological effects seem to increase with age, at least through adolescence.

Severity of crippling is another factor. Children with either severe or relatively slight defects often have the most difficult adjustment. Obviously, a child born without a leg, or one whose entire face is deeply burned, will confront great difficulties. On the other hand, a mild handicap, as opposed to a "middle-sized" handicap, has its hazards too. For instance, the child whose motor coordination is poor enough to make him extremely awkward at games but not obvious enough to arouse understanding may face constant rebuffs. He tries to compete with normal children, never having fully realized that he is unable to meet their standards. A more severely handicapped child would have the perception of his condition forced upon him, compelling him to accept it and to live within its limitations. The totally blind child receives all sorts of consideration; the partially blind, often none. When the latter accidentally shoves another child, he receives a scowl or even a blow in return. In school he turns in messy papers and upsets bottles of ink, incurring both low grades and the teacher's displeasure. Gradually, he comes to feel sorry for himself and to reject others (Walman, 1958).

In cases of the severely handicapped, reactions vary greatly:

> I am the parent of a handicapped child—beautiful of countenance, brilliant in mind, the soul and understanding of an angel, but with a body condition which is revolting to most people.
>
> There is no need to mention the agony, the tears, the time, the energy expended, the insults, the expense of doctors, nurses, clinical therapists, of the merciless caustic remarks of even those who should know better. But when your child (who is considered to be one of the "best adjusted" in this area) cries out that perhaps suicide is the answer, your heart and soul are rent into a million pieces [Boroson, 1965, pp. 35–36].

> I approached Steve—an 18 year old boy whose fingers grow out of his shoulder and who has other anomalies. I asked Steve would he rather not have come into this world in the shape God had given him? A squawking protest was his immediate reply: "Gosh, think what I would be missing if I hadn't made it." My only response was to think what others would be missing if this boy "hadn't made it" [Boroson, 1965, p. 31].

A factor sometimes neglected in assessing the seriousness of a handicap is its susceptibility to correction. Many defects, such as moles, burns, or harelips, may be wholly or partially repaired by plastic surgery or other treatment. In one study, analysis of figure drawings before and after surgery by persons suffering facial disfigurements revealed dramatic changes in some cases, though less in others. In general, however, the self-concept was improved (Abel, 1953).

A major factor in such widely different reactions to handicap is the attitude of significant persons in the child's life. Of these, the parents' attitude is most important. A mother may overprotect the child, depriving him of independence. Preoccupied with taking care of the child, she martyrs herself, becomes socially withdrawn, and neglects friends, husband, and other children. She may also have feelings of guilt, somehow believing the child's handicap a punishment for some failing of her own. The father often perceives the child as a liability, and may not be proud of him (Boles, 1959). Siblings may resent having to take care of the child and find him an embarrassment among their peers. They may also resent the mother's preoccupation with him.

Dealing with handicapped children. Certain general recommendations can be made for the proper treatment of the handicapped, although these points must be adapted for each individual case. Overall, a happy, wholesome environment is crucial. Parents should treat the child as normally as feasible, while unobtrusively making due allowance for his handicap. They should make every effort to build his self-concept, because the child who accepts himself is more likely to be accepted by others. For example, note this brief exchange between Dick, a child born without a left arm, and another boy. Other boy: "What happened to your arm?" Dick: "Oh, I was just born this way." Other boy: "O.K., let's get going." . . . And they went off to play (Strang, 1965).

• MOTOR DEVELOPMENT

The importance of **motor development** has long been recognized. Note this fifteenth-century pediatrician's advice about the newborn:

One should also know that after the bath, before the child is wrapped up, the legs should be bent backwards, and also the feet brought forward to the head, especially in boys, so that their joints will be the more supple [Bartholomaeus Metlinger, as quoted in Rührah, 1925, p. 77].

Motor development affects children's adjustment in various important ways—for example, by modifying physical health. Physical play and other activities stimulate respiration and circulation, thus providing better nourishment for the cells and more effective removal of wastes. Through strenuous play, the child also improves his muscle tone and rids his body of pent-up energy that might otherwise produce tension. Another bonus is entertainment. Motor activity is fun—with all the exhilaration and relaxation of recreation. Motor skill also makes possible solitary play, such as carpentry, painting, or crafts. These same activities provide cognitive training; for instance, building a doghouse involves mathematical concepts and computations.

Another benefit is experience in socialization, for children's peer relations are built about physical play. Physically weak or clumsy children are forced to play alone or with children younger than they. In time they become defensive, either withdrawing into themselves or becoming aggressive. Such reactions, once habituated, tend to persist into adult life.

In the following paragraphs, two teen-agers recall problems of motor development experienced in childhood:

Because of my awkwardness I felt inferior to other children in grade school. When we chose up teams for relay races, no one wanted me and I was always chosen last. (Female)

I have always felt inadequate in motor skills, swimming especially. Numerous times I was enrolled in classes, but never learned to swim. One instructor asked me to drop from his class. He returned my parents'

money and said I'd never learn to swim. (Female)

Boys' social acceptance is linked more closely than girls' to motor skills, though less so than formerly. Even now, the boy who fumbles and bumbles at play is not only socially neglected but rejected (Bull, 1958).

Finally, motor development is related to self-concept, for reasons already suggested. An individual's concept of self hinges on his adequacy to cope with his world, either material or

Skillful handling of the body enhances the image of self.

social. Coping techniques involve motor skills as well as cognitive components. Skillful handling of the body permits more effective solution of many problems while enhancing the image of self. A healthy self-concept, in turn, promotes skilled motor development, thus providing a circular reaction. The shy child, for instance, hesitates to try new skills, whereas the child who is skilled will be sought as a companion and, hence, will be less shy.

The Normal Course of Motor Development

Although children vary vastly in motor skills, there are certain common features in their motor development. To begin with, it has been suggested that kinesthetic drive is basic to the organism (Kulka, 1960). This is expressed initially by the free movement of the fetus in its fluid environment. However, for the first few months after birth, the infant is grounded while sight and hearing acquire their range. Later on, progress in motor skills proceeds irregularly, with periods of progress followed by periods of dormancy.

Throughout childhood certain basic laws operate in motor development. For instance, progression of bodily control is both **proximodistal**—that is, from the center of the body region to the extremities—and **cephalocaudal**—from head (cephalic) to foot or, in animals, to tail (caudal) regions. The cephalocaudal order of development is quite clear in infancy, when children are much more skillful with arms and hands than with feet. By 18 months they can throw a ball with fair accuracy, but they don't kick as well.

Also, recall that growth proceeds from the mass to the specific; that is, as practice proceeds, mass responses become progressively displaced by more specific responses. For example, stimulation of the foot at first evokes activity from the entire body; a few weeks later, however, it evokes merely a purposeful withdrawal of the foot. In other words, early responses are both stereotyped and generalized; but with time and practice they become increasingly differentiated. The infant first makes larger movements, then smaller, more precise ones. Sweeping motions with the arm gradually give way to precise coordinated use of hands and fingers. These progressions proceed simultaneously and correlate closely with neural development. As this individuation occurs, proportionately less expenditure of energy is involved, and less cross-purpose action. The tendency is toward minimum muscular involvement. Originally, the baby may flail arms and legs and twist his entire body in maneuvering to grasp his bottle; later he simply extends his hands and arms, while the rest of his body remains still.

In time, specific movements and skills become integrated into more complex skills. Thus, growth also proceeds from specific to mass, in the sense that processes become reintegrated into increasingly more complex patterns even as they become differentiated from simpler ones.

The Maturation-Learning Controversy

From the foregoing discussion, one may be tempted to conclude that motor development proceeds spontaneously, in ways predetermined by genetics. This is the so-called "maturationist" view. However, learning also plays a significant, though much-debated, role in motor development.

The maturationists' position. At first, the maturationists seemed to have the better of the argument. In consequence, Shirley's classic chart of locomotion, which shows the child's progress stage by stage, as though following an unvarying timetable, became a textbook favorite. On Shirley's chart, the child was shown sitting alone at 7 months, creeping at 10 months, and walking alone at 15 months.

In supporting the primary importance of maturation, certain authorities compared Hopi infants, cradled during the early months, with others permitted the free use of arms and legs (Dennis and Dennis, 1940). The infants who had been cradled walked as early as those who had never been thus restrained.

Another study supporting the same position was the classic study of Johnny and Jimmy, originally believed to be identical twins but later found to be fraternal. Johnny, who was physically inferior to Jimmy at birth, was stimulated and helped in acquiring motor

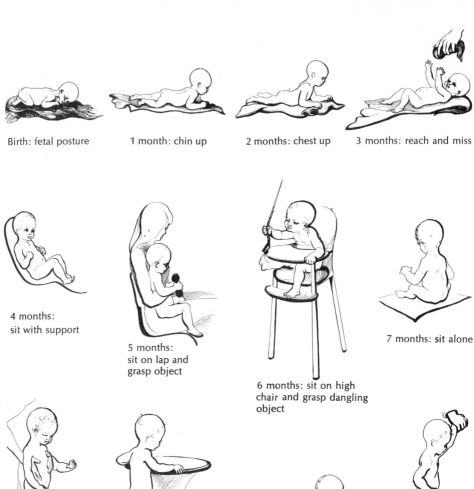

Birth: fetal posture

1 month: chin up

2 months: chest up

3 months: reach and miss

4 months:
sit with support

5 months:
sit on lap and
grasp object

6 months: sit on high
chair and grasp dangling
object

7 months: sit alone

8 months:
stand with help

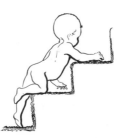

9 months:
stand holding furniture

10 months: creep

11 months:
walk when led

12 months:
pull to stand by
furniture

13 months:
climb stair steps

14 months:
stand alone

15 months:
walk alone

Shirley's developmental sequences. Adapted from M. M. Shirley, The first two years, a study of twenty-five babies, I, intellectual development, *Institute of Child Welfare Monographs,* Series No. 8. University of Minnesota Press, 1933. Used by permission.

skills of all kinds and encouraged to be self-confident in coping with obstacles. Meanwhile, Jimmy played unhindered, with no special training in physical skills. Periodically, the boys were compared with each other and with other children serving as controls. Although Johnny had had practice in stepping movements from the age of 20 days, both twins took their first steps when 9 months old. Johnny could roller-skate and swim by 16 months but despite considerable effort could not be taught to tricycle until three months later. Finally, when the twins were 22 months old, Jimmy was given two and a half months of intensive practice in the identical activities formerly reserved for Johnny. At the conclusion of this training, he still did less well at roller-skating than Johnny but easily mastered other activities, such as tricycling, in a briefer time than Johnny had required at an earlier age. As compared with a group of 57 infants who had received no special training, Jimmy proved no better than average in these skills.

During their third year, the twins' training was stopped, but their performance in these skills was checked at intervals until they reached six years. At that age both boys showed deterioration in roller-skating, in which their greater weight was a handicap; however, neither did less well in tricycling, where bodily changes were not so important. Overall, results were construed as underlining the significance of maturation. That is, the study seemed to prove that a skill could not be taught until the stage of maturation permitted, and, presumably, that children would spontaneously learn basic locomotive skills without special training (McGraw, 1939).

The environmentalists' position. Since 1940, however, authorities have increasingly stressed the importance of training. Their position is amply supported by research. For example, young chicks fed artificially from a spoon for two weeks after hatching never developed a pecking response. If progress toward pecking had simply been a function of maturation, this early deprivation would have made no difference (Padilla, 1935).

Among human infants, Dennis (1960) found severe retardation among children in certain Iranian institutions who had received little handling. Attendants had failed even to place them in sitting and prone positions. The absence of experience in these positions was believed related to retardation in sitting and locomotion.

In the study of the twins Johnny and Jimmy, reported above, it was now pointed out that daily life activities had provided both boys with training in the basic patterns needed for tricycling; hence, Jimmy was able to catch up quickly at this task. Besides, the twins were found *not* to be identical, so maturational factors for the two boys could not be assumed to be identical.

Evaluating the evidence. Recently the meanings of all these studies have been reasonably well reconciled. For example, Shirley's norms for progress in locomotion are met only under favorable environmental conditions. In Dennis' study of Iranian institutions, not only was sitting retarded, but in many cases creeping did not occur. Instead, an alternative form of locomotion was employed. This finding would indicate that experience affects not only the ages at which forms of locomotion occur but also their very form. Undoubtedly the maturation of certain structures, as yet unidentified, is required before certain responses can be learned; but experience, too, plays a part.

In the Hopi study, which showed infants progressing satisfactorily despite swaddling, other factors should not be overlooked. While on the mother's back, the infant was exposed to a rich variety of auditory and visual inputs. Having a variety of things to listen to and to look at is probably important for overall development, including locomotion, in the first year of life (Fiske and Madde, 1961).

In other words, it has been wrong

to seek the effects of experience only in the practice of the function to be measured. The existence of an epigenesis of intellectual function implies that the experiential roots of a given schema will lie in antecedent activities quite different in structure from the schema to be observed. Epigenesis in this case refers to the emergence of new properties that are not contained in earlier stages of the organism's life history—although such emergent properties are somehow related to those earlier stages. Thus, antecedent practice at tower-building or buttoning may not be important for later skills; but unhampered chances to throw objects or to manipulate in a variety of situations may be important (Hunt, 1964).

After surveying the literature, Fowler (1962) concluded that studies were often subtly structured to support the maturation hypothesis and to minimize the effects of training. The fact that training experiences almost invariably exerted some effect was often glossed over. Furthermore, behaviors in which training was given were often uncomplicated acts. In simple activities the impact of training was vastly diluted. Also, the training tended to be brief and to deal with meaningless material for which motivation might be minimal. Finally, psychosocial and personality factors were often slighted in interpreting results, although they are now widely considered to be highly potent influences in the learning process. For instance, children's progress in motor development would be affected not only by practice in relevant skills but also by personality variables, such as the degree of responsiveness or emotional stability of the children involved.

Factors Related to Motor Development

Although children follow the same basic pattern of growth, there are significant individual differences. Both prenatally and postnatally, babies differ in their rates of achieving specific motor behaviors (Carmichael, 1954). They also differ at both periods in amount and vigor of activity (Kessen et al. 1961).

Various factors correlate with or modify individual progress in motor development—for example, prenatal growth. Correlations have been found between fetal activity and postnatal motor skills. Thus the active fetus is likely to be more advanced in motor behaviors as an infant (Richards and Newberry, 1938). How much of prenatal activity derives from maturation—that is, the unfolding of genetic factors—and how much from prenatal environment is uncertain.

Traits like height and strength are at least partially the result of maturation, or the unfolding of genetic factors. However, the acquisition of new behaviors in the child's repertoire depends on the interaction of maturational phenomena with appropriate experience. The baby sits alone at six months partly because he has matured sufficiently and partly because of certain learning experiences. His head, in proportion to torso and legs, is smaller and more manageable, and his back muscles are stronger. Meanwhile, he has practiced constantly. He has reared up from his stomach, using his arms for props. He has practiced balancing his head, used his legs, and often attempted to lift himself by his hands and arms. Finally, through integrating these separate skills, a new skill—partly the result of learning, partly of maturation—emerges, and he sits alone.

Both race and intelligence have been cited as factors affecting motor development. Investigators have reported, for example, that gross motor behavior is accelerated in Negroes. However, Pasamanick and Knobloch (1966) have failed to verify this finding. Infants of both races, according to their 1950 data, proved comparable in motor development and significantly advanced over the past two decades. Although child-rearing methods may have been responsible, no definitive explanation exists. Sex differences are more clear-cut; boys are generally more active and vigorous than girls. However, there are great intra-sex differences and a considerable overlapping between the sexes (Richards and Newberry, 1938).

Principles of Sound Motor Development

Current attitudes and practices. A factor directly affecting motor development is child-rearing. At least in practice, adults assume three different postures relative to children's motor development. Some simply leave this component of children's behavior to chance, perhaps because they believe the child thrives best who engages in motor activities as he pleases. Or they may simply take this aspect of children's behavior for granted, ignorant of the part it plays in development. Others merely believe in setting the stage; that is, they provide facilities for play and then leave children to their own devices. Having provided Junior with a souped-up tricycle and a bat twice his size, they assume that health and athletic powers will follow. Still others favor

actively arranging for motor development, though few would advocate so strenuous a program as some communist countries have. In China, everyone—old and young—must tumble out and exercise every morning at five. Perhaps the best program involves elements of all three attitudes just described.

Adapting the program to the child's needs. Certainly not every program of physical development, whether formally or informally conducted, is sound. Adults who lack training in this area are prone to err, as illustrated here:

> My family lived at Jones Beach where the water was rough. When I was a child, my parents would take me into the deep water and hold me in a prone position. I remember screaming and crying because I was afraid my parents would drop me.

In school physical education programs, certain common but unfortunate practices are followed. Teachers often

Adults can help the child develop motor skills.

79

take more interest in the skilled than in the unskilled, and some of them embarrass the child who is poor at physical skills by calling attention to his ineptness in front of the others. Few of them possess the insight to realize the dangers of choosing up sides, or of the sort of competition involved in interscholastic sports.

A good program must be carefully planned. It must respect each child's level of maturation and recognize that motor development cannot be left to chance. Ample research suggests that severe restriction of activity lessens both physiological and "psychological" tonus (Anderson, 1960). This point requires special emphasis in an age when labor-saving devices deactivate muscles, diets become the casualties of high living, and automobiles make extended walking obsolete.

Having acknowledged the need, home and community must make available suitable places and equipment for play. In many cities, safe opportunities for strenuous play scarcely exist. Even in suburbs, land is denuded of trees and houses divested of stairs to climb. Housing developments concede each house only a tiny lawn. Where indoor space is provided, play areas are often slippery, drafty, dirty, and small.

Little research tells what facilities best serve children's physical needs. For example, does nursery school equipment provide the challenge desired? Is it too stereotyped to allow for individual differences? Does it permit progression through successive stages of motor development?

Another consideration is quantity and type of equipment. A certain amount is basic to stimulating activity; too much may rob a child of initiative. Some toys, like swings and slides, encourage vigorous activity; others encourage fine motor coordination. For uninhibited activity, there should be swings, slides, and places to run. For finer coordination, plus social and cognitive development, there should be families of dolls or play animals, blackboards and chalk, or construction sets.

Both facilities and program should be adapted to the child's stage of development. A school-age child needs plenty of physical activity, but he is still a child and not ready for highly organized competitive athletics. When a child's muscle growth is greatest, he should be especially active. All indications are that muscle growth is promoted by suitable activity when muscles are forming. At the same time, the program should be continuous, not spotty. Strength, endurance, and ability to avoid straining muscles depend on the regularity of their use. Furthermore, overall muscle-tone and coordination depend on developing the total musculature, not merely specific muscle groups; hence diversified activities are recommended.

However, individual differences in experience and developmental patterns should also be respected. Has the child been ill recently? He may need milder exercise. Is he in excellent condition, with a history of vigorous play? Then he can sustain hardier activity than many others. Has he hurt himself recently? While reasonable precautions should be taken, he will become anxious if adults are excessively concerned. Is he a timid, self-conscious child? Too great prodding in his case may simply alienate him from physical activities.

A final factor is attitude—that of both children and adults. Fortunately, children possess a natural affinity for motor activity. Note the neonate's gyrations, or the child's efforts to walk. Forcing activities on children, regardless of their readiness, may kill or dim this enthusiasm. Facilities should be available and participation encouraged; but, within reason, children should pace themselves. Sometimes a child simply has no appetite for the form of activity at hand. Children who dislike activity will more readily overcome this distaste if permitted some choice in what they do.

Handedness

Theories about hand preference. A special case involving the basic principles of sound motor training is the establish-

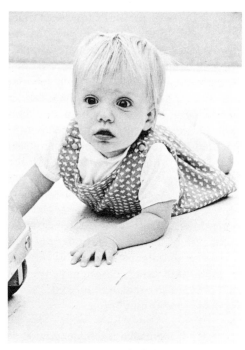

Children possess a natural affinity for motor skills.

dence provided by cultural artifacts, all civilizations have been prevalently right-handed. Second, the fact that infants do not immediately manifest a preference is no disproof of hereditary influence. Many hereditary traits, such as baldness, appear long after birth. Besides, even when parents provide a right-handed setting, some infants strongly persist in predominantly left-handed behavior.

Dominance, where it exists, manifests itself quite early. Some children show a preference as early as six months, and by 12 months dominance is clearly evident. Others report distinct hand dominance by nursery school age (Brown, 1962).

The question of changing handedness. The next controversy hinges on the question of whether left-handed children, regardless of possible predisposition, should be converted to right-handedness. This question, in turn, involves another: How great a handicap does the left-handed child face?

Many problems attributed to left-handedness seem to have arisen from the common failure to adapt handwriting instruction to the left-handed child. In consequence, the child imitates the right-handed model, and uses awkward, inefficient movements that produce fatigue and tension. Similar problems are involved in acquiring other motor skills — for example, playing field hockey, or playing the violin. Instruction and equipment are structured for right-handers, while the left-hander must work out his own adaptations. A less assured child may become self-conscious about being different. Later, as an adult, he may encounter job-seeking and on-the-job difficulties. Rightly or wrongly, some employers report left-handed workers to be slower and harder to train and more accident-prone (*The New York Times*, August 2, 1959).

However, the "lefty's" handicaps may be exaggerated. The severity of difficulty has been a matter of assumption rather than proof. After questioning students informally over the years, the au-

ment of handedness. Unfortunately, the cause of preferred handedness is not fully understood, although various theories have been advanced. According to one theory, handedness depends on the particular cerebral hemisphere that is dominant; right cerebral control supposedly leads to left-handedness, and left cerebral control to right-handedness. In some people, however, the hemispheres may be approximately equal, so that neither hand is clearly preferred.

Others attribute the choice of handedness to environmental influence. Left to himself, they assert, the child may become right-handed, left-handed, or even ambidextrous. Most children, they believe, become right-handed because they are born into a right-handed world. They cite the infant's early readiness to use either hand until experience leads to a preference. Hildreth (1950) claims that in "an unbiased world, left-handedness would be as common as right-handedness, for the play of chance factors would be equal for the two sides."

However, the dominance theory seems more reliable despite the preceding arguments. First, to judge from the evi-

thor has concluded that few "lefties" have found their handedness of any special significance for adjustment. While they may have experienced minor problems, almost none had found it emotionally upsetting. Rarely had they been embarrassed, and some, as children, had even enjoyed their difference as a mark of distinction. Moreover, left-handed children write as well as right-handed ones if they have consistently used the left hand and originally learned to do so correctly (Trankell, 1956). In conclusion, Jersild (1960) reports: "Whatever difficulties the left-handed child may suffer in a right-handed world are minor compared with the problems of the child with a strong bent for left-handedness who is compelled to shift to the right hand."

Pending resolution of the dispute over the causation of handedness, adults must somehow decide how to handle the problem of handedness. Other things being equal, it would seem that right-handed children might adjust better to a right-handed world. Hence, adults can subtly set the stage — for example, by placing objects in the infant's right hand. However, if the child shows a distinct preference for the other hand, adults should encourage use of that hand and adapt their instructional methods accordingly. Difficulties often arise because they pursue inconsistent policies.

Several factors should determine whether a child's handedness should be shifted once it has been established. Factors that seem to favor a successful change are (1) if the child is under six and uses both hands interchangeably; (2) if he is agreeable to change; (3) if he is above average in intelligence; and (4) if a trial period has revealed no serious difficulty (*Journal of Genetic Psychology*, 1950).

Psychological difficulties resulting from change depend on the type of child concerned, the methods used, the degree of natural dominance, and how well handedness has been established. A child with mixed dominance will normally experi-

ence less confusion in making a change. An especially high-strung child might develop nail-biting, stuttering, or thumb-sucking, especially if handedness has been well-established. These behaviors are not inherent in the changing of handedness, but they can be a concomitant of the process when it is poorly handled. For example, a child may feel so insecure when encouraged to divorce himself from a familiar habit that his behaviors reflect the resultant tensions. Hence the decision in any specific case boils down to this: Do the probable advantages of change warrant chancing whatever problems may be involved?

The following cases indicate the different results that attempts at changing handedness may bring:

My kindergarten teacher explained to my parents that left-handed people face many difficulties and suggested that my handedness be changed. My parents said they would leave it to me, so I refused. At school, the teacher still tried, but I never gave in. For a time I felt very conscious of being different and hated being called a southpaw. However, by the third grade I realized there were other southpaws and didn't feel quite as odd.

I learned to write with my left hand, but in the second grade the teacher taught me to use my right. Then I injured my right hand and used the left again. After that, I printed with my left hand but used my right for longhand. When I wrote very rapidly, my right hand would tire, and I'd feel an urge to use the left hand. My writing was now much poorer than originally when I used my left hand. In other skills, I was left-handed and proud of being different. Now, years later, I am a switch artist, using first this hand, then that, with equally dismal results.

•SUMMARY

Growth refers to the quantitative changes in body size and structure involved in progression toward maturity, while **development** refers to the complex process of integrating body functions. In general, the growth process is consistent and coordinated, although various parts of the body may grow at different rates. Each individual's growth is target-seeking, and when it strays from its own unique course some **catch-up mechanism** takes over until the normal growth pattern is restored. In fact, every individual has his own rate of maturing and his own distinctive body make-up and economy. Such individual differences suggest that statistical norms must not be taken as standards for individuals. However, a particular individual's deviation from the norm signals the need to determine whether such variation is optimum for him.

Varying combinations of genetic and environmental factors modify physical growth. Intelligence affects growth in that brighter parents make better provision for their children's physical development. Race is a factor in certain physical characteristics; but when environmental factors are controlled, many physical characteristics attributed to race diminish. Some slight relationships have been found between **body build** and personality traits, perhaps because body type contributes to the development of certain traits or because the same genetic factors modify body build and basic temperament. The child's **body image,** or perception of his own body, depends partly on the cultural ideal and partly on his own goals.

Homeostasis, or the process that regulates all the functions of the child's body, is controlled by the **autonomic nervous system** (smooth muscles) and by the **endocrine system (glands).** Upsets in homeostasis may lead to various disturbances, such as dwarfism, and may be temporary or permanent. To an unknown degree, upsets in homeostasis may affect weight, but perhaps societal affluence and psychological factors are the chief offenders. Either an excess of high-caloried foods or personal tensions may cause children to overeat. Problems of either over- or underweight suggest treatment on both physical and psychological levels.

A related problem, **malnutrition,** implies failing to obtain the necessary food requirements. Not merely how much the child eats but what he eats is important. Especially during childhood, malnutrition may have serious and partially irreversible effects. Problems resulting from inadequate sleep and rest may be equally devastating.

Illnesses, accidents, and physical handicaps may also prove upsetting, their effects depending greatly on the type of child and the manner of handling by adults. Unless it is unwisely handled, ordinary illness leaves little effect. However, if the child is overprotected or his illness prolonged, he may miss valuable social experience and resist getting well if he receives too much attention. Accidents may involve similar hazards and may also bring physical handicaps that result in varying combinations of self-pity, resignation, resentment, or compensatory behaviors. In general, children adjust better to congenital handicaps than to those acquired later on. In cases of illness, accident, or physical handicap, the attitudes of significant adults in the child's life are especially important in determining the child's adjustment.

Motor activity is important for building both physical and psychological health. Both cognitive and social training are often facilitated when combined with motor activities. Motor skills contribute to children's social adjustment and feelings of personal and social competence, as well as to their physical well-being.

Progress in motor development depends both on maturation and training. Progression of bodily control is **proximodistal** (from the center of the body to the extremities) and **cephalocaudal** (from head to foot or tail regions). Motor development also proceeds from mass to specific and from specific to mass; that is, mass responses differentiate into more specific ones, which in turn reintegrate into more complex and sophisticated behaviors on successively higher levels.

A certain amount of controversy concerns whether motor development hinges on maturation, proceeding spontaneously in ways determined by genetics, or on learning. In certain motor skills, children apparently progress about as well without special training as they do with it. However, such studies have ordinarily involved short training periods and relatively simple activities.

Motor development correlates with fetal activity and depends somewhat on genetic factors affected by heredity, including height and strength. Racial differences in motor development are still uncertain, except where obvious physical factors such as height make a difference. Sex differences are more apparent, but how much such differences are genetically or socioculturally based is in question.

A sound program for children's motor development must be well-planned and must include suitable places and equipment for play. Facilities and equipment should be geared to the child's stage of development. A sound program will build the sort of attitudes required to spark a child's continuous interest in motor skills.

Considerable controversy has surrounded the question of establishing handedness in motor skills. Some persons attribute dominance in handedness to genetically based cerebral factors; others attribute it to environmental ones. But its cause is not yet fully understood. In general, adults might best set the stage for the infant to use his right hand; however, if the child shows a clear preference for the left, he should be encouraged to use that hand and instructed in how to use it properly. Adults who direct any aspect of the child's motor development require a blend of concern, tact, skill, and patience.

• SUGGESTED QUESTIONS AND ACTIVITIES

1. Answer each of the following questions on a separate slip of paper, identifying yourself only by sex. These slips of paper may be collected and discussed before the class, either by the instructor or by committees assigned to analyze the various questions. (a) Describe the image you held of yourself physically as a child. How keenly were you aware of this image? (b) When you were a child, how much did your physical characteristics contribute to or hinder your personality development? (c) Compare how you felt about your physical traits in childhood and in adolescence. (d) List those of your physical traits that you liked best and least as a child. How was your adjustment positively or negatively affected? (e) What part has some specific physical factor — such as height, weight, health, or motor coordination — played in your life? (f) List the most and least effective ways that home and school have affected your own physical development. (g) Tell how an accident or illness has affected both your short-term and long-term adjustment. (h) Appraise the adequacy of provisions in your own home and school for health education and physical fitness.

2. Write a fictional episode, in the first person, imagining that you are a child with some specific type of physical handicap.

3. Discuss this question: If you had a child who was blind, or deaf, or badly crippled, would you place him in a special class or school in his early years, or would you keep him at home?

4. Should plastic surgery or other operations be performed on a child with a cleft palate, a crooked nose, a mole or birthmark in a conspicuous place, or any other facial blemish? What age would be optimum for such an operation? If the parents refused to have such an operation performed on the child, should they be compelled to do so?

5. What might be done to improve the adjustment of the physically handicapped child? (a) Should a teacher talk to children about the way they should treat a handicapped child? (b) To what extent should parents and teachers treat the handicapped child differently from other children?

6. Should a fifth-grade child's handedness be changed: (a) if he is strongly dominant for left-handedness? (b) if he is mildly dominant for left-handedness?

7. Since early nutrition is especially important, would it be wise for mothers to feed their children pre-packaged, balanced meals especially prescribed for the child by a physician?

8. Should schools provide all children with well-balanced breakfasts and lunches free of charge?

9. Discuss ways that home, school, and society might more adequately provide for children's physical needs. For purposes of discussion, try to devise some truly imaginative ideas on this subject.
10. Should physical-fitness activities be required of everyone in the community? If so, what might such a program include?

•SUGGESTED READINGS

Clements, F. W., ed., *Child Health: Its Origin and Promotion.* Philadelphia: Williams and Wilkins, 1964. A small volume discussing the emergence of homo sapiens and his evolution as he develops a society and culture. Sections are devoted to such topics as "Health and Well Being," "The Child and Disease," and "Education for Health."

Haldane, J. B. S., "Biological Possibilities for the Human Species in the Next Ten Thousand Years," in Gordon Wolstenholme, ed., *Man and His Future.* Boston: Little, Brown and Company, 1963, pp. 337–361. Fascinating speculation involving alternative possibilities for man's future biology.

Kagan, J., "Body Build and Conceptual Impulsivity in Children," *Journal of Personality,* Vol. 34 (1966), pp. 118–128. This paper summarizes three independent attempts to assess the relation between conceptual impulsivity on the one hand and body build on the other.

Lipton, E. L., A. Steinschneider, and J. B. Richmond, "Physiologic Disorders in Children," in Lois W. Hoffman and Martin L. Hoffman, eds., *Review of Child Development Research,* Vol. II. New York: Russell Sage Foundation, 1966, pp. 169–220. This excellent review of psychophysiologic disorders treats relevant genetic and developmental factors and discusses psychological as well as purely biological and physical variables involved.

Simpson, G. G., "The Biological Nature of Man," *Science,* Vol. 152, No. 3721 (April 22, 1967), pp. 472–478. Considers the question of how man's basic biology limits his development.

Tunley, R., "America's Unhealthy Children," *Harper's Magazine,* Vol. 232 (1966), pp. 41–46. Describes what the United States should do to provide proper medical care for children. America, the author contends, lags behind much of the world.

Walker, R. N., "Body Build and Behavior in Young Children: II. Body Build and Parents Ratings," *Child Development,* Vol. 34 (1963), pp. 1–23. In this study, the body builds of preschool children are classified on variables similar to those employed by Sheldon concerning endomorphy, ectomorphy, and mesomorphy, and are then related to personality traits.

4
PERSONALITY

The popular concept of **personality** reflects the term's origin in the Latin word *persona,* meaning a mask worn by Roman actors. Personality, in this sense, means the individual as seen by others. An individual is thought of as having a personality, rather than being one. In the psychological sense, however, personality is all that one is—the summation of his traits, uniquely organized through the blending of heredity and experience.

In the course of attempting to satisfy his various needs, each individual finds that some forms of behavior work better than others. These behaviors, or **traits,** having proved successful, are used over and over until they become characteristic of a person. Some of these traits prove fundamental to his pursuit of goals; these are called *central* or *core traits.* Others, called *secondary* or *peripheral traits,* are less important in satisfying his needs.

In the individual, traits interact with and affect each other, becoming organized into patterns appropriate to his roles. **Roles** are "sets of socially expected behavior patterns associated with an individual's functions in various social groups" (Rogers, 1962). Most important in childhood are family, sex, age, peer, and pupil roles, but the individual plays numerous other roles during the course of his life. In his family role, a child learns to make his bed, to play off one parent against the other, and to cope with an older brother. As a pupil, he learns to do his homework, to accommodate to a succession of varied teachers, and to make the thousand-and-one other adaptations required to move smoothly up the educational ladder.

• THE SELF-CONCEPT

Common to all the child's roles, and transcending all of them, is his **personal role.** This role is reflected in the common values, goals, and interests that color all his roles. For instance, regardless of whether he is playing his role as student, child in the family, or child in the peer group, he may be highly goal-directed,

or determined to succeed. He strives for grades and provides able leadership for his gang.

Meanwhile, each child comes to feel some way about his roles. He concludes that he plays them well, or poorly, or just moderately well. In short, he acquires a **self-concept,** which embraces all his impressions and beliefs about himself. When a child says, "I'm a dumbbell," or "Lookit, Daddy, how high I can swing!" we glimpse the way he sees himself. A healthy self-concept can be a child's greatest asset; a poor self-concept, however, can become a hammerlock on his progress.

Coexistent with each child's self is an **ideal self,** which is the projection of his dreams. Both consciously and unconsciously, he continuously strives to close the gap between his **real self**—or the self he perceives himself to be—and his ideal self. In the process, he finds some behaviors effective and practices them until they become habitual. Others he discards as inappropriate to his goals. Hence his behavior becomes increasingly refined and organized in ways to further the attainment of his ideal. Thus a child's self-concept develops a persistent core, which unifies his behaviors, preventing a chaos of traits. Nevertheless, the self-concept continues to change, albeit with increasing resistance to change as successive stages of development are reached.

Significance of the Self-Concept

Having briefly examined the basic concepts involved in the organization of personality, let us take a closer look at the self-concept as a key factor in child development. Much evidence supports the view that the child's behavior in any specific context is determined largely by the way he perceives himself. He may try hard to ignore experiences that do not enhance his self-concept; or he may distort them so that they don't conflict. The boy who perceives himself as a good athlete believes the umpire wrong who rules him out. The girl who sees herself as bright judges the teacher unfair who gives her low grades. Neither the boy in the first case nor the girl in the second can readily accept a judgment that conflicts with what he or she wishes to believe.

The self-concept is crucial to mental health (McQuitt, 1950). Frances, for example, possesses an unrealistically high self-concept and is constantly rebuffed when others reject her attempts at leadership. By contrast, Tommy's self-concept is so weak that he constantly concedes to others' judgments (Spivack, 1956). As a result, he never quite knows just who he is or why. One unkind remark is enough to convince him he is unworthy. A weak self-concept also permits a child to be manipulated by others. Ralph, who is self-assured, readily persuades Pete, who undervalues himself, that he should steal some fruit from the shopkeeper. If Pete had a higher opinion of himself, he might pit his own judgment against Ralph's and reject the notion as unwise.

A strong self-concept, by contrast, helps a child believe in and rely upon himself. In the face of life's complex problems, he feels less insignificant; he finds the world friendly rather than threatening. In brief, a healthy self-concept strengthens the child's capacity to cope with his environment. When confronted with an obstacle, he does not meekly surrender, but sets about removing it, provided that it can be removed and is worth the effort. In general, he both persists longer and makes more progress than children with weaker self-images. Moreover, if he fails to make progress toward some goal, he does not feel like a failure. He simply concludes that his abilities are better adapted to an alternative choice. A child who is unsure of himself tends to perceive his lack of success as a function of his own inadequacies rather than as an indication of failure to articulate properly his capacities and goals.

A child's reactions toward himself shift somewhat, no matter how stable he is. As he plays with this or that group, or participates in this or that activity,

his feelings about himself fluctuate. The common factor that prevents his becoming a diffuse, disorganized aggregate of relatively discrete traits is the **self.** The self (**ego**) is the integrating core of the personality; it mediates between needs and reality. The centrality of the self in mediating adaptations stems, on the biological level, from the integrating influence of the nervous system. On the operational level, integrity of self stems from the fact that the self has the function of denying or repressing information incongruent with it. For example, the child who perceives himself as healthy has difficulty recognizing that he is ill. He plays even when he has a fever, and does not rest until he is ready to drop.

Development of the Self-Concept

The child is born without any feeling that could properly be called a self-concept. His original sense of self, as we understand it, is simply a composite sense of either well-being or stress. It is indistinct, amorphous, and largely physical in nature. A normal infant gradually acquires a self-concept, however, which is both physical and psychological. The following illustrates a step in this direction:

> Tiny Sammy toddles over to a cake on the table, and sticks a finger tentatively into the icing, then hastily withdraws it, looking furtively for his mother. "Sammy bad boy," he says aloud, making a mild concession to his absent mother, before succumbing and licking the icing anyway. Already Sammy is introjecting ideas of himself as good or bad [Woodcock, 1941, p. 44].

For at least three reasons, the child probably fails to develop a true self-feeling until the second or even the third birthday. Since the self is essentially an abstraction representing the common factor from all one's personal memories, it depends on an adequate development of memory function. Second, the infant lacks the repertoire of experience to dis-

89

tinguish self from not-self. Finally, self-awareness depends on language. Only through speech does a child attain the symbols for ordering his mental processes and differentiating self from environment (Stagner, 1961).

In time, the child has many experiences involving awareness of himself. He experiences himself as hungry, tired, or excited; he sees himself doing things ineptly or successfully. He also views himself in terms of the roles he plays, as a boy or girl, son or daughter, pupil or gang member, and so on. Self-awareness emerges as the common factor in all these contexts, and is by that very fact independent of them.

The self-concepts that gradually emerge are varied and sometimes strange, as indicated by college students' recollections from early childhood:

> All I remember is a "me" on a smaller scale, with the same relationships as now to my parents, my sister, and others.

> From my earliest recollections, I was quite conscious of self. I felt that I was a very special person, with unique experiences and feelings.

> When I was very small my brother tried to convince me that I was a tablet. He believed this to be true because during my mother's pregnancy she took pills daily.

Factors Affecting the Self-Concept

Factors affecting the self-concept may be as numerous as the stimuli to which the organism is equipped to respond. The very fact that one responds at all indicates he has somehow related himself to a stimulus, either on the conscious or unconscious level. However, those experiences to which one relates himself most readily—that is, with which he identifies—have the most impact.

Effect of others on the self-concept. The experiences to which the child is said to be ego-related involve his most

important roles, such as child in the home, pupil in school, or child among his peers. Among these, his role in the family is most important. Here the child first differentiates himself as liked or disliked, wanted or unwanted, acceptable or unacceptable, able or unable, worthy or unworthy (Combs and Snygg, 1959). Parents who are too strict, insufficiently protective, or overly critical may interfere with his attainment of a mature self-concept. They try to write the child's life script when he should be writing his own.

This childhood recollection reveals both a strong self-consciousness and a keen awareness of others' reactions:

> What stands out strongest in my memory is the belief that I was being watched all the time. I felt that I was part of an experiment—the whole world was a big stage where I was the person being tested. I believed I was being watched all the time by hidden cameras. The walls had cameras in them, and so did mirrors, lights, and everything else. Also, I was being recorded at all times. I felt that as soon as I walked away from a particular place, men came out and took the scenery away. I used to run back to a place I had just left to see if I could catch the people in the act. This feeling left me at about the age of nine.

Effect of age on the self-concept. Also influencing the self-concept is age role, which often may have either positive or negative effects. Young children's activities are relatively noncompetitive and thus without great threat to security or ego. Besides, most adults treat little children kindly, making them feel accepted. Having been defined by adults as having worth, children perceive themselves that way. In general, however, children perceive themselves as less important than adults; they view adults as powerful and children as powerless (Emmerich, 1961). Furthermore, the child lives in a world designed for older people and run by older people. He often stubs his toe, figuratively speaking, because he has not yet learned to solve his problems without constant assists from adults. Yet if he is over-assisted, he is deprived of the crises required to crystallize his identity.

During middle childhood, the child's self-concept may decline. No longer is he a sweet little thing, pampered and petted by his elders. He encounters competition and failures at school and tactless treatment by insensitive peers. He attends an age-graded school where adolescents are automatically accorded higher status than younger children. In short, he is outgrowing his role as a child and is eager for the greater independence and status accorded his older brother.

But the child's self-concept is not fully restored in adolescence, for teenagers often suffer from marginal status. Being neither child nor adult, the adolescent finds his role diffuse and uncertain. However, by early adulthood the individual has supposedly established an identity and a reasonably consistent set of values. From this time on, at least for some years, his self-concept improves and then declines. In one projective study in which subjects were asked to draw the human figure, males drew increasingly larger figures until age 30 and thereafter smaller ones, while females drew increasingly larger figures until age 40 and then smaller ones (Lehner and Gunderson, 1953). If human figure drawings are, as conjectured, the projection of a self-concept, these findings suggest that the self-concept normally grows until sometime in young or middle adulthood and then declines.

Effect of sex on the self-concept. Sex is a confusing factor in the self-concept. Everyone's personality represents a blend of masculinity and femininity, although each sex possesses a relatively greater proportion of traits appropriate to its own role. However, Bennett and Cohen (1959) suggest that, within the American culture at least, the stronger factors in the self-concepts of both sexes are more characteristically feminine ones. Since both sexes spend their early years under the guidance of a mother and women teachers, feminine aspects of the self-concept become more sharply defined. According to this theory, maleness is a secondary accretion picked up in later childhood. Masculine traits, then, are viewed as less fundamental than feminine traits. For instance, when a boy becomes disturbed, he may finally cry, his masculine — and relatively more superficial — self-control breaking down.

Despite the primary nature of femininity, society places a premium on masculine traits, especially for males but also somewhat for females, since girls are also expected to be reasonably positive and independent. In fact, both sexes respond to the premium placed on male characteristics. The boy is rewarded for escaping his original feminine behaviors — crying, clinging, and so on; but the girl's self-concept remains confused. On the one hand, she views herself as warm, friendly, and dependable — for which she is praised; on the other hand, she is perceived as helpless, timid, and inferior, because even as a child she is treated that way.

Self-Actualization

The child of either sex proceeds in certain main ways to improve his self-concept — that is, to close the gap between the self he believes he is and the self he would like to be. One of these ways is **self-actualization.** Self-actualization involves the constructive development of individual potential through progression to increasingly higher levels of motives and organization (Maslow, 1954). It implies finding a way of life congenial to one's own needs and traits, rather than slavishly imitating others. It also implies the enthusiastic pursuit of goals. However, it is not always equivalent to the individual's achievement of his own goals, which sometimes conflict with his own best interests. A child may succeed in uniting his small friends

91

Self-actualization helps in establishing identity.

as an individual and provided with the kind of environment in which he can flourish.

> A flower or a tree cannot tell us articulately what it needs for growth, but it can still tell us a great deal. We ask only that the child be watched as closely as a flower or a tree would be when new soils, new methods of handling are being considered. . . . The demands of many a child's environment are sometimes too much for him, sometimes too little, and . . . hand in hand with the realization of inner potentials goes the rebuilding of the world in such a way that more children can more adequately realize what is inarticulate within them [Murphy and Murphy, 1960, pp. 215–216].

To find out what the child needs, we must learn from his choices what his interests and talents are. He may need help in sustaining an interest and in learning the techniques required to develop it. But if it is *his* goal, the chances of his achieving it will be good. The child should also be helped to select goals that are achievable without undue expense of energy or strain, and he should be helped to find areas of maximum pay-off in terms of personal satisfaction and socially recognized accomplishment.

If the need to *actualize* — that is, to close the gap between the real and the ideal self — is to be successful, personal weaknesses standing in the way must be removed. The child with a hot temper will find small cooperation in meeting his goals. To achieve his goals, he should be helped to think of self-actualization in terms of becoming his best self. Unfortunately, many parents and teachers, swayed by unrealistic social standards, pressure children toward goals incompatible with their ultimate best interests. For instance, parents often browbeat or coax their sons to win prestige, even in the earliest school years, regardless of the emotional hazards involved (Kahl, 1953). Every child — and not just the child who presents a special challenge, whether it be

against their teacher, but we would hardly cite this feat as an example of self-actualization. By contrast, the following recollection involves evidence of genuine progress toward self-actualization:

> When I was in grade school I made the rounds with my father as he inspected his widespread properties managed by tenant farmers. Meantime, I led my neighborhood gang in various activities including building a clubhouse and peddling vegetables. As a man I gradually acquired properties myself and directed a large number of workers.

Assisting children with self-actualization. Any child can be helped in his efforts to achieve self-actualization. First, however, he must be understood

92

cultural deprivation or special talent—should be helped toward maximum achievement. In making what they called an "individual-centered plea," Murphy and Murphy (1960) express concern not only for the unusual child but also for the "everyday" child.

Achievement Orientation

Like self-actualization, **achievement orientation** implies the existence of goals; unlike self-actualization, it suggests nothing about the worth of those goals. The essence of achievement orientation is simply the need to accomplish, a strong drive constantly pushing one to pursue goals. Since achievement orientation is so basic a value in this society, at least for boys, it deserves some discussion.

Achievers, as achievement-oriented persons are called, are characterized by high levels of ambition, energy, and independence. They possess the ego-strength required to make decisions and pursue courses of action with vigor. They prefer moderate risk to certainty, and jobs that present a challenge to less difficult ones. The two individuals quoted below were obviously achievement-oriented, feeling a compulsion to drive ahead no matter what the goal:

In middle childhood, I used to set up contests for myself. I would say to myself that if I didn't perform a certain task before something else happened, something drastic would happen to me. For example, I had to reach a certain telephone pole before an approaching car did, or I would fail the test. Some of the tasks were much more drastic, with correspondingly graver consequences. (Male)

As a child, I was constantly setting goals for myself, and became a compulsive finisher. For some months I ran around the block twice each morning to strengthen my leg muscles; and I would never stop on the first lap, no matter what arose. In school, I had to be the leader. Even when our physical measurements were taken at school, I was terribly chagrined that I could not stretch sufficiently to measure taller than all of my classmates. (Female)

Achievement orientation is most often measured by having subjects relate stories about people in the process of making decisions. Subjects who relate stories in which the main character is ambitious, makes plans for the future, and expects to forge ahead are said to show high n Ach (achievement orientation); those who see the central character as yielding to pressures, failing in his undertaking, or preferring to remain with his family instead of setting forth to make a life for himself are said to show low n Ach (Lindgren et al., 1966).

The significance of achievement orientation. Before either encouraging or discouraging the development of achievement orientation, one should consider its worth. First, the trait is socially approved, especially in males; so boys who possess it feel more in tune with their society. With the firing of the first Sputnik, achievement was re-established, displacing adjustment as the highest goal of American life. Also, it is a necessary adjunct of sheer ability if goals are to be reached. Beyond the minimum ability required, achievement motivation becomes the deciding factor, especially in academic achievement. In one nation-wide study of high school students, 54% of the lowest quarter in ability ranked in the highest third academically. Also, 42% of college entrants with an aptitude (AGCT) score between 95 and 104 graduated, as did 27% of the entrants whose aptitudes were between 85 and 95. Keep in mind that the average for all persons is 100 and that college work is presumably geared to the cream of the crop (Green and Harbeck, 1962).

Achievers' success can be explained, in part, by the fact that achievement orientation provides the motivation required to sacrifice short-term gratifications for long-term goals. Among Negro children in Trinidad, children high in achievement motivation proved 93 more willing to forego smaller immediate rewards for greater future ones (Mischel, 1961).

Achievement orientation is also related to self-concept. Over-achievers consistently rate themselves higher than under-achievers (Peppin, 1962). More than likely, the effect is circular: a high self-concept encourages high achievement, and high achievement improves the self-concept.

On the other hand, achievement orientation also has its hazards, because unusual sacrifices are often involved. The child who obsessively pursues personal goals may alienate family and peers. First-generation immigrant parents may feel scorned by the child who rejects their way of life for something he deems better. Increasingly, as the child attains the speech, manners, and education that achievement requires, the social distance between child and parents widens.

The achievement-oriented child may also alienate his peers — for instance, by shunning group activities in favor of purely personal pursuits, such as plugging for high grades or working in his shop.

Still another hazard of achievement orientation is this: it is all too easy to become obsessed with the need to reach goals, regardless of means. A boy may pilfer money to treat the fellows in a futile effort to win the leadership to which he aspires. Or a girl may cheat to maintain her place at the head of the class. Achievement orientation per se is neither good nor bad; its significance derives from the way it functions in a person's life.

Achievement orientation in boys. Probably because achievement orientation is considered more appropriate for males than for females, most research on the topic applies to them. In a study of eight-year-old boys, those who told many achievement stories (for example, "A boy is sitting at his desk trying to do his homework so he can get all A's") had

mothers who demanded independence and mastery of their sons, especially during years four through seven. The mothers of such boys also rewarded them more often with hugs and kisses for demonstration of achievement and mastery (Winterbottom, 1958).

Similarly, McClelland (1961) reported that parents who were successful in developing achievement orientation in their sons possessed high standards and expectations but kept emotional ties loose and permitted the child to master the environment in his own way. True, they made certain restrictions, but they reduced these restrictions markedly after age eight, presumably after the child had mastered the most basic skills.

McClelland added, however, that when parents' demands became excessive, the child's achievement orientation was reduced. In one study, mothers of German boys with weak achievement

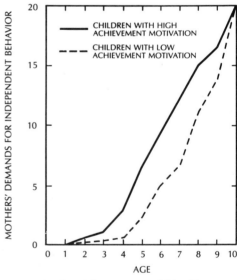

Maternal demands versus child-achievement motivation. Mothers of boys rated high or low were asked at what ages they demanded of their sons 20 kinds of independent behavior, such as doing well in competition, performing well in school without help, and staying home alone. From D. C. McClelland et al., *The achievement motive.* New York: Appleton-Century-Crofts, 1953. Adapted by permission.

were found to place great stress on obedience, cleanliness, and politeness. Presumably, whatever achievement aspirations the boys had were stifled by their mothers' extreme insistence on compliance.

Rosen and d'Andrade (1959) differentiated the roles of mother and father in a son's motivations. Mothers of achieving boys were vitally interested in their sons' performance and highly demanding that they do something well, but they were permissive about what their sons did. That is, the son could do what he liked as long as he did it well. Fathers of achieving boys put less pressure on their sons than did fathers of less motivated boys. The powerful father who demanded that the son meet his standards was seemingly perceived as an invincible competitor. On the other hand, the demanding mother was apparently perceived as a source of attainable reward.

While parents are primary in determining their son's achievement orientation, Simpson (1962) notes that boys are also influenced by their friends. Generally, children react more strongly to peer influence on approaching the teens.

Achievement orientation in girls. The data relating to girls' achievement orientation are fewer and somewhat different. Above all, the mother's influence is crucial. In one study, girls whose mothers rewarded their intellectual development during the first three years showed substantial increases in IQ between the ages of 6 and 10 and a high concern for mastery and competition. For instance, a girl with an achievement-rewarding mother responded to the picture of a boy with a violin by saying the boy was practicing in order to be good enough to play in Carnegie Hall. A low-motivated girl with a non-rewarding mother said the boy didn't want to practice but wanted to go out and play (Moss and Kagan, 1961).

Lower-status mothers with better-than-average education are especially likely to pressure their daughters to achieve. Their daughters, more often than girls generally, daydream of personal achievement rather than of homes and children. They aspire to jobs normally engaged in by males, which carry high status and require a good education. Apparently, the lower-status but better-educated mother who has failed to realize her own status quest in marriage projects her dreams onto her daughter, along with the middle-class values that will be instrumental in achieving them (Douvan and Adelson, 1966).

Achievement orientation in both sexes. Several studies have attempted to differentiate achievement orientation in girls and boys. Kagan and Moss (1959) found that the mother's concern for her child's achievement at age three was strongly related to the older daughter's achievement fantasy but not to the older son's. Even in early childhood, the girl is more prone than the boy to adopt maternal attitudes and values.

Shaw and Dutton (1962) also reported a greater effect of parental attitudes on daughters' achievement orientation than on sons'. However, underachievement in boys was associated with the mother's confinement to the homemaking role and with suppression of the boy's sexuality. Mothers of underachieving girls typically fostered their daughters' dependency and discouraged any expression of tendencies toward aggression. Fathers of under-achieving girls suppressed their expressions of sexuality and manifested little affection toward their daughters. In general, fathers are concerned chiefly with their sons' performance and show less concern for, and appreciation of, their daughters' achievements (Tasch, 1952).

In view of the far greater emphasis placed on male achievement, it is hardly surprising that boys, more often than girls, believe they will succeed. Boys also show closer correlations between IQ and achievement than do girls. One reason for this may be that girls are more often rewarded for a "good try" and even criticized for stating high aspira- 95 tions, even when they are realistic, on the grounds that achievement is unfeminine. Some of them develop a passion for passivity and anonymity and concede without a struggle. Whatever the reasons, the normal linkages between achievement motivation and performance, including realistic readjustment to successes or failures based on past performance, are often missing among girls (Crandall et al., 1962). Douvan and Adelson (1958) conclude further that mobile boys (those who aspire to higher status), as contrasted with mobile girls, have less energy tied to the resolution of conflict. Since boys are expected to achieve, they can channel their full energies into the task. On the other hand, girls who draw disapproval for aggressively forging ahead may develop anxiety, which interferes with achievement.

Parenthetically, it should be noted that first-borns of both sexes rate higher than later-borns in the need to achieve. Since they receive greater responsibility training and more experience in playing the adult-surrogate role, they presumably establish more rigid standards for success (Sutton-Smith et al., 1964).

Social class as a factor in achievement orientation. Also related to achievement orientation is social class, especially when mobility — that is, rising to a higher social class — is considered a main goal within the society. The working-class child, who encounters frequent frustrations and more economically precarious conditions, is less willing to take chances — and risk-taking is basic to achievement (Hyman, 1953).

Age as a factor in achievement orientation. A longitudinal study by Kagan (1961) revealed certain relationships between age-stages and achievement motivation. Achievement between ages 6 and 10 correlated more highly with adult achievement than did that of any other similar span of years. Children were rated on recognition-seeking be-

haviors for four age periods: ages 0 to 3, 3 to 6, 6 to 10, and 10 to 14. Achievement-striving for the age period 6 to 10 correlated most highly with similar behaviors in adulthood. Involvement in intellectual activities from age 10 to 14 also showed high correlation with adult achievement, although athletic involvement revealed no correlation at all with later achievement. It would seem, therefore, that certain age-stages are critical in the development of achievement motivation.

• IDENTITY

Both self-actualization and achievement orientation assist in establishing **identity,** which Erikson (1959) asserts is the basic need of our time. At the outset, note that identity is not the same as the self-concept. The self-concept embraces an individual's total picture of himself, while identity refers to his feelings of distinctiveness from others. An individual with a strong sense of identity feels that he is of one piece, with an integrated rather than confused, or diffuse, self-concept. He is aware of himself as an entity with a unique role in life. Identity should also be distinguished from **identification,** which implies merging one's goals and purposes with those of another, or modeling them after that person. If carried too far, identification obstructs attaining an identity.

However, a mere sense of identity is not enough; it should be a healthy one. A child who is constantly ridiculed may feel quite distinctive, in that he feels like a clown among his peers. Another child is the family scapegoat, a special person in the worst sense. In the positive sense, identity means autonomy as a person, and confidence in oneself. It implies the ability to establish and maintain independent judgments without continuous reference to external sources (Dyk and Witkin, 1965). The child with a strong sense of identity insists on his right to be himself; the child with a weak one only plays at being himself.

When college students were asked to indicate various factors that somehow affected the early establishment of their identities, these were some of their answers:

> What first gave me a strong sense of identity was our family garage. Ours was the only one in the neighborhood and served as the neighborhood playhouse. As a result, I felt like a somebody.

> I felt distinctive largely because of my musical ability. For instance, I was chosen to play the piano at assemblies and to sing in the choir. Adding to my feeling of distinctiveness was the fact that my father was the school bus driver and everyone was crazy about him.

> To be the only blonde in a large family of dark-haired, brown-eyed individuals made me feel distinctive. I felt I didn't belong, and even imagined I was treated differently. Friends and relatives often remarked to my parents: "Where did you get that one?"

Clark and Clark (1952) cite an example of the negative aspects of identity:

> A colored child revealed a negative self-identification when he explained the dark color of his skin by saying, "I burned my face and made it spoil."

Problems in Establishing Identity

The complexity of modern life hampers the establishment of a stable identity. A child bombarded by conflicting pressures and values may have trouble deciding who he is, what he thinks, or what he wants to be. Even as he is struggling to stabilize his position in his environment, that environment is constantly shifting. Hence maintaining an identity is a lifelong process of preserving a stable anchorage in a whirlpool of confusing influences.

A second problem is maintaining the courage to be oneself despite tremendous social pressures on every hand to "go along." The child may not dare to pit his judgment against the collective views of peers or elders. He may simply avoid the whole matter of decision-making by taking refuge in the group. As a result, his behaviors are ready-made, tendered him by adult authority figures and peer leaders.

A third problem, a product of recent times, is that of maintaining distinctiveness in a world so populous that one person seems infinitesimally small. The child's "world" is now conceived as a rapidly expanding universe, of which his own habitat, earth, seems an increasingly smaller part. The following description, written by a teen-age boy, expresses this view:

> In late childhood, I used to think the whole world was contained in a drop of water on a larger scale, on some other plane of existence. That is, since things are relative, we — that is, everything on the planet and in the universe — were actually a molecule of water or some other element on some other level of life. There were millions and billions of these molecules making up this higher form of life — thus, there were thousands of other planets with life on them, but we were so small we had no contact with any of them. I also felt that little worlds existed in all the molecules around us, and that each atom had a little world within it.

Development of Identity

To some extent identity is earned, to some extent assigned. Through his own efforts, a child may come to perceive himself as a very special person in his group. However, his identity is partially assigned. He has no choice about his membership in a specific sex, race, or ethnic group, and he comes to ascribe to himself whatever traits society assigns persons who play these roles. The extent to which a child's race enters into his identity depends on how much his experience projects his racial self-image upon him. For instance, since whiteness represents status in Western culture, the lighter a Negro, the higher, often, his status and self-concept. A dark Negro child, who is quickly recog-

97

The child's identity is partially assigned.

nized and invariably treated as a Negro, sees himself as a Negro more consistently and at an earlier age than does a very light one (Clark and Clark, 1952). For him the life space soon becomes structured in terms of black and white. He acquires a racial identity that is different from that of the dominant group (Radke et al., 1949).

Identification

Whereas identity involves a sense of distinctiveness from others, identification involves the dissolution of barriers between oneself and another. A child identifies by equating himself with someone he admires or by imitating that person's behaviors. Unconsciously, or sometimes consciously, he mimics his model's actions and values. Although identification may interfere with the development of identity, it can also promote self-identity. For example, if the child simply copies his model's traits and behaviors he reduces his own

98

individuality; but if he integrates those traits and behaviors into his unique behavioral organization, he is actually helping himself achieve his own goals.

Many authorities, especially the psychoanalytically oriented ones, view identification as a defensive process. A child may try to become like his parents in order to reduce his anxiety. If he is like them, he believes he is assured of their affection (Bronfenbrenner, 1960). And because he is little and comparatively helpless, the boy, at least, identifies with the parent who holds greater power. In one experiment, when one adult controlled access to toys and the other played with them, the child tended to imitate the former (Mussen and Distler, 1959).

Oldest and only children are more likely than other children to identify with the mother, perhaps because mothers are prone to make oldest children assistant parents and to provide only children with greater nurture. Besides, both oldest and only children have the mother all to themselves, at least for a time (Heilbrun and Fromme, 1965). Understandably, first-born girls show the greatest mother identification of any children in the family.

The child mimics his model's clothes, actions, and values.

Identification does not always proceed in the oversimplified, straight-line manner often suggested. A child may identify with either parent or with certain traits of both parents. He may incorporate strong traits or weak traits, whole patterns of traits or quite insignificant tendencies. He may pick up traits here and there, identifying partially with many people or largely with one individual. He may incorporate a parental trait he especially dislikes, perhaps because his intense reaction has focused his attention upon it. However, because he is capable of selectively excluding from his self-concept those aspects that conflict with his self-ideal, he is often totally unaware that he has introjected a disliked trait. In any case, whether identification is conscious or unconscious, it will importantly modify the child's development.

Identification also works in reverse, when the parent lives out his dreams in his child. A weak father may impose a gang-buster image on his son to make up for the strength he himself lacks. Such a child may have trouble developing an authentic identity.

Mass media and identification. Among other important sources of identification figures are the **mass media,** including books, movies, and television. Note these childhood recollections:

> The first movie I ever saw, and still remember vividly, was *Sergeant York.* I recall his conflicts as a conscientious objector and his bringing in all those German prisoners. He was a real-life hero, and not the made-up James Bond type we see in movies and comics. I still identify with heroes of biographies and movies. They act like a hypo and make me feel I could become great if I tried.

> I devoured every adventure story I could find, and dreamed of going to exotic places and of undergoing hardships and conquering obstacles. These stories struck a wild chord in my nature, and their heroes provided examples to follow.

Autonomy

An important part of achieving identity is establishing **autonomy,** or self-direction. The externally directed

individual lives as though he wore a receiving set on his head to get signals from others telling him how he should live and what he should believe. By contrast, the self-directed man does not blindly accept social values; he evaluates and searches. He forms a frame of reference and style of life appropriate to his own needs while still contributing to the group.

The child who is making progress in autonomy can disagree with his parents without unreasonable hostility if he feels his percepts are accurate.

Autonomy is basic to the development of identity.

He distinguishes between his parents' love, which is central, and their disapproval of his act. Even when pressured by parents and peers, he increasingly makes his own decisions. He possesses a strong self-image, which permits him to value his own views enough to believe in and defend them.

Children differ widely in the ways in which they demand autonomy. Boys are far more likely than girls to assert "their rights" aggressively; but even some girls actively manipulate situations to satisfy their needs. Other girls assert autonomy

99

simply by resisting, or by evading a situation; and since passive resistance is less likely to provoke counter-aggression, it often proves more effective.

In the following illustration, Sheila demonstrates active autonomy, Vivian passive autonomy:

> *Sheila,* age 2 years 8 months, busily moving and arranging equipment according to *her* plan, accompanied by continuous soft, low, babyish chatter, impatiently refused to be bound by any prearranged adult plan ("No, I wanta make it zissaway. I want to make a choo-choo"), and often expressed annoyance with repetition or petulance with difficult, frustrating motor tasks, which she attacked with vigorous non-functional pushing and squeezing, culminating in angry scattering or shoving away.
>
> *Vivian,* age 2 years 3 months, beautifully and expensively dressed, but wide-eyed and vacantly staring, with mouth open and drooping, seemed more like a fashionable children's store mannequin than a real, live child. She rarely spoke and avoided the examiner's direct gaze; but she made it quite clear that she preferred performance items to verbal tasks, which she firmly but quietly refused. At the slightest hint of difficulty she usually became immobile and mute, with only an occasional sad or faintly resistant "I don't know" [Moriarty, 1961, pp. 65–67].

• PERSONALITY: SOME BASIC CONCEPTS

Whatever the means or combinations of means that the child uses to enhance his self-concept, he will hardly develop an adequate one unless it is consistent with his total personality. It is the special way in which an individual's traits become organized, or patterned, that accounts for the uniqueness of his personality.

Traits, remember, are characteristic ways of behavior and are classified as either central (core) or secondary (peripheral). In general, core traits are fundamental to the pursuit of an individual's goals, while peripheral traits are less essential. Both types may be either biologically or environmentally determined, although practically all derive from some combination of heredity and environment. Biological origins are often overlooked, largely because their influence is hard to measure. They become obscured by the environmental influences that blend with and hide them. Nevertheless, considerable evidence indicates that heredity does indeed provide a basis for personality.

Genetic Bases of Personality

But is the emphasis on heredity often too extreme? Are core traits firmly rooted in heredity, or are they determined largely after birth, perhaps in the infancy period? Does the child enter the world a neutral mass of protoplasm, completely without personality, or does he already possess personality characteristics that manifest themselves independently of social interaction? Let's examine the evidence.

Among lower animals, characteristics analogous to human personality traits are obviously inherited. In a classic experiment, Stone et al. (1932) bred rats for wildness, developing strains with clear-cut differences in this characteristic.

Among humans, the evidence for genetic bases of personality is less definite but still significant. Ausubel (1957) identified six main categories of distinct and stable individual differences among infants during the early months of life: placidity or irritability, activity level, tone length and vigorousness of crying, tolerance of frustration or discomfort (including reaction to stress situations and overstimulation), differential sensitivity to stimulation in various sense modalities, and social responsiveness. Still other traits may be rooted in heredity and not become overtly identifiable until later. For example, introversion-extroversion can first be manifested only after a certain degree of maturity is reached.

Such early traits as persist, despite environmental influences that would normally produce quite different results, are probably genetically based. For instance, excitability and outgoingness resist change and may result from genetic factors such as autonomic balance or body type rather than from strictly social forces (Digman, 1963).

A second and perhaps better source of evidence concerning the effect of heredity on personality comes from studies of twins. Identical twins, as we saw earlier, have the same heredity, while fraternals are no more alike genetically than ordinary siblings. Whatever differences are found in identicals who have been reared apart can be ascribed to their different environments. Evidence abounds from such studies. Vandenberg (1962) reported more similarity between identicals than fraternals in degree of self-confidence and of stubbornness and in response to music and color. Other traits, such as being easygoing, bold, sociable, or withdrawn, are also found more often in identical than fraternal twins (Cattell et al., 1955).

In another study, twelve pairs of Danish identical twins, separated in childhood, were reunited only after they reached some stage of adulthood. One pair had been reared apart from infancy in two very different types of homes. One had received only elementary schooling while the other had attended medical college. Yet when tested they were found to differ little in mental ability, and both lacked self-confidence, found it hard to achieve emotional contact with others, and presented similar neurotic, hypochondriacal symptoms.

In a twin study by Newman (1937), twins Edwin Iske and Fred Nestor were separated in infancy, reared apart by different foster parents, and reunited through a remarkable coincidence. Both were working as telephone repairmen in communities a thousand miles apart. After company representatives noted their startling resemblance and brought them together, they proved amazingly alike in both mental ability and personality.

In another case, male identicals were separated in infancy, one being reared by an Italian family in New York State, the other by a Jewish couple in Florida. They were unaware of each other's existence until repeated instances of being mistaken for each other led to their reunion at the age of 23. They were amazingly similar in looks and physique. They were both 6 feet, 3 inches tall and weighed about 200 pounds. When tested, they proved to have very similar IQ's and aptitude for clerical work. However, their personalities seemed quite different. The one reared in the Italian home was more extroverted and self-assured; the one from the Jewish home more sensitive and impressionable (Lindeman, 1964).

On the basis of available evidence, most psychologists grade hereditary influences in this way: Most likely to be influenced by heredity are such basic abilities as intelligence, speed of reaction, motor skills, and sensory discrimination. Somewhat less likely to be influenced by heredity are temperamental traits, including emotionality, alteration or evenness of mood, and activity or lethargy. Least likely to be influenced by heredity, if at all, are attitudes, beliefs, values, and characteristics in which training or conditioning are the major factors (Scheinfeld, 1965).

The indirect effects of heredity on personality have already been noted. For instance, the short man may grow sensitive after years of being called "Shorty" and may manifest compensatory defensive behaviors, such as taking long steps, smoking cigars, or affecting authoritative gestures.

Instincts

Other controversial and closely related concepts in personality theory are those of instinct, imprinting, and the critical period. What implications, if any, do these concepts have for humans? The first of these terms, **instinct,** has long occupied an important, though now declining, role in developmental psychologists' deliberations. In the pre-experimental period, it was commonly believed that children were composed of a bundle of "instincts," or inborn behaviors. Humans were supposed to have dozens of instincts, including fighting, mothering, keeping clean, making war, and hosts of others. Then, for a long time, psychologists simply discarded the term, largely because semantic confusion made it all but useless. They relegated it to oblivion after making bumbling attempts to write its obituary. More recently, instinctive behavior patterns have been defined as behaviors produced by maturation rather than learning. In this sense, an instinctive behavior is inborn, the product of heredity, though it may not appear until months, even years, after birth. However, it is expected to appear full-blown the first time an adequate stimulus is presented. It is this factor that distinguishes the present from the former concept of instinct, which postulated instincts as operating without reference to any specific environmental stimulation.

To qualify as instinctive, behaviors must satisfy certain other conditions, too. They must be generally characteristic of the species; otherwise the genetic base is in doubt. Also, they must be relatively complex and continue for some time in the absence of the conditions evoking them. This latter condition distinguishes them from reflexes, which are automatic reactions to stimuli.

Instincts among animals. Since the body develops on a pattern laid down by the genes, instinctive behaviors are claimed to appear at any time from birth onward. An example of a so-called instinctive behavior is the maternal behavior of the mother rat. The pregnant rat builds a nest before the young are born and cleans them afterward. If they wiggle out of the nest, she retrieves them. While these behaviors vary a bit from one species of rat to another, they are relatively unvarying within the species. These behaviors occur at the time of the first litter, without any chance of their having been learned through observation. Note also, however, that they could not occur without the presence of appropriate environmental conditions.

Nevertheless, even among animals it is difficult to distinguish behaviors that are truly innate from those that are learned or from those that are largely reflexive responses to stimuli. For example, nightingales' songs are so similar as to seem instinctive; however, every juvenile male bird must learn the song individually (Tinbergen, 1951). At other times, neurosensory mechanisms, triggered by certain highly specific stimuli, give rise to relatively unvarying responses that *seem* to be instinctive. For instance, the male moth responds to the sexual odors of the female and may attempt to mate with any object emitting this scent. The male English robin, which reacts aggressively to the dull-brown breast of an intruding bird, reacts even more violently to a simple tuft of red feathers. In fact, many so-called instinctive behaviors of animals, when analyzed, simply prove to be highly specific neurological reactions to certain stimuli, which, because of their specific properties, are adequate to provoke a reaction (Tinbergen, 1951).

Views about instincts among humans. Where humans are concerned, most present-day developmental psychologists pass over the instinct concept lightly. They judge it of little value either because they believe humans have extremely few, if any, instincts or because they find the concept relatively useless for explaining child behavior. Ruch (1958) says instincts among humans are "rare," but he fails to name even those few. Morgan (1966) concludes that, with the possible exception of a few behaviors that mature without practice (he does not name these behaviors), we cannot say with certainty that there are any instinctive behavior patterns.

These two writers, like most psychologists, believe that humans possess such great innate adaptability to their world that instinctive behaviors, whether nonexistent or slight, are relatively unimportant. The much slower maturation of humans than of animals makes learning of transcendentally greater significance than any so-called inborn behaviors.

Pending more definitive evidence, perhaps we should reject altogether the notion of complex innate behavior patterns, as opposed to purely reflex reactions. Activities that occur spontaneously and resist modification are essentially "biological action" rather than behavior. An unlearned biological action is simply a response to certain object properties whose stimulus significance derives from the biological character of the organism. That is, so-called instinctual behavior is simply determined by the biological sensitivities and momentary organic state of the organism.

Furthermore, apparently "unlearned" action may not be unlearned at all. Behaviors may be acquired as the result of a single experience. For instance, we may say the child has an instinctive fear of falling because he cries as he falls. In the very process of falling, he is learning what it is to fall. Anyhow, the experience is not entirely new because the infant's reaction derives largely from having come, even prenatally, to depend on physical support.

Certain other behaviors, such as birds' flying south in the winter, represent, at least partly, the integration of more basic activities already learned, such as the ability to fly and to establish direction.

Especially in the early days, the term "instinct" was merely a convenience to explain what was not understood (Schwartz, 1963). An adequate explanation of so-called instinctual behaviors must await more intensive study of both biological and psychological equipment and development of different organisms.

Imprinting

Of more immediate concern are two relatively new and closely related concepts, imprinting and the critical period. **Imprinting** implies learning that may occur only during a specific, and usually rather brief, period in the early life of the organism. Theoretically, the behavior, once learned, sets about as firmly as though it were innate, and is almost as irreversible. However, imprinting differs from instinctive behavior in that it definitely depends on learning. It is probably the most dramatic of all the evidence supporting the long-held belief that early experiences have the most pervasive and enduring effects on development.

As a concept, imprinting is not completely new. Husbandmen have known for centuries that the young of certain animals, if deprived of their natural mothers early in life, will reject those mothers if restored to them later on. They have also observed that infant animals tend to become attached to whatever stimuli are present in their environment immediately after birth or hatching. Only recently have such behaviors been scientifically controlled and tested. In a typical experiment, male bitterns in a zoo were imprinted through exposure to the zoo director and were deprived of any contact with other bitterns during the brief critical stage. The bittern thus imprinted would chase his mate from the nest when the zoo director appeared, and would show by his actions that he expected the director to sit on the nest with him to incubate the eggs (Lorenz, 1955).

In another study, the experimenters set up a wooden model of a duck and by remote control made the duck move around a track emitting sounds of "gock, gock, gock" (recorded on tape from a mother duck). Ducklings, exposed to this wooden duck within a few hours after hatching, learned to follow it instead of their own mother (Ramsay and Hess, 1954). However, those exposed 30 hours after hatching failed to imprint at all.

Other studies of ducklings' behavior have shown that the duckling is easily imprinted with a decoy; that the duckling

103

will follow the male in preference to the female if he has been imprinted with the male; that ducklings imprinted with a decoy will congregate around the decoy in preference to a live adult duck; and that the duckling will overcome obstacles to reach the decoy (Hess, 1958).

The Critical Period

Implicit within the concept of imprinting, and related to it, is the **critical-period** hypothesis: that certain experiences are likely to have a far more profound effect at certain periods than at others. In the following excerpt from *Witness,* by Whittaker Chambers, the narrator tells of a time in childhood that he believes to have been critical:

Then my mother told me to go and kill the first chicken. The thought of hurting anything so helpless and foolish was too much for me. I said: "I can't." My mother did not even answer me. She took a sharp knife and pressed the handle into my hand. "I will not have any man in this house," she said fiercely, "who is afraid of blood." I knew that she was thinking of my father.

I caught a chicken. I sat down with it in the coop, stroked its feathers and tried to quiet its alarm. It was a sunny day. It was the thought that from the bird's bright eye that world of light must now fade that unnerved me. Why must I darken it? So that the live, free creature could pass through the bowels of a gross person? It made no sense.

I tied the chicken's legs and hung it, head down, from a nail, and as quickly and as mercifully as I could, severed its head. The knife fell as if gravity had jerked it from my hand. Then I hid [Chambers, 1952, p. 123].

The critical period and imprinting hypotheses differ in several ways. For one thing, imprinted learning can occur only early in life, whereas critical periods, theoretically, can exist at any time (with increasingly less frequency) until maturity or even beyond. Moreover, imprinting is characterized by a brief period of time and very rapid learning, whereas a critical period may span some months or even an entire age-stage, such as infancy or adolescence. In fact, there may

be many critical periods, with different ones for different functions. In every case of imprinting thus far reported, the period when it may take place is quite brief. Between the ages of 9 to 20 hours, ducklings can be imprinted in only 10 minutes to react to the wooden decoy duck as a mother; and forever after the duckling will respond to the decoy duck in preference to the mother duck (Hess, 1959). Among partridges, pheasants, and mallards, the period when such associations may occur lasts only several hours, beginning just after the young have dried. If the crucial period is missed, even by a few hours, young mallards cannot be taught to follow humans in preference to a mother duck (Lorenz, 1957).

The discovery of an imprinting period among infants would depend on close observation and complete control of the environment; otherwise, it would be hard to determine whether, in fact, they experience learnings that correspond to imprinting in animals.

By contrast, critical periods may occur at any time. Stendler (1952) proposes two critical periods in the establishment of overdependency: toward the end of the first year of life, when the child first begins to test the mother to see whether he can depend on her, and during the two- to three-year age period, when the child is subject to basic training in socialization. Conversely, if a child *fails* to have certain experiences at a critical period, the behaviors normally accruing to such experience may never occur. For instance, an illegitimate girl named Anna was confined to her bedroom from age one and a half through five. The mother fed the child but did not bathe, fondle, or socialize with her. She was then removed from home, and by the time she died at age 10 she had had almost five years of training. However, she never learned to speak better than the normal two- to three-year old. The critical period hypothesis might suggest that she simply missed the period for learning speech (Davis, 1940).

Critical periods tend to occur earlier

in animals than in humans. Consider puppies, for instance. Before three weeks of age, a puppy is highly insulated from its environment by the immature development of its sense organs, which prevents conditioning. From three to seven weeks, the puppy's sense organs and cerebral cortex are still not fully developed, but it has acquired extremely sensitive emotional reactions and is capable of making associations. This is the time when it is easiest for the dog's owner to establish a strong special bond. Since important maturational changes continue to occur in humans for a considerably longer period of time, the critical periods that relate to them may occur at least until adulthood, perhaps later. Puberty, for example, may be a critical period for the establishment of heterosexuality; and early adulthood may be critical for the organization of much later experience.

The behaviors that involve imprinting are typically simpler and more firmly rooted in the nature of the organism than are those related to critical periods. For example, imprinting depends on the organism's being developed to the point of being impressionable, yet still sufficiently immature to make the reaction automatic. Hence imprinting by any object whatsoever between the size of a bantam hen and a big rowboat, if it moves and emits noises of a wide variety of pitches, can release certain responses in the greyleg goose. Obviously, there has been a simple conditioning process, so that each of these stimuli simply activates some innate releasing mechanism (Lorenz, 1956).

By contrast, the critical-period hypothesis may involve learnings on any level of complexity, from very simple to very complex. Imprinting itself, basically a simple process, occurs during a critical period, but so may such complex behaviors as the learning of language or fractions. By extension, curricular planning may be thought of as research for critical periods in cognitive development and of relating the learner's psychological growth to the most appropriate materials and methods.

The persistence of learning acquired during later critical periods has not been examined, but it is probably more variable than that acquired during imprinting. As already indicated, imprinted learning is supposedly either irreversible or highly stable, largely because it is rooted in the biological nature of the organism itself. Greyleg goslings reared by human hands continue their attachment to the adopted parent even when placed with a goose family. However, human learning during critical periods, though more persistent than that which occurs at other times, theoretically can be reversed, even if it occurs relatively early (Thompson and Schaefer, 1961).

Significance of the critical period. Among humans, the concept of critical periods has thus far proved more fruitful than that of imprinting. While imprinting relates to very early, simple learning, which occurs during some quite brief time not long after birth, the critical-period hypothesis suggests that "golden times" for learning may occur at various times during life, the specific time dependent on the type of learning involved. For instance, we have always assumed that the optic nerve develops regardless of light stimulation; however, chimpanzees reared in darkness develop organic defects (Riesen, 1951). Even if they receive a small amount of light each day, this still inadequate visual experience prevents them from learning to distinguish different persons on a purely visual basis.

Similarly, congenitally blind persons, after cataracts are removed late in life, fail to learn certain visual discriminations despite an intact optic apparatus. They can distinguish light from darkness but have trouble with form (von Senden, 1960). Von Senden suggests that many aspects of vision are permanently impaired by lack of visual experience during some critical period, probably between birth and age four.

105

Apparently, stimulation of whatever kind, whether pleasant or unpleasant, may constitute an adequate base for later learning. Infant rats disturbed in their nests later manifested greater willingness to explore a strange area than did unstimulated rats (Meyers, 1962). In another experiment, such subtle effects as those involved in transporting an infant mouse from its nest to the shock apparatus and back proved sufficient to modify its learning score when it became an adult (Denenberg and Bell, 1960). Such studies suggest these questions: Do we overprotect human infants? Does the currently prevalent "kid-glove treatment" militate against the degree of toughness and alertness optimum for later learning? Do boys have an advantage because parents "rough-house" with them more than with girls? If so, what amount of "rough-housing" is optimal? Forcing a child to strain for success, concludes Vernon (1961), is crucial for "internalized processes." However, instead of driving the child to action, it is probably better to create conditions that challenge him to take action. In any case, the function of early experience is to build mediating processes, which, once established, make possible the more rapid learning of maturity.

We do not know just how early human experience relates to later function; nor do we know the neurophysiological mechanisms involved. However, such evidence as exists suggests that free access to a highly varied environment is extremely important for later development. One might then ask: Is it possible that designing the infant's quarters to provide widely varied sensory stimuli and maximum opportunity for unhampered exploration would produce relevant effects? To date, most people have resisted the idea of manipulating tiny infants simply to make them better scholars sometime in the hazy future. Mothers, especially, reject the idea. Babies are to cuddle and to care for, not to mold into efficient learning machines. In view of such obstacles to research, the only wholly justifiable conclusion to emerge

so far is that early learning proves hard to alter, perhaps because it is inaccessible to conscious memory (McClelland et al., 1951).

At least where animals are concerned, the nature and quality of stimulation seem relatively unimportant. It is the quantity of stimulation that plays the decisive role. However, after the critical period is passed, both the nature and quality of the stimulus interact with the intensity and quantity of stimulus to determine the effect (Denenberg, 1961). In consequence, one might raise this question: Because type and quality of stimulus *apparently* make no difference among infant animals, can we conclude that they make no difference for human infants? The animal's nervous system is further developed, hence less susceptible to differential stimuli; we might then err in exposing human infants to a barrage of stimuli with little concern for their quality. Research now pending may throw light on this question.

At any rate, psychologists ought to give due consideration to this whole question. To what extent are doors closed, in succession and forever, to an individual because appropriate experiences are missing at critical times? Perhaps the deprivation of adequate experience creates permanent living difficulties, besides deficient or atypical cognitive-affective development (Zupansky and Leiderman, 1963).

Can deficiencies be made up? Let us conclude this topic by raising still another question: Do the apparently irreversible effects of failure to provide suitable experience at critical times simply reflect our failure to find methods of making up deficiencies? In another case in which an illegitimate child was found after having been hidden away during infancy and early childhood, intensive training restored the badly deprived girl to normal. By coincidence, Isabelle was found only nine months after the discovery of Anna, whose case we discussed earlier. Isabelle had been locked up by her mother's family for six and a half years in a darkened room with her mother, a deaf-mute. Though Isabelle had communicated with her mother by simple gestures, she was unable to speak and made only a strange croaking sound when discovered. Her legs were so badly bowed by rickets, owing to lack of sunshine and proper diet, that the soles of her shoes came nearly flat together. This condition was later corrected surgically so that normal walking and running were possible.

When she was found, Isabelle's behavior toward strangers was like that of a wild animal, full of fear and hostility. She spent the first two days crying, and refused to eat anything but a little milk and crackers until Dr. Marie K. Mason, a psychologist from Ohio State University, was able to win her confidence. Though at first Isabelle was believed to be wholly uneducable, Dr. Mason, aided by other psychologists and student teachers, decided to try to teach her. After interesting her in a doll, a watch, and a ring by the use of gestures, and after working hard with her for a whole week, Dr. Mason succeeded in getting Isabelle to say "ouh" for "ball" and "ah" for "car." This occurred on November 25, 1938. By the following February 8, Isabelle was using such sentences as "That's my baby." Early in March she showed that she was developing social manners by asking Miss Mason to "Say please" when making requests. By that time she could identify the words "blue" and "yellow" in printed form and match them with the appropriate colors. She continued this rapid progress until at the end of a year she knew many printed words and sentences, and could write well, count to 20, do addition to 10, sing "with gusto and accuracy," and re-tell a story she had heard.

At the end of 22 months in her new environment, Isabelle was regarded as normal in intelligence. The latest report on Isabelle was at the age of 14, when she had just passed the sixth grade. She was participating freely in a variety of school activities and making an excellent social adjustment.

On the face of it, Isabelle's response

to training suggests that original deficits may be overcome. Indeed, new learning procedures yet to be devised, or even treatment on the biochemical level, may restore now hopeless cases. On the other hand, one could also ask: Might not Isabelle have been far brighter than "just normal" had she been reared in a normal environment? Probably we should proceed on two fronts: to determine the optimum times for learning, and to seek means of minimizing the loss if critical periods are bypassed.

Many other questions remain to be resolved relative to critical periods and imprinting. If imprinting-like phenomena do occur among infants, *when* do they occur? On the basis of such evidence as we have, we might expect them to begin as early as a month or six weeks after birth, or perhaps as late as six months. How long do critical periods in infancy last? For primary socialization, certainly as long as the period of complete dependency on the mother. What are the physical bases or behavioral mechanisms for critical periods? Among animals, we look for certain stages of maturation within the sensory, motor, and neural organization and the central nervous system. We are still unclear on these points about humans. We do not, for example, know just what neurophysiological changes undergird the shift to heterosexual orientation. However, since considerable current research involves such questions, additional data should be forthcoming.

• THE ORGANIZATION AND DYNAMICS OF PERSONALITY

The Personality Syndrome

Each child's traits are unique, and they become patterned in unique ways. That is, the child is said to have a typical **personality syndrome.** This pattern, different for each child, originates because in the process of development some traits prove more useful than others and are habituated. Those traits closely related to the preservation and

Not even twins have personalities exactly alike.

enhancement of a child's self-concept are especially crucial and become the bases for less fundamental traits. Thus a girl may identify closely with her mother and vaguely feel like a little mother herself. With great solicitude she tends her little brother; with complete conscientiousness she helps clean the house. These traits — motherliness, nurture, and conscientiousness — become the cornerstones of her personality. In time, she develops other traits, too. For instance, she may be so home-bound that she becomes relatively reserved and overly serious. One readily sees, therefore, that traits do not arise in random fashion. All are part of a pattern that is integrated by central goals and values.

Confirmation from research. The foregoing concept of personality organization is confirmed by research. In a classic study of the life histories, from birth to adulthood, of 25 individuals, each had preserved a central stability, or center of gravity that did not change (Roberts and Fleming, 1943). In another study, teachers rated preschool children on 231 common traits. Intercorrelations among the teachers' ratings were low, but when the teachers starred ratings of traits that were of central importance in the children's personalities, the agreement rose sharply (Conrad, 1932).

Note, too, that certain dominant traits may become associated with other important, although less central, traits. The creative child, for instance, is often less anxious, less defensive, and more willing to concede faults (Reid et al., 1959). Creative children tend, in addition, to be unconventional and sensitive to the feelings of others (Drevdahl, 1958). Aggressive children also show certain typical traits. They tend to be more expansive, for example, and require more space. In a study in which children were divided into groups aged 4, 6, 9, and 10, both the more aggressive and the older ones used more room space and words (Lebo, 1962). In another study, the more creative children also manifested greater cultural interests, were more self-sufficient and independent, and were less concerned with maintaining close ties with social groups; moreover, they adhered less closely to sex role, disregarding barriers normally imposed on their sex (MacKinnon, 1962).

Persistence of Traits

Implicit in the concepts already discussed are certain beliefs about the stability or permanence of personality traits. Research studies on this question are mounting fast. The following thumbnail sketches, extracted from one such study, demonstrate how certain traits of two small children persisted over a period of time:

A. J. had admirable leadership qualities but was also forcefully domineering. During the second year, when he did not have his way, he would become very angry, and sometimes bite. In his third nursery school year, he would scratch other children who interfered, or attack viciously. Again, between the ages $8\frac{1}{2}$ to 9, we find this typical comment: A. came in feeling very mean and threw his coat up on top of the rack. I told him he was crushing C's hat. He said, "Well, that's my sister's hat anyway; so what do I care?" While I went after him to see that he hung his coat up another boy left his on the radiator. I asked A. whose coat it was, and he said, "What do I care? That isn't my business. I'd like to sock that guy anyway." Then he rushed toward some little fat fellow with glasses and began to strike him. . . .

By contrast, B. R. was submissive. At age 2, he sucked his thumb habitually, and kept in the background. At age $2\frac{1}{2}$ he pretended he could not climb on the slide. He was very timid and attached himself to his father. At around age 4, he began playing more with bigger boys and even holding his own with the others, but his promise of a new trend toward more self-assertiveness

did not materialize. At age 11, he continued to show compliance to the wishes of others [Stott, 1957].

Research evidence. How typical are these children? Do most children, like these two, demonstrate great persistence of basic traits? Or do children generally manifest greater change? The answer is clear-cut: persistence is the rule.

Two such studies indicated consistency of certain traits during the infancy period. One of these identified among infants the following "primary reaction characteristics": activity level, rhythmicity, approach or withdrawal, adaptability, intensity of reaction, threshold of responsiveness, quality of mood, distractability, attention span, and persistence. All these traits, among the 118 infants studied, proved remarkably stable through the first two years of life (Birch et al., 1962).

In a similar study, nursery-school children continued over a two-year period to manifest the same amounts of aggression, dominance, dependency, autonomy, achievement, and friendship affiliation. That is, each child maintained his position in the group with regard to the relative frequency of such behaviors. At the same time, each child's behavioral profile was unique; and for four children out of five, it remained stable over the period studied. It appears as though each child has his own "behavioral economy," which persists through time. Admittedly, he modifies his behavior, but only in search of enduring goals (Martin, 1964).

Other studies have revealed a similar constancy, at least in certain traits, over a much longer period. For women, traits that proved stable from early childhood to maturity were passive withdrawal from stressful situations and dependency on the family; for men, ease of anger arousal and sexual behavior; and for both men and women, involvement in intellectual mastery, sex-role identification, and spontaneity. Among these variables, the persistence of

109

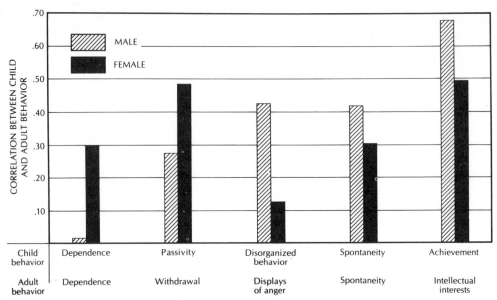

The persistence of personality traits. The height of the bars indicates the percentage of correlation between the behaviors of the same individuals as children and later as adults. The children rated for dependence, passivity, and disorganized behavior were aged 6 to 10; those rated for achievement and spontaneity were aged 10 to 14. From J. Kagan and H. S. Moss, *Birth to maturity.* New York: Wiley, 1962. Reproduced by permission.

spontaneity was the most impressive, since it was stable and predictive for both sexes (Honzik, 1965). For about the same period, birth to age 18, Bayley and Schaefer (1963) reported as most stable the broad dimension "active, extroverted versus inactive, introverted."

For certain other traits, adolescence appears to be critical; that is, certain traits which stabilize at that time persist into adulthood. Furthermore, certain traits, observed then, prove more highly predictive of adult personality than do childhood ratings in those traits. For instance, the correlation between the birth-to-age-three ratings on aggressive retaliation is only .19; but by the age period 10 to 14, the correlation is .47. In fact, in the Fels study (Kagan and Moss, 1962), only a few of the behaviors observed in the age period 3 to 6 years were predictive of related behaviors in early adulthood; however, the ages 6 to 10 proved critical in determining the child's later behavioral organization. These findings suggest that the so-called *latency period* (middle childhood) is more critical in

development than is sometimes believed.

Two other categories of behaviors — those relating to sex and dependency — stabilize in early adolescence and remain highly persistent, at least through the early adult years. However, there is less stability for behaviors that deviate from social norms. For example, dependent behavior in men and aggressive behavior in women, both of which are disapproved of in our culture, show less stability from adolescence to adulthood than do the same traits in the opposite sex. That is, girls who are aggressive in adolescence are not necessarily aggressive as adults, because society discourages aggression in females. Similarly, dependent adolescent boys sometimes become independent adults because of cultural pressures. However, adolescent behaviors that are not subject to strong social punishment are often a good index of behavior 10 to 15 years later. Striving for intellectual competence and mastery behaviors, which are not discouraged for middle-class children of either sex, are highly stable from high-school years through early adulthood, at least for most adolescents (Kagan and Moss, 1962; Tuddenham, 1959).

Apparently, basic traits tend to persist through adult life. Among 300 engaged couples studied between 1945 and 1948 and then again 20 years later, basic traits changed little, although more narrowly defined characteristics and behaviors were sometimes modified. Little or no relation was shown between these changes and known forces in the subjects' immediate environment. In short, significant changes may occur—not large enough to threaten continuity of self but of sufficient magnitude to offer some basis of hope for continued psychological growth during adulthood. However, desirable basic traits should be established as soon as possible, because they tend to persist throughout life.

The sleeper effect. A significant finding from the Fels study was the existence of the so-called **"sleeper effect."** Apparently, a trait that is depressed for a while may later reappear. For instance, behaviors such as passivity and fear of bodily harm in the age period birth-to-three years were found to be more predictive of love-object dependency in adult men than were later assessments of this childhood variable (Kagan and Moss, 1962).

Similarly, Stott (1957) found that children might demonstrate temporary changes in traits but tended to revert to earlier patterns. In fact, he found that four-fifths of a group studied in nursery school and again 12 years later showed no consistent changes. Children who were originally aggressive, dominant, submissive, dependent, or independent tended to remain so. In effect, each child is stalked by a past that may overtake him at any time.

Further questions to be answered. The foregoing research suggests various questions that require further investigation. For example, how much is the persistence of behavior patterns due to genetic factors and how much to constant factors within the environment?

How much could such traits be changed, if especially intense stimuli were applied at critical ages? One must not lose sight of the minority of children whose traits do change. Again, what hope, if any, exists for making long-term predictions for specific children? Escalona and Heider (1959) reported an attempt to predict what individual children, first studied at eight months of age, would be like several years later. They studied case materials on the infants and made specific predictions about the kinds of behavior that might logically be expected of these same children prior to their starting school. These predictions were matched with actual descriptions of each child made independently by other investigators about four years later. Although some traits, and some children, proved more predictable than others, 66% of 882 predictions proved to be essentially correct.

The constancy of personality and its susceptibility to change are important to all those concerned with child behavior. If core traits are highly rigid, the child must be helped to accept those traits and build on them. If core traits can be changed, however, he can be helped to revise the traits that are less useful to him.

Developmental Tasks

The developmental-task concept. Any child's adjustment within an age-graded society—and all societies are age-graded in varying degrees—depends on the continuous mastery of new tasks appropriate to successive age-stages. The infant, for instance, must learn to walk and talk before he is prepared for childhood. The child, in turn, must learn basic academic skills before he is ready for the more complex intellectual tasks of adolescence.

Havighurst (1953) and Erikson (1963) have popularized the concept that a child must master the tasks appropriate to his current age-stage before he is ready for the next one. Some tasks, asserts Havighurst, arise mainly from physical maturation; others stem primarily from cultural pressures. For example, getting along with the other sex is a task dependent on physical maturation, while learning to read is required by social pressures. A third source of developmental tasks is one's personal value system. A boy who spends time developing his body probably aspires to become an athlete.

Erikson defined life tasks somewhat differently, in terms of personality characteristics. In infancy, said Erikson, the child must develop a basic *sense of trust.* Periodically, he feels discomfort from cold, hunger, or pain. However, if he discovers that he can rely on older people to restore his comfort, he develops confidence, both in the world and in himself. On the other hand, if he finds his world unstable and confusing, he will feel helpless and insecure.

The second year is characterized by the child's growing *autonomy.* When the child is trained in basic patterns of eating, sleeping, or toilet-training, he is permitted some alternatives. Thus he acquires feelings of freedom and personal dignity. Next, during early childhood he develops a *sense of initiative,* as he begins to undertake more activities without the direct aid of his mother. During adolescence, which Erikson calls a period of role confusion, there gradually emerges a *sense of identity.* The younger adolescent must decide who he is, the older one what to do about it. Self-diffusion becomes a danger as when genital maturity floods the body with vague new feelings. Such feelings, in turn, must be offset by the sorts of experience that will foster a unified and healthy sense of self.

Adulthood brings the *need for intimacy.* However, in a culture that subordinates sexuality and sensuality to work, duty, and worship, the sense of intimacy is hard to establish. Next comes the need for *parental sense,* which is never truly acquired if the parent exploits his children or becomes their rival. Ideally, through caring for and guiding his children, the parent

should find fulfillment. The final crisis of development, which continues throughout adulthood, is the conflict between despair and integrity. Only through achieving a *sense of integrity,* does one acquire the capacity to defend his own life style.

Pitfalls of developmental-task theories. Although such theories as Havighurst's and Erikson's help to order life tasks, they also pose certain dangers. Mastery of specific tasks may indeed be more crucial at certain stages; however, such tasks should not be thought of as discrete and belonging solely to a specific stage. A task can hardly be mastered successfully if the groundwork for its accomplishment is not laid earlier. For example, an adolescent will hardly establish an identity at adolescence unless he has made considerable progress toward that goal earlier. The developmental-task theory also encourages the perception of development as a lock-step process: one performs Task No. 1, then Task No. 2, and so on, in that order. Actually, progress in mastering developmental tasks is overlapping and relatively continuous, and setbacks are normal. Moreover, the identification of such tasks, in so precise a fashion, tends toward crystallizing the life-curriculum prescribed for children, thereby obstructing the sort of critical re-examination and continuous modification needed in a rapidly changing society. For instance, to the period of adolescence we may assign the goal of establishing satisfactory heterosexual relations. However, if the child society continues its present trend toward admitting both sexes in childhood activities, then tomorrow's child, in order to be well-adjusted socially, may need increased interaction with opposite-sex peers at an earlier age.

Finally, the concept of developmental tasks may be wrongly interjected as implying that each life stage is simply an apprenticeship for what follows. Thus, the child's role would simply be an audition for the role he will play as an adult. However, although it must provide a healthy base for later stages, each stage is important for its own sake.

• STATUS OF PERSONALITY RESEARCH

From all the research just reviewed, notice how many questions about personality have not yet been resolved. The truth is that personality research is unbelievably complex and still in its infancy. The concepts involved, such as self and traits, are inherently elusive and complex. Nor is there any real agreement about the desirability of specific traits, such as unconventionality or aggressiveness. In order to resolve such dilemmas and to establish an empirical base for theory, researchers have devised various measures of personality. However, these tests suffer from the same confusion as do the concepts they supposedly measure. For instance, projective tests, which are designed to prevent deliberate distortions and to expose the deeper layers of personality, predict little of importance about the individual (Thorndike and Hagen, 1961).

It is hardly surprising, therefore, that most authorities concede only small progress to date in personality research. One may try out different soils for growing different plants, writes Murphy (1956), but children are more subtle. In sum, we have only made a beginning in defining the laws that control behaviors. Nevertheless, bit by bit significant findings are emerging, and research on the topic is increasing in volume and sophistication. Only time can determine the worth of present efforts; perhaps certain data that are of small apparent relevance now may someday constitute a breakthrough to significant new ways of dealing with children.

• SUMMARY

One's **personality** represents the summation of all his **behaviors** as uniquely organized through the inter-action of his heredity and experience. In satisfying his own unique needs, each individual finds certain behaviors effective and habituates them. These characteristic behaviors, or **traits,** may be either *central (core)* or *secondary (peripheral).* Traits, in turn, become organized into socially expected behavior patterns appropriate to the individual's roles or functions in life. The feature common to all of an individual's roles is his **personal role,** or self-in-action. A child's **self-concept** represents how he feels about the way he plays his roles. His self-concept determines his behaviors, the nature of his goals, his mental health, and his relationships with others.

The child's self-concept, at first amorphous, becomes differentiated through his experiences with self and with others. Meantime, fluctuations in self-concept relate partially to the relatively different status of age roles in the society. Ordinarily boys have a stronger self-concept than girls, reflecting their higher status in society. The female's self-concept may be somewhat confused, reflecting pressures both to marry and to have a career.

Among ways of improving the self-concept is **self-actualization,** which connotes the constructive development of one's potential. Adults can help children toward self-actualization by providing the sort of environment in which they can flourish. Like self-actualization, **achievement orientation** requires the existence of goals; but unlike self-actualization it suggests nothing of their worth. Individuals who make satisfactory progress toward their goals are called **achievers;** those whose goals are nebulous or whose progress toward them is uncertain are called *non-achievers.* Achievers ordinarily have healthy self-concepts; however, such individuals may overreact by making undue sacrifices or alienating others.

Various factors relate to the degree of achievement orientation, including the child's sex, social class, and age. Achievement during the first four grades, at ages 6 to 10, seems especially critical for later achievement. At any age, middle-class children, especially boys, receive far more encouragement and prodding to achieve than their lower-class counterparts. In fact, boys are generally far more achievement-oriented than girls.

Also basic to achievement orientation is the establishing of an **identity,** or a feeling of uniqueness. Whereas self-concept is defined as an individual's total picture of himself, identity refers to one's feelings of distinctiveness from others, or his "*me*-ness." Identity differs from **identification,** which suggests merging one's own goals with or patterning oneself after another person. Various factors may hamper the attainment or preservation of a healthy identity. A child may identify with someone else so thoroughly that he sacrifices his own distinctiveness, or he may identify with unhealthy traits. In addition, the very complexity of modern life may hamper development of a stable self-concept. Meantime, pressures to conform interfere with remaining true to oneself. Besides being subject to the foregoing hazards, children who are handicapped or of lower social status face special identity crises. It is hard to take pride in who they are when others hold an unfortunate image of them.

Another critical process of development is the establishment of **autonomy,** requiring self-direction rather than direction from without. Ordinarily, parents automatically grant boys increasing autonomy but keep girls on the leash into adulthood.

Other controversial subjects in personality theory are **instinct, imprinting,** and **critical period.** Traditionally, *instincts,* or inborn behaviors, are said to appear full-blown whenever appropriate stimuli are present. Even though certain animal behaviors seem to be innate, most psychologists have discarded the idea of instinct. Of more current concern are the concepts of *imprinting,* which involves learned be-

havior that is indelibly adopted only during a specific, rather brief period in the early life of the organism, and *critical period,* which suggests that certain experiences have a more significant effect at certain periods than others. Whether imprinting occurs in human infants is uncertain, but critical periods have been claimed for various functions. For instance, infants apparently require early sensory stimulation as a base for later learning. Supposedly, once the critical period is past, deficiencies incurred at that time may never be fully compensated for; however, this aspect still needs much research.

It is important to remember that every child is unique, with his characteristic pattern of traits, or **personality syndrome.** Certain of his traits are basic, are apparent from birth, and persist through life. Sometimes a trait, depressed for a while, reappears; this phenomenon is called the **sleeper effect.**

Regardless of his personality, the child must adapt his personality traits to society, which requires his mastering of appropriate **developmental tasks** at successive age levels. However, such tasks should not be regimented or they may constrict the child's development. The naming of such tasks has been somewhat arbitrary, as has much theory relating to personality. The whole topic of personality is unbelievably complex; nevertheless, personality research is burgeoning and significant findings are gradually emerging.

• SUGGESTED QUESTIONS AND ACTIVITIES

1. Can infants, at birth, be said to possess personalities? If not, at what age do they acquire them?
2. How does the fact that an individual begins by playing infant and childhood roles affect the development of self-concept and personality?
3. Which type of child do you believe would have a more clearly defined self-concept: The conformist or the deviate? The bright child or the dull child? The introvert or the extrovert? The city child or the farm

child? Give reasons for your choices.

4. In what specific ways might provision be made for children to achieve autonomy at a faster rate than is now customary, without undesirable side effects being produced?

5. What are the best ways to encourage achievement orientation in children without making them feel anxious and overly sensitive to failure?

6. What factors in the American culture today, as they impinge on the child, tend to enhance or retard his progress toward self-actualization and the establishment of identity?

7. Discuss those factors most likely to reduce or enhance the child's self-concept (a) on the playground, (b) in the home, (c) at school, and (d) in society at large.

8. Analyze current television characters, especially those popular with children, in terms of their possible effects on children's identities, self-concepts, or personalities in general.

9. Answer the following questions on an unsigned sheet of paper, labeled only with your age and sex. These slips can be collected and read to the class for discussion, or they can be analyzed by class committees and the results reported to the class. (a) Indicate the approximate ages at which you first incorporated into your self-concept your sex, race, and nationality roles, respectively. What factors led to such recognition? (b) When were you first aware of having any special identity as a person? What gave you that feeling? (c) With what persons did you identify as a child? (Include characters in books, movies, or television.) (d) What specific incidents, experiences, or age-stages did you find most critical in your own childhood? Why? (e) As a child, what specific factors were most significant in giving you a sense of distinctiveness, or a feeling of identity? (f) As a child, did you tend to perceive yourself as a little speck in the universe or did you think of the universe as revolving around you? Give reasons. (g) In what ways did your parents affect your establishment of autonomy? What restrictions did they place on your freedom? How did you react? (h) To what extent are you achievement-oriented? What childhood experiences have especially modified your achievement orientation? (i) In what respects did your parents differentiate their efforts to "push" their daughters or sons toward achievement? (j) Discuss how you compared as a child with society's ideal child, and how the degree of difference affected your development.

PERSONALITY

• SUGGESTED READINGS

Bloom, B., *The Stability and Change in Human Characteristics.* New York: John Wiley & Sons, Inc., 1964. Summarizes and critically examines a large number of longitudinal and cross-sectional studies, both classic and recent, to discover the forces affecting stability of development from infancy to maturity.

Caldwell, B. M., "The Usefulness of the Critical Period Hypothesis in the Study of Filiative Behavior," *Merrill-Palmer Quarterly,* Vol. 8, No. 4 (1964), pp. 229–242. On the basis of available data, Caldwell concludes that critical periods indeed exist and that the significance of such periods deserves more analysis and recognition. She stresses especially the importance of laying foundations in very early childhood for later cognitive development.

Chethik, M., E. Fleming, M. F. Mayer, and J. N. McCoy, "A Quest for Identity," *American Journal of Orthopsychiatry,* Vol. 37, No. 1 (January 1967), pp. 71–77. Discusses the effect of being treated in an otherwise all-white treatment center on the self-concepts of several Negro children. Describes staff reactions, peer relationships, specific problems, and methods of therapy

Cohen, S., "The Problem with Piaget's Child," *Teachers College Record,* Vol. 43, No. 3 (1966), pp. 211–218. An interesting critical analysis of Piaget's model of child development.

Hunt, J. McV., "Traditional Personality Theory in the Light of Present Evidence," *American Scientist,* Vol. 53, No. 1 (1965), pp. 80–96. Examines the most critical new evidence relating to motivation and personality. Concludes that all behavior is motivated, that emotional factors are indeed more important than cognitive factors in psychological development, that emotional attachments derive from gratification of libidinal needs, and that stress in infancy produces a proneness to anxiety.

Kagan, J., and H. Moss, *Birth to Maturity: A Study in Psychological Development.* New York: John Wiley & Sons, Inc., 1962. Report of an important longitudinal study and the persistence of certain traits.

Kessen, W., "Research in the Psychological Development in Infants: An Overview," *Merrill-Palmer Quarterly,* Vol. 9 (1963), pp. 93–94. Provides a critical overview of the most significant personality research relating to infants. There emerges the picture of a "competent," active infant as opposed to the image of a "passive receptacle."

Murphy, L., and collaborators, *The Widening World of Childhood.* New York: Basic Books, Inc., 1962. Treats the concept of "coping" in terms of anecdotal material from situations in which 32 preschool children were observed. Evidence for existing hypotheses is examined and new ones suggested.

Scott, J. P., "Critical Periods in Behavioral Development," *Science,* Vol. 138, No. 3544 (November 1962), pp. 949–958. Of his own and other research Scott concludes that the concept of critical periods is highly important for human and animal welfare. Once the dangers and benefits for each period of life are known, he believes it possible to avoid the dangers and take advantage of the benefits.

Sears, P. S., and V. S. Sherman, *In Pursuit of Self Esteem: Case Studies of Eight Elementary School Children.* Belmont, Calif.: Wadsworth Publishing Company, Inc., 1964. Two clinicians, experts in the case-study method, consider children's self-esteem in relation to their school life and work. The focus is on normal children in a moderately well-to-do suburban community.

Wickes, F. G., *The Inner World of Childhood,* 3rd ed. New York: Appleton-Century-Crofts, Inc., 1966. A newer edition of a classic in analytic psychology. Discusses different aspects of child life, including early life, imaginary companions, fear, sex, dreams, and fantasy.

Yarrow, L. J., ed., "Symposium on Personality, Consistency and Change: Perspective from Longitudinal Research," *Vita Humana,* Vol. 7 (1964), pp. 65–146. This issue is devoted to a symposium on consistency and change in personality. Reports are given concerning three longitudinal studies (the Berkeley Growth Study, the California Guidance Study, the Fels Study of Human Development), and one non-longitudinal study (the Topeka "Coping Project").

5
MENTAL DEVELOPMENT I

In this chapter and the following one we shall treat certain basic concepts and issues related to mental development. To begin, let us review some of the terms commonly used to describe mental functioning. Wechsler (1958, p. 7) defines **intelligence** as the "global capacity of the individual to act purposefully, to think rationally, and to deal effectively with his environment." Intelligence is global in the sense that it is a characteristic of the individual's behavior as a whole.

Hebb (1959) recommends distinguishing between Intelligence A—an innate potential to develop a given capacity—and Intelligence B—an average level of performance at a specified time in one's developmental history. Obviously, at any specific time there is a gap between innate and measured potential.

In either sense, intelligence constitutes one's capacity for **learning,** or modifying one's behavior as a consequence of experience. Learning may be very simple, as in simple conditioning, or extremely complex, as in cognition. **Cognition** refers to the higher mental processes involved in understanding and dealing with one's world. It embraces such concepts as perception, language, thinking, concept formation, abstraction, and problem solving.

Considerable controversy has raged over the question of how intelligence, which is basic to all these processes, is organized. Spearman (1927) portrayed mental abilities as involving a G-factor (general intelligence) and S-factors (an unspecified number of specific abilities), which are closely related and function as a unit. In general, Cattell (1946) supported Spearman's theory. However, he argued not for one general factor, as did Spearman, but for a number of general abilities.

Later controversy centered on whether intelligence is the sum of varied and unrelated abilities (multifactor theory) or of several constellations of capacities, each bound by a common factor (cluster theory). Perhaps the most widely accepted theory today is Thurstone and Thurstone's (1941), which posits a large number of special or primary abilities having some central organizing factor underlying all of them.

All studies of children, asserts Avakian (1961), reveal an appreciable correlation between primary abilities. In the early years these abilities are closely integrated, but they gradually become differentiated into relatively independent abilities.

Basic to the issue of mental ability, of course, is the old question of heredity versus environment. Is intelligence an innate capacity, determined by heredity, or is it molded significantly by environment? This controversy is discussed in Chapter 2. You will recall that hereditarians point to evidence that intelligence correlations between pairs of individuals decrease regularly with decreases in the degree of blood relationship (Kimble and Garmezy, 1963). Environmentalists argue that identical twins reared in different environments often show significant differences in IQ (Newman, 1932; Anastasi, 1958). This controversy has now subsided somewhat, however. Most psychologists now acknowledge hereditary limits beyond which environmental influences are ineffective; but they also acknowledge the complex interaction of heredity and environment in every phase of human development.

• MEASURING INTELLIGENCE

Intelligence tests were developed around the turn of the century. In 1904, the French minister of public instruction became concerned because certain children, ostensibly of lower ability, had failed to profit from academic instruction. To identify such children, Alfred Binet, a psychologist, was invited to devise some objective measure of intelligence. He collaborated with Simon in producing and standardizing a graded series of tasks, which has since been

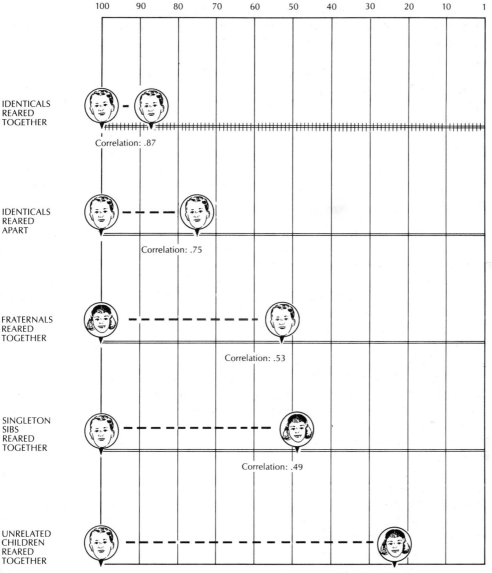

How close are twins' IQ's? This chart shows the IQ correlations (degrees of closeness) between various pairs of twins as compared with other paired children. "Unrelated children" refers to foster children of different parents reared in the same home. Figures given are averages derived from an analysis of intelligence test scores in 52 studies, covering thousands of twins and nontwin children, as reported by Drs. L. Erlenmeyer-Kimling and Lissy F. Jarvik in *Science*, 1963, **142.** From A. Scheinfeld, *Your heredity and environment*. Philadelphia: Lippincott, 1965. P. 371. Reproduced by permission.

progressively revised and refined into the Stanford-Binet test. Its scores are reported in terms of an **intelligence quotient (IQ).** The IQ is a measure of a child's rate of development up to the age at which he is tested. It is computed by dividing the **mental age (M.A.)** — as determined on a standardized test of intelligence — by the chronological age (C.A.).

The Reliability and Validity of Tests

Intelligence tests have been devised for all ages, from infancy through adulthood, and they vary greatly in both reliability and validity. A test is **reliable** if the same results are obtained time after time. It is **valid** if it measures what it is supposed to measure — in this case, intelligence. Intelligence tests have proved reasonably reliable and valid for children of school age but much less so for infants. Bayley (1955) found no relation between infants' mental performance in the first few months of life and scores earned at the end of the first year.

We say: "Boy is to trousers as girl is to what?"

The first two drawings are alike except the second one has a dot inside it. Which drawing goes with the circle in the same way as the first two drawings go together?

Find the picture that shows two boys running.

Find the circle that has the largest star inside it.

Sample items for second and third graders from the Otis-Lennon Mental Ability Test. At this age level the person giving the test reads the instructions to the group of children; at older levels the children read the instructions for themselves. Copyright 1967 by Harcourt, Brace & World, Inc. Reproduced by special permission of the publisher.

In fact, no available measures, when administered under 20 weeks of age, have proved of predictive value for later intelligence. However, if environmental conditions are relatively stable, test scores for infants aged 20 weeks to two years may prove better than guesswork in predicting later scores (Escalona and Moriarty, 1961). In any case, a clinical appraisal based on total test performance on two or more instruments is a better predictor of the child's later performance than scores obtained from a single test.

The reliability of mental tests increases steadily from ages two through six, remains stable in later childhood, and then declines. Schools tend to provide children with the common core of experiences on which mental testing depends; but adulthood provides no such common base. One is left with this

problem: How much are changes in an individual's IQ score due to differences in the types of test administered at each age and how much to actual changes in intelligence with age? Pinneau (1961) ascribes such changes both to differences in what tests measure and to actual changes in intelligence.

The validity of intelligence tests has also been questioned, despite the growing IQ mystique. First of all, tests vary somewhat in the components of intelligence measured, and in the weighting of each component in the overall IQ score. For example, the number of memory items may vary from test to test. If you believe memory constitutes about a twentieth of overall intelligence, you will include five items; if a tenth, 10 items. The test scores of the child who possesses an excellent memory but does only moderately well on reasoning will thus vary with the number of items testing each trait. Note that intelligence tests have traditionally attributed small importance to creativity, and have included only a few items to measure those traits that presumably contribute most heavily to it. Hence the correlation between current tests of creativity and those of intelligence is not very high. Torrance (1962) estimates that if gifted children were identified solely on the basis of intelligence tests, fully 70% of our most creative individuals would be missed.

Another hazard to a test's validity is culture bias. Standard intelligence tests are based on the assumption that the children who take them possess a reasonably equivalent core of knowledge. But what about the child in a remote area who lacks exposure to much information that most children take for granted? Some years ago an investigator presented a standard test item to a child from the hills of Tennessee:

Tester: If you went to the store and bought six cents worth of candy and gave the clerk ten cents, what change would you receive?

Child: I never had ten cents and if I had I wouldn't spend it for candy, and anyway candy is what your mother makes.

The examiner tried to reformulate the problem as follows:

Tester: You have taken ten cows to pasture for your father and six strayed away. How many would you have left to drive home?

Child: We don't have ten cows but if we did and I lost six, I wouldn't dare go home.

Groggy but game, the examiner made one more try.

Tester: If there were ten children in the school and six of them were out with measles how many would there be in school?

Child: None, because the rest would be afraid of catching it, too [Pressey, 1933, p. 237].

Actually, culture may affect every phase of testing. A paper-and-pencil test given Samoans was misleading because the children had never before seen pencils. Again, among a group of American Indians, there was such a strong desire for certainty that guessing was unthinkable. Also, to do anything hurriedly was deemed bad manners — a formidable handicap in taking timed tests (Klineberg, 1935).

Also threatening the validity of intelligence tests is the built-in rigidity of such tests. To increase reliability, each examiner is supposed to measure replies by well-defined standards. In one test, a picture is shown in which the smoke from a chimney is blowing one way and the trees are blowing another. The child is asked, "What's foolish about that?" One bright child insisted: "It's not foolish. Currents may eddy and conflict with each other, thus causing air currents to whirl in opposite directions." Was the examiner to use his own judgment and mark the child's reply correct? While examiners may indeed score as correct the answers obviously deserving such credit, some replies fall in a "gray area" where it is hard to make a decision.

The examiner is also prone to judge the child from the grown up's frame of reference. Why should a child's reply be judged incorrect just because, when asked to define a dress, he insists that "A dress is a dress"? A child's world is of the immediate; he has little of the adult's need for analysis, prediction, and comparison (Smillie, 1958).

Notwithstanding all these pitfalls, Honzik (1965) notes that when the measuring instruments such as intelligence tests are carefully chosen and administered, the results of longitudinal studies of mental growth in various research centers are remarkably similar. Furthermore, present trends reflect greater flexibility in basic concepts of testing. Current emphases include more attention to individual patterns and less judgment of the child's total developmental pattern in relation to group criteria. Also emphasized currently are the variations in mental-growth pace among individuals and the influence of experiences that may depress or stimulate the utilization of abilities.

• THE DEVELOPMENTAL
VIEW OF INTELLIGENCE

All relevant research indicates a gradual growth in mental capacities over the years. In a study by one British researcher, children's growing ability to reason inductively was revealed in tests involving the choice of correct answers from among alternative hypotheses.

At seven years, for instance, children could solve this problem: Tom runs faster than Jim; Jack runs slower than Jim. Who is the slowest, Jim or Jack or Tom?

At eight years, the children solved a problem such as this, which likewise called for elimination of untenable hypotheses: I don't like sea voyages, and I don't like the seaside. I must spend Easter either in France, or among the Scottish Hills, or on the South Coast. Which shall it be?

Not until near the end of the elementary-school age, however, were children able to solve a problem requiring the discovery of a general rule from a number of particular instances, such as: One pound of meat should roast for half an hour; two pounds, three-quarters of an hour; three pounds, one hour; eight pounds, two-and-a-quarter hours; nine pounds, two-and-a-half hours. From this, can you discover a simple rule by which you can tell from the weight of a joint how long it should roast? [Burt, 1919, pp. 68–77; 121–127; 358–359].

Mental-Growth Curves

Intelligence tests have revealed two **mental-growth curves,** one a composite describing the so-called typical pattern, the other individual, varying from one person to another. The composite curve is derived either from averages of the longitudinal growth curves of many individuals or from cross-sectional investigations of groups of persons representative of different age groups. There is general agreement about the overall pattern of mental growth from birth to the mid-teens. Intelligence rises rapidly at first and continues to increase (but at a declining rate) into the teens (Munn, 1966). There is also general agreement that most intellectual functions "peak" somewhere between early adolescence and age 30; they then remain on a relatively flat plateau — declining slightly in duller individuals, remaining even for average ones, and rising slightly for brighter ones — until the approach of old age, when all groups show a rapid decline. Two major questions have not been resolved: Approximately when does the peak occur? And when does the plateau change into rapid decline?

Early studies suggested that the peak occurred in the early teens. However, there is probably no single peak age or specific age for onset of rapid decline. A study of individuals over the first 25 years of life indicated that some individuals reached their peaks in adolescence, while others continued to increase throughout the period, though at a declining rate (Bayley, 1955). In another study, Bayley (1955) found that superior adults demonstrated increasing abilities through middle adulthood, especially in tasks involving verbal concepts and abstractions. In still another study, spanning the years from preschool to age 25, the mean IQ rose by 10.8 points, with almost all the increase occurring during the late adolescent years (Bradway et al., 1958).

Individual Differences

Most of the studies above relate to people generally, and to overall intellective function. The picture is somewhat different for individuals, subgroups, and different mental factors. For example, brighter individuals show mental decline later than others. More growth occurs after adolescence in abstract reasoning and in vocabulary than in rote memory and practical reasoning (Bradway and Thompson, 1962). Also in brighter individuals, number ability continues to improve until middle life, although other functions have already diminished. Vocabulary remains at a high level throughout life, while new learning and reasoning undergo a rapid decline. In fact, reasoning begins to decline even in the twenties (Fox and Birren, 1950).

•CONSTANCY OF THE IQ

A central controversy in intelligence testing concerns **IQ constancy** within the same individual. If IQ were completely constant, and if 1,000 children of the same age were tested every year, their rank order would never change. Practically speaking, no one assumes perfect constancy, given the random errors inherent both in measuring instruments and in the testing situation. Besides, there is always a gap of unknown size between innate potential and demonstrated intelligence.

The real question at issue is this: Is a child's intellectual capacity largely the result of heredity, so that the basic factors underlying mental performance develop in a somewhat regular fashion? If mental capacity is largely hereditary, and if growth patterns are similar within the species, the individual child's status in his age group should remain roughly the same. Those who oppose the constancy theory argue that environmental influences are of such overriding importance that they make the question of constancy irrelevant. Besides, IQ is demonstrably inconstant, they claim—so much so as to make the genetic underpinnings of little importance.

The Argument for Constancy

Let's take a closer look at the two positions, beginning with those who, especially in the first half of the century, believed intelligence to be relatively constant. A valid IQ score was considered to measure accurately the child's cognitive status. Mental growth was believed to proceed mainly through maturation and to resist alteration in its course, except in unusual conditions. Fluctuations in IQ scores were ascribed to poor motivation, disturbance in the child being tested, or other factors. Besides, tests measured different capacities at different ages, concentrating on motor function in infancy and verbal functions later on; hence fluctuations in test scores reflected differences in function measured rather than basic changes in the individual's capacity. Variations might also stem from testing during a specific period when the individual under consideration was experiencing a brief, atypical "jog" in a generally consistent mental-growth pattern.

Some investigators have demonstrated a strong underlying constancy, at least after infancy. There is some shifting of position, reports Bayley (1955), but the changes are gradual over rather long intervals of time.

In short, the advocates of constancy, while acknowledging the obvious fluctuations in test scores, argue that brain cells and nerve tissue cannot be created or, once destroyed, regenerated. Furthermore, they believe that maturation results in relatively even growth, although each individual's growth pattern has distinctive characteristics. Some children's growth will proceed faster, others' more slowly; some children will peak out earlier than others. For some children, the growth curve is relatively smooth; for others, more irregular; but in the long run, argue the constancy advocates, a child's standing relative to other children remains relatively stable, if it can be assumed that environment is held constant. Obviously, however, environment cannot be held constant. Hence IQ scores do change, sometimes markedly, not because of shifts in innate ability but because of differential influences that permit greater or lesser development of potential.

In short, those believing in the relative constancy of intelligence would acknowledge the possibility of making an individual's intellectual potential more functional, but they would argue that heredity inevitably sets limits. If in fact a child's IQ should rise greatly, the hereditarian simply says that, on the first test, factors operated to prevent his potential from manifesting itself; or perhaps, on the later test, ways had been found of permitting his potential—there all the time, but hidden—to reveal itself.

The Argument against Constancy

The foregoing point of view, which is advocated by the author, has been all but obliterated by the vast majority who currently emphasize environmental factors. This latter group rejects the view that intellectual potential is fixed, preferring to believe that experience, if provided at propitious and properly sequenced stages, can have an almost unlimited effect on an individual's capacity to deal with his world. Many studies appear to support this position. In one such study, which tested the same children at intervals from a few months of age to 10 years, over 60% showed measurable fluctuations in IQ. Decreasing levels of performance were attributed to a passive infantile dependency pattern and, in the female, to a passive role that offers no motivation to achieve. Progressively advancing performance was attributed to a competitive independent pattern with an "aggressive, self-assuring mastery of tasks" (Sontag et al., 1955, p. 562).

Others who question the fixedness

of intelligence point to differences in IQ by subculture. They note, for example, that Jews manifest increases in verbal scores. They argue that mental functions will improve if they are valued in a specific subculture (Levinson, 1961). On the other hand, is it possible that constant intermarriage among the Jews, coupled with selective cultural factors that have caused more verbal Jews to survive and propagate their kind, have led to superiority in those parts of the nervous system conducive to greater verbal facility?

Present Status of the Constancy Controversy

Miller (1962) sums up the current points of view. Test results, he asserts, can be interpreted to support either side of the controversy. If a child shows a sudden spurt, the hereditarians, or constancy advocates, simply argue that some maturational effect is just now manifesting itself. Environmentalists look for external influences. However, note that some children respond to stimulating environments by showing substantial increases in IQ, while others show none. In support of constancy, one might argue that influences did not "take" in some cases because maturational factors were not ripe.

Informed opinion now supports the anti-constancy position. Psychologists who should know better plot smooth curves of mental growth, suggesting that a child's mind grows like a potato. They have apparently forgotten they are dealing with a composite of many separate curves for distinct skills. The convenience of a single number, or IQ, is simply too great to resist (Miller, 1962).

• FACTORS RELATED TO CHANGES AND DIFFERENCES IN IQ

Personality Traits

Changes in demonstrated intelligence, whether basically constant or not, relate to a wide variety of factors, one being personality. In one study, those who showed largest gains in IQ were relatively more independent, competitive

and verbally aggressive. Those who gained also worked harder in school and tried to master challenging problems (Sontag et al., 1958). In another study, the ascenders were characterized by independence, mastery, and an attitude that competition was emotionally satisfying. IQ descenders were characterized by dependence, lack of parental love, and a dislike of competition.

In still another study, children were told to make up stories about pictures from the Thematic Apperception Test. In this test, commonly called the T.A.T., the subject is asked to make up a story about each of 20 pictures, telling what led up to the scene in the picture, what is happening, and how it turns out in the end. Stories told by children who had gained in IQ reflected a desire to be superior and to perfect talents and skills. For example, one picture shows a young man on a rope. A child whose IQ has risen might say something like, "He's in a rope-climbing contest and is trying hard to get to the top so he can win the race." The child whose IQ has declined might be more apt to reply, "He's escaping from prison and people are shooting at him" (Kagan et al., 1958). Summing up, Kagan writes, "Perhaps the most accurate generalization is that for middle-class children with average or above IQ levels, strong achievement, competitive and curiosity needs may facilitate IQ gains by motivating the child to master intellectual skill."

Level of Intelligence

Another characteristic relating to changes in IQ is level of intelligence. By age six, brighter children have normally made greater gains (Pinneau, 1961). By contrast, the IQ's of low-IQ children tend to decline (Wheeler, 1942). In either case, fluctuations correlate with the degree of environmental stimulation. By and large, bright children live in more intellectually stimulating environments than do dull children.

Race

Race as a factor in intelligence has long been a subject of controversy. Nowadays the issue is largely ignored, partly because of the current interracial situation. Even to study the question would suggest that the investigator doubts that all races have equal potential, in effect defying the popular assumption that all men are created equal.

Valid comparisons among races and ethnic groups, whether dealing with intelligence or any other trait, are difficult. Where does the American investigator find an average sample of Italians to test? Italian-born Americans hardly represent a random sampling of all Italians, since they reflect selective factors that determined their migration. Even if the researcher chooses a random sampling in Italy, how can he compare the results of persons taking the test in Italian with those of persons taking the test in English? Many studies indicate that language controls to some extent the way concepts are defined or handled.

Nevertheless, among very young children, no valid differences are found between races. Pasamanick (1946) studied 53 Negro infants and found that at 26 weeks their norms on the Yale Developmental Examination were little different from those of white infants. Bayley (1965) found no significant differences between Negro and Caucasian infants aged one to 15 months. Since racial differences are repeatedly found after age four, Bayley suggests that the experiences of very early childhood may be critical in determining differences in mental function among socioeconomic and cultural groups.

What is the status of the question today? McKeachie and Doyle (1966), who reflect the point of view most popular among psychologists today, declare psychological similarities among races to be so great that we must look to individuals rather than to races to discover the hereditary factors accounting for differences in behavior. However, Klineberg (1963) notes that, although there is no scientifically accepted evidence that ethnic groups differ in innate abilities, this does not necessarily mean that there are no differences in abilities. Interpretations may also be questioned, since

scarcely anyone undertakes investigation in this field without some bias (Dreger and Miller, 1960). Unfortunately, it is commonly assumed that racial differences, if established, would necessarily show a hierarchical order, thus branding members of each race as better or poorer types of humanity. Instead, racial differences might simply prove that each race, due to centuries of inbreeding, possesses certain strengths in greater measure than other races. Racial characteristics may thus come to be viewed qualitatively across a broad spectrum rather than hierarchically or in terms of narrow cultural value judgments.

Sex

In many ways, the conflict about sex differences is similar to the one about race. Undoubtedly, the sexes do differ in mental performance and abilities. A typical study reports that twice as many boys as girls show large gains in IQ. And after reviewing available research on basic intelligence patterns, Ruch concluded that boys excel in spatial intelligence and most kinds of problem solving; girls excel in memory, reasoning, word fluency, and numerical ability. Furthermore, in most studies, girls have been found to do better than boys in school (Ames and Ilg, 1964). Since each sex excels in some primary abilities, the differences cancel each other when general tests are used (Ruch, 1963).

What, if any, innate factors account for such differences is uncertain. Girls' early superiority in certain mental functions, such as language, may partially derive from their relatively faster maturation. Thus, faster growth may give girls an initial advantage; however, males eventually catch up and may even profit from the extra year or two required for physical maturation (Bieri, 1960). Learning has a relatively greater impact on the still maturing than on the fully mature organism.

A Summary of Differences

At least among very young children, aged one to 15 months, Bayley (1965) found no relation between intelligence-test scores and sex, birth order, education of either father or mother, or geographic residence. Among older children, intelligence was found to vary with a great many related factors, not only the ones just mentioned but also size of family, season of birth, health, nutrition, and prematurity of birth. In each case, it would appear that intellectual growth and performance are the complex resultants of inherent capacities, emotional and material environment, encouragement, and opportunity. In short, concludes Bayley, "I suspect each child is a law unto himself." That is, each child's mental performance represents the unique blending of his heredity and an assortment of experiences.

• CATEGORIES OF INTELLIGENCE

In recent years, psychologists have come to feel increasingly less confident of their ability to pigeonhole children in various mental categories. However, as a frame of reference we can define mental categories as follows: The *bright* child we shall classify as one who performs above average (over 120) on currently respected intelligence tests. On the Stanford-Binet scale, this category would include roughly the highest 12.6% of the population, or about one child in eight (Terman and Merrill, 1960). *Below-normal* (but not defective) children we shall define as having IQ's of 70 to 90; these children number about 21.1% or about one in five. The *mental defectives,* with IQ's below 70, constitute 2.6% of all children, accounting for one child in 46. Most children—roughly three out of five—fall either in the *average* (90–110 IQ), or *high-average* (110–120 IQ) group. Another group, who are usually but not always bright by current IQ standards, are the *creatives,* who possess unusual capacity for novel solutions. The number of creatives is unknown.

Bright Children

The most important knowledge we have gained about bright children derives from a classic and still continuing longitudinal study that originated in 1921. In that year, a quarter of a million school children were tested to locate those with the highest IQ's in the state of California. From these, the approximately 1,000 chosen for study had IQ's of 135 or above and represented the highest 1% of the school population. Their mean age at the time was 10, and they have been under observation periodically ever since (Bayley, 1968).

The findings from this study have exploded many old myths about the bright (Terman and Oden, 1959). Apparently, the bright individual is not anemic and maladjusted, as once believed. On the contrary, the subjects of this study have had better health than the average and fewer adjustment problems. As adolescents, fewer than average proved delinquent; and as adults, fewer have become alcoholics.

These individuals have also proved far superior to the average both in scholastic and vocational accomplishment. Most of them entered college and obtained degrees, many of them graduate degrees. Those who performed less well scholastically than expected from their IQ scores were apparently handicapped by lack of parental emphasis on accomplishment or by home tensions. Even these individuals gathered steam as young adults, however, and partially overcame the adverse effects of their earlier handicaps. One can only speculate how much greater their achievements would have been had they not had early disadvantages. Among the group generally, a steadily increasing number have emerged as eminent in their respective vocational fields.

In all ways, the group at mid-life are still superior and, relative to the general population, are becoming more so. All continue to score among the top 1% of the population. Among the men, 86% fall in one of the two highest occupational categories: either the professions and semi-professions or higher business. Most of the women are housewives but have made many times the creative contribution of women generally.

Creative Children

Almost 30 years ago, in their book *Child Psychology*, Stoddard and Wellman noted that creative aspects of intelligence were grossly neglected; however, this neglect persisted until mid-century, when Guilford began trying to measure creativity. Since then, much effort has been directed toward this goal; and a veritable cult of creativity has grown up since. Nevertheless, no test yet devised is generally viewed as an adequate measure of creativity. However, this area of psychometrics is still young and bears watching. Typical of tasks currently used for distinguishing creatives are the following: (1) The subject may be asked to give as many definitions as possible of fairly common stimulus words, such as "bolt," "bark," or "sack." Scores depend on the absolute number of definitions as well as the number of different categories into which the definitions might be placed. (2) The subject is asked to give as many uses as he can for objects customarily having a stereotyped function, such as "brick" or "paper clip." Scores are based on both the number and the originality of uses suggested. (3) Subjects are presented with four fables in which the last lines are missing. Scores depend on the appropriateness and uniqueness of the endings (Getzels and Jackson, 1962).

Many studies have been devoted to determining what the creative child is like. In one study, primary-grade children were asked, "Who in your class has the silliest or wildest ideas?" and "Who in your class has the most ideas for being naughty?" In this strange competition, the creative boys won the sweepstakes handily (Torrance, unpublished). In a study of fourth-grade pupils, creative children scored significantly higher than controls on strength of self-image; and on the Rorschach inkblot tests, they showed a tendency toward unconventional, unreal percepts, and a fanciful treatment of the blots (Weisberg

and Springer, 1961). Similarly, Hammer described the truly creative child as less ego-defensive and manifesting a frank and open flooding of inner feelings onto test stimuli (Hammer, 1961).

Creative children seem to find difficult problems challenging. They pursue goals enthusiastically and search for the meaning of life. Since they often seek and live with tension and possess considerable psychic freedom, they are able to accomplish relatively more than

The creative child is independent and has the ego strength to withstand societal frustrations.

others. However, they tend to view society as coercing them into conformity. Nevertheless, asserts Torrance (1961), they maintain their perspective and their sense of humor despite the alienation of peers and teachers. He suggests that counselors should help creative children solve their social problems without sacrificing creativity (Torrance et al., 1960). It is questionable, however, whether creative children do tend to alienate their peers. One study that distinguished the most creative boy and girl in each of 23 classrooms reported high social acceptance of creative children (Wallen and Stevenson, 1960). These children were also distinguished by unusual productivity of off-the-beaten-track ideas, and by humor and playfulness.

In summarizing data on the topic, Cronbach describes the "creative thinker" as:

> . . . marked by an active approach. He enjoys exploring and rearranging possibilities. He finds pleasure in variety and in anticipating "what would happen if . . . " He is, then, independent; he does not wait for someone to show him what to do. He is free to fail; when his idea proves worthless, he loses no self-respect. Much that is known about the creative process can be summarized by saying that the creator is playful. He does not take any one trial seriously. He enjoys the activity even when he is behind in score. His creations emerge from large amounts of "waste-effort" — but no one throwing himself into a game tries to conserve his energy [Cronbach, 1963, p. 390].

High-IQ versus highly creative children. Given a minimum IQ of 120, higher scores seem irrelevant in affecting creativity (Barron, 1963). Many persons with high IQ's are not especially high in creativity, and vice versa (Gough, 1961). In consequence, Getzels and Jackson became interested in comparing children superior in IQ but just normal in creativity with those high in creativity but only average in IQ. In general, the high-creatives proved more humorous and intellectually playful, less conforming socially and intellectually, and more aggressive in their fantasies. The high-IQ's were oriented toward obtaining right or customary answers, the high-creatives toward diverging from the customary. The latter seemed to enjoy the risk and uncertainty of the unknown.

The high-creatives do as well scholastically as the high-IQ's; but the creatives are less well liked by their teachers and less success-oriented than the high-IQ's, at least in terms of commonly accepted standards of success.

Parents of the high-creatives tend to be less vigilant, less "bookish" in the academic sense, less obsessional, and less critical of their children than do parents of the high-IQ's (Getzels and Jackson, 1962). It would seem that society in general, and schools in particular, are congenial to high-IQ's but less so to creatives. Fortunately, the creatives have the ego strength to withstand the societal frustrations imposed upon them.

In one study, children were shown pictures and asked to write stories about them. The first story below was written by a child with a high IQ but just average creativity, the second by an unusually creative child with only average IQ. The stimulus picture for both was a picture ordinarily perceived as a man working late (or very early) in an office:

> There's ambitious Bob, down at the office at 6:30 in the morning. Every morning it's the same. He's trying to show his boss how energetic he is. Now, thinks Bob, maybe the boss will give me a raise for all my extra work. The trouble is that Bob has been doing this for the last three years, and the boss still hasn't given him a raise. He'll come in at 9:00, not even noticing that Bob has been there so long, and poor Bob won't get his raise.

The same picture elicited the following response from a child high in creativity but not in IQ:

> This man has just broken into the office of a new cereal company. He is a private eye employed by a competitor firm to find out the formula that makes the cereal bend, sag, and sway. After a thorough search of the office he comes upon what he thinks is the current formula. He is now copying it. It turns out that it is the wrong formula and the competitor's factory blows up. Poetic justice! [Lindgren et al., 1966, pp. 263–264.]

Of course, it must be remembered that creativity and IQ are not necessarily either/or characteristics. Many creative children have impressively high IQ's.

**Mentally Retarded
Children**

Mental retardation may be the result of either social deficiency or biological deficiency. Biological deficiency, which involves pathology within the nervous system, may be caused by environmental factors, such as injury or disease, or by

You will recall that these include genetic factors, prenatal influences, and mechanical trauma sustained in the birth process.

Some studies have designated maternal deprivation as another factor in the etiology of mental retardation. However, Stott (1962) argues that in

The culturally deprived child may seem as retarded as the organically retarded one.

hereditary influences. Such a deficiency would have to be remedied, if possible, by repairing or making up whatever biochemical or structural deficiencies might exist. Social retardation, or pseudo-retardation, might simply result from environmental deficiencies that prevent either a reasonably adequate adjustment or the effective utilization of inborn capacities. Sometimes the two types are confused. The culturally deprived child may, to all outward appearances, seem as retarded as the organically retarded one.

The various causes of mental deficiency are discussed in Chapter 2.

most such cases prenatal stress is also present, making the fetus, later on the infant, especially susceptible to disease. Diseases, in turn, can be associated with backwardness in school.

Lower-level retardation is generally thought to stem from either a defective genetic combination or an environmental trauma; upper-level retardation, however, usually results from the natural combination of genes from dull parents.

The problems of extreme defectives are quite different from those of lesser defectives. Very extreme cases represent no great problem to society for three reasons: percentage-wise, there are very few of them; they almost never reproduce; and they are generally placed in institutions (Farber, 1959). Upper-level and borderline defectives pose a greater social problem than do the more extreme types. They are substantial in number; and they marry and have children. Many are led into prostitution and crime, or clutter relief roles. As children, they pose a problem both to parents and to schools.

Despite their handicaps, however, many moderately subnormal individuals ultimately adapt to their condition and perhaps to some extent outgrow it. A follow-up study of a group of mentally retarded individuals whose mean IQ, as children, was 85.7 indicated that all but 22.1% were employed, and that only 16.9% had received any relief help during an eleven-year mid-life period. Over 96% were self-supporting (Miller, 1965). In another study, 3% of the early school population was classified as mentally retarded, whereas less than 1% of adults over 20 were so classified (Hartung, 1966). However, since the death rate for subnormal individuals is higher, the significance of this differential is correspondingly reduced.

Since few people understand these problems, government-sponsored programs, both national and local, should provide the assistance required. However costly such help may be, it is less costly than permitting these individuals to become lifelong charges of society. To cope with biological causes, heavy outlays are required for research, which in time may eliminate many types of mental deficiency. Where the retardation stems from social causes and is classified as pseudo-deficiency, remediation should involve environmental enrichment, special educational procedures, and perhaps psychotherapy. Until the 1950s psychotherapy was deemed of little use for mental retardates; however, since then such treatment has been reported as beneficial, at least for selected cases (Kisker, 1964).

• ISSUES RELATING TO MENTAL DEVELOPMENT

Mental Status at Birth

The study of mental development has involved many complex issues, one being the infant's mental status. William James (1890) described the newborn's world as "one great, blooming, buzzing confusion." Is this view valid? Are the infant's perceptions completely amorphous? Is the infant himself simply a compound of cells, a mass of pulsing flesh, helplessly reacting to whatever stimuli impinge upon him? What, in fact, is the newborn's mental repertoire?

During recent years, opinion on this point has reversed dramatically. Pavlov and Watson viewed the infant as a receptive organism; more recently, Piaget has portrayed children, including infants, as interacting with their environment. Their reactions seem differentiated, rather than diffuse, and selectively adaptive to various forms of stimulation (Richmond and Lipton, 1959).

Cognition at birth. In short, cognitive development may not begin "from scratch" at birth. Prenatal life undoubtedly involves conditions and "experiences" that indirectly modify postnatal cognitive development. At birth, the lower, noncortical brain centers are well developed, though higher (cortical) ones do not function well for several months. After the noncortical state comes a transitional stage, followed by the cortical stage, in which the cortex is dominant. Thus the infant passes from simple awareness to awareness plus meaning—in other words, to perception. Experience is the catalyst by which the infant ultimately attaches significance to the stimuli that impinge on him.

The newborn's sensory status. The neonate's sensory-response system, especially, is quite sophisticated. Even at birth, all his senses are fully operating. True, he fails to respond to soft sounds or pure tones; nor can he differentiate certain differences in pitch. However, these impairments are only the result of the outer ear's being plugged with amniotic fluid at birth. Actually, the child can respond to higher pitches than can an adult; and he can probably respond to sensitivities in pitch better at birth than ever after (von Bekesy, 1957).

Authorities differ concerning infants' sensitivity to taste. Most experiments report that infants react first to sweetness, only later distinguishing salt, sour, and bitter tastes. By two or three months, babies notice and react to changes in formulas. If the adult makes his own distaste for foods evident, the infant will refuse them. Otherwise, he will accept a wide variety of strong-tasting foods, including cod-liver oil and turnips.

Until a decade ago, opinion about the infant's visual experience was largely speculative. However, Fantz, among others, has provided significant data and conclusions. The following excerpts constitute a concise summary of his chief findings and views on this topic:

Long before an infant can explore his surroundings with hands and feet he is busy exploring it with his eyes. What goes on in the infant's mind as he stares, blinks, looks this way and that? Does he sense only a chaotic patchwork of color and brightness, or does he perceive and differentiate among distinctive forms? The question has always fascinated philosophers and scientists, for it bears on the nature and origin of knowledge. At issue is the perennial question of nature versus nurture. On the one side is the nativist who believes that the infant has a wide range of innate visual capacities and predilections, which have evolved in animals over millions of years, and that these give a primitive order and meaning to the world from the "first look." On the other side is the extreme empiricist who holds that the infant learns to see and to use what he sees only by trial and error or association, starting, as John Locke put it, with a mind like a blank slate. It has long been known that very young infants can see light,

color, and movement. But it is often argued that they cannot respond to such stimuli as pattern, size, or solidity; in short, that they cannot perceive form. This position is the last stronghold of the empiricist, and it has been a hard one to attack. How is one to know what an infant sees? . . .

When we set out to determine the visual abilities of helpless infants, the only indicator we could find was the activity of the eyes themselves. If an infant consistently turns its gaze toward some forms more often than toward others, it must be able to perceive forms. . . . [However] the work described so far does not answer the second question posed earlier in this article: whether or not the infant's innate capacity for form perception introduces a measure of order and meaning into what would otherwise be a chaotic mass of sensations. . . .

[At any rate, in the infant's world] people have an importance. . . . Facial pattern is the most distinctive aspect of a person, the most reliable for distinguishing a human being from other objects and for identifying him. So a face-like pattern might be expected to bring out selective perception in an infant if anything could. We tested infants with three flat objects the size and shape of a head. On one we painted a stylized face in black on a pink background, on the second we rearranged the features in a scrambled pattern, and on the third we painted a solid patch of black at one end with an area equal to that covered by all the features. We made the features large enough to be perceived by the youngest baby, so that acuity of vision was not a factor. The three objects, paired in all possible combinations, were shown to 49 infants from four days to six months old. The results were about the same for all age levels; the infants looked mostly at the "real" face, somewhat less often at the scrambled face, and largely ignored the control pattern. The degree of preference for the "real" face to the other one was not large, but it was consistent among individual infants, especially the younger ones. The experiment suggested that there is an unlearned primitive meaning in the form perception of infants. . . . Innate knowledge of the environment is demonstrated by . . . the interest of young infants in kinds of form that will later aid in object recognition, social responsiveness, and spatial orientation. This primitive knowledge provides a foundation for the vast accumulation of knowledge through experience [Fantz, 1965, p. 71].

Characteristic differences in perceptual response. Not only do all normal neonates respond selectively to their environment; they also manifest highly individual modes of response. Even within the first five days, some children respond vigorously to stimuli, some moderately, some only mildly. In general, those who respond to some stimuli vigorously do so to all; and between the second and fifth days, the typical mode of response is well-established (Birns, 1965). In describing specific infants, Brown (1964) portrayed infant Felicia as very interactive with her environment, in contrast to Dorothy, who was hardly reactive at all. Felicia, who was relatively placid, also differed from Charles, who was active and tense.

Unresolved questions. By now the reader is probably inclined to agree with André-Thomas (1960), who declared that "the neonate is not a neophyte." However, Kessen (1965) counters with the question, "If the human newborn is so capable, why is he so stupid?" There is early adaptation, but is there early learning? Indeed, he possesses simple reflexes, such as respiratory movements of the thorax, swallowing, peristaltic movement, and sucking, some of them present even before birth (Hooker, 1943). Moreover, he can pick up an approaching stimulus and reduce the distance to it quickly, as in finding the approaching breast or bottle. However, by contrast with other organisms, the human infant has a limited repertoire of responses for dealing with his world. How, therefore, can we reconcile the view that the infant's behaviors are largely reflexive with the evidence that the infant's innate equipment is pretty sophisticated? How do we reconcile the fact that babies adapt their sucking styles to feeding routines with the difficulty that investigators have had in

demonstrating learning in newborns? Two observations have a bearing here: First, the newborn's neurological immaturity may prevent such early learning; and second, definitive explanations of infant learning are lacking (Kessen, 1965).

Conceptual Stages—Piaget's Theories

However sophisticated or unsophisticated the neonate's original mental equipment may be, it rapidly proceeds to develop and to become involved in acquiring concepts. In general, **concepts** are built by a "process of seeing relationships, categorizing, discriminating, and generalizing about those things which the child sees, hears, and feels in his environment" (Wann and Liddle, 1962, p. 10). By what pattern the process occurs is still unknown. The most widely discussed theory was propounded by Piaget and his collaborators, who, working with Swiss children, reported four main stages of development.

Stage 1: sensorimotor activity. The first stage is said to last about two years, and is subdivided into six phases (Flavell, 1963). During the first month, the child shows little besides reflexive behavior; then, from one to four months, reflexive activities become modified by experience and coordinated with each other. For instance, eye movements and hand movements become increasingly coordinated. From four to eight months, the infant begins to anticipate sequences of action toward objects and to notice events outside his own body. Moreover, he can intentionally repeat responses that produce interesting results. For instance, a baby will kick his legs to swing a toy that is suspended over his head. In effect, he is beginning to exhibit goal-directed activity. In the next phase, 8 to 11 months, he begins to differentiate means from ends. If a toy is hidden, he will search for it and remove the obstacle. The fifth phase, 11 to 18 months, involves active experimentation, variation, and modification of be-

Between 11 and 18 months the child becomes interested in novelty and manifests curiosity.

havior. The child is interested in novelty and manifests curiosity. He will drop objects simply to watch them fall. The period from 18 months to two years is characterized by emergence of the capacity to respond to or to think about objects not immediately observable. Some degree of problem solving is possible, too. A child may use a stick as a tool for drawing an object toward him, even though he has never seen one used for that purpose before.

Stage 2: preoperational thought. This stage is divided into two periods: *preconceptual* (ages two to four) and *intuitive* (ages four to seven). During the preconceptual stage the child is egocentric, using himself as the standard of judgment and failing to understand the viewpoints of other people. He also categorizes on the basis of single characteristics of objects; for instance, he cannot take into account the height and width of an object simultaneously. Moreover, he regards a stimulus as representative of other objects. A tree stump may be perceived as a castle, a twig as a machine gun.

During both the preconceptual and intuitive stages, the world is magical and perceived in animistic terms. That is, the child endows inanimate objects with life properties, which by age 11 he will attribute only to animals or plants, or even to animals alone. Commonly,

such "animistic" concepts have been adjudged the product of the child's immaturity and prelogical thinking. However, Klingensmith (1953) found that children from kindergarten through grade 7 who attributed life to inanimate objects meant something quite different from what adults mean by "animate." Contrary to common belief, children rarely conceive of objects as knowing or wanting things, or as feeling pain.

From approximately ages four to seven, the period of intuitive thought, the child conceptualizes more, constructs more complex thoughts and images, and groups objects into classes. Sometime during this period, perhaps between ages four and five, a developmental shift occurs from associational to cognitive verbal function (Kendler and Kendler, 1962). Henceforth, instead of identifying appearance with true reality, the child acquires the notion of conservation. This theory, that physical qualities are invariant (conservation theory), becomes more fundamental to him than the way the world looks. Something far away looks small, but he has formed a theory, based on cumulative experience, about size as related to distance. In brief, he has reorganized his world and cannot even recall his old concepts, perhaps because lower-level ones are simply absorbed by higher-level ones. This cognitive evolution may help account for childhood amnesia.

Stage 3: concrete operations. Even at age seven, the child's theories are still limited in their range of application. He cannot state, in so many words, any particular theory he has adapted but must rediscover it in new contexts. For instance, a child may be given two balls of modeling clay, one of which is then mashed flat. "Which contains more clay?" he is now asked. A young child, impressed by sheer density as he holds the ball in his hand, may say the ball holds more, or, if he is impressed by visual extent, he may say the pancake holds more. An older child, however, will say they are equal. But when asked which weighs more, even the older child may not know, and may be surprised to find they weigh the same. Even after he has mastered this concept, he may still expect the pancake to displace more water than the ball. Conservation of volume is not understood until the eleventh or twelfth year, after concepts of size and weight have become familiar (Miller, 1962).

During the years seven to 11, the *concrete-operations* period, reasoning processes begin to be based on logic. Classification at this stage consists not merely in labeling a set of stimuli but in imaginatively compiling objects within a class. When asked to sort objects, the child perceives similarities on the basis of perceptual factors such as structural similarities. He may group all items that have legs or black specks. Later still, he shifts to conceptual or categorical labels, including animals, tools, and the like (Sigel, 1963). The children described below exemplify the concrete-operations period.

> A group of seven- and eight-year-olds were asked to classify human figures such as fireman, cowboy, and nurse on the basis of similarity. They tended to use labels descriptive of part of the stimuli. For instance, a child might pair the fireman and the soldier because both had uniforms, or the boy and girl because both wore shoes. Also, they sorted familiar objects by functional or class labels. Hammer and saw, for instance, might be paired with cow, sheep, or chicken, because they can be used to build structures in which these animals might live [Sigel, 1961].

In sum, during the second and third stages, ages four to 11, the child uses logic and reasoning in an elementary way and applies them to the manipulation of concrete objects but not to verbal propositions. He may order sticks by height but have trouble with a problem such as "Edith is taller than Susan; Edith is shorter than Lily; who is the tallest of the three?" (Mussen, 1963).

Stage 4: formal operations. This final period, during which truly logical

thinking emerges, occurs between ages 11 and 15. The child now takes the final step toward abstract thinking and conceptualization. He can now consider general laws and can think about what is hypothetically possible as well as what is real. He can speculate, and his specu-

Curiosity is crucial to cognitive development at all stages.

lation is governed by logical rules. By age 15, he can use logical operations in an adult manner to solve problems.

Earlier, the child organized knowledge in terms of concrete operations with actual objects. Often he knew the rules but not how to communicate them. A boy might have been an expert at catching a ball but unable to explain anything about its trajectory. The girl could ride her bicycle yet be unable to explain the concept "center of gravity." We might say that they knew more than they understood. Now, in the logical stage, the implicit becomes explicit; what is known is understood. Never will everything that is understood become explicit; but the adolescent begins to move in this direction and to codify his knowledge.

The ability to make tacit knowledge explicit holds several advantages. The expression of facts in terms of symbols permits relating different propositions, or generalizing knowledge. Different situations, summarized symbolically, can be perceived as variations on a single theme. A formal core, or single scheme, expressed and manipulated symbolically can be transferred to other situations fitting the same schema.

Symbols also permit the communication of knowledge (Miller, 1962).

Conceptual stages as revealed in projective tests. As the same child is tested over the years, changes in cognitive-expressive dimensions are reported. Children under age 10 are likely to adopt a more concrete, descriptive approach to stimuli, while older ones tell more elaborate stories, involving motives and feelings (Gurin, 1953). The following three stories, in reaction to T.A.T. card No. 3 BM, are from the same "normal" boy at three different ages. They illustrate typical stylistic changes:

Protocol 1: Age 8 years 9 months: Well the boy — is that a boy? I'll have it be a boy and he's got his head laying on a step and he had black hair. And he's — the boy is crying because he's at home by himself and his mother and dad have went away and he came home from school and there wasn't anybody home. And that looks like a sword laying beside him and the house is white and his shoes are all colors and his belt is the same color as his shoes.

Protocol 2: Age 9 years 10 months: What's that right here? Looks like a gun. Well this little boy — his mother and dad, well, they went away and he's here all by himself and they told him to lock the door and he didn't. He thought he'd be O.K. Somebody came along and they had been mean to this little boy. They went in the house and this little boy was all frightened and scared. They had a gun and he didn't know it. These men were robbers. And they had seen his mother and father come out of the house and leave him there. And so these men — this boy was frightened — these men shot the little boy and he was laying up against the bench when his mother and father come home.

Protocol 3: Age 17 years 6 months: This young man has just tried to commit suicide. He shot himself and he isn't dead. And they find him later on and they save his life. And they turn him against trying it again. He turns out to be a great success. He suicided because he and his parents didn't get along and he had no place to go [Blum, 1960, p. 108].

The "benign" critics. The foregoing age-stage theory, as pronounced by Piaget and modified somewhat by others, has aroused considerable controversy. The question was a long time coming to a head, and Piaget's contributions were slow to attain widespread recognition. They extended over more than three decades, 1930 to 1960 and beyond, but have made their impact in America only in the last portion of this period. The delay was undoubtedly due to problems inherent in adequately translating research from another language, and to Piaget's originally casual approach to experimental design — since greatly improved. Even now Piaget is interpreted in somewhat different ways. More favorable critics place a less rigid interpretation on his work. Baldwin (1955), a "benign" critic, perceives certain main Piagetan themes: (1) Changes in children's thinking and behavior are continuous and progressive. (2) Successive structures make their appearance in a fixed order, but the rate of change is a function of the environment. (3) Thought processes are conceived as originating through a process of internalizing reactions, and intelligence is modified accordingly.

Another "benign" critic, Miller (1962), denies the common contention that Piaget believed all children go through unvarying age-stages. Rather, Piaget said that in the normal Swiss environment they appear to follow certain stages. In a different environment, or with special coaching, the results might be different (Bruner, 1960).

Other critics who support the age-stage view construe Piaget's writings as lending support to their position, although they may explain the bases for their position differently. Some persons believe the sequential order of age-stages to be the invariant result of heredity (Gesell and Armatruda, 1941). Others claim that a fixed sequence in behaviors is the natural outcome of interaction between organism and environment (Hunt, 1961). Even those assuming a fixed order accept the position that the appearance of age-stages will vary with hereditary potential and experience (Tanner and Inhelder, 1960).

Opponents of the conceptual-stage theory. At the other extreme, many individuals completely reject the age-stage concept as either invalid, misleading, or lacking in value. Ezer (1962) reports that clear-cut stages simply do not exist. For example, sequences may vary, and the rate and quality of change depend on particular kinds of experience (Ausubel, 1957). Furthermore, while Piaget acknowledged the possibility of modifying the pace of acquiring concepts by providing appropriate experiences, he failed to suggest how radical such changes might be. Within only three one-hour sessions, investigators moved children of ages five and six through sequential concepts of specific gravity that theoretically should have required two or three years (Ojemann and Pritchett, 1963).

Moreover, Piaget's "straight-line" concept of stages failed to take account of early learning stages that might in effect be related to later learning even though on the surface the two might appear different. That is, early concepts may be transitional, serving as bridges for later concepts. In one experiment, first-graders failed to achieve an operational capacity to measure area, even with instruction, but they nevertheless gained insights that would expedite proceeding to the more advanced operational level. Early and later stages thus appear to be inevitably related to each other (Beilen and Franklin, 1962).

Another problem is that stages overlap, causing wide variation within a given age range. For instance, Piaget's discussion of five-year-olds rarely takes into account that there are very bright and also very dull five-year-olds, so that the same generalizations will not apply to all these children. Besides, although types of thinking may be more characteristic of one stage than another, they may nevertheless occur at other stages. For example, children show the ability to reason long before the age of seven—

the age assigned by Piaget as the beginning of such advanced conceptualization. Moreover, many adults still show evidence of preconceptual thinking and egocentric speech. The line between child and adult mental processes is less distinct than Piaget implied (Calvin, 1961). Finally, there is apparent continuity in mental development, rather than observable gaps or turning points (Laurendeau and Pinard, 1962). In other words, growth appears to proceed gradually rather than in the leaps-and-bounds fashion suggested by Piaget and his followers.

Our debt to Piaget. However Piaget may be interpreted, he cannot be denied a highly significant place in cognition research. Some of his terms and classifications have proved descriptively useful. His efforts have fired the imagination and stimulated quantities of research. Moreover, he has suggested many fruitful hypotheses for investigation, and his research has demonstrated the value of highly flexible, global-type procedures for unearthing such hypotheses (Thompson, 1962).

Readiness

Another confusing issue related to cognitive development is **readiness.** This concept may be interpreted in two quite different ways. Most often readiness has been construed to mean the state of maturation that permits a learning experience to "take hold." However, a contrasting interpretation of readiness holds that an experiential background must exist sufficient to permit the successful acquisition of a designated concept.

Let us examine these two positions. On the one hand, consider the argument that a level of maturational readiness must be attained before learning can take place. Those who hold this view cite research showing that children cannot learn concepts before they are "ready." They demonstrate further that concepts ripen in unvarying sequences;

for example, readiness for learning quantity, weight, and volume presumably proceed in that order. In consequence, proponents of this position suggest that curricular materials should be arranged accordingly.

Others question this sort of research. They claim that the failure to learn may derive not from any immaturity but from insufficiently long training periods or from inappropriate training techniques. The method employed simply might not have provided the proper sequences, including the laying of groundwork. Besides, the best sequence involves no single, precise ordering of learning experience; it varies somewhat according to the method employed.

As a case in point, a group of experimenters sought to determine whether five-year-olds could be taught specific gravity (Ojemann and Pritchett, 1963). First, a group of children were asked: "Do you think it would be worthwhile trying to find out why things float? Why should anybody spend time worrying about why things float?" Among other reasons given were these: "We want to know how things work." "It would help us to know what will happen when things are put into water." "It might help us to find a way to learn about things."

The investigators then showed the children a plastic ball and placed it in the water, where it floated. "Why did it float?" they were asked. Replies were "Because it's light" and "Because it's made of plastic." One child responded: "Because it's big." Then the children were shown articles of different weights, made of different materials, and varying in density and size. These articles, placed in the water two at a time, included a rectangular piece of iron and a metal jar lid; a plastic lid and a dime; a wooden block and an iron piece. Soon the children discovered for themselves that their previous explanations, when applied to each of these groups, brought inconsistent results. They learned that you could not base conclusions solely on qualities of heaviness, or plasticity, or softness, or size.

Next the experimenters showed the children that something placed in water pushes the water away. As the children watched the water level rise, the experimenters asked: "How much water do you think rises?" The children had no idea, so the investigators filled a beaker to the spout with water, put a tube of shampoo in it, and caught the overflow in a plastic container. They demonstrated with other objects as well. Each time the youngsters measured and weighed the amount of water and the object. The experimenters then tested the children on questions and materials used by Piaget: "Will it sink?" "Will it float?" "Why will it sink?" "Why will it float?" It was quite obvious, from their replies, that the children had acquired concepts of displacement. They behaved at age levels far above those that might have been predicted from Piaget's norms. In fact, some of the children had progressed through three stages of concept development, and were functioning at the "logic stage" reported by Piaget as attainable only by ages 11 and 12.

A perspective on readiness. In substance, the writer agrees with Ojemann and Pritchett, although with certain qualifications. First, "mastery" of a concept is not attained at a single point; rather, it is continuous. Since mastery suggests the ability to apply general insights to new situations, the concept itself grows and broadens as the child develops more and more applications. Second, however imaginative the methods employed, the learning of any concept depends on the maturation of relevant neural and physiological structures. One cannot teach fractions to even the most precocious neonate. Concept learning also requires certain prior experience, whether directly relevant or of such a nature as to establish the necessary foundations for the new learning. For example, in Ojemann's experiment, described above, the children who had had experience handling many kinds of materials in various contexts already had some notion about related concepts. That is, they had "base" experiences on which further learning could build. For children who had had little such experience prior to the work by the experimenters, the proper sequential arrangement of experiences within the teaching experiment itself made up for gaps in the children's prior experience. In either case, certain experiences are required before the child can master particular concepts.

What would seem to be necessary is the determination of three things: (1) what sort of relevant experiential base each child brings to the teaching situation; (2) whether he has matured sufficiently—that is, brings to the situation the basic biological equipment required; and (3) whether the results make the effort required to teach the concept at this stage worthwhile. Obviously, not every concept can be taught at once. The problem in arranging the curricular sequence is to determine the periods of greatest pay-off. Actually, some sort of circular organization might be best, in which the same concepts are taught on varying levels of complexity, at successive stages, as the child both matures and acquires greater experience. Even then the child will select and reject current offerings according to fluctuations in motivation; learning experience cannot be dished out with the dispatch of a short-order cook.

To sum up, it seems impossible to determine the specific stage either in maturation or in experience that is optimal for learning a given concept. The reason is simply this: one may teach a concept on various levels of complexity, and by many techniques. While maturational factors dictate a very rough general order by which concept learning may proceed, the pace and level of acquiring concepts, within that framework, depends on how experience is organized.

Early Sensory Experience

The basic need for sensory stimulation. Related to readiness is the question of early sensory experience, since some writers have suggested that there is a critical period during which sensory stimulation should be introduced. A good illustration to open this topic is a cartoon that appeared in *The Saturday Evening Post.* It shows a boy, apparently just returned from school, standing before his father, who has been interrupted from his paper. The boy, fixing his father with an accusing glare, is saying, "Somebody goofed. I'm improperly motivated!" The basic assumptions involved here are that behavior must be motivated and that adults must somehow organize a child's environment to provide the required motivation (Hunt, 1965). On the other hand, if motivation is inherent within the organism, it may be sufficient simply to "set the stage" by providing the necessary tools for accomplishment.

Indeed, certain evidence suggests that organisms are self-motivating. For example, two well-fed, well-watered monkeys worked repeatedly at a difficult puzzle for 10 consecutive hours without losing their apparent enthusiasm (Harlow, 1950). Again, rhesus monkeys have been shown to learn quite complex discriminations when rewarded only by a peek through a glass window (Butler, 1953).

Humans, no less than monkeys, appear to abhor sheer boredom. Note how infants ceaselessly explore the circumscribed world of their crib or playpen. As one boy recalls:

I was an early explorer. My very earliest memory is of the "thrill" I received from rocking my crib around the room and just peering around at anything and everything. One day I found the open box of the light switch in our new house. A sudden jolt of 110 volts ended my early exploring career.

In a now classic study at McGill

University, students were paid $20 a day for each 24 hour day of doing nothing. They lay on comfortable beds and could plan, daydream, or sleep to their heart's content. However, their eyes, ears, and hands were shielded to minimize stimulus variation. They could hear nothing and could see only their own bare cubicles. Few subjects could endure more than two or three days of such emptiness. They developed an overwhelming desire for variation (Bexton et al., 1954).

Apparently, humans have some sort of drive, whether innate or acquired, to be doing something. Piaget remarked repeatedly on children's enthusiasm for, and repeated performance of, such skills as standing, sitting up, or manipulating a toy. Moreover, an individual needs not only to be doing *something* but to be doing something that poses a challenge. Gordon cogently describes this need as follows:

> The youngster who has mastered the elements of bike riding tries to do it with "no hands"; the prospective Little League star chides the novice with the cry that "two hands are for beginners"; and the adolescent with the newly acquired driving license is not content merely to drive, but engages in "drag races" and games of "chicken." The adult, in turn, climbs Mount Everest "because it is there."*

Hebb expresses much the same view in this way:

> When you stop to think of it, it is nothing short of extraordinary the trouble people will go to in order to get into more trouble at the bridge table or

*Ira Gordon, "New Conceptions of Children's Learning and Development" (Washington, D.C.: Association for Supervision and Curriculum Development, 1966), *Learning and Mental Health in the School*, 1966 Yearbook. Walter B. Waetjen and Robert R. Leeper, editors. Washington, D.C.: Association for Supervision and Curriculum Development, 1966, p. 67. Reprinted with permission of the Association for Supervision and Curriculum Development.

on the golf course; and the fascination for the murder story or thriller and for newspaper accounts of real-life adventure or tragedy is no less extraordinary. This taste for excitement must not be forgotten when we are dealing with human motivation. . . . Risk and puzzle can be attractive in themselves, especially for higher animals such as man. If we can accept this, it will no longer be necessary to work out tortuous and improbable ways to explain why human beings work for money; why children should learn without pain; why a human being in isolation should dislike doing nothing [Hebb, 1955, pp. 250–251].

However, people obviously vary greatly in their degree of manifest activity, perhaps partly for genetic reasons. The level of arousal, or degree of activation, probably depends on functions of the brain stem, which in turn relates to general blood chemistry, which is affected by fatigue, poisons, hormones, and drugs (Magoun, 1958). Life experience, too, such as the activating effect of goals or the deactivating results of frequent failure, modify activity.

Importance of early stimulation. One of the best-supported findings of recent years is the discovery that supplemental sensory experience, specially designed, effectively enhances cognitive development in animals and probably in humans. For animals the evidence is clear-cut. Supplemental experience actually alters the nature of the brain and nervous system. The brains of rats that were reared in cages filled with "toys" and given extensive opportunities to run mazes, when compared with the brains of rats raised in ordinary laboratory situations, had thicker, heavier cortical areas. By contrast, noncortical areas of the brains of the "culturally favored" rats were actually smaller than similar areas in "deprived" rats. Furthermore, the brains of the environmentally stimulated rats were richer in the chemicals that activate and deactivate the synapses.

Possibly, enriched experience increases the number of synapses while concomitantly stimulating the production of chemicals that facilitate function of the synapses. Overall, the study would seem to imply that brain development is susceptible to environmental influences, thus supporting physiological theories of learning and perception (Bennett, 1964).

Not surprisingly, the same sort of sensory experience that produces biological changes reveals accelerated learning and concept formation. For instance, rats that were permitted to roam as they please outdistanced their "culturally deprived" cousins, the rats reared in bare cages, in maze learning and complex behavior (Barnett, 1963). In another experiment, a group of rats was raised in culturally enriched cages with two black triangles and two black circles on the walls. A control group was raised in similar cages, identical except for plain white walls. After 90 days, the enriched-environment group learned to discriminate between triangles and circles significantly faster than did the controls (Walk and Gibson, 1961).

In another example, one of a pair of kittens was yoked to a gondola that moved the other, restrained in a suspended cage, around a track. Both obtained similar visual stimulation, but the yoked kitten's visual experience was fused with active, self-initiated movement. The kitten that simply went along for the ride suffered greater deficits in subsequent tests for paw placement and visual cliff reaction (Held and Hein, 1963).

It would seem that both animals and humans need not only stimulation but complex stimulation. For still more evidence, consider the research on attention span, long considered purely a function of maturation. In 1932, Van Alstyne obtained mean attention spans of seven minutes for two-year-olds, which would suggest that attention span is largely, or wholly, a function of maturation (Van Alstyne, 1932). How-

ever, in a later study of attention span, children played much longer with carefully designed, relatively intricate toys than with a simple toy, a red plastic automobile. Attention span proved to be more a function of the sort of toy used than of age. Even very young children have long attention spans if the tasks involved are sufficiently challenging and interesting (Moyer and von Gilmer, 1955). In one study, children overwhelmingly chose more complex tasks over simpler ones (May, 1963).

However, after a point, risk and challenge have negative value. Moderate risk activates; abnormal risk deactivates. A puzzle that suggests the possibility of solution is challenging; one impossible of solution would simply be ignored.

The implications of the foregoing research are highly significant although, in some respects, still unclear. The most consistent conclusion is that supplemental sensory experience enhances a possibly innate need for activity.

Time and quantity of stimulation. If additional sensory experiences are to be provided, when should such enrichment begin? The infant lying in his crib, moving his arms and eyes, making random noises, urinating, defecating, and being held, fed, and bathed is having a variety of sensory experiences. But are these experiences enough? In Chapter 10, "The Infant in the Family," we shall see that infants raised in certain unstimulating foundling homes seem less reactive than infants raised in normal homes. Wouldn't it be possible, even in private homes, to organize the infant's sensory experiences in such a manner that sounder foundations could be laid for later cognitive development? Apparently so; at least recent studies of infants suggest this conclusion. So simple a matter as the way infants are handled may account for differences in very young infants' demonstration of visual attention (White et al., 1964). Again, Castler (1965) found that infants aged four to five weeks who were provided with two 10 minute sessions of tactile stimulation each day did better on language and social items than did a control group who received no similar stimulation. Such findings, in the aggregate, may constitute the basis for a more intelligent and conscious control of children's early cognitive development.

If it should be determined that sensory experience may accelerate cognitive development, how much of this experience should be provided? Should the infant constantly be bombarded with whatever compound of stimuli research has concluded is desirable? Agreement is consistent that up to a certain point various stimuli, including sensory experiences and motivating properties such as complexity, risk, and puzzlement, may have an integrating effect on motivation, and that selected stimuli, especially sensory experience, may provide a wholesome foundation for learning. However, at some point not yet determined, the same stimuli, if continued, begin to induce negative reinforcement (Hebb, 1955). The child's individual characteristics should be taken into consideration, as well as the intangible adult attitudes that inevitably limit the effect of whatever environmental setting is arranged.

A final question: Does deprivation result in irrevocable mental deficits? Apparently, subsequent "enrichment" may result in the rapid improvement of environmentally retarded infants (Sayegh and Dennis, 1965). However, we have no evidence whether these children might have been more advanced had enrichment been provided earlier. Nor do we know how late such enrichment can be added and still overcome earlier deficiencies.

Significance of other experience. The question of early sensory experience should not obscure the significance of all types of experience and the ways in which experiences are perceived and organized in the child's daily life.

The illustrations below indicate how new concepts relate to earlier experience; they suggest the importance of arranging a wealth of early experience. The first is from the author's files.

> A young teacher was in her kitchen preparing a "cloud in a bottle" for use as a demonstration in her kindergarten class next day. Her own four-year-old son watched with great interest while she tried to make the cloud by placing a flame in the bottle. Next morning the child looked out the window and a veritable blizzard was blowing. "Look, Mother," he exclaimed, "I think your cloud got out of hand!"

> A little girl, having heard the background in her Mother Goose book designated as "sky," called a tablecloth "sky" in the background of a photograph of a table setting [Kidd and Rivoire, 1966, p. 310].

Support for the assertion that rich experiential background facilitates mental development comes from a study in Virginia, where five communities differed greatly in their accessibility to the outside world (Sherman and Henry, 1933). In the most remote one, Colvin Hollow, people lived a very primitive life. They could neither read nor write. In Needles Hollow, connected with the outer world only by a mountain trail, a few men were literate, and occasional meetings were held in a combined church and school. A third community, Oakton Hollow, had a post office, a general store, and some contact with the outside world. In the fourth community, Rigby Hollow, people had larger houses, more money, and received mail daily. School was in session seven months a year, and 75% of the people were literate. In Briarsville, a typical small community, all the familiar trappings of civilization were present. Although the racial stock in the five communities was very similar, children's intelligence-test scores related directly to their contact with civilization. In a test about losing a ball in a field, the mountain children, who had never seen a ball, failed miserably. Also, since they lived in a wooded region with plentiful stumps, they had little concept of a field.

This study simply underscores the need to provide programs of cultural enrichment for the disadvantaged. Meantime, let us not forget the disadvantaged children of well-off parents who for various reasons may fail to provide the sort of early intellectual stimulation needed.

• SUMMARY

Certain terms are central to the study of children's mental development. **Learning** is the modification of behavior as a consequence of experience. **Cognition** refers to the higher mental processes and functions involved in understanding one's world. **Intelligence** is the capacity to act purposefully, think rationally, and deal effectively with one's environment. Just what constitutes intelligence is unclear. However, current research indicates that there is a considerable correlation among primary abilities. Whether these abilities are determined mainly by heredity or by environment is also unclear. Psychologists commonly acknowledge that heredity sets limits, but they emphasize that environmental experience is highly significant in determining the individual's functional level of intelligence.

Formal efforts to gauge mental performance originated near the turn of the century. Intelligence tests, from which scores called **intelligence quotients (IQ's)** are derived, now exist for all ages from infancy through adulthood. The IQ scores indicate how each individual's demonstrated mental ability compares with that of others at the same developmental stage. Of course, there is always a gap of unknown width between the individual's actual ability and his demonstrated ability. Intelligence tests are considered **valid** to the extent that they measure what they are supposed to measure; they are **reliable** to the degree

that the same results are obtained time after time. There is still some question about the validity of intelligence tests. The reliability of such tests has been shown to increase through early childhood, remaining stable in later childhood and then gradually declining, especially in later years.

Certain important controversies have arisen concerning intelligence, one being the nature of the **mental-growth curve**—the composite pattern of mental development. Psychologists generally agree that intelligence grows rapidly from birth to the mid-teens, but they are uncertain about when and how much it tapers off after that. The picture varies somewhat for different individuals and subgroups and for different mental factors. Test norms that fail to account for such variations often distort the true picture.

Also controversial has been the matter of **IQ constancy** within the same individual. If IQ were constant, the child's own rank within a group of children would remain the same year after year. The vast majority today take the anti-constancy position, pointing to widely differing scores obtained at successive ages from the same individual.

Changes in demonstrated intelligence relate to personality, especially the traits of independence and mastery. IQ **ascenders**—those whose IQ's rise with the years — are more often male, independent, and high achievers than are those whose IQ's fail to rise. Bright children typically make more IQ gains than do duller ones. Just how race or ethnic origin relates to intelligence is unclear, although most psychologists discount its significance. Each child's mental performance depends on the unique blending of many factors, including inherent capacities and emotional and material environment, integrated by his own neural mechanisms and modified by his experience.

Psychologists have become increasingly less confident of their ability to pigeonhole children in mental categories. However, such categories may roughly be defined as including *mental defectives* (IQ's below 70), *below-normals but not defective* (IQ's between 70 and 90), *average children* (IQ's between 90 and 110), *high-average children* (IQ's between 110 and 120), and *bright children* (IQ's above 120). *Creative children* (a characteristic not necessarily related to IQ) possess unusual capacity for novel solutions. *Highly creative children* are characterized by nonconformity, humor, unusual productivity, and unusual ideas. *High-IQ children* are characterized chiefly by their superior achievement, both scholastic and vocational. At the other extreme, *mentally retarded children* face severe social problems, but if given suitable help they can learn to cope successfully with their conditions.

The view of the infant's mental status has changed considerably. Formerly, his perceptions were considered nonexistent or completely amorphous. But now infants are viewed as actively and selectively responding to their environments.

Piaget perceived cognitive development as progressing by age-stages; however, others insist that clear-cut stages do not exist. They argue that sequences vary and that the rate and quality of change depend on experience.

Another issue concerns **readiness,** or the particular state of maturation that must exist before specific learning can take place. Perhaps maturational factors do indeed suggest a rough general ordering of conceptual learning, but within this broad outline the acquisition of concepts hinges on the way in which experience is organized. How basic early sensory experience is for later concept development is uncertain. In fact, it is unclear when—or even whether—specially arranged sensory experience should be provided. In the case of the disadvantaged, however, supplemental enrichment seems essential.

Note: The Suggested Questions and Activities for this chapter are com-

bined with those of the next chapter. See page 169.

• SUGGESTED READINGS

Bayley, N., "Research in Child Development: A Longitudinal Perspective," *Merrill-Palmer Quarterly,* Vol. 2, No. 3 (1965), pp. 183–208. Uses results of the Berkeley Growth Study to demonstrate the sort of information that may be obtained on the same individuals through longitudinal studies. Shows developmental trends in various traits, including mental scores.

Boehm, L., "Exploring Children's Thinking," *Elementary School Journal,* Vol. 61 (1961), pp. 363–373. In simple language, the author interprets Piaget's conceptual-stage theory of children's development. She also suggests implications of this theory for educators.

Caldwell, B. M., "What Is the Optimal Learning Environment for the Young Child?", *American Journal of Orthopsychiatry,* Vol. 37, No. 1 (1967), pp. 8–21. Judging from available data, Caldwell identifies conditions that provide an optimal learning environment for the young child. She believes the whole topic requires far more and better research than is currently available.

Fowler, W., "Cognitive Learning in Infancy and Early Childhood," *Psychological Bulletin,* Vol. 59, No. 2 (1962), pp. 116–152. The author critically examines representative studies on cognitive learning in early childhood and shows how the neglect of certain key problems has contributed to psychology's low estimate of the young child's potential for such learning.

Hunt, J. McV., "How Children Develop Intellectually," *Children,* Vol. 11, No. 3 (1964), pp. 83–91. First discusses how and why psychologists have come to believe that experience can be manipulated to produce an increase in IQ. Suggests implications of these changes for experiments designed to provide corrective early experiences and to feed back information on ways of counteracting cultural deprivation.

Kessler, J. W., "Environmental Components of Measured Intelligence," *School Review,* Vol. 73 (Winter 1965), pp. 339–358. An analysis of the relationship between intelligence and four environmental factors: prenatal and paranatal conditions, early maternal care, sociocultural influences, and individual personality characteristics.

McCurdy, H. G., ed., *Barbara: The Un-*

conscious Autobiography of a Child Genius. Chapel Hill, N.C.: University of North Carolina Press, 1966. A well-written and fascinating account of a child prodigy.

Newman, H. H., et al., *Twins: A Study of Heredity and Environment.* Chicago: University of Chicago Press, 1937. A classic report on the mental and physical similarities of twins reared together, compared with twins reared apart.

Oden, M. H., "The Fulfillment of Promise: 40-year Follow-up of the Terman Gifted Group," *Genetic Psychology Monographs,* Vol. 77 (1968), pp. 3–93. Over 40 years ago Lewis M. Terman undertook a monumental study of gifted children whose IQ's placed them in the highest 1% of intelligence in the school population. This article describes a follow-up study of subjects from the original group. The first part of this report indicates in what respects the group has changed over the years; in the second part, a study of success among gifted men based on their case-history data yields correlates of vocational achievement.

Ojemann, R. H., and K. Pritchett, "Piaget and the Role of Guided Experiences in Human Development," *Perceptual and Motor Skills,* Vol. 17 (1963), pp. 927–940. This report describes an experiment designed to test Piaget's theory that cognitive development proceeds by conceptual stages. Results indicated that age levels as suggested by Piaget do not hold for a significant proportion of child subjects when a planned learning program is applied.

Reger, R., "Myths about Intelligence," *Psychology in the Schools,* Vol. 3, No. 1 (1966), pp. 39–44. The author, a member of the Board of Cooperative Educational Services, Buffalo, New York, briefly examines the "folklore" of intelligence, involving the basic concept of IQ, constancy of IQ, and terms used to describe low-performing children.

Skeels, H. M., "Adult Status of Children with Contrasting Early Life Experiences: A Follow-up Study," *Monographs of the Society for Research in Child Development,* Vol. 31, No. 3, Serial No. 105 (1966). This report is "concerned with the question of whether, and for how long a time, mental development is affected by major changes in early environment." It provides evidence concerning the effects of deprivation and poverty on the young child's ability to learn.

Stott, L. H., and R. S. Ball, "Infant and Preschool Mental Tests: Review and Evaluation," *Monographs of the Society for Research in Child Development,* Vol. 30, No. 3, Serial No. 101 (1965). Reviews research concerning intelligence and its measurement, especially at infant and early childhood levels. Surveys current practices in testing infant and preschool intelligence, and analyzes the content of five of the most widely used tests in this field.

Terman, L. M., and M. H. Oden, *The Gifted Group at Mid-Life.* Stanford, Calif.: Stanford University Press, 1959. Reviews the research done by Terman in his longitudinal study of the behavior and traits of 1,000 gifted individuals from their childhood in 1921 until the mid-1950s. Clarifies the relationship between childhood and later stages and between mental factors and other aspects of development.

Zigler, E., "Mental Retardation: Current Issues and Approaches," in Martin L. Hoffman and Lois W. Hoffman, eds., *Review of Child Development Research,* Vol. 2, pp. 107–168. New York: Russell Sage Foundation, 1966. Reviews and analyzes available research on mental retardation.

6
MENTAL DEVELOPMENT II

• CONCEPT FORMATION

Acquisition of Basic Concepts

Although overall patterns of cognitive development are apparent, the modes of acquisition of the various basic concepts are sufficiently discrete to justify separate treatment. This chapter, therefore, deals with the acquisition of certain significant concepts, beginning with the properties of objects.

Color. Color as a basis for response has sometimes been considered more primitive than form. And it is true that two-year-olds can match colors for which they do not even know the names (Cook, 1931). However, other studies indicate earlier discrimination on the basis of form than of color. After an initial preference for form discrimination, color becomes preferred from ages three to six, when form predominates again (Brian and Goodenough, 1929). Perhaps color becomes less relevant in the world of objects because it affords a poorer clue to identification. The form of almost any object—for instance, a chair or a bed—is more significant than its color.

Form. Concepts of form may take shape very early. In fact, infants distinguish patterns as early as three weeks, which suggests that aspects of form perception are innate (Fantz, 1958). By six months, an infant may be taught to choose correctly between two differently shaped blocks when one of them is sweetened (Ling, 1941).

Often, form perception is intertwined with more complex experience. For instance, children must learn to distinguish forms within widely different contexts—a familiar face, perhaps, within different groups. However, they become capable of relatively involved discriminations at an early age. As young as 15 months, they can differentiate a cross from a square, even when the object's position and the color of the background are varied (Munn and Steinung, 1931).

This capacity to distinguish form or other characteristics despite changing

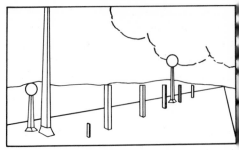

Perceptual constancy. The block of wood and the lamp post at the right appear much bigger than the block of wood in the foreground and the lamp post at the far left; actually the two lamp posts and blocks of wood are exactly the same size. In the process of concept development we learn to correct for distortions commonly experienced in our environment, but when faced with a novel situation (as here) we realize the problems a young child has in learning to deal with his world. From N. F. Beeler and F. M. Branley, *Experiments in optical illusion.* Copyright 1951 by Thomas Y. Crowell Company, New York, publishers. Reproduced by permission.

contexts is called **object constancy.** It permits familiar objects to be perceived as we think they should be rather than as sensory input might otherwise lead us to see them. For example, a coin such as a nickel, seen from the side, casts an elliptical image on the retina. Nevertheless, we perceive the nickel as round because experience has taught us that a coin does not change shape merely because it changes position.

Size. Size is a less functional clue in the young child's perceptions than are color and form. However, in certain situations size conception is obviously required. A child attempts to pick up a pebble but not a piano. He has no trouble with extremes, as in the pebble-piano problem, although he does often have trouble with lesser distinctions (Thrum, 1935).

Judging from available data, the concept of size seems hard for children to learn even though they begin to acquire form discriminations very early. That is, they find it hard to abstract size from other properties such as form, color, distance, and the like. Our knowledge on this topic is still sketchy, although data concerning children's concepts of size as related to other factors such as form, similarity, difference, and distance are being accumulated and pieced together — for example, by Charles C. Spiker and his associates — and often reported in the *Journal of Experimental Child Psychology.*

Space. To illustrate the young child's concepts of space, Piaget (1957) tells of an experimenter's passing a window outside which a child was playing on a balcony. The experimenter appeared from the left, went behind a screen placed in the middle of the window, and reappeared on the right. The child was astonished, having expected the man to be where he originally was on the left. Only later, says Piaget, do objects continue to have existence for the child, or definite locations, when out of sight. Progress from the more primitive to this more advanced concept of space proceeds, according to Piaget, by fairly specific stages paralleling progress in maturation.

However, Dodwell (1963), who reapplied Piaget's tests, found no such invariable stages. Children's drawings executed after the launching of the Sputniks indicated a similar variability. That is, children of different age levels demonstrated no clearly distinctive levels of sophistication or complexity. The drawings were multidimensional, showing the satellites in relation to earth, sun, and other parts of the solar system; and the majority had some relation to reality, despite the children's lack of information about satellites at that time (Metraux, 1961).

Distance. The concept of distance is closely related to that of space. Basically, the distance concept is this: the farther away an object is, the smaller is its image, the less definite its outlines, the slower its apparent movement, and the less saturated its color. However, preschool children atop a high building sometimes fail to realize that the "toy world" below them is actually a real-life world of life-size people and cars. Distance distinctions, then, are acquired by experience. Moreover, such concepts

Drawing by Dawn, age 8. Note especially her concepts of form and distance. From the author's files.

don't develop all at once, but rather advance like a "joggling shuttle" as children work back and forth between more and less complex ideas and in terms of their own world.

At least in America, children gain distance concepts earlier than they formerly did. Even children aged three to five may know that New Jersey is closer to New York than to California; and in playing train, they often call cities in proper sequence (Wann et al., 1962). Concepts of constancy, of both form and distance, have been reported at much earlier ages, especially when appropriate training techniques were devised (Whorf, 1956).

Nevertheless, even at age eight, says Witkin (1959), children remain strongly dominated by the visual field. They accept as "up" whatever looks "up." Only later, after more experience, do they learn to anticipate the future position of objects. Still later they learn to attend to internal cues and to ignore irrelevant stimuli that distort perception. It should be noted, however, that Witkin's conclusion derives from a specific experiment and is hence contingent on its special characteristics.

Undoubtedly, concepts of both space and distance are related to the child's personality and experience. Evidence from projective techniques indicates that the four-year-old has simple concepts of up, down, round, beneath, and inside—all related to immediate experience—but little concept of space as related to distance. He can still believe that TV performers, who may be hundreds of miles away, are shut up inside the set.

Time. The sense of time, like the foregoing concepts, hinges on both personal factors and experience. It varies to some extent with body conditions and also with emotional states such as boredom, excitement, or concentration. Some individuals have poor internal clocks, others good ones. In any case, experience is important. Few of us have any more than a vague concept of a light year in distance or a million years in geological time.

Young children understand time largely in terms of activities. Bedtime means more than 8 P.M. "I will be back in a half hour" is meaningless to a small child. However, "I will go across the street, deliver the milk, and be right back" may carry meaning, especially if the child has accompanied the parent on similar expeditions (Ames, 1946).

Many of a child's questions, if patiently answered, help sharpen time concepts. Here is a conversation typical of the process:

Child: I'm four, aren't I?
Mother: Yes, four years.
Child: What's a year?
Mother: (Explains.)
Child: Is that a long time?
Mother: Quite a long time.
Child: How long?
Mother: It's hard to explain, but it is a lot of days, 365, and that's many.
Child: Well, but how long?
Mother: Well—you know when it was Christmas.
Child: Oh, yes, and I had a tree, and once I had the tree in the corner, and once I had it on the table.
Mother: Well, that was twice, and it takes a year to have a Christmas. You see we have Christmas, then the time between that Christmas and the next is a year.
Child: Well, that's a very long, long time. When I was very small we had a Christmas. Is a year a birthday?
Mother: Well, you have one birthday, then the time between is called a year, then you have the next birthday.
Child: Yes, three then four—then five . . . say how old are you?
Mother: Thirty.
Child: How did you stretch up? [Rust, unpublished.]

Body concepts. Concepts of body, like those of time, are a gradual acquisition. A child's experience, especially in the area of physical or psychosomatic disorders, importantly affects the way he perceives his body. Since children's experience is limited, their body concepts are correspondingly distorted. In one study, some of the youngest children (four to eight years) said the reason for skin was "to not make us see the blood and bones"; "so people can't see the other part of us"; and "if we didn't have skin we'd look funny—our face would be all red." Other children perceived the skin as holding the body together ("so the blood won't fall out; it helps keep everything in") (Gellert, 1962, p. 345).

nately from above and below the table, for some moments [Woodcock, 1941, p. 44].

Lena was three years old (accuracy unchecked). Lena localized herself in the body, at first. As we continued exploring, in order to check the consistency of the response, Lena appeared in her lower right jaw. She was not in the hand, arm, or leg, nor in the eye, head, nor other (left) jaw. Lena seemed fixed in her lower right jaw. The definiteness of this localization may be indicated by her petulant response when we touched her right cheekbone and asked, "Is this Lena?" "What is the

Self-figures drawn by children with lower-extremity disability following poliomyelitis. Adapted from A. B. Silberstein and H. A. Robinson, The representation of orthopedic disability in children's figure drawings, *Journal of Consulting Psychology*, 1956, **20**, 333–341.

The following illustrations indicate two children's body concepts. In the first, the child is beginning to comprehend her body parts as all of a piece. The second shows the relation of self-concept to the body.

Meg lay over a table on her stomach and peered under. Exclaimed, "Fee [t]!" then raised her head and turned to look at her feet from on top . . . Kept at this activity, looking at her feet alter-

matter with you?" [she replied]. "I told you three times this (pointing to lower right jaw) is me" [Horowitz, 1935].

Other children designated the abdomen, the head, and so on. Most adults tended to locate the "self" in the head, brains, face, and eyes, but a few indicated other parts of the body. The locus of self varied considerably among both children and adults.

149

Death. A child's concept of death, like that of the body, is personal and to some degree emotionalized. Nagy (1948) reports three stages in the child's attitude toward death. Between ages three and five, the child denies death as a regular and final process; death is merely a temporary change in existence. From five to nine years, the child personifies death. He knows it exists but erects defenses against it. He engages in death phantasies, such as "people who die may be carried off by deathmen." At about age nine, the child begins to conceive of death as a process, the result of dissolution of bodily life; thus ultimately he accepts death as inevitable and becomes more realistic in his views.

This conversation indicates a mother's effort to help a small child acquire a more intelligent concept of death.

Child: (four and a half years old): Mummy, what means a dead mother?

Mother: A woman that has died and does not walk or talk any more.

Child: But what will the children do?

Mother: Well, if a mother should die, the father would take care of them and maybe an aunt.

Child: Will you be a dead mother some day?

Mother: Why yes, though I don't expect to be for a long time.

Child: A very long time?

Mother: Yes.

Child: But I don't want you to die; I want you here like this.

Mother: Well, you probably will be quite grown-up before that happens.

Child: A long time?

Mother: Yes.

Child: But what means dead, Mummy?

Mother: Well, your heart stops beating and you lie still without breathing.

Child: And what do you do with the talking part—you know, the inside talk?

Mother: I'm not sure, but some people think you live in another world, and of course, some don't.

Child: I guess we do (excitedly). Yes! And then you die in a long, long time—a very long time, and then I die and we both hug each other and then you won't have any wrinkles—Oh, look at that cute pussy. Isn't she darling? (Runs off) [Rust, unpublished].

Childrens' Concepts as Revealed in Behavior and Conversation

Children are continuously in the process of forming concepts. A good way to appreciate their conceptual development is to observe and listen to them. Consider this example:

A philosopher was visiting for the first time in the home of his two-year-old granddaughter. At their first meal, the little girl studied his bald head from the elevation of her high chair, and said in a friendly manner: "You don't have to part your hair, do you?" [Landreth, 1958, p. 276].

Piaget might have termed this prelogical thinking. Actually, it was quite logical. Nor is this sort of thinking limited to children. An older child or even an adult of the especially atypical or creative sort might have had the same thought in passing but would have suppressed an impulse to say it. Many of an adult's thoughts are simply "screened out" by restraints imposed by convention. The young child, not yet "socialized," expresses himself more freely.

When we come to think of it, much of children's spontaneous symbolism represents a freedom from the conventionality that stifles and devitalizes expression. The following is an instance of this:

Betty covered her ears as a huge truck rumbled by the school, then drew it—a black rectangle, with wheels beneath. She then seized a red crayon and covered the whole of it with great scrawls. "See the truck I made," she said happily. "It has lots of wheels," commented the teacher, tracing a red spiral or two with her finger. "That's the noise," corrected Betty [Strang, 1959, p. 143].

Landreth (1958, p. 261) suggests that children's concepts reflect progressively more stimuli as the passing years bring greater experience. In early childhood, she says, their drawings indicate a limited and selective attention to whatever stimuli currently dominate their attention.

> Before Christmas, John and David were painting. John said, "I'm going to paint the baby Jesus." "Is he a real person?" inquired David. "Yes," replied John, completing a circle for a head, and attaching a larger one. "He had a stomach, too." "Now," he said, "I'll draw the Virgin Mary!" "Is she a real person?" inquired David. "Does she have a stomach?" "Yes," replied John; "Jesus was in her stomach." John finished the second figure, then said, "Now, I'll draw God." "Is he a real person?" asked David. "No," said John, this time drawing only a head, and then removing his painting to dry.

Obviously, children's drawings reflect both their own intellectual maturity and their parents' teachings, modified by individual interpretations.

• LANGUAGE DEVELOPMENT

Early communication can be divided roughly into pre-speech and post-speech. Perhaps the infant's crying and cooing only incidentally serve the function of communication. These early sounds are explosive in nature, caused by air being expelled from the lungs and crossing the vocal folds. Crying, which soon comes to serve a communicative purpose, may also be associated with gastro-nervous tension, thumb-sucking, and enuresis. Parents often ignore a child's crying, intending to teach him he cannot get what he wants in this way. However, he cannot understand why he is ignored and feels insecure, so he cries more, causing the family to react unfavorably to him. Since the infant cannot tell the adult observer how he feels, these con-

jectures are somewhat speculative, but such possibilities should not be ignored (Lakin, 1957). Anyhow, since crying is a form of communication, it usually diminishes as the child's ability to speak proceeds.

Crying, babbling, and gestures are all important forms of pre-speech communication. Often a child's babbling assumes a conversational tone, as though he expects a response.

Hurlock (1964) calls 12 to 18 months the period of speech readiness. The child speaks his first word, usually, by 12 months. Delay in speaking, however, is not necessarily predictive of articulatory defectiveness, unless it extends beyond 18 months (Darley and Winitz, 1961).

The earliest speech is less intellectual than motor and involves rather intricate muscle coordinations. Speech with meaning must await further development of the association areas of the brain, as well as a greater accumulation of experience. At first, sounds are mere repetitions conveying little meaning. Note, for instance, this two-year-old's speech:

> Pat walked up and down a plank, chanting "Doggie piggie, doggie diggie loggie," and "Lig a loggie, dig a poggie, a la boggie poggie boggie" [Woodcock, 1941, p. 94].

The association of meaning that follows this stage is a matter of "conditioned reflex." Parents repeat certain sounds the baby uses, and these he learns to associate with objects, people, and situations. For example, if the mother says a word while handing the infant an object, he learns after several repetitions that that combination of sounds stands for the object presented (Hurlock, 1964). Only later does the child learn to generalize—that is, to apply meanings to categories.

The pattern of speech development is much the same for all children. There is little variation in the age of learning to talk, although the rate is accelerated by native endowment and environmental stimulation. The overall pattern is marked by spurts of rapid learning and plateaus when little new learning occurs. Especially when new motor skills are being established, there is a temporary plateau of speech development. For instance, when the baby is mastering the skill of walking, between 9 and 18 months, the urge to walk seems stronger than the need to talk. After walking is established, talking follows.

The Rules of Child Language

Does the speech of early childhood possess its own special characteristics and rules, as sometimes claimed? If so, what are they? Many writers, among them Piaget (1959), have asserted that children's speech, to age seven or eight, is more egocentric than that of adults. At first, asserts Piaget, the child doesn't care to whom he is speaking, or whether he is being listened to. Only later does he engage in genuine interchanges of thought and take into account the listener's perspective. However, McCarthy (1954) declares that it has not been demonstrated that children's speech behavior is more egocentric than that of adults or that egocentrism declines with age.

Nevertheless, children's speech is distinctive. For one thing, the child uses objects as action symbols, as in this recording of four- and five-year-olds:

> Mashed potatoes are to give everybody enough.
> A face is so you can make faces.
> Dogs are to kiss people.
> Hands are to hold.
> A hole is to dig [Krauss and Sendak, 1952].

Maccoby (1964) provides an interesting analysis of children's "grammar." She claims that many strange-sounding rudimentary sentences spoken by young children—for example, "There horsie" or "That daddy car"—have their own rules and do not merely represent random word combinations.

The child's confusion reflects inadequate experience with language and a lack of knowledge of the rules, but it often conceals excellent reasoning beneath. Here are examples:

> Stella, taking nails out of the box to pound into her block, was asked not to take "too many." Later she showed two nails to an adult, saying, "I didn't take any more of the manys" [Woodcock, 1941, p. 108].

> Joe's father had a twin who looked a lot like him. Once when they were together, Joe looked at the two and said "Two daddies!"

The Logic of Child Language

Because children have their own ways of expressing themselves, adults may underestimate their understanding. Adults have been trained to follow fairly logical sequences of thought. By contrast, young children's thinking often manifests a lack of precision and logical connection between successive observations. For example:

> Some children were "going to have a wedding," and there was much talk as to whether Priscilla would marry Frank or Dan, who were the two rivals for her affection. Frank said, "You can't marry Dan, because daddy must be bigger than mommy." They argued about this and appealed to Mrs. I. as to whether "daddies are always bigger than mommies." She said, "Well, let's ask everyone about it," and we asked each child in turn whether his mommy or his daddy was the bigger. The others all decided that "daddies must indeed be bigger than mommies," whereupon Dan said, stamping his foot, "Yes, you see, I shall be bigger than Priscilla." The logic in this case seems to proceed from the major premise, "Men are bigger than their wives," to the minor premise, "Dan is not bigger than Priscilla," to the conclusion, "Dan cannot marry Priscilla." However, Dan focused upon his own needs in the situation; hence, he reasoned, "I shall marry Priscilla; men are bigger than their wives; so I shall be bigger than Priscilla" [Isaacs, 1933, p. 158].

Since children receive constant verbal feedback from older children and adults, they gradually eliminate the illogical and often, unfortunately, the more imaginative and flexible aspects of expression as well. Of course, in some cases what appears to be imaginative speech to an adult may simply be a faulty attempt on the part of the child to communicate. In others, however, it may represent a genuinely novel approach to thought. A problem for parents and educators is this: how can one encourage the freshness, spontaneity, and color of young children's expression while at the same time effecting needed refinements?

Factors Affecting Language Development

Biological factors. A great many factors affect language development, among them the unique characteristics of the individual child. Intelligence surely plays a part, for the intellectually gifted child usually speaks earlier and more efficiently, while the mentally defective child speaks later and articulates poorly.

Normal language development also assumes integrity of the sensorimotor and central nervous systems. Factors that may interfere with normal language development include sensorimotor defects, such as deafness and blindness, and central nervous system damage, such as that related to aphasia, cerebral palsy, or mental deficiency. The deaf child lacks an aural model, and the blind child a visual model, of how words or sounds are formed. Conditions such as aphasia and cerebral palsy interfere with the muscular control and motor coordinations involved in forming words.

Maturation. Maturation as a factor in language development can hardly be separated from experience, which also increases with time. However, the various stages of language development hinge on adequate maturation of relevant neural and structural mechanisms. To illustrate, let us note certain ways that maturation affects the acquisition of language.

Many think of language development as beginning when the child uses his first word, but it actually begins much earlier, with the mastery of certain preliminary skills. For example,

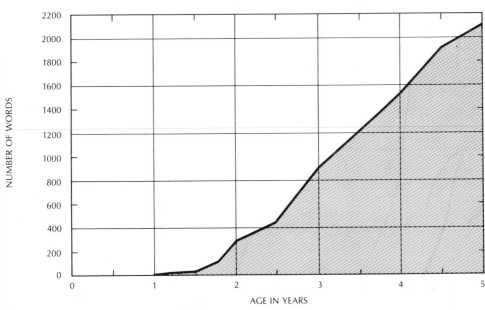

Increase in vocabulary in relation to age. From M. E. Smith's (1926) University of Iowa study, as shown in L. P. Lipsitt, Learning processes of human newborns, *Merrill-Palmer Quarterly,* 1966, **12,** 45–71. Reproduced by permission.

breathing, sucking, and swallowing must be well-established to leave breath for speaking. Also, chewing solid foods, by affording exercise, may help develop the speech mechanisms. The establishment of postural control is another factor. Babbling, which begins at about seven months, coincides approximately with sitting up, and the first real words with standing. The relation between the development of motor skills and progress in vocalization is cyclical. While babies are busy with a new skill, such as learning to sit up, they may be relatively silent, and babble freely only after the skill is mastered.

At every stage in language development, adequate structures, sufficiently matured, must be present. For example, the formation of consonants and post-dental sounds must await the period 6 to 28 months, which involves dentition. Before then, the child has no front teeth to serve as a front wall for the oral cavity (McCarthy, 1960).

Emotional status. The bearing of emotional factors on language development is unclear. Melanie Klein (1932) claims that an optimum amount of anxiety, as well as the capacity of the emerging ego to tolerate anxiety, assists with symbol formation and language development generally. However, McCarthy (1960) notes that language development may be obstructed by severe anxiety.

Interaction with family. Of special significance in language development are family relationships. The availability of adults is especially important. The mother and older siblings provide important feedback, so that the child hears his words repeated, corrected, and modified (John and Goldstein, 1964). Words become the infant's means of gaining operant control over others; and as his verbal efforts are rewarded, they naturally increase.

The child's first language teacher is his mother. It is her voice he echoes, her smile that elicits cooing and prelinguistic utterances. In one experiment, on days

Words become the infant's means of gaining operant control over others.

when the experimenter smiled, patted, and made "tsk" sounds, as contrasted with maintaining an expressionless face, the infant's vocalizations increased (Rheingold et al., 1959). Perhaps one sign of the adult's importance in language learning is that only children talk better and earlier than those with siblings (McCarthy, 1960).

Singletons versus twins. Twins and other multiple-birth children are typically retarded in language development. One reason for this occurrence may be that they receive little individual feedback from their speech because they share the mother. Another reason may be that they develop forms of private communication and hence require less attention from others (McCarthy, 1954). The reason may also be biological: both multiple-birth and premature infants sustain greater-than-average brain damage at birth.

General nature of home environment. Institutionalized infants also receive little reinforcement of their speech by older persons (Yarrow, 1961). Hence they, like twins, are retarded in language.

Whatever the environment, whether home or institution, special training helps. In one experiment, working-class mothers were instructed to read daily to their children, aged 13 to 30 months, from illustrated baby books. The mothers pointed out objects, named them, made up stories about them, and talked frequently to the children. The experimental infants made considerably more progress in language than did a control group whose parents, also of the working class, received no special instruction (Irwin, 1960).

Television. In recent years, television has increasingly affected language development. The medium undoubtedly increases a child's information, and presumably his vocabulary, although lower-class children profit more than upper-class children. To appreciate the differential effect of television on different socioeconomic backgrounds, consider these two hypothetical situations:

Child A, five years old, comes from a lower-economic group. Because of pressures, his parents spend little time with him, hence seldom serve as models or reinforcers of his speech. Moreover, their vocabulary is relatively impoverished anyway. The child himself spends much time with siblings, aged two, three, and six, who have a combined vocabulary of 2,500 words. In addition, the child watches television 25 hours a week. Counting comic strips and comic books, which have vocabularies of over 10,000 words, he is now exposed to a vocabulary of over 15,000 words. However, his environmental handicap is not completely overcome, for reinforcement seems likely to determine both quantity and quality of verbal behavior.

Child B, also aged five, is the only child of a nonworking mother and a father who is a physician; both are college graduates. Each has a speaking vocabulary of about 30,000 words, and both spend much time talking with the child and reading to him. The child is also exposed to visitors, grandparents, and neighbors, many of whom have similar vocabularies. The introduction of a television set into this child's life might actually reduce the quality and amount of verbal stimulation he has been receiving [Rheingold et al., 1959, pp. 68–73].

Speech Problems

We have already touched on speech problems deriving from various environmental factors. Even more serious are the problems of the child with disordered speech, for other children may taunt him or teachers may grow impatient as he stumbles through responses to questions. Not surprisingly, Solomon (1961) reported that children with speech defects differ from normal-speech children in overall adjustment, peer-group relations, and fears and anxieties.

Speech disorders may derive from varying combinations of biological and environmental factors, including those already discussed. Speech retardation may stem from partial or complete deafness. Or it may derive from brain injury, as involved in cerebral palsy (Irwin, 1962). The causation of stuttering is more complex. Stuttering is repetitious speech accompanied by spasms of the muscles of the throat and diaphragm. It results from the disturbance of normal breathing rhythm because of either partial or total failure of speech muscles to coordinate.

Among young children, stuttering can be considered normal, at least in Western culture. Probably the child is trying to say more than he knows how to say or can readily find speech to say. Such stuttering fades away if parents are patient and do not nag at the child (Bloodstein, 1960).

One must look for other causes among children who stutter abnormally or persistently. It is currently held, for example, that persistent stuttering usually derives from tension. The practice appears most often during ages two-and-a-half to three, and later about the time of school entrance — both times when the child is being trained in basic social patterns. Besides, stutterers, more often than other children, have been subjected to pressures during the processes of weaning and toilet-training (Johnson et al., 1959). The illustration below indicates still other kinds of experience that may precipitate stuttering:

One small boy began to stutter when his baby sister was brought home from the hospital. He never tried to pinch or hit her, but simply acted uneasy.... Another child, a two-year-old girl, began to stutter when a new maid came. . . . After she became accustomed to the maid, she stopped stuttering for a while, but resumed the practice when the family moved to a new house. Again she stopped, again began when her father was called into the Army. In each case the mother was also tense, which is a factor that seems to intensify the child's stuttering [Spock, 1946, p. 273].

Among American Indians, where no impatience was shown with children's speech, and where infants were not subject to unusual stress during socialization, stuttering was so rare that the language lacked a word to describe it (Johnson, 1944). One long-popular theory held that a change of handedness would lead to confusion in cerebral dominance, and its supposedly inevitable sequel, stuttering. However, if a physiological mechanism causes stuttering, why do most stutterers stutter when with adults but not when they are with animals or babies or when alone? True, the onset of stuttering may coincide with change of handedness, but the problem probably derives from the method employed. Between 90% and 95% of children thus converted do not become stutterers (Hutt and Gibby, 1959).

Status of Research on Language Development

Literature in the field of language development is vast and perplexing. Traditionally, efforts have concentrated on developing norms to show when the child first coos, imitates sounds, employs his first word, joins two words in speech, and so on. Thus language has been treated as a unidimensional process, limited to vocal utterances (Zigler et al., 1964). Such an emphasis equates language with speech and ignores a central aspect of language behavior—that is, the ability to understand and cognitively manipulate symbols, which in the preverbal child is called "passive language."

Although current researchers also make use of the normative and descriptive approaches, much of their work is breaking new ground. For instance, while early investigators charted developmental trends in children's usage of adult grammatical categories, the question is now raised whether early phases of language possess syntactical rules of their own.

Beginning with three children aged 18 months, Braine (1963) identified a primitive grammar made up of two parts of speech—a so-called "pivot word" plus a single word used with the pivot word. For example, "sentences" uttered by one of his subjects included: "more high," "more sing," and "more toast." In this case, "more" was the pivot word.

Efforts are also being made to determine the underlying significance of language research data, rather than merely to catalogue it. For example, a child demonstrating acceleration on a speech scale may prove to have been coached, rather than to have been innately endowed with a special gift of language. What is needed is a language model sufficiently valid or complex to explain the developmental aspects of language behavior. While there are various theories of language, none of them definitively explains children's speech behaviors or affords a valid measure of language development.

• INFLUENCES ON COGNITIVE DEVELOPMENT

Cognitive development progresses at a different rate for each child. The factors modifying such development cannot easily be categorized because they are overlapping and interrelated. However, largely for convenience we shall divide them into three broad classes of influence: biological influences, personality factors, and more purely environmental influences. Some biological influences were discussed in Chapters 2 and 5. You will recall that they include both genetic factors—especially those determining native intelligence and sensory capacities—and maturational factors. Two biological influences—age (in the sense that it is involved in maturation) and sex—should be discussed in more detail here.

Age

The creative years. Lehmann (1953) has listed 65 persons who effected outstanding achievement prior to age 20, including Galileo, who arrived at the principle of the pendulum at 17, and Bryant, who wrote "Thanatopsis" at age 18. Nevertheless, in our own society, adults between the ages of 20 and 70 account for all but a very small fragment of significant human achievement. It might be well to ask: How can the cognitive timetable be accelerated to permit earlier creative achievement, and what can be done during childhood to lay a proper foundation for such achievement? In commenting on the fact that most creative work is produced before age 40, Terman (1954) stressed the need to train the young for their life work before too many of their creative years have passed. Perhaps nurseries should be programmed for learning, so that the infant's first word will become "why" instead of "mother."

The debate over early training. The real question is this: Just how early should cognitive training be initiated? Does delay doom a child to a lifetime of mental mediocrity? Would more formalized efforts at infant education capitalize on the sort of intellectual curiosity revealed in the following recollection?

> I was about one and a half years old when my family was renting a room, pending construction of a new house. The walls had many holes in them that had been made by rats. In my infant's mind, I imagined the holes were small tunnels leading into each other. I decided to try an experiment to prove my theory. I took my favorite spoon and dropped it down a hole and waited for it to reappear at a different hole, but nothing happened. I was dejected, not only because I lost my spoon, but because my theory about holes was wrong.

Popular opinion has it that early intellectual stimulation may cause emotional damage. The young child is deemed too fragile, autistic, disorganized, irrational, and egocentric to absorb any substantial amount of perceptual-conceptual data. Any fare more solid than nursery lullabies is believed shattering to the infant psyche. Many even maintain it to be a question of neural immaturity, and suggest that an appropriate "ripening" must occur before the child is "ready," for example, to learn to read. To resolve these issues, let us examine attempts to teach young children to read, a fairly complex cognitive skill.

Over a period of nine months, Fowler (1965) gave his two-year-old daughter intensive, daily stimulation in reading, besides general intellectual and psychosocial guidance. Pre- and post-training measures were taken, and a daily log was maintained. In time she acquired an extensive repertoire of meaningful, out-of-context recognition vocabulary, entailing fine discriminations as well as a functional use of phonics. She also read meaningfully a few two-, three-, and four-word sentences, in isolated form and in preprimer contexts. How much fluency and autonomy in reading texts could be achieved remained in doubt. In sum, she learned to read two or three years ahead of norms, while sustaining very slight social-emotional maladjustment. This last may have been related more to a serious adjustment difficulty in a nursery peer group than to the training itself. Subsequent success with reading appeared to have been greatly enhanced as a result of the early training.

Fowler also gave reading instruction to a group of three-year-old identical twins and triplets. Of the four whose mental age was at least four, three learned to read fairly fluently within five months. They were well-launched in a typical first-grade-level primer program and read with evident comprehension and achievement-oriented enjoyment.

A third group whom Fowler involved in reading instruction were slow learners with a mental age of less than two. Over a few weeks, they came to recognize a number of words and letter signs (phenomic values), but they never reached a level at which they could read a single sentence independently. They made least headway not in quantity of items recalled but in conceptualization.

A perspective on early training. What conclusions can be drawn about early learning? First, the child must spend an "apprentice" period acquiring elementary discriminations and generalizations about his physical world. Because he lacks prior experience to serve as a frame of reference, these primary percepts and concepts require considerable time to build. All this is a part of learning how to learn.

The learning process used is also important. One must take into account both the language patterns used by parents and teachers and the amount of material to be learned. Training must be progressively paced in a shallow gradient within the young child's growing capabilities. The simplification and ordering of material is not a matter of mere reductionism, but of relating parts to wholes, of analysis and synthesis. The presentation must be adapted to the complexity of the material and to the child's level of comprehension. In general, the principles involved are the same as those used with older children, with certain modifications. For instance, motivation is of primary importance, as it is at any age; but with young children, the play approach is more vital than later on. Also, learning must proceed by what would seem to an adult to be very tiny, insignificant steps.

Overall, early cognitive training would seem desirable, if carefully adapted to the child. Many studies indicate that such early intellectual stimulation actually enhances social adjustment in later years (Miles, 1954). Very few three- and four-year-olds with at least average IQ have suffered emotional ill effects when given early training in

reading, and in some cases they appear to have benefited. Physically, early and prolonged stimulation in fine visual, perceptual motor discriminations, such as involved in reading, produces no evidence of eye injury or other physical disability among children aged two to five (Fowler, 1965).

In sum, available data offer promise of considerable success in training very young children to read. Success in this area suggests the need for determining the effects of early training in other areas—for instance, in science and mathematics. Perhaps the greatest ultimate gains will come from learning how to build attitudes and experiential foundations that provide conditions for later, more complex learning. For example, the young child may not be ready to learn how to solve problems in arithmetic, but playing with blocks and construction sets may provide the concepts that will help him when he is later exposed to formal arithmetical training. Such experiments are, in fact, under way; and significant insights are emerging. Perhaps brain trusters will replace baby sitters in tomorrow's nurseries!

Sex

The differences defined. As noted already, sex differences in specific mental functions are consistent, although small when compared with the total range of individual differences (Kagan et al., 1963). Boys excel in spatial intelligence and most kinds of problem solving; girls excel in memory, reasoning, word fluency, and numerical ability (Ruch, 1963). Boys are capable of more open-ended thinking and are less bound to a set; girls are less able to break down percepts and to deal with elements apart from the whole (Witkin et al., 1962). Girls are also given more to yielding in the face of disagreement (Tuddenham, 1961). Such tendencies hinder the development of creative thinking (Maccoby, 1963).

Some reasons for differences. What, we may ask, accounts for differences in the cognitive development of the sexes? First, let's view the situation longitudinally. Girls get off to a good start in their early years. They say their first word at an earlier age, combine words into sentences sooner, and count accurately sooner. In early school years, boys learn to read later and have more reading problems. There is no consistent difference in vocabulary; but after the fifth or sixth grade, boys do as well as girls in reading comprehension, though girls continue to excel in spelling, punctuation, and verbal fluency. In mathematics skills, the sexes do not differ consistently in early or middle school years; but by college age, boys excel far more in the mathematics area than girls of the same age do in language skills (Maccoby, 1963).

Apparently such differences stem from differential social sex roles, including patterns of child-rearing, rather than from genetic differences. Children of both sexes who do well in mathematics and science have been encouraged to assume initiative, and trained to be independent. In the same vein, Witkin (1962) found that children who do well on the rod-and-frame test, which relates to mathematical performance, have been encouraged to assume initiative and given freedom to explore their environment.

Traits of intellectually superior girls. In other studies, it has been found that girls who do better in mathematics and science typically identify with their fathers. They are low in acceptance of authority—another evidence of the importance of autonomy in analytic thinking (Bieri, 1960).

At Stanford, Maccoby and her associates (1962) found that fifth-grade girls who were best on spatial relations were more masculine and aggressive than other girls of similar IQ's; they were also rather withdrawn socially from their age-mates. Girls best in numerical tasks were highly competent in organizing and less likely to ask their parents for help when in difficulty. Girls good at verbal tasks more often asked their mothers for help.

A perspective on sex differences in intellect. We can summarize the findings on this subject as follows: (1) Research indicates that intellectual development is not an isolated unfolding process but responsive to a network of interpersonal relations; and certain modes of thought depend on aspects of personality rather than on qualities of intellect. (2) Methods of child-rearing that foster dependence and passivity, such as those typically used with girls, have the same effects whether used with boys or girls. These methods encourage obedience and create children who do well in subjects such as language and spelling, which depend on rules. In general, a conformist upbringing snuffs out the twin candles of curiosity and creativity that burn in young children's minds.

At least two questions arise: What blend of child-rearing would permit both boys and girls to be good at both types of subjects, those depending on rules and those requiring creative thought? Would either sex lose any essential element in sex-appropriateness in the process? Does the woman's wife-role, including child-bearing, require dependent behaviors, for which independence training in childhood would be maladaptive? Research up to now has rested largely on theoretical and often highly prejudicial grounds; pending better answers, parents and educators must arrive at their own answers for the dilemma. They may rear the girl as a tomboy and provide a better chance for intellectual development; or they may encourage her to be tractable and better adapted to her sex role while dissipating her intellectual potential. Still another alternative exists: the sex roles themselves could be altered to permit each sex to develop its talents more fully without violating social dicta.

Personality Traits
Traits positively related to cognitive effectiveness. Certain specific personality

traits seem to be especially significant for cognitive development—for instance, activity. Since some children who possess high IQ's and demonstrate high-caliber intellectual performance are very active and others much less so, the real significance of activity for cognitive performance seems to hinge not on sheer activity as such but on factors contingent to its use. In other words, what is important is the child's capacity to adapt activity to the situation. This observation has been borne out by research. Capable nursery-school children can either inhibit movement when required or attack a problem with energy.

Personality is significantly related to cognitive development.

They are not characterized by a single level of gross activity. They are exploratory, but some forms of exploration involve gross activity, others do not. Both sedentary play (drawing, working puzzles, constructing things with blocks) and kinetic play (constructing things with hammers and saws, playing cops and robbers, exploring a nearby wood) may be functional for intellectual activity (Maccoby, 1965).

A personality trait related to and contingent upon both activity and cognitive performance is curiosity. The curious child seeks rather than avoids complex problems. He also retains answers better than other children. Other traits related to activity as well as to effective intellectual performance are initiative, resourcefulness, competitiveness, and aggressiveness (Sontag et al., 1965).

These recollections from childhood, related by college freshmen, exemplify relationships between special personality traits and cognitive development.

Curiosity: One day my father was repairing an electric pump that carried water into our home. It was in a damp cellar. I was standing by, watching with curiosity. When he was nearly finished and about to cover two exposed wires, he left to get certain materials he needed. He warned me, "Now don't touch those wires; they're dangerous." Nevertheless, curiosity got the better of me. I poked them, and the next thing I remember was my father picking me up on the other side of the cellar.

Resourcefulness: Since my father was a physician, I had all sorts of curiosity about medical matters. However, he was a very busy man, and could spend little time explaining things to me. I "borrowed" butcher knives from my mother's kitchen and cut up a cat, and caught a large barn rat, and cut it up, too, to see what was inside.

Activity: I was a very lively youngster and generated a terrific amount of energy. I was everywhere, into everything. I chatted with tramps who passed along the street and listened to their weird stories. I watched construction workers by the hour. When tourists stopped in my father's shop, I bombarded them with questions. I tried grafting fruit trees, attempted to revive a drowned cat (unsuccessfully), and did infinite other things. Life was a ball, the world my oyster!

Traits negatively related to cognitive effectiveness. Also related to cognitive effectiveness—in the negative sense—is anxiety, which tends to inhibit action and stifle curiosity. The anxious child is often too fearful of his environment to explore it. Low-anxious children, older children, and boys prefer greater novelty than do their opposites; and taste for novelty correlates with creativity (Mendel, 1965).

Factors That Distort Perception

Any condition that blocks perception will reduce the accumulation of data from which concepts are formed. One such factor is prejudice, which prevents a child's taking into account all available data. Prejudiced children have greater difficulty handling abstract concepts than do less prejudiced ones. In one study, a group of seven-year-old boys and girls first indicated their agreement or disagreement with statements rated as intolerant or prejudiced concerning Mexicans, Catholics, Jews, and Negroes. After being categorized as relatively prejudiced or unprejudiced, the children were given tasks to determine their approach to problems and their ability to solve them. The prejudiced children, as compared with the unprejudiced, had more difficulty solving the problems, persisted longer with poor hunches and hypotheses, and indicated an inability to make effective use of hints from the experimenter. They performed especially poorly when the problem was ambiguous and they had to structure its meaning. The author of the study concluded that the prejudiced child tends to look for simple solutions and has difficulty shifting from his original approach (Kutner, 1958). In short, the rigidity of attitude characteristic of the prejudiced individual is reflected in his approach to intellectual problems.

Also poor in concept acquisition is the autistic child, who is nonresponsive to his environment, and hence is incapable of interpreting stimuli that originate outside himself. Such a child selectively hears and sees what he wants to hear and see; and although an adult may switch from an autistic mode of perception to an unautistic one without much trouble, a child has more difficulty separating his feelings from his perceptual world. However, some degree of autism is desirable for creative work. "A scientist or an artist uses fantasy, imagination, and the not-yet-real to generate research and theory. He uses hunches based on feelings to guide his intellectual endeavors at some times and tough-minded logic at other times" (Solley, 1966, p. 285).

Cognitive Style

The unique blend of traits that constitutes one's method of organizing his environment is called **cognitive style.** It represents any or all of an individual's special ways of perceiving, organizing, and labeling various dimensions of the environment. It is the preferred use of a specific class of conceptual responses (Kagan et al., 1960). Sometimes the term is used broadly to encompass the individual's overall approach to mental tasks; sometimes it refers to more specific ways of relating to the problem at hand. In the following discussion we shall use the term interchangeably to apply either to total approach or to more limited types of response.

Individual styles can be distinguished in infancy; and available evidence indicates that these styles tend to persist. While they may be viewed as the result of the interaction of biological and environmental factors, their characteristic flavor derives from basic traits, such as the tendency to be passive or aggressive, which are apparent in the first months of life (Rutter et al., 1963).

Cognitive style inevitably reflects the person who employs it. It is the trademark of the person-in-action. For example, Corwin (1965) notes those traits most characteristic of the scientist. The scientist possesses both playful curiosity and objectivity. He considers alternative points of view, and can entertain perspectives contrary both to his personal predispositions and to popular assumptions. He has no axes to grind, and no predisposition to be either respectful or disrespectful toward a subject.

Typical styles. Cognitive styles may be classified in various ways. For instance, Getzels and Jackson (1962) speak of two basic cognitive or intellective modes. One involves retaining the known, preserving established values, and maintaining the status quo; persons employing this process tend to demonstrate the usual and expected behaviors. The second mode involves revising the known; this is the mode employed by persons who prefer the novel and the speculative. The first mode favors certainty, the second risk.

Individuals may also be classified as **field dependent** or **field independent,** a field-dependent person being described as one likely to change his stated views on an issue in the direction of authority. Witkin (1959) and his associates attached a rod to a frame in such a manner that both parts could be moved independently of one another. The frame could be tilted at various angles while the subject was asked to maintain the rod in a vertical position. Certain individuals, who were called field-dependent, were strongly influenced by the position of the frame; others remained independent of it. The investigators found that the two groups were also characterized by related behaviors, all part of a total pattern or style of life.

Analytic versus global thinking is a dichotomy used almost interchangeably with field independence versus field dependence. In either case, a child's status on these traits typically involves a particular cluster of behaviors. The global thinker tends toward generalizations, the analytical thinker toward taking things apart to see what makes them tick. Compared with the nonanalytic child, the analytic one tends to be self-sufficient, almost to the point of isolation, and to show greater IQ gains. The nonanalytic child is more impulsive, less able to inhibit urges to action, more distractible, and less capable of intense involvement in tasks requiring concentration and motor passivity. For instance, verbally analytic children are also likely to be quiet, contemplative, willing to

play alone for extended periods, and likely to approach new situations cautiously rather than impulsively (Kagan et al., 1963).

Honkavaara (1958) identifies two other cognitive types: color reactors, who prefer to organize on the basis of color, and form reactors, who prefer form. Form reactors have lower IQ's, are more practical and socially conforming, and are more often found among women. Color reactors are more perceptive and sensitive to other people.

Kagan (1965) introduces still another dimension, that of speed. Children with fast conceptual tempos impulsively report the first classifications that occur to them. Reflective children, on the other hand, actively consider alternatives before making an evaluation. However, the reflective child is not necessarily the brighter child. Nor may one assume either style to be inherently superior to the other. Each has areas in which it functions better than the other. Kagan suggests that new pedagogical presentations should be tailored to the child's preferred style.

To date, cognitive styles have been classified according to many dimensions, including activity level, threshold of responsiveness, rhythmicity of functioning, adaptability, intensity, approach-withdrawal, mood, persistence, and distractibility. As yet, however, there is no standard way to classify either cognitive styles or specific features of style. An individual's style is unique—a blending of all the characteristic modes of reacting mentioned above, and more.

Here two college students describe their cognitive styles and indicate the persistence of these styles from childhood:

From the time I was very small I liked to tinker with things. I always liked to work from diagrams and instructions. I guess I'm a combination of kinesthetic- and eye-minded. I like to have the feel of things even as I inspect them closely. Before I tackle a project, and at intervals during its execution, I simply loaf around and let the idea incubate. I am a deliberate, methodical worker. I've had this pattern from childhood, the chief change being that I've developed a block about finishing things. So many people have tried to speed me up that at a certain point I give up. (Male)

Early in childhood I was developing a way of attacking intellectual problems. Already I was a block-type worker and enjoyed tackling work in chunks. Also, I brainstormed problems — that is, my brain welcomed any idea that wanted to come in no matter how wild it was. Then I sifted out the ideas I'd collected and refined them. I did a lot of doodling as I worked, which in effect helped me to organize my ideas. (Female)

Family Influences

Among environmental influences on the child's cognitive development, none is more important than family experience. Although research data do not support the contention that a child develops a specific ability because his parents have selectively trained him in it, the manner of child-rearing and the quality of the parent-child relationship have been found to limit the intervening conditions that stimulate or suppress differential abilities (Bing, 1963). The parent's attitude toward his child as a thinking individual is important, too. Some parents worry if the child knits his brow. Childhood must be carefree, they believe; hence they view the intellectual child as an introspective neurotic.

Certain modes of dealing with children correlate with specific types of cognitive development. For instance, a high interaction between mother and child relates to verbal facility (Bing, 1963). Fostering dependency makes for children who are less motivated to achieve and more likely not to gain in IQ (Sontag et al., 1958). Also associated with verbal skills, and possibly impeding numerical and spatial skills, is a warm, positive family atmosphere. Spatial ability probably develops from interaction with the physical rather than the interpersonal environment (Bing, 1963).

The intellectual climate of the home is important, too, whether stimulating or dull, work-oriented or dedicated to relaxation. Some homes are so drab and lifeless that the child is little better off than the laboratory mouse confined in his cage.

Adult Manipulation

Not only in the home but throughout society, adults manipulate the environment in all sorts of ways that modify children's perceptions. In one case, the adult's capacity to instill biases into children was experimentally demonstrated as follows. A color preference for "yellow" was established simply by rewarding children who consistently chose objects (rectangular blocks) of this color. Thereafter, these children showed an increased preference for yellow eggs, yellow toy cars, or yellow shoes, as compared with pre-training preferences. Obviously, anything colored yellow would have greater impact on these children (Rhine and Silun, 1958).

Sociocultural Factors

Language. Among the most important cultural influences on concept formation is language. Apparently, language determines how the environment is perceived, how perceptions are organized, and what kinds of abstract concepts can be invoked (Johnson, 1962). In Yiddish, there is a term encompassing the relationship between two mothers-in-law; in English there is not. English-speaking children, excluding those who also know Yiddish, are rarely even aware that such a relationship exists.

Similarly, societies differ in their expressions of such concepts as time and color. Time-oriented societies, like those in the Western world, relate events to the past, present, and future; and their language reflects this fact. Others, like the Hopi, are more oriented to the present and have no past or future tense in their language (Whorf, 1940). Similarly, the Zuni have trouble distinguishing orange and yellow, apparently because they have only one name for both colors (Lenneberg and Roberts, 1956).

163

Since the 1950s there has been a growing recognition of the role of language in concept formation and problem solving. In one study, subjects who were required to state a plan of attack before embarking on a problem performed better than those who silently went about the job (Ray, 1957). Another study indicated that subjects who learned the names of the component parts of a pressure regulator proved more adept at assembling the machines (Saltz and Newman, 1960).

Social class. Even within the same culture, children of different social classes acquire distinctive perceptions determined by their different needs. In one instance, a group of 30 ten-year-olds manipulated an apparatus consisting of a wooden box with a screen at one end and a knob at the lower right-hand corner. By turning the knob, the children could vary the diameter of the circle of light shining on the screen. Two groups of children, one rich and one poor, matched the size of the circle of light to the size of coins of various denominations; a control group matched the light to the size of cardboard circles. The coins, socially valued and hence more in line with children's needs, were judged larger than the discs. Moreover, the poor group overestimated the size of the coins to a much greater extent than did the rich group, apparently because they attached correspondingly greater value to them (Bruner and Goodman, 1947).

Television. An important modern influence on cognitive development is television. In some households, the one-year-old's playpen is in the same room as the television set, and there are cases where the child's first word is the name of a television star or some advertised product. Perhaps more sophisticated programs would constitute a painless way to produce infant eggheads.

One school survey reported kindergarten tots spending roughly half as much time (14.2 hours a week) at tele-

vision sets as at school. In another study, 51% of one group said they would prefer a sound spanking to the blackout of a favorite program (*Time,* March 24, 1958, p. 62). Over the calendar year, children spend more time with television than with all other mass media combined, and more time than they spend in school (Hess and Goldman, 1962).

With increasing age, reports Schramm (1961), the time spent watching television varies as follows: In the first three grades, a child views television 15 or 16 hours a week, with the time gradually increasing until grades 6 and 7, when he watches 22 hours a week. After that, the average time declines through the high school years.

What appeals to children, Schramm observes, also varies with age. In America, the young child likes variety shows and adventure programs, especially science fiction and children's westerns. Thereafter, interests come to include crime programs and situation comedies. On approaching adolescence, the child shows interest in popular music and variety shows. During high school years, a small minority become interested in current events and public affairs programs.

Television undoubtedly contributes heavily to the young child's fund of knowledge, and children relate what they see to their own experience. For example:

> Two four-year-old boys found a worm on the playground. They noted it was the same shape as a snake, and one of the boys told of large rattlesnakes he had seen on a television program. "Even the man couldn't touch those snakes," he said, "because they were poison. See, I can hold the worm; it's not poison" [*Childhood Education,* May 1954, p. 434].

Whether the rise in children's televiewing has been paralleled by a reduction in their reading is unclear. About 57 million juvenile books were sold in the United States in 1947, and close to 270 million in 1957 (Cerf, 1958). However, the sheer number of books sold may possibly reflect growing affluence rather than increased reading.

Perhaps television's beneficial effects are confined largely to early years and to lower-class households. Children previously exposed to television enter

Televiewing has been suspected of unduly limiting time available for developing other interests; however, studies made since the advent of television indicate both the persistence of old hobbies and the appearance of new ones (*Television and Youth*, 1954).

The effects of television on the child's mind have not yet been fully determined.

school with a vocabulary about one year advanced over those lacking such experience. However, after the first year or so, these effects disappear. Moreover, there is little sign that television is raising taste; and perhaps it may crystallize in children a value level based on its own common-denominator standards (Schramm et al., 1961). For one thing, children tend to see things as all black or white and to ignore motives for action. Children whose exposure to television is high more often agree with statements like: "People are either all good or all bad" or "There are only two kinds of people in the world, the weak and the strong." Note that children also generally manifest some increase in stereotyped behaviors after reading comic books under experimental conditions (Bailyn, 1959).

Similarly, Witty (1960) found that television had not brought a reduction in outdoor play, hobbies, sports, and creative activities; nor did heavy viewers get lower grades.

Most authorities recommend learning to live with television because it has come to stay. Activities should be balanced and better programs encouraged. More realistic programs should be brought to television to break the barrier between passive fantasy and actual experience. Adults should help children learn to differentiate good and bad, authentic and superficial (Schramm et al., 1961).

• STATUS OF RESEARCH

In concluding our treatment of cognitive development, it might be well to appraise the current status of research, including where we have been and where we appear to be going. Psychologists have long been concerned with cognitive processes, especially learning. In general, they have focused on the process itself—on the minimal conditions necessary in order for learning to take place, and on the conditions that serve to facilitate or obstruct learning.

Studies of children's learning date from early in the century and include two periods of high-volume activity (White, 1963). The first, during the 1930s, coincided with the rise of the child-development movement and focused on this question: In what respects is childhood learning unique? Such topics as classical conditioning, reminiscence, and learning versus maturation were examined in terms of their special significance for childhood. Perhaps the most basic conclusion was that children's learning processes are not unique and are not distinctively different from those of adults or animals (Munn, 1954). Given optimum environments, little children can think big.

Current Trends

The second wave of activity began in the 1950s and is still rising. Recent study of children's learning has been closely tied to research with animals as well as adults. That is, work on various topics—operant behavior, discrimination learning, learning set, and transfer of training—is proceeding simultaneously among all three groups, each contributing to the other. No one theme encompasses the scope of research activity. As principles emerge from studies of simpler forms of learning, they become tentatively integrated into more comprehensive theory, although no one broadly based theory has attained universal acceptance (McCandless and Spiker, 1956).

Researchers were initially disposed to view learning in stimulus-response terms, assuming that mere association is sufficient to stamp environmental effects onto children, who were themselves

perceived as uniform in type and passive in nature. However, this emphasis is being displaced by a developmental one. Investigators are showing how such factors as attention, strategy, and cognitive style vary with the child and evolve in terms of his own unique development.

Another recent emphasis is on cognitive development during infancy. Until recently, asserts Deutsch (1960), we have conceived of children "as always on the verge of some disease process"; and we "have assigned ourselves the role of protecting the child in the same manner that a zoo-keeper arranges for the survival of his charges."

In short, the study of children's learning and cognitive development is in a stage of furious ferment. New data are emerging which permit broader, deeper insights into the learning processes of children. Many conclusions have resulted from pooling the findings of innumerable small studies, unprepossessing and limited when taken alone, but nevertheless in the aggregate forming the backbone of current research. Their great strength is their speed and precision of execution. When used intelligently in continuous research programs, their flexibility and self-correcting power seem to outweigh drawbacks contingent on their limited scope and brevity (White, 1963).

Inevitably, the concern with basic processes will lead to hypotheses about the biological bases of maturation, sensory development, brain function, emotion, and attention. Substantial help on this score should come from animal study, physiology, and biochemistry. Concurrently, as data accumulate, there will be continuing efforts at integration; and ultimately, broader and more significant conceptual schemes should emerge.

Application of Research Data

Organizing curriculum. Research findings about children's concept development hold significance for both school and home training. For example, if concepts can be acquired only in a precise, unvarying order, the curriculum should be ordered accordingly. Indeed, there does appear to be a rough ordering of concept development, to the extent that concepts on successively more complex levels require relatively greater increments of maturation and experience. Hence, the curriculum should comprise flexible, roughly sequential units, while taking fully into account the great differences among children.

Motivation. Of late, psychologists have become increasingly more interested in the motives behind curiosity, stimulation-seeking, and exploration. Apparently, some rewards work for no other reason than that they are "interesting." When a lever was placed in a nursery for about an hour a day, children pressed it for one or two days in an exploratory fashion, then ceased responding. However, when pressing the lever was then made to turn on a light, the children resumed pressing the lever for about a week (Antonitis and Barnes, 1961).

Children, especially boys, also like a challenge. They prefer to resume work on a puzzle on which they have failed rather than select another (Crandall and Rabson, 1960).

One aspect of motivation involves providing the sort of stimuli to which children will respond. Quite different stimuli may be used to teach the same concept, yet these stimuli will vary in their appeal for different children. One child might respond more readily to auditory stimuli, thus learning effectively from tape-recorded materials. Another might respond better to tactual stimuli; he would want to get his hands on the problem—literally. Moreover, some children can learn to discriminate more easily between solid objects than between flat shapes and patterns (Stevenson and McBean, 1958). On the basis of such evidence, it would seem wise to learn more about the child's sensory capabilities and what sort of stimuli

inherently possess the greatest impact. The material aspects of the child's environment, including tools, toys, and educational materials, should be modified accordingly. Only research can separate the functional from the foolish in designing more stimulating environments for children.

New approaches. Finally, we can hope that research will reveal methods of sharpening the child's capacities in just the right way to permit flexible and imaginative approaches to problems. Coping with today's world is a far more complex matter than it was a few decades ago. Today's student will hardly come to understand atoms on a field trip through the local milk factory—or even an atom plant. Nor can modern theories of economics be comprehended via simple household budget models. The acquisition of such concepts hinges on the ability to think symbolically and to organize thoughts into meaningful patterns. It takes imagination to engineer the sort of environment that will fire the child's imagination and help him gain a better understanding of his world.

• SUMMARY

Basic to the child's cognitive development is the acquisition of certain significant concepts, especially concepts of the properties of objects. Infants become capable of relatively involved discriminations at an early age. Apparently, form is more important than color in object discrimination, and size less important than either. Such concepts, as well as those of space, distance, and time, depend heavily on experience. In addition, the concept of time depends on body conditions such as boredom, excitement, or concentration. Body concept itself is considerably altered by psychosomatic and physical disorders. Both body concept and concept of death are strongly emotionalized.

Many attempts have been made to describe the nature of children's concepts, particularly as expressed in their speech. Early communication may be divided into pre-speech and post-speech. *Pre-speech*—that is, babbling and gestures—serves as a basis for speech. First sounds are mere repetitions, but when parents repeat certain sounds that the baby uses in conjunction with particular objects, the child learns through association. Later he learns to generalize or to apply meaning to categories.

Various efforts have been made to describe children's language. The common assumption that children's language is more egocentric than adults' is not completely substantiated. Children's grasp of an idea may over-reach their capacity to express it. Sometimes more logic underlies their remarks than is grasped by adults, who are often boxed in by their own formal rules of expression. Undoubtedly, there is also considerable illogic, which gradually disappears.

Language development depends on many factors, including the integrity of the sensorimotor and central nervous systems. At every stage, maturation must be such that adequate structures are present. Family members, especially the mother, provide important environmental stimulation. Apparently, television also facilitates language learning in the young child, especially the child whose family is relatively uneducated. However, it may retard language development in children of educated families who might otherwise be involved in higher-level intellectual experience. Much remains to be done in the language area, for not yet is there a language model sufficiently valid or complex to accommodate all aspects of such behaviors.

Various factors may account for individual differences in cognitive development. Principal among these are biological factors, particularly heredity. Age also serves as a limiting factor, but just how is unclear. Perhaps formal cognitive training might proceed, without detrimental side effects, at an earlier age than is ordinarily assumed. The methods used would be the same as those used with older children, but with shorter steps and more of the play approach.

The significance of sex as a factor in learning is also unclear. Typically, each sex excels in certain areas, probably because of various social and motivational factors. Children of either sex who are encouraged to show initiative and granted greater freedom tend to do better in mathematics and science. Those who are urged to abide by the rules and encouraged to be dependent ordinarily do better in language and spelling. Thus, intellectual development relates to aspects of personality and, ultimately, to methods of child-rearing. Traits of special significance for effective cognitive performance include initiative, resourcefulness, competitiveness, aggressiveness, activity, and curiosity. On the other hand, a weak ego and anxiety appear to obstruct clear thinking. In fact, the whole individual seems to participate in every intellectual act.

Also important is the way the individual organizes his environment; this is sometimes called his **cognitive style.** The bare outlines of an individual's cognitive approach can be discerned in infancy. An important dimension of individual style is the degree of global or analytic thinking. *Global thinkers* tend toward generalizations, *analytical thinkers* toward taking things apart. Individuals also differ in reaction to form versus color and in pace of work.

Among the environmental influences on children's cognitive development, none is more important than family experience. Both the intellectual climate of the home and the parents' attitude toward intellectual achievement rub off on the child. Among the sociocultural factors affecting cognitive development are (1) language, which limits the sort of thoughts that may be expressed, (2) social class, which limits the child's experience, and (3) television, which provides a fund of knowledge and helps build vocabulary.

Psychologists have been interested

in children's cognitive development for a long time, and activity in this area continues to increase. Two areas of current concern are early childhood learning and the learning of the disadvantaged. The integration of data from innumerable smaller studies should permit the formulation and testing of broader hypotheses that will advance the understanding of basic mental processes. Hopefully, there will emerge more effective ways of helping children to learn.

• SUGGESTED QUESTIONS AND ACTIVITIES

1. Might it be possible to devise special tapes or films for infants' rooms to provide desirable visual and auditory stimulation?

2. Bring to class a toy catalog and discuss the contents in terms of their possible impact on children's mental development.

3. Do you believe that long-playing records might be devised to stimulate language development in infants?

4. Since the early years seem to be the "golden" years for establishing cognitive style, what special qualities and training should teachers of younger children have?

5. Suppose an infant school has opened in your community, and it provides the latest scientific care, including various cognitive and emotional experiences designed to enhance mental development. Will you enroll your one-and-a-half-year-old child, assuming he will be at "school" eight hours a day? List the pros and cons. Should enrolling children in such schools be required by law?

6. Would it be better (a) to send babies one-and-a-half to three years old to special schools, (b) to require that one of the parents take a short course in the mental training of infants, (c) to proceed as we are now, or (d) to follow some other plan (which you should be prepared to outline)?

7. Relate to the class incidents or remarks of very young children which give special insight into their early cognitive development.

8. Does it seem reasonable to assume that critical periods in human development could ultimately be charted to provide optimum efficiency both in formal and informal education? What changes would be required in present approaches to method and curriculum?

9. In what ways do the more traditional schools tend to inhibit the development of creativity?

10. Is the present-day "mental diet," which involves so much televiewing and spectator sports, so passive as to undermine children's creative development? If so, what should be done about this situation?

11. Would it be wise to have a "foster parent" system whereby infants of underprivileged parents might be placed in more stimulating homes about two hours each day?

12. In today's automated world, is there a place for the dull and the feeble-minded? Should they be sterilized?

13. As a class, discuss your own early experiences by answering these two questions: (a) What factors contributed most to your mental development? Appraise the relative importance of each. (b) What is your own cognitive style? Attempt to explain its origin and development.

• SUGGESTED READINGS

Almy, M. (with E. Chittenden and P. Miller), *Young Children's Thinking: Studies of Some Aspects of Piaget's Theory.* New York: Teachers College, Columbia University, 1966. Tests Piaget's theories and reviews the literature dealing with the development of quantitative concepts.

Church, J., *Language and the Discovery of Reality.* New York: Random House, Inc., 1961. Summarizes the child's cognitive and linguistic development, combining ideas, research findings, and personal interpretation. An entertaining book directed both to better educated laymen and to scientists.

Church, J., ed., *Three Babies: Biographies of Cognitive Development.* New York: Random House, Inc., 1966. Life histories of three babies, birth to age 2 (in one case, almost to age 3), as recorded by their mothers, and stressing cognitive development.

Hess, R. D., and V. Shipman, "Early Blocks to Children's Learning," *Children,* Vol. 12, No. 5 (1965), pp. 189–194. Describes research under way at the Urban Child Center at the University of Chicago designed to test two hypotheses: first, that the behavior leading to social, educational, and economic poverty is socialized in early childhood—that is, it is learned; and second, that the central factor involved in the effects of cultural deprivation is a lack of cognitive meaning in the mother-child communication system. Suggests implications of findings to date for school programs.

Hunt, J. McV., "How Children Develop Intellectually," *Children,* Vol. 11, No. 3 (1964), pp. 83–91. Hunt reviews changes in traditional beliefs about the development of human capacity and motivation, and recommends a creative approach, including proper evaluation of programs of preschool enrichment.

Kidd, A. H., and J. L. Rivoire, eds., *Perceptual Development in Children.* New York: International Universities Press, Inc., 1966. Authorities review and interpret research relating to various areas of perceptual development.

Sigel, I. E., "The Attainment of Concepts," in Martin L. Hoffman and Lois W. Hoffman, eds., *Review of Child Development Research,* Vol. I. New York: Russell Sage Foundation, 1964, pp. 209–248. Excellent review and interpretation of the literature on the development of concepts.

Stevenson, H. W., ed., "Concept of Development: A Report of a Conference Commemorating the Fortieth Anniversary of the Institute of Child Development, University of Minnesota," *Monographs of the Society for Research in Child Development,* Vol. 31, No. 5, Serial No. 107 (1966), pp. 40–108.

Torrance, E. Paul, "Scientific Views of Creativity and Factors Affecting Its Growth," *Daedalus,* Vol. 94 (1965), pp. 663–681. Torrance critically appraises views on creativity and offers his own opinions.

Vernon, P. E., "Ability Factors and Environmental Influences," *American Psychologist,* Vol. 20, No. 9 (1965), pp. 723–733. Summarizes research concerning various categories of environmental influences on mental development.

Wallach, M. A., and N. Kogan, "Creativity and Intelligence in Children's Thinking," *Trans-action,* Vol. 4, No. 1 (1967), pp. 38–43. Describes research designed to determine the relationship within individual children between intelligence and creativity.

Wallach, M. A., and N. Kogan, *Modes of Thinking in Young Children.* New York: Holt, Rinehart and Winston, 1965. Intelligence and creativity are treated in relation to each other, and to the areas of education and research.

Witkin, H. A., et al., *Psychological Differentiation: Studies of Development.* New York: John Wiley & Sons, 1962. An important study of the personality correlates of cognitive behavior.

7
EMOTIONAL DEVELOPMENT

Emotion refers to a "complex feeling-state accompanied by characteristic motor and glandular activities . . ." (English and English, 1958, p. 176). It has three main aspects: a mental component, since it is a conscious experience involving feelings such as happiness, anger, and fear; a physical component, since it involves a complex of muscular, chemical, glandular, and neural changes; and a motive component, since it induces continuous readaptions to problems. The motive is often the core of the individual's emotional state.

Emotional states may also be described as having certain dimensions: intensity of feeling, ranging from a "bare twitch" to powerful passion; strength of motive, or impulse to action; hedonic tone, or degree of pleasantness or unpleasantness; and complexity, or the extent to which basic emotions such as love, hate, and anger become intertwined. Emotions may also be integrative or disintegrative—that is, maximizing or interfering with an individual's effectiveness, and lending pleasant or unpleasant overtones to his experience. Disintegrative emotions typically include grief, mental confusion, hostility, and fear; integrative emotions include love, hope, wonder, and joy.

• SOME BASIC CONCEPTS

Emotionally Healthy Behavior

The individual whose behaviors promote integrative emotions may be characterized as follows:

He accepts his right to be human; he laughs with gusto; he expresses normal anger or fear without feeling guilty about it. He does, however, discriminate between appropriate and inappropriate circumstances for showing emotion. He controls his emotions; they do not control him. He experiences an inner freedom derived from confidence in his ability to utilize emotions properly. Expression for him is no all-or-none affair; he can express feelings in whatever graduation required. If the door is stuck he does not smash it down. He also discriminates between positive and negative aspects of emotion. He recognizes that mild fear, worry, and anxiety may be stimulants to the right actions; his goal is not mere cowlike contentment. He does, however, avoid the excessive tension that paralyzes action [Rogers, 1962, pp. 108–109].

Emotional Health and Adjustment

Emotional health may also be defined in terms of **adjustment,** which represents continuous readaption to changing demands and establishment of the sort of relationship between self and environment that allows the maximum self-actualization consistent with social welfare and external realities. In this sense, adjustment does not mean meekly fitting into the group. It simply involves recognition of the fact that an individual must seek his goals within the sociocultural framework. While short-term considerations may precipitate conflict between individual needs and social welfare, the best solutions generally work to the ultimate advantage of both.

Often we hear a person referred to as normal or abnormal, indicating healthy or unhealthy adjustment; but this concept needs careful consideration. Note that the term "adjustment" is often qualified with such modifiers as "adequate" or "moderate." These terms are necessary because normal adjustment is itself relative. Every child suffers some anxiety and displays some unacceptable behaviors. It is when a maladaptive behavior becomes excessive, or habitual, that it becomes a matter for concern.

The most effective adjustment may imply something quite different from the usual notion of normality as a condition of euphoria or homeostasis. Sheer euphoria may produce flabby relaxation, instead of the sense of positive well-being conducive to enthusiasm and action. Homeostasis, in its true sense, implies an optimal, not a zero, state of tension. Nor is it to be conceived merely as absence of intrapsychic tension, because a certain amount of stress may be necessary for physical well-being (Golden et al., 1964). In fact, individual children may thrive on widely different amounts of tension. One child may need his current state of tension reduced; another may need his increased (Buhler, 1951). One child thrives when life grabs him by the throat; another must remain safely within the comfort spectrum. Probably all children need at least some tension, however.

Richter (1959) suggests that in our current civilization we are paying for our cumulative absence of stress by increases in arthritis and similar ailments, as well as by lessened stimulus to creativity and imagination. Conflict has sparked many advances in thought. For example, Freud's theorizing was undoubtedly shaped by his own psychological structure, which certainly reflected considerable ideological conflict (Jones, 1957). In short, the sheer reduction of tension, unless it is extreme, is hardly a goal to be sought.

Again, consider the traits "absent-mindedness" and "well-roundedness" as illustrations of adjustment clichés. We lament absent-mindedness; yet the disregard for irrelevant stimuli and the capacity to ignore the trivial permit concentration on what is important. Many an "absent-minded" child is simply preoccupied with the sort of fantasy that helps lay the basis for creative productivity. We also praise "the complete child" who is "well-rounded." However, not only is the complete realization of a child's potential impossible; it may be socially undesirable. The selective development of a child's potential permits him to focus his efforts on those aspects of his potential which hold prospects of the greatest pay-off. Standards of emotional well-being are an individual matter, although everyone must establish a modus vivendi within his society.

Another error is to forget a child's age. Any specific behavior must be viewed in terms of the developmental pattern. In our culture, most children suck their thumbs for shorter or longer periods; and stuttering represents a disequilibrium in growth often found among growing children. For another instance, note that many children aged 6 to 18 months rock themselves to sleep, but few indulge in strenuous body rocking to the point of physical exhaustion. It must be determined whether a child's behavior is normal or unduly exaggerated for his age, and whether he is divorcing himself from it at a satisfactory rate. We may also inquire whether the culture itself needs readjustment. For instance, we consider a certain amount of night fear normal and almost inevitable—but is it? The substitution of stories that produce pleasant associations with darkness for certain frightening favorites about witches and goblins might help liquidate "normal" night fears within this culture.

Other problems occur simply as a result of growth. No child can escape the universal problems of development, such as learning to eat solid foods, or to sleep in a full-size bed. Nor can a child escape the necessity of adapting to continuous changes within his own body.

Often a child's maladjustment is a parental or sociocultural artifact. The parent holds the image of the ideal child in his own mind; and to the extent that Junior fails to approximate that ideal, the parent deems him maladjusted. Again, society may arbitrarily depict as mentally ill anyone who fails to fit snugly into the rigid confines of that society. A few years ago, a young man declared his desire to give up his American citizenship and become a world citizen. Another man gave away all his property. Both were popularly declared "nuts" in a society dedicated to patriotism and capitalism.

A major problem is that standards of adjustment are often imposed by the majority, whose claim to authority derives chiefly from their numbers. The concept of adjustment becomes a sort of social fantasy. Many great crusaders who have fought social injustice, like Florence Nightingale or Susan B.

173

Anthony, were adjudged maladjusted persons in their own times.

Actually, terms like "mental illness" and "pathology" should merely be used descriptively to connote failure to adapt to a particular time and place, rather than as a stigma on the person himself (Szaaz, 1961). For instance, a Navajo boy calls a robin's egg green, but he is neither color-blind nor ignorant. He is simply designating colors in the manner of his culture. When a Mexican boy says he has an angel whispering in one ear and a devil in the other, he is neither emotionally disturbed nor poetic. He is merely voicing his culture's expression of inner conflict (Witmer and Kotinsky, 1952). However, if the boy's family should move to Chicago, he would have to change such expressions or else cope with the general impression that he is "mentally sick."

In short, the usual concepts of normality have been too confining. The writings of psychiatrists and philosophers, as well as those of behavioral scientists, indicate that many distinctly different personality patterns must be judged as mentally healthy (Jahoda, 1958). Murphy and Murphy (1960, p. 213) lament "our often bleak, rigid, mechanical concepts of normality (or concern with the 'normal range') [which make] individuals feel self-conscious and embarrassed by relative weaknesses in one or more areas."

• FACTORS THAT MODIFY EMOTION

Biological Factors

Biological mechanisms. Underlying emotional behaviors are significant biological functions and mechanisms, including the brain centers, which help regulate feelings of fear and anger, aggression and submission. Certain cerebral operations can make cats so placid that it is impossible to anger them, while other operations can turn them into raging beasts (Bard and Mountcastle, 1947). Also important is the **autonomic nervous system,** composed of the sympathetic and parasympathetic nervous systems. The **parasympathetic system** is more concerned with the everyday, ongoing functions of the body; the **sympathetic system** becomes dominant in times of stress. At such times, the sympathetic system mobilizes the body for defense, a process that involves numerous reactions, including increased oxygen consumption and the release of energy-providing glucose into the blood. So long as the sympathetic system is dominant, the body's normal functions, such as digestion and elimination, are correspondingly depressed; but when the emergency is over, the normal sympathetic-parasympathetic balance is resumed. Ordinarily, no damage has been done; the process hurts the body no more than the occasional speeding-up of an automobile to avoid some obstacle hurts its engine. However, if stress is prolonged, and the sympathetic-parasympathetic balance too long upset, the biochemical processes involved work in ways injurious to the body. It may be said the body is equipped for hot wars but not for cold ones.

Biological influences. The specific influences of biology on emotion are unclear. However, several tentative findings from research have been reported. For example, Jones (1960) found that differences in emotionality among infants and children varied according to differences in functioning of the autonomic nervous system. Similarly, Block (1957) reported that children with a parasympathetic dominance manifested more emotional inhibition, less emotional excitability, a lower frequency of activity, and less fatigue; they also proved to be neater and more patient than children with a sympathetic dominance. However, a child's specific emotions are determined by his perceptions, which are learned. That is, a child may be prone to excitable reaction, but whether he will react at all to a strange dog will be determined by whether or not he perceives the dog as threatening.

Other studies demonstrate the glandular bases of emotion. For instance, when injected with epinephrine, or adrenaline, subjects feel more emotional; but this emotion may readily take forms ranging from euphoria to anger. In such cases, subjects report that their emotion seems not quite like the real thing (Schachter and Singer, 1962).

A third study, summarized below, supports the conclusion that biochemical differences predispose individuals toward more or less emotionality and affect the quality of their emotional experience. However, remember that learning inhibits or exaggerates emotional effects and even determines what sort of emotions are aroused and what stimuli will produce emotion.

In severe stress situations, students were insulted, harassed, and hurried by the experimenter. In one, they were asked to tell a story as rapidly and accurately as they could, but found themselves speaking into sonic confusers that relayed the sound of their voices to their ears after a fifth of a second. Whenever they stopped or slowed down, they received a mild electric shock. All the while, they were lying on their backs, strapped down by ballistocardiograph equipment used to measure the movement imparted to the body by the heartbeat.

The subjects showed three main patterns of response. The "anger-outs" reported feeling angry, irritated, or annoyed. The "anger-ins" indicated anger, but turned the feeling inward upon themselves. The "severe anxiety" subjects reported feeling panicky, frightened, and apprehensive. The anger-outs showed least difference in pre- and post-stress patterns, the anxious subjects the most, and the anger-ins somewhat in between. Both anxiety and anger-in states were accompanied by increases in the amount of epinephrine, or adrenaline, in the blood. Epinephrine stimulates metabolic activity, thus producing a faster heartbeat, muscle tension, and the like. The anger-outs released more nor-epinephrine (nor-adrenaline), a substance that does not produce much increase in metabolic activity and only slight physical disturbance.

The manner of emotional reaction also related to the manner in which the subjects had been reared. The anger-outs described their fathers as figures of authority, stern and difficult, often angry and seldom showing affection; their mothers had little authority but showed much affection and understanding. They generally admired their fathers, and described them as having the same sort of reactions as themselves. The anger-ins saw both parents as affectionate, and the roles of father and mother were not sharply contrasted. The anxiety group reported family relations in which the mother was the main source of authority and affection and the prime model for the child's behavior. Fathers of more than half of this group were missing through death or divorce [Funkenstein et al., 1957].

Hereditary bases. The simple fact of bodily involvement in emotion is no proof of its genetic origin. For instance, a child may have emotional outbursts because of extreme fatigue; but the fatigue may stem from prolonged malnutrition rather than some native organic weakness. However, considerable evidence does support the role of heredity in emotion. For example, studies of animals indicate that various breeds of dogs have distinctive patterns of emotional behavior.

The autonomic balance. Evidence suggests that each child has a characteristic autonomic balance, which remains fairly constant from year to year (Wenger, 1947). Besides, infants differ constitutionally in all sorts of ways that indirectly modify emotional patterns. For instance, females are more sensitive to pain than are males—a reaction that may contribute, at least subtly, to girls' feeling more threatened and insecure (Lipsitt and Levy, 1959). Also, infants who possess the most robust physiques, the best energy resources, and the smoothest vegetative functioning prove least insecure (Heider, 1966). Variations in stress tolerance, concludes Stagner (1961), reflect individual differences in function of the autonomic

175

nervous systems, striped and smooth muscles, endocrine glands, and miscellaneous biochemical processes.

The uniqueness of each individual's biochemistry has been further corroborated by Williams (1956). In a study of 10 "normal" young men, he reported one consistently below the acceptable level of blood sugar, another high on blood uric acid, and a third consistently below the normal range in serum amylase values. Some of the men showed high variability from day to day, others extremely little. The effects of these differences on emotion are still unclear. But in the long run, the differential sensitivity that causes a boy to react badly to family stresses that leave his brother unaffected may derive from biochemical differences. Williams' major contribution, says Stagner, lies in his systematic undermining of the concept of the "average" individual. There is no such thing, for not one of Williams' subjects possessed a biochemistry that even faintly resembled the hypothetically normal. It would seem to behoove authorities to spend less time on developmental stages through which all children pass and more on variations in sequence; less on uniformity of perceiving and more on distinctive ways of perceiving (Stagner, 1961).

Prenatal influence. Prenatal factors in emotion are unclear. Among newborn infants, Hauer (1914) found a positive correlation between the infant's frustration tolerance and the mother's, but not the father's. Since heredity would be equally determined by mother and father, the possibility of prenatal influence is suggested here. That is, the mother's emotionality, via the common glandular pool shared by mother and fetus, leads to increased emotionality, and presumably to reduced frustration tolerance in the neonate (Marquis, 1931).

The birth trauma. As noted in Chapter 2, the emotional effects of birth trauma are indirect, since the cortex is insufficiently developed to absorb distinct impressions. However, the organism sustains a tremendous shock, which in turn affects the infant's tension level. Bolin (1959) reported that infants whose birth processes were prolonged manifested more fears later on. However, this report is difficult to interpret, one complication being that prolonged birth may have colored the mother's attitude toward the child over the years.

Maturation. Not all genetic influences on emotion are manifest early in life. "Time genes" operate sequentially and in conjunction with experience to organize patterns of development. For instance, at puberty glandular changes preordained by heredity may result in heightened emotionality. Even more significant is the delay in maturation of cortical control, a process not completed until adulthood. Note that if an individual's frontal lobes are removed, his emotions lack depth and shift rapidly. Similarly, incomplete development of the cortical centers, especially the frontal lobes, probably accounts for the immature emotional behaviors of children (Bousfield and Orbison, 1952).

Nutrition. A physical factor of especial importance to emotion is nutrition, partly because it affects energy level. The child who lacks energy is prodded and scolded, and becomes depressed, irritable, and unsocial (Bell, 1958). Significantly, when nursery-school children are given fruit juice and regular rest periods, they have fewer emotional outbursts.

Emotional Patterns

Primary reaction patterns. Emotional patterns are both unique and persistent. In one study (Chess et al., 1960a), newborn infants demonstrated distinctive and enduring styles of reaction. Infants who reacted rapidly to loud sounds reacted rapidly as older children. While the nature of stimuli initiating reactions varied among the fast reactors, they had this fast style in common. The investigators identified five basic reaction patterns that

Children differ in their styles of emotional reaction.

played significant parts in the infants' emotional adjustment. One type of infant was nondistractible, with a high threshold of response. Children in this category would not be disturbed by stimuli that might impinge strongly on others. A second type demonstrated irregularity, nonadaptability, high intensity of response, withdrawal, negative mood, and high activity level. Such children are certainly predisposed to maladjustment (Chess et al., 1960b).

Children also manifest a somewhat constant capacity to deal with frustration. In one study, children were asked to perform a simple and boring task—

packing spools in a box. When a child demonstrated boredom with this task, he was given a similar task, packing blocks in the box. Shortly thereafter, the child was permitted to play with attractive toys, and then prevented by a barrier from playing with them. In the process, the children demonstrated great differences in capacity to stand frustration. Those unable to tolerate it became less constructive in playing with ordinary toys, and kicked at the barrier when the toys were removed (Block and Martin, 1955).

The same investigators also noted that such patterns tended to persist over time. In a longitudinal study, children manifested persistent tendencies to flee or fight. Girls aged seven and eight who consistently withdrew from anxiety-producing events continued to do so in adult life. Conversely, those who attacked obstacles retained the habit whenever crises arose during the years that followed (Kagan and Moss, 1962). The fact that certain traits, as reported here, are highly resistant to change, while others are more easily modified by experience, would seem to indicate varying ratios of hereditary and experiential factors.

Determining and dealing with emotional patterns. New situations, such as a child's first experience on the toilet or his first experience with solid food, often reveal identifying emotional patterns. If genuine reaction patterns exist, each child might be expected to react to all these experiences in an individually consistent manner. Chess and his associates (1959) found that this was indeed the case. However, the mere existence of such patterns is no proof of their innate character. Nevertheless, the researchers were inclined toward believing the patterns intrinsic rather than experientially determined.

To whatever extent practicable, children should be helped to recognize and live with their own special patterns of emotional reactivity. For in-

177

stance, the quick reactor must learn to "cool off" before he takes action. The "emotional child" might discharge his feelings in pursuing a photography project instead of just as energetically pursuing alley cats and abusing them.

The Impact of Childhood Experience

Now let us examine the ways experience affects emotion. A recent and still unresolved issue is this: What sort of infant experience proves functional for later emotional health? For some years, many clinicians argued that children must perceive their early environment as friendly if they are to deal confidently with future problems. In fact, it was assumed that the more painful or threatening experiences a child encountered early in life, the greater would be his tendency to respond with anxiety to frustrating or threatening situations in the future. Although this hypothesis has lacked any real test among humans, it has been supported by findings from animal research. For example, studies have shown that shocked rats tend to avoid shock later on (Finney, 1961).

Nevertheless, Hunt (1965) has argued that this viewpoint may lead to the overprotection of infants, a danger supported by certain recent research. In one study, infant rats, subjected to various stresses, but also handled by humans to give them body contact, failed to show any disturbance in adulthood (Levine, 1960). Infant rats that were not handled developed at a slower rate anatomically and physiologically, and were less tame and much more fearful. When placed in unfamiliar surroundings as adults, they cowered in corners or crept about cautiously, often urinating or defecating. This suggests that rats, and presumably other creatures, may only develop a capacity for handling stress if provided body stimulation in infancy.

In another study, in which dogs competed for a bone, normally raised animals dominated those confined to opaque cages for seven to 10 months after weaning (Thompson and Heron,

1954). Even in cases where the normally reared animals were younger, they proved dominant (Thompson and Melzack, 1956). As much as 10 to 12 months after their release, the restricted dogs still made more diffuse responses than the free-environment dogs (Melzack, 1954).

On the basis of the foregoing research, certain tentative conclusions seem justified. If an animal does not learn appropriate tension-reduction patterns in infancy, it may never acquire such behaviors as an adult. In other words, a long period of well-organized experience involving emotion-arousing stimuli is essential for the development of adjustive behaviors such as avoidance and aggression.

The incongruity-dissonance theory. The adaptive potential of early stress is sometimes explained in terms of **cognitive dissonance.** One of the clearest expositions of this theory is Hebb's (1959). The child may have no ready response for the new stimulus, says Hebb, because it differs too much from any prior experience. In other words, he lacks relevant cortical firing patterns as residuals of early experience. For instance, the individual who has been overprotected finds himself without relevant responses when confronted with problems. The gap, or dissonance, between response patterns that proved functional in early stress-free environments and those required for later stressful situations is too great. In effect, extreme anxiety seems to be the natural consequence of unusual incongruity.

Let us note one of the many studies that support this position. Levine (1956) compared the adult behavior of rats that had been shocked or petted daily for 20 days after birth with the adult behavior of rats left continuously in their nests with their mothers. Originally, he expected to find that the traumatic effects sustained by the shocked animals would be reflected later in heightened emotionality and in damaged capacity to learn adaptive responses. On the contrary, the shocked rats as well as the handled animals gained weight faster than those left in their nests. As a result of early experience, the shocked and petted animals had presumably acquired cognitive structures with which new receptor inputs would be congruous.

The incongruity-dissonance theory provides one explanation of infant anxieties — for example, the anxiety associated with the absence of the mother. According to the theory, this anxiety occurs simply because the child lacks cognitive pathways for readily dealing with the new situation.

However, the dissonance issue is not fully resolved; important questions remain to be answered. For instance, which sorts of stimuli may prove beneficial and which harmful for laying the bases for later adjustment? How may such stimuli be adapted to individual needs? How much stimulation is needed? There is always the danger of overloading, which lowers efficiency and induces irritability; in fact, in extreme degree it completely disorganizes behavior (Miller, 1961).

Trauma. Certain experiences, called **traumas,** are so shock-producing that no one denies their damaging effects. Early stresses are especially likely to leave their mark because children lack both the capacity for critical evaluation and the self-defenses to cope with the situation. Besides, early wounds, though apparently healed, may be reopened by later stresses, which otherwise would invoke a far milder reaction (West, 1958).

The effect of trauma on a particular child will depend on his perception of the situation. The child who has had little contact with his father may not be disturbed by his death. Moreover, what is traumatic to the adult may be viewed quite impersonally by the child, who feels no relevance to the situation. For instance, after Kennedy's assassination, children unthinkingly told such jokes as this one: "What did you get for your birthday, Carolyn?" "I got a Jack-in-box" [Wolfenstein, 1965, p. 67].

The following incidents, recalled from childhood, would seem of little consequence to most adults:

When I was about four years old, my parents took my brother and me to Coney Island. When I had to go to the bathroom, my father took me into a restaurant, and stayed at the counter, while sending me to the restroom. Completely confident, and armed with the nickel he gave me, I went in. The door, which reached to the ceiling, jammed, and I was locked in. I screamed and screamed, and finally the manager and my father came. Finally, someone had to come with a blowtorch to open the door. Today, sixteen years later, I still dislike going into elevators or any confined areas. (Male)

When I was eight, I was riding a horse when its colt was hit and killed while running across the road to join us. Ever since, I've been afraid of animals close to the road, and am extremely cautious about crossing streets. (Female)

The effect of trauma will also depend on the total impact, including frequency of occurrence. A certain amount of stress, if handled properly, may increase resistance to later stresses; but intense or too-frequent trauma may markedly reduce the child's capacity to handle later stresses (Denenberg, 1959). Similarly, animals given mild shocks during infancy manifest above-normal capacity for dealing with adult stresses, while others given more intense shock manifest excess emotionality and poorer learning ability (Gauron, 1964).

The child who experiences successive traumas may develop a pattern of heightened emotional response. In time, this pattern may become a generalized emotional state in which any stimulus related to some earlier tension-producing one may give rise to anxiety. This implies that a wide range of stimuli may acquire tension-producing effects. For instance, the child abused by his parents may later become terribly disturbed any time a teacher, policeman, or other authority figure speaks firmly to him.

179

Certain traumas, by their special character, have unusual effects. In one case, six Jewish refugee children, aged three, had been transferred from camp to camp before arriving at a country house in England. Since they had been mistreated by adults, and had found their only solace in each other, they felt an intense solidarity among themselves, and viewed all adults with suspicion and hostility. Toward the staff they behaved with cold indifference and active hostility. At times, the children would not even look up when staff personnel entered the room; at others, they would hit, bite, or spit on them. It took weeks of sympathetic help before they developed emotional ties with adults (Freud and Dann, 1951). Another instance of children's reaction to a traumatic event occurred in 1953, when a tornado struck the small city of San Angelo, Texas, causing 11 deaths, injuring over 150 people, and destroying or badly damaging 500 homes. Afterward, residents were interviewed, with special attention to children. The child's reaction was importantly affected by his own personality and his own family relations. In some cases, children's dependency needs were reactivated, causing them afterward to cling to parents and home. "They won't go anywhere without me," said one parent, "except to school. They didn't sleep well. They'd get up and ask me to sleep with them, and I would. . . ." Another parent said, "If the wind blows or there is a cloud, he shakes all over — just scared to death. . . ." Few victims, whether adult or child, required hospitalization for psychiatric causes. However, it was concluded that an indeterminate number of the children suffered a reduction in anxiety tolerance (Perry et al., 1956).

However, the child's personality or current condition may determine whether a serious emergency becomes an adventure or an ordeal. A child who is self-confident and otherwise emotionally healthy can sustain major traumas without apparent long-term damage.

Child abuse. Child **abuse** is usually defined as bodily harm done to the child. Cases of child malnutrition, starvation, or sexual misuse would not be so classified unless bodily harm was done.

For various reasons, genuine cases of abuse are hard to prove. Despite the problems involved in proving abuse, the bulk of evidence suggests that infants and young children may be brutalized, even killed, through the negligence or assault of their caretakers (Gwinn et al., 1961). In some cases, parents may simply overdo their discipline, not really meaning to harm the child. Even if they do mean to harm the child, they may attribute his injuries to other causes.

Obviously, parents who abuse children are seriously maladjusted. They may see the child as a burden, or as a competitor, who must be destroyed or at least made to suffer. Or they may intensely dislike the child for certain traits. Parents themselves may rationalize that children are their own private affair. In any case, the child reacts with various emotional symptoms, including bed-wetting, fire-setting, withdrawal, and truancy. The long-term effects are not known.

Unfortunately, the present status of the situation is not encouraging. The U.S. Children's Bureau has drafted a recommended wording for state laws affecting the abused child. This law would require that physicians and institutional authorities report evidence of abuse. Some states already have such laws, but objective guidelines for child protection have not been firmly established (Elmer, 1963).

Television and emotional health. One might facetiously suggest that the continuous and uncritical exposure of children to television is closely related to child abuse. However, authorities differ among themselves as to the effect of television on children's health, attitudes, and emotions. Schramm and his associates (1961) reported little or no evidence of harmful physical effects such as eyestrain, loss of sleep, or loss of energy. In the behavioral area, a Senate committee hearing on mass media in 1955 produced impressive evidence that criminal activities constitute one of television's central themes, and that the criminal is sometimes presented sympathetically and the law-enforcement officer unsympathetically.

Nevertheless, the meaning of relevant data is not clear. Research indicates that the amount of televiewing does relate directly to a child's heightened state of excitement. However, note that it is the shy, insecure, withdrawn child with few friends who watches TV most (Himmelweit et al., 1958). More frequent viewers also tend to have high levels of antisocial aggressiveness (Schramm et al., 1961). Maccoby (1964) concludes that highly aggressive or pleasure-seeking children may be more motivated to watch television; television then reinforces their pre-existing behavioral tendencies.

Considerable research has revolved around this issue: Does television reduce pent-up negative emotions by draining them off, or does it increase them? While the issue is so far unresolved, later in the chapter we shall see that the bulk of evidence is against the "drainage" hypothesis. Apparently, television does more to activate tendencies than to drain them off.

The Influence of Parents

Among primary-group or more intimate relationships, parental influence is by far the most significant in the child's emotional development. The family constitutes the child's rear echelon of defense in emotional skirmishes, and it neutralizes the trauma in his life. Altman (1958) found a consistent relationship between children's happiness, as rated by a psychiatrist, and their mothers' marital contentment. Similarly, Liverant (1959) reported that parents of children referred for psychiatric help were more maladjusted than parents of normal children.

In a study of preschool children, Lafore (1945) reported a consistent relationship between children's emotions and parental behaviors. Parents who dictated to their children received the most hostile reactions from them. Children of parents who blamed, hurried, punished, and interfered with their activities had the greatest tendencies toward crying, while children whose parents ignored them showed tendencies toward teasing and nagging. Children whose parents manifested least affection were rated least secure. Those who were frequently encouraged academically made the highest grades. Children most often cautioned scored low on resourcefulness. Children frequently threatened scored high on fearfulness. In brief, it would seem that parents simply reap what they sow.

Sullivan (1963) assessed the parental influence this way, where neurosis is concerned: An individual who passes from childhood to maturity with unresolved problems is still engrossed in solving them and behaves in childish ways. If the child is to attain emotional maturity, he must learn what to expect from others, particularly his parents, and must have a satisfying relation with them. Otherwise, the child engages in a form of anxious overlearning that prevents highly discriminative perceptions.

The overall pattern of child rearing appears especially significant. In one study, disturbed subjects had received more authoritative treatment and less approval than had healthy children (Kearsley et al., 1962). In another study, the parents of infants who cried excessively apparently wavered uncertainly between over-stimulation of the children and comparative neglect (Stewart et al., 1954). Emotional coldness proved especially dangerous, contributing to feeding problems, persistent bed-wetting, and high aggression (Sears et al., 1957). The following case represents not so much coldness as active hostility:

Since Ron continued to fall asleep in class, his teacher investigated. His

181

mother, who had "mental troubles," often became angry with him. She would shoot at him with a shotgun—but over his head, Ron said. One morning, when the school bus passed, Ron's mother was on a tractor chasing him across a field, shooting at him. All the teachers believed the situation deplorable, but no one would take any action.

At the other extreme, overprotection is equally harmful. The child cushioned against minor blows is crushed by a crisis. The overprotected child is encouraged to focus attention on himself (Banham, 1951) and also develops low frustration tolerance. He has had no experience with delay in need satisfaction or with denial of gratification. When he leaves the narrow orbit of his parents and teachers, he finds frustration wellnigh intolerable (Heyns, 1958). Bereft of his platoon of caretakers, he feels helplessly exposed.

The father's influence. The father's role in the child's adjustment has been so generally overlooked that it warrants special attention. In a study of children referred to a clinic, the fathers of children with conduct problems (hyperaggressive behavior) were weak and ineffectual; those of children with personality problems (shyness and inferiority) were dictatorial and unconcerned about them (Becker et al., 1959). In another study, the fathers' attitudes were found to be more intimately related to maladjustive tendencies in their children than were those of the mothers. The major finding was that harshness and aggressiveness in the fathers related to both sorts of problems in their children (Peterson et al., 1959). Here is such a case:

Mike, now aged 16, has just served a stretch in a training school for boys. Throughout childhood he was regularly beaten by his father, for no apparent reason. The father was a chronic alcoholic and the mother a heavy drinker. Mike always became particularly frightened when his father played with live hand grenades he had gotten in the war. At intervals, when his parents didn't want him around, Mike was placed in different homes. When his father got drunk, Mike rolled him for money, which was the practice his mother used to obtain funds for running the household.

Children's Roles and Adjustment

Age role. In case histories such as Mike's, we see how childhood adjustment influences adjustment at other age-stages. Often the progress of adjustment is predictable. For example, the child who holds his breath in infancy may have temper tantrums in early childhood and fits of sullenness or arguments during adolescence (Rosen and Gregory, 1965). Other age-related emotional patterns have been identified but not yet fully explained. In one study, adolescent adjustment was found to be inversely related to adult adjustment. Significantly, some of the individuals who seemed remarkably well-adjusted during adolescence appeared to be "brittle, discontented, and puzzled" at 30. On the other hand, many of those who endured strain-producing experiences during adolescence became well-adjusted, highly competent, and emotionally mature adults (Macfarlane, 1963).

For the great majority, emotional growth connotes cumulative integration and is probably not too reversible (Bloom, 1964). That is, the quality of emotional maturity appears to remain pretty consistent. Hence the establishment of proper foundations in childhood is crucial. The child who is moving in the direction of emotional maturity becomes more stably organized, and increasingly better able to resist and recover from disorganizing effects.

Sex role. Sex as a factor in emotion probably derives more from social sex roles and the stresses they produce than from inborn differences. Whatever the cause, it is worth noting that girls show more general stress and anxiety than boys, although there is a great deal of overlap in distribution between the sexes

(Pressey, 1957). Specifically, girls are more nervous, shy, anxious, and jealous, while boys are more aggressive and unruly (Jones and Burke, 1936). Moreover, psychiatric clinics see two or three times as many boys as girls, probably because boys are more prone to aggressive and delinquent behaviors.

Emotional differences characterizing the sexes vary somewhat according to age. Even at the age of two, however, boys are markedly more aggressive than girls, and girls more fearful (Hattwick, 1937). In a study of children in grades 6 through 12, girls were found to have greater fear of noises at night, being left alone in the house at night, walking along the edge of a cliff, nightmares, thunder, lightning, earthquakes, singing by themselves, and attending a music class (Tryon, 1939). In some cases, such as going down a dark street, boys showed a decrease and girls an increase of fear with age. Not surprisingly, such differences persist into adulthood. Women prove consistently more emotional than men when galvanomic readings are employed (Berry and Martin, 1957).

In general, it may be said that girls appear to adjust better before grade 5 and boys better after that. Apparently, our society's formula for sex development favors girls in early childhood and boys later on. At all ages, boys manifest more of the sort of problems that lead to clinic referral, including withdrawal and antisocial behavior (Peterson, 1961). The biological bases for sex differences in emotion are unclear. Some writers believe them due largely, if not almost solely, to cultural factors. Tryon (1939) ascribes such differences to differential sex roles and treatment by adults. Girls are taught to perceive the world as a more threatening place; and less is done to develop in them the ego strength or skills required to cope with problems. Instead, they are taught that they are the weaker sex and that males will take care of them.

Peer-group role. Also affecting the child's adjustment is his peer-group role; in fact, his relation with his peers is an especially good weathervane of his current emotional adjustment. In one study, one of the best auguries of adult adjustment was acceptance by peers in childhood. If a child is judged a problem by adults but is accepted by his peers, his chances for making a satisfactory adjustment are good (Roff, 1961).

Less Personal Influences

Sociocultural influences. Among the more diffuse, impersonal influences on children's emotions are culture and subculture. A given problem may not even develop unless relevant sociocultural factors exist. For instance, in certain primitive cultures, there is no truancy because there are no schools. In others, children suffer no conflicts over masturbation because the practice is sanctioned. Thievery occurs only in cultures with property rights. Where no such emphasis exists, as among the Kaingang Indians of Brazil, stealing is absent (Henry, 1947).

The sociocultural environment varies somewhat with the times, thus providing relatively better or poorer "climates" for emotional health. In one study, 4,457 children, aged 9 to 17, wrote essays on "Who I Would Like to Be Most (Least) and Why." Comparisons with similar studies dating back to 1901 indicated acceleration of today's children in the realm of practical intelligence but retardation in the ethical realm. This gap between practicality and ethical sensitivity helps explain certain children's proneness to succumb to conflicts (Englemann, 1962).

Physical environment. Physical features, either of community or home, affect the child's adjustment, although just how or to what extent has not been firmly established. Sheer noise, whether from factories round about or from too many children confined in the same small apartment, may prove irritating. The baby in the quiet environment whose needs are met consistently is less likely to suffer nervous tension than one among noisy, exciting surroundings (Lakin, 1957).

The aesthetic effect is even more subtle, but significant. In one study, the effects of a beautiful room (indirect lighting, mahogany furniture, paintings, and so on) were compared with those of an ugly room (a naked overhead bulb, straight-backed chairs, tin-can ashtrays, and so on). Subjects were placed in the rooms and then asked to rate the energy and well-being of faces in photographs. Neither the examiners nor the subjects were aware of the experiment's purpose. Subjects in the beautiful room ascribed greater energy and well-being to the persons in the photographs. Moreover, examiners in the ugly rooms were quicker to complete the tests. Observational data indicated that examiners in the ugly rooms experienced monotony, fatigue, headache, sleepiness, discontent, irritability, hostility, and a desire to avoid the room. In the beautiful room, they experienced comfort, pleasure, importance, and energy (Muntz, 1956).

• INTEGRATIVE EMOTIONS

Having examined various factors affecting emotions, now let us look at emotions themselves. The emotional reactions of the neonate are diffuse, representing varying degrees of excitement or quiescence. Gradually, as the child grows older, early diffuse states differentiate into a variety of emotions. Extremely little research has been done on children's **integrative emotions** — those emotions that produce a sense of personal satisfaction and harmonious adjustment — perhaps because adjustment has been treated largely in clinical settings. Nevertheless, we should not ignore them if we expect to maintain a constructive and not merely preventive approach. Two typical integrative emotions are generosity and sympathy.

Research proves that the child's desire to give is quite as important as his need to receive; and his generosity is neither the artificial product of teach-

ing nor the sheer desire to repay what has been received — that is, to liquidate a debt or get rid of a sense of guilt. The child may enjoy sharing as greatly as he does anything in life (Murphy and Murphy, 1960).

The child may also enjoy expressing sympathy, but rarely in very early years. In one case, children under three, when shown pictures of people with black-and-blue wounds, were unmoved (Murphy, 1937). In like vein, Landreth (1958, p. 228) relates this incident:

Recently in a nursery school a police dog entered the yard where the children's pet rabbit was nibbling the grass. The teacher rushed to the scene. Anxious to spare the rabbit and children an unpleasant experience, she quickly got the dog outside the gate. Immediately the boys gathered angrily around her. "We wanted to see what the dog would do to the rabbit," they complained. Looking into their faces, the teacher realized that had the dog turned on her, at least some of them would have watched the outcome with objective detachment.

Nevertheless, sympathetic behavior may be observed even in very young children. It may represent a child's desire to please someone else in the group, or it may simply constitute the projection of his own anxiety. In other cases, it may represent genuine warmth and friendship for a hurt or injured friend. Instances of adult sympathy, though more sophisticated, may stem from similar motives.

The following examples of various integrative emotions show that such behaviors need much more recognition and research so that they might be encouraged.

[Incident from a mother's diary revealing sympathy and confidence that good will prevail:] September 16, 1957. Read the boys the story of the three bears tonight for the first time. Mark loved the drama of it, and almost fell into the book sympathizing with the wee little baby bear whose porridge got eaten and whose chair was broken.

Little research exists on integrative emotions, such as wonder.

Steve assured us both that the mamma bear would make the baby bear some more tomorrow [Piucci, unpublished diary].

[Incident involving humor:] Frances began to pound on the painted newel post with her hammer and was asked not to do so. She then began to ask about one place after another:

"Can I hammer on 'at?"
"No."
"Can't I hammer on 'at udder sing?"
"No."
"Can I hammer on my han'?" doing so with a little grin [Woodcock, 1941, p. 251].

[Incident indicating wonder and awe recalled from childhood:] One day I wandered off alone and found myself before a high hedge that I had never seen before. It was so tall that I could not see over it and so thick that I could not see through it. But by lying flat against the ground, I wriggled between the privet stems.

I stood up, on the other side, in a field covered from end to end, as high as my head, with thistles in full bloom. Clinging to the purple flowers, hovering over them, or twittering and dipping in flight, were dozens of goldfinches — little golden yellow birds with black, contrasting wings and caps. They did not pay the slightest attention to me, as if they had never seen a boy before.

The sight was so unexpected, the beauty was so absolute, that I thought I could not stand it and held to the hedge for support . . . [Chambers, 1952, p. 117].

• DISINTEGRATIVE EMOTIONS

There is plentiful research on **disintegrative emotions** — the quality of feeling that produces personal dissatisfaction, disorganizes behavior, and in general obstructs healthy adjustment. Nevertheless, we shall be able to view the dynamics involved more clearly by concentrating on a few: fear, anxiety, guilt, aggression, and jealousy. All arise as a result of an individual's relationship to his environment, both interpersonal and physical, and all represent apprehensions of malaise and threat. Fear and anger are directed at a particular object, while anxiety is more diffuse and its cause not easily identified. Fear and anger are more sharply defined than anxiety and trigger action, whether withdrawal or attack, to cope with an immediately threatening situation. Anxiety is pervasive and more enduring in time, leaving its victim feeling helplessly exposed to a vague, yet unidentifiable threat. The anxious person knows something is wrong, but causal factors are either so intangible or so diffuse as to obscure the wise course of action. Inaction or vacillation is the inevitable result. Guilt, like fear and anxiety, typically involves withdrawal, although active efforts may be made to atone. Jealousy may have components of anxiety, guilt, and aggression. Hence it becomes evident that all these emotions are related, often blending with and overlapping each other.

Fear

"Normal" fears versus phobias. Let us now concentrate on **fears,** which may be classified as (1) normal, (2) disturbing but not extreme, and (3) intense, or abnormal. A normal fear suggests that the feeling of apprehension is appropriate to the threat involved. The child who is afraid when his clothes catch fire is hardly manifesting a pathological fear. A disturbing though not intense fear might be a fear of heights. The individual concerned does not get all worked up when riding along mountain roads, but feels quite uncomfortable, and avoids such experiences when convenient. In still other cases, fear develops out of all proportion to the threat involved and proves highly disturbing to the individual concerned, who is said to possess a **phobia.** Here are cases of normal fears, mild fears, and phobias:

[Normal fear:] I lived in a run-down neighborhood where there had been riots and gang wars. I was afraid to venture far, and mostly clung close to home.

[Disturbing but not extreme fear:] I dreamed of snakes and reptiles. They were always chasing me, but never caught me. I was even terrified to stumble on a picture of a snake in a book.

[Extreme or pathological fear:] When I was a child, there was a flash flood, and I ran into the yard to rescue the baby chicks. Some I rescued, others drowned. Since then I have had a terror of feathered creatures. Whenever a bird or chicken approaches me, I scream in terror and become paralyzed with fright.

Among the most serious childhood fears is school phobia, which affects about three pupils in a thousand. It is more prevalent in the primary grades and may be associated with a combination of conditions, including concern over being separated from an overprotective or dominant mother, pervasive feelings of inadequacy in peer-group situations, communication to the child of the mother's anxiety when he enters school, and traumatic events, such as being beaten up by the school bully (Leton, 1962).

How fears are acquired. Contrary to what many people believe, fears are not "inborn" or "instinctive." In one

"But being in the woods SCARES us! Goldilocks met the bears there, Red Riding Hood met the wolf, Snow White met the witch..."

Fears of young children often originate from mass media. Drawn by Bill Keane. Adapted from "The Family Circus," *The Philadelphia Evening Bulletin,* August 5, 1965. Used by permission of the Register and Tribune Syndicate.

study, only two out of 15 infants, whose average age was 15 to 21 months, showed definite fear of a six-foot harmless snake, although 60 out of 90 college students showed fear of the same snake even after being assured it was harmless (Jones and Jones, 1928). Fears are also commonly assumed to be acquired through conditioning, or association, a process illustrated by a now famous case:

Albert, a remarkably happy small boy, had rarely been seen to cry. After a number of tests had indicated that nothing but loud sounds and loss of bodily support would evoke fear responses in the child, an effort was made to condition in him a fear of a white rat — a fear he had never shown previously, because he had always manifested a liking for it. In the experiment, just as Albert's hand touched the white rat, a metal bar was struck behind the child's head. The boy was obviously startled, but he didn't cry. Again he reached for the rat, and again, just as he touched it, the bar was struck. This time the boy whimpered and jumped violently.

A week was permitted to elapse before further efforts at conditioning were tried. Then, on the first trial, the animal was presented alone without the sound. Albert reached for the animal hesitantly and, after just touching it, withdrew his hand suddenly. Several additional trials followed, each of these again accompanied by sound, and each time Albert exhibited startled response. On later trials, he whimpered or cried. Finally, the rat was again presented alone without the sound. However, the child began to cry immediately, and he turned and moved quickly away from the animal (Watson, 1926).

In effect, new objects come to elicit emotional responses which originally aroused no negative response. By a process of stimulus generalization, the child learns to fear more and more objects as his experience broadens. Children come to acquire many irrational fears in this manner, because they are acquired without conscious realization. For instance, a fear of inoculation may spread to white coats, and through generalization, to anyone in a white coat, such as a barber, or even to haircuts (Levy, 1960).

It might therefore be assumed that children could, through this process of association and generalization, come to fear almost anything. However, a psychologist who succeeded in conditioning a child to fear a caterpillar failed with opera glasses (Valentine, 1930). This experiment suggests that there is a hierarchy among emotional stimuli of emotion-arousing properties. At one end of the continuum are such stimuli as loud sounds and loss of bodily support, which elicit fear responses the first time they are presented. This is not to say that these fears are inborn; instead, the stimuli involved—such as falls, loud noises, or bites—are inherently tension-producing or unpleasant, or else somehow related to early experiences. For instance, the fear of loss of support may spring from the fact that the infant has always been supported, while the fear of loud noises may come from the fact that the infant is unaccustomed to them. Consider the case of noises louder than those typically heard but not so loud as to be painful. If from birth the infant has been exposed to increasingly louder noises, but never to the painful point, the above-average noise might never attain fear-eliciting properties.

Anyhow, certain objects apparently lack any tie-up either with prior experience or with biological bases of stress—such as opera glasses, toward which it is difficult, or perhaps impossible, to build fears. Finally, there are such objects as rats, rabbits, snakes, dogs, and caterpillars, which children can, with a few trials, be conditioned to fear. The nature of the stimulus, therefore, as well as the nature of the child, appears to play a definite role in determining conditioning effects (Ruch, 1953).

However, it is well to reserve opinion on the question of what items can become conditioned objects of fear. It may simply be that the children used in the experiments possess the sort of adjustment or past experiences that block the inculcation of such fears; or the processes of conditioning may be ineffective. Anyhow, many individuals report extremely strange fears. One girl had acquired a fear of bookcases because she once saw a movie in which the bookcase suddenly moved away from the wall and the murderer, with a gun in his hand, stepped forth (Rogers, 1957). What if the murderer, in this case, had had a pair of opera glasses in one hand and the gun in the other? Might not the girl have acquired a fear of opera glasses instead of, or perhaps in addition to, a fear of bookcases?

Influence of age on fears. Even within the same culture, children of different ages report somewhat different fears, probably because of differential experiences at different age-stages. The small child may fear witches because he has too little knowledge to distinguish real from imaginary. In one study, children aged four reported fears of animals and of the supernatural, but these fears were reported by very few adolescents (Pratt, 1945). In cultures where little scientific knowledge exists, however, a child will retain such fears. In another study, 80% of children aged five and six reported fears of one or more animals, especially snakes, lions, tigers, and bears. Sixty percent or more of children aged 7 to 12 answered similarly, but after age 12 such fears were rare. Oddly enough, children rarely mention certain objects they are taught to fear, among them traffic, germs, and kidnappers. Nor are they generally afraid of punishment, war, or the atom bomb, although the answer might be different if they were asked directly, "Do you fear . . .?" As children grow older, their fears become diverse, unique, and related to their personal experiences and concerns.

At any age, the results of questionnaires must be interpreted with caution. An answer may result from a fleeting mood, or some current, but unimportant stimulus. A passing hearse may elicit the answer "fear of death" in a child who actually has little such fear.

Fear and cognitive dissonance. Let us see how fear can be explained in terms of cognitive dissonance. For example, consider fear of the dark among children accustomed to night lights. In this case, fear need not imply some painful association with darkness; it may mean, rather, that the child has no ready cortical patterns for dealing with it.

Either of the following instances of fear could be explained in terms of cognitive dissonance because the children involved had no relevant experience for dealing with the situations.

> When I was about four or five, whenever I entered a room where there was a stuffed deer head on the wall, I ran from the room terrified. Finally, my mother got me to touch the deer head, so I could see it would not hurt me.

> When I was about five, I had my tonsils removed. When the nurses wheeled me into the operating corridor, leaving my mother behind, I became very frightened. The nurse attempted to quiet me by explaining the operation used, and showed me the instruments used. This frightened me all the more, so that it took the surgeons a while to quiet me enough to give ether. I still remember fighting the anesthetic, and I can picture the operating room.

A classic study by Jersild and Holmes (1935) also illustrates this point. It was arranged that preschool children could obtain toys only by going into a dark room and removing them from a chair near a woman dressed in a large floppy black hat and a long grey coat. Some of the children started immediately for the toys; others hesitated, but ultimately went ahead. Some would go only if accompanied by the examiner. Others refused to go at all. Hunt (1965) suggests that those children who were less fearful

had had greater experience with such situations previously. As a result, they had "cerebral circuits" that permitted them to accommodate to the new.

The incongruity-dissonance theory could also be used to explain the differentiation of fears by sex and social class. For instance, lower-class children report only half as many fears as upper-class children, and boys fewer than girls. It might be argued that children both of the lower class and of the male sex have had more painful experiences than their opposites, and hence adapt more easily to subsequent stresses.

Persistence of fears. Simply because children of different ages report somewhat different fears, it must not be assumed that time itself dispels fear. In some cases, a child may receive conscious and intelligent assistance in getting rid of his fear. In others, the passing years may simply involve the sort of experiences that ultimately permit the fears to dissolve. Otherwise, fears may, and often do, last a lifetime. In one study, two-fifths of childhood fears relating to personal failure, inadequacy, and ridicule persisted into adulthood (Holmes, 1935). Hence adults should never simply write off children's fears in the belief that they will outgrow them.

Effects of fear. Fear can have disturbing effects. For one thing, it is unpleasant. The fearful child is rarely self-respecting or respected. The Junior Milquetoast is a displaced person in children's rough-and-tumble world. Fear also acts as a brake on usable intelligence by narrowing the perceptual field. Suppose a child is extremely afraid of men teachers. He is so concerned over having a male teacher that he cannot "take in" his studies, nor the evidence that this particular male teacher is kindly. Again, consider the child who falls into the water, but is so disturbed that he can neither see nor hear the person on shore who is shouting instructions. The fearful child also suffers a narrowing of experience in areas related

189

to his fear. If he fears water, he avoids swimming, fishing, and canoeing. Furthermore, if he feels very insecure, and comes to perceive his environment as generally threatening, he will be less likely to initiate any new experience, whatever its nature. In such a case, even minor experiences can leave long-term effects, as indicated below.

> The earliest experience I can recall was looking out of my crib and seeing a coiled snake two or three feet from the crib. I lay there in terror, without moving, until my mother came in and turned on the light. The snake was a pair of black shoes. I am still afraid of snakes and of darkness.

Such traumatic experiences do not inevitably leave fears, especially on emotionally healthy children. Note this example:

> When I was seven, a mad dog bit me. Shortly afterward, some men with guns came along chasing it. A servant split open a live chicken and applied it to my arm "to draw out the poison." Over the next three weeks I had 21 antirabies shots in my stomach. But I developed no fear of dogs, partly because I had a a firm concept of myself as a fearless, adequate child. Also, I was very healthy, and perceived myself as a problem solver capable of dealing with my environment.

Prevention of fear. Since it is easier to prevent than to cure fears, it is wise to avoid their development. Fortunately, the present-day emphasis is on creating an emotionally healthy environment, as opposed to the rather grim, severe circumstances under which children grew up in colonial times. Take a single example — death. Today, children are helped to perceive death as the completion of a self-fulfilling life, with as few morbid overtones as possible. In Puritan days, death was often portrayed in somewhat ghoulish terms, as in these rhymes for children:

Child:
> Tell me, Mamma, if I must die,
> One day as little baby died,

And look so very pale and lie
Down in the pit-hole by its side.

Mamma:
> 'Tis true, my love, that you must die,
> The God who made you says you
> must.
> And every one of us shall lie,
> Like the dear baby in the dust [Taylor and Taylor, 1948, p. 60].

Here lie both the young and the old,
Confined in the coffin so small,
The earth covers over them cold,
The grave-worms devour them all [Taylor, 1948, p. 21].

To prevent fears from originating, several general principles should be followed. The child should be given such diverse experience that he learns to deal with many situations. This approach would seem especially appropriate if cognitive dissonance is in fact the basis for fears. Moreover, adults should manifest confidence in him, because his picture of himself as competent or otherwise reflects in large measure the attitudes of significant adults toward him. Finally, remember that sound mental health is the best general safeguard against developing fears.

Once a fear has developed, it is not wise simply to recommend that the child face whatever he fears. Perhaps he is not ready to deal with it, in which case his fear will simply be reinforced. The best approach is to make success possible so that pleasant associations may be established. Success is more likely if the child is taught techniques for dealing with the situation, and if he is encouraged to tackle it of his own accord. Finally, parents, especially the mother, should control expressions of fear as well as they can in front of their children. Typically, children look on their parents as pillars of strength, and are especially shaken when they betray fear. For example:

> Alice had a strong fear of mice and thunder, instilled in her by her mother. Whenever her mother saw a mouse, she would scream and jump on top of a chair or a table. And during thunderstorms, the mother would huddle all

the children together and sprinkle them with holy water.

Anxiety

Anxiety differs from fear in several respects. It is less clear in its feeling components, chiefly because it is a blend of many emotions. Fear ordinarily relates to a present situation that can be perceived, but the anxious child is often unaware of the cause of his malaise, which may result from past, perhaps forgotten, experiences. Moreover, anxiety is generalized, providing a feeling of intense discomfort and impending doom. The anxious person is like a broken-field runner, expecting to be tackled from all sides.

A child may demonstrate anxiety in various ways. He may go to sleep, even though he is not tired; or he may withdraw into fantasy, overeat, or revert to infantile forms of behavior (Broida and Thompson, 1954). His thinking is fragmented, and his behavior shredded with indecision. Typically, girls react by daydreaming and developing feelings of inadequacy, expressed in withdrawal behavior; boys, who consider anxiety unmasculine, compensate by acting rebellious or annoying (L'Abate, 1960).

Origins of anxiety. Many sorts of experience, especially within the family, may create reservoirs of anxiety. In infancy and early childhood, impulses to masturbate or to suffocate a new sibling may be blocked, leaving a residue of anxiety. The whole parental pattern may have some dominant characteristic—such as domination, over-indulgence, eroticism, or indifference—which gradually instills in the child a basic anxiety (Horney, 1955).

The parents' own adjustment creates an aura of either insecurity or security, which envelops the child. On anxiety scales, daughters and mothers show a consistently positive correlation. The son-mother scores show a lower relationship, but higher than between son and father. Since the girl is more often confined at home, and identifies more closely with the mother, she natur-ally reflects the quality of her mother's emotional states (Adams and Sarason, 1963). In short, the ways that parental influence may relate to the child's anxiety are endless. Murphy tells of a child who became very disturbed through hearing her parents talk of moving. Vague anxieties kept her disturbed. After about two months, Molly began to cry when prospective buyers began to look through the house, saying, "I don't want those people to live in my room" (Murphy et al., 1962).

Factors related to anxiety. Several factors relate to anxiety. Not surprisingly, unpopular children are more likely to be anxious than are popular ones (McCandless et al., 1956). Lack of success also leads to anxiety (Sarason, 1957). However, once a child has developed a generalized state of anxiety, any situation that somehow threatens his security tends to activate it (Lipsitt, 1958). Probably the most common variable disclosed in studies of anxiety is sex (Jensen, 1958); girls consistently experience greater anxiety than boys. Also, Negro children experience more anxiety than do Caucasian children (Palermo, 1959).

Positive and negative features of anxiety. Most authorities differentiate between normal and excess anxiety. Some anxiety is desirable, it is claimed, because it leads the individual to take sensible precautions against danger and encourages acceptable patterns of behavior. However, anxiety is essentially a negative and highly dangerous way to motivate the individual. It all too easily gets out of hand. Moreover, it is painful. Again, by narrowing the perceptual field, it prevents considering all aspects of a problem. It also leads to feelings of personal inadequacy, making a child susceptible to group persuasion. This is especially true of socially oriented anxiety, which is characterized by shyness, fear of ostracism, and low self-confidence (Walters et al., 1960). In conclusion, those who would deliberately instill anxiety in a child, whether for the purpose of motivation or for other reasons, should be fully cognizant of the harmful by-products of this emotion.

By way of illustration, let us consider anxiety as a stimulus to academic achievement—a long-standing source of controversy. In one study, high-anxious boys did less well academically and were more insecure with their teachers than were low-anxious boys (Sarason et al., 1958). By contrast, another study reported that boys scoring in the middle range of anxiety made better school marks than did those scoring at either extreme of the scale (Cox, 1960). The best learners, concludes Lindgren (1965), maintain sufficient anxiety to identify and respond to relevant stimuli; but they are not so tense that they do not respond at all.

The writer questions the virtue of debating which anxiety level constitutes the best academic incentive. The fact that students who possess moderate anxiety make better grades than those at either extreme of the anxiety scale is no argument for its desirability. The existence of moderate anxiety among a majority of moderately successful students may simply reflect the average teacher's failure to devise better means of motivation. Pupils with strong interest in what they do, and with the sort of ego-strength that requires standards, would probably do better work than any of the groups described above (Lindgren, 1965).

Dealing with anxiety. Foolproof formulas for treating anxiety are lacking. The literature on this topic is probably permeated with as much theoretical formulation as any other aspect of personality research. However, authorities agree on certain general principles. Children are not helped by being told there is nothing to worry about. If told there is no reason to feel miserable, they are simply confused.

Success in reducing anxiety ultimately hinges on discovering basic causes. In the process of this search, repression may prove to have been partial, so that causes are fairly easily uncovered, or it may prove so thorough that the individual concerned feels ill at ease, with no idea why. To whatever extent possible, causes should be eradicated. Professional assistance may sometimes be required; but in any case, the arrangement for manifold successful, pleasant experiences will help any child perceive his environment as warm and friendly, and will gradually reduce his reservoir of anxiety.

Guilt

The nature of guilt. The emotion of **guilt** must be viewed in the context of **conscience.** Conscience is a conditioned anxiety response—a sort of policeman that enforces the internalized standard by which an individual judges and controls his own behavior (Eysenck, 1960). Originally, the child simply introjects his parents' teachings, but the more mature individual, at least, gradually assumes greater personal responsibility for making judgments.

Meantime, if the child does not measure up to his standard, he feels guilty; that is, he experiences a negative self-evaluation. However, before guilt can develop, at least three conditions must exist: (1) the child must accept certain standards as right and wrong; (2) he must accept the obligation to regulate his behavior by those standards; and (3) he must have sufficient self-critical ability to recognize the discrepancy between his behavior and his internalized standards (Ausubel, 1955).

Guilt is to be contrasted with shame, which is a self-judgment derived from a negative evaluation by others, and which constitutes a self-depreciation in relation to the group. Guilt relies on internal and external sanctions, shame on external sanctions alone. Jimmy may have no guilt feelings about cheating, unless caught and punished, but he may feel ashamed when caught and reprimanded before the group.

The significance of guilt. It is often argued that guilt serves various important functions. For one thing, a child cannot be watched all the time—hence, the significance of the internal watchdog. Guilt constitutes a means of social control, because the child can be so taught that he assumes society's standards as his own, and will believe he is acting solely on the basis of personal reasoning. Guilt also protects the child against his own dangerous impulses—in psychoanalytic terminology, the id. Thus, no matter how much in need of money, the child does not rob the teacher's pocketbook, even when she leaves it in her desk.

However, the potential dangers of guilt seem far greater than its presumed values. It easily gets out of hand, so that the individual may feel guilty out of all proportion to his misdeed. Moreover, the individual's need to alleviate guilt may cause him to focus on his own misery, thus perceiving less clearly the effect of his behavior on others. When Janie drops her baby sister, she feels guilty. Might she not, without realizing it, have held the baby more carelessly than she should? To overcome her guilt, Janie caters to the youngster to an unwise extent. Actually, she has humored herself, by using the child to appease her own painful feelings.

The following incidents clearly reveal that guilt may arise from incidents both large and small, and may sometimes leave enduring effects:

> When I was about five, I was chasing a frog to get a better look at him, and accidentally rolled a rock onto him and killed him. I felt very guilty, because he had done nothing to me.

> When I was eight, I stole 39¢ from a toy store. I have felt very guilty ever since, and have never told anyone.

> When I was five, I stole a large balloon from a store, and told my mother I found it. But I worried that the police would come and get me, and I felt so guilty that I gave it to my little sister to satisfy my guilt.

A perspective on guilt. Unfortunately, guilt feelings are very common in Western society, and parents deliberately foster guilt in children when they err. Most psychologists follow the party line. They defend a measure of guilt as normal and even desirable as a stimulus to socially approved action. However, the writer believes that the virtues of guilt as a control of behavior have been overstressed and overrated. Perhaps guilt feelings may serve as a crutch, unless or until better controls can be developed, but they should be removed or dispensed with whenever and to whatever extent possible. Guilt feelings solve nothing; in fact, they can so confuse and immobilize the individual that no action, or the wrong action, may be taken. Guilt feelings cause a negative self-evaluation, which is unwholesome, and result in less constructive, less assured action. Far better is it to inculcate in children the sort of self-concept that will cause them to select behaviors they are proud to identify with themselves. At the same time, the individual should be helped to achieve the sort of emotional well-being and regard for others that will make him desire to do what is best for others. If he internalizes this standard, he will not need guilt to drive him to do "the right thing."

Hostility

Patterns of hostile behaviors. Unlike anxiety and guilt, **hostility** is active and seeks an object. Its expression is often stifled, however, and may take the form of fantasy, as when an unhappy young boy exclaimed, "If I had a locomotive I would rush down the street at 100 miles an hour and knock everybody over in a heap" (Kisker, 1964, p. 152). At other times, it is completely repressed and makes its presence felt chiefly in dreams. No other form of social interaction occurs more often in dreams (Hall and Domhoff, 1963).

The typical cause of hostility is thwarting, especially in infants, who respond with a diffuse, chaotic outburst.

193

The response is neither purposive nor directive but consists in crying and threshing about. Later, aggressive responses to frustration become less random and more purposive and retaliative. The child hits, kicks, or bites the frustrating agent. With increasing experience, the child discovers that an indirect attack is often more strategic than a direct one. Consequently, the child may hide or break his big brother's toy to retaliate for some offense.

Next in the sequence is a shift from the indirect physical to the symbolic level. Thus, with the onset of language, a verbal attack may be substituted for either direct or indirect retaliation. The boy calls his brother names or otherwise berates, him. The final shift in aggressive responses is to the indirect symbolic or verbal level. Instead of calling his brother names to his face, the child says things about him behind his back or casts aspersion by innuendo.

At any age, expressions of anger may be classified into two major categories: impulsive and inhibited. Impulsive expressions, commonly labeled **aggression,** consist of responses directed outward against a frustrating agent. Most such expressions are extrapunitive, or directed against others, although some are intrapunitive, or directed against oneself. The intrapunitive child becomes the victim of the anarchy of his own feelings.

Inhibited responses are those that are kept under control, or "bottled up." The child withdraws, removing himself from the offending object. Then he becomes apathetic, perhaps pretending to himself and to others that he is not disturbed. Feeling that resistance is futile, he conceals his anger rather than running the risk of counter-aggression if he attacks.

Here is the case of a boy who generally inhibited his anger but under provocation manifested impulsive hostility:

We had an old, wet-eyed female dog that used to follow me on errands to the village. One day the dog and I, going home, met one of my school-mates going to the store. By way of making himself agreeable, he kicked the dog in the stomach. Then he went on.

My first reaction was stunned astonishment that anybody would do such a thing to an animal. My next was anger, which, as usual with me, mounted very slowly until there was little else in me but anger. I sat down on a stump . . . and waited for the boy to come back. I waited some time. When he reached me, I got up and slapped his face. Then I waited until he put down his mother's groceries, then we fought. The battle ended when I punched his vulnerable nose. The blood ran down very satisfactorily and he began to blubber. My anger was gone. I felt only regret. I helped him pick up his bundles and tried to comfort him. He shrugged me off [Chambers, 1952, p. 114].

Foundations of hostility. Among environmental factors that affect children's hostility, family influences are crucial. Note, for example, how the child's status in the family relates to his emotional pattern. Boys with girl siblings, only children, and babies of large families all tend to use impulsive forms of aggression, while children who need affection and attention more often use inhibited expressions of anger (Levin and Sears, 1956).

Another familial factor is the form of control and punishment. In general, extremes of either permissiveness or punishment correlate with high hostility. In such cases, young children typically act overly hostile. Older ones, when harshly punished, tend either to repress their hostility or to express it quite aggressively. Among boys, even medium punishment can generate hostile feelings (Hoffman, 1960).

The overall pattern of child-rearing may tend either to increase or reduce hostility. Interparental inconsistency in dispensing punishment relates to higher crime rates, and erratic discipline by either parent to heightened hostility in the child (McCord et al., 1959, 1961). On the other hand, certain forms of child-rearing have the reverse effect. The way to produce nonhostile children, says Sears (1957), is to make crystal clear that hostile and aggressive behavior is frowned upon, and to stop it, but to avoid punishment. Either tolerance or severe punishment makes children angry. In summarizing several studies, Becker (1964) suggests that internalized reactions to hostility in the form of guilt or the acceptance of responsibility for misdeeds will be more likely to occur if the child feels that the parent's love has been withdrawn.

Another factor determining hostility is the sheer weight of frustration. At any given moment, the tendency to repress anger or to release it hinges on what has gone before. If the child has been frustrated time and again, a very mild stimulus may trigger a reaction.

Many factors limit the modes of counter-aggression a child may use when punished. Boys, more often than girls, fight successfully against restrictions imposed by their mothers. Girls often react with hostility toward their mothers as much as boys do, but with less success. Girls are also more likely to inhibit hostile feelings in the classroom (Sears et al., 1957). Severely punished children of either sex may generalize their hostility toward parents or all persons in authority; but feeling powerless against adults, they find scapegoats among weaker peers on whom to vent their pent-up anger (Siegel, 1956).

Sex differences in hostile reactions are large—this being the single most thoroughly documented finding on the topic of child hostility (Buss, 1961). Parents make a sharp distinction in handling their sons' and daughters' aggressive behaviors. Any overt aggression on the part of the girl is strongly discouraged. Boys are permitted more chance for aggression, though not permitted to fight with brothers and sisters. To many mothers, being boylike means being aggressive (Sears et al., 1957).

In consequence, the sexes express their hostility differently. Boys characteristically act out their destructive impluses, while girls repress them. In consequence, girls express anger in somewhat inhibited forms such as crying, daydreaming, or making critical remarks, while boys employ more direct forms, especially physical assault. When girls make a direct attack, it is usually in the form of ridicule or scolding, rather than physical attack (Sears and Sears, 1951).

Whatever the form of hostility used, the girl is more likely to feel anxiety afterward, especially in late childhood and thereafter. By then she is feeling the pressures to become ladylike (Sears, 1961). She has also identified with her mother, which encourages the inhibition of hostile impulses. Moreover, having introjected the mother's values, she is self-punitive when the mother reprimands her. In short, the girl's impulses become converted into avoidance behaviors, guilt, and somatic symptoms.

The drainage hypothesis. Let us now illustrate the so-called **drainage hypothesis,** which is frequently applied to hostility, although its principles would also apply to other emotions. This hypothesis implies that the venting of antisocial impulses in safe ways will reduce the need to assert them in undesirable ways. When under stress, the body mobilizes its defenses, and the physical concomitants involved upset bodily homeostasis unless some sort of emotional release can be found. When it is not possible to release tension directly, the body is cleared of pent-up energy in some alternative fashion, a process called **catharsis.** Dorothy Baruch (1949, pp. 38–39), a major advocate of the catharsis theory, asserts that "when pus accumulates and forms an abscess, the abscess must be opened and drained. If it isn't done, infection spreads. Just so with feelings, the 'badness' must come out."

The form of catharsis is important; for example, strenuous physical activities may only temporarily reduce tension, although they may limit its injurious effects. Other types of release experience relating directly to the behavior areas involved may have more direct effects. If the child is having trouble with a sibling, doll play therapy, in which dolls represent the child's family, may be helpful. Instead of smothering his baby sister, Tommy "kills" the infant doll, thus effecting a drainage of hostility and reducing the need to smother his baby sister. Thus release therapy uses the child's play as an instrument for expressing his destructive wishes. The play therapist is permissive and accepting while actually interpreting little of the child's behavior (Maslow and Mittelman, 1951).

Advocates of release therapy admit that catharsis may be inadvisable in some cases, as in long-term frustrations, perhaps involving a broken home or chronic friction within the family. In such cases, the instigation to aggression persists, and release could have only temporary value. The apparent improvements following the release experience might prevent recognition of the need for more basic measures.

In other words, advocates of the drainage hypothesis make no claim that letting off steam will change the child's point of view or remove the source of stress. They liken the process to treating digestive disorders. When the body is poisoned through failure to rid itself of waste products, a laxative will purge the body, and the individual will feel better temporarily. However, unless the factors blocking elimination are identified, he will shortly feel uncomfortable again.

The reinforcement hypothesis. A counter-theory, the **reinforcement hypothesis,** holds that the unleashing of a specific emotion can either increase or decrease its expression in the future, depending on the consequences. In other words, if an act of aggression proves tension-reducing, it will probably be repeated; if tension-producing, it will tend to be repressed, suppressed, or diverted into some other channel. For instance, if the child fights and wins, he will probably fight the next time he becomes frustrated; but if he loses, his tendency to fight later on will be correspondingly reduced (Berkowitz, 1958).

The bulk of empirical evidence thus far supports the reinforcement hypothesis. In one experiment, preschool children exposed to aggressive models reproduced aggressive behaviors resembling those models (Bandura et al., 1961). Note, too, that fathers who are punitive and less emotionally inhibited tend to have aggressive, rather than withdrawn, sons (Bandura and Walters, 1963). Also, Lovaas (1961) reported that the mere exposure of children to film-mediated aggression apparently stimulated hostile behaviors. Mussen and Rutherford (1961) found similar results. They used two matched groups of children, one of which saw an aggressive cartoon. Afterward, when each child in both groups was invited to play with and pop a large yellow balloon, children who had seen the cartoon proved far more likely to break the balloon. In still another study, children listened to stories and records with aggressive themes and played with objects such as guns, chosen to stimulate the expression of aggression. Observers failed to note any overall decrease in aggressive play, as the drainage theory would have predicted (Feshbach, 1956).

In short, it seems that aggressive experience is more likely to enhance than to reduce subsequent aggression. However, several points remain to be considered. Perhaps aggressive release to some point, or with some children, may prove helpful. The inhibited child, especially, may profit from aggressive incentives that would overstimulate an already excitable child. Moreover, the form of release is important. Perhaps certain forms of aggression-release might prove hostility-reducing, others hostility-enhancing. Thus far, experiments have been too superficial to justify sweeping conclusions, especially for individual children.

Jealousy

Another emotion often arising from children's interpersonal relationships is **jealousy**. A child is jealous when he feels envious of another who possesses something he himself desires. This emotion often occurs in conjunction with feelings of inferiority and anger. A child may be jealous of a favored sibling, or of a playmate who has nicer toys.

Jealousy is more common among girls than boys, and among more intellectual than less intellectual children. It is also more common among children who are less sure of themselves or who are less favored in terms of looks and ability. Or it may arise from age difference, the older child resenting the attention accorded the younger one, or the younger child resenting the greater privileges of the older one.

Reactions to jealousy. Children's reactions to jealousy vary greatly. A child may assume a proprietary attitude toward someone whose affection he desires, and become angry if this individual pays attention to someone else. Another child, finding himself unable to compete, may withdraw from direct competition, yet find some indirect way to hurt his rival. Ten-year-old Dinah resents Joan, whom she believes to be the teacher's pet. Joan has everything Dinah desires — pretty clothes, plenty of spending money, and popularity. Dinah herself is unattractive and unpopular, and says unkind things about Joan whenever she gets the chance. Other children simply feel sorry for themselves, and retreat into fantasy, where they always come out on top. Bobby, who is constantly snubbed by the star athlete of the neighborhood, daydreams of fighting him and emerging the victor, while the vanquished ex-hero slinks home in shame.

Reactions to jealousy may be direct or indirect. Young children, especially, may physically attack the rival by hitting, kicking, biting, or scratching. The attack may be so severe that it poses a real danger, partly because children have little concept of how much harm they may do. Joey may impulsively grab a pair of scissors and throw it at a sibling, putting out his eyes. Terry may throw the baby to the floor or smother him.

Indirect reactions to jealousy are more common, perhaps because they help avoid guilt feelings or punishment. A child may suck his thumb or wet his bed. He may be generally naughty and destructive, or resort to tale-bearing and name-calling. Sometimes he displaces his hostility, venting pent-up feelings on the family pet or smaller children. In such cases, it is not easy to identify jealousy (Jersild, 1960).

Jealousy among children may take many forms, as illustrated here:

> Seven-year-old Sandra was extremely fond of her father, and would become extremely jealous and "throw fits" when she saw him kissing her mother. The father died, and the child did not even want to live with the mother. The feeling persisted even into adulthood, and after the stepfather died, Sandra put her mother into an old people's home.

> Mr. Jones presented his wife a parakeet on her birthday, and the wife spent many hours teaching the bird to do things. After a few months the son, a three-year-old, broke out in a rash. Getting rid of house plants and providing a special diet did no good. However, when the bird was disposed of the boy speedily recovered. It was conjectured that the boy was jealous of the bird, and that his jealousy had precipitated the allergy.

Assisting the jealous child. If the jealous child is to be helped, he himself must be made to feel secure. He must receive his share of attention and affection. Every means must be used to give him satisfying experiences, to divert attention from himself, and to build his ego. When he believes in his own worth, is convinced he is loved, and leads a full

197

life, he will have little reason to envy others.

• PSYCHOSOMATIC DISORDERS OF CHILDHOOD

In past centuries there was little recognition of the part emotions might play in children's physical disorders. For example, in the fifteenth century, enuresis, or involuntary wetting, was treated wholly in physical terms.

Of Pyssyng in the Bedde

Many times for debility of vertue retentive of the reines or blader, as wel olde me as children are oftentimes annoyed, whan their urine issueth out either in theyr slepe or waking against theyr wylles, having no power to reteine it whan it cometh, therfore yf they will be holpe, fyrst they must avoid al fat meates, til ye vertue retentive be restored againe, and to use this pouder in their meates and drynkes.

Take the wesande (traches) of a cocke, and plucke it tha breanne it in pouder, and use of it twise or thryes a daye. The stones of an hedgehogge poudred is of the same vertue.

Item the clawes of a goate, made in pouder dronken, or eaten in pottage.

If the pacient be of age, it is good to make fyne plates of leade, with holes in them and lette them lye often to the naked backe [Thomas Phaer, as quoted in Rührah, 1925, pp. 185–186].

The pendulum has swung so far in the other direction that now we are likely to go to the other extreme, ignoring biological factors and explaining all sorts of disorders, including enuresis, in largely situational terms. Actually, specific disorders may be due largely to **genogenic** (hereditary) or to **physiogenic** (physical), or to **psychogenic** (mental and emotional) factors, or to varying combinations of these three, depending on the individual case. The relationship between physiogenic and psychogenic factors is reciprocal. Good physical health promotes sound emotions and vice versa. The chroni-

cally ill child is more likely to be unhappy; and unhappiness will make the sick child feel even worse.

The relationships between mind and body suggest the term "psychosomatic"; for psychosomatic symptoms are bodily manifestations of psychogenic origin. Traditionally, **psychosomatic illness** has connoted any emotional disturbance that results in somatic dysfunction in organs controlled by the autonomic system. However, mind-body interaction is so pervasive that psychosomatic medicine is coming to concern itself with all aspects of the personality-illness relationship.

Varying combinations of genogenic, physiogenic, and psychogenic factors determine the nature and location of somatic complaints. There may be an inherited or acquired weakness in a specific organ. For instance, the child may be predisposed to suffer from asthma because of bronchial structure. Or the specific manifestation may result from life experience. According to Grinker (1953), the frustrated infant functions with everything it has, including crying, salivating, regurgitating, defecating, and becoming red in the face. To cope with the situation, parents use arsenals of special diets, laxatives, enemas, and medications, which tend to subdue some functions and overload others. Thus, through conditioning, protective reactions become individualized. For instance, if the parent concentrates on special diets, at the same time manifesting great emotional concern for the infant, future stresses may automatically arouse gastric reactions.

Treatment of Psychosomatic Illness

First, a physical examination is indicated to determine whether an illness is psychosomatic or organically based. Even if the disorder is largely psychogenic in nature, medical treatment may be needed. For instance, neurotic-like symptoms may arise from serious malnourishment, which may require special diets by the doctor, as well as advice from a psychiatrist. However, the child's symptoms of apathy, depression, and irritability — all concomitants of prolonged malnutrition — may have become so thoroughly habituated as to require psychotherapy.

The child may simply need help in releasing and dealing with repressed emotions. Marked help may be achieved by freeing a child's blocked impulses, such as the hypertensive's simmering anger or the asthmatic child's desire to cry. However, the only enduring cure derives from locating and treating the basic causes of stress, which often lie so deep that professional help is required. For instance, a child who began having spells of nausea proved to have a deep-seated fear of her school teacher.

Treatment of psychosomatic illness in childhood is especially important. For one thing, such disorders, once habituated, tend to persist and to become reactivated whenever the individual is under stress. For another, long-established psychosomatic patterns are hard to cure, and children respond to treatment more readily than do adults. Again, physical difficulties, whether physiogenic or psychogenic in nature, have a correspondingly greater effect on the growing child. Until eliminated, psychosomatic symptoms are signposts indicating that the child's adjustment is askew, at a time in life when basic personality patterns are being formed.

• EMOTIONS AND MENTAL HEALTH

The Extent of Emotional Problems

The incidence of emotional problems, especially among children, is still unknown. If, as assumed, adult adjustment reflects child experience, we may gain some idea from statistics for adults. One study estimated that 8% of college students require psychiatric help each year (Funkenstein, 1959). In a densely settled section of Manhattan, about half the adult population was judged to be

in some psychiatric difficulty (Srole et al., 1962). Only 18% were considered really well. During World War II, about 6% of the selective service registrants were so seriously disturbed that they were rejected for military service.

Among children, severe maladjustment apparently reaches about the same proportion. In the public schools, says Kaplan (1959), about one child in 12 may be regarded as severely maladjusted. In another study, three children were adjudged emotionally disturbed in the average classroom in grades 4 through 6, and emotional disturbance increased with grade level (Bower, 1957). It is also wise to recall the unknown legions of children who linger in the twilight zone between fairly adequate and exuberant emotional health. We must not confuse the child who manages to keep his head above the water with the vigorous swimmer.

Subcultural variations in adjustment. Adjustment differs vastly among subgroups. For example, twice as many 10-year-old children in Israel expressed pessimistic responses as did children in a comparable group in Michigan (Rabin, 1959). The Israelis were also more suspicious of their friends. Among the phrases the children were supposed to make into sentences was this one: "When I'm not around, my friends . . ." The Israeli children more often gave negative responses, such as "Call me names," while the Americans more often gave positive ones, such as "Look for me."

Again, consider the Hutterite sect, an isolated rural group of Canada and South Dakota. They stress religion and internalize their aggressive drives. Both children and adults develop strong guilt feelings and depression. However, the adults manifest little schizophrenia or antisocial behavior (Weil and Eaton, 1955).

A perspective on the magnitude of mental health problems. Any interpretation of this data must be qualified, since

199

for many cultures we have no figures at all, and for none are they highly reliable. Such figures as we have are hard to interpret. When a child is reported as maladjusted, how extreme is the condition? Moreover, estimates of maladjustment, often based on referrals to clinics, are misleading. To quote Kanner (1957):

> The high annoyance threshold of many fond and fondly resourceful parents keep away from clinics and out of reach of statistics a multitude of early breath-holders, nail biters, nosepickers, and casual masturbators, who, largely because of this kind of parental attitude, develop into reasonably happy and well-adjusted adults. But, in clinic statistics, these same symptoms, figuring among "the traits" found in the histories of "problem children," are apt to be given too prominent a place, far out of proportion to their role as everyday problems or near-problems of the everyday child.

Finally, the magnitude of the mental health problem would attain vast proportions if it included those large numbers who exist in the shadowy realm of passable but not excellent adjustment. Subclinical conflicts and anxieties undoubtedly snuff out or lessen the potential of innumerable children, causing them to live the rest of their lives somewhat uncomfortably and ineffectively. Lesser problems, in the aggregate, sentence them to a life term of less-than-major but nevertheless crippling fears and inadequacies. They may never commit suicide, but they probably wallow in orgies of worry and self pity.

Individual Solutions

The problem-solving approach. The ideal way for a child to reduce tension when goals are blocked is through **problem solving.** In problem solving, one takes rational steps to overcome obstacles; or if he perceives they cannot be removed, he finds other satisfactions. When Susie first moved into the community, she sought to win friends by

impressing them with her importance. When she found herself rejected, she tried another, sounder device. She dropped her artificial behaviors and invited the girls to her house, where they had a good time. Probably, she did not reason out her course of action in the manner of adults; nevertheless, on her level, she achieved success through actively rejecting one approach for another.

Sometimes, as in the following case, children's efforts at problem solving are ingenious but inappropriate, because children often lack the experience necessary for making proper judgments.

> Trudy had heard her parents discuss selling the house, and, as a result, became quite disturbed. Finally she devised a plan for solving the problem. She smeared mud all over the freshly scrubbed front porch. When asked why she did it, she replied, "Well, you said no one would buy the house if it wasn't pretty, so I put mud on it so it wouldn't look pretty" [Murphy et al., 1962, p. 72].

Ego-defensive mechanisms. Like Trudy, children in general feel constrained to ease their tensions as best they can. If a rational solution is lacking, they seek alternative ways, collectively called **ego-defensive mechanisms,** to reduce their tensions. To paraphrase Cameron (1947), these are habitual methods (other than direct attack on, or simple withdrawal from, the frustrating object) of circumventing, overcoming, avoiding, escaping from, or ignoring frustration, in order to reduce the tensions of anxiety, suspense, thwarting, and conflict.

One of these mechanisms is **repression,** which, strictly speaking, means not dealing with the problem at all. If the child who uses the problem-solving approach withdraws, he knows what he is doing and has chosen withdrawal as the wise course of action. However, the child who represses is unaware that the problem exists. He simply excludes from his consciousness thoughts that are too painful to bear. For instance, a girl who has been taught that sex is wholly evil is molested by an uncle. After several weeks of acute terror and anxiety, she "forgets" the whole incident, partly by avoiding anything that might constitute a reminder.

If repression protects the ego from anxiety, why is it not an adequate solution? The girl who was molested no longer worries about it. However, in avoiding situations that would reinstate her anxiety, she is doing nothing to resolve a basic conflict—her desire to marry as opposed to her anxiety that sex is bad and men fearsome creatures. Later on, if she does marry, she may view sex relations with loathing, perhaps never understanding why. Moreover, repression is rarely complete. Repressed thoughts subtly creep into gestures, words, and behaviors. In this case, the girl probably shrinks from people who tell sex jokes or quickly changes the subject when the topic comes up.

Another escape technique is **fantasy,** or wishful imagination. It is not necessarily bad. It makes frustration bearable; and the child who finds consolation in daydreaming is less likely to commit a rash act. Coleman (1964) tells of the child who imagined he owned a tame lion, which he could control but which terrified everyone else. This fantasy was of extreme importance to the child and had assumed endless variations. The lion was his constant companion and support. Similarly, a lonely child, or an only child, may have a daydream companion who is with him at all times.

While a certain amount of fantasy is completely normal, and even desirable, excess fantasy is a symptom that the child is finding inadequate satisfactions in his small world; and by daydreaming, he delays solving his problems. Instead of creating an imaginary lion, a weak boy might better spend his time developing his body and thus eliminating the cause of his tension.

Still another form of evasion is **regression,** which means retreating to more childish ways of behavior, or behaving in a more primitive manner. When other boys tease him, Johnny throws a tantrum and rages at them uncontrollably, in the manner of a wrought-up two-year-old.

Regression is common among young children.

Regression is often observed in young children. When the infant is learning to walk, he often regresses to crawling when tired. Even animals regress. Bear cubs and young chimpanzees suck their toes when they are scolded or neglected.

Whether regression represents simply a return to previously learned patterns or the destructuring of behavioral organization (**primitization**) is uncertain. Lewin (1937) states that people under stress "regress" to a more primitive level. Primitization, in this sense, does not represent "regressing" to previously learned habits; it represents a destructuring of the personality due to frustration. Destructuring occurs when behaviors become less unified and organized, less under conscious control and more subject to repressed needs and impulses.

In a classic study, children aged two

201

to five were separated by a wire screen from toys they had previously played with. The children were provided with less attractive toys but could easily see the forbidden ones. As a result of the frustration, behavioral ratings indicated an overall regression in constructiveness of play. On the average, the children four and a half years old regressed to the 22 months level in constructiveness of play, and the children of two and a half to the five months level. The amount of regression was related to the strength of frustration (Barker et al., 1941).

Regression is not wholly bad and may serve a useful purpose. There is a certain release, often harmless, brought about through acting immaturely at times. The big boy may gain some harmless release through rolling on the floor with his baby brother. After a scuffle with the other boys, he may somewhat shamefacedly seek a hug from his mother. That is, as long as regression is used consciously, not too often, and in restrained ways, it may be helpful. However, when used habitually, it is unfortunate. Basically, it represents a retreat from reality; moreover, it can make the child ridiculous before his peers.

An especially common mechanism is **rationalization,** in which a person uses false but logical-appearing reasons to justify his acts both to himself and others. To keep from facing the truth, he often convinces himself these are the real reasons. Sammy thinks he failed because the teacher didn't like him, not because he neglected his work.

Sometimes we need to save face with ourselves until we have the ego-strength to face up to our weaknesses. However, rationalization easily becomes habituated as a way of dodging realities that cry out for attention. Emma believes that her classmates reject her because her folks belong to a minority group—something she can do nothing about. Actually, she is disliked because she is crabby—something she has not had to face up to, because she has found another reason for the rejection.

Instead of escaping his problem, a child may make some sort of compromise. If he cannot gain a specific goal, he settles for a substitute. When Lester fails to become gang leader, and becomes the leader's lieutenant, he has coped with disappointment through **substitution.** Other forms of substitution are more indirect and sometimes unhealthy. The unhappy child who has failed to find anything to interest him may listlessly sulk, while biting his nails, picking his nose, or pulling at his skin (Kisker, 1964).

Substitution may sometimes prove quite sensible, as when the child who failed to receive the toy he wanted "makes do" with another one. However, a child may form the habit of relinquishing any goal as soon as he meets an obstacle and settling for a lesser one. Consider the child who abandons projects in the school shop whenever the going is hard. On the other hand, some children unwisely persist in pursuing goals long after the prospects for success have faded.

One form of substitution is **compensation,** in which an individual tries to make up for some real or imagined deficiency. Tommy compensates for his very small size by boasting and swaggering. Some forms of compensation are healthy, especially when they lead to the development of strengths that otherwise might be ignored. Roy has a club foot and hence cannot earn self-esteem on the playground; but he is good at school work and works long hours. This solution is good, unless he overcompensates. Dominated by his goal to lead the class, he may resort to cheating when a new boy arrives and threatens to outshine him.

If an individual substitutes a socially unacceptable behavior for a socially acceptable one that fulfills the same need, the mechanism is called **sublimation.** A very active child who has worked off excess energy by picking on younger children may divert his extra energy into constructing some project. The boy who bullies younger boys to gain prestige may gain even more status by leading them at games.

Miscellaneous ego-defensive behaviors. Actually, all sorts of behaviors may be used in ego-defensive fashion. Note, for example, the following:

Lanny had had a dozen minor accidents in his eight years, including accidentally killing two pet birds, bruising his penis on a rocking horse, and suffering numerous cuts and falls. He was fearful, enuretic, prone to having nightmares, and retarded in school. His most frequent defense, except for flight, was identification with the aggressor, such as growling like a lion [Kessler, 1966, p. 349].

As a child I had two beautiful English setters that I loved more than anything else in my life. However, when my older brothers picked on me, I would use the dogs for punching bags [the mechanism of scapegoating]. Then I would feel terrible, and hug them, and feel ashamed of myself [from the author's files].

Eight-year-old Nancy was prone to daytime wetting and soiling; but her friends had been cautioned to say nothing about it. Once, when she attended a Girl Scout meeting with soiled pants, and no one said anything to her, she took this as proof that no one could tell. Since she had managed to "arrange reality" to suit herself, she was insufficiently aware of having a problem to benefit from treatment [Kessler, 1966, pp. 448–449].

Whenever anything happens in school, Tommy, a second grader, who is accustomed to being accused of whatever goes wrong at home, immediately yells "I didn't do it" [from the author's files].

One eight-year-old boy, referred because of excessive bullying of his classmates, drew a man who was menacing in every aspect: bared teeth sharpened to a point, a club in one hand, the other hand coming to an end not in conventional fingers but in a clear depiction of what looked like the ends of scissors, a weapon which might shear off and do damage to vital parts of the subject. The social worker's investigation of the father revealed that he was a despot in every way—cruel, punitive, and domineering. The bullying attitudes the subject had picked up suggested that he had already begun to defend himself against the threat of destruction through the universal mechanism of **incorporation.** In an understandable self-protective maneuver, he donned his enemy's cloak so that he could put himself out of harm's way. He became the bully, rather than the bullied. The process of incorporation became the bridge across which the subject sought to travel to comparative safety [Rabin and Haworth, 1960].

A perspective on ego-defensive mechanisms. Certain generalizations apply to ego-defensive mechanisms collectively. First, they are neither good nor bad of themselves; their value depends on their use. Whether the behavior employed is integrative or disintegrative depends on its significance for the individual and on how it functions in a particular situation. Second, there is no distinct boundary between these mechanisms; several may be used at once, in complex and interrelated fashion. Third, although temporary employment of ego-defensive mechanisms is normal and sometimes desirable, they all too easily become habituated and exaggerated. Whenever possible, defensive behaviors should be displaced by problem-solving behaviors, which provide the same benefits without the concomitant dangers.

• HELPING CHILDREN WITH EMOTIONAL ADJUSTMENT

Whatever the child's own efforts at preserving emotional stability, his parents become involved, too. Typically, they resort to negative methods to "stamp out" their children's problems. However, the child who is punished by any strongly emotion-arousing method cannot think clearly, since among the autonomic by-products of intense emotion are a blocking of thought and disturbance of motor controls (Davis, 1958).

203

Another method of dealing with children's emotional problems that is sometimes resorted to is the use of tranquilizers. Most pediatricians discourage their use in children; however, some may prescribe sedatives for infants and preschoolers to stop crying and to reduce "nervousness." Sometimes, a physician recommends tranquilizers to control moods and behavior of school children. The writer recalls speaking at a school where the teachers reported frequent prescription of tranquilizers for children sent to the school clinic. In another school, Esty reported witnessing an incident in which a six-year-old girl in a euphoric but dreamy state was brought to the school health office and laid on a couch. The nurse explained that the mother had apparently given her too many tranquilizers again to keep her from being a nuisance in school (Esty, 1966).

Another danger in tranquilizers is that they may mask symptoms that should be identified and treated. Hence, they should be used for children very sparingly and only when prescribed by competent authorities, preferably psychiatrists who specialize in children's problems.

Detecting and Treating Maladjustment

Certain general rules may help to maintain or restore emotional health in children. For example, the adult must recognize the importance of rapport, which implies a comfortable relationship involving mutual trust. Otherwise, the child will not feel free to show himself to the adult, who then cannot obtain the evidence needed to help him. To establish this confidence, the adult must show that he perceives the child's blunders as products of misjudgment and anxiety, not of perversity. Unfortunately, the adult's own emotions often blur his vision of the child's problem. The adult's approach should be somewhat nondirective, or just directive enough to protect the child from making too many mistakes. Assistance may be given but should be reduced as the child begins to take hold.

When the child errs, the adult should also be careful to distinguish causes from symptoms, which, like the visible tip of an iceberg, give little idea of what lies underneath. The same overt symptom may have quite different meanings. A child may beat up his friend and feel good about it, or he may feel guilty about it. He may beat him up without provocation or after prolonged provocation. All the adult may see is the beating. In fact, the child's overt reaction may indicate just the opposite of his true feelings. He may strike back at the parent whose affection he desperately wants. He may talk very big, chiefly to overcome a feeling of unimportance. As children shift from more obvious to more subtle forms of expression, it becomes harder to judge their inner feelings. It becomes increasingly hard to detect their need and to help them.

Any one symptom may be unimportant in itself; it is the total pattern that is significant. Especially when several nervous habits (thumb-sucking, nose-picking, head-scratching, face-rubbing, head-banging, body-rocking, facial tics, and frequent urination) occur together, chronic maladjustment is indicated. Because symptoms are so indirect and diffuse, however, the source of conflict may be hard to find.

The symptom must also be dealt with, of course, because the symptom is what others see and react to. Every child must constantly cope with the image he creates and with the effects of his acts. No matter how justified a child's ill temper may be, his peers will reject him for it. Therefore, assistance should involve dealing with symptoms as well as treating causes.

Getting at Underlying Causes

More basic help can proceed in several ways. Children may be assisted to express their impulses in healthy ways.

For example, aggressiveness may be a core trait of the child, but it can assume either socially approved or disapproved forms. The aggressive behaviors of a predelinquent child could be expressed in debating issues in the classroom, in tackling projects in a shop, or in competitive sports (Bloom, 1964).

The direct attack often eliminates one symptom while giving rise to another. Junior, when punished for masturbating, begins biting his nails or bed-wetting. Besides, if the cause is deep-rooted, surface approaches such as mechanical devices for thumbsucking, rewards for "being good," or reminders (such as "Stop!" or "Now don't get into any trouble!"), will simply increase the strain.

should spend more time praising progress made than calling attention to undesirable behaviors that recur.

More Formalized Approaches to Therapy

There are also more formalized approaches to therapy, one being **environmental engineering.** In this method the environment is manipulated so as to elicit from a child more suitable behaviors—or, indirectly, to produce in him a better adjustment. For instance, one elementary teacher set down this plan for an excessively inhibited girl:

> One of the goals for Yvonne is to get her to relax and have a little more fun in life. Therefore, I decided to seat her in a rather lively social setting. At

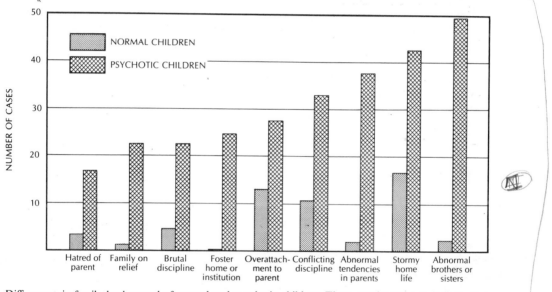

Differences in family background of normal and psychotic children. These results seem to indicate that psychoses are strongly modified by environmental factors. From E. C. Yerbury and N. Newell, Genetic and environmental factors in psychoses of children, *American Journal of Psychiatry*, 1943, **100**, 599–605. Reproduced by permission.

When children react to parental injunction with defiance, sneaking, or resistance, they may be telling the adult they are unable to change a behavior just yet, without undue strain. In such cases, the so-called breaking of one habit will probably result in the appearance of another. Therefore, it is important that adults think of pacing improvement and not expect new patterns at once. They

first she resisted the temptations all about her, but slowly she has loosened up a bit, and once or twice I have watched her pass a note or whisper (rather self-consciously). When she notices me watching her she looks very guilty and waits for my reaction. She seems to be waiting for some censure, but I have been merely smiling and letting her enjoy some of the social goings-on in the classroom [Sears, 1957, p. 324].

205

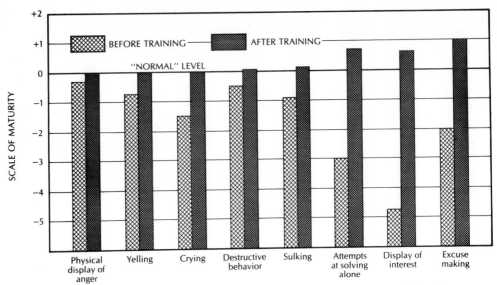

The results of training in frustration tolerance. A group of 12 children who had shown higher-than-average frustration and various immature behaviors when confronted with difficulty were given special training to increase their tolerance for frustration. After training, the group that originally behaved more immaturely when faced with frustration made better scores in some kinds of behaviors than did the originally more "normal" group. The experimenters encouraged the "frustrated" children to complete simpler tasks and showed them ways of attacking problems constructively without the help of adults. From R. Updegraff and M. E. Keister, A study of children's reactions to failure and an experimental attempt to modify them, *Child Development*, 1937, **8**, 241–248. Reproduced by permission of the Society for Research in Child Development, Inc.

Improving Children's Problem-Solving Techniques

Another method is devising ways to help children learn to handle problems more effectively. A classic experiment by Updegraff and Keister (1937) showed that children could be taught to cope more effectively with frustration. In one problem situation, children were required to fit objects into an overly snug bag; in another, a very heavy box weighing 60 to 90 pounds was placed upside down over several attractive toys, and the children were told they could play with them if they could get them. The children's responses varied widely. Some attempted vigorously to solve the problem; some made no overt effort whatsoever to do so. Other reactions included requests for help, rationalizing failure, laughter, crying, whining, and hostility.

The children who showed the more immature reactions were provided training designed to produce more mature responses. They were encouraged to persist in the task longer, to be less dependent on adults, and to think more constructively. They were given simple tasks such as completing picture puzzles and creating three-foot-long toys out of colored blocks. These were graded according to difficulty, so that the child would experience success before moving on to more complex problems.

Following training, the immature children, as compared with a control group of equally immature children who had received no such training, more often attempted to solve problems without help, cried less, and showed greater interest in the tasks. Also, they ceased to sulk and cry or to show their former violently emotional behaviors.

The value of therapy. Actually, we do not know how effective most currently used therapies are. Undoubtedly, a large percentage of troubled and maladjusted children either improve through some self-healing processes of the highly flexible human organism or continue their deviant and self-defeating behaviors into adult life (Levitt, 1957). If therapy is being used, we are inclined to credit to it any improvement that occurs. It is possible that similar, or even better, results would sometimes have been achieved by leaving the child alone.

• SUMMARY

Emotion refers to a stirred-up state of the organism, and involves both motive and feeling components. Emotional health, in terms of adjustment, represents those adaptations to changing demands most consistent with personal happiness, effectiveness, and social welfare. The most effective adjustment for the individual may violate common notions about normality. Some children thrive on a degree of tension that demolishes others. Sometimes it is the environment, rather than the child, that needs adjustment. Terms like pathology and mental illness often reflect society's biases and should be used with care.

Basic to emotional behaviors are certain biological functions and mechanisms, including regulatory centers in the brain and the **autonomic nervous system.** The **parasympathetic** division of the autonomic system controls the everyday functions of the body, while the **sympathetic system** is dominant in times of stress. When stress is prolonged, the balance between these divisions is upset and works in ways harmful to the body.

Studies of both animals and humans suggest that autonomic balance is highly individual, and that these constitutional differences coupled with subsequent experience determine emotional patterns. Individuals differ both in predisposition to emotionality and in the intensity of emotional experience. Maturation plays a part, too, through glandular changes largely preordained by heredity. Presumably prenatal factors, including the mother's emotionality and the birth process itself, modify the infant's emotions. The significance of sex in emotion is unclear; for example, to what extent the female's greater neuroticism and the male's greater aggressiveness are due to biological or sociocultural factors has not been fully resolved.

Even at birth, infants manifest differences in their capacity to handle frustration and in their emotional patterns in general. Whatever their patterns, children should be helped to live with them comfortably. Postnatally, each child's unique blend of experience further modifies his original pattern. It is debatable how much tension the infant needs in order to establish adjustive patterns. It is known, however, that the child is upset when he has no ready response for a new situation; this condition is described as **cognitive dissonance.** The theory of cognitive dissonance would explain the particularly disruptive effects of **traumas** – which are stresses beyond the usual ones. To what degree the vicarious stresses of television drama are upsetting is unclear, and the degree probably depends on the child's emotional stability and perceptions.

Among the interpersonal influences on children's emotions, the child-parent relationship is dominant. In fact, a consistent relationship seems to exist between child-rearing patterns and the child's adjustment. The father's very real impact, both directly and indirectly, through the mother, is likely to be overlooked. Nor has sibling influence received due attention. However, since the quality of emotional maturity, once established, is pretty consistent, all these familial experiences are crucial.

Among the more diffuse environmental influences on emotions are culture and subculture. The nature of a culture may tend either to encourage or to depress particular emotional conditions. The effects of physical environment are equally important, as industrial psychologists have shown many times. Unfortunately, little research relates to positive emotions, including sympathy, humor, and the like. Far more studies concern **disintegrative emotions,** including fear, guilt, aggression, and jealousy. Such emotions exist in everyone in limited amounts, but they easily get out of hand. An unhealthy fear, out of proportion to the threat at hand, is called a **phobia. Anxiety** is a generalized apprehension of discomfort and impending doom, and differs from fear in that the cause of disturbance and the feeling components of the emotion itself are unclear. Perhaps because of its diffuse nature, anxiety is particularly devastating. The origin of **guilt** is more clear-cut: guilt occurs when one does not live up to some standard that he has been taught is right or that he has come to believe is right. Unlike anxiety and guilt, **hostility** is active and seeks an object. It is especially damaging when repressed and turned against oneself.

In theory, it is easier to prevent negative emotions than to cure them. One theory of emotions is the **drainage hypothesis,** which suggests that the venting of negative emotions in safe ways will reduce the need to assert them in undesirable ways. Thus, to prevent a fearful experience from leaving a serious imprint, the child should speedily relate it to someone else. To forestall aggression, he should release hostile impulses in vicarious ways—for example, through boxing or seeing western films. Most research, however, suggests that such experiences tend to build up the negative emotion rather than dispel it. Nevertheless, the issue has not been fully resolved.

Only recently has much research been done on children's **psychosomatic disorders.** Traditionally, such disturbances connoted somatic dysfunctions in organs controlled by the autonomic nervous system. However, the term now refers to all aspects of the personality-illness relationship.

The scope of children's emotional problems and the best approach to treating them are somewhat uncertain. In general, children should be helped to reduce tensions through **problem solving,** which means taking rational steps to overcome obstacles. However, many individuals resort to **ego-defensive mechanisms,** which are habitual methods of circumventing rather than removing the basic causes of frustration. These mechanisms include **repression,** which means automatically excluding from the consciousness whatever is unpleasant; **fantasy,** or wishful imagination; **regression,** or retreating to more childish or primitive ways of behavior; **rationalization,** or the use of false, but logical-appearing reasons to justify one's acts; **substitution,** or the acceptance of an alternate goal; **compensation,** or the effort to make up for some real or imagined deficiency; and **sublimation,** or the substitution of a socially approved behavior for a socially unacceptable one. The value of such mechanisms depends on their use.

The adult's most effective approach to children's emotional problems is helping to prevent them. If they arise, symptoms should be distinguished from causes. While the symptom may require treatment, basic help necessitates getting at underlying causes. Treatment may be somewhat formalized, as in **environmental engineering,** in which the environment is manipulated to produce a satisfactory adjustment, or it may be informal and involve intertwining therapy with the child's day-to-day experiences. Just how much observed improvement in children's adjustment is due to consciously planned therapy and how much to the child's own initiative or to some self-healing process is uncertain.

• SUGGESTED QUESTIONS AND ACTIVITIES

1. As a class, pool recollections of very young children's demonstrations of sympathy, wonder, awe, and other positive emotions. Then try to arrive at some generalizations concerning the way children experience and handle their emotions.

2. Try to think of some less obvious ways of reducing children's anxiety, fear, and hostility.
3. People often refer to childhood as "happy." Is this characterization appropriate?
4. To what extent should we try to make children "well-rounded"?
5. Does emphasis on "normality" encourage mediocrity?
6. Does the individual who will probably be creative later in life tend to be an "oddball" as a child?
7. What traits or behaviors often observed in children do adults often deplore as abnormal? Which of these may actually prove functional in children's lives?
8. Enumerate episodes that are perceived as trivial by most adults but that might prove upsetting to a child.
9. What are some of the most common ways that children manifest regression, sublimation, rationalization, fantasy, and compensation?
10. Would it be wise to encourage boys to cry when disturbed?
11. Should children's frustration tolerance be built up by slightly and regularly increasing their frustrations?
12. What changes in the manner of rearing girls might reduce their later tendencies toward neuroticism?
13. In terms of the incongruity-dissonance theory, would later adjustment be easier if infants had a less consistent environment, both physical and interpersonal?
14. Should parents be furnished with guides to television programs that give some indication of their potentially stress-producing effects?
15. Should children be safeguarded against such tension-producing experiences as seeing horror films, hearing frightening stories of witches and goblins, going to funerals, and hearing adults' morbid conversations?
16. From your own experience and observations, do you believe that films showing aggression tend to relieve or to increase children's feelings of hostility?
17. Analyze several popular children's programs on television in terms of the probable emotional impact involved.
18. Answer each of the following questions on a slip of paper, indicating sex but not name on each slip. Papers may be collected and the most significant ones read to the class for discussion. (a) Describe an incident from your own childhood involving some specific emotion, such as hostility, anxiety, or worry. (b) Recall the earliest incident that aroused your emotions strongly. (c) How did emotional upsets affect you physically as a child? (d) What sort of defense mechanisms did you typically use? Give examples. (e) Describe your own emotional pattern during childhood—that is, any tendency to be emotional, hostile, or whatever. Give examples. (f) Describe your worst emotional problem as a child—for instance, a tendency to cry or to have a hot temper. (g) Analyze how various factors, such as family life or school experience, affected you emotionally while growing up. (h) Can you name any generally disapproved behavior or trait that nevertheless seemed to function well in your life? (i) Describe briefly an unusually well-adjusted child you have known. (j) Describe some childhood incident involving sex behaviors. Include attitudes and reactions of both children and adults involved.

• SUGGESTED READINGS

Axline, V. M., *Dibs: In Search of Self.* Boston: Houghton Mifflin Company, 1964. Follows a small boy's progress in therapy until he emerges as a highly intelligent, gifted, happy child.

Bandura, A., D. Ross, and S. A. Ross, "Imitation of Film-Mediated Aggressive Models," *Journal of Abnormal and Social Psychology*, Vol. 66, No. 1 (1963), pp. 3–11. The study provided strong evidence that exposure to filmed aggression heightens aggressive reactions in children. Subjects who viewed aggressive human and cartoon models on film exhibited nearly twice as much aggression as did subjects in the control group who were not exposed to the aggressive film content.

Despert, J. L., *The Emotionally Disturbed Child—Then and Now.* New York: Vantage Press, 1965. Surveys the status of the child, and attitudes toward him, from biblical times through the nineteenth century, followed by sections on "The Emotionally Healthy Child," "The Emotionally Disturbed Child," and "Reflections on the Family."

Epstein, R., "Social-Class Membership and Early Childhood Memories," *Child Development*, Vol. 34 (1963), pp. 503–508. Demonstrates that recall of early memories is related to social class. Lower-class children have more memories of anger, aggression, and sexual behavior; middle-class children have more recollections involving euphoria and parent and sibling relationships. The relatively late age of

209

memories recalled by the lower class is ascribed to defensiveness.

Feshbach, S., "The Stimulating versus Cathartic Effects of a Vicarious Aggressive Activity," *Journal of Abnormal and Social Psychology,* Vol. 63, No. 2 (1961), pp. 381–385. The purpose of this study was to test the hypothesis that exposure to aggressive fantasy in an animated cartoon may intensify children's impulses to aggression. Findings supported the hypothesis.

Harlow, H. F., and M. Harlow, "Learning to Love," *American Scientist,* Vol. 54, No. 3 (September 1966), pp. 244–272. In this paper the Harlows discuss three of the affectional systems in the primate order: the maternal or mother-infant affectional system; the infant-mother affectional system; and the age-mate or peer affectional system.

Hartley, R. E., "A Developmental View of Female Sex-Role Definition and Identification," *Merrill-Palmer Quarterly,* Vol. 10, No. 1 (1964), pp. 3–17. A discussion of the early dynamics involved in acquisition of female sex roles, and the relation of certain published findings with these dynamics and with each other. Hartley concludes that sex-role differentiation takes place through a variety of highly complex processes, each of which contributes to a particular facet of status-related personality formation, perceptual sharpening, and response reinforcement.

Hebb, D. O., "On the Nature of Fear," *Psychological Review,* Vol. 53, No. 5 (1956), pp. 259–276. A review of research concerning emotion, with special attention to research involving primates, in an attempt to derive a theory of emotion. Hebb concludes that fear is distinct from other emotions and originates in a disruption of organized cerebral activities.

Johnson, M. M., "Sex-Role Learning in the Nuclear Family," *Child Development,* Vol. 34 (1963), pp. 319–333. The writer advances the thesis that it is identification with the father, in the sense of internalizing a reciprocal role relationship with the father, that is crucial for producing appropriate sex-role orientations in both males and females.

Kessler, J. W., *Psychopathology of Childhood.* Englewood Cliffs, N. J.: Prentice-Hall, Inc., 1966. Deals with children's problems as encountered by teachers, psychologists, speech therapists, social workers, and others. Problems are considered in the context of normal child development and psychological factors accounting for them.

Kreitler, H., and S. Kreitler, "Children's Concepts of Sexuality and Birth," *Child Development,* Vol. 37 (1966), pp. 363–378. Report of a study, done in Israel, of ideas held by children aged four to five and a half years, about creation and the birth of babies. A survey of the results indicated that children's sexual concepts deviated in essential points from the concepts ascribed to them by Freud and Piaget.

Lynn, D. B., "The Process of Learning Parental and Sex-Role Identification," *Journal of Marriage and the Family,* Vol. 28, No. 4 (1966), pp. 466–470. A summary of the author's theoretical formulation concerning identification, much of which has been published piecemeal in various journals. Previously published hypotheses have been revised and placed in a more comprehensive framework.

Sarason, S. B., et al., *Anxiety in Elementary School Children.* New York: John Wiley & Sons, Inc., 1960. A report of research studies conducted over a six-year period at Yale University.

Seymour, L., "Stimulation in Infancy," *Scientific American,* Vol. 122 (1960), pp. 80–86. Shows that both painful shocks and gentle handling enhance the development of normal stress responses in infant animals, whereas the absence of such treatment leads to behavioral disorders when the animal matures.

Wolfenstein, M., and G. Kliman, eds., *Children and the Death of a President.* New York: Doubleday & Company, Inc., 1965. A collection of studies, mostly psychoanalytic in orientation, of children's and adolescents' reactions to the Kennedy assassination.

8
PSYCHOSEXUAL DEVELOPMENT

Closely related to emotional development is sexual development. First we shall discuss the child's biological sex role, which involves the emergence of masculine and feminine attitudes as the psychobiological consequences of sex drive, sex awareness, and sex interests. Then we shall deal with the broader behavioral patterns appropriate for each sex — that is, the social sex roles. Within the context of this chapter, **sex roles** refer to the patterns of behavior deemed appropriate for each sex, and **sex drive** is the psychological condition that causes the organism to desire and to be receptive to sexual stimulation.

• THE BIOLOGICAL SEX ROLE

The Biological Sex Drive

There is plentiful evidence, such as illustrated in the testimony below, of the significance of biological sex in childhood.

> At age 10 I tried to have intercourse with the girl next door. (Male)

> My first experience with sex was kissing a girl in a locker when I was in kindergarten. (Male)

> I was sitting next to my sister on our parlor couch when my penis was brought to erection and it was obvious when looking at my pants. I called my sister's and father's attention to it. He told me I could show something like that to him but not to my sister. (Male)

> My first awareness of sex was noting differences between me and my brother when mother bathed us together in the bathtub. I felt a certain anxiety over the difference. (Female)

The feelings accompanying such situations are rooted in each individual's experience. In fact, the infant is born with neither sex drive nor sexual emotions; instead, he is born with a capacity to develop both. Sex hormones, secreted by the gonads, have powerful effects, and their relation to sex drive in subprimate mammalian species is fairly constant. In the primates, too, sex drive is originally dependent on the hormones, and when either humans or animals are deprived of sex glands before puberty, sex interests fail to develop. Moreover, if an individual is shielded from sex-arousing stimuli, so that sex awareness never enters the psychological field, heterosexual feelings may remain latent throughout life. However, once generated, sex drive becomes extremely insistent, with considerable variation from one individual to another.

The hormonal substrate itself sets no goals, and the sex structures permit wide variations in the practices that satisfy sex drive. In short, sex drive may be satisfied in a wide variety of ways, involving both sexes, all ages, animals, and inanimate objects.

Research suggests that childhood play may be essential to the final emergence of adult sexual patterns. In one study, monkeys raised in individual cages and deprived of play with their agemates failed to develop normal sex behavior, even under the tutelage of an experienced mate (Harlow, 1962). A few did become pregnant, but proved totally inept at motherhood. Among humans, it is possible that the suppression of childhood sex play may adversely affect sexual behaviors in adulthood. Thus, sexual behavior is another pattern in which genetic and environmental patterns both contribute to the final product.

The outcomes of sexual behavior are related to certain fundamentals of group living, such as marriage, parenthood, inheritance, and property laws. At the same time, the nature of the organism is such that sex drive can be frustrated to an extent not possible with other basic drives. For all these reasons, every society has regulated sex drives to a greater extent than other drives. In fact, rules governing sexual behavior are enforced with such vigor that they come to seem "natural."

The child may adapt to societal restrictions simply by denying his sex feelings, and thus prevent full personality development, which requires fulfillment of all basic needs. Moreover, any need that is blocked assumes exaggerated importance in relation to other needs; and energies that should be channeled toward constructive activities ᵃ sipated in the form ⸺ by guilt and re ⸺ sion of sex dri ⸺ dividual's relati ⸺ others. The chil ⸺ that "handling ⸺ may lose self-res, ⸺ not control the hat ⸺ is attacked by a ma ⸺ ing distrust of men ⸺ undo the damage, ⸺ tudes tend to persis. ⸺ fects of sexual stre ⸺ emphasized. Sometim ⸺ is merely symptomati ⸺ more general maladju ⸺ 1962). Besides, the or ⸺ vive and be quite hea ⸺ sexual intercourse is completely denied (Beach, 1956).

The following recollections suggest the varied ways that sex experiences may affect different children.

> Maybe I'm abnormal, but I don't think so. Anyhow, I can't remember anything about sex from childhood. Not that it was considered shameful or hidden. I just can't remember any sex incident or sex feelings from then. (Female)

> When I was seven, I told a girl she could ride my new three-wheeler if she would take her pants off. She did and I was quite taken aback at seeing her private parts. I still avoid that neighborhood for fear of seeing her. (Male)

> When I was about nine, a boy told several of us how babies were made. I disagreed emphatically, because I was shocked and couldn't believe it. Finally I asked my mother, and after she explained, it didn't seem quite as revolting. (Male)

Sex Practices Viewed Cross-Culturally

The best way to gain perspective on our own sexual practices and atti-

tudes is through cross-cultural comparisons. In a world-wide survey, Ford and Beach (1951) classified societies according to perᵐⁱ siveness of sex pracᵗⁱ ⸺ more restrictive ones ⸺ Africa, the Kwomas ⸺ and the Cunas in ⸺ e Ashantis, fathers ⸺ asturbate or to en- ⸺ Similarly, Kwoma ⸺ against handling ⸺ ile urinating; and ⸺ esses a boy with ⸺ to beat his penis ⸺ children remain ⸺ ters—as far as ⸺ ncerned—until ⸺ age ceremony. ⸺ en permitted ⸺ nely permis- ⸺ ᴴopi and Siriono, ⸺ take a highly permissive attitude toward all sensual behaviors, at least until puberty, while the Kazak adults excite the young ones' genitals by rubbing and playing with them. Among the Pukapukans, all members of the household sleep under the same mosquito net. Although parents wait until they believe their children are asleep, the children often observe adult sex activities. Lesu children are completely free to observe adults copulate, with the specific exception that they may not watch their own mothers having intercourse. On Ponape, children are given sex instruction from the fourth or fifth year.

Stages in Psychosexual Development

In any specific culture, patterns are so organized that most people follow the same general stages in psychosexual development. These are the stages originally proposed by Freud and his followers. At each stage, sexually approved behaviors are rewarded and disapproved ones punished.

Narcissistic stage. The pattern of psychosexual development characteristic of Western culture is commonly con-

213

ceived as involving four stages. During infancy, the child is described as **narcissistic;** that is, he obtains sensual satisfaction from his own body. Pleasure gained from the anus (bowel movements), from the sex organs (masturbation), and from the mouth (nursing), often leads to tumescence (Haverson, 1938). Among a sample of 317 male infants two to 12 months old, one-third experienced erection (Kinsey et al., 1948).

The question arises whether infants experience purely biological, or partly sensual, satisfaction. Kisker (1964) supports the latter position. The infant's urges are undifferentiated but satisfy sensual as well as purely organic needs. The infant nurses because he is hungry, not because there is a sex urge. But when he uses his thumb as a pacifier, he is no longer satisfying hunger; he is seeking sensual pleasure. Similarly, when he first has a bowel movement, he is merely relieving organic tension. Yet most children come to the point where they prolong the toilet experience, presumably for pleasure. The infant also discovers pleasant sensations when he handles his sex organs. Henceforth, normal children, especially boys, engage in intermittent masturbation.

Although Kisker writes in terms of sensuality instead of sexuality, he does not make the difference completely clear. Ausubel (1962) makes a sharper distinction, denying that erotic significance derives from phenomena collectively categorized as "infantile sexuality." Instead, infantile sexuality is chiefly erogenous sensuality, indulged for its own sake or to relieve tensions deriving from frustration and anxiety. It also involves elements of manipulative activity and curiosity. Psychoanalytic confusion about this activity, asserts Ausubel, is easy to explain. First, we overemphasize the fact that the same bodily parts are involved in both infantile and adult sexuality. This superficial resemblance is misleading; pre- and post-pubertal individuals do not gain the same sort of satisfaction from masturbation simply because they stroke the same organ.

Again, consider the sensual pleasures connected with anal and bladder evacuation, "remembered" as having erotic significance, but ordinarily having no part in adult sexual expression. When genital activities do acquire erotic significance in mature years, adults retrospectively superimpose sexual interpretations onto children's anal-urethral sensuality. Certain Neo-Freudians admit that "infantile" and adult sexuality are not phenomenologically the same, but they interpret eroticism broadly enough to encompass sensuality and affectional expressions as well as sexual behavior in the literal sense. However, asserts Ausubel, this broad interpretation only results in unnecessary semantic confusion and loss of scientific precision.

True eroticism, according to Ausubel, is a form of self-expression in which the individual perceives himself in a biological sex role. Prerequisite to this role is hormonal facilitation, as well as recognition of oneself as a sexually mature person. Since these conditions cannot be fulfilled prior to puberty, the erotic behavior of children cannot be regarded as qualitatively comparable to adult sexuality.

Nevertheless, infant sensuality is of importance for several reasons. For one thing, it fosters sensitivity in the genital area, thus laying the foundation for later sexuality. Second, it attains significance from the fact that in certain cultures, among them ours, people often react negatively to this kind of behavior. If the mother slaps the baby's hands, frowns, or says "No, no" when he handles his genitals, he learns to associate that part of his body with fear and shame—an association that may constitute a foundation for later maladjustment.

Oedipal stage. During early childhood—the **Oedipal** period—the child supposedly becomes attached to the parent of the opposite sex. The boy, upon observing the father's attachment to the mother, is jealous. Inherent in his unconscious, it has been claimed, is a potent libidinal drive for incestuous sexual union with the mother, accompanied by hatred of the father as a sexual rival (Gesell and Ilg, 1943). Besides, the boy identifies with the father and envies his status and power, thus reinforcing his jealousy. In the opposite sex, the girl is jealous of the mother and attached to the father—the so-called **Electra complex.**

A number of arguments militate against the validity of the Oedipal hypothesis. The majority of studies indicate the mother to be the preferred parent of children of both sexes, undoubtedly because she attends their needs more often (Simpson, 1935). Moreover, no indisputable evidence exists that either the boy's or girl's emotional response to the parent of the opposite sex is sexual in nature. Besides, note that overtly affectionate relations between mother and son, or between daughter and father, are regarded as appropriate in this culture, while overt affection between father and son is frowned on. Thus the mother-son relation becomes more overtly affectional than the father-son relation, even when the son loves his father equally. If some sexual component should exist within the relationship, it is likely to have originated with the parent, whose biological sex role has matured, rather than with the child, who lacks the hormonal base to support it.

Conversely, a son's conflict with his father can more logically be credited to the father's authority role, especially with relation to the son, than to competition for the mother's affection. Traditionally, the father is sterner toward the son than toward the daughter, which would tend to divert the son's tender feelings to his mother. In matrilineal societies where the maternal uncle enforces discipline instead of the father, the boy resents the uncle in much the same way that some boys resent their fathers in this culture.

Homosexual stage. In the next period, the **homosexual** stage, the child is weaned from dependency on his parents. When he goes to school, much of his time and attention become diverted from parents to peers. At the same time, culturally prescribed differences in play patterns tend to separate the sexes. Boys play with boys and girls with girls; but the relation is hardly homosexual, at least in the erotic sense. Such sex play as exists involves both sexes equally. Moreover, sex play at this stage typically represents exploratory needs, or perhaps the desire to act grown-up, rather than erotic behavior. Here are several such instances:

> When I was about eight, we would go down into a ditch near my house and undress and look at our sexual differences. We didn't think anything of it because we were first cousins. We didn't touch each other, but it was an exciting, naughty thing to do.
>
> I recall exploring two girls' sex organs, and once I was caught by my parents. They were terribly upset, and told me it wasn't nice.
>
> When I was about six years old, my buddy and I and a girl our age went into a garage and stripped. Then we lay on a rug and began to "fool around." My feelings seemed directed by impulse because I had never heard of, or done, this sort of thing before.

Heterosexual stage. The final, or **heterosexual,** stage is initiated after puberty, and normally persists through life. Heterosexuality simply connotes sexual attraction to members of the opposite sex. After years of conditioning to a sexually dichotomous society, most individuals will pursue this pattern, when hormonal changes provide the base for it. Besides, heterosexual activity presumably provides greater tension reduction, at least for the male. Complementary anatomical features encourage compatibility between the sexes on the physical level, while cultural demands and the institution of the family promote it on the psychological level. However, arrival at the heterosexual stage does not automatically bring good adjustment. Heterosexual behavior, too, can become highly distorted, as, for instance, when a man makes advances to small girls.

A perspective on psychosexual-stage theory. It is doubtful that everyone goes through all four of the foregoing stages, or in the order given. Sex development is a complex process involving all sorts of emotions and various kinds of love objects. Probably only through sociocultural sanctions and the prospect of related rewards, such as family and children, do such a large majority manage to "muddle through" and establish reasonably satisfactory marriages. A sizable number never attain a mature heterosexuality, probably because—according to the theory—they have become "arrested" at some earlier stage. The individual arrested in the narcissistic stage may ultimately marry someone like himself, and seek sex solely for his own pleasure. Even the homosexual relation, it is claimed, may derive from unresolved narcissism, because the sex partner is a mirror image of oneself. Again, the individual who never moves beyond the Oedipal stage may remain with his parents the rest of his life, unable to make a break, or he may get married but choose a wife who resembles his mother.

Sex Interests and Concepts in Childhood

Whatever the degree of sensual feeling involved, it cannot be denied that children often show intense interest in sex (Kisker, 1964). In addition to sexual curiosity, Isaacs (1933) frequently observed exhibitionism (exposing the genitals), voyeurism (looking at others' genitals), and other sex activities. Among Isaacs' anecdotal records are such items as the following:

When the children were playing a family game with the puppy as baby, Duncan said: "Undress him." Priscilla: "Yes, Duncan; and then we can see his bim-bom." There was great laughter and excitement among the children, and all repeated, "see his bim-bom." Priscilla undid the rug in which he was

wrapped and called others to look: "Come on, come on, look underneath." The puppy stood on its hind legs near Priscilla. Duncan: "Oh, he tried to get to your wat-d'ye-call-it."

Jane and Conrad went with Mrs. I. to the ethnological museum. . . . When looking at a human figure made of bamboo, Conrad pointed out the prominent penis, giggling and saying, "What is that funny thing sticking out? We know, don't we?" They whispered and giggled about it [pp. 141–142].

In the foregoing illustrations, note that the children's sex vocabulary is notably unscientific; nor are older children much more knowledgeable. In a study involving seventh- and eighth-grade boys, only 22% fully understood the term wet dream, 11% intercourse, 6% scrotum, 2% menstruation, and 0% uterus (Ramsey, 1943). Parents themselves continue to use private family designations, often baby terms or vague euphemisms such as "it," "down there," and "not nice" (Sears et al., 1957).

Not merely in vocabulary, but in matters of sex generally, children are inaccurate or vague. Two Russian children were reported discussing the question "Where do babies come from?" in this way:

"My mother has gone to Moscow to buy me a little sister."
"Silly, it's only in America that people buy children. Here they come out of the womb."
"That's untrue. In America children are made by monkeys" [Tchoukovsky, 1959, p. 568].

In America, many very young children believe women become pregnant through something they have eaten. Some believe children are born from the intestines. Others think the female has a male sex organ, or that the sex act is painful (Kisker, 1964).

Katcher (1955) had preschool children identify the sex of figure drawings of children and adults, both clothed and nude. The same outline—a compromise between the male and female figure—was used in all pictures, and adult nude figures were cut off at the waist. The children were asked to identify the figures' sex from various cues, including hair, breasts, clothes, and external genitals. In general, errors decreased with the subject's age, and no significant socioeconomic differences were found. The cue that children most readily used to differentiate sex was clothing, followed in order by hair, genitals, and breasts. No subject over eight years of age made errors in identifying the genitals. Overall, girls were more accurate than boys. At ages four and five, when the phallic phase is supposed to be in operation, over half the children still made mistakes on genital cues. Although breasts are presumably less traumatic than genitals, they nevertheless elicited more errors.

Sex Problems of Childhood

Masturbation. Among those sex behaviors that cause parents special concern is masturbation, or the fondling of the genitals for the sake of pleasure. It is almost universal among infants, especially boys. Mothers of children aged five and six reported that about 60% had been observed masturbating (Sears et al., 1957). In another study, 92% of adult males admitted to having masturbated at one time or another (Kinsey et al., 1948). Mead (1939) suggests that masturbation is more common among boys than girls because the females' genitals are less exposed; Kinsey postulates a basic difference in sex drive; and Mussen and Conger (1956) emphasize the greater cultural suppression of female sexuality.

The child's attitudes toward the practice reflect those of his culture. In societies where it is accepted, he fondles himself, or is fondled, and thinks nothing of it. However, in this culture, which misunderstands and condemns the practice, even young children experience deep-seated guilt. This reaction, by an adolescent, is typical, especially for girls:

Even as I write I am becoming nervous; my stomach is knotting up, and I think I will die if anyone finds me out. When I was 9 or 10, and I had already been practicing masturbation for a while, I slept with a friend. I wondered if she did, too, and clumsily inquired. She didn't even know what I meant. Later I tried to explain to my mother. She didn't scold but brushed it aside as unimportant. From then on I never mentioned it to anyone but masturbated intermittently. Each time I started I felt thrilled, but later guilty and dirty. Nevertheless, I had no will power to stop [Rogers, 1962, p. 292].

Typically, boys experience less guilt over masturbation than girls. Some, like the one quoted here, feel no anxiety at all.

I didn't think of masturbation as sex. It was just a pleasurable experience for my body, a good sensation. I felt it was my right—and why not? I didn't know the name for it, but it was a favorite activity at about age 12.

Attitudes toward masturbation have changed greatly over the years. In the early 1900s, a physician addressing the American Medical Association advised boys that "If in an unguarded moment [anyone] tries to entice you to masturbatic experiments . . . strike him at once and beat him as long as you can stand" (Hall, 1905, p. 470). As late as the 1930s, outcomes popularly attributed to the "sin of self-abuse" included cancer, insanity, loss of weight, insomnia, pimples, weak eyes, and loss of potency (Spock and Huschka, 1938). Today, people generally "play ostrich" with the topic. Masturbation is still widely regarded as "not nice," although it is not considered as sinful or fraught with horrible outcomes as formerly. Psychologists hold that it is normal and has no ill effects except those generated by feelings of tension and guilt, which are derived from societal attitudes. A few say that it is quite desirable in centralizing sexual impulses in the genitals and permitting safe catharsis for sexual feelings.

217

Ordinarily, parents would do best to avoid any overt emotional reaction upon noting it; in fact, a child may need reassurance that he will not be harmed. Since compulsive masturbation is a symptom, help in such cases should involve seeking and treating basic difficulties.

Homosexuality. The causes of homosexuality, and the age-stages at which it originates, have been widely debated. There are some arguments for a genetic base. If one identical twin is homosexual, the other almost always is—although this is not necessarily the case with fraternal twins (Kallman, 1953). Another argument for a genetic base is that homosexuality is also found in animals, who would hardly reject a dominant mother or have problems of identification with weak fathers.

Other evidence indicates that sexual proclivity may be determined within the womb. In one experiment, injections of male hormone into pregnant monkeys appeared permanently to have altered their female offsprings' behavior. Normally, female monkeys begin to act shy and retiring within a month after birth, averting their heads when challenged by a male. However, these female monkeys wrestled, tugged, and bit in the best-approved masculine fashion. There was no sign of hormonal imbalance, nor had any hormones been given them since birth, suggesting that predisposition toward one or another form of psychosexual behavior might be determined chemically in the fetus (*Newsweek,* 1965).

Despite such evidence, the overwhelming majority of psychologists accept the environmental theory. According to this theory, the individual is born with sex drive but without specific sex goals. In some instances, male homosexuals have been given male hormone in an attempt to induce appropriate sex feelings. Apparently, these injections produce diametrically opposed effects on different persons, perhaps due to interaction with other glands and the

pre-existing psychological balance (Benedetti, 1957). In general, however, such injections merely increase erotic feelings toward whatever sort of stimuli the subject has found sex-arousing already.

The specific causes of homosexuality, say the environmentalists, relate to family life and child-rearing. Conditions such as these are said to encourage homosexuality: (1) marked hostility toward a parent of the opposite sex; (2) inharmonious marital relationships on the part of the parents; (3) strong attachment to a parent of the same sex; (4) rearing the child as if he were one of the opposite sex (sissy, tomboy); (5) unsatisfactory social relations with members of the opposite sex; and (6) feelings of inadequacy (Katz and Lehner, 1953).

Much evidence could be interpreted to support either side of the argument. In one study, "passive homosexuals," or those preferring the "female" role in erotic activities, more often reported atypical paternal relationships as children and close relationships with their mothers than did "active" homosexuals. In such cases, however, which is cause and which effect? On the one hand, a boy's femininity may be attributed solely to identification with his mother. However, it could as easily be argued that a boy whose femininity is genetically based may simply find his mother a more congenial person with whom to identify.

Actually, such ambiguous evidence abounds. Kisker (1964) points out that there are no distinctive features of homosexual physique, but that many male homosexuals can be recognized by what Sheldon (1940) called secondary gynandromorphy. In such cases, are physique and homosexuality genetically related, or has type of physique simply encouraged a homosexual role? For example, secondary sex factors such as femininity of face, voice, and mannerisms are associated with male homosexuals (Kisker, 1964). One may argue either that the possession of such traits causes a male to be viewed as a sex object by other males, or that the traits themselves are genetically sex-related.

Whatever the cause, Money (1963) believes that the basic heterosexual orientation is established by the age of six. If that be the case, certain questions should be raised. For instance, efforts are often geared toward assisting the homosexual child to "change." However, if the child's sexual orientation is already firmly fixed, perhaps he should simply be encouraged to accept himself and helped to adapt to a sexually dichotomous environment. On the other hand, if sexual orientation is "imprinted" in early years, how can the proper sort of "imprinting" be assured? At present, this whole area of research requires more objective treatment.

In conclusion, let it be noted that it is easy to confuse incipient homosexuality with normal exploratory sex activity or with close friendships between members of the same sex. On the surface, we cannot say which was involved in these cases:

When I was 8 or 9, a girl of about 13 was visiting in our home. The three of us were in the barn, when she and my sister performed a homosexual act. She invited me to participate, but I felt revulsion and refused. (Female)

When I was a child, from age 7 on I had crushes on a series of girls. They were my idols, and in fantasy I thought of them often. (Female)

As a child, I felt especially ill at ease with girls, and could not possibly imagine what my older brother saw in his girl. I had an older boy chum with whom I experimented a bit. (Male)

Trauma. Sex difficulties also arise from traumatic experiences. A common one involves the concept of "primal scene," or observation of sexual activities between parents or other adults. Such events are often traumatic because the child is unprepared to understand or to control his own emotions (Kisker, 1964). Also greatly disturbing to children are sexual advances made to them,

especially by older persons. Here is such a case:

I recall only one sex incident from childhood, which occurred at age seven or eight. A boy of perhaps 15 came to our house, which was just being built. I can remember standing behind the house, with him kneeling before me and holding onto my arms with his hands. His fly was open and his organ was visible. It scared me and left a deep imprint on my memory. Since sex was a forbidden and shameful topic in my home, my anxiety about this incident was strengthened. (Female)

Early reactions to physical differences between the sexes may be exaggerated in retrospect. In one study, only 17 of 50 children had been disturbed by the discovery of such differences (Conn and Kanner, 1947). Among 200 children, only 10 boys and 11 girls thought of the differences in terms of loss or castration (Conn, 1940). Possibly the apparent absence of castration thoughts resulted from the researchers' failure to gain rapport with their subjects, or to break through their defenses to deeper levels. But without more definitive evidence, it would appear that disturbance over genital differences, and consequent castration anxieties, are neither universal nor inevitable in this culture.

However, there is plentiful evidence that traumas such as rape or sexual molestation by adults may have great impact on psychosexual development. Books on abnormal psychology are full of such cases.

• ADULT INFLUENCES ON PSYCHOSEXUAL DEVELOPMENT

Parents' reactions to children's sex behavior are generally negative, embracing various combinations of evasion, denial, repression, rejection, and shock. Evasion takes the form of simply avoiding the recognition that such behaviors take place, or, when recognition is unavoidable, evasive discussion. The child who is discovered handling himself is told it is "not nice." The mother who

219

hears the children playing "doctor" pretends that nothing unusual is going on. Some mothers practice distraction; for example, when the child is seen masturbating, his hands are moved or he is given something else to do. When children's sex behaviors are extreme, parents normally demonstrate shock and instill in the child a sense of sin and humiliation. Here are two cases in point, recalled from childhood:

> After my sister caught me in the barn performing "experiments" on a girl, she told my mother, while I hid behind a door, afraid. I was not punished, but shamed. (Male)

> When I showed my father the picture of the cross-section of a pregnant horse I had found in a medical book, he was horrified and slapped my face. It was my first knowledge (age 10) that storks didn't enter the picture. Later he berated my mother for having given me pamphlets about the birds and bees. The sex act was unknown to me until I happened on a small booklet owned by the hired man. For some time afterward, I couldn't imagine how ministers and other straight-laced people could perform the act and produce children. To me it appeared wicked. Later on, my parents got a divorce, and my father married a 16-year-old girl four days before their first child was born. (Female)

Overall, prohibition of sex is the rule, with no sex substitutes offered. Conditions may simply be arranged to prevent stimulation, such as providing separate sleeping rooms for children of each sex, separate bathing hours, and closed doors for toileting. Much "sex" training takes the form of modesty training (Sears et al., 1957).

Parents almost always superimpose sexual interpretations onto the child's sex-related behaviors. However, on the basis of his clinical experiences, Plant (1950) insists that children's apparently sexual behaviors are usually motivated by other factors. These may include the need to break taboos, including sexual ones, the desire to act grown-up, the urge to satisfy curiosity, and the like.

Because parents overreact, so do children. Children may feel that all sex is evil and reject any form of sexuality, however innocuous. Unless this attitude is prolonged into the middle and late teens, assert Stuart and Prugh (1960), it can be looked upon as a phase in development. However, the author would take issue with this conclusion. "Phase of development" connotes normality, when actually the negative feelings toward sex instilled in children by adults are unhealthy. As any psychiatrist can testify, children with such feelings often never get over them. A statement made some time ago by Groves and Blanchard (1930, pp. 142–143) is equally appropriate today: "In every case of a child who comes to the attention of a psychiatrist, psychologist, or social worker because of maladjustment in the field of sex, unsatisfactory parent-child relationships are to be found a fundamental factor."

Sex Education

In view of the foregoing, it would seem wise to provide sex education for children both as children and as future parents. As early as 1900, authorities were complaining about the indirection and subterfuge in sex instruction. Note this observation by G. Stanley Hall (1905, p. 469):

> Some think, at least for girls, that all that is needed can be taught by means of flowers and their fertilization, and that mature years will bring insight enough to apply it all to human life. Others would demonstrate on the cadaver so that in the presence of death knowledge may be given without passion. This I once saw in Paris, but cannot commend for general use.

Parents hesitate to discuss sex with teen-age children and even more so with younger ones (Remmers and Radler, 1957). When one group of teen-agers was asked about sex education received during childhood, these replies were typical:

As a child, I can't recall that sex existed. My father never mentioned the subject, and my mother was embarrassed and treated it as though it did not happen except in the married state. When I was 10 or 11, her first and last bumbling attempt to explain anything about the subject was when she tried to tell me about the menstrual cycle. (Female)

My parents never told me anything; and I never stopped to think about where people came from. I assumed it just happened naturally. (Male)

Even today parents do little about children's sex education. Such teaching as they undertake is mostly negative in nature, consisting in the transmission of their own anxieties whenever they stumble on the manipulatory and curiosity behaviors that inevitably occur. Since these attitudes begin before children have mastered verbal skills, their significance is not apparent. Consequently, parts of the body and curiosity-exploratory impulses become focuses of anxiety (Bandura and Walters, 1963).

Sex education in the family. Parents probably evade the responsibility because they don't know what to do. Two questions often raised are these: When should children first be provided sex education? And what form should it take? Whether parents intend it or not, their child's sex education begins in infancy. The mother who removes her son's fingers from his genitals is teaching him: This part of me is shameful. The father who berates his wife teaches his daughter to distrust men. Years later, after she marries, she cannot adjust sexually because deep down she rejects men as beasts.

Unfortunately, most parents think of sex education in purely physiological terms. This part of sex education is relatively simple, involving certain principles. Such teaching should begin early and continue on graduated levels of complexity, as the child's maturity and adjustment permit. Since the child will rarely initiate such discussion, the par-

ent may take advantage of natural situations, such as when a pet gives birth, to introduce incidental information. His manner should be quiet, composed, objective, and neither humorous nor emotional. He should use correct vocabulary and clear, simple explanations. What he says may be supplemented, both at home and at school, by suitable pictures and readings. The parent should avoid inculcating fear, guilt, or shame, but rather rely on realistic instruction concerning the way society feels about such matters.

Far more important than the physical facts are attitudes relating not merely to biological sex behaviors but to all intersex relationships. Often, proper sex attitudes are thought of negatively in terms of avoiding "dirty jokes," pornographic reading, and sex "experiments." Instead, healthy attitudes should connote positive feelings that sex, if rightly used, is both normal and good, representing the finest in adult human relationships. The following conversation between a mother and small daughter illustrates an informal and enlightened episode in sex education.

Child: When I'm thirty will I be a mother?
Mother: If you have a baby you will.
Child: Do all womans have babies?
Mother: No.
Child: Why?
Mother: Some are not strong enough, some are too busy doing other things – some . . .
Child: Well, in three or six weeks when I'm thirty, I shall have a baby – where do babies come from?
Mother: Seeds.
Child: Where do the seeds come from?
Mother: The father and the mother.
Child: Where does the father keep his?
Mother: They are in his body.
Child: Oh, is he keeping them warm same as the mother does the baby?
Mother: He doesn't have them there to keep them warm, but because they belong there.
Child: Well, when I'm six I'll marry you because you're so cute.

Mother: But—(Father comes in.)
Child: Hello, Daddy. Did you buy me something?
(No further questioning) [Rust, unpublished].

Sex education at school. Teachers, like parents, generally ignore sex education. Among students whom the author perennially polls on the subject, very few report having received sex education from parents, and practically none from teachers. A woman graduate student who attempted sex education among seventh- and eighth-graders in 1964 had children turn in questions they desired answered. Here are the children's questions, with their own spelling retained:

When the sperm goes into the vagina does it always produce an egg? When the male does this, does he always make you pregnant when he is doing it?

Is there any pain when the male and female unite?

Does it hurt when the doctor cuts the umbellical cord?

Do making out and kissing make you pregnant?

When a woman has her baby I hear my mom say something about "breadking water," what does that mean?

How long do the male and female have to stay united?

Why doesn't the man have a baby instead of a woman?

Before birth does a human baby have a tail?

Is a Caesarian birth always because the Vagina is too small?

If the mother wanted to see the baby born would doctors set up mirrors or something for her to see it?

How come you can't have a baby until you get married?

Do the sperm always leafe the boy's body at night?

Do the boy and girl both know when sexual intercourse takes place?

Does the male have to put his penis inside the vagina or just on the outside touching the vagina?

Why don't boys have mensturation?

I read in a book that when a woman looses her virgintry it hurts as much as labor and there is a possibility the male might break a blood vessel in the female—is this true?

Can you get pregnant through clothing?

How does the baby come out such a small opening?

How far does the boy's penis go in to the girls vagina and does the boy put it in by force or musale?

Why didn't the boys have this unit with us because it consens them?

Is a doctor's present necessary when two people have sexual intercourse?

Why is the father always so surprised when his wife says "I'm going to have a baby" after this has happened?

At the conclusion of the course, the teacher asked the children for a frank evaluation of the course. Here are two replies:

Mrs. F. explained everything and was not scared. A lot of people would be ashamed and scared to do so. I like the way you did it.

I think this was a very good course and I hope the boys will take the course also because if we know about them they should know about us. I think if they took this course some of them wouldn't be so nasty!

In conclusion, it may simply be said that sex education, even in this "enlightened" age, is largely a myth. Mostly, children obtain their knowledge haphazardly, as best they can.

• THE SOCIAL SEX ROLE

Turning now from the biological to the social sex role, let us note that research on the latter topic hardly existed prior to mid-century. One reason lies in the history of psychological theory. Both of the major comprehensive schemes for understanding human behavior—the behavioral and the psychoanalytic—had needs at the center of their systems; and basic needs, such as food, security, and love, are common to both sexes. Neither system directed attention to sex differences in the patterning of these needs (Kagan, 1964). However, from about mid-century on, research on the social sex role has proliferated, although reasons for the spurt are not clear. Perhaps attention was called to the topic by the evidence of sex differences that emerged in the course of various longitudinal studies.

For proper orientation to this topic, we should become acquainted with certain concepts. Recall that **sex role** refers to those psychological characteristics and behavioral patterns characteristic of each sex. It consists of behaviors socially defined as appropriate to one's status as male or female. It represents the abstracted concept of the ideal male or female as defined by the culture. A **sex-role standard** refers to approved characteristics for males and females.

An individual may relate to his sex role in several ways (Lynn, 1959). His **sex-role preference** indicates perception of one role or the other as more desirable. It may be measured by asking a child whether he ever wanted to belong to the other sex, or whether he prefers objects associated with that sex. A boy may overtly deny that he would prefer to be a girl but clearly demonstrate such a preference by eschewing rough-and-tumble games for hop-scotch and weaving.

Sex-role adoption involves actually taking the behavioral characteristics of one sex or the other. Normally, each child adopts the socially ascribed sex role, although certain children, to a greater or lesser extent, may not. Susie plays the boy role wherever allowed, in clothes, manner, and gesture; Tommy dares adopt only a few girl patterns, such as wearing relatively frilly clothes or playing with girls.

Whatever a child's behaviors, **sex-role identity** indicates how he feels about himself. It comprises a complex set of beliefs and attitudes about himself. For instance, a boy may affect "all-boy" behaviors yet secretly prefer the girl's role. He secretly identifies with the other sex but for expediency's sake plays the role assigned him.

In every culture, the sexes play distinctive roles, whether because of physical differences or accepted power relationships. Since males are typically dominant, they tend to preëmpt for themselves the higher status, leaving the more humdrum activities to the weaker sex.

Significance of the Social Sex Role

Social adjustment necessitates a child's learning the behaviors appropriate to his sex and knowing those expected of the other sex. Inwardly, he may reject society's differential patterns, but in most cases he effects some sort of compromise with them. For instance, he is expected to adapt his behaviors to whichever sex is present. Joey may muss Arnold's suit but not Bonnie's dress. He may talk tough to Jack but must speak politely to Jenny.

Similarly, others modify their behaviors toward the child according to his sex. Whatever his picture of himself, he must somehow cope with the image he creates in the eyes of others. Tony identifies with girls, but his relatives insist on giving him boys' toys for Christmas. Moreover, a child inevitably, albeit unconsciously, absorbs something of societal concepts into his self-image. Regardless of how much he may imitate girls or identify with them, the boy's self-identity will reflect in substantial degree society's treatment of him as a male.

The social sex role is especially important in countries with high sex polarization—that is, where behaviors appropriate to each sex are highly differentiated. The first question asked at birth is: "Is it a girl or a boy?" Henceforth, sex role modifies a child's total life pattern. It defines daily activities: Bill plays football; Judy knits. It delimits privilege: Tim can use tough language; Sally can cry. It determines early occupational fantasy and identifications: Clarence plays cowboy; Debbie plays nurse. It permeates all a child's perceptions, competencies, prejudices, and reactions

223

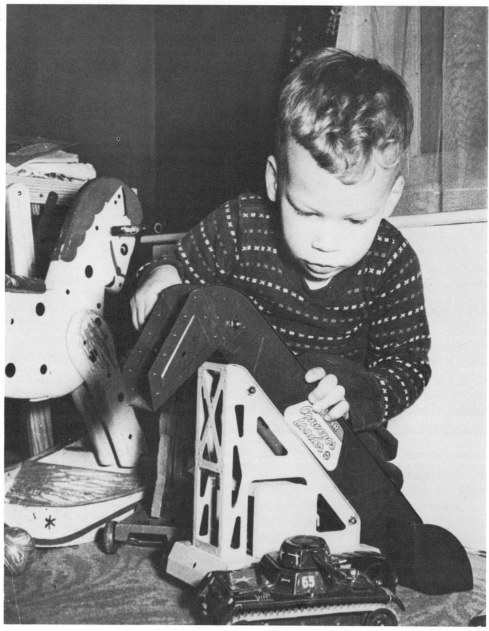

The stage is set to elicit sex-appropriate behaviors.

in all sorts of subtle ways. In one study, when the content of problems was altered to make them more typical of both sexes, sex differences in problem solving were reduced (Milton, 1959).

When the whole society is sexually polarized, most of our attitudes and actions are colored by our sex roles. A boy may resent women teachers, believing they cannot appreciate tough guys. A girl may automatically vote for George rather than Grace to be class president because "chief executives" are typically male.

The wisdom of strict polarization is dubious. For one thing, it is based on a fallacy: that the physical bases of behavior are distributed bimodally between the sexes. In addition, each sex is compressed into a mold and thus deprived of certain behaviors for no other reason than custom. Mary would rather take shop than sewing, and the current cost of household repairs would make such a choice highly functional. However, school policy dictates that she take sewing instead. Polarized sex roles also lead to rivalries and jealousies. Albert resents the greater leniency shown his sister, while Nancy is jealous of her brother's exemption from dish-washing chores. Meantime, the establishment of a satisfactory heterosexual orientation is impeded. Even though children's roles are less polarized than those of adolescents, they nevertheless lay the foundation for later husband-wife roles. The girl who resents the preference shown her brother may become the wife who is sexually cold and belittles her husband. Moreover, the child who dislikes the sex role assigned him may resist polarization altogether. Soured by squabbles with the other sex, he resolves never to marry and will probably keep his resolution.

Age-Stages in Sex-Role Development

Infancy and early childhood. Authorities disagree on the significance of the early years for sex-role differentiation. On the one hand, Sears and associates (1957) found few dimensions on which very young boys and girls were differentially treated. Only about 4% of the parents said they stressed sex role in child-rearing, while about 5% claimed that sex made no difference whatsoever. The vast majority acknowledged placing some weight on it, but not a significant amount. From such reports it would seem that early years are not highly significant in determining sex role. Nevertheless, in an informal survey, mothers of children aged one to five reported fussing with their girl babies' hair and dressing them in feminine fashion, while rough-housing the boys (Hartley, 1964). Also, the young child is exposed from birth to all sorts of sex-related symbols: style of wearing hair, depth of voice, posture at the toilet, and characteristic behaviors of each parent in the home (Kagan, 1964). In short, children become oriented to their respective sex roles in hundreds of subtle and constantly recurring ways.

Here four college students tell when and under what circumstances they first became especially aware of their own sex roles:

> I first realized I was a girl when I was in the first grade and a boy kissed me in the cloakroom. I told my mother, who said he was a naughty little boy. I shied away from boys after that, and was aware of sex for the first time.

> My sex role was first brought home to me at age five, when I visited the dentist. "You are a big boy now," he said, "so show us you are a big boy!"

> Father became ill, and I took over being the man of the house as a boy of seven would in a situation like this.

> I became conscious of being a girl chiefly through restrictions placed on me because of my sex; I was encouraged not to play football; I had to wear silly little dresses instead of jeans; I was expected to wash the dishes and mind my baby brother. When I heard that kissing my elbow would change my sex, I strove nightly to do just that.

The evidence suggests that sex-role differentiation proceeds gradually, probably beginning in the second year and becoming definitely established by age three (Sears et al., 1957).

While ideas *about* sex role are not clearly crystallized by age six, there is already a considerable overlap between standards of first-grader and adult. In the next few years, ages six to 10, sex roles become pretty clearly delineated, with girls increasingly conformist and boys asserting more leadership (Tuma and Livingston, 1960).

Comparison of pre- and post-adolescents. By adolescence, sex identification has become clearly fixed. The change is thrown into focus by comparing pre- and post-pubescents. As the body becomes distinctly more masculine or feminine, the individual gradually reacts to others' intensified perceptions, strengthening his self-image as male or female. On

225

standardized tests, post-pubescent boys and girls make higher scores typical of their sex than do pre-pubescent persons of the same age (Terman and Miles, 1936). In drawing the male figure, pre-pubescents endow him with such masculine objects as cigars, pipes, cigarettes, scars, masks, and accentuated adam's apples. Post-pubescents more often than pre-pubescents draw neckties on the male figures, indicating that maleness at this stage is associated with social proprieties (Smith, 1953).

From birth to adulthood, only one age span for each sex — birth to age three for girls and birth to age 10 for boys — appears significantly related to adult sex-typed interests. Whatever tendencies each sex shows during these years is predictive of related interests in adulthood (Kagan and Moss, 1962).

The Male Role in Our Society

Advantages. We have already discussed some aspects of male and female sex roles, but now, for better perspective, let us focus on each. It is commonly acknowledged that the male's role carries greater advantages. The girl is in effect punished for being a girl, through being accorded a lower status and denied equal autonomy (Hubert and Britton, 1957). She is treated as a child until she is handed over to her husband. The male's role, on the other hand, carries with it broader opportunities. If funds for education are limited, they go for the boy's education, not his sister's. It is a man's world, ordered by men; and it is men who carry the power and prestige. In consequence, the masculine role brings much ego-satisfaction. Masculinity is idealized; for example, in royal families more cannon shots herald the arrival of boys than of girls. The boy's superior status permeates every aspect, minor and major, of the culture. Prizes in breakfast cereal typically have masculine appeal. Even the most basic social institutions perpetuate the pattern of masculine aggrandizement. The Judeo-Christian faiths involve worshipping

God the "Father" and Christ the "Son" (Brown, 1958).

Both Freud and Adler stressed the superiority of masculinity. Freud referred to penis envy, or the girl's desire for the male organ, which symbolizes masculinity and, indirectly, the boy's higher status. Adler pointed to the driving force both in males and many females to achieve the ultimate — that is, the masculine.

The boy also holds a strong sex advantage. His sex feelings are considered legitimate. He is unencumbered by as great a need as weighs on the girl to suppress sex urges. And while such feelings are hardly insistent before puberty, basic sexual attitudes are in process of establishment.

The boy is also granted more individuality. His questioning is healthy curiosity, the girl's willfulness. To question authority and kick over the traces is masculine. Certain traits widely acknowledged as contributing to enriched living — initiative, independence, curiosity, and activity — are encouraged far more in boys than in girls. Small wonder, then, that boys like the role accorded them. Far more girls would like to be boys than boys would like to be girls (Winker, 1949). Here boys tell some things they like about their role:

I like it cause I don't have to do the dishes, and can play ball. (age 9)
I wouldn't want to be a girl because they're sissy. (age 8)
I'm glad I'm a boy because I don't have to babysit. (age 9)
I'm glad I'm a boy because boys have more fun, and can go places more. (age 10)
I'd rather be dead thin to be a gril. (age 7)

Disadvantages. Nevertheless, the masculine role is both ambiguous and narrow. The boy's peers condone rough behavior; his mother, perhaps secretly abetting the same pattern, overtly praises gentle behaviors. Thus, if the boy fights he is punished; but if he shrinks from fighting he is branded a sissy. Meanwhile, since his father is absent from home during most of his waking hours, and most of his early teachers are women, he lacks mature male models.

The image of the ideal boy is also narrow. He must be a "red-blooded gentlemanly go-getter, and any confessions of doubts or insecurities about himself would tarnish his image and render him suspect of femininity" (Gillin and Gillin, 1944, p. 172). Nevertheless, only a fraction of all boys fit this image completely. Few are altogether strong, self-sufficient, brave, and self-confident. Nevertheless, the pressure is so great that the male tries hard, though futilely, to achieve this overidealized image. Anxious lest he fail, he avoids femininity like the plague and overstrains to be masculine (Gray, 1957).

In overreaching for masculinity, many boys are driven to excesses. To appear properly tough, some become delinquent. They have difficulty discriminating between acceptable "all-boy" behavior and unacceptable delinquent behavior. Others feel compelled to prove themselves sexually, because sexual aggressiveness represents both "grown-upness" and masculinity. Thus a boy may become involved in forms of sex play that lay the bases for future neurosis, perhaps at the same time exploiting other children.

In the vocational area, the boy's role is discontinuous — that is, it is so unlike the adult role that it provides neither transition nor adequate training. He is trained to be autonomous, self-sufficient, and status-seeking, but most jobs are routinized and directed by a boss. Nor is there room at the top to accommodate the armies of little boys endowed by their parents with an insatiable desire to get there.

Despite these disadvantages, only the rare male dislikes his role. Here are two such exceptions:

My father was indifferent toward me although I was the first-born son. Since he never showed me any affection, I had very much to do with my mother, and grew up imitating her and wanting to be like her. For a time I wanted to be a girl, but became resigned to my role.

As a child, I always felt the male's role was a limited one. I was forbidden to strike girls, even when I was mad at them.

The Female Role
The female's questionable advantages.
The female's role, like the male's, is said to carry with it certain advantages; however, inherent in nearly every one of these so-called benefits are potential dangers as well. For instance, the girl is said to be more secure from life's strains, because she is sheltered as a child and upon marriage simply transfers her dependency from parent to husband. However, this same protection makes new situations appear threatening, so that the female finds the world a more frightening place than the male. Moreover, the sheltered life is hardly the full life or the creative life.

The girl is permitted to cry, while her brother is confined to a certain stoicism. Theoretically, she is thus permitted a catharsis her brother is denied. In actuality this is not quite the case. The male's outlets are different, but they are fully as diverse and probably healthier than the female's. He gives vent to his feelings in vigorous, large-muscle activities like fighting or sports, which substantially reduce the negative effect of strong unpleasant emotions. Besides, crying, though perhaps involving some cathartic benefit for the female, casts her in the image of a child. Whatever benefit she gains from release is offset by appearing immature. Similarly, the female is permitted a warmer, softer disposition, but this trait pattern, unless blended with a certain firmness and toughness, easily degenerates into weakness. Girls are also allowed considerable latitude in sex role. The boy is required to be all-boy, while the girl is permitted more other-sex behaviors, perhaps because striving for male status is understandable.

Most girls, even small girls, adjudge the privilege of motherhood their sex's greatest gift. It is ego-strengthening to look forward to being the focal point of the young child's existence. However, the woman who makes motherhood the core of her existence may find her life empty after the children leave home. Besides, the concentration on motherhood often results in excess mothering, which robs children of initiative and self-reliance.

Whether through rationalization or genuine conviction, most girls ultimately accept their role and fail to perceive the dangers inherent in many of its so-called advantages. Here two girls tell why they like their role:

> I always liked being a girl because I enjoyed dressing up in my mother's old clothes and pretending I was a big girl. I never enjoyed baseball. I'm more the housewife type.

> My father took a great deal of pride in me. He was strict about my being neat and clean and acting like a little lady. His attention made me glad I was a girl, because my older brothers were not thus pampered.

Clear-cut disadvantages. Other aspects of the female role are less ambiguous and more clearly handicapping. Informal studies by the author have revealed that elementary teachers find little boys more likable and interesting than little girls. Moreover, at Ohio State University, fully 91% of the men and 66% of the women expressed a preference for a male child if they could have only one (Dinitz et al., 1954). The knowledge of this differentiation undoubtedly undermines the female's self-respect (White, 1950).

The female also suffers a sex disadvantage, in the psychobiological sense. Sex pleasure is deemed a male prerogative, from childhood onward. The boy can acknowledge his sex drive, but the girl must repress hers. When children engage in sex play, the girl is blamed more even as a child. Also, the girl is supposed to acknowledge the boy's superiority, although she is conceded the right to manipulate him. It may be questioned whether such duplicity and inferiority can be reconciled with the ideal of a mature personality.

In still other ways, the female's role obstructs wholesome personality development. The girl is often busy housecleaning and baby-tending while her brother plays ball. He wanders the neighborhood at will, while she must report every move. The effect on the female personality is devastating. In comparison with men, women feel less adequate, less mature, more fearful, more anxious, and more inferior (Bennett and Cohen, 1959).

Here two girls tell why they dislike their role:

> I lived in a neighborhood with all boys. My father taught me to fight, though mother objected. For a time, I was better at sports than most of the boys. However, when I was about 10 the boys gradually eliminated me from their games because I was a girl. It was hard to try to adjust to the feminine role after climbing trees and playing ball with the boys.

> I hated being a girl because I loved to climb trees and wanted to live in my tree house.

While certain of the female's disadvantages become operant only in adolescence or adulthood, the flavor of her later role filters into the small girl's life. Diffusely, though no less significantly, adult manifestations of sex role affect the growing girl's self-concept, aspirations, and morale. Her childish and perhaps distorted perceptions of her future role undoubtedly affect her sense of personal well-being. Besides, at all ages she suffers the repercussions of whatever discontent her mother feels with her role.

Significantly, girls who delay assuming the traditional feminine role are more likely to develop career interests than are those who accept it at age six or younger. It is early masculinity of interest that relates to the development of the career pattern. While most girls eventually resign themselves to the traditional feminine role, delay in accepting it relates to interest development (Tyler, 1964).

Sex Roles Compared

In some respects, the sex roles can best be examined simultaneously. The entire culture is subtly divided into two "subcultures," each with its own way of life. Simply to dramatize this statement, imagine living just one day as someone of the other sex. In many languages, even inanimate objects are endowed with sex. In our own culture children associate inanimate objects more often with one sex than the other. Thus knives, boats, planes, trucks, and cement mixers are regarded by school children as masculine, while dolls, cribs, dishes, and nurses' equipment are regarded as feminine (Honzik, 1951). Daily activities, including games, are heavily differentiated. Boys are associated with sports, machines, speed, and power, while girls are associated with kitchen, home, personal attractiveness, and fantasy, in which they play subordinate roles to males.

When one group of children was asked which sex should perform each of certain tasks, the results were as follows: 74% of the boys compared with 44% of the girls believed the girl would bring a drink of water to mother. Almost the same ratio, 73% of the boys and 39% of the girls, indicated that the boy would protect a little girl. Almost all (95%) of the lower-middle-class children designated tree climbing for girls, but scarcely half (47%) of the upper-middle-class sample did. Both sexes assigned boys to emptying the waste basket, but more girls than boys saw both sexes performing this chore (Hartley and Hardesty, 1964).

Game preferences become increasingly sex aligned with age. From ages nine to ten, girls' preferences are more variable, while boys show increasing preference for male-oriented games with age. Many girls aged three to ten prefer masculine activities, while it is unusual to find boys who prefer feminine activities during this period. This difference in game preference is matched by the considerable number of girls stating a desire to be a daddy rather than a mother when they grow up (Honzik, 1951).

Another differentiation between the sexes concerns the qualities that flavor various activities. Girls' play is less violent and less varied than boys'. Girls keep house and cook, though seldom including adult male figures among their dolls. They enjoy caring for little children of either sex, like little mothers (Josselyn, 1955).

Boys are more aggressive. They are given license, even encouragement, to attack when threatened by another male. Every study of preschool or school-age children indicates aggressive behavior to be more characteristic of boys than girls (Bandura et al., 1961).

Behaviors are also sex-typed in terms of dependency, passivity, and conformity, with girls permitted greater license in these respects. In addition, girls are more preoccupied with people and interpersonal relations (Goodenough, 1957). They also show more submissiveness than boys, fewer overt signs of sexual desire, and greater cultivation of domestic skills (Harris, 1959). Whereas a socially oriented self-image would not connote instability or lack of self-esteem in the girl, it would in the boy (Carlson, 1965). For males, such characteristics as independence, interpersonal dominance over both sexes, initiation of sexual behavior, and acquisition of money and power are sex-typed requirements (Bennett and Cohen, 1959).

Many writers have differentiated the two roles categorically as either nurturant or instrumental. The female's orientation is toward pleasing others, while the male cannot be primarily oriented toward emotional reactions because his role involves the disciplined pursuit of goals that transcend the social situation (Johnson, 1963). To be nurturant, the female must cultivate attractiveness, effective social poise, and friendliness. By contrast, males are urged to be aggressive and independent in problem situations and to suppress strong emotions, especially anxiety (Parsons, 1955).

• FACTORS AFFECTING SEX-ROLE DIFFERENTIATION

Biological Factors

The part that heredity plays in differentiating sex traits and behaviors is surrounded by confusion. Boys are discouraged from looking toward careers as elementary school teachers because they are said "by nature" to lack the patience and gentleness required. Women are said to be less well fitted for responsible jobs because they are naturally more neurotic than men (Gordon, 1953). On the empirical level, males prove superior in problems that require restructuring, or reorganizing facts in new ways (Sweeney, 1953). Such differences, whether real or imagined, raise the question: Do sex-role differences rest on biological bases? A quotation from Scheinfeld tends to confirm the significance of biology in sex role, at least among chimps:

> Among the sex contrasts [one trainer] reported were these: "Little ape females are more docile, gentle, and ever so much more sociable; the boy chimps are apt to show aggressiveness very early (they bite more, for one thing) and are more active, restless and destructive. . . . The little girl chimp sits still and occupies herself much more than the male with activities not requiring a lot of moving around or strenuous exertion. She is more adept with her hands, it being far easier to teach little girl chimps to thread a darning needle. The strangest fact is how the little girl chimps take an interest in clothes, loving to be dressed up and responding eagerly to colors. The male is utterly indifferent to what you put on

him, and as like as not will rip his clothes off [1965, pp. 518–519].

Other data relating to animals confirm the existence of clear-cut sex differences. In corroboration of the findings reported above, Harlow (1962) reported self-grooming among monkeys to be a distinctively feminine behavior, rarely practiced by males. It is also well-known that castrated horses, bulls, and hogs are more docile, less aggressive, and less active than unaltered ones.

Among humans, the evidence for biological sex differences is less clear. However, one investigator reported parallels between the ovarian hormone cycle and emotional attitudes. Different periods of the cycle related to such emotions as flightiness, irritability, and introversion-extroversion (Benedek and Rubenstein, 1939). Note also that in cases of castration the individual experiences a reduction in energy level and emotional responsiveness. However, his reactions may derive at least partly from feeling "unsexed" and incapable of a normal love life.

If biological effects are indirect, however, they are no less real. For instance, masculinization is facilitated in young boys by their higher activity levels and greater freedom of movement. The girl is handicapped, at least mildly, in sports by the somewhat disadvantageous angle at which her legs attach to her body. In sum, however, biological differences would seem to play an insignificant part in sex role, at least on the human level. On the basis of data obtained by Bayley, by Gilkinson, and by Terman and Miles, Anastasi (1958) concludes that correlation between masculinity-femininity scores and physical characteristics have been generally low and insignificant. Such correlations as have been found, she says, are probably the result of social effects of conspicuous physical characteristics, rather than of underlying biological factors.

Contrary to popular opinion, no primary genetic or other innate mechanisms preordain psychosexual differentiation; nor do the internal organs directly affect sex role and identity. We find evidence of the foregoing assertion in the annals of pseudohermaphroditism, or cases in which the child has been reared as a member of the other sex. Usually, the sex role and psychosexual identity simply agree with the sex of assignment. Nevertheless, when mistakes in sexual identity are made, the "incorrect" gender role becomes indelibly imprinted and as irreversible as if innately preordained (Money, 1963).

Where problem solving is concerned, Taylor (1954) has shown that sex differences are primarily a matter of attitude and disappear with equal training. In fact, almost all personality traits and behaviors typically associated with males or females, with the possible exception of aggression, would seem to be more socioculturally than biologically determined.

Influence of Primary-Group Relationships

Basic processes involved. The most important environmental influences on acquisition of social sex roles are primary-group relationships. Within this framework, the sex-typing processes may include reinforcement, canalization, identification, and system of child-rearing. **Reinforcement** implies either "stamping in" or eliminating a behavior through reward or punishment. A girl's sex role may be positively reinforced by saying, "That's a good girl," when she has behaved in a ladylike manner, and a boy's negatively reinforced by punishing him when he cries.

Even more subtle is the effect of **canalization**—the process of arranging the child's environment so as to elicit sex-appropriate behaviors. Tommy is given toy soldiers, his sister a doll. Minnie's dress-up clothes are so fragile that she must exercise restraint to prevent tearing them, while Tom's clothes are far sturdier and permit uninhibited action. In addition, the child's life is

filled with infinite subtle reminders that he lives in a heterosexual world. He notes differences in his parents' voice tone, clothing, gestures, hair styles, and affectional-aggressive patterns. He sees restrooms labeled "Women" and "Men" and shops catering solely to one sex.

Another particularly basic process is **identification.** The child copies some respected same-sex image, until in his ideal's absence he acts as though he were present. Such identification is constantly fostered, often in subtle ways. Girls are told they will grow to be like

The girl depends largely on her mother for a model.

Mommy if they act like Mommy. Identical clothes are supplied for mother and daughter. If the girl wants to play at shaving, she is told "Mommies don't shave; daddies do."

In other cases identification is with some composite or stereotyped ideal of male or female as portrayed in books or on television. Without realizing it, the child involuntarily and unconsciously comes to imitate heroes and heroines carefully chosen to represent society's current masculine and feminine ideals.

Various theories have been proposed concerning the nature and degree of identification. Freudian theory has it that the boy's early identification with his mother makes him, in effect, his father's rival. He therefore becomes vulnerable to retaliation from the father. The theory holds that the boy switches identification to the father in order to feel as powerful as he can and thus protect himself from the fantasied threat his father poses. At the other extreme, the social-learning theorists say that the boy imitates his father simply because he loves him (Kimble and Garmezy, 1963). Mussen and Distler (1963) agree that nurturance strengthens identification but believe the crucial aspect to be salience, or paternal "impact." Investigators conclude that most boys perceive their fathers as power figures capable of dispensing either reward or punishment. Heilbrun and Fromme (1965) reported a positive correlation between good adjustment in children of both sexes and high masculinity in their fathers. Similarly, Hetherington and Brackbill (1963) found that boys identify with a dominant father but not with one who holds less power than the mother.

From a synthesis of these data it may be inferred that the boy who regards his father as both nurturant and powerful is highly motivated to incorporate the parent's qualities. By generalization, he tends to view other adults of the same sex in the same way and emulates their behavior. As a prevention against inappropriate identification, Mussen and Distler (1959) suggest that the child whose like-sex parent is weak might be placed in a foster home.

From the foregoing it would seem that the boy whose father is missing, either in the physical or psychological sense, will suffer. However, father-absence has a lesser effect on boys' identification than does mother-absence on girls'. Most boys in our culture see their father in but few aspects of his adult role. The father's occupational and sexual roles are all but a closed book to many boys. Much of his life is lived in secret as far as his son is concerned. In consequence, boys often identify with males outside the home, including their male teachers and male heroes of sports and fiction. By contrast, girls usually choose for their ideals women whom they actually know (Crane, 1955).

Age and sex interrelate as factors in identification. At first, boys as well as girls identify with their mothers, but boys soon shift to the paternal model. In doll play, girls more often use the mother doll, boys the father doll (Payne and Mussen, 1956). Moreover, among small girls, aged five, such traits as obstinacy, orderliness, and parsimony relate to the same traits in their mothers; however, no such relationship exists between these traits in sons and fathers, perhaps because they see little of each other (Hetherington and Brackbill, 1963).

Significance of identification with the parent. The foregoing data imply that identification with the like-sex parent is crucial; however, this is a debatable hypothesis. Let us first consider the view that such identification is necessary. Given a positive father-son relationship, assert Mussen and Rutherford (1965), no specific family socialization techniques are required for the boy to achieve an appropriate sex-typing. Similarly, they assert, a positive mother-daughter relationship is of paramount importance in establishing the girl's role. McCandless (1961) suggests that the daughter's best available sex-role model is a self-accepting mother. A major reason that the girl's maternal identification is so crucial is the weak support provided by society. While the boy is subtly propelled toward male identification by the higher status accorded males and by the presence of many outstanding male images outside the home, including politicians, athletes, and historically important persons, the girl depends largely on her mother for a model.

On the other hand, the girl's parental identification may be less important than the male's simply because her sex identification is less crucial. The girl's identification is less important, says Gray (1957), because the criteria for femininity are less easily specified. The ideal of femininity is more diffuse, embracing contrasting images of mother and career woman; and the girl who over-identifies with her mother may be at a disadvantage. Besides, the girl with a more masculine identification actually makes a better overall adjustment (Heilbrun, 1962).

Angrilli (1960) found results that have special implications for the preceding discussion. He reported many intertwined determinants of psychosexual development, not merely identification with the like-sexed parent. In his study, he found no relationship between the child's psychosexual orientation and either weak or strong parent-identification. Slater (1961) would seem to support Angrilli's position. It makes little difference for sex-role adoption, he says, with which parent the child identifies more. An adequate personal identification with both parents presupposes a satisfactory climate for making the correct choice. The choice itself will be made through the internalization of cultural norms held by both parents, which are conveyed to the child in many ways.

In sum, most psychologists accept the identification theory, at least in principle, as basic to normal sex-role acquisition; however, the theory may assume somewhat conflicting variations. By way of illustration, the following statements show that children may identify with parents of either their own or the other sex, and that the identification may operate in varied ways:

> From early childhood, I helped my mother bake and clean house; and I often thought how much fun it would be to have my own house and be a mother. (Female)
>
> I wanted to be a boy because I knew my father wanted it. I tried to do things

he admired. For instance, he was very proud of my running ability. (Female)

> I felt good about working with my father outside and being physically dominant over women, like God intended. Housework (dishes, washing) was girls' work, according to my parents; and strenuous work, requiring muscles, boys' work. (Male)

Differences in family sex-typing of boys and girls. Whatever the process involved, sex-typing for boys and girls differs in certain essential ways. In the beginning, sex-typing favors the girl, later on the boy. During early childhood, both sexes live in a female-dominated world, at home and at school, which

During early childhood, both sexes live in a female-dominated world.

would seem to favor the girl and disfavor the boy, who must somehow shuck off his original feminine identification. Later, as both sexes relate more to the larger world, the boy comes to perceive his sex as dominant and the girl to perceive hers as secondary, even inferior.

At any rate, the female's role is more continuous—that is, more steadily consistent with adult function. From the

233

very beginning, the girl lives in the home, which will always be her chief domain, while the boy's role, on reaching adulthood, will change drastically. Moreover, domestic chores are deemed feminine; and since the father often helps out, the boy may have trouble discriminating his parents' roles. As a result, says Schoeppe (1953), the male's identification is harder to accomplish. Girls grow up by evolution; boys are forced to grow up by revolution.

the types of reinforcement required for learning. The more social, overt type of responses expected of the girl require others' reactions. Without feedback, the girl cannot assess whether she is attractive, socially poised, or effective with others. The boy, on the other hand, develops many sex-appropriate behaviors on his own—for example, perfecting gross motor and mechanical skills. Observe the boy shooting baskets or repairing his bicycle. On the basis of

Boys live in a society that encourages aggressiveness as a masculine trait.

A further major difference in boys' and girls' sex-typing is this: The girl's identification is more family-bound, the boy's more externally determined. The girl is confined more closely to the home, thus reducing potential outside influence. By contrast, the boy is affected more by the standards of his peers. Also, since his father is usually absent during his waking hours, he is more influenced by the cultural image for his sex (Benedict, 1938).

Differential reinforcement of sex roles. Sex roles also differ in respect to

such experiences, he strengthens his masculine self-image. Moreover, independence of others' attitudes is itself a masculine trait. Therefore, the typical boy attempts to suppress anxiety over social rejection, because easy surrender to social pressures is considered unmasculine in this culture.

The sex roles differ also in respect to the strength of reinforcement they receive. The boy's role is more strongly reinforced, both positively and negatively, than the girl's. On the one hand, the boy lives in a male-oriented society, where masculinity is encouraged with countless status rewards. However, he probably gravitates toward masculinity less for the rewards involved than to escape femininity, for which he may be severely punished. That is, his role is defined less in terms of what he should do than what he should not do. If he plays with dolls or wears dresses, he is strongly ridiculed. In consequence, he avoids any appearance of femininity, thus acquiring a certain perceptual rigidity. Moreover, if he incurs disapproval for any feminine behavior, such as crying, he is anxious because he does not fully understand the reasons (Mussen and Rutherford, 1965). In consequence, boys become as sensitive to the female role as girls do—an awareness produced by an extreme need to avoid it. As a result, many males overstrain to be masculine and virtually panic at being caught doing anything traditionally defined as feminine (Hartley, 1959).

Differential roles of parents. Parents play different roles in the child's sextyping, in ways already implied. The father takes a more direct part in sextyping the child than the mother, who thinks of both sexes more as children (Goodenough, 1957). The father usually seeks to foster quite different traits in his children of each sex. He pushes his son toward the masculine role by being demanding, whereas he rewards his daughter just for being good and attractive. Through demonstrating high masculinity himself, he emphasizes her contrasting role. Moreover, by providing his daughter with a male sex model to relate to, he facilitates her heterosexual adjustment. Unfortunately, the father's frequent absence leaves both sexes without an adequate male model and may contribute toward the feminization of society (Mussen and Rutherford, 1965).

The mother plays an important role in the daughter's sex-typing, and a lesser but perhaps still significant one in the son's. The girl identifies with her mother directly, sharing in the mother's work and learning from her first-hand what women do as wives and mothers. The mother's effect on the boy's sextyping is much less direct. His sextyping seems unrelated to any specific relationship to his mother, or to the personality structures of either parent, or to parental encouragement of specifically sex-typed activities (Mussen and Rutherford). Nevertheless, argues Heilbrun (1962), the mother's influence, as compared with the father's, holds potential dangers for the boy. On the one hand, he absorbs the idea that the mother's affection is all-important and that the father's significance is negligible. On the other, if he fails to throw off the maternal yoke and become firmly masculine, he finds himself at variance with strongly held mores and susceptible to unhappiness and delinquency. This differential emphasis might not be inappropriate in a society that tolerated effeminacy and homosexuality in males, but it is hardly sound in our own. In other words, there may be a dissonance between the mores of our society and the measures provided to meet those needs.

Specifically, the mother may unwittingly encourage traits that the child will find maladaptive. She is more prone than the father to overprotect the children; and parental overprotection is a major predictor of nonmasculine sex-role interests in boys. Overprotection may also make the girl seem more feminine, but in the worst sense of the term—that is, through emphasizing weakness and dependency (Kagan and Moss, 1962). Here is testimony on how parents may affect the sex-typing of their children:

> My mother dressed me in brightcolored, fancy dresses, and spent a lot of time plaiting my hair into braids and putting on ribbons. She also let me watch her dress. She looked very nice and I wanted to be like her. (Female)

> My father wanted a son, and since there was none, my father treated me and my sister as boys. We were given boys' toys and boys' work to do. (Female)

235

My father wanted me to be all boy and taught me to act like a man. He hated "pretty, nice guys." I feel the same way, and am proud of it. (Male)

My mother was a wonderful woman, and I found her traits much more admirable than my father's. I'd say my traits are a blend of those I tried to copy from my mother and those I unwittingly and unwillingly acquired from my father. (Male)

Influence of other significant persons. The child's sex identification is influenced somewhat by all his primary relationships, including those with peers and with family members other than the parents. The sex of siblings is especially important. The child of either sex who has an older brother will be more masculine (Sutton-Smith et al., 1964).

Grandparents may be especially important, often holding up outmoded ideals for the sexes. The grandfather may take a dim view of Tommy's chemistry sets, believing his grandson should engage in more red-blooded activities. Significantly, the larger the number of adults in the household, the greater the sex differentiation, since "a greater number" usually indicates the presence of grandparents, who grew up in a more sexually polarized society (Barry et al., 1957).

Sociocultural Influences

Culture. The specific ways that primary groups induct children into their sex roles are largely determined by, and specific to, the culture. For in every culture and subculture there are cultural prototypes of the ideal male or female that constitute standards against which members of the society gauge the appropriateness of their sex-typed behaviors. The heroes of myth and song, the folklore of primitive tribes, television and magazines in modern societies — all convey the image of what males and females should ideally be. While parents constitute the original prototypes of ideal male and female, the child gradually accommodates his definition of sex appropriateness to the values of the broader community.

A survey of 110 cultures indicated a widespread tendency for the female prototype to be obedient and docile and the male to be more self-reliant and achievement-oriented (Barry et al., 1957). However, personality is plastic, and sex roles may undergo extensive variations (Mead, 1935). Among the Tchambuli of New Guinea, little girls of 10 and 11 were bolder and more alert than the boys. The women had shaved heads and served as managers and providers. It would appear that in many sub-cultures sex becomes an arbitrary device for the ascription of duties and status (Mead, 1939).

Even those traits considered incontrovertibly masculine or feminine may undergo drastic cultural modification. Apparently, the critical age for such characteristics is early childhood. The die is cast by age six, after which realignment of sex-role identity is rare (Money, 1963). Even aggressiveness, a cornerstone of masculinity, is modifiable. Boys whose fathers are away from home are slower to develop the aggressive behaviors associated with their sex (Sears et al., 1946). After checking available research, Tyler (1965) concluded that any individual of either sex may possess any degree of psychological masculinity or femininity.

Within different cultures, **polarization,** or distinctiveness between social sex roles, varies greatly, generally being greater in North America and Africa and least in Oceania. Where economics are dependent on physical strength, such as in many primitive societies, sex differences are wide (Barry et al., 1957). By contrast, in New Zealand, girls participate in only slightly less vigorous sports than boys. As a result, there is little observable concern over demonstrating sex masculinity or femininity by indulging in, or refraining from, sex-appropriate activities (Landreth, 1963).

Most cultures delay specific sex-typing until after infancy. In 92 out of 96 cultures, sexual differentiation of infants was deemed unimportant. Often babies constituted a single status undifferentiated by sex, although the "boy" and "girl" designations were still used (Barry et al., 1957).

Since biological differences in childhood are slight, perhaps these neutral social-sex statuses would normally persist into puberty. However, social pressures influence boys and girls to conform to their respective roles. It may be that relearning as late as puberty would prove too difficult to effect the transition to polarized statuses.

Social class. Cultural influences on sex-typing are modified somewhat according to subcultural variations. Lower occupational groups differentiate sex roles earlier and to a greater extent than do middle economic groups. They distinguish the boy's and girl's statuses and behaviors somewhat rigidly; middle-class children, on the other hand, are dressed and treated much alike. Middle-class children of both sexes are dressed similarly for play, and girls are given tricycles and guns if they wish them. When a girl plays with wagons, trucks, and toy soldiers, the situation apparently does no violence to her sex-role cognition, and it would be wrong to interpret a girl's liking for such things as rejection of sex role (Hartley, 1964).

The boy's position relative to the girl's is best in the lower class, because the higher the social class, the narrower the status distinction between the sexes. Moreover, working-class, as compared with middle-class, jobs (for example, bulldozer operator versus auditor) are conducive to masculinity in the traditional sense (Rabban, 1950). Hence, the lower-class boy's father is likely to perform a distinctly masculine work role.

The girl's situation improves among the higher social classes. In the lower class she is closely restricted to what is deemed appropriate for her sex. However, in the middle class her sex role provides greater room for maneuvering than does the boy's. He cannot play with dolls, but she can play football. Perhaps middle-class mothers, often dissatisfied with their own sex role, delay their daughters' sex-typed training (Komarovsky, 1946).

Reactions to One's Own Sex Role

Family influences. Individually, children vary widely in how they feel about their sex roles, the most important determinant being family experience. The father who desired a son may label his daughter "Daddy's boy." She, in turn, attempts to play the part. In such cases, peer education is insufficient to offset the parent's subtle influence.

Another factor is the special quality of the parent-child relationship. A child who possesses a poor relationship with his like-sexed parent may dislike the sex role that the parent exemplifies. Girls, on noting that society accords their father higher status, may become anxious about their own sex role (Kagan and Lemkin, 1960).

The child's feelings about his sex are also affected by the parents' differential treatment of sons and daughters. The son whose parents express a special liking for boys finds his own self-image enhanced; but if the parents frequently beat him, while catering to his sister, he may reject his sex role as undesirable.

Nor should we forget the sibling influence. The girl with an older brother often comes to view his sex role as more desirable than her own. She is more likely than the girl with an older sister to have a male cognitive profile, showing interest in economic items such as life insurance (Sutton-Smith et al., 1963).

Sociocultural influences. Societal values are important too. Cultural notions of male superiority, for example, are inculcated by both sexes. In one study, children aged eight to 15 were asked to state whether boys or girls possessed to a greater degree a list of 237 desirable or undesirable traits. Both sexes rated boys more favorably, and the older the group, the more favorable the rating given the boys (Smith, 1939). Undoubtedly, the girl's inferior status is one reason more girls than boys dislike their sex role.

The effect of social class is perhaps clear, in view of what has been said elsewhere. Boys of all classes, especially the lower class, are relatively content with their sex-role status. Presumably, the middle-class girl is happier than her lower-class counterpart because her status is relatively higher; however, an alternative hypothesis presents itself: perhaps the lower-class girl is more content, simply because her role is rigidly defined and hence less ambiguous; the middle-class girl may have just sufficient status to desire more. A comparable situation may be said to exist among black people, who began to fight for equality only after they had had a taste of it. To date, data are lacking to support these hypotheses.

Cross-cultural comparisons of reaction to sex role are lacking; therefore, the status of such reaction must be inferred from the relative status accorded the sexes within the cultures concerned. In Russia, women repeatedly expressed to the author their satisfaction with the economic opportunities accorded them. However, the author noted little tendency among middle-class Russian males to assist with housework. In primitive societies, where the author has traveled extensively, sex roles appeared relatively inflexible. However, this is not the same as saying that inflexibility creates discontent. It may well be that the reverse is true. One is hardly concerned with facts that he can do nothing about.

Personality factors. Perhaps the most basic factor in reaction to sex role is the individual's congeniality with that role. Sometimes a child is biologically ill-adapted to his role. A girl should be pretty and small, a boy tall and strong,

with a large muscle mass (Cobb, 1954). Hence the male weakling will be a cast-off on the playground, and the girl with unattractive features will be less well accepted than her more attractive peers.

Personality traits are perhaps more significant still. An independent girl may resent the female's passive role, while a mild-mannered boy may shrink from rough-and-tumble play. The happy, secure child will be favorably disposed to all adjustments required of him, including sex-role adaptation. Another factor is past success in playing one's role. The boy who is regarded as "all boy" is approved by others; hence he tends to find his role more gratifying. The girl who lacks the graces expected of her sex may find her social role uncomfortable.

Age. Another factor modifying the child's attitude toward sex role is his age. Among very young children, sex roles are commonly so undifferentiated that extreme distaste for one's own role is uncommon. However, Hartup and Zook (1960) reported that by age four boys identified more closely with their role than girls did with theirs. Brown (1956) found similar results, using an ambiguous child figure called "It" to test children's attitudes toward sex role.

Between ages three and a half to ten and a half, boys expressed a stronger preference for the masculine role than did girls for the feminine role. Among the boys, 85% in kindergarten and 95% in grade 3 indicated that "It" would rather be an Indian chief than an Indian princess. Girls aged three and a half to six and a half gave more heterogeneous answers. About half had "It" preferring cosmetics, half shaving articles. Between the sixth and ninth years, most of the girls showed a strong masculine preference. Boys at all ages showed a strong preference for the masculine role. At age eight and thereafter, between 90% and 95% said "It" would rather wear a shirt and trousers than a dress. In sum, Brown reported the girl to be feminine-oriented before age three and somewhat less so from then until age 11. Originally, the girl identifies with her mother, but exposure to a masculine-oriented culture apparently breaks down this identification.

During this interim between ages three and 11, significant changes take place. At first, girls are accorded approximately the same freedom and privileges as boys; however, by grade 3 they become vaguely aware of subtle pressures toward feminization. Some girls persist in the tomboy role but are concerned about it and show a peak of anxiety. Those who manifest trends toward more ladylike behavior show correspondingly less concern (Sutton-Smith and Rosenberg, 1963).

This girl's unusual testimony indicates how feelings about sex roles may change.

> When I was age 10, I was permitted to have a kitten, which proceeded to grow into a cat. I took her to a vet to have "her" spayed, but was told "she" was a tomcat. I scorned the cat for being a male, and loved it much less than when I'd believed it to be a lady cat. Until then I always believed females the superior sex; but as time went on, I came to believe them inferior, in terms of what society does to them today.

During this same period, boys manifest a steady increase in masculine sex identification. Among a group of boys aged five to 12, more of the younger than older boys drew same-sex figures first when asked to draw both sexes. By college age, 91% of a group of males drew the masculine figure first, while only 67% of the females drew the feminine figure first (Smith, 1953).

Changes in reaction to sex role may also be due either to changes within the individual himself or in his interpersonal relationships. The frail, pretty little girl who finds herself persona non grata in vigorous childhood groups may often wish she were a boy. However, after puberty she may discover her helplessness and fragile beauty assets in attracting males, and thereafter she may enjoy her femininity. Similarly, the boy whose father always favored his sister may find being a boy more pleasant after his mother remarries. His step-father, having no son of his own, caters to the boy and ignores his sister, the erstwhile family pet. Again, when parents who wanted a son but got a daughter gradually shift from rejection to acceptance, the girl may accordingly achieve greater self-acceptance, including acceptance of her sex role. Or the boy who is vaguely unhappy because he performs poorly at football may become better adjusted after his father teaches him to hunt and fish.

• A PERSPECTIVE ON SEX ROLE

A proper evaluation of the foregoing discussion should take into account the fact that social sex roles are in a state of flux and that disagreement exists concerning their present status. Some people see a narrowing gap between the sexes. In America more than in most European countries, sex differences are blurred (Clausen and Williams, 1963). For instance, in many communities, everyday dress has become almost identical for both sexes, while feminine frills are reserved for dress-up occasions. Children's games, too, like baseball and basketball, are now neuter, at least in grades 4 through 6. While males play few traditionally girls' games, in 1960 girls reported far greater interest in masculine activities than in 1926. In fact, the feminine self-concept has become generally more masculine (Rosenberg and Sutton-Smith, 1960). The greater sharing of activities has also increased the number of cross-sexed friendships (Broderick and Fowler, 1961). For further evidence of depolarization, note that in 1926 Terman and Miles found that women became more feminine with age. More recently, Kelly (1955) reported women's masculinity to increase with age. Since

239

the latter was a longitudinal study, it may have reflected the general reduction in sex-role differences in American society in recent decades.

Meantime, the male's sex role is widening and becoming less self-consciously masculine, at least in the middle class. The frontier, rural, hair-on-the-chest version of masculinity has failed, Denny (1963) asserts, and females are glad. One of the most observable shifts since World War II has been toward the "subtle, the Italianate, the pale, and the pensive. The frontier blonde and stubbled football player are out" (p. 144).

The reasons for decreased polarization may be several. Boys and girls receive the same education; the modern home permits little difference in tasks assigned each sex; and modern life simply makes sex differentiation less necessary. Both the so-called "masculine" tasks and the distinctly feminine ones have been taken over by machines.

Other factors, however, raise doubts concerning the basic nature of the change. Girls by and large do not desire a life of robust and vigorous masculinity. Similarly, boys, though accepting the virtue of being gentle and kind, balk at attitudes that would suggest sentimentality. Conversely, they are willing to grant females considerable latitude but are unwilling to concede them the more basic masculine attributes such as action, vigor, and achievement effectiveness (McKee and Sherriffs, 1957). Children continue to believe that aggression, dominance, and independence are more appropriate for males, and nurturance and **affect** for females (Hartley, 1960).

In sum, many persons believe that the homogenization of the sexes is proceeding apace; others acknowledge change but insist that the core of sex-role stereotypes — traits such as male aggression and female passivity — will change last, if at all.

• SUMMARY

The child's **psychosexual development** involves the psychobiological consequences of sex drive, interest, and awareness, as distinct from the broader behavioral patterns that constitute social sex roles. Infants are born with neither sex drive nor sex emotions but with the capacity to develop them. The hormonal substrate sets no goals, and the sex structures permit wide variations in means employed to satisfy sex drive.

Sex drive and behaviors hold significance both for the individual and for society. Sexual behaviors relate to fundamentals of group living, including marriage, inheritance, and property laws. Although the individual himself can survive and be healthy without sex behaviors, any felt need that is blocked may assume an exaggerated importance.

In Western culture, the normal pattern of psychosexual development is sometimes portrayed as involving four stages, beginning with the **narcissistic** stage, when the infant obtains sensual satisfaction from his own body. During early childhood, or the **Oedipal** stage, the child presumably becomes attached to the parent of the opposite sex. In the third, or **homosexual**, stage, the child under-associates primarily with members of his own sex and sometimes engages in exploratory sex behaviors. The final, or **heterosexual**, stage, which normally begins after puberty and persists through life, involves direction of mature erotic feelings toward the opposite sex. However, it is doubtful that everyone goes through all the foregoing stages, or in this order, because sex development is a complex process involving various kinds of love objects and various blends of sex feelings and behaviors.

Children may have a variety of sex experiences, including **masturbation**, or the fondling of one's own genitals for the sake of pleasure. Except for the emotional effects caused by adult attitudes about it, masturbation is normal and harmless, although compulsive masturbation may be a symptom of tension. A deviant sex behavior, **homosexuality**, or erotic attachment to members of one's own sex, possibly has its origin in childhood. In fact, John Money believes that an individual's basic sexual orientation is determined by the time he reaches age six. Among determinants of unfortunate sex orientations may be various sexual traumas, or shock experiences, such as molestation by an adult.

Parental influences undoubtedly affect children's psychosexual development strongly. Most parents simply prohibit their children from sex behaviors and offer little wholesome advice or education. Parental overreaction to sex creates a corresponding overreaction in children. Such slight sex education as is provided, either by family or school, typically ignores the more subtle psychological aspects of sex. Exactly what information should be taught, or at what age, or by whom, is in dispute.

The child's social sex role is much broader than his biological sex role and involves the patterns of behavior and characteristics deemed appropriate for his sex. The **sex-role standard** refers to approved characteristics for each sex. **Sex-role preference** refers to perception of one or the other role as preferable, and **sex-role adoption** to assuming the behavioral characteristics of one sex or the other. An individual's sex-role identity indicates aspects of his self-concept that concern sex attitudes and the way an individual incorporates sex into his own self-image.

The individual's sex role and the way he relates to it help pattern his life and determine his adjustment. The whole of society is sexually polarized, so that individuals of each sex are expected to adhere to the sex role assigned them. This prescription results in jealousies between the sexes and in unhappiness for those who find aspects of their role distasteful.

Acquisition of sex role begins during the second year and becomes established by age three. By adolescence, sex-role identification is clearly fixed and can probably not be significantly changed. Among the factors that influence children's psychosexual development, biol-

ogy plays an important part, although just how important is unclear. Biological factors would seem to affect sex differences significantly in animals but much less so in humans. No primary genetic or other innate mechanisms decree one's psychosexual identification; in fact, in cases of pseudohermaphroditism, where mistakes in sexual identity have been made, the individual's psychosexual identity simply agrees with the sex of assignment. Once gender role becomes imprinted it seems irreversible.

The sex-typing processes themselves include **reinforcement** — that is, stamping in or eliminating specific behaviors through reward or punishment; **canalization,** meaning setting the stage to elicit the approved behaviors; and **identification,** or the copying of a respected same-sex image, usually the parent. In general, the girl identifies more often with her mother, the boy with his peers and men outside the home. The boy's role is reinforced both positively and negatively more than the girl's. That is, he is rewarded for being "all boy" and punished for being any-part girl. Presumably, the mother tends to treat both sexes more as children, while the father strongly differentiates between daughters and sons, hence playing a significant part in their sex-typing. Undoubtedly, siblings and other relatives within the home, especially grandparents, affect the child's sex-typing, too.

Society itself tenders to parents the pattern for their children's sex behaviors. In every culture and subculture there are prototypes of the ideal male and female. Cross-culturally, the female prototype is obedient and docile, the male more self-reliant and achievement-oriented. Otherwise, traits considered masculine or feminine vary widely with the culture, as does the degree of **polarization,** or differentiation between male and female. In general, polarization is more rigid in the lower than in the middle or upper classes. The girl's situation relative to the boy's improves among the higher social classes.

Each sex role carries both advan-

241

tages and disadvantages, though the male role holds relatively higher status and rewards. Males take great satisfaction in the freedom and high status accorded them, even in the very considerable burden of having to run the world. By contrast, the female's role obstructs high achievement and healthy personality growth. Not surprisingly, far more females than males are dissatisfied with aspects of their sex role, although many of them deem it an honor to have the privilege of motherhood. In specific cases, an individual's reaction to his sex role depends somewhat on his success in playing that role and on his congeniality with that role. An individual's reaction to his own sex role may vary somewhat with the years, in terms of experiences in playing that role.

At present the social sex roles are in a state of flux, and disagreement exists concerning both the present status of sex roles and the direction they should take. Whether society should consciously modify sex roles in order to reduce disadvantages involved is in dispute. Anyhow, it is often averred that the differences between the sexes are becoming blurred, perhaps because today's society makes strong polarization either undesirable or unnecessary.

• SUGGESTED QUESTIONS AND ACTIVITIES

1. Observe several parents whom you know, and set down anecdotally any differences you note in their treatment of daughters and sons.
2. Observe an elementary school classroom and note differences in the teacher's treatment of boys and girls.
3. Analyze boys' and girls' toys in mail-order catalogs in terms of their differential effect on personality development. Does either sex miss anything essential through being denied toys associated with the other sex?
4. Look at comic strips, television programs, and children's readers and analyze boy and girl characters in terms of sex-role stereotypes portrayed.
5. Analyze in terms of sex role the boy and girl characters in several children's stories and cartoons.
6. Obtain children's readers of earlier years and compare with recent ones in terms of sex roles portrayed.
7. What effect do you believe each of these practices has on the boy's and girl's respective sex-role identification: the father's helping with the dishes; the mother's working; the child's attending a private boarding school catering only to one sex?
8. What do you believe accounts for the greater latitude in the female's than the male's sex role?
9. Should boys be given dolls so that they may more easily be inducted into their father role later on?
10. To provide more dynamic, vigorous sex-identification figures for girls, should history books include more achievements of outstanding women?
11. Should there be an equal number of male and female teachers in nursery school through grade 3 so that boys and girls will be adequately exposed to identification figures of both sexes?
12. Would children establish more natural heterosexual relationships and achieve fuller self-realization if the sexes were not segregated in childhood play situations, such as in physical education classes and "Y" activities?
13. In what ways, if any, should boys' and girls' sex roles be modified?
14. Do you believe the world of the future will call for sex roles that are more or less polarized than at present? What do you believe to be the trend in sex roles?
15. Have committees compile and analyze the results of these questions, answered by the class anonymously but with sex indicated: (a) If you could have only one child, would you prefer that it be a girl or a boy? (b) Who has the better of it in this culture, girls or boys? (c) Did you ever want to belong to the other sex? At what age? Why? Have your feelings about your sex role changed? (d) Relate to what extent, and in what ways, your own parents demonstrated differential treatment of sons and daughters. What other factors modified your feeling about your sex role? (e) Relate incidents or describe situations that first gave you a sense of sex identity.

• SUGGESTED READINGS

Beach, F. A., *Sex and Behavior*. New York: John Wiley & Sons, Inc., 1965. A number of experts present research about sex involving various species of animals and man and the approaches of different sciences to sex problems.

Erikson, E. H., *Childhood and Society,* 2nd edition. New York: W. W. Norton & Company, Inc., 1963. See Chapter 2, "The Therapy of Infant Sexuality" for a psychoanalytic treatment of early psychosexual development.

Johnson, M. M., "Sex-Role Learning in the Nuclear Family," *Child Development,* Vol. 34 (1963), pp. 319–333. Attempts to explain the roles of father and of mother in their children's sex-role identification. Johnson's hypotheses support the findings of a number of studies that do not fit any previous theories.

Kagan, J., "Acquisition and Significance of Sex Typing and Sex-Role Identity," in M. L. Hoffman and L. W. Hoffman, eds., *Review of Child Development Research,* Vol. I. New York: Russell Sage Foundation, 1964, pp. 137–167. Excellent survey of research on this topic.

Lansky, L. M., "The Family Structure Also Affects the Model: Sex-Role Attitudes in Parents of Preschool Children," *Merrill-Palmer Quarterly,* Vol. 13, No. 2 (April 1967), pp. 139–150. Parents' sex-role attitudes, especially those concerning the sex of their children, are studied in terms of family structure.

Maccoby, E. E., ed., *The Development of Sex Differences* (Stanford Studies in Psychology, V). Stanford, Calif.: Stanford University Press, 1967. Treats differences between the sexes in areas other than that of specifically sexual behavior. Suggests explanations for sex differences in temperament and ability among young children.

Money, J., ed., *Sex Research: New Developments.* New York: Holt, Rinehart & Winston, 1965. Reports important symposium concerning frontiers of sex research.

Mussen, P., and E. Rutherford, "Parent-Child Relations and Personality in Relation to Young Children's Sex-Role Preferences," *Child Development,* Vol. 34 (1963), pp. 589–607. Tests several hypotheses relating to the boy's father identification and the girl's mother identification.

Sutton-Smith, B., "Development of Sex Differences in Play Choices During Preadolescence," *Child Development,* Vol. 34 (1963), pp. 116–126. Reports results of a play inventory for children in midwestern townships in grades 3 through 6.

9
MORAL AND RELIGIOUS DEVELOPMENT

Evidence abounds that moral and religious questions play an important part in children's lives. Among trespasses college students recall having committed in childhood are these:

Girls:
Broke into houses that were being built.

Played with street-corner light buttons and held up traffic.

A girl friend and I stole things from the five-and-ten until age 11, when we were caught stealing dolls. The owner threatened to call the police and informed our parents.

Called people on the telephone and offered them phony deals.

Boys:
Mugged people, especially old women.

Played at Peeping Tom in girls' windows.

Hid in a stolen car; gang war; shoplifted clothes and candy.

Shot out street lights; stole a wheel and axle.

At age nine got caught with other kids breaking window in factory. Stole rubber bands at dime store to shoot bobby pins at girls in schools.

All I can remember is stealing a dime, at age five, from my own piggy bank.

On the basis of the foregoing sample, we can see that childhood morality is not simply a matter of dealing with pre-delinquents. It also involves distinguishing those factors that cause some children progressively to achieve mastery over antisocial impulses and others to persist in socially disapproved behaviors throughout life.

Student testimony indicates that moral situations in childhood may have long-term effects:

In the second grade, I was lectured before the whole class for cheating on a spelling test. I never cheated again. (Female)

At age eight, I swiped a book on yo-yo tricks from a ten-cent store, but my conscience bothered me so much I told my parents. They were very understanding and did not punish me, but I never did such a thing again. (Male)

Certain central concepts enable us to understand such episodes better. Among them is the concept of *moral-ethical values,* or generalized guides by which individuals judge the reasonableness and appropriateness of their relationships with mankind. **Morals** are standards of right and wrong determined by the values of the culture and subculture of which the individual is a part. The goodness or badness of an individual's **character** is merely a generalized reflection of the value judgments of his associates in a specific subculture (Thompson, 1962). *Moral behaviors* comprise those actions that hold special significance for the welfare of society and that may be judged to be supportive of the social good. An individual is judged as moral if his behavior conforms to the values of the dominant group, which serves as arbiter. Moreover, since what is deemed good depends upon, and grows out of, situational factors, standards of morality vary with time and place.

An individual's morals are reflected in his **ideals,** which represent standards toward which he strives. However, his actual behavior will depend on his concept of what an ideal means. Take, for example, honesty. A child who would not take money from his mother's purse may, without violating his conscience, copy another child's paper. In the latter situation, he reasons that no damage is done the other child; in the other case, he realizes that his mother would lack what she requires to pay the milkman.

The Nature of Moral Maturity
No standard criteria exist for moral behavior. However, Peck and Havighurst (1960), employing some 30 test instruments, found six separate factors that kept turning up on one test or another. (1) One of these was *outward conformity to rules.* At one extreme of this dimension is the person who cheerfully follows most regulations; at the other is the sullen delinquent who regards every social requirement as some-

thing to be evaded or violated or as something that does not apply to him. (2) A second dimension, *friendliness in outward behavior,* implies at the one extreme outward friendliness and helpfulness to others, and at the other, coldness, indifference, and condemnation. (3) *Freedom from inner hostility* suggests inner good will as opposed to sullen hostility. (4) A fourth dimension, *zestful spontaneous commitment,* implies doing good or evil in a wholehearted, positive fashion rather than approaching life half-heartedly, with feelings of futility and impotence. (5) *Susceptibility to inner controls* connotes behaving properly in the absence of external authority, as opposed to satisfying selfish needs whenever possible. (6) Finally, understanding the implications of behavior implies *rational self-criticism* as opposed to blind failure to perceive the outcome of one's acts.

Another dimension that might be added to this list is moral strength or courage, which connotes an individual's ability to maintain his own version of moral beliefs in the face of pressure from peers or adults. It would mean placing a higher pricetag on conscience than comfort and being willing to make a real sacrifice to uphold one's beliefs. It may have been commendable to be a freedom marcher in 1966, but hardly courageous, for such marches were in vogue.

Problems in Developing Morality

Children face many problems in developing morality, and the problems derive partly from the nature of morality itself. Moral distinctions are abstractions, and the capacity for abstraction must await an adequate level of intelligence and experience. While not specifically age-related, they nevertheless depend to an extent on maturity. They do not spring full-fledged into being; a long gestation is required. Furthermore, moral standards are relative, varying with circumstance. But until the child has lived for a span of years and associated with a variety of groups, the relative nature of morality is meaningless.

Another problem derives from the fact that the child *is* a child. Since the child's status is unequal, the parent does not feel compelled to reason with him. The parents' "do this" and "don't do that" are underscored with authority, not reason. Given all these obstacles, it is hardly surprising that many persons never attain a truly mature morality. They lack a proper base, established sufficiently early, to support it. They fumble their way through life, and when confronted by hard value judgments, beat a retreat into the safe and secure.

Another problem relates to the degree of generality or specificity of moral behavior. A heterogeneous society would seem to require constant adaptation to groups who sanction many variations of a general code. However, the Hartshorne-May studies (1929) reported moral traits to be specific, and recommended training in specific behaviors, such as particular ways of being honest, truthful, and the like.

Let us consider the evidence from this research. The tests were elaborately designed to simulate moral choices in real-life situations. Each child was placed in situations designed to elicit choices that would indicate various moral traits, such as persistence and truthfulness. The children tested in these situations revealed no generalized tendency to behave in specific moral ways. For instance, a child might cheat when supervised by a teacher he considered unfair but refrain in the case of one he liked.

The Hartshorne-May conclusion, that moral training must be specific to a situation, may be criticized on two grounds. First, certain of the test situations employed might raise some question. In one test, a child's persistence was judged by the length of time he could stand on one foot without leaning against an object, touching the foot to the floor, or losing his balance. Might not a child's ability to maintain this

247

posture depend more on motor control than on will to persist? Besides, how important a goal—simply to stand on one foot—is being tested? A child who might persist at length in a meaningful task might give up an artificial one as silly.

Second, discreteness of behavior—the apparent relevance of moral behavior to a situation—may reflect the investigator's perception rather than the child's. The child who cheats in the room of a disliked teacher may not have violated his concept of himself as an honest child at all. His goal might simply have been to outwit the teacher; he was not trying to get something to which he was not entitled. He had concluded he would receive low grades anyhow, because the teacher disliked him (Rogers, 1962).

• THEORIES OF MORAL DEVELOPMENT

Historical Perspective

Theories of moral development naturally reflect the times, and for best appreciation require a historical background. During Puritan days, it was believed that children were born with a burden of sin. Natural man was wholly vile, corrupt, and prone to evil; he could do no good without God's assistance. He thoroughly deserved to broil in hell for eternity, and would do so if he did not grasp the hand of grace offered him by a merciful Christ (Morison, 1936). Even in the poems and stories written to guide the young, we find the themes of threat and retribution. Children were led to believe that wrongdoing would inevitably bring punishment, certainly in the world hereafter, and most likely on this earth. Object lessons permeated children's literature. In one rhyme, a little boy who caught fish in a forbidden pond met swift punishment as he sought to place the fish on a shelf at home:

But as he jumped to reach a dish,
To put his fishes in,
A large meat hook that hung close by
Did catch him by the chin.

Poor Harry kicked and call'd aloud,
And screamed and cried and roared,
While from his wounds the crimson blood
In dreadful torrents poured.
[O'Keefe and Taylor, 1948, p. 22]

For centuries such dire threats were deemed necessary because it was believed that children were inherently evil. Children were to be rigidly trained, regardless of any resistance they might show. Parents who gave in to their cries would produce young monsters. The idea was to install moral codes much as a workman installs plumbing. However, by the 1930s psychologists had long accepted the idea that children were born neither good nor evil but were easily led astray.

The 1940s saw a dramatic change as psychoanalytic writers cautioned against overrestraining the child. Frustration, they said, would produce neuroses and the persistence of infantile wishes. Only his strong ego might safeguard a child against cruel overconscientiousness, which is the inner residue of the child's inequality with his parent (Erikson, 1965).

With the 1950s, the pendulum began to swing back again, but indecisively. Love and attention were necessary, but children should not be gratified continually. From within the framework of this intermediate position, two somewhat opposing doctrines have evolved. On the one hand, present-day Freudians agree on the need for both loving and training the child. The Neo-Freudians advocate extreme permissiveness in the name of Freud, although Freud himself believed some frustration was necessary both for individual personality development and the good of the social order. Strength of character, he believed, must be forged by trial. Presumably Ego, or self, should strike a balance between Id, or the primitive impulses, and Superego, or conscience. Similarly, Neo-Freudians, while emphasizing relative permissiveness, also see the need for an adequate Superego.

An opposing doctrine maintains that

if children's basic needs are not thwarted, an inherent growth process, or self-actualizing tendency, will lead them into paths of creativity and genuine morality. This concept is generally associated with Neo-Freudian or Gestalt-phenomenological theorists such as Fromm and Maslow. However, it dates from the romantic notions of the eighteenth and nineteenth centuries, when many French philosophers assumed goodness to be the original state of man.

Piaget's Contributions

Piaget (1932) perceived three forces as interacting to produce moral change: adult constraint, peer-group cooperation, and the changing character of the child's mind (maturation). These forces determine the child's progress through the two main stages of development. The first stage, from birth until about age seven, is characterized by *objective morality*. The term used to describe this stage, **moral realism,** applies solely to one feature characterizing it—judgment by the child of a deviant act in terms of the damage done. Other features of this age seem to refute Piaget's designation, however. For example, the child at this stage sees adults as dominant and omnipotent and rules as unchanging and to be obeyed without question.

During the second stage, the child comes to see rules in terms of their intent and what they are supposed to accomplish (**restitution**); but he still judges all people absolutely alike. Only later does he grasp the need for the differential application of principles (**equity**) to ensure real justice—realizing, for instance, that the lame boy should be given a handicap in running. In brief, the stage of moral equity involves concern for the details of a situation. It is further marked by the weakening of adult constraints as the child gains increasing autonomy and self-respect. He no longer sees laws as immutable or adults as omnipotent. He realizes that rules can be altered.

To illustrate the foregoing theory, consider two hypothetical situations employed by Piaget. (1) A little boy, John, is called to dinner. Unknown to John, behind the door to the diningroom is a chair on which there is a tray holding 15 cups. As he enters the room, the door knocks against the tray, and all the cups are broken. (2) One day a little boy named Henry tries to get some jam out of a cupboard while his mother is away from the house. He climbs on a chair but can't reach it. While he is trying, however, he knocks over a cup, which breaks.

Using moral realism, children in the youngest stage responded to these stories by saying that John was naughtier than Henry. After all, he had broken 15 cups, whereas Henry had broken only one. Older children, aged nine and ten, labeled Henry the naughtier, because he had intended to commit a misdeed. That is, they considered the intent more important than the material damage done. In another story, of a boy who had broken his little brother's toy, the older children said he should pay to have it mended. They now believed that punishment should entail putting things right (Berkowitz, 1964).

Re-tests of Piaget's theories have yielded uneven results (Whiteman and Kosier, 1964). Some studies support Piaget, at least in principle. For instance, Boehm and Nass (1962) found that children below age nine did indeed display moral realism in the story of the broken cups, and those over nine considered subjective responsibility. Other studies, however, indicate that different forms of judgment may occur at the same age level. Using a wide variety of verbally described situations eliciting moral judgments, Bandura and McDonald (1963) found that children between five and 11 exhibited highly discriminative moral judgments; that is, the developmental sequence proposed by Piaget proved by no means invariant. In short, criticisms of Piaget's conclusions about moral development are similar to those of other Piagetan theory, especially theory involving the age-stage concept.

For another thing, Piaget minimized the influence of the child's social environment. His subjects were children from the poorer section of Geneva; and studies of children with more diverse backgrounds have yielded correspondingly varied results. After reviewing the literature, Bronfenbrenner (1962) concludes that there is less and less empirical support for Piaget's formulation the further one goes from Europe.

The Family and Moral Development

More recent theories of moral development hinge on familial influence, which research indicates is basic (Hartshorne et al., 1930). Since moral values are critical, parents take a firm hand, generally depriving a child of his right to self-determination in this area. In fact, the family is the cornerstone of most theories of moral development. In one extensive study, children tended to resemble their parents on all values studied (Fisher, 1948). Family background had become indelibly etched in child character.

Parents shape children's moral behavior in many ways, one being the provision of mature models. Inherent in this concept is the implication that the parent serves as a sort of external superego. For instance, if an adult fails to punish an act, a child may assume an action good. In one study, preschoolers showed an increase in aggressive play when watched by a permissive adult but not when that adult was absent. As far as they were concerned, her failure to clamp down was equivalent to approval of their morally ambiguous aggressive behavior (Siegel and Kohn, 1959).

Some parents afford their children socially unacceptable models. When parents are rejected by the majority of their socioeconomic group, they may form a mutually supportive circle of deviant adult models who transmit their atypical behaviors to their offspring. This phenomenon is clearly evident in delinquent subcultures, in deviate religious or culture cults, and among some extremely impoverished groups (Festinger et al., 1956). An American vice-consul in Calcutta told the author that parents in certain Indian villages deliberately maim their children so that they will make better bait when begging. It is inconceivable that the children of such parents would ever acquire decent moral-ethical standards.

It is possible, of course, to exercise an effect contrary to familial influence even after a child has borne the impress of his family for years; but such experiences are seldom intensely enough or personally enough exerted to make any significant change (Peck and Havighurst, 1960).

The Sears study. Sears and associates (1957), in a study of family influence on character, defined high conscience as "inner control with resistance to temptation based on genuine acceptance of parental standards, the violation of which caused the child to feel guilty and ashamed." They interviewed 379 mothers of five-year-olds of all social classes. One question was: "When the child has deliberately done something he knows you don't want him to do, when your back is turned, how does he act?" Some mothers responded in this fashion: "Oh, I can always tell! Whenever he comes in with this sort of hang-dog expression and sort of stands around and looks at me and has a kind of sad look, I know he's done something wrong." Another child might sidle over to the mother with a shoulder-wiggling kind of behavior, get up close and say, "Mother I love you," then with tears streaming down, confess. Some children would open their remarks with, "Mother, I haven't done anything wrong." Other children, by contrast, showed fear and hostility. Some would be irritable toward the mother, muss her work, or snap off the television program she was watching. Still others showed signs of fear, perhaps disappearing for the afternoon.

Children who reacted by confessing, apologizing, or trying to make restitution were judged as having high conscience; those who reacted with hostility or aggression were classified as having low conscience. Three types of maternal behavior or attitudes correlated with high conscience. First, the mother wanted children. Second, she disciplined her children by love-oriented methods. That is, she deprived the child of the attention and affection to which he was accustomed, by sending him to his room, or saying "I don't think you have really thought about how I feel," or getting tears in her eyes and turning away. Such techniques, including withdrawal of love, worked only in the case of warm, affectionate mothers. Among cold mothers, the threat of withdrawal of love had no effect on conscience. "Apparently," stated Sears, "one cannot withdraw what isn't there." A third maternal behavior that related to high conscience was the use of reasoning, such as "Well, when he does something wrong, we sit down and talk about it, and I try to explain how I feel." However, this "understanding one another" can mean smothering the child into believing that he thinks the same way his mother does (Sears, 1960).

On the basis of this study, Sears derived a theory of conscience development. He noted that strong conscience failed to develop if the parent failed to meet the child's needs or to point out conditions of approval, or if, on performance of a disapproved act, the parent failed to withdraw approval or to set the limits firmly. The first stage in the development of strong conscience would thus be forming a reasonable emotional dependency on the parents, reinforced with affection, and creating an atmosphere of mutual trust. Since the mother's presence is rewarding, the child learns to imitate her and to do what she wishes — that is, to take the parental role himself. In short, he identifies, such identification being strengthened by the mother's warmth and love-oriented discipline tech-

niques. When the mother withdraws approval of certain acts, the child withdraws approval from himself when he performs those acts, even if she is absent. Here is an example:

> A couple brought with them for a visit to a friend's home their bright 17-month-old youngster. She explored the livingroom eagerly, twice almost knocking over a floor lamp. Each time her father said, "Martha, don't touch."
>
> After the second interruption, Martha began exploring again, several times stopping to glance at her father. Once she deliberately stepped toward the lamp, lifted her arm a little jerkily, then said sharply, commandingly, "Don't touch."
>
> There was an instant of silence, then she turned, stumbled across the room, flopped on the floor, and laughed excitedly. Her father, laughing with her, and obviously adoring, hugged and snuggled her. Apparently, it was not simple fear of her father which caused Martha's withdrawal from the lamp. She did not even look at him firmly, or whimper or waver in her decision. She clearly looked to herself for guidance, not to her father. She had accepted her father's standards as her own [Sears et al., 1957, pp. 365–366].

This incident gave no opportunity to judge the child's conscience operating in the face of temptation when no one was present, nor to determine the extent of guilt feelings when the temptation was not overcome. These two conditions, control in the face of temptation when no one is present, and guilt, are alleged by Sears and his associates to be the hallmarks of conscience control. Perhaps Martha would have been too young to have met these conditions fully anyway.

In general, reports Sears, the three-year-old is trustworthy, but only to a point; the four-year-old somewhat more; and the five-year-old still more. Even when the children involved in the study had reached the ages of five or six, 34% of their mothers reported no evidence of the development of conscience; that is, the child still hid and denied his infractions and did not seem unhappy when naughty. By contrast with the psychoanalytic school, who believe that superego, or conscience, is largely formulated during infancy, these investigators concluded that the critical period for learning internal control occurs mainly between the ages six and ten. Whatever happens then, they aver, determines the extent to which conscience will operate the rest of one's life.

Those children whose mothers gave evidence of rejection showed less complete conscience development. Typically, these mothers relied on physical punishment, deprivation, and material reward more, while mothers of high-conscience children used withdrawal of love and isolation as punishment, together with verbal praise as reward (Levin and Sears, 1956).

The Peck-Havighurst study. Using a somewhat different frame of reference, Peck and Havighurst (1960) arrived at reasonably similar results. They discriminated five character types, or motivational patterns, although any given child would rarely constitute a pure type. (1) The **amoral** type, corresponding to the clinically defined psychopathic person, is typical of infants. This sort of individual follows his impulses without regard for their effect on others. (2) The **expedient** type is primarily self-centered and considers others' welfare only to gain personal ends. Such a pattern is characteristic of many young children (ages two to four) who have learned to respect the rewarding-punishing power of adults, and to behave correctly whenever an adult is around. In the absence of controls, they lapse into doing whatever gratifies their selfish whims. (3) The **conforming** individual is ashamed only when others find him violating the rules. Violation is not wrong in itself, but simply because others say it is wrong and their approval is at stake. This individual's attitude differs from the expedient person's in that social conformity is accepted as good for its own sake. It constitutes a crude conscience, since departing from the rules brings

discomfort. This pattern is visible in middle and late childhood. (4) The **irrational-conscientious** individual judges a given act by his own internal standard of right and wrong. Such a person rigidly adheres to principles regardless of their effect on others. His is the blind, rigid superego at work. At this stage, children have internalized parental rules, but have not attained awareness that the rules are man-made and intended to serve a human, functional purpose. This level of morality is considered normal among children aged five to ten or beyond; but adults, too, often fixate here. They are said to have strong character but their judgment is faulty in complex situations. (5) The **rational-altruistic,** or highest, moral type has a stable set of moral principles, but evaluates behavior in terms of its effect on others as well as himself. This sort of individual may make evaluations either consciously or unconsciously, since the issue is not awareness, but the quality of his judgment. He is capable of self-sacrifice, but only if it genuinely helps others, not for neurotic self-satisfaction. Supposedly, this type of person is largely confined to adults, although sometimes he is found among adolescents.

The relationship between moral types, as just defined, and child-rearing methods proved to be a close one. Familial relationships of amoral children were chaotically inconsistent, and so lacking in trust and affection as to be deemed actively rejecting. The families of several such children were autocratic and severe, of others lenient and almost laissez-faire in discipline. The parents of expedients approved their children and granted them indiscriminate freedom, but treated them in unthinking, inconsistent ways. The conformists had autocratic parents who punished them consistently but severely. The irrational-conscientious children came from very harsh families; these families, however, differed somewhat from each other in characteristics other than harshness. The rational-altruistic type had loving, democratic parents who were consistent and lenient in their punishments. They were given opportunities to experiment in making decisions and to develop and trade ideas with others. Their families were by no means child-centered, in the manner characterized as progressive. However, they manifested a tendency to increase the child's autonomy as his judgment became more competent.

Each child's personality and character were found to be linked to his family experience in an almost inexorably logical way. Disorganized parents produced disorganized children with weak ego functions. Hostile, rejecting parents bred children who were hostile and rejecting of others. Undisciplined, uncaring parents resulted in children with little incentive to internalize an effective conscience. Parents who were lazy and uncritical had children who were selfishly expedient. Contrariwise, harshly autocratic but consistent parents produced overly submissive children, who would take over the rigid rule-transmitting role themselves upon attaining adulthood. During childhood, the child's overt compliance might seem the opposite of the parents' autocratic domination; but even by late adolescence, the harshly disciplined child showed a restless need to break away in order to establish and boss his own family.

In predicting results for specific children, a complication arises from the fact that few parents treat all their children alike. A parent's immaturities, such as unfulfilled wishes or repressed feelings, often emerge in the form of highly polarized attitudes toward different children. One child becomes "Mamma's pet," another her scapegoat. "In retrospect," reported one ex-child scapegoat, "I felt I had the face that launched a thousand lickings." The mechanism at work here is projection onto different children of different aspects of the parent's personality. For such reasons, Peck and Havighurst defined parental treatment by the way a particular child perceived it.

Tangentially, this study disclosed that mothers in most families have a more profound, direct influence on the child's character than do fathers, probably because the major responsibility of child-rearing is assigned the mother. There appeared no generally harmful effects of this matriarchal pattern on the development of character per se; but children of highly matriarchal families showed defects in capacity to develop solid emotional intimacy with members of the other sex.

MORAL
AND
RELIGIOUS
DEVELOPMENT

• FAMILY DISCIPLINE AND PUNISHMENT

One aspect of parental control that plays a critical role in moral development is discipline and punishment. For one thing, punishment has been the parents' primary mode of coping with children's moral infractions; and in no other interpersonal relationship does one person possess so much power over another as does the parent over his child. Any sort of parental authority short of outright brutality is sanctioned, or at least overlooked, though the naked use of parental power has markedly diminished. A century ago the doctrine "Spare the rod and spoil the child" reigned supreme. In fact, punishment is so firmly rooted in our folklore that infrequently punished children have traditionally been regarded as spoiled, and their parents viewed askance (Sanford, 1965). Sadism, masked as firmness, has maimed many a child while society sat complacently on the sidelines.

How, one may ask, do parents justify punishment, often to the point of child abuse, in the name of moral development? Apparently, they feel that if bad behaviors are systematically and forcefully stamped out, good behaviors will remain. At successive levels in the child's growing up, those behaviors inappropriate to each level are blotted out by some force or punishment. All too few parents utilize the positive-reinforcement method of rewarding good behaviors; instead, most parents seem to take good behaviors for granted.

253

Factors Related to Discipline

The complex nature of the influences that determine disciplinary techniques long defied analysis; however, with the aid of computers and the data emerging from certain longitudinal studies, the intermingled factors relating to discipline are becoming unraveled. As yet, however, their implications are poorly understood.

Among the most significant factors relating to discipline are individual differences, sociocultural factors, and sex. In general, rural parents are more authoritarian than urban, fathers more than mothers, older parents more than younger, and foreign-born more than native-born (Rapp, 1961). Also, better-educated parents are less coercive and more likely to justify their punishment, a factor that lessens the child's anxiety (Kagan and Freeman, 1963). All parents, of whatever group, show less warmth and more punitiveness after the child's second year.

Sex of parent. More specifically, where sex of parent is concerned, patterns of discipline have changed. In colonial times, the father was the disciplinarian; now the mother has assumed this role. Nowadays, the mother disciplines the girl almost exclusively and the boy most of the time, although the father may assume charge of the boy when he is home (Bronson et al., 1959).

Some fathers discipline their sons much more than others. Fathers who are closely supervised on their jobs tend either to supervise their sons very closely or to neglect them, especially if they resent the supervision they themselves receive. Closely supervised boys, in turn, act as role enforcers of their peers. That is, they insist that their peers play their assigned group roles with precision (Maccoby, 1961).

Naturally, the fact that parents play distinctive roles as disciplinarians causes their children to perceive them differently. The father is viewed as more fear-arousing, strict, and likely to use physical punishment, especially with sons; the mother is perceived as more nurturant, loving, and prone to use psychological control, especially with daughters. The same-sex parent is seen as less benevolent and frustrating, especially by older children, while the opposite-sex parent is rated as more likely to grant autonomy (Becker, 1964).

The child's parental identification will be correspondingly affected. If the mother assumes full control of the children and disparages the father, the boy may have trouble identifying with him. On the other hand, if the mother uses her authority to support the father, the child's image of the male parent is quite different (Helper, 1955).

Social class. Parental disciplinary patterns also vary according to social class, in not clearly defined ways. Research on this topic is largely confined to the middle class (professionals, proprietors, managers, white-collar workers) and the working class (skilled minor laborers with steady jobs). Little attention has been paid the lower-lowers or the upper class. Discipline employed in middle and working classes tends to differ, though less so than formerly. Kohn (1963) found that parents of both classes use physical punishment rarely, reserving it for extreme situations. However, the definition of what is extreme varies between classes. Such differences as exist Kohn attributes to differences in life conditions of each class, and the resultant values. The working class, which still has to find its place in the sun, must be concerned about conforming to external prescriptions. Middle-class parents, having attained status and a higher education, place more value on self-direction. Besides, the working class typically are employed by others, while the middle class tend to be leaders within their community—hence must make their own decisions. Simply following the rules is the more functional pattern in the one case, flexibly interpreting rules in the other.

In general, working-class parents are more inclined to use ridicule, shouting, physical punishment, and strict rules on their children. The working-class parent grants adolescents, especially boys, greater freedom from parental control than does his middle-class counterpart (Psathas, 1957). Whether mere freedom from adult supervision can be classed as permissiveness is questionable. On the other hand, it seems equally unwarranted to classify it as rejection or neglect. By contrast, middle-class parents tend to use love-oriented techniques. They use reasoning, isolation, show of disappointment, or guilt-arousing appeals in disciplining the child, as in cases of aggression toward parents, table manners, neatness and orderliness, bedtime rules, and general obedience. They accord much greater permissiveness than formerly to young children—for instance, with regard to toileting and masturbation (Bayley and Shaeffer, 1960).

Patterns of power orientation also vary by social class. In the lower class, the power-motivated father behaves assertively toward both his child and his wife, while she displaces her resentment onto a safe target, the child. Middle-class parents may attempt to control each other, but in more indirect, restrained ways. In dealing with their children, middle-class parents balance power motives with child-rearing norms, a balance sometimes disrupted by the accumulated resentment of muted power struggles with each other (Hoffman, 1963).

In general, the higher the family's status, the less the boy is punished or the girl overprotected (Bronson, et al., 1959). Also, the higher the social class, the greater is the tendency for the mother to discipline the boy as well as the girl. As a result, Bronfenbrenner (1961) argues, boys thrive more under lower-class authority patterns, girls under middle-class rearing. Boys in an aggressive society are undermined by the love-oriented socialization accorded them in the mother-dominated middle class, while girls of that class acquire

more of the freedom they need. Furthermore, boys thrive more in a patriarchal climate, such as the lower-class household, and girls in a matriarchal one, such as the middle-class home. However, Bronfenbrenner concludes that both sexes thrive best in the democratic family, which is neither patriarchal nor matriarchal but equalitarian.

Parental personality. Patterns of discipline also reflect the personality traits of the parents. Those who are restrictive in one area tend to be so in other areas. However, exceptions to this general rule occur. For instance, a parent may be relatively more restrictive or permissive concerning sexual behaviors than with aggressive ones. Or he may punish a son's aggression toward himself, but encourage him to "slug it out" with his peers (Becker et al., 1962).

Sometimes parents are so unsure of themselves that they establish no feeling of moral stability within the home. Their views possess no sinew; and their pronouncements on values have the consistency of cooked spaghetti. Again, parents may be of the type who strive so hard for *the* answer that they never come up with *an* answer. They become so confused in philosophical debate that their decisions are little more than wild speculation.

Effects of Punishment

The effects of disciplinary practices are hard to distinguish, because parents employ complex blends of methods instead of easily identifiable techniques. However, most parents use characteristic overall patterns, at least with a particular child. Patterns of punishment may be classified in various ways—for instance, as love-oriented or power-oriented. In **love-oriented discipline,** the parent relies on reasoning and tries to explain why the child's behavior is wrong. Control involves subtle emotional manipulation rather than tangible rewards or concrete punishments such as deprivation of privilege or spanking. In **power-oriented discipline,** the parent

Patterns of discipline inevitably reflect the personality traits of individual parents.

simply lays down the law and expects to be obeyed. The child who disobeys is summarily punished. The following type of incident is not uncommon:

> At age seven, I was treasurer of our neighborhood club. In a treasure hunt, I hid the box of club dues, and later could not find it. The other kids yelled at me, so I replaced the money from my mother's pocketbook. I was restored to their favor, and was quite happy until my mother discovered her loss. I owned up, and was lectured at length by my mother, then by my father. Moreover, my mother deprived me of peanut butter and jelly sandwiches, which I liked very much, for a whole week. I was furious, and got my friend's mother to make me one. (Female)

Effect of power-oriented punishment. The power-oriented approach, which commonly involves physical discipline, is still often employed, although its dangers are poorly understood. Some authorities suggest, at least by implication, that it may be desirable. One study reported the lowest crime rate to occur where both parents had been consistently punitive during the child's early years (McCord et al., 1959). In another study, physical punishment was described as more effective than psychological punishment for controlling very young children. Observations of four-year-old nursery-school children suggested that severe physical punishment tended to produce children somewhat resistant to temptations to cheat. Perhaps they were too young to realize what they might get away with in the laboratory (Burton et al., 1961).

However, one might ask: What are the concomitant effects of such punishment? What fears, insecurities, or losses in self-esteem do children suffer in the process? Does martial rule on the home front traumatize or merely civilize? Is the "good" child simply a conquered child? Young children may indeed require physical punishment when life is in danger, or injury imminent, especially before they are sufficiently mature to comprehend reasons. However, if such punishment is given for all sorts of infractions, it will lose its value in emergencies.

In any case, research provides little basis for approving physical punishment for older children. It is often part of the child-rearing pattern that eventuates in delinquency. Adult reprisal also prevents children from performing effectively on problem tasks (Kagan and Freeman, 1963). Furthermore, contrary to popular opinion, punishment for aggressive behavior tends to generate in children further aggressive activity (Eron et al., 1963). For example, Bandura and Walters (1959) found that parents whose sons had gotten into trouble with the law were more likely to use physical punishment and less likely to use reasoning. However, compared with parents of law-abiding youngsters, they did not differ in the extent to which they threatened the child with loss of love. Also, the parents of delinquent children made greater use of material rewards, while parents of the others were more affectionate. Among boys at least, punitive discipline appears to produce socially deviant behavior (Winder and Rau, 1962). And where severe discipline is accompanied by rigid moral standards, it results in a highly repressed, rigid child who lacks spontaneity and warmth, and wastes his energy controlling his unacceptable impulses. In another study, physical punishment was associated with fewer confessions; that is, the child who had reason to fear punishment kept his transgressions to himself. Punishment also fostered aggression toward the parent who dispensed it, thus preventing the sort of identification with an authority figure that results in internalized guilt.

However, the effects of power-oriented punishment remain ambiguous. Apparently, physical punishment induces aggression in children under five but inhibits it in children past the age of 12 (Sears, 1961). Physical punishment administered to boys produces resentment coupled with dependency and submission (Douvan and Adelson, 1966). The paternal power relation, especially, leads to a son's aggression. Unable to strike back at his father, the boy may displace his anger onto siblings or peers. With girls, the effect of the power relation is somewhat different. While boys respond with rebellion, girls simply succumb. Bronfenbrenner (1961) concluded that lack of discipline makes boys irresponsible, but that high discipline is debilitating for girls, whose dependency behaviors are constantly reinforced.

Love-oriented versus power-oriented techniques. Power-oriented techniques are thrown into focus when compared with love-oriented techniques. Love-oriented methods utilize love, including praise and reasoning, as the instrument of reinforcement, whereas power-oriented methods utilize force or punishment. Love-oriented techniques generally correlate both with internalized reactions to transgression, such as guilt, and with nonaggression. Power-asserting techniques are more likely to correlate with fear of punishment and aggressive reactions (Becker 1964).

These recollections from childhood illustrate types of reaction to power-oriented techniques:

> At age three, I poured my mother's perfume over our cocker spaniel, who I thought smelled bad. I was severely spanked and became very frightened. (Female)

> When I was caught throwing rocks at cars passing our house, something similar to a Senate investigation followed, with seeds of dissension sown among all parties involved. I developed long-term grudges, anger, and frustration, because my parents' methods of punishment were uncalled for, and disgusted me. (Male)

Bronfenbrenner cautions against believing love-oriented techniques unqualifiedly good and power-oriented techniques invariably bad. Boys who have learned how to counterattack may adapt better to their peers. Discipline that strongly inhibits such behavior could foster adjustment problems for boys. On the other hand, power-oriented methods might go too far in generating anger responses. Where love-oriented methods are concerned, there is no evidence that positive methods have undesirable consequences; but threats of withdrawal of love may jeopardize independence.

Love-oriented discipline may be either permissive or the reverse. Permissive discipline suggests relatively flexible and relaxed controls, but it shouldn't be confused with ultra-permissive discipline, which means simply the absence of controls. Extreme permissiveness apparently leads to a lack of concern for others and a decline in gratitude, guilt, and other emotions of personal involvement. After all, a genuine concern for others is the root of morality (Henry, 1961).

Here is testimony by boys and girls whose parents used love-oriented techniques:

> I hurt myself when playing in a house under construction, but told my parents I had fallen while playing. I felt miserably guilty, and several days later told my mother. She did not get angry, but simply explained why I should stay away from houses under construction. (Female)

> I was brought up on the "look method." I was praised often and scolded little. If I erred there was that "look." Many times I wished I'd been spanked, but am glad now my parents followed this method. (Male)

> When I erred, my mother would simply look at me, without saying a word. I could have crawled into the hole of any particularly undernourished rat. Since my self-respect was thus undermined, a great wall grew between me and my mother. (Male)

Obviously, it is no simple matter to assess the effects of love-oriented techniques.

Currently the most widely approved techniques are relatively permissive, involving love-withdrawal rather than physical punishment, scolding, or threats. The father's role is increasingly more affectionate and less authoritarian, while the mother has assumed greater

importance as an agent of discipline, especially with boys. This disciplinary pattern, claim Miller and Swanson (1958), produces greater adaptiveness, unaggressiveness, and sensitivity to rejection, while discouraging independence, initiative, and self-sufficiency.

Whatever the form of discipline used, random reward and punishment will prove unusually disruptive. Inconsistency is often disturbing and makes selecting an appropriate response difficult. For example, in Pavlov's experiments, the requirement that a dog make a distinction between an ellipse and a circle—a task apparently beyond a dog's sensory capacities—produced a breakdown in behavior and led to aggression. The animal would indiscriminately bite himself, his harness, or the researcher. Similarly, the child incapable of determining right answers in an ambiguous situation becomes confused.

A strange though fairly common reaction to punishment is learning to like it. A child may come to seek punishment if parents follow it by guilt-inspired demonstrations of affection. Sometimes the only way a child can win the undivided attention of his parents is through requiring punishment.

On the basis of the foregoing, punishment wins few laurels. After a large-scale study of child-rearing practices and their long-term effects, Sears and associates declared that punishment just did not work. Its unhappy effects ran "like a dismal thread" through their findings. Mothers who punished children for aggression had more aggressive children. Mothers who punished children for toilet accidents ended up with bedwetting children. Harsh punishment created child aggressiveness and feeding problems. As a result, the researchers branded it ineffectual for eliminating any specific behavior toward which it was directed (Sears et al., 1957). True, punishment occasionally stopped a specific act, such as a boy's picking on his sister; but in the long run it was not effective.

Recommended Patterns of Discipline

Certainly, it would seem wise to employ those methods of reinforcing socialization that leave in their wake as few harmful by-products as possible. Therefore, it is fortunate that many authorities agree upon certain principles of proper discipline. If a child is uncertain, or tends to disregard boundaries, a degree of order is deemed reassuring. Such children, it is said, welcome the firm hand and function better with well-defined guidelines (Herin and Phillips, 1962). They should also be encouraged, bit by bit, to accept more responsibility. The reins should be slackened as the child proves himself able to accept responsibility and to tolerate a measure of ambiguity.

The so-called love-oriented techniques are themselves merely means of preventing "bad" behavior instead of reinforcing good behavior. Whether power-oriented or love-oriented, punitive behaviors leave in their wake a plethora of neurosis-inducing effects: fear, guilt, insecurity, dependency, and reliance on external control. Love-oriented techniques are claimed to eventuate in internal controls; but the individual disciplined in such a fashion is never quite free from guilt when he behaves differently from the way in which he was reared. In fact, often such a person never quite grows up. Whether or not his parents are present, they direct his behavior. To do anything that conflicts with their views is to reject them and invoke their disapproval. Perhaps no individual can be thought of as fully mature until he can have confidence in his own perceptions and behave in ways directly contrary to his parents' teachings without feeling undue stress.

The alternative favored by the author would be plentiful reinforcement of socially approved behaviors, with a sparing use of power-oriented techniques in case of emergency. A great many minor infractions would be ignored, although the stage would be set to encourage their displacement by more acceptable behavior. Instead of scolding the child for being irritable in the evening, the parent might introduce an afternoon nap to circumvent the problem. At the same time, every effort would be made to teach the child such respect for himself that he would desire to do what he could for the mutual good. Since he inevitably associates his behavior with himself, he would come to behave respectably because he pictures himself as respectable. Moreover, his parents would constantly show him the reasons for behavior, so that decisions might rest on a logical rather than a purely emotional base. This approach has been reported as successful in eliminating various disapproved behaviors, including temper tantrums and noisy behavior (Williams, 1959).

It might also be well to take note of certain other cultures whose members merely note when an act occurs, rather than judging it. Among certain Eskimos, for example, even the most permissive parents, by American standards, would seem like autocrats. The Eskimo child, in some tribes, is punished neither for errors in judgment nor for bad behaviors. Disapproved behaviors are simply not reinforced; they thus fall into a vacuum. Perhaps the technique is slow, but it is more efficient in the long run than punishment (Osgood, 1952).

Whatever techniques are employed—power-oriented, love-oriented, the reinforcement of approved behaviors, or others—one thing should be noted. The saying "Example is better than precept" appears psychologically sound; therefore, parental example is important.

• EXTRAFAMILIAL INFLUENCES ON MORAL DEVELOPMENT

Peer Influence

In general, the peer society tends to reproduce the moral atmosphere established by the parents. That is, peer influences act to reinforce or crystallize behavioral influences already present. However, the peer group performs special functions as well. It provides

Peer influences are strong in the slums.

the best opportunity for the rational testing of moral behavior and its consequences. Moreover, agemates may constitute effective models, especially where the child has a poor relationship with his parent, or the parent is of doubtful worth as an identification figure. In some cases, where a child is from a chaotic, unloving family, the peer group may be used as an unwitting treatment agency, under the guidance of a skilled adult (Peck and Havighurst, 1960).

The following incidents reflect peer influences on conduct:

Twelve-year-old Billy went with a friend to view the remains of a burned-out restaurant. Tempted by his friend, and unwilling to appear cowardly, Billy went inside with him and took some smoke-laden glasses and plates. That night Billy confessed to his parents, who told him he had been guilty of both trespassing and stealing. Also, they said the restaurant might have collapsed upon him. Billy prayed to God for forgiveness and vowed never to do such a thing again.

Jim, a newcomer to the neighborhood, found himself among a group of lively children who had gobs of imaginative fun but stopped short of vandalism and meanness. When Jim tried to beat a little dog, they quickly ordered that he stop. When Jim began breaking out street lights, he was again abruptly stopped. He learned that further infractions of the group's code would make him an outcast, and mended his ways.

School

In the early days of our country, considerable effort was made to forestall wrong behaviors through moral-laden stories. The idea was to produce an automated conscience and a blueprint of behavior for every moral situation. In most cases, the retribution recommended made no allowance for the mischievous nature of normal children. For example, in a story prefaced by the remark "Children are very apt to be cruel," an account was given of a small boy who, during a ride in a cart with other children, yielded to the temptation of "pricking the poor horse on the

back to make him go faster." With lightning speed his punishment came, for "the poor animal plunged with pain and darted suddenly around a corner, where the boy was thrown out and crushed to death." The author concluded the grim tale with this moral: "The boy had gone out from his parents' house in sound health and spirits, but he was now returned a stiff cold corpse. And cruelty to an animal caused his sad death" (Kiefer, 1948, pp. 62-63).

Exhortations to children in an Early-American book, *The School of Good Manners*, reveal the ideals of juvenile conduct of Puritan days:

1. Let thy Thoughts be Devine, Aweful, and Godly.
2. Let thy Talk be Little, Honest, and True.
3. Let thy Works be Profitable, Holey, and Charitable.
4. Let thy Manners be Grave, Courteous, and Cheerful.
5. Let thy Diet be Temperate, Convenient, and Frugal.
6. Let thy Apparel be Sober, Neat, and Comely.
7. Let thy Will be Compliant, Obedient, and Ready.
8. Let thy Sleep be Moderate, Quiet, and Seasonable.
9. Let thy Prayers be Devoute, Often, and Fervent.
10. Let thy Meditations be of Death, Judgment, and Eternity [Kiefer, 1948, pp. 72-73].

Well into the present century, schools taught morals very directly. However, a content analysis of children's readers in the United States showed a steady decline in direct moral teaching over the period 1800-1950 (de Charms and Moeller, 1962). Today, no effective effort seems to be made to help the child resolve knottier moral issues. In this area, write Peck and Havighurst (1960), the school can only hope for one-tenth the influence of the home. Insofar as the school is effective, he adds, it probably produces a morality built around a safe but irrational conformity to rules. It hardly undertakes to

261

foster the more responsible and mature, but also more risky, morality that comes from rational altruism. Others are concerned that the morality stressed by the schools emphasizes passivity at the expense of more positive, venturesome aspects of character.

This is not to say that today's schools are totally unaware of moral development as a goal. Some educators recognize that the school may be the only place some children can find an ethical anchorage; and if the school does not teach morals, the child is thrown onto hedonistic peer values. However, the teaching of morals nowadays is typically incidental rather than direct. For example, instead of expounding directly on the virtues of truthfulness, a history teacher may have a class evaluate the ethics of political propaganda used in a specific presidential campaign.

Mass Media

As for the much-debated effect of mass media, an English study involving 1,800 matched groups of TV viewers and nonviewers between the ages of 10 and 14 indicated marked effects on children's thought processes and values, more on girls' than on boys'. However, the kind and degree of effect varied with the traits of the child concerned (Himmelweit et al., 1959). In another study, mass media apparently did little to change values already learned from the parents. However, they seemed to serve some purpose in providing catharsis, or the fantasied solution of problems (Warner and Henry, 1948).

There are many explanations for the inconclusiveness of research on media. For one thing, communication media have changed so fast that large-scale studies are out of date before they are completed. Again, much of the influence of media consists of unconscious conditioning that extends to all segments of behavior. Finally, it is hard to determine their significance for any specific child. Each individual sees something different in a program, depending on his needs and background. The boy with repressed needs for aggression concentrates on the TV badman; the boy who admires his policeman father follows every move of the marshal.

Culture

The effects of overall cultural influences are still more pervasive. Parents primarily transmit socially approved values, as they perceive and interpret them. Such influences can best be appreciated by making cross-cultural comparisons. Some cultures, such as those in most Christian countries, encourage children to feel guilty if they do wrong; others—for instance, the Japanese—teach the child to practice socially approved behaviors to avoid being shamed by others. In the one case, the child uses internalized controls; in the other, he relies on external controls (Hsu, 1961).

The data become even more illuminating when comparisons are made of corresponding subgroups within the countries or cultures being compared. One such comparison of American and Korean children revealed no differences in either the severity of moral judgment or the hierarchical arrangement of various morally prohibited activities. However, Korean males were more severe than American males, and there was a greater difference between males and females among the Koreans (Rettig and Pasamanick, 1959).

Actually, every agent involved in modifying the child's moral development—whether parent, teacher, peer, or television personality—himself reflects the culture. All transmit socially approved values as they perceive and interpret them. Thus, influences on morals are filtered through the unique personalities of the individuals transmitting them and the children receiving them. The residue is a unique blend of ideas, values, and judgments that become the child's way of ordering his life, and that he in turn will transmit consciously or unconsciously to others.

Self-Influence

Personality traits. Also related to moral development are characteristics of the individual himself. The child's overall personality apparently affects his moral development. For instance, the more maladjusted the child, the less mature his moral judgment, and the greater the likelihood that it is based on concepts of absolute authority (Shumsky, 1956).

Not only do personality traits affect moral behaviors; moral behaviors, in turn, apparently modify personal attitudes and traits. For instance, Mills (1958) demonstrated how a child's experience in situations involving morals may affect his judgments of others. Children who decided not to violate a moral standard became more severe in their attitude toward cheating, while children who continued to cheat became more tolerant of the practice. Perhaps in each case the child who resisted wanted to be sure no one else profited from such undeserved spoils either. Or, possibly, by hearing himself condemn others he managed to reinforce his own superego. Conversely, the child who "gave in" may have reassured himself that by tolerating the same behaviors in others he was taking no unfair advantage himself.

Sex. Of special and only recently appreciated significance in shaping morals is the child's sex. Girls may be thought of as more precocious in their moral development than boys if we simply equate morality with the interjection of socially approved standards of behaving. From earliest years, girls are taught simply to conform. They hear it from parents, television, everywhere — that nice girls do what they are told. Therefore, even as children they develop "high" or "automated" consciences; whatever rules are imposed by authority figures are right and must be obeyed. However, we would not say that girls are more moral than boys if we think of moral maturity as insightful handling of moral situations rather than as compliance to rules. As we shall see, the opposite may be the case.

Girls move directly from their passive, childlike acceptance of authority to identification with their mothers, the transition being effected without any intervening phase of rebellion. That is, as children they obey the parent because they believe nice girls should. At the same time, the girl identifies closely with her mother, who communicates the rules. During adolescence, as the girl looks toward marriage, she comes to identify with the wife-mother role; hence her adherence to rules is further reinforced. Conformity becomes an internal adapter, and power figures the monitors of her ideals.

Other factors, too, explain the conformist feminine pattern. The girl's role is oriented toward others, therefore she is more sensitive to her mother's approval (Douvan, 1960). Also, less pressure is placed on her to define herself as an individual, so she feels less need to differentiate her values. Moreover, her protected role places her in fewer situations where crucial moral decisions are required. She is more often in the home, where she simply relies on her mother's views. Her mother's morality becomes her own, just slightly warmed over.

The situation with boys is quite different. From their earliest years, they are granted greater autonomy and expected to "kick over the traces." Even while parents punish the errant son, they are often privately pleased that he is masculine enough to assert himself. He is expected to question; and when he does so, mothers, especially, feel constrained to give him a reason.

Small wonder, therefore, that boys have quite different feelings from girls toward rules and authority figures. Far more often than girls, boys question rules and rely on their own judgment in determining whether rules are fair and deserve to be kept. Moreover, boys are likely to react somewhat violently, in keeping with the more externalized, aggressive patterns considered appropriate for them. One boy, when asked whether he would be willing to confront authority directly, stared at the interviewer in disbelief and asked, "You kiddin', lady?" (Douvan and Adelson, 1966). Even when girls reject authority, they often do so quietly and covertly, while outwardly maintaining a ladylike conformity.

Actually, the boy changes far more in his moral development than does the girl. He undergoes a real metamorphosis from the rowdy "all boy" to the youth who holds firm beliefs about what is right and wrong. His decision-making runs a collision course between practicality and idealism. As already noted, while the girl tends simply to learn rules, the boy often develops true moral maturity. He establishes his own controls after testing and refining them. The girl deals in specifics—it is wrong to do this, right to do that—while the boy thinks more in terms of "whys" and principles. As a case in point, McDonald asked 472 children, representing a wide range of ages and backgrounds, to judge which of two actions, stealing from an individual or from a corporate owner, was worse and why. Half of the children judged both actions equally serious because they were stealing. Where children made a distinction, they considered the presumed effect on the owner, the assumed value of the objects taken, and the possibility of detection. Girls were more likely to evaluate actions—in this case, stealing—categorically; boys judged more often in terms of the value of the objects stolen (McDonald, 1963).

In short, we may say that internalized standards, dependent on internal rather than external control, result from autonomy and are more commonly a masculine pattern. Children employing this pattern—that is, most boys and a few girls—show high achievement, activity, and self-confidence levels combined with realistic self-criticism, independence, and effective ego-functioning.

Intelligence. The relationship of intelligence to moral development is clear-cut, though its significance is not. In summarizing the results of 300 investigations, Wiggam (1941) asserted that brains and character are definitely correlated. Even more recently, researchers concluded that the ability of children to assess and judge behavior maturely is a function of higher levels of IQ (Whiteman and Kosier, 1964). However, Unger (1964) questions the significance of such findings. Perhaps morality is not a function of intelligence as such but of certain other factors. For instance, parents may reason with brighter children, while not bothering to explain to duller ones, even on their level of comprehension. If we used suitable methods to convey abstract reasons, the moral differences between intelligence levels might be reduced.

• THE CHILD AND HIS RELIGION

Turning from morality to religion, we find considerably less research. When William James wrote his *Varieties of Religious Experience,* observes Allport (1950), he expressed himself brilliantly and freely on the subject, but could hardly bring himself to mention sex. By contrast, today's psychologists freely describe the sexual styles of mankind but blush and grow silent when religious fashions come into view. Scarcely any modern textbook devotes as much as two pages to the subject, even though religion, like sex, is of almost universal interest to the human race.

This observation, made by Allport 19 years ago, holds equally true today. Especially where children are concerned, research on religion hardly exists. Presumably, this absence of data reflects the problem of finding representative groups of children whom researchers may question. School administrators, especially, have well-trained reflexes for dodging this sort of research. Although many studies of college students' values and religion are available, those for children are rare. Therefore, the author embarks on this section somewhat hesitantly, admitting that it rests on inadequate and sometimes outdated research.

The Influence of Religion on Moral Development

There are several ways that religion relates to moral development in childhood. First, adults may use God to help them enforce morality. The child becomes imbued with the idea that if he "does wrong" God will frown on him. The young child, especially, may believe that accidents and misdeeds that befall him are God's way of punishing him for having gone astray (Medinnus, 1959).

Religion may also become a reinforcer to the child's superego or conscience. That is, if the child believes that a supreme being is watching everything he does, he is less susceptible to succumbing to temptation. However, religion wrongly used may prevent his progression toward moral maturity. To the extent that he associates religious authority with moral behaviors, he may conclude that such areas of his conduct are no longer subject to examination and must remain intact. To question their rightness is to question the religious authority with which they have become associated.

The following retrospective reports by adolescents show some of the ways that religion influences moral development:

Religion was very meaningful to me. I will never forget the day, when I was about nine, that I ran to church in the rain. When I finally entered the church, I had an exalted feeling. (Female)

For me, religion was a strong deterrent to immorality. Hell was a burning furnace with people instead of coal used for fuel. (Male)

My family was closely knit, and religion was the basis of our happiness. Religion will always be the foundation of my life. (Female)

Religion was something copied from my parents—a ritual. It was going to church, and saying prayers to statues, and blessing myself with holy water. It meant doing something simply because God said it was good. I pictured my soul as sort of like my heart inside, and when I sinned a black mark was made across it. People said a soul was white, but I pictured mine as covered with black—and dirty. (Male)

Children's Religious Concepts

For some adults, religion may be little different from a philosophy of life; for others, religion may represent a more conventional pattern of practices, rites, and beliefs, defining their relationship to God or a supernatural realm. For children, religion is largely a matter of concrete beliefs, transmitted to them by parents and Sunday School teachers, coupled with familiar religious observances such as church attendance.

There is no consensus on the pattern of religious development; however, the patterns outlined by Harms and by Hirschberg are typical. Harms (1944) hypothesizes three stages: the fairy-tale stage, during which children have fanciful beliefs; the realistic stage, when they reject early imaginings and formulate explanations in terms of natural phenomena; and the individualistic stage, during which they select from religion to fit their own needs. Hirschberg's (1956) account is similar. In early years the child's religious ideas relate to his everyday life and to experiences within his family. God is vividly alive. In later childhood, religion becomes less egocentric. It provides a secure, non-compulsive control of impulses. During adolescence, however, a reconstruction and re-evaluation of religious beliefs occur, often producing areas of conflict. Children depend for their religious beliefs on parental authority, while adolescents acquire an independent maturity in their views.

Some earlier views. Now let us consider researchers' reports of common religious beliefs held by children. The following material, paraphrased from G. Stanley Hall (1893, pp. 39–40), is representative of children's concepts of God,

God, Flying through the night with his cape on and his cross.

Drawn by Pam Abu-Jaber, age 9. Children's religious concepts are influenced by impressions from many sources.

heaven, and hell in the late nineteenth century:

> God is a big, perhaps blue man, very often seen in the sky, on or in the clouds, in the church, and even street. . . . He makes lamps, babies, dogs, trees, money, etc., and the angels *work for him.* When people die they just *go* or *are put in a hole,* or a box or a black wagon *that goes to Heaven,* or they *fly up* or are *drawn* or *slung up* into the sky where God catches them.
>
> When children get there they have candy, rocking-horses, guns, and everything in the toy shop or picture book, play marbles, tops, balls, cards,

hookey, hear brass bands, have nice clothes, gold watches and pets, icecream and soda water, and no school.

> The bad place is like an *oven* or a *police station,* where it burns yet it is all dark, and folks want to get back and God *kills* people or *beats them with a cane.*

Later concepts. More recent concepts are hardly less primitive, though brighter children from better educated, more sophisticated families, especially those with more liberal religious affiliations, may hold relatively less concrete and more mature views. In 1950 Merry

266

and Merry reported that children thought of God as someone to appeal to for toys, food, and clothing. Heaven was a very real place of beauty, either "in the ground" or "in the sky." A six-year-old girl believed it was a creek; and a boy of nine thought it was "smoke, water, and air." A seven-year-old girl asserted that Jesus made candy; and another said that "He makes you well when you are sick."

In another study, children were asked to imagine what God looked like and to picture on paper whatever came to mind. The children were astonished at the request, but immediately went to work, often patterning their pictures in the manner of fairy tales (Harms, 1944). Even older children sometimes retained more primitive concepts. A 12-year-old altar boy thought of God as someone with "just a head and shoulders sticking out of the clouds."

In 1955, McCann summarized children's religious concepts as "concrete, based on pictures and stories." They perceived God as a person, made of flesh and blood. He appeared very large, with either a kindly or stern face, was old, wore long white flowing garments, and had a white beard. Some children conceived of God as wearing a crown or having wings. They believed he could see everywhere, and spent his time watching how people behaved. If they were bad, he punished them, although they could make special pleas in their prayers. While practically all children conceived of God as all-powerful, some thought of him as kind, others as somewhat terrifying and awe-inspiring.

Typically, concepts of Jesus rest on similar bases: stories, pictures, and Christmas dramas. Children see him:

... not as an ideal grown-up who helped people, but as a little baby, whose mother put him in a straw thing in a barn instead of a crib; and to whom queer-looking men in striped gowns brought presents no baby could use. They learn, too, that there was a bad

king, with a ferocious face, of whom the baby's mother was afraid, so that she had to take him a long way from home, riding on an animal that is not seen in the city, nor even in the zoo [Murphy, 1956].

More recent concepts. Despite the more sophisticated thinking of children in recent years, primitive concepts persist, shifting to relatively abstract, indefinite concepts in adolescence. In 1966, the author questioned teenagers about how they viewed God as children and later as adolescents. Here are typical replies:

As a child, I vividly pictured Him seated Indian style on a cloud watching me, and checking everything I did that was wrong. Santa Claus sat on the same cloud, checking his book to see if I had been good enough to get any presents at Christmas. My present ideas are a question mark. I'm afraid to say I don't believe; but for two years I've had no definite concept, nor any conviction that there has to be a God. Nevertheless, God is the only aspect of religion I cling to, because Bible stories are no more than fables or a book of etiquette. (Male)

As a child, God was an all-good Being, whom people should try to imitate. Now I feel God was created by man for his own uses. (Female)

As a child, I saw God as intangible, omnipotent, and able to move the world with a slap of his hand. (Male)

To me, God was an invisible disciplinarian, but I never had a solid concept and often wondered what he was like. He was portrayed as infinite — that is, "what was in the beginning, is now, and ever shall be." It is hard to imagine someone who is without beginning or end. (Female)

My earliest ideas of God fluctuated between picturing him as an old man, in the style of the Jesus pictures, and picturing him as nothing and everything — nothing because I couldn't picture him physically, everything when I visualized him as the universe — a flower, a tree, a baby, stars ... God was made up of all these things. (Female)

God was a fearful monster, a sort of

Santa Claus who always watched and put our sins on a big score card. Now I don't know what he is or does, but I do think God exists. (Male)

On the basis of all the students' replies, it became apparent that children still hold somewhat stereotyped pictures of God, Christ, heaven, and hell. During adolescence, concepts are more varied, abstract, and confused. Even those who "believed" had about as much difficulty defining their concepts as those who did not. In general, concepts of heaven and hell are consistent with children's views of their respective masters. Heaven is a place where people have what they want, especially what they failed to get on earth. On arrival there, people become winged angels and wear long flowing garments. Hell, by contrast, is a place of fire and deprivation of all pleasures. It is presided over by the Devil, a crimson-colored creature in the form of a man with horns and a tail and equipped with a pitchfork. He is red all over (Allport, 1950).

The child's communication with God. Concepts of prayer are equally unsophisticated. Children under age eight believe prayer permits talking to God; and they agree to be good if God will come across with what they want. They chiefly request material things, usually whatever they have been unable to get for themselves. The older child, far more often than the younger, will ask forgiveness for wrongdoing or thank God for his help (Kuhlen and Arnold, 1944). On the whole, however, children's prayers are a "begging ritual," with emphasis on pennies from heaven (Jersild, 1960).

Children's communications with the infinite often betray a certain light touch and other signs of the times. In a charming little volume called *Letters to God,* these signs are apparent (Marshall and Hample, 1966). One child requested of God that He "do something quick" to prove He is real—*if* He is. Another wrote God that Church "is alright but you could sure use better music." And

a third child congratulated God for having a book with so much "zip" in it.

The meaning of church and denominations. Children readily proclaim their religious affiliations but have little idea what they mean, as indicated by this first-grade teacher's anecdote.

A child in my room lived with her father and grandmother. Just before Easter she told me she and her grandmother were going to church together next Sunday, and about the new clothes they would wear. "Isn't your father going, too?" I inquired. "No," she replied, "my grandmother's a Catholic, but Daddy's a prostitute." "You mean a Protestant," I corrected. "That's what I said," she answered, "a prostitute."

When the child goes to school he begins to acquire at least a fuzzy concept of his religion, partly through comparisons—however immature they may be—with the concepts of others. Around ages five or six, most Jewish children know they are Jewish; however, the concepts of what it means to be a Jew and what the term Jew means are undifferentiated, except in the sense that Jews somehow differ from Protestants and Catholics. Between ages seven and nine, they conceive of Jews as behaving in a certain way, as attending synagogue or celebrating Jewish holidays. Between ages 10 and 11, they develop an abstract concept of a Jew as an individual who believes in one God and worships in a way different from persons of other religions. A similar pattern has been found among Catholic children (Elkind, 1961, 1962).

Meanwhile, children come to realize that church membership relates to social status (McCann, 1955). Note this example:

From childhood I recall three churches in our small town, though one didn't really count. The upper crust, who would be classified as middle-middle class in the larger American society, were Methodists and worshipped in a nice brick church. The

Baptists were just a shade lower in social status and occupied a somewhat smaller wooden church. The Wesleyan Methodists, having no relationship to the Methodists, were lower class and met under a large wooden tabernacle. In a small nearby mill town a still lower-class group, the Holy Rollers, met in an unpainted shack, where the congregation assembled in their cheap, but gaudy Sunday best.

Factors Related to Religious Concepts

Various factors relate to children's religious concepts, among them the language used, which bears only vague meaning for the child. Jersild (1960) tells of the child who told his mother about Jesus' 12 bicycles (disciples) and who was puzzled about the "consecrated cross-eyed bear" (consecrated cross I'd bear). Children understand concepts relating to special religious days and places, such as Christmas, church, and Sunday, better than those relating to more purely spiritual experiences, such as conversion, cross, and Christian (Josephina, 1961).

The child's concepts also reflect his own experience. His idea of God the father will undoubtedly be colored by his feelings about his own father. Similarly, his ideas about sin and forgiveness will be affected by the way he has been told to behave and the way he is punished when he has erred (McCann, 1955). In cultures where children are punished harshly, they are likely to perceive their God, or Gods, as aggressive rather than benevolent (Lambert et al., 1959).

Not surprisingly, the differences in the way boys and girls view religion reflect their respective patterns of child-rearing. Girls conform more closely to conventional ways of viewing religion, while boys raise questions or become downright negative toward it (Estvan and Estvan, 1959).

Children's Doubts about Religion

Despite their differences, most children of the Christian faith hold certain fundamental beliefs. They accept the idea of miracles and believe God can do anything. Sunday is a holy day, and going to church makes people good. Good people say their prayers and can expect them to be answered. God wrote the *Bible,* which is completely true, and to doubt it is sinful. What happens after death depends on what kind of life one lives here on earth (Alexander and Adlerstein, 1958; Gilliland, 1953; Remmers and Radler, 1957).

Most young children accept such teachings implicitly, although many occasionally express doubts. Even when a child questions, which is more often the case with bright children of better educated families and more liberal religious affiliation, he reacts unemotionally and objectively. He does not worry about religion because his "Day of Judgment" seems very remote and unreal (Kuhlen and Arnold, 1944).

In an informal study by the author, many college students acknowledged having had doubts, most often arising in high school or college, though often in junior high, and occasionally before then. Here are replies typical of those who doubted before adolescence:

My relatives were very religious—didn't smoke, swear, or drink—according to my aunt, real goody-goody. However, I found they had merely put up a front. One uncle and one aunt had to get married; and both were quite the boozers. This awakening made me reject religion. I wish I could believe, because when I did I had nothing to worry about. Now I have to solve my own problems. (Female)

As a child religion was a bore; I preferred to stay home from church and watch TV. I was told it would help, but I couldn't see what it did. If it does nothing, is it useful? (Male)

As a child I attended church, but those who went didn't seem to be any better than I was. I said to myself, "Who needs Him?" (Male)

I never doubted God, but was puzzled by many things that happened. For example, an innocent three-year-old girl in my town was murdered. Also, a German Shepherd police dog slashed

269

my little sister's cheek. I still wonder about God's reasons for such tragedies, but suppose we humans on earth aren't supposed to know. (Female)

I saw some regular church-going men beat a colored person for trying to move into their neighborhood. Then, when my best friend, the only true friend I ever had, died of cancer, that was the final blow. (Male)

Needed Research on Moral and Religious Development

If we are to provide children with sound guidance in their religious and moral development, we must have more adequate research. Considerable research was done in both these areas in the 1930s and 40s; then the topic slipped out of sight. Only recently has interest revived, chiefly in that aspect of the topic concerned with values. To date, findings are inconclusive, reflecting the basic problems of conducting this type of research.

One problem is the determining of criteria against which to measure moral growth. Morals involve complex abstractions, varying with the groups and subgroups involved. Who decides what moral behavior is, or the gradations that represent theoretical steps toward its achievement? The times are changing so rapidly that standards are in a constant state of flux.

Researchers have taken refuge in oversimplified criteria of morality, such as the presence of guilt feeling, which is supposed to correlate in straight-line fashion with resistance to temptation. However, in one study, when children were given a chance to cheat, children who yielded to temptation often exhibited guilt feelings at home. They were fully aware of moral standards, which nevertheless failed to prevent their wrongdoing (Rapp, 1961).

To establish a manageable experimental situation, researchers often test very simple types of moral conduct in highly controlled artificial situations; generalizations based on such simple tests far exceed justification. In one test,

children were asked to operate a "raygun" shooting gallery and then were tempted to transgress the rules to win a badge. The extent of the children's conformity to the rules was taken as an index of conscience. This gross oversimplification ignores the realities. Some of the children might desire the badge, others not. Some might have believed both the game and the rules silly, hence not worth obeying. Besides, following the rules of such a game would hardly predict moral performance in the far more serious and complex crises of life (Grinder, 1962).

Where real-life situations are studied, as in the home, attention is too often focused on extremes of behaviors, because only thus are clear-cut differences obtained. However, most parents use a variety of practices that fall somewhere between these polar positions. For this reason, it is difficult to determine relationships between child-training techniques and moral outcomes.

Available research is also limited in its content. It relates mainly to boys, and moral values themselves are masculine-tinged, because the great writers and philosophers are men. Hence generalizations about girls' moral status are even less reliable than are conclusions about boys' (Hoffman, 1963).

Research has failed to keep pace with the times. It has been intermittent in a time when continuous measurement is needed. The pace of change has quickened so that moral evolution often becomes revolution. Morals are inexorably linked to time, place, and circumstance, and research that fails to take these factors into account can produce only distorted impressions.

• SUMMARY

The study of children's moral development involves certain concepts — for example, **morals,** or standards of right and wrong, and goodness or badness of **character,** or the generalized reflection of value judgments of the child's associates. **Moral behaviors** embrace actions of particular significance to society and reflect the individual's **ideals,** or standards toward which he strives.

There are many unresolved questions surrounding morality. For instance, what constitutes moral maturity? It has been defined as including such dimensions as rational self-criticism, spontaneous self-commitment, and susceptibility to inner controls. Another question relates to the relative desirability of specific or generalized moral training. Perhaps today's society requires a generalized training to permit constant readaptation to changing social codes.

Ideas about children's morals have fluctuated with the times. For centuries children were believed inherently evil and were firmly controlled. However, in recent decades psychoanalysts have preached permissiveness and gentle handling of the child. Now the pendulum is swinging uncertainly, tending toward permissiveness, but with hesitant moves toward firmness.

There have been several well-known studies of children's moral development. Piaget, the most influential of recent child-study theorists, perceived children's moral development as progressing by stages. The young child interprets wrong in terms of amount of damage done, the older one in terms of motives and principles. In one study, by Sears and his associates, certain maternal behaviors were shown to be associated with high conscience (confessing, apologizing, or making restitution). These included the use of reasoning, the setting of firm limits, and the withdrawal of approval for disapproved acts. Children whose mothers relied on physical punishment and material reward showed incomplete conscience development. Another major study, by Peck and Havighurst, portrayed five character types, from the lowest, or **amoral,** to the highest, or **rational-altruistic.** The child's character proved

closely linked to his family experience. Parents who used harsh discipline produced submissive children; uncaring parents produced undisciplined children.

Especially critical in moral development is the mode of discipline employed. Formerly the father was the disciplinarian, and is still viewed as more strict than the mother. Parents of the lower social class are more concerned about conforming to external prescriptions, while those of the middle class place a higher premium on self-direction. Lower-class parents more often use **power-oriented techniques,** which often involve physical punishment, while middle-class parents tend to use **love-oriented techniques,** which involve reasoning and withdrawal of love when the child disobeys. Power-oriented techniques result in various blends of aggression, submission, repression, and other unfortunate traits. Love-oriented techniques, however, tend to produce such traits as guilt and dependency. Most parents probably use some blend of methods instead of polarized extremes of power or love. Punishment of any kind and degree, if frequently used, leaves a residual of negative effects, including fear, insecurity, and dependency. In general, girls react to such techniques by submitting and boys by rebelling. For either sex, perhaps it would be better to reserve power-oriented techniques for emergencies, while otherwise concentrating on reinforcement of approved behaviors. The stage would be set for making approved behavior easy, and wrong behaviors would be ignored as far as practicable. Whatever the philosophy, it should be generally consistent, since the practice of random reward and punishment is especially disruptive. Meantime, the child should be helped to acquire such respect for self and for others that he would desire to do the right thing.

Among extrafamilial influences on moral development, the child society affords a testing ground for moral behavior and its consequences. Peer influences generally reinforce socially approved behaviors. The school's effect is also important but largely indirect. Instead of deliberately planning lessons on morals, today's teachers integrate moral teaching with the regular curriculum. The effect of culture is pervasive, because teachers and parents for the most part simply interpret what the culture approves. Mass media, too, sanction societal values, but with what effect is in dispute. The values transmitted change gradually with the times, although perhaps at a greater pace today than society can readily absorb.

Moral development also depends on the individual himself, his personality, and his sex. In general, the poorly adjusted child is less mature in his moral judgments. Girls obey rules more rigidly and are more passive in their acceptance of authority than boys. Boys are granted greater autonomy and encouraged to reason more. In short, boys rely more on internalized authority and girls on external controls. Brighter children of both sexes appear to be more mature morally, perhaps because they can reason better and understand the issues involved.

Another aspect of the child's moral development is the development of ideals. Children may imitate individuals they have seen on television, read about in books, or known in real life. As children grow older, they shift from fantasy toward reality in their choice of persons with whom to identify.

The identification figure permits the child to try out different roles, and with them different values and ideals. The child may identify with certain traits without introjecting the whole pattern. Sometimes he identifies with someone of questionable character and as a result acquires unhealthy ideals. However, there is very little research on conscious efforts to upgrade children's ideals.

Also, little research exists on children's religious development. Harms (1944) portrays children as moving from a fairy-tale stage to an individualistic stage, when they choose religion to suit their own beliefs. In later adolescence a re-evaluation of beliefs may produce conflicts.

Children's religious concepts are somewhat primitive except in the case of brighter children from more sophisticated families, especially those with liberal religious affiliations. Children's concepts of religious figures are somewhat stereotyped, adolescents' views abstract and varied, but confused. In prayers children beg for handouts in exchange for promises to be good. Their notions of religious denominations are hardly more sophisticated. Most children cling to traditional beliefs, such as beliefs in God's goodness, Sunday's holiness, and everlasting life.

Distortions in religious concepts stem partly from the language used and partly from the manner of child-rearing. Girls, especially, who are reared to be dependent, picture God as an authoritative yet nurturant protector. Help for remedying children's religious confusion is hampered by the general taboo on such research. Researchers take refuge in safe but somewhat superficial questions that fail to get at the more basic factors. For too long this significant area in children's adjustment has been all but ignored.

• SUGGESTED QUESTIONS AND ACTIVITIES

1. Do the levels of morality delineated by Peck and Havighurst seem logical to you? That is, does each stage, as defined by these writers, seem to represent a logical progression toward moral maturity?

2. Do girls typically develop too strong and boys too weak a conscience?

3. Devise an appropriate moral dilemma and ask children of your acquaintance for a solution. For example, children might be asked, "When Tommy finds a quarter in the school yard, what should he do with it?" Or, "If Laura sees Johnny cheating on an examination, should she tell the teacher?" Report your findings in the class.

4. Outline ideal rules for family discipline.

In each of the following situations, how would you suggest that parents discipline the child who (a) runs away, (b) steals candy from a store, (c) picks on a younger sibling, (d) talks back to a parent, (e) refuses to do his share of the household chores?

5. Which of these forms of morals reinforcement would you favor: punitive action for disapproved behaviors, love-oriented discipline, or positive reinforcement? Why?

6. Analyze the differences, from your own observations, in the mother's and father's roles in morals training and punishment.

7. Is the elementary school teacher's personal moral code "his own business," or should he always constitute an identification figure beyond reproach?

8. Which, if any, of the following situations should a sixth-grade teacher discuss with his class? (a) A local high school boy has been apprehended for stealing a car. (b) A local citizen has been arrested for murder, ostensibly in self-defense. (c) A child in the class has been caught cheating. (d) A sex deviate has been caught molesting girls in the community.

9. Would it be advisable to supply children with attractively written children's stories consciously designed to inculcate socially approved moral standards?

10. Analyze several children's comic strips and television programs in terms of the moral concepts involved.

11. Should television programs, children's books, and comic strips be censored so that only socially accepted moral standards are presented?

12. Have committees compile, analyze, and report to the class the results of these questions, answered anonymously (but with sex designated) by the class: (a) Recall the earliest morals conflicts you can remember and the circumstances involved. (b) Describe a childhood incident when you felt you did wrong, including your feelings, your parent's reactions, and so on. (c) How did you perceive yourself morally as a child? Why? (d) Relate a childhood incident that indicates how you reacted as a child to punishment. (e) What general form of discipline did your parents use: power-oriented, love-oriented, or simple reinforcement of "right" behaviors? Describe the apparent effects on you. What sort of authority roles did each parent play? (f) Name specific factors that somehow affected your moral code during childhood.

13. How can religious teachings in childhood and adolescence be properly articulated to prevent confusion?

14. Would it be best for parents to take their children to several Sunday schools or churches so they might decide for themselves what religion to follow?

• SUGGESTED READINGS

Berkowitz, L., *The Development of Motives and Values in the Child.* New York: Basic Books, 1964. A brief book that summarizes and analyzes the very considerable research literature of the last decade on achievement orientation and moral development in childhood.

Boehm, L., "Social Class Differences in Conscience Development," *Child Development,* Vol. 23 (1962), pp. 565–574. Reports a study of the effects of social-class differences on conscience development. In general, the study supported Piaget's hypothesis that moral development depends on maturation and proceeds through successively more mature stages.

Bronfenbrenner, U., "The Role of Age, Sex, Class, and Culture in Studies of Moral Development," *Religious Education Research Supplement,* Vol. 14, No. 4 (July–August 1962), S3–S17. Bronfenbrenner examines available data relating to age, sex, class, and culture as factors in moral development, identifies gaps remaining in such research, and suggests directions that future research may take.

Elkind, D., "The Developmental Psychology of Religion," in Aline H. Kidd and Jeanne L. Rivoire, eds., *Perceptual Development in Children.* New York: International Universities Press, 1966, pp. 193–225. Reviews the somewhat scanty research available on this topic.

Hoffman, M. L., "Childrearing Practices and Moral Development: Generalizations from Empirical Research," *Child Development,* Vol. 34 (1963), pp. 295–318. Pulls together research findings concerning effects of parental practices on the child's moral development and points up tentative generalizations, gaps, and inconsistencies that can be used as guides in further research. The studies examined are those that were designed primarily to investigate parental antecedents of moral variables and that meet current methodological standards.

Kohlberg, L., "Development of Moral Character and Moral Ideology," in Martin L. Hoffman and Lois W. Hoffman, eds., *Review of Child Development Research,* Vol. I, pp. 383–431. New York: Russell

273

CHAPTER NINE

Sage Foundation, 1964. Excellent interpretation of available research on the topic of moral development.

Kohlberg, L., "Moral Education in the Schools: A Developmental View," *School Review,* Vol. 74, No. 1 (Spring 1966), pp. 1–30. An outstanding authority reviews moral research and relevant issues, and concludes that moral education does not "imply the imposition of a curriculum upon the teacher." However, the teacher must be concerned about the child's moral judgments and the sort of values that should be encouraged.

McDonald, F. J., "Children's Judgments of Theft from Individual and Corporate Owners," *Child Development,* Vol. 34 (1963), pp. 141–150. Children were asked to judge which of two actions, stealing from an individual or from a corporate owner, was morally more reprehensible, and why. The results were evaluated in terms of age, sex, intelligence, and social class.

Rosen, B. C., "Family Structure and Value Transmission," *Merrill-Palmer Quarterly,* Vol. 10, No. 1 (January 1964), pp. 59–76. This study relates the acquisition of values to various factors within the family structure. Independence training and methods of discipline are found to be of special importance in value transmission.

10
THE INFANT IN THE FAMILY

• THE IMPORTANCE OF
THE FAMILY

Before introducing the infant, let us first have a look at the institution in our society in which practically every newborn finds himself automatically enrolled—the family. Psychologists agree on at least one point: that the family is the greatest single influence on the child's development, in two irrefutable ways. First, parents provide the child with his biological heritage. Second, they organize his life, selecting from an infinity of possible combinations of child-rearing patterns those with which to shape their child's life. These choices are especially significant because the child's character structure correlates more closely with specific modes of child-rearing than with parental personality (Behrens, 1954). This same fact makes it important that parents receive special training for their role. For too long we have assumed that girls have an "instinct" for motherhood and have ignored boys' future parental role altogether. Perhaps training boys for fatherhood would help to prevent situations such as this girl endured:

My father was a severe disciplinarian toward us girls, was extremely unfair to my mother, and conspicuously favored my brother. My parents' arguments and fights made me cry many times. My brother would stick up for my father, my sisters and I for my mother. Things are better now since my parents have separated, but I still can't stand to see people fighting, even verbally. To avoid the fighting and anxiety it causes, I simply don't stick up for my rights.

The family also shapes the child's values, more in some areas than in others. Intrafamilial resemblance is high for religious values, somewhat less for economic (practical) ones, and even lower for aesthetic standards, like "love of truth" (Fisher, 1948). An especially important value, instilled within the home, is the child's "instrumental activism," which refers to mastery of the environment and development of re-

sources, rather than passive resignation to things as they are. Among the components of this trait are achievement and efficiency, both of which are vital for adjustment in a competitive society, and both of which depend heavily on parental encouragement (Parsons, 1965).

Another factor that greatly increases the impact of family life is the family's continuous reinforcement of selected behaviors in the child's most impressionable years. That is, family environment possesses a certain consistency, so that the impact of the same basic values, individuals, material objects, and the like is felt over and over (Schaefer and Bayley, 1960). Parental influence may not be strongly felt in a specific situation, but the attitudes and ideas expressed day after day inevitably leave their mark. In effect, the family is a postage-stamp-sized society, or subculture, in which the child learns the basic principles of social interaction. The child rehearses life roles in miniature, where he can afford to be himself without paying the consequences.

However, despite its undoubted influence—in fact, partly because of it—we may come to overemphasize the home's significance. There are roles it does not perform. For instance, no longer do older children obtain their chief recreation at home; nor does the boy learn his vocational role from his father. Primary socialization experience in the family may be so overstressed as to obscure recognition of secondary social factors like world affairs or political and social movements. And parents, who are blamed for everything that happens to the child, will do well to recognize the limitations of their role. They will feel less overwhelmed by their responsibility, and less guilty when children fail to live up to their expectations, if they know they are not omnipotent.

• THE FAMILY AND
CHANGING TIMES

Family structure has changed radically since colonial times and is still changing. From 1890 to 1960, the proportion of American farm families was reduced from almost half to less than a tenth. Meantime, the authoritarian, economically integrated, self-sufficient family, traditionally adapted to rural living, became obsolete.

All these changes, rooted in the Industrial Revolution, brought concomitant problems (Nash, 1965). Instead of the whole family's working together, the father became the chief bread-winner. Then, as labor-saving devices increased, mothers followed fathers into the workaday world. The concurrent shift from an authoritarian to a democratic family structure brought certain gains. Decisions were now made by consensus in which children participated from an early age. And while joint parent authority, instead of father domination, created some problems of decision-making, the democratic structure was essentially healthier (Rosen and Gregory, 1965). No longer was the child on the lowest rung of a rigid household hierarchy.

In short, modern family life is probably less decaying than different. Indeed, now more than ever the family concentrates on the personality development of its members. It also provides warmth and sanctuary from the anonymity of urban existence — services no other social agency is prepared to offer. Such family disorders as exist are due partly to growing pains, which are inherent in adaptive change.

• THE FAMILY VIEWED CROSS-CULTURALLY

A cross-cultural survey would reveal many relatively distinctive patterns of family life. Nevertheless, for all their diversity, the world's cultures share certain universals. Most people, in time, belong to two families: the family of orientation, in which they grow up, and the family of procreation, in which they become parents. Equally universal is some sort of kinship system, involving relatives beyond the immediate family.

In many cultures, modes of child-rearing are fairly rigid. However, in a complex modern society, conflicting theories of child-rearing may exist simultaneously. A case in point is the 1966 court battle over the custody of Harold Painter's seven-year-old son Mark. After the death of Painter's wife and daughter in an automobile accident, he placed Mark in the home of his own foster parents in Santa Rosa, California, and took a newspaper job there. When this did not work out, Painter took his son to stay with his late wife's parents in Ames, Iowa. Painter then returned to California, took a good job as a designer, and remarried. Now able to provide a home for Mark, whom he had not seen for a year, Painter returned to Iowa to get the boy. The grandparents, who had never approved of their daughter's marriage, refused to give Mark up, on the grounds that Painter could not provide a suitable upbringing for their grandson. Painter applied to district court and won custody, but the grandparents appealed to the Iowa Supreme Court, which reversed the lower court. It based its decision partly on testimony that Harold Painter was "bohemian," "atheist or agnostic," and "a political liberal," and that his way of life was "romantic," "arty," and "unstable." The court declared that Mark would be better off with his grandparents, who were "conventional, middle-class, dependable, middle-west" people. Painter continued the battle for his son and wrote a book called *Mark, I Love You*, which increased the already widespread publicity on the case. Eventually the grandparents relented and gave Painter custody of his son.

While there is certainly more to this case than is contained in this brief summary, the situation as outlined raises several questions. First, should a father's rights to his children be deemed as fundamental as a mother's? Second, should society have the right to decide a custody case even partially on the basis that the father's life is "bohemian" and somewhat atypical? Might it not be argued that the child's creative potential would have a better possibility of realization under the guidance of a highly intelligent, creative, and loving father and stepmother?

For a better perspective, let's look at the family as a social institution. In Western countries, the kinship system is decaying somewhat, though it still thrives in much of the world. The largest such groups are the joint families of India, the Middle East, Africa, and the Balkans, where a household economy like that of ancient Rome still persists. Here a family founder, his sons, his son's sons, and all their wives, children, grandchildren, and servants live out their lives in a compound of many rooms with common fields and gardens, under a central authority.

However, in the Western world's open society, where parents must be free to move with their jobs, the small family is more functional. Families are increasingly isolated, not merely from familial ties but from ties with others in the community. The typical group is composed of parents and minor children, or parents without children at all. We even speak of childless couples as "families." Family "shrinkage," meanwhile, has brought greater emphasis on independence and on self-realization, as opposed to self-sacrifice on behalf of the family group. Each individual must be free to "go it alone" and set his own path, free of entangling kindred. However, recent studies attest to the persistence of reciprocal relations such as gift giving, visiting, and mutual aid between grandparents and parents, nuclear family and kinfolk. And most people still turn to relatives more often than to friends when crisis strikes (Hill, 1960).

A concurrent change, arising from the **nuclear family** pattern has been age separation, with older people living separately. No longer do they importantly influence either their children's or their grandchildren's daily lives. However, the parents themselves do not wield the authority once held by the elders of the family group. Authority has been divided among the members of the nuclear family, with even the children's interests and prejudices taken into consideration. The modern father is not so much the mentor and model for his son, as his pal, often away performing his important nonfamilial work role, while women and children are left at home. On the other hand, fathers have far more time at home nowadays because of the shorter work week and longer vacations. One may even question whether children might not profit from more salutary neglect by both parents, which would permit greater self-initiative.

By now this point should be clear: The current parental role, viewed culturally, has become not so much diluted as different. The nuclear family requires that parents simultaneously play many roles, including spouse, householder, family head, and amateur psychologist. Nevertheless, the burden is somewhat attenuated by the shortened time it is borne. Nowadays siblings are born close together, and upon completing high school take jobs or go to college, never to join the family of orientation again. Thus most people play the parental role only 20 or so years of their lives.

• INTANGIBLES OF FAMILY LIFE: WAY OF LIFE, VALUES, AND CLIMATE

Thus far we have talked of the family in terms of the society and culture in which it exists; however, in a sense, every family is a miniature, unique subculture. For instance, every family has its characteristic way of life, such as indoor or outdoor, intellectual or sports-loving, social or isolated. Some families are close-knit; some seem like unrelated strays who accidentally took refuge under the same roof. Some families run Do-Drop-Inns; others maintain closed corporations. Whatever the family life style, it rubs off on its members, affecting each in a different way. The lazy child feels like a stranger in the hardworking home, while the diligent child grows impatient with a family that prefers a playful way of life.

Distinctions in family value-orientations might be multiplied endlessly. Some families emphasize dedication to the worth, dignity, and personal development of family members. Others accentuate the outer façade of the family, or its image in the eyes of the community. Some stress present pleasures; others concentrate on past memories or future goals. Families may be dominated by one major value, like power, or status, or money; or by several values; or by hardly any values, so that children merely drift (Ackerman, 1958).

Here we glimpse values that dominated particular families, as reported retrospectively by adolescents:

My parents were domineering and had but meager education. Our house was nice, but no one was ever in it, because we were all out working to support it. I would rather have lived in a smaller house and found out what my parents were like. As it was, money — and putting up a front — were all that counted.

My family is a highly competitive unit, and each child has maintained high honors in school. Each tries to impress the rest of the family by something well done. Games that we play as a family involve such tasks as factual recall and giving word meanings. Our main forms of humor are esoteric jokes and riddles.

Physical Climate of the Home

Each family also has its characteristic "climate," derived from a blending of material and psychological factors. Physical climate embraces such factors as space, lighting, color, arrangement of rooms, design, odors, cleanliness, and resistance or openness to sound. It involves whether the house is old or new, whether it has an attic or a basement, and whether there are adaptations for the children at their respective age levels. Physical climate also derives from many subtle factors such as the height and size of windows, the sturdiness of furniture, the number of books, and the condition of fixtures and plumbing. The way these factors, either singly or blended together, affect each family member depends on his own needs and personality.

The home should meet certain physical standards if it is to fulfill children's needs. First, it should be healthful, providing fresh air, proper temperature, and protection against disease — essentials often taken for granted but sometimes lacking.

Another requirement is adequate space. Pending more definitive research, we must guess at standards from what we know about children. Certainly, a child wants a place of his own, where he has room to grow. He needs boxes or shelves for his belongings, to reduce tensions over "what's mine or thine," and to enhance his own consciousness of being a distinct personality. In fact, the entire home space should be zoned, to permit the most effective life patterns. There should be places for noise and places for quiet, places for getting together or for being alone, places for work and places for play. (Unfortunately, some houses afford the privacy of Times Square, the quiet of a boiler factory, and the spaciousness of a nest of telephone booths.) In short, the home should lend itself to supporting each family member, rather than constitute an obstacle to his activities and a factor conducive to unpleasant moods.

Let's look at a home occupied by a family that has taken these factors fully into account. On the main floor there is a living area consisting of living-room and diningroom combined, sufficiently large and flexible in design to permit the entire family, or the parents and their friends, to be together. The full basement is divided into areas, the largest one for the children, smaller ones for Mother's laundry and Dad's study and shop. In the children's area there are toys and tools appropriate to each child's age, and bulletin boards on which they can post whatever they wish.

Each of the two children also has a small bedroom for which he is responsible, and which he can organize within flexible limits set by the mother.

Few families are affluent enough to be able to have such an ideal situation; but every family can make adaptations as children move through successive age-stages. Babies will grow up less inhibited if provided places where they can freely explore their environment. Otherwise, they face barrages of "don't do this" or "don't touch that," which produce a gradually constricting influence on their tendency to explore and their curiosity to know. Small sets of garden or shop tools may be purchased for children whose small hands cannot cope with grown-up ones. And low hooks may be placed where the toddler can easily hang his things. However, parents should guard against maintaining the trappings of babyhood too long. Graduation from the crib to a grown-up sized bed may assist a child to mature. The ideal is simply this: to make such adjustments as may help children deal effectively with their environment at different growth levels.

Parents also determine whether the family dwelling is simply a house or a home. Murphy (1946) speaks of the "house beautiful standard of living." The house and grounds are decorated according to good taste and must be kept just so. The appearance of the house is placed ahead of the needs of the child. The child becomes a little adult because he cannot live in the unrestrained, informal fashion of childhood. He also learns to attach more importance to things than to people (Rogers, 1957).

On the other hand, the home should be as attractive as the family budget will permit—one that children will enjoy and of which they will be proud. Children need a place to entertain their friends, as this illustration shows:

> From the time I was born until I reached the sixth grade, my family was very poor. We lived in a rented house that was dilapidated and leaked. We children were so ashamed of the house that we never brought our friends home. After my father died, my mother got a job, and we had more money and a better place to live. My younger brothers now began bringing home their friends. I was jealous because I had never been allowed to do so, and indeed would have been ashamed to do so. (Male)

A child is especially self-conscious if he lives in a fringe area of dilapidated dwellings and goes to a school largely attended by middle-class families. While feelings of pride or shame are strongest at adolescence, even younger children are affected. Rogers and Rice (1947, pp. 112–114) tell how home visits helped them to understand better the behavior of children in an underprivileged community:

> Another activity these children indulge in is just sitting and looking out the windows. All children do this to a certain extent, but many of these boys and girls will spend as much as an hour at the window, quietly looking out and apparently enjoying the experience immensely. . . . After visiting in the dirty, overcrowded, smelly little apartments where so often the one window in the room faces a dark wall of another apartment house, it is apparent why the low windows in our sunny schoolroom attracted these children.

One subject yet to be researched properly is the impact of physical characteristics of the home on children's emotions. However, drab colors probably have a depressing effect; and small rooms and low ceilings may produce hemmed-in feelings. Presumably, too, nervous tensions are increased by thin walls that permit sound to reverberate through the house.

Significance for the individual child. Of course, an individual child's reactions are his own. One child may love the ancient family homestead, which is despised as an outdated relic by his sibling. Note this individual's reactions to his home:

We live in a duplex whose two sides are identical. The rooms are large and square, with high ceilings. Their openness offers no privacy. In fact, I used to spend much time in my bedroom closet, or the attic stairway, having made these areas into something of an office — just to gain some feeling of privacy. The house must have been built by a mathematician who likes the shape of squares. I would not live there if I had any choice [Rogers, 1962, p. 305].

The sensitive child, especially, may react to the physical features of his home to an extent more ordinary people can scarcely comprehend. Note Whittaker Chambers' description of his childhood home:

It was big, built like a nest of boxes and painted a faded yellow. Over the years, the paint faded still more and peeled off in an incurable acne. The shutters, that had once been green, weathered to a washed-out blue. Some became unhinged and had to be taken down. That made some of the windows look like lashless eyes. . . .

The paper on most of the walls was faded and browned and sometimes bubbled and peeled off. . . . a sizable piece of ceiling fell down one day, exposing the laths. My mother . . . donned over-alls (rather a daring act in those days) and stretched and glued cheesecloth over the hole. My brother and I admired her skill. We were even more interested by the fact that mice soon nested behind the cheesecloth [Chambers, 1952, pp. 102–103].

A perspective on physical factors. Few houses can meet all standards completely; however, parents who adapt facilities and decoration as well as they can, enhance their children's enjoyment and effective potential. A child who senses that his parent tries to make the house a home will find his confidence in his parents strengthened and his own security feelings enhanced. Even less affluent parents should realize that several gallons of paint, coupled with children for cheap labor, can transform a drab interior into a sunny one.

Fortunately, research in this area is beginning, at least in a small way. In Baltimore, a five-year longitudinal study of housing and family life was completed in 1959 (Wilner et al., 1960). A test group of low-income families, who were moved to a modern housing project, was compared with a matched control group. The test group, after several years, had had fewer accidents and less illness, besides attaining improved morale. When planning a house, the researchers concluded, psychophysiologic and social factors, as well as technical ones, should be considered.

Emotional Climate of the Home

Emotional climate, unlike physical climate, has received much attention from researchers. In a sense, it embraces all research about family relationships. However, the concept of emotional climate has features distinctly its own. Emotional climate derives from a blending of many factors; and while intangible, it is nevertheless very real, spilling onto and infecting all family members. In a study of well-adjusted children, home climate was clearly apparent in the way parents spoke of their children:

They spoke of making the child feel wanted. "He has always known he was 'our boy' and 'greatly beloved.'" "You have to let children know they are wanted or they turn mean. We sure let him know it." "We have always told her how happy we are to have her and she loves the story of how her father's headache, the day she was born, disappeared when he saw her."

They spoke also of appreciation, trust, and confidence. "He's such fun, he's a real pal." "He has never failed us and I know he won't." "We would trust her anywhere." [Stout and Langdon, 1950, p. 458].

Just the opposite type of climate is evident in this girl's testimony:

My parents constantly fought, and though their anger was never directed at us children, I was terrified. They gave us much attention, and took care of our needs, but I felt I lived on a battleground. If my marriage turns out like that, I'll get a divorce.

281

In another study, which involved analyzing 132 biographies, an effort was made to determine how specific factors related to different types of personality. It was concluded that something more than specific parental practices accounted for personality differences — that something being good family morale and an atmosphere of good will between parent and child (Stagner, 1937).

In general, family climate reflects such oft-cited variables as warmth, confidence, security, and their opposites, besides many less obvious factors, such as "double-bind" situations. A child may be placed in situations where he can't win; for instance, his mother complains of his lack of regard for her, yet freezes when he is affectionate (Bateson, 1960). A highly emotional mother may overwhelm children with her hysteria. A gloomy father may create a graveyard aura each evening on coming home from work.

Complaints that family climate is deteriorating may not be justified. Older people often object to today's more casual family life, perhaps because parents are less strict and have their own interests outside of family responsibilities. However, as parenthood has become more of a hobby, it has also become more of a profession. Children are desired more and more for their own sake, not as extra hands. Whether current modes of family life are of the type best adapted to today's world, research has not determined.

• THE STATUS OF THE INFANT

Having gained a view of the family as a unit, and of certain of its problems in present-day Western society, let us now examine the status of the infant. As we shall presently see, no other period in human development poses more critical issues or presents a more dynamic challenge to researchers than infancy; however, authorities differ on the questions of which early experiences are most critical, and how persistent their effects are. Animal experiments are less equivocal, and clearly show long-term, irreversible results of early experience. They show, for example, that hunger, electrical shock, and other traumatic experiences in infancy leave permanent traces (Levine et al., 1956). Psychiatrists have pointed out the lasting effects of early trauma on humans. According to Baruch (1952), fantasies may show up in personality far removed from where they started, their beginnings completely disguised. One little boy, Baruch asserts, held in his bowel movements in order to punish his mother, and became a man who held onto his money and was stingy with his wife.

While many if not most psychologists would question Baruch's interpretation, much empirical evidence exists for the long-term effects of infant experience, especially basic-habit training and the infant-mother relationship. According to some data, a satisfying relationship with the mother apparently strengthens the child's capacity to cope with stress (Yarrow, 1963). In fact, child-rearing practices seem related to susceptibility to emotional illness, though just how is not clear (Kisker, 1964).

However, the long-term effects of the infant-mother relationship are not clear-cut. The same child-rearing pattern may be associated with completely different types of adult personality. In certain simple societies, notably in Haiti and Kaska, babies are fed on demand, often comforted, and rarely disciplined, yet Kaskans are introverts and Haitians extroverts (Underwood and Honigman, 1947).

Nor are effects always of the "straight-line variety"; the seemingly "logical" effects of some early experience sometimes may not follow. Contrary to expectations, only a low positive correlation was found between an infant's social initiative and the social stimulation he had received (Yarrow, 1963). Still other infant characteristics show little relation, either direct or indirect, to environmental influences. In fact autonomy and adaptability show only low positive, or even negative relations with all postnatal environmental variations (Yarrow, 1963). The reason for this may be that hereditary or prenatal influence determines these traits.

In view of the foregoing, one may well ask: To what stimuli are infants sensitive, and how persistent are their effects? Some authorities perceive the infant as highly vulnerable and aware of subtle shades of feeling; others see him as a vegetable, sustaining little impact in the first months. However, Stevenson (1957) simply dismisses this question. It is unnecessary, he states, to posit a special impressionability or vulnerability of children. The *quality* of early experience is not so important as the relatively unvarying *quantity* of any particular type of experience.

Apart from any special vulnerability or lack of it, infants and young children naturally feel the effect of special influences. Their very helplessness and lack of coping techniques make them susceptible to certain traumas. For example, the young child hurts himself because he is incapable of assessing environmental hazards accurately. The world is rigged for adults, not for him. The small child whose eyes are at the level of his father's knees sees a far different world from that encompassed by the adult.

Some writers emphasize the infant's primitiveness and his utter dependency. The repertoire of the four-week-old child "still seems to be eating, crying, and eliminating, prompting one observer to portray an infant as an 'alimentary canal open at both ends'" (Gesell and Armatruda, 1947).

Allport (1955, p. 28) confirms this picture of a dependent, primitive creature:

Even at the age of two, the child is, when measured by standards applied to adults, an unsocialized horror. Picture, if you can, an adult who is ex-

tremely destructive of property, insistent and demanding that every desire be instantly gratified, helpless and almost totally dependent on others, unable to share his possessions, impatient, prone to tantrums, violent and uninhibited in the display of his feelings.

By contrast, young monkeys are dependent only a few weeks, and baby chimpanzees remain with their mothers only three to six months. The infant's longer period of plasticity permits greater behavioral modifications; in fact, it accounts for the wide variations in world culture. However, the infant is no mere sponge, soaking up whatever his environment dispenses. He is "reactive, competent, and in reciprocal interaction with

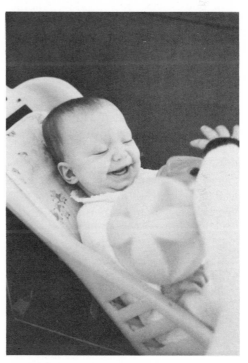

The infant is reactive and reciprocating rather than passive.

the environment," not "an undifferentiated passive recipient of stimulation" (Kessen, 1963); and he quickly develops his own distinctive tempo, rhythms, and coordinations—internal and external, perceptual and motor. He has his own level of readiness to discharge tensions and achieve satisfaction in relation to oral experiences, body contact, warmth, sound, taste, and movement. Environmental experiences are filtered through his own highly individual traits; and he reacts to a social environment constantly modified by what he himself is.

• THE INFANT-MOTHER RELATIONSHIP

Maternal Attitudes

Reactions to pregnancy. To the shock and surprise of many people, not every baby is highly desired and welcome when he crosses the threshold of life. In one study, 64% of the women questioned reported delight with their first pregnancies, but only 34% welcomed later ones (Sears et al., 1957). Another researcher reported only slightly more than half of a group of women pleased at being pregnant (Cobliner, 1965).

Various factors are related to the mother's feeling about pregnancy. In general, the fewer children a mother has, the more pleased she is with the knowledge of pregnancy. Favorable response also correlates positively with the length of time since the last child was born. Sex makes a difference, too. A girl may be welcome in an all-boy family, or vice versa. Also, parents are often more willing to assume responsibility for another child if they have only girls, assuming that girls are easier to rear in early years; while having only boys discourages mothers from inviting further burdens. Surprisingly, the mother's age does not relate to her attitude toward pregnancy (Sears et al., 1957).

Feelings about pregnancy also vary with physical and emotional characteristics of the mother. Levy (1952) found a positive correlation between length of menstrual flow and "mothering," suggesting either a constitutional basis of maternal attitudes, or conversely, physical changes stemming from such attitudes. Indicators of "mothering" included such factors as playing with dolls in childhood, taking care of babies, baby-carriage peeking, number of children wanted, and anticipation of care and breast-feeding of their own babies.

Emotional health is a factor, too, for the mother with high self-esteem as a woman and wife usually greets her new baby with a generous measure of maternal love (Bibring et al., 1961). If, on the other hand, a woman's love experiences have been disappointing and her self-esteem is low, her gift of maternal love will hardly be adequate (Ourth and Brown, 1961).

The welcome accorded the newborn also varies with socioeconomic status. The lower classes may view parenthood as the price they must pay for sex relations, while the middle and upper classes more often regard parenthood as marital fulfillment and children as their pride and joy. In general, lower-class men resent responsibilities for child care, while their middle- and upper-class counterparts take pride in being family men, and willingly make sacrifices of time, energy, or even vocational advancement for their children (Bossard, 1953).

Factors modifying reaction to pregnancy are endless and are often subtly intertwined. A woman may feel the family cannot afford another child; or she may be overworked already. If the child is illegitimate, she may be afraid his status will be found out. Or if she is party to a shotgun wedding, she may view the child as the cause.

The following testimonials betray women's attitudes toward pregnancy:

My feeling toward my unborn child was almost total happiness. I never had any of the distressing pregnancy symptoms I have read about. I only worried when I read about babies being born deformed and retarded.

During my first pregnancy, my husband and I were still in college, and we could not afford a child. I resented the pregnancy, especially the limitations it placed on me, while also thinking of the baby lovingly. I accepted the second pregnancy more quickly, because by then we could afford a child. Besides, I had learned from experience and had fewer fears.

Maternal feelings toward the infant. Of course, a mother's attitude may change after the child is born. Many "other than happy" mothers claim they eventually accepted their babies, after many fluctuations (Cobliner, 1965). However, it may well be that feelings of rejection have been merely repressed, as a defense against guilt feelings.

To the impartial observer, mothers' attitudes, whether recognized by the mothers or not, are often clearly apparent. Cobliner (1965) reported a wide variation in the way they fed, burped, and handled their newborns. During the process of feeding, some mothers talked continuously to their babies, pinched their mouths, handled their heads, rocked their bodies rhythmically up and down or sidewise, and played with them afterward. Others remained apathetic and listless, regardless of the baby's temperament. A considerable number seemed anxious to hurry along the feeding. Many of them seemed unnecessarily to interrupt the process, taking the bottle from the baby's mouth, often unexpectedly, to check the milk level. Small wonder, concludes Cobliner, that some children may have a chip-on-the-shoulder from birth. They find themselves shackled to mothers they had no choice in selecting.

Factors modifying maternal attitudes. There are various reasons for mothers' postnatal attitudes. It may be that the child fails to correspond to maternal expectations. Hochberg and Lambert (1958) found that college girls' concepts of babies were far from typical of what babies are actually like. Their ideal corresponded to the perfect child or "baby card" type. Here college girls tell what sort of babies they want:

I'd like one with a spirit of its own. I wouldn't mind its crying, if it weren't a sickly thing. Of course, you get what you get, and then it's up to you.

I want a decent-looking baby formed with all parts in good condition. An ugly baby would have a hard time growing up. However, I'd love the baby as much as if it were perfect, even if it wasn't.

I want my baby to weigh seven or eight pounds, and to be happy, seldom crying, and always smiling and gurgling. I want him to be a fast learner (early in walking, talking, and toilet training).

Levy (1958), who observed mothers' differential attitudes toward children as revealed during feeding, concluded that the condition of the baby was the main factor in determining the presence or absence of maternal greeting. Only one in three mothers greeted babies who were whimpering or crying; all greeted those who were awake and quiet. An expressive baby will have an effect on the mother that a phlegmatic infant fails to elicit (Cameron, 1963). Obviously, therefore, the baby's autonomic stability, which is basic to his emotional stage, will strongly affect the mother-child relationship.

Obviously, too, some babies seem more lovable than others. Most babies are soft and easy to cuddle, but some seem stiff and bony. It is one thing to mother a mildly active, highly adaptive child, and quite another to cuddle a wiggly child who cries a great deal (Thomas et al., 1963). Ackerman (1958) notes that a child may be rejected either because of specific characteristics he possesses or because the parent would have rejected any child. For example, a mother may reject a particular child because he is hairy and she has had a lifelong anxiety about hair on her legs and breasts. Or she may be vain about her figure, and reject the child regardless of his traits because of the change after birth in the contour of her breasts.

Much depends, too, on the compatibility of mother and child. An active, sensitive mother may be continually disappointed by a slow-moving, unreactive infant; a phlegmatic mother may find an energetic baby disturbing. The buxom

285

Much depends on the compatibility of mother and child.

mother with a lady wrestler's physique can hardly accept the sickly premie who barely made it—and looks it. Greedy feeders may actually frighten some mothers; they seem like attacking little monsters. Other mothers may simply find them amusing. The apathetic little feeder may arouse sympathy in one mother and annoyance in another.

A common, though often obscure, factor in determining both parents' attitudes is the infant's effect on their relationship. The father, especially, may fear that the baby will usurp the affection he has erstwhile enjoyed by himself.

The woman's job status is another consideration. Mothers with professional experience may find motherhood an unwelcome interruption of their careers. In fact, women with status occupations tend to regard themselves as more sick during pregnancy than they actually are (Bibring, 1959).

The Infant's Role in the Infant-Mother Relationship

Basic to recent research on infant-mother relations is a new theme: the child's interaction with his mother. For many years the child had been portrayed as a passive, receptive organism simply soaking up, unresistantly, influences from his environment. This model was inherited from Pavlov and Watson, and supported by Thorndike and the connectionistic learning theorists. It was assumed that all children would react similarly to the same environmental influences. A rigid set of rules for bringing up baby resulted.

The current approach is vastly different. Infants are seen as reactive and differing among themselves in their kinds of response. One group of researchers found two broad general classifications of infant "reactors": one characterized by ready adaptability, easy distractibility, and high-level rhythmicity, and the other by high intensity and a tendency to resist environmental stimuli. Some children are far more subject to environmental impact: highly distractible and readily adaptable. Others are very intense, persistent, and not easily distractible—the infant version of the inner-directed man. In the main, concluded these researchers, the reactive characteristics of the child, and not the attitude of the mother, determine the course of events (Thomas et al., 1963).

Other writers warn against exaggerating the young infant's capacity for environmental perceptions. His very immaturity, they assert, insulates him from the influence of parent attitudes. According to Levy (1958):

> He does not perceive his mother as an object at all. He does not have the means necessary for recognizing her as a separate being who watches over him, feeds him and cares for him, makes him comfortable and safe. Before birth he floated aimlessly in the amniotic fluid; after birth he is adrift in a shoreless world without objects of any kind. He can in no way reciprocate the love he gets; he is unable to return love or even to long for it. All that he can contribute is his own body; and he is not even aware that he has one. His mother is vividly aware of motherhood; whereas the child at first has no self to be aware of, and he cannot know that he is a child.

General Significance of the Infant-Mother Relationship

After many years and hundreds of pamphlets on the subject, to doubt the paramount importance of the infant-mother relationship would be equivalent to doubting that the earth is round or that democracy is good. It is comparatively easy to support such orthodoxy. Both sexes have a close relationship with their mother in infancy. They rely on her for food, comfort, affection, and sociability. Even when they grow older, they seek their mother when comfort and assurance are needed. She becomes their temporary ego in protecting them from the consequences of their own activities, when, because of inadequate experience, or imperfect motor coordination, they fall prey to physical dangers and emotional stresses (Finney, 1961). It is the overwhelming theoretical consensus, concludes Yarrow (1963), that the mother is the single most important

factor in the infant's life, although authorities differ in defining the extent and persistence of her influence.

However, animal studies have raised certain significant questions about the infant-mother relationship, and have placed certain "truths" in jeopardy. For example, the feeding experience was long conceded the crucial role in establishing affectional bonds, but studies with monkeys indicate that "contact comfort" may be even more crucial (Harlow and Zimmerman, 1959). Eight newborn baby monkeys were separated from their mothers and placed with artificial **mother surrogates.** Half had substitute mothers made of wire, the others of cloth. The wire mother's body was a wire-mesh cylinder; the cloth mother's was wood covered with terry cloth. Bottle-holders were placed in the upper-middle part of the "mothers' " bodies, permitting them to nurse. Thus both mothers dispensed food, but only the cloth mother provided contact comfort. Four of the monkeys were provided food by the wire mother, the other four by the cloth mother; but clearly all eight preferred the cloth mother. Furthermore, when confronted with fearful objects—for example, a moving toy bear—the monkeys sought the cloth mother for security.

One cannot be certain that data based on animal research will apply in like manner to humans. While the developmental pattern of monkeys closely approximates that of humans, monkeys are further advanced at birth. And since human infants are fully dependent on their mothers for food, feeding may assume a correspondingly greater significance in their social-affectional behavior.

Other evidence on the question of the mother's importance is unclear. Monkeys reared in total isolation for two years failed subsequently to display normal social or sexual behavior. Isolation for shorter periods produced lesser deficits. In fact, infant monkeys isolated for the first 80 days showed only mild effects. Again, monkeys raised by

When infant monkeys were given a choice of a wire or a terry-cloth surrogate mother, they showed a strong preference for the contact comfort provided by the cloth figure. (From H. F. Harlow, Love in infant monkeys, *Scientific American*, 1959, **200**, 204.)

live mothers achieved more advanced social and sexual behaviors than did monkeys subjected to wire or cloth mothers—all of which, one might argue, proves the importance of early mothering. However, when monkeys subjected to the surrogate mothers were placed in a more stimulating playroom situation, they developed normal social and sexual behavior (Harlow and Harlow, 1962).

What Should the Infant-Mother Relationship Be?

Having noted the significance of the infant-mother relationship, we might ask: What ideally should it be? From Chapter 1, recall that the behaviorists advocated stern treatment, while their successors of the 1940s and later years recommended plentiful "mothering," which included physical contact, succor, social stimulation, and ladling out of love. Which approach is better, the stainless steel approach, the warm-mother outlook, or something between? The issue is not yet fully resolved, but let's consider the evidence. Warmth was one of seven distinct clusters of traits that Sears and his associates (1957) found in child-rearing practice. The warm mother showed much affectional interaction with the baby, found ample time to play with him, accepted his dependency, praised him when he showed good table manners, and used reasoning as a method of training. Maternal coldness, characterized by the absence of such behaviors, was associated with behavioral difficulties, including high aggression, feeding problems, and bed-wetting. Brody (1962) found that infants whose mothers showed conspicuous ability to accommodate to their needs demonstrated social responsiveness, superior confidence in bodily movement, and interest in mastery of objects. Accommodation was measured by the mother's sensitivity, consistency, and attentiveness.

Ausubel (1958), among others, questions the infant's need for effusive mothering. In all instances where in-adequate mothering has been associated with harmful effects, the children have been deprived not merely of ideal mothering but of minimally sufficient care as well. In general, infants lack the cognitive capacity to perceive highly differentiated interpersonal responses. Indeed, older infants merely require sufficient interpersonal attention to ensure a feeling of confidence in their environment. Nor does it matter whether mother, mother surrogate, or several different adults minister to the child's needs. Whenever separation from a single mother figure has had damaging consequences, the infant has been conditioned to derive his security from her alone. In many primitive cultures—for example, the Hopi—infants seem just as content when cared for by older siblings or relatives who help the mother (Eggan, 1945).

Consider further the argument that mothers must provide the child adequate motor and sensory stimulation (Foss, 1961). Albanian infants ordinarily spend most of their first year bound to a wooden cradle board in a dark corner of the room, with no apparent ill effect (Ausubel, 1958).

Reservations are also sometimes expressed about the quantity of mothering needed. The neglected child may be deprived of a chance to explore his world and may have trouble defining his self—separating the "me" from the "not me." However, the mother may maintain contact beyond the optimum, especially if she has failed to achieve a separate identity herself. Her manner of handling the child reflects her needs, not the child's; she often believes she is fulfilling his needs when she is actually inventing them. "Perhaps I do baby my 10-year-old," she explains, "but he's frailer than most" (Witkin et al., 1962).

Excess mothering can make tyrants of children. Having been catered to in all things large and small, they rule their parents' lives and prove obnoxious to others (Dinkmeyer, 1965). Children may also become excessively dependent and disturbed at even the briefest separation from mother, as in the following description of a scene that took place during a mental examination:

> Timmy [aged three] was brought by his mother. He began sobbing, "I want Mamma!" the moment his mother left and kept this up for nine minutes in the playroom. He then gradually subsided but kept worriedly questioning the observer, "Mamma come back soon? After num-num (dinner) Mamma come back?" or attempting to bolster up his courage by saying, "No Timmy c'y" (apparently meaning to convey the thought "Timmy will not cry"). But his voice continued to tremble, and his brow never lost its pucker [Murphy et al., 1962, pp. 48–49].

While authorities differ as to the quantity of mothering required, they agree more closely on the importance of consistency and quality of mothering. At least minimal consistency is required if the infant is to count on his environment. The correlation is low, but positive, between maternal consistency and such aspects of infant behavior as developmental progress, social initiative, and capacity to handle stress (Yarrow, 1963).

Beyond minimal consistency, however, the quality of contact seems most important. In fact, it is a mistake to assume that a parent's influence on the child is directly proportional to the amount of time he spends with the child. His influence depends, rather, on the sort of relationship he has with the child. One small boy, aged four months, when shown pictures of the human face, paid attention only to the male face, cooing and trying to touch it. "He's Daddy's boy," explained the mother who spent far more time with him; "I'm just the diaper changer" (Sibliger, 1963).

Whatever their differences, authorities agree that ideal standards of mothering vary with the child's age and cognitive maturity. Until he acquires a functional concept of self and can comprehend threats to his safety, the infant's

own immaturity probably shields him from such psychological traumas as personal inattention or maternal separation. However, between the ages of nine months and three years, the child seems especially susceptible to such traumas, and child-care patterns must be adjusted accordingly.

The ideal pattern of mothering will also vary with the culture. Extreme mothering may be appropriate in Okinawa, where the culture is simply organized and noncompetitive, and may help account for the low incidence of psychosis there. However, when Okinawans practice the same patterns in the highly stratified Hawaiian culture, they manifest a higher incidence of psychosis (Wedge, 1952).

Pending better solutions, warns Spock (1957), it is better to make a few mistakes than to become stalemated from indecision or to do everything letter-perfect because of undue concern. Child-rearing methods that reflect a blend of love and popularized child psychology gleaned from a magazine at the corner grocery store build invisible trellises that determine the direction of children's lives. While it behooves parents to maintain as relaxed and wholesome a frame of mind as possible, they should also keep abreast of the very considerable, and highly significant, research on this topic.

• PARENTAL DEPRIVATION

While opinions about child care vary, parents are generally deemed significant, and concern is felt for children who are deprived of either mothers or fathers. This problem, typically called parental deprivation, may have relevance to any age; but it has aroused most controversy where infants are concerned. Overall, parental deprivation involves many children; for approximately 7,000,000 children in the United States live with only one parent or with neither parent: 4,900,000 with the mother, 600,000 with the father, and most of the others with relatives (Rutledge, 1960). These numbers would be multiplied several-fold if more subtle forms of parental deprivation were included, such as parental neglect or constant parental absence. Mrs. Jones may ignore her child so completely that, in effect, she is hardly there, except in the negative sense of making the child feel terribly unimportant. Mrs. Brown dislikes the housewife's role, to which her husband insists that she be confined, and is constantly out of the house visiting or on errands, leaving her children to their own devices.

Maternal Deprivation

The problem of **parental deprivation** has been related chiefly to mothers. To question the virtue of mothering became the worst heresy since Stokes challenged our kinship with monkeys. Great concern has been aroused over various forms of maternal deprivation— for example, when a mother's death required institutionalization of the infant. Certain studies, especially one by Spitz (1946), heightened interest in the problem. Among children who had been institutionalized as infants, Spitz reported a significant retardation in physical development and motor and language skills, as well as a high mortality rate. The cause of these untoward consequences, asserted Spitz, was inadequate mothering, a mere one-twelfth to one-fifteenth of what infants normally receive. However, Spitz failed to report all sorts of relevant data, such as the details of institutional care or the infants' heredity and socioeconomic backgrounds.

One might ask whether the picture presented below might be somewhat different in a well-run, adequately staffed institution:

Infants below the age of six months who had been in a certain institution for a considerable time manifested a typical syndrome. In appearance they were pale and emaciated, having failed to gain weight despite diets which seemed adequate. They slept poorly, had frequent stools, and lacked nor-mal sucking habits. Not surprisingly they appeared unhappy, and unresponsive to stimuli such as smiles and cooing [Coleman, 1964, p. 129].

The differences in views about maternal deprivation—and there are many—derive from varying combinations of confusion over terminology, poorly designed research, inadequate data, overgeneralization, and inadequate reporting. The terms "mothering" and "maternal love" are poorly defined, and some of the critical variables, such as age when separation occurred, are seldom accounted for. Also, few studies report the reason for separation or provide an adequate description of the post-separation environment.

Factors limiting the effects of separation. Nevertheless, available data suggest several conclusions. For example, the impact of separation seems to depend largely on an infant's capacity to interpret environmental stimuli—a matter on which authorities disagree. Shaffer's (1958) data indicate that it is hard to determine just how the infant feels. His findings suggest that the lack of strong overt protest in a young infant may not be taken as evidence that he is unaffected by an experience.

If maternal deprivation does affect the infant adversely, various factors may limit the strength of impact, one being the quality of the mother-child relationship prior to separation. In some cases, separation actually proves beneficial to the child. Children long exposed to dislike or indifference from their natural mothers gain by separation if they fall into kind and sensible hands. Also, the effect is diluted where the child has been cared for by several older people, as in primitive cultures and families where grandmothers babysit while mothers work (Mead, 1962). A second major factor is the sort of environment in which the child is placed after separation from the mother. Separation may involve placing the infant in an institution, a foster home, or a residential school.

In still other cases, the child may stay with relatives or remain in his own home. Ill effects may be considerably reduced by a certain amount of environmental engineering—for example, providing the hospitalized child with familiar toys, or maintaining accustomed schedules for the child placed in a foster home.

The effect also depends on circumstances surrounding the event. If a mother's death simultaneously removes a major portion of the family income, thus precipitating financial crises, it is hard to distinguish the effects of separation from those of poverty.

The impact of separation also depends on certain of the child's characteristics, including his age, temperament, and prior experience. Younger children, reported Faust and his associates (1952), responded more adversely to separation involving hospitalization for tonsillectomies than did older ones, but neither group suffered much. Children most seriously affected had had other traumatic experiences or poor relationships with their parents.

The effect of maternal absence will be intensified where other problems exist. Wooten (1962) notes that children subject to severe separation experiences typically come from families with a higher-than-normal incidence of mental deficiency and psychological disturbance. In addition, the residual effects of separation depend on what came before and what follows. For example, note the results in this case:

> I first attended a religious boarding school, which I disliked intensely. It operated by the law "survival of the fittest." However, in retrospect, I think the experience was beneficial compared to what might have been the case. My mother had a nervous breakdown and was permanently removed from home; my father was illiterate and knew nothing about raising a child. Besides, the neighborhood was predominantly a biracial slum.

In any case, the effects on children will vary, some children possessing much greater resilience than others. Some "come back" after the severest sorts of experience, but we tend to lose track of those who recover. In a study of severely deprived adolescents, remarkably large IQ increments occurred after just one year's remedial work (Clarke and Clarke, 1959).

Some authorities emphasize the importance of when deprivation occurs. In summarizing the literature bearing on maternal deprivation, Ainsworth (1962) concludes that children may be most sensitive between six months and two years, when affectional relationships are normally established, and less affected later, when less dependent. Similarly, Bowlby (1958) argues that a child is especially vulnerable at about eight months, after he has learned to depend on a particular person, usually the mother. Besides, he is at the stage when he is trying to locate the world outside himself and people he can count on.

In view of their changing vulnerability, it is important to remain aware of infants' developmental sensitivities and of focal conflicts typical of different ages. For example, hospitalization for surgery may be most critical when a child is especially concerned about body integrity (Yarrow, 1963).

Orlansky (1949) emphasizes the significance of a break in the continuity of child-care patterns, especially at critical times. For example, in some cultures children are carried on their mothers' backs, in others not. In some they are weaned early, in others late. Whatever the pattern, asserts Orlansky, infants adjust, provided the plan is consistent. However, in cases of maternal deprivation, practices to which the child has grown accustomed may be abruptly changed.

Casler (1961), who reviewed all the foregoing arguments at length, concluded that emotional, intellectual, and physical deficits may not be caused by deprivation itself; such ill effects as follow separation—and often none do—may be due to stimulus deprivation.

Certainly, some of the institutions where these studies were made could hardly be classified as enriched environmental situations.

The problem of "multiple mothering." The other side of the coin is excessive mothering. Can a child have too many mothers? Some evidence seems to indicate this—for example, when older sisters or grandmothers play the role of mother as well. Contrary evidence comes from cultures like the Hopi, where several women minister to the same child's needs, and are all given the name of mother. Discipline tends to be less harsh in such families and most harsh where the mother is the sole adult (Whiting and Whiting, 1960). In a more modern culture, among the Israeli kibbutzim, infants are tended by a mother figure called the *matapelet* while receiving regular visits from their own mothers. Infants show some developmental retardation, which disappears by middle childhood. In fact, in one study such children proved superior in overall maturity and ego strength to controls who lived with their own mothers. And while there was a tendency for the children's relationships to be the same with parents as with peers, such a pattern might actually prove functional in a communal culture, where primary identification is with peers rather than family (Rabin, 1958).

In effect, a similar situation was produced during the London bombings of World War II, when infants were separated from their parents for a period of three years and placed in residential nursery schools. These same individuals, when studied as adults, were making a normal adjustment, with a notable absence of the sort of affective and cognitive disturbances reported by Goldfarb and others for early-institutionalized children (Maas, 1963).

Other studies involve children who, as infants, lived in home management houses on university campuses prior to being placed in adoptive homes. Student mother-figures took turns, each for a few days, assuming full charge of the child. Some continuity was provided by the instructor, who also assumed some share in the infant's care. Usually the infants received much more than normal stimulation from the several mother-figures. When the children were studied later, and compared with matched controls, no differences from normally reared children were found in school achievement, or in personal, social, and emotional development (Gardner et al., 1961). In short, the bulk of evidence would seem to justify the conclusion that multiple mothering, per se, seems to do infants no damage, and may even prove more functional for some cultures.

Paternal Deprivation

Studies of maternal deprivation vastly outnumber, and tend to obscure, studies of paternal deprivation. Yet a Norwegian study suggests that father absence may have negative effects, too (Lynn and Sawrey, 1959). Sailors' children showed higher-than-normal dependence, **pseudo-maturity,** and idealization of the absent fathers. In general, boys showed greater immaturity, compensatory masculinity, and peer adjustment, and girls greater dependency than children generally. As Tiller (1957) points out, father absence for the child also means husband absence for the wife, whose adjustment vitally affects that of her children. Sailors' wives participated less than average in the community, tended to be overprotective and to stress obedience and politeness to a greater-than-normal degree.

In a study of war-born children, Stolz (1954) also found negative effects of father absence. She found feminine fantasy behaviors among boys, both during the father's absence and after his return. The boys had trouble in their relationships both with peers and adults, and showed higher-than-average levels of anxiety in doll-play experiments. Nor did they readily adjust to their fathers after they returned from service. The

293

father's unfamiliarity with the paternal role and his attempt to establish a paternal role with a son unaccustomed to such a relationship often brought friction.

Other studies have confirmed Stolz' findings about the feminizing effect of father absence on boys. McCord and her associates (1962) reported a correlation between paternal absence and feminine (though not overtly homosexual) identification, aggressiveness, anxiety about sex, and oral tendencies. Similarly, Sears (1951) found more girl-like behavior among boys whose fathers were absent, mostly on war service. They differed less from girls than did controls in frequency of aggression, and emphasized less the maleness of the father and boy dolls.

Carlsmith (1964) reported a somewhat different feminizing effect of father absence on boys. Such boys, he found, do better in verbal areas than in mathematics. Recall from the chapter on mental development that typical patterns of girl-rearing tend to produce more skill in verbal areas than in science and mathematics.

Other studies report a connection between father absence and delinquency. One group of delinquent boys, aged 11 to 15, as contrasted with a control group of non-delinquents, had failed to identify with their fathers (Andry, 1960). However, the effects of father absence are linked with other factors and hence difficult to assess. In the McCord study, cited above, boys whose fathers were absent showed neither increased delinquent activity nor heightened anxiety. And such ill effects as were apparent seemed to result not from father absence per se but from such family characteristics as parental conflicts, rejecting mothers, and the like. In fact, it is always difficult to untangle the effects of father absence, as such, from factors that accompany or account for his absence. For instance, the child of divorce may suffer from a lack of

certain material needs associated with loss of the father's income.

Naturally, children will feel the effect at some ages more than others. Boys whose fathers are absent during their early childhood may have trouble establishing sex identity, and later on may manifest overcompensatory masculine behaviors.

Overgeneralization in this, as in all areas of behavioral research, is unjustified. Where the father-child relationship is poor, separation from the father may even have a salutary effect (Bradburn, 1963). Moreover, the mother may be reasonably successful in acting the father's role as well as her own. In any case, concludes Stolz (1954), apparently ill effects do not always prove lasting.

Almost all the foregoing has pertained to the effect of paternal absence on sons; little attention has been paid to its effect on daughters. However, the following cases indicate that the effect on girls may be considerable:

> After we gave up our apartment and took a house in the suburbs, my father had to take a second job to support it. I only saw him on week-ends, and when he'd yell at me, I'd think, "I do without you all week long, and I could do without you on weekends, too." I love him, but I still feel this way. I guess I don't understand him because I never knew him.

> Since Joan's father held two jobs, she rarely saw him and established a close relationship with her mother. When her parents argued, she developed a deep resentment of her father. He made overtures to regain favor, but it did no good.

Parenthetically, studies of paternal deprivation have made little attempt to differentiate its effect on the sexes. Such research as exists shows a far greater effect on boys than on girls. For example, where fathers were in military service, Sears (1951) found that boys' doll play was affected, but not girls'.

Dealing with Cases of Deprivation

By now, it is obvious that children separated from one or both parents feel various effects. Just as clearly, all possible should be done to minimize whatever ill effects may result. Yet research on ways to reduce separation trauma is almost nonexistent. Well-meaning efforts at reducing negative effects, without empirical verification of their worth, may do more harm than good. For example, is it better for a child to attend a parent's funeral or not? Is it better to permit an anxious mother to remain with a child before and after an operation? There is a faint line between providing sufficient catharsis and arousing emotions that cannot easily be handled.

Fortunately, preventive and therapeutic approaches to dealing with children's traumas are currently being tried in varied settings. If the factors that cause damage can be identified, perhaps separation from parents can be accomplished without significant damage (Alpert, 1959).

• ISSUES IN BASIC-HABIT TRAINING

Toileting

Other important issues in infant care relate to basic-habit training—for example, toileting. Toileting assumes various forms even within our culture:

My mother took toilet-training so seriously that she would ask us if we had to go no matter where we were. Many a time I went to the bathroom right in the street.

Jimmy, aged three, is the youngest of four children. Since his parents believe toilet training should come naturally, Jimmy is still not trained, and refuses to go to the toilet when he should.

Physical factors involved. To understand the problem, it is necessary to recognize the physical factors involved. However anxious the mother, the child's toilet-training must await the maturation of certain brain centers. None of the cerebral cortex, where these centers are located, functions very well prior to six months (McClellan, 1939). Beyond this elementary fact—that toilet-training cannot succeed until then—the practice lends itself to infinite variations. It may proceed rapidly or slowly, leniently or rigidly. In our culture, sphincter control is generally established between the second and third years; but in some cultures, where incontinence is severely punished, control may be established between six and nine months. In still others, the toilet is as big as all out of doors, and the child's own plumbing a matter of little concern.

Toileting viewed cross-culturally and historically. In general, variations in toilet-training down the centuries and around the world reflect widely differing emotional attitudes toward this so-called "natural function." Many cultures have indeed treated it as a natural function, while others have shrouded it with an aura of shame and secrecy. In the Balinese culture, writes Mead:

Elimination is treated very lightly. No fuss at all is made over urination by an infant; children urinate playfully into their baths; little boys learn to make elaborate patterns in the dust. Adults simply turn aside from a group to urinate. . . . A child's chief learning from culturally-imposed elimination habits is to watch where it is and to move away from inappropriate spots [Mead and Macgregor, 1951, pp. 47–48].

By contrast, in Western cultures, including America, toilet-training has been treated with prudishness and characterized by strict regulation. And while the following excerpt, written in not-so-distant 1929, may seem a trifle strict today, American mothers are still eons away from their sisters, the Balinese. Some readers of this book may recall reading advice like this:

How may a child be trained to be

regular in the action of the bowels? By endeavoring to have them move at exactly the same time each day. At what age may an infant be trained in this way? Usually by the third or fourth month if training is begun early. What is the best method of training? A small chamber about the size of a pint bowl is placed between the nurse's knees, and upon this the infant is held, his back being against the nurse's chest and his body firmly supported. This should be done twice a day, after the morning and afternoon feedings, and always at the same hour. . . . What advantage has such training? The regular habit formed in infancy makes regularity in childhood much easier. It also saves the nurse much trouble and labor [Holt, 1929, pp. 183-184].

Appraisal of psychoanalytic claims. Psychoanalysts of the Freudian stamp deplore such rigid practice and warn of dire consequences—a sort of anal determinism or fatalism. Anal evacuation, they argue, is sexually gratifying, and bowel training a threat to erogenous satisfaction. If training is especially severe, the child may renounce hedonistic pleasures altogether, and acquire such traits as stinginess, perfectionism, self-punitiveness, and rigidity (Freud, 1924). However, research has failed to confirm these sweeping claims. Toilet-training affects the child's development in much the same way as teaching him to use proper speech or table manners. It involves curbing his impulses and imposing demands at an especially impressionable age:

> For some children, the toilet-training experience may be the first time that strong anxiety is associated with the mother. If the mother has been nurturant during the first year of life, her positive value might be sufficient to neutralize some of the negative feelings produced by socialization demands without a marked change in the perception of the mother. But if the mother has been cold and rejecting, then use of strict toilet training is much more likely to have a deleterious effect on the child, and lead to negative feelings toward her [Sears et al., 1955].

In addition, children—especially girls—often come to associate toileting with shame and concealment. Parents reprimand children for making references to the habit before others, insist that children, while toileting, screen themselves from others' view, and employ euphemisms to avoid correct but embarrassing terms. Besides, parents communicate anxiety about sex to the child, who becomes self-conscious about evacuation simply because of the proximity of the body parts involved in sex and elimination.

In short, the child reacts to the overall interpersonal context and not to specific training techniques as such; seldom can any relationship be found between manner of training and broad personality variables. After reviewing the literature, Hetherington and Brackbill (1963) conclude that "too early, too late, or too severe training" bears no relationship to obstinacy, orderliness, and parsimony. Instead, any relationship between toilet-training and personality derives from maternal behaviors, especially dominance, displayed in this and other socializing situations. Or anxiety may simply stem from excess emphasis on cleanliness, even by an intelligent mother:

> A two year old rather abruptly developed a fear of going to sleep, and began waking in the night. When she awoke she demanded to be taken to the bathroom, which the mother interpreted as a stalling operation, or a technique to get her to come.
> Upon inquiry, the social worker learned the child's symptoms began shortly after she had been toilet trained; and decided the child was fearful of wetting or soiling the bed. After the mother acted on the advice to assure the child that it did not matter if she had an accident during sleep, the child's symptoms disappeared [Kessler, 1966, p. 447].

Infant Feeding

Infant feeding viewed cross-culturally and historically. Still other controversies surround infant feeding, a practice lending itself to infinite cultural variations. Certain American mothers who seem convinced there is only one way to feed their young might well consider how such practices may vary. Among the Bajoeng Gede in Bali, for example, baby-feeding falls into two categories: (1) suckling, in which the infant, after it is a few weeks old, is held high above the mother's breast and nurses down, and (2) giving solid food to the infant, which is done in the bath:

> The mother prechews a mixture of rice and banana and builds a mound on the baby's face. When it opens its mouth to protest, she pushes some food in. When older children are given food, they display related behavior, pushing the food into their mouths with the flat of their hands, or turning their coconut shell plates straight over their faces. Feeding is something done to a baby and later something that one does to oneself [Mead and Macgregor, 1951, pp. 46–47].

Concern about infant feeding is far from new; however, ideas about it were relatively primitive even as late as the nineteenth century. Eating butter was believed to "obstruct the glands" and cause a breaking-out. Pickles and fruit were not recommended. Fish was to be avoided by children because bones might stick in the throat. "Confectionary" was believed to destroy "the tone" of children's minds (Kiefer, 1948).

Mothers around the world and down the ages have fretted over what to feed Junior and how. Some issues, like breast versus bottle feeding, have never been resolved, and wax and wane with the times; others, like wet nursing, have faded away, at least in our culture. The scientific approach to such problems is speedily dispatching many an old-wives' tale—or in many cases, physician's tale—of other days. Octogenarians today can remember when wet nurses were carefully chosen lest they transmit to the infant diseases "known to be hereditary," like cancer, insanity, and defi-

ciency in mental power. Blondes and redheads were to be avoided because their passionate temperaments were said to produce deterioration in the quality of milk (Routh, 1879).

Self-demand versus regulated feeding. One of the most volatile controversies in the history of feeding problems relates to self-demand versus regulated feeding. Certain practical considerations are obvious. **Self-demand feeding** places a heavy strain on the mother, who depends on schedules for getting her work done. Besides, she has difficulty distinguishing hunger cries from other signals of stress, and may feed the child too often. In consequence, the child may lose his ability to choose foods in accordance with his physical needs.

Proponents of self-demand feeding claim that young infants know what they need. In support of their position, they cite Davis' (1939) classic study of newly weaned infants eight to nine months of age. These children were permitted to choose whatever foods they desired from a large array placed before them. Meal by meal, the children's choices failed to meet recommended requirements, but in the long run they balanced out. Sometimes the children went on "jags," concentrating on one food, such as bananas, for days at a time. However, they got the essential foodstuffs, even when the latter were obviously distasteful, as in the case of salt, which some of the infants took straight, despite many grimaces. They paid no attention to what should go with what, and might eat their way backward from dessert to appetizers (Davis, 1939). Obviously, claimed the proponents of self-demand feeding, infants possess a true wisdom of the body. (However, they ignored the fact that Davis' menu included no cake or candy.) Furthermore, they asserted, infants who are thus fed develop healthier personalities—a claim that research has failed to support (Sewell and Mussen, 1952).

The wisdom of permitting infants a

free choice of foods is questionable. For one thing, it is hardly practical for parents to provide widely varied foods at each meal. Besides, we do not know how to determine just when and how much cultural influence corrupts the body's wisdom. The author observed an anemic-looking woman gobble a box of candy and then pick at her next meal—proof that the infant's body wisdom may fail over the years!

Early versus late weaning. A second problem that has worried mothers down through the years is weaning. In the fifteenth century, Heinrich von Louffenburg advised mothers concerning how best to wean their children:

> In case the child be unwilling to give up the mother's breast promptly, one must pound some myrrh and mix it with crisp mint. From this mixture a poultice should be made and placed on the mother's breasts. The bitter taste of the poultice will make the child lose its desire for the breasts [Rührah, 1925, p. 486].

Perennial argument has focused upon whether the child should be weaned early or late. The early-weaned child, says psychoanalytic theory, has a tendency to hoard food, and becomes the overcompetitive, arrogant adult, while the later-weaned infant acquires a generous, optimistic disposition (Fenichel, 1945). However, Sears and his associates (1957) failed to find that early weaning produced emotional disturbance or nervous habits such as thumb-sucking. Furthermore, on a priori grounds, no compelling reasons exist for believing the infant has any innate need for obtaining nourishment from any specific external source.

True, forcible separation from an accustomed feeding pattern, along with whatever contact and affection the mother's personal supervision provide, will surely produce immediate frustrations. And if the weaning process is timed to coincide with generally stricter parental regulation in other areas, as

often happens, the disturbance will be proportionately greater. Lasting effects on personality are another matter. Any permanent effects of weaning on personality probably relate not to the technique used but to maternal attitudes underlying the practice and to the child's capacity to perceive them.

Breast-feeding versus bottle-feeding. Furor over the foregoing topic is mild compared to that over bottle- versus breast-feeding. Infants have sucked their way through centuries of controversy. Back in 1545, Thomas Phaer, in *The Boke of Children,* strongly recommended that the mother nurse her own child, but suggested that the practice could have ill effects:

> Wherefore as it is agreing to nature so is it also necessary and comly for the own mother to nourse her own chylde. Whiche if it maye be done, it shal be most comendable and holesome, if not ye must be well advised in taking of a nource, not of yll complexion and of worse maners; but such as shal be sobre, honeste and chaste, well fourmed, amyable and cheareful, so that she may accustome the infant unto myrth, no dronkard, vycyous nor sluttyshe, for suche corruptethe the nature of the chylde [Rührah, 1925, p. 158].

A century later came this advice concerning proper procedures for infants' nursing:

> From the twin Fountains let the Nectar flow,
> Greedy he'll suck, and to your Bosom grow.
> First with weak Lips the swelling Breast he'll pull;
> Help him, and squeeze it 'till his Belly's full.
> But let him not be glutted with the Feast,
> A medium in the flowing Meal is best.
> Sometimes deny the Nipple, sometimes grant;
> But too much wat'ring drowns the sprouting Plant [Rührah, 1925, p. 509].

Typically, breast-feeding has been

portrayed as natural, and bottle-feeding as somehow inhuman or downright immoral. In 1817, an angry physician named Davis stated the case in uncompromising tones. The mother's breast, he asserted conclusively, is an infant's birthright, and suckling a sacred duty which, if neglected, is fatal to the child.

Questioning the merits of breast-feeding. More recently, Newton (1955) recommended breast-feeding as a highly commendable shared relationship, which usually provides pleasurable sensations for both mother and baby. Of course, continued Newton, not every feeding is automatically pleasant. If the "let-down" reflex is working well, as will be the case when the mother is favorably disposed toward the experience, she will receive a pleasant, sensuous sensation. The let-down reflex affects not only breast but also uterus, which continues to contract rhythmically for as long as 20 minutes after feeding. The same sort of uterine contractions occur, according to Moir (1934), during sexual excitement.

But breast-feeding has its drawbacks—one being its obvious threat to modesty, sometimes a matter of concern. One early twentieth-century invention contained a tube that led from the mother's fully draped breast to the mouth of the child. Other reasons for using the bottle rest on more practical grounds: the mother holds a job; or lacks a sufficient supply of milk, or, for whatever reason, finds the practice inconvenient or distasteful. In such cases, breast-feeding would hold little satisfaction for mother or child.

While research fails to show any psychological superiority of formula feeding, neither does it support the contention that it proves damaging. Note, for example, the arguments that mother's milk is best because it is richer in vitamins, cannot become bacterially contaminated, is less allergenic for human infants, and contains antibodies that

protect against disease. Such arguments have become increasingly irrelevant as methods of milk handling and vitamin enrichment have improved. Besides, canned breast milk and synthetic substitutes are available for infants who may have special needs. In fact, bottle-fed babies tend to survive as well as breast-fed ones, to weigh as much or more, and to be less often underfed (Douglas, 1950).

Nor does breast-feeding prove superior where personality factors are concerned. After analyzing all available research on the topic, Heinstein (1963) concluded that neither practice seemed significantly related to specific personality factors. The few differences that have appeared are the reverse of what psychoanalytic theory would predict; for example, boys and girls at age 18 who had been bottle-fed were less aggressive than those who had been breast-fed. Recall, too, the study that showed that monkey infants preferred the soft terry-cloth mothers to the milk-giving ones. If the significant factor is having some object to cling to, perhaps fathers can prove as adequate for dispensing the bottle as mothers, except for the restrictions that their jobs impose (Heinstein, 1963). In fact, a warm, accepting father may be a very effective "mother," and perhaps his lack of mammary glands is no real disqualification for child-rearing, as commonly believed. So much for the sacred cow of breast-feeding.

Sex of infant as a factor in breast-feeding. What does seem crucial is the interpersonal context in which feeding occurs. The worst maladjustments are suffered by boys nursed for long periods by cold mothers. A distant mother, who nevertheless fosters dependency, produces a conflict situation. For girls as well as boys, if the mother is warm, breast feeding is better; if she is distant, formula feeding is to be preferred. Therefore, the choice of the nursing regime must have reference to the sex of the

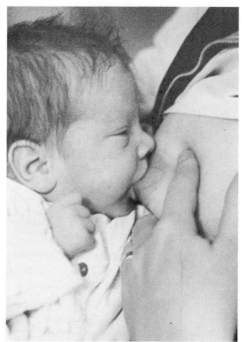

The crucial factor in feeding is the mother's attitude.

child, the mother's personality, and the general atmosphere of the home during the nursing period (Heinstein, 1963).

Differential sex reactions to feeding are hardly surprising when one notes this startling fact: that mothers accord boy infants a degree of autonomy in the feeding situation commonly denied girls. They follow their rhythms of starting and stopping; and they build into them the feeling that they have mastery over the situation—an important foundation for later freedom of activity. Girl babies, by contrast, are more hovered over and fiddled with. Mothers are more apt to take the mother-knows-best attitude, subtly imposing on the girl baby a pattern of conformity. Nevertheless, not all girl babies acquiesce to efforts to make them conform. Sally's mother, reported Murphy and her associates (1962), tried to treat her in a feminine way, but she demanded and won independence.

A perspective on breast- versus bottle-feeding. To sum up, let us acknowledge that definite conclusions hardly exist. It is difficult to show con-

sistent relations between nursing habits and either child or adult personality. Fragments of evidence supporting one practice or the other are not convincing, because of failure to control all pertinent factors, such as the amount of physical intimacy accorded non-breast-fed subjects (Caldwell, 1964). Other variables have not been adequately considered, such as the mother's own feelings about the matter. Typically, it is the warm, motherly woman who wants to breast-feed the child and is able to do so. Hence, the significant variable may be the sort of person who chooses to breast-feed the child rather than the practice itself (Finney, 1961; Klatskin et al., 1950).

While direct relations between the feeding technique employed and personality variables are doubtful, feeding difficulties may indeed complicate the infant's adjustment. Parents may precipitate problems of infant gastronomy in many ways: by failing to acknowledge individual differences in children's tastes and needs; by harboring narrow notions about diet and table manners; and by utilizing the feeding situation as a battleground for proving their superior strength. In such cases, the feeding situation may contribute toward poor parent-child relationships. Also, where children come to associate eating with unpleasantness, they may become picky eaters and develop nutritional deficiencies (Ausubel, 1958).

Cross-Cultural Variations in Infant Care

Throughout the foregoing discussion we have seen that mothers differ greatly in their approaches to infant care; but they also tend to reflect the broad general patterns of their social classes and cultures. Viewed cross-culturally, variations in infant care are wider still. In fact, one of the best ways to gain perspective on child-rearing methods is to survey practices in cultures radically different from ours. For example, in Uganda babies are reared with great solicitude. They are constantly stimulated with cuddling, tickling, and soft words. Even during her pregnancy, the mother's interest is the child. In consequence, infants show unusual precocity, an attribute much less apparent among higher-class families that have become somewhat westernized (Geber, 1958).

One might naturally ask: Why not import such an obviously successful method of child care? Simply because child training must fit the culture concerned. Note the differences in the manner of dressing infants. In certain primitive cultures—for example, in Panama and the Fiji Islands, infant boys often wander around freely, wearing nothing below the waist. In our own culture, infants are clothed very loosely. By contrast, infants in various Eastern cultures are swaddled, or wrapped tightly as in a cocoon. Swaddling may be practiced to ward off violent impulses of the child, or to prevent his touching his genitals, or to provide maximum protection. In different countries, the same practice may represent quite different attitudes toward the child, each of which will become communicated to the child in infinite, subtle ways (Benedict, 1949).

Overall Effects of Infant-Care Practices

What are the effects of infant-care practices? It is hardly surprising that psychoanalysts of the Freudian stamp differ from others in assessing the long-term effects of infant-training practices. As already noted, certain traits in adults, like stinginess, are attributed by certain analysts to early training. However, Sewell and Mussen (1952) found no support for those who maintain that breast-feeding, demand schedules, and gradual weaning promise better adjustment than bottle-feeding, regular scheduling, and abrupt weaning.

Similarly, a study of 25 middle-class mothers revealed no significant relations between infant-rearing practices and infant adjustment. However, Behrens (1954) did find a significant correlation between child adjustment and the "total mother person"—a score based on ratings of the mother's underlying attitudes and character structure, her handling of the maternal role, and her conduct toward the child. Thus, the quality of the child's socialization relates more to what the mother is like than to what she does.

Caldwell (1964) notes certain basic weaknesses in prevailing interpretations. First, data are viewed from adult frames of reference. From the adult's point of view, the infant snuggled against his mother for repeated breast feedings ought to feel more secure than the one abandoned to his own sucking struggles with an indifferent bottle. The baby picked up whenever he cries should gain feelings of power over his environment. Thus, prevailing interpretations of the meanings of such experience gain ready acceptance merely because they fit the adult's frame of reference (Hoffman and Hoffman, 1964).

Caldwell notes further that little attention has been paid differences in infant reaction to child care. A training technique, when imposed on a docile child, works, and is thus pronounced a good one. The same plan tried on a resisting child may be abandoned as bad after the third bowel movement has been deposited in the middle of the living-room or the neighborhood supermarket. In conclusion, writes Caldwell, ideal studies of child-training effects must involve both attitude and practice, as well as the multiple experiences through which a specific practice is filtered before becoming a significant influence on the child's life.

• STUDYING THE INFANT

Unfortunately, laymen—and some professionals—fail to realize present weaknesses in infant research. Popular columnists blandly prescribe for whatever ails Junior, without acknowledging gaps in present knowledge. Even pediatricians, prodded by anxious mothers who demand answers, may find themselves coerced into voicing opinions that have yet to be sustained by research. The mothers, in turn, believe that the pediatrician who can prescribe for mumps and measles will surely know what to do about "crying it out" and thumb-sucking (Ausubel, 1958).

Thus, pronouncements about infant care often reflect the brilliance of a five-watt bulb. Definitive statements about many aspects of the topic are premature. For example, no known studies have permitted the intensity of

How does the father's role—and his attitude toward that role—affect the infant? More research is needed.

maternal contact to vary while controlling for other factors such as maternal personality and type of paternal contact. Besides, research conclusions are based on loosely defined concepts and faulty data. Researchers often speak of children as "toilet trained," but exactly when is it achieved? They fail to specify. Does it mean the time after which absolutely no accidents occur, or when relatively few occur?

Infant research, especially, is subject to retrospective error. The subject cannot recall his own infant experience;

hence, reports must be obtained from highly biased parents. Through the distorting lenses of his love, the parent often perceives the barely average child as an infant Edison or latter-day Socrates. Direct observation obviates this problem, but is hardly feasible except for brief periods. Even then, the adult observer interprets infant motivations from his own adult frame of reference. Again, how long must one await the effects of infant experience? An effect may not show up immediately, but appear later on. It is hard to show a causal relation between events far removed in point of time.

After a realistic appraisal of such difficulties, it is hardly surprising that many topics remain controversial. For the time being, however, the psychology of infancy profits from being in a state of theoretical disequilibrium; and the diversity of ideas about all these questions will undoubtedly yield important empirical advances (Yarrow, 1963).

• SUMMARY

Research supports the long-held belief that family influences are critical in shaping the child's development. The family continuously reinforces selected behaviors during the child's most impressionable years. It also constitutes a miniature society in which the child practices his roles and obtains his primary experiences in socialization. Over the years the family has shifted from authoritarian to democratic in structure. Mothers have been freed of much of their former drudgery, so that they have more time for their children and consequently represent a greater psychological impact. In short, although the family is changing, its influence may be as important as ever.

Of course, the family is no homogeneous entity affecting all its members at all times and places alike. Family influences vary with time and culture. Families of both working and middle classes urge their children, especially their sons, to achieve. Middle-class parents are more concerned with their children's ideals, lower-class parents more with specific behaviors. Cross-culturally, child-rearing practices reflect the values of the societies concerned; and in complex Western societies they are as varied as the subcultures involved. A common characteristic of such societies is the **nuclear family**, composed only of the parents and minor children or perhaps of the parents alone.

Certain of the more important intangibles of family life are way of life, values, and climate. Every family has its characteristic mode of living—indoor or outdoor, introverted or extroverted—and its distinctive value orientations. Every family has its particular climates, derived from material and psychological factors. Contributing to physical climate are such factors as space, noisiness, and attractiveness of dwelling. Emotional climate stems from all family interactions. The effect of family climate depends to some extent on the sort of child involved and the way he himself experiences the family climate.

The newcomer to the family is especially vulnerable to its influence. Yet he is also his own man, in the sense that such influences become modified as they filter through his own embryonic personality. At one time the infant was viewed as a helpless vegetable simply soaking up the physical and psychological nutrients bestowed upon him. Lately, the infant is being viewed as interacting with his environment, both affecting and affected by those around him.

The infant-mother relationship begins before the child is even conceived, in that the mother dreams of what her child should become. During pregnancy her concern becomes intensified, especially if she has otherwise been emotionally upset. If she is happy about having the baby, it is more likely that her hormonal function will be satisfactory and not react unfavorably on the unborn child. After the child is born, mothers vary greatly in their attitudes and actions toward their children. Meantime, the baby's and mother's traits interact. Although some writers question the child's capacity to interpret his mother's attitudes, others merely say that the impact of the mother's behaviors depends on how the infant perceives them. The author suggests that original interpretations are relatively undifferentiated though important reactions of unpleasantness or pleasantness, which become increasingly differentiated.

Just how important the infant-mother relationship is and what in fact it should be are the subjects of some controversy. It is universally acknowledged to be important. But how? Might machines be rigged to give whatever the mother dispenses, including periodic pats on the back, diaper changes, and other varied sensory experiences? Might we even have glossed over the possible ill effects of excessive mothering?

One way to gauge the significance of mothering is to study the effects of maternal deprivation. Various studies have cited the sad condition of many institutionalized youngsters. Much would seem to depend on the characteristics of the mother and child involved. Children might be better off without certain types of mothers. Children might also be affected more at certain ages than others. Perhaps much of the reported damage stems not so much from maternal deprivation as from the lack of certain things that the mother normally provides, especially sensory stimulation. Research suggests that if care is taken to make up for what mothers normally provide, children will not suffer especially. At the other extreme it is also questionable whether a child suffers from having too many mothers.

The effect of paternal deprivation is likewise in dispute. Perhaps problems presumably chargeable to the father's absence may relate not so much to father absence, per se, as to factors that sometimes accompany it, such as maternal loneliness. Apparently the effect of paternal absence on girls and boys is

303

somewhat different, but inadequate research exists to determine exactly how.

Basic-habit training—for example, toilet-training and feeding—have also proved significant for later personality. Controversy has focused on certain pertinent questions. For example, how early should the child be toilet-trained, and what method should be used? Should the child be bottle-fed or breast-fed, and how early should a breast-fed child be weaned? Longitudinal studies have failed to show any straight-line relationships between specific child-training methods and later personality. Instead, the mother's total personality and attitudes subtly modify the emotional climate in which training occurs. Socialization practices are filtered through complex attitudes and interactions.

In sum, much research relating to the infant's development has been done, but much remains to be done. Progress is already being made; and a growing body of empirically derived data is available. The researcher's approach has become less dogmatic and sentimental, more cautious and scientific. Certain new emphases are also apparent. Formerly, the effects of a single factor, artificially isolated, were studied. Now the trend is toward analyzing large matrices of relationships, an approach made possible by computers. Caldwell (1964) observes that the computer era will make "a vigorous eclecticism possible for the first time." Hopefully, infant care may become more of a science and less a matter of psychological brinkmanship.

• SUGGESTED QUESTIONS AND ACTIVITIES

1. Criticize the American family as an institution. For example, is it too close or too loosely knit? Is it too mother-centered? In what ways does it fail to meet the needs of society currently?
2. Call on a mother who has a small infant and report, anecdotally, what you observed relative to the following: the degree of apparent "compatibility" of mother and infant; the mother's apparent feelings toward the infant; the reactions of siblings toward the infant; and any other items of interest.
3. Has the importance of mothering during the infancy period been overrated, and overemphasized?
4. Is the quantity of mothering of any real significance so long as the quality is good? Does the 24-hours-a-day regimen detract from the quality of mothering? How early do you believe it is all right for a mother to return to her job after a child's birth? In such a case, what is the best arrangement for the child?
5. In what ways would the placement of infants in public nurseries supervised by highly trained personnel about seven hours each day be of advantage or disadvantage both to mothers and infants? Take into consideration that the average work day for parents of the future may be considerably less than now.
6. Can the father perform the infant caretaking function as well as the mother? To what extent should he involve himself in infant care? Ideally, what should his role be?
7. Are girls overtrained, and boys undertrained, for their respective future roles as parents?
8. Clip from newspapers and popular magazines columns of advice to mothers about the care of infants. Bring to class and criticize in terms of the research reported in this book.
9. Are the possible merits of breast-feeding sufficient to offset the handicaps thus imposed on the mother?
10. Evaluate the merits of demand versus scheduled feeding; of relatively late versus relatively early toilet-training.
11. Look up the way infants are treated in some other culture. Compare with this culture in terms of advantages and disadvantages for later adjustment.

• SUGGESTED READINGS

Bijou, S. W., and D. M. Baer, *Child Development, Vol. II: Universal Stage of Infancy.* New York: Appleton-Century-Crofts, Inc., 1965. Examines human behavior from about the twenty-eighth week of gestation until the end of the second year, utilizing principles of learning and reinforcement.

Brackbill, Y., and G. G. Thompson, eds., *Behavior in Infancy and Early Childhood.* New York: The Free Press, 1967. A book of readings embracing various areas of infant and early childhood development.

Caldwell, B. M., "The Effects of Infant Care," in M. L. Hoffman and L. W. Hoffman, eds., *Review of Child Development Research,* Vol. I. New York: Russell Sage Foundation, 1964, pp. 9–87. Excellent summary and interpretation of available research on infant care.

Foss, B. M., ed., *Determinants of Infant Behavior.* New York: John Wiley & Sons, Inc., 1962. Four papers dealing respectively with neonate behavior, animal experiments, social behavior, and theory.

Heinstein, M., "Behavioral Correlates of Breast-Bottle Regimes under Varying Parent-Infant Relationships," *Monographs of the Society for Research in Child Development,* Vol. 28, No. 88 (1963), pp. 1–61. Report of a study designed to ascertain over a long age span (21 months to 18 years) the behavioral correlates of breast and bottle nursing under varying personal-social environments.

Landreth, C., *Early Childhood,* 2nd ed. New York: Alfred A. Knopf, Inc., 1967. A comprehensive and excellent review of the child's early years.

Ribble, M., *The Rights of Infants,* 2nd ed. New York: Columbia University Press, 1965. This second edition updates a volume first published 20 years ago. Concerns physical vulnerability and early problems of infants as well as roles of parents.

Stevenson, H. W., E. H. Hess, and H. L. Rheingold, eds., *Early Behavior.* New York: John Wiley & Sons, Inc., 1967. Comparative and developmental psychologists and ethologists, working with different organisms but on related problems, present current research on the behavior of young organisms of different species.

11

THE CHILD IN THE FAMILY

• FAMILY PATTERNS
AND RELATIONS

Murphy and Murphy (1960) call the family a growing organism, because it changes in size and complexity while its members function both individually and as part of the family unit. In consequence, family members, and the family as a unit, should be studied as the family grows. While the same general pattern of relationships tends to persist, subtle changes may occur. For example, on arrival at puberty a boy may attain relatively greater privileges than an older sister, thereby creating tension.

unperceptive observer assumes that the mother's and child's problems are related simply because they exist concurrently in time. Understanding, says Loevinger, will come only through a more subtle and differentiated approach.

Similarly, Hurlock (1966) describes the family as a complex interactional system, which becomes more complex with the arrival of each new baby. At first there are three family members — mother, father, and child. This means five interactions. With the arrival of a new sibling, there will be 11. If another comes, there will be 26. If the grand-

The family inhabits a world of its own making.

Loevinger (1962), too, emphasizes the dynamic nature of family relationships. She warns against expecting simple correlations between such factors as "problem mothers" and "problem children." For example, a mother may consciously avoid imposing her problems on the child who is suffering from rejection by his father. Yet the

mother comes to live with the family, the number jumps to 57. Furthermore, each family group is composed of individuals of different ages and different sexes. The masculine sex may predominate; the two sexes may be equally represented; or the family may be predominantly feminine. These variations influence the behavior of each member.

In many families, relatives, roomers, or servants become a part of the enlarged family group. Even a boarder in the house can wield a considerable influence. An individual's impact is not determined by closeness of kinship, but by the needs of the child and the satisfactions he derives from each relationship. A family may have an elongated pattern—perhaps with members of four generations represented from both sides. However, all evidence points to the fact that the nuclear family—that is, parents and children only—plays a more important role than the elongated family in the child's development.

Ackerman (1958) describes the family in terms of homeostatic relations; that is, the mother and child achieve an equilibrium, which is constantly modified by interactions between the mother and father. The husband and wife also establish an equilibrium, which may be upset by economic factors, changes in the community, or many other influences. Meantime, the child must defend his internal equilibrium, especially in times of physical stress, like accident or illness. The very fact that the welfare of all family members is a single objective serves to integrate goals and harmonize activities.

• FAMILY ROLES

Family roles—the functions each parent and child plays in the family group—derive partly from custom and partly from factors within the specific situation. By custom, the oldest girl is expected to take care of younger children; but a specific older girl may be sickly and hence freed of such duties.

Roles are complementary and reciprocal, each individual's function depending on and affecting all the others. For instance, an older girl assigned the role of assistant mother can hardly carry out her role unless younger children accept her as such. Or an especially independent youngest child may simply refuse to become the family pet.

Roles also vary in impact. In a very small family, a child may play an important part simply because his parents direct toward him a relatively large degree of attention and project on him more of their goals than they would in a larger family, where their impact would be more diluted.

For the sake of simplification, family roles are often designated by such names as assistant parent, pet, spoiled brat, and the like; but roles cannot be so simply categorized. They consist of so complex a fusing of functions that any specific designation is likely to omit salient features and to fail to capture the true and often subtle essence of the role.

• THE CHILD'S ROLE IN THE FAMILY

In general, the child's family role is modified by his sex, age, ordinal position, and individual traits, as well as by external factors, such as the family's social class. Boys often play a less vital role in the family than girls, simply because they remain outside more. In one study, only one boy in 10, even in adolescence, participated in family economic activities such as paying bills or financial planning (Johannis, 1958).

The child's age is another factor. The older child is more likely to become the assistant parent than a younger one. However, children's roles may change in subtle ways as they grow older. In time, a strong younger brother may throw off the role of scapegoat earlier assigned by a less vigorous older brother.

Individual traits modify role assignments, too. An especially dependable child, perhaps an older boy, becomes the pillar of the family, a role unlikely for a more shiftless boy. An especially submissive, conscientious child may become the family scapegoat, or servant, constantly called upon to do the more arduous family chores.

Other factors external to the child also affect his role—for instance, the family situation. After his divorced father leaves home, the boy may become a father substitute. Or an older child may die and his role fall to a younger one. The father may have viewed his eldest son as the heir who would achieve what he himself had tried but failed to do. After the oldest son dies, the father automatically assigns this goal to the second son, imposing stringent standards to which the younger boy has not been accustomed. If the father himself dies, the oldest son's role may be altered drastically:

> Tom's father died when he was only 12, but he immediately became the man of the family. Instead of doing the things a boy his age normally does, he went to work after school, not because his family badly needed the money, but because this was the role a man should play. He was no longer a carefree school boy, but a serious "little man."

Not surprisingly, social class is another modifier of family roles. In lower-class homes, the son is expected to respect and please his parents, and later on, to contribute to the family's support. The girl helps with the household, and assumes a role subservient to her brothers. In middle-class families, the daughter has fewer responsibilities, and the son is largely dependent financially on the family. Any money the boy earns is his, for spending as he likes.

Numerous other factors and blends of factors serve further to modify children's family roles—for example, the times. Implicit in the following item of juvenile etiquette is children's lowly family status in the nineteenth century:

> As soon as thou shalt be moderately satisfied; or whensoever thy Parents think meet to bid thee, rise up from the table, tho' others thy Superiors sit still. . . . When thou risest from the Table, take away thy Plate; and having made a Bow at the side of the Table where thou sattest, withdraw, removing also thy seat (if removable.) When thanks are to be returned after eating, return to thy Place, and stand reverently

till it be done; then with a Bow withdraw out of the Room, leaving thy Superiors to themselves (unless thou art bidden to stay) [Moodey, 1948, p. 75].

Whatever the age, a child fulfills a specific role within the family, which is the derivative of countless factors, including his own personality, his ordinal position, and the family situation. Here a girl describes her childhood family role:

> We were a close family, and all of us—parents, older sister, younger brother and I—did everything together. Whenever I returned from a trip or visited relatives I brought them something. When I was 14, another baby was born, and my self-concept changed very much. Already I had felt like an important member of the family, but with the added responsibility, I felt much more so. Also I was the "funny" girl in the family, and was relied on to reflect my happiness on the rest.

Problems Related to the Child's Family Role

Role-playing within the family brings many problems, some already implied. Family members may disagree concerning the assignment of roles. The mother may assign a daughter the job of assistant housekeeper, a function middle-class girls may resent. The boy without sisters may be delegated the chore of babysitting, which he resents as sissified.

A child's adaptation to his role can vary from enthusiasm to resentment, depending on numerous factors. Much, of course, depends on the parents' attitudes. If parents attach importance to the child's role, it will have more importance in his own eyes. If his siblings relegate him to the role of scapegoat or "baby," he may dislike his role exceedingly (Henry, 1961). The critical factor in determining the impact a child sustains from his role is whether it obstructs or enhances his development as a person. A child may be assigned so time-consuming a function that he has little opportunity to become an individual and develop his own special talents. Or the role may simply be imcompatible with what he is like and hence fail to reinforce his best traits. Often a father assigns an aesthetically oriented son heavy out-of-door work, which the boy dislikes. Many parents unconsciously designate the child's role according to their own needs or their own ideal of what a child should be rather than according to the child's own special traits. Sometimes parent and child are mismatched, as though the genes were juggled. In such cases it is hard to work out successful family roles.

Family Size

The child in the small family. A factor of special significance for the child is family size. The small-family child feels the impact of family crises more acutely and is more likely to be overprotected and to gain an exaggerated sense of his own importance. Also, the parents may focus too much attention on the children, which obstructs full development as individuals.

In the main, however, the small-family child is fortunate. The family atmosphere is usually democratic, with the children participating in decision-making. With so much invested in each child, parents encourage them to attain success, and provide the wherewithal for its accomplishment. Emphasis is on achieving "the full life," through participation in many social and cultural activities, and through achieving vocational and social mobility (Douvan and Adelson, 1966). Indeed, a major reason for the limitation of family size is to permit a higher standard of living and greater opportunities for the children (Rosen, 1956).

In consequence, small-family children are consistently superior in physical, emotional, and social adjustment to children from large families. They also have consistently stronger ego-development. They identify with their parents and absorb parental perspective, but not unthinkingly. Family discipline, usually administered by the mother, is psy-

chologically rather than punitively oriented (Douvan and Adelson, 1966).

To summarize, the relationships between family size and adjustment are generally straight-line, in the sense that strength of ego traits correlates inversely with the number of children (Douvan and Adelson, 1966).

However, the impact of family size is modified by other factors. For example, lower-class girls and middle-class boys seem most affected by family size, and younger children more than older. The lower-class girl, for instance, would have an unusual number of duties in the large family, and the middle-class boy much less than the usual freedom accorded him. "Small fry," especially, would suffer from neglect by mothers with several below-school-age youngsters to tend (Elder and Bowerman, 1963).

The child in the large family. The child with few siblings is apparently more fortunate than the one with a greater-than-average number. The cases below suggest the problems that may arise in the large family; while the problems related in the second illustration did not necessarily stem from size of family, they were undoubtedly accentuated by it:

I was one of nine children, and was often excited about the prospect of doing something with my father that he'd promised to do. But somehow he never quite found the time and I always ended up disappointed. He'd have to work at some second job, or do chores around the house.

I was next to the youngest in a family of nine children. I hated my father for the way he drank and licked us for no reason at all. We were poor, and he drank up the money while Mom worked to feed us. Later on, time mellowed him, and he wanted us to love him, but we couldn't.

Such cases are not unusual in the very large family. Nevertheless, many well-adjusted and even eminent persons

The child of a large family encounters more handicaps than benefits.

have come from large families, and research reveals a few actual advantages of having a greater-than-average number of siblings. Children in large families learn to cooperate and to carry out responsibilities from sheer necessity. They also develop a certain flexibility, through adjustment to crisis and repeated readjustment to changes in responsibility and status. As each new addition arrives, the child must establish his own beachhead in the home. Left to work out things for himself, he develops a certain maturity and resourcefulness. At the same time, he always has brothers or sisters to turn to when parents are busy or unavailable. Moreover, he is unlikely to become overly dependent or jealous, because there is little chance for parental cuddling.

However, the child of the large family encounters more handicaps than benefits. For one thing, he has little choice over his role, which is usually determined by order of birth. The first-born girl is mother's little helper, the first-born boy the father's assistant in masculine tasks of the household. If something happens to the parent, the oldest boy or girl assumes the vacated role, even to the extent of foregoing higher education to support the family. The baby becomes the spoiled one, waited on by the others and contributing little to the family's welfare (Bossard and Boll, 1960).

Furthermore, the large family is often not planned, and children may arrive at especially unfavorable times— for instance, during the family's economic or emotional crises. Large families are more susceptible to such strains anyhow (Bossard and Sanger, 1952). And while family members learn to adjust to recurring crises and to family additions, the attitude easily becomes one of hopeless resignation.

Parents of large families are often more authoritarian, employing fewer psychological control techniques than parents of average-sized families (Bell, 1965). They tend to be more traditional

and more punitive in their exercise of authority, and the children are less likely to have a say in making rules. Authority is usually wielded by the parents, but often by an older brother or sister. Indeed, such control may be necessary to insure the best utilization of limited family resources—money, housing space, and time. In fact, the authoritarianism of colonial days may have been due, at least partially, to the larger families that then prevailed. However, whether necessary or not, domination discourages the growth of individual initiative and achievement and damages the emotional climate.

Whatever the cause—whether family size per se or factors associated with large families, such as poverty or poor housing—large families contribute heavily to Selective Service mental rejectees. According to the President's Task Force on Manpower Conservation (1964), although only a third of the nation's children come from families with four or more children, about 70% of rejectees (those performing at fifth-grade level or less) come from such families. More striking is the fact that 47% of the rejectees represent the relatively rare individuals (11% of all cases) with six or more siblings. Not surprisingly, these men fare poorly by income, occupational, and educational standards; and four-fifths are school dropouts.

Of course, the effect of family size will vary according to the sex of the child, ordinal position, and family income. Boys adjust better than girls, and in-betweens better than the oldest or youngest child. The oldest child, especially the girl, is the most poorly adjusted. Such testimony as this is typical:

"From the time that I was five," writes the oldest of eight, "I can remember taking care of the children. I used to lie on my mother's bed and push my little brother back and forth in his carriage until he fell asleep. Mother kept on having babies. Many problems beset us. By the time I was in the third grade, I was helping mother while the others played with the neighboring children. This made me old beyond my years, serious, and quite responsible for all that went on in the household. . . . At night, I bathed six children, washed their heads, and tucked them into bed. Saturday nights continued like this until I rebelled. I wanted to have time for dates like other girls had" [Bossard and Boll, 1956, pp. 159–160].

Individual adjustment hinges on the specific family situation. The parents may either enjoy or dislike large families; the family income may be sufficient, just adequate, or completely inadequate. The home may be spacious and on a large farm with plenty of land, or small, permitting no privacy at all. Therefore, the effect of family size on a particular child must be judged in terms of his own circumstances.

The only child. Traditionally, the only child has been believed to play an unfortunate family role. A 1927 book on child guidance suggested that the only child was handicapped and incapable of the adjustment that sibling relationships provide (Blanton and Blanton, 1927). More recent doomsayers—namely, Maslow and Mittelmann (1951)—claim that he is domineering, egotistical, weak in character structure, and insistent on being the center of attention. These "sad sacks," as some traditionalists call only children, fall into two categories: the spoiled, egocentric, antisocial children commonly called brats; and the sensitive, nervous children overly dependent on parents, often branded "mice" (McGuire and White, 1957).

Such dire views of onlies belong to old wives' tales, as research amply shows. The only child is not so much a lonely child as a juvenile VIP. There is no evidence that only children are more emotionally unstable or have more scholastic problems than other children (Montague, 1948). Nor are they problem children; on the contrary, they manifest fewer delinquent tendencies than do children from large families (Nye, 1958).

Both outside and inside the home, they make better adjustments than children in homes plagued by sibling rivalries and jealousies (Bossard and Boll, 1960).

In several ways, onlies have distinct advantages. They are less likely to suffer economic hardship, an especially important factor in a materialistic society. And since they use adults as their models, they are maturer for their age than children with siblings. Their greater maturity, in turn, facilitates social adjustment and leadership. And perhaps because of their more intensive relationships with adults, onlies are more advanced in language and more likely to achieve intellectual and scientific eminence (West, 1960).

Onliness also affects self-esteem, with 54% of only boys possessing high self-regard as compared with 44% of boys with siblings. They live in a strong sun and flourish. However, the difference among girls is very slight, with 47% of only girls holding high self-esteem compared with 44% of girls with siblings (Rosenberg, 1965). At least one researcher, however (Campbell, 1933), reported generally greater effects of onliness on girls. The mean scores of girls were higher on neuroticism and introversion scales and lower on scales of dominance and self-sufficiency. This finding Campbell attributed to boys' greater freedom, which permits them to associate more freely with children outside the home.

The oldest child. The significance of being the oldest child is widely recognized. One often hears parents say, "I learned on my first child," implying that they had made mistakes, corrected with later-borns. To some extent they may be right, because the oldest does, indeed, reflect parental uncertainties and anxieties. But he holds advantages, too, thus becoming a child with conflicting tendencies. He is overprotected, yet given unusual responsibilities; he is humored, yet prodded to achieve. His parents overprotect him because they are uncertain about how to care for him, or what impacts he can sustain; yet they make him an assistant parent when younger children arrive. At the same time, they are eager to validate their worth as parents, and constantly prod him to achieve. Perhaps for this reason, besides the fact that he is constantly looked up to by younger siblings, he is more likely to achieve eminence.

Since parents are initially more intense in their "parenting," the oldest child identifies more closely with them and their values than the younger ones do. He is closer to their age besides. Partly because of this identification, he often incorporates an overly strong superego, which makes him more sensitive, withdrawn, and less popular with peers (Douvan and Adelson, 1966). Perhaps, too, serving as an example for the younger children compels him to examine his own values more closely.

For a time at least, his parents are more available to him, and he receives greater warmth; but later he must share that love with younger children. Some older children effect the adjustment to later-borns easily; others develop hostilities that persist through life.

Data relative to the oldest child's personality traits are somewhat conflicting. After reviewing the literature, Mussen and Conger (1956) reported the oldest child to be relatively less self-confident, more sensitive, introverted, passive, worrisome, and anxious to escape blame, besides possessing more nervous symptoms. In a later study, however, interviewers rated first-borns high on poise, self-confidence, and attractiveness, which may reflect their ease with adults (Douvan and Adelson, 1966).

As always in human relations, there are mitigating factors—for example, social class. The first-born girl in the large, low-status family tends to be emotionally disturbed and to reject her feminine role, while the first-born from the large but high-status family shows no signs of difficulty (Douvan and Adelson,

1966). Perhaps lower-class parents are more prone to lean on the oldest girl, while higher-class families, either because of more funds or more enlightened views on child-rearing, usually avoid such imposition.

Second and middle children. Apparently, the second-born child is better adjusted than the oldest (Altus, 1959). He is spared much of the parental anxiety experienced by the first; since the mother feels more confident and less tense, a more relaxed mother-child relationship exists. In consequence, the second-born is less neurotic and introverted, more fun-loving and humorous than his older brother. However, if he uses the first child as a pacemaker, and cannot keep up, he may feel inadequate.

Literature concerning the middle child, in a family of three, is somewhat inconsistent (Elkins, 1958). Apparently, he is somewhat neglected and lacking in aggressiveness. He is also generally gregarious and craves affection. However, more middle children prove very unpopular than those in any other ordinal position.

The youngest child. The youngest child occupies a relatively secure position (Mussen and Conger, 1956). He is pampered by his parents and older siblings, and often he has more than one older sibling as a pacesetter, providing a variety of models. As a result, he may form closer and more significant relations with siblings than with parents. Because of their security-reinforcing influences, he is more striving, self-confident, and persevering than other children.

Koch's study of ordinal position. Koch (1956a) made an important study of the relative effects of ordinal position and spacing of siblings. Both affect the child's range of interests; especially, the wider the spacing, or age difference, the greater the number of interests held. Also, the second-born holds more interests than the first-born, and is generally influenced by the older one's own preoccupations

315

and companions. However, even when the age gap is minimal, first-borns are better planners than second-borns. Perhaps the first-born's greater responsibility may be attributed to the necessity for maintaining his superior position.

Ordinal position also affects language development, Koch found. First-born children consistently speak more articulately than second-borns; and the greater the gap, the better the older one's articulation tends to be. There is some indication that stuttering is related both to sex of sibling and to the gap between the children's ages. These factors may produce jealousies between the children, which in turn modify amount of stuttering.

Nevertheless, one can easily overgeneralize about the impact of a specific ordinal position. Many factors, including size of family, sex of sibling, spacing, and social class limit the effect of ordinal position. For example, Rosen (1956) found that oldest children tend to have higher achievement motivation than younger ones in large-sized middle-class families but that the reverse is true in lower-class families. Only when findings are based on larger, more carefully chosen samples, and replications are established, can interacting effects be disentangled.

Sibling Relationships

Byproducts of sibling interaction. Often overlooked, because of the concentration on parent-child relations, are the very real effects of **siblings** on each other. The following cases illustrate how varied these effects may be:

> I do not recall these incidents, but my parents have told me of them. I was two when my baby brother was brought home from the hospital, and I was very jealous. When he began crawling, I slapped and pushed him; and when he toddled, I pushed him off balance. Throughout childhood my relations with him were strained. (Female)

> When I was three, my sister was born, and I felt very affectionate toward her. I wanted to take care of her

and saved up nine cents and bought her some bubble gum. (Male)

> I was so distant from my brother, who was four years older, that I felt like an only child. (Female)

Clearly, sibling relations have broad-ranging effects. For example, the first boy to arrive after several girls have been born is highly valued. In one group of such boys, 56% held high self-esteem as compared with 48% of older boys with younger sisters and 31% of boys whose siblings were mostly brothers. On the other hand, the girl's self-esteem is not enhanced by having only brothers. In fact, whether her siblings are boys or

Sibling relationships may have broad-ranging effects.

girls has little effect on her self-acceptance (Rosenberg, 1965). As for intellectual development, children with male siblings score higher than those with female siblings on certain mental tests. Perhaps boys' greater competitiveness and aggressiveness create a more stimulating environment for the sibling.

Sibling relations also affect children's adaptation to sex role (Koch, 1956b). The boy with a slightly older sister is rated as relatively less aggressive and more sissified, a trait that diminishes with increased age-space between them. She may be jealous of him, and hostile, causing him to become nervous and to underachieve.

Conversely, the girl with an older brother is rated as more tomboyish (Koch, 1956b). In addition, she is more likely than a girl with an older sister to be aggressive, persistent, and decisive with problems. She is less sensitive than girls with older sisters, and learns to take the teasing boys engage in without getting her feelings hurt. If all her siblings are boys, she either becomes a tomboy or comes to feel that all males should do her homage (Strauss, 1951). When siblings are of both sexes, parents expect the daughters to be relatively more feminine than in a two-girl combination; and in the two-girl family, the younger daughter is not discouraged from assertive competition. The parents may even encourage the masculine-aggressive pattern, through disappointment at not having a son. The child herself may adopt the role more readily because she is denied the more feminine surrogate-mother role her older sister has assumed. Out of simple need to distinguish herself from her more advantaged older sister, she may find the aggressive-assertive role satisfying (Douvan and Adelson, 1966).

Siblings also develop special feelings about each other. In a girl-girl combination, there is more jealousy than in a boy-girl or boy-boy combination. Boys fight more with their brothers than their sisters, partly because of parental restraints against aggression toward girls. Instead, older brothers often resort to teasing, which girls absorb with fewer hurt feelings than teasing by older sisters (Strauss, 1951).

Parents' differential relation to opposite-sex siblings, however, is not static. Before the child is born, the father typically wants a boy, but afterward caters to the girl and disciplines his son. The mother prefers her sons, especially the first-born, thus producing sibling frictions that increase throughout childhood. Older children pick on and nag the younger ones, while the younger ones make fun of the older sibs or project their aggression onto still younger children. In an age-graded society, children feel less comfortable with vertical relationships, such as sibships, than with horizontal ones, such as peer relations.

Ruptures in sibling relations are not only common, but often serious. A new baby may be poked, slapped, or dropped by an older sister. In Levy's (1943) classic study, a four-year-old twice tried to throw her baby sister out of a window. Yet it is too much to expect young children, who are natural rivals for the same life space, love, and material objects, to understand the meaning of infants' rights or family situations.

Koch's study of sibling relationships. Koch (1960), in a study of 360 five- and six-year-olds, studied many aspects of sibling relations, including children's choice of siblings as companions. Boys, who felt less protective than girls toward younger children, associated less with younger siblings. However, both sexes (61.6%) preferred to play with other children. About a third said they would be happier with no sib, usually when the sexes were different. Second-borns, particularly, wanted to be free of them, especially where the age disparity was great. First-borns, by contrast, tended to find siblings friendly, though not always interesting, companions, and often a nuisance. Among reasons children gave for being glad they had a sibling were these: "I am used to him." "She helps me fight." "He is silly and fun to play with." "My brother is gooder than anyone." Those who would be happier without a sibling offered such reasons as these: "He always dreams and makes noises so I can't sleep." "She hits. She's mean." "He acts wild and crawls around." "I wanted a brother." "She scratches me." "She bothers me when I have a toothache."

Since quarreling is believed to be a significant part of sibling interaction, Koch asked children whether they quarreled, and how much. Of all the children, 28.4% indicated severe and frequent quarrels, 38% occasional quarrels, and 35.5% rare altercations. No sex differences proved significant, though it had

317

been anticipated that males would squabble more. About half the children said they typically came out of the fracas on top, while only 29.2% admitted initiating fights.

About 37% expressed a desire to change places with a sibling, the second-born more often than the first, who doubtless saw advantages in greater size, power, and ability. However, the infant's status sometimes held appeal for the first-borns. One five-year-old girl confessed: "Yes, I would like to change places with my baby brother. Then I could yell my head off and my mamma would take care of nobody but me."

Second-born boys were more likely to desire metamorphosing into an older male than a female sibling, but second-born girls, when the spacing was close, were more likely to want to exchange places with an older brother. In fact, more girls than boys wanted to change places with an opposite-sexed sibling. Here were reasons children expressed for desiring to change places: "I like her rubber knife." "She doesn't have to have her hair cut." "She has a fancy hanky." "Then I could get even." "I like her name better." "She doesn't have to go to school." "So I could hit him." And here are reasons children said they would not want to change: "She makes in her pants." "She is a little creb." "He gets more lickings." "He is naughty." "She is icky." "She has to wash the dishes." "She has tooth cavities." "She has snarls in her hair."

Factors modifying sibling relations. Certain factors, including sex, age, and spacing have relatively greater effect than others on sibling relations. The sex of a given sibling has relatively strong effects on adjustment, while ordinal position relates more closely than either age or sex to mental abilities. Boys affect girls more than girls affect boys; and first-borns affect later-borns more than later-borns affect them. When the age difference is greater between siblings, whether of the same or opposite sex, a correspondingly more affectionate, friendly, and cooperative relationship exists. An exception may be when the older child is expected to take care of the younger (Macfarlane et al., 1954).

Spacing has other effects, too. When the spacing is large, parent-child relations, as compared with sibling relations, have relatively greater impact. The first-born child with a close sibling becomes reserved. He is afraid he will be punished if he reacts to the younger sibling in an aggressive manner. Second-borns are encouraged to defend themselves, and hence are less hesitant to express their anger directly (Macfarlane, et al., 1954).

In general, it may be said that the narrower the spacing, the more generally a child's emotional characteristics may be imputed to sibling interaction; and the wider the gap, the greater are the influences of the child's interactions with his parents. Moreover, as the spacing between siblings increases, each child's tendency to go his own way also increases (Koch, 1956c).

• PARENTAL ROLES

The Mother's Role

Already we have considered the mother's role within the specific context of infancy. We shall now examine her much broader role as parent in the family. It is sometimes claimed that the mother's role is currently diminishing; but it is still primary, says Parsons (1955), though concentrated within a few years. In other years, he asserts, women were denied achievement in the workaday world and relegated to household management, a sort of pseudo-occupation not highly valued. As a result, many disgruntled women sought other roles, such as the masculine career pattern, in direct competition with men. Others chose the glamour pattern, seeking to establish feminine sexual attractiveness as equal to or even more important than occupational status. Still others assumed the good-companion pattern and participated heavily in community affairs.

More recently, pursues Parsons, all this is changing. Women do not feel compelled to choose between the domestic pattern and the glamour or good-companion roles. Instead, many have their children early, bearing their last child by age 27, and then resume their careers. As a result, mothering today is focused on the young child, while the older child, increasingly, receives a diluted form of mothering different, though not necessarily inferior, in quality.

Of course, the mother's personality is significant in defining her function. Women with high aggression scores, for example, show their children less overt affection, more criticism than approval, and fewer intense contacts. Others with strong nurturance needs bestow on their children more solicitude, and tend to over-protect them (Crandall and Preston, 1961). They indulge in frenzied mothering, often termed "smother" love, because they have dedicated their lives to motherhood. By contrast, some mothers have a talent for converting warmth, love, and intelligence into genuine parental craftsmanship, while maintaining a wholesome perspective and preserving their own and the child's individuality.

The effects of differential patterns of mothering vary with the child, for the relationship is reciprocal. The mother's attitudes, motivations, temperament, and compatibility with a specific child are part of a field which is significantly affected by the child's own traits (Witkin et al., 1962).

The Father's Role

Because the father is so often neglected, we shall accord him special attention. "Father" has been the missing person from human development literature. The word "father" does not even appear in an article entitled "The Search for Significant Concepts in a Study of Parent-Child Relationships" (Nowlis, 1952). Nor is the term "father" found in the index of Carmichael's (1954) comprehensive *Manual of Child Psychology*. A survey of 160 publications, dated from 1929 through 1956, revealed 160 articles about the mother-child relationship, and only 11 about the father-child relationship (Peterson et al., 1959). Fathers Anonymous has become a well-established institution.

Even among writers who accord the father a mention, few concede him any significant role in child-rearing. According to Bowlby (1951), the father affects the child only indirectly, though providing emotional and economic support for the mother.

Children, too, tend to think of the father as less significant in the family circle than the mother. Young children, especially, are so completely the charge of their mothers that they may have only a hazy idea of their fathers' role. Woodstock (1941, p. 136) relates this incident about a two-year-old:

> Donald heard [the researcher] use the word "mamma" and said that he had a mamma, then added, "I have a daddy to eat wid me—in duh restaurant." After [the researcher's] acknowledgment of this remark, he said, "Why have we daddies?"

There are several reasons for this neglect of the father, one being the problem of incorporating him into research studies. Ordinarily, research interviews are conducted during the daytime, when fathers are at work. Besides, the American society delegates to the mother the care and training of both sexes. By contrast, in many primitive cultures, the sex division of labor is rigid, giving rise to values emphasizing maleness and femaleness. Father-son and mother-daughter relationships are the rule, with each parent teaching like-sex offspring their respective roles (Hogbin, 1946).

However, in America, says Gorer (1948), the mother has "arrogated to herself, or has had thrust upon her, the dominant role in the rearing of her children." Small wonder, he further asserts, that American society is epitomized as the "Motherland." In addition, motherliness is conceived as having deep psychological roots, while fatherliness hardly exists as a psychological entity. In fact, mothers often extend to fathers the same sort of maternal attitude they accord their children. Fatherhood, by contrast, is vestigial, a mere social obligation (Josselyn, 1956).

A major reason for such attitudes is merely this: In post-colonial times, fathers moved out of the home into offices and shops, leaving mothers behind with the babies. No longer did sons merely follow in their fathers' footsteps, learning their trade. Instead, fathers became so wrapped up in the pursuit of success that they largely abdicated control over their children's upbringing. And mothers, increasingly freed from domestic chores by labor-saving devices, had nothing else to do but pamper their children (Kluckhohn, 1949).

pating in the family's leisure-time pursuits. And while the mother's day-by-day influence on the children is more direct than his, she depends heavily on her husband for emotional support. In consequence, the whole quality of the mother-child relationship is importantly colored by the father-mother relationship (Bartemeier, 1953).

The child's relationship with the father is often a better index of family integration than his relationship with the mother, and the child's relationship with both parents more accurate still (Landis, 1962). Perhaps the reason is this: The mother's relationship to the children is nearly always a warm one, while the father's attitude is more variable, and hence constitutes the distinguishing factor.

The father, by assuming a more intimate role in caring for the young child,

The father's role may be far more significant than is commonly conceded.

Others, however, argue that the father's role is far more significant than commonly conceded. Shorter hours and longer vacations have restored him to the family, not in the colonial role as domestic worker, but as a father participating in

320

may importantly affect his psychological structure, especially his cognitive development. Recall from Chapter 6 the differential effects of parental identification on type of mental development. If the father spends more time with the infants, both sexes may become more flexible, field-independent, and creative—qualities enhanced by paternal influence (Fowler, 1962). This new type of father is conceived of not as an emasculated petticoat papa but as a healthy male who insists on being a father in more than the biological sense.

Nash (1965) even objects to viewing our society as matricentric, at least in effect. If it were, he hypothesizes, most males would be either homosexual, delinquent, or disturbed—which is not the case. Perhaps, he suggests, boys differ in susceptibility to feminizing influences, so that only the less resistant ones are overtly affected. An analogous situation exists with regard to disease, when factors, sometimes unknown, confer immunity on some individuals, while leaving others susceptible.

The father's perception of his role. Of significance, too, is how fathers see themselves. Only recently have fathers been called on to assess their own status in regard to function and significance.

To determine how fathers see their role, Tasch (1952) interviewed 85 in all, along with a total of 160 children. They were from the greater New York area, and represented a diverse sampling of national origins, educations, and occupations. These men did not see themselves as "vestigial" or as secondary to the mother. Instead, they viewed child-rearing as an integral function of fatherhood, and themselves as active participants in child-care routines. Nor did they resent these functions, but found them deeply satisfying. Those who had failed to establish good relationships with their children found the situation a major cause of discontent. In short, the father refuses to perceive himself as a very minor family official and has promoted himself from corporal to captain. This sort of paternal reaction is typical:

What I see most important about my status as a father is being needed and depended upon. I had hoped for a boy, but decided I would settle for either sex, if healthy. Got a girl, and love her to pieces. I feel I must not get lost in my role as a breadwinner, but rather spend time with the family and enjoy them. As the only male in the family, I must be even more so, to assist my daughter to identify, in a positive manner, with other males in the future.

Other researchers report variations in the father role according to social class and national origin. In general, Rosenberg (1965) found that middle-class fathers were more supportive of their sons than were working-class fathers; but middle-class fathers were only somewhat, if at all, more likely to be supportive of their daughters. Middle- and upper-class boys have always been found to possess high self-esteem, which may result from their closer relationship to the father. Fathers of the middle class tend to seek involvement in child-rearing, while lower-class fathers abrogate such responsibilities (Kohn, 1959). Middle- and upper-class fathers hold the developmental concept of child-rearing, which emphasizes understanding children and doing things for and with them to prepare them for the future. The lower-class father, by contrast, tends to be authoritarian; he is the provider, disciplinarian, and head of the house. If he teaches his child, it is by example rather than precept. He treats his sons harshly, often making bullies of them, because to love them, openly at least, would emasculate them (Bartemeier, 1953).

Parental Roles Compared

Subcultural differences notwithstanding, Johnson (1963) perceives the present role differential largely as one of function rather than authority. The mother's role, he asserts, involves giving pleasure and easing tensions in the family. Her efforts are relatively undifferentiated where the sexes are concerned. The father shapes the boy's personality by being demanding and using techniques that promote initiative and independence, qualities required for his instrumental role outside the home. The part each parent plays represents a mutual *accommodation a deux,* which may shift somewhat with increasing experience and current needs.

The following recollections indicate what varied forms parent authority may assume:

> My mother was a giant of a woman, while my father was small and hen-pecked. Mother never doubted that "mother knows best." Once in a while Dad made a futile, whining protest, which The Great Authority quickly subdued. We children—and Dad—lined up like so many buck privates to do our Commander's bidding. (Male)

> My parents operated as a team, and always talked over what their policies would be. As we grew older they incorporated us in the process. In fact, we "got incorporated" from the time we could think at all, and always perceived decisions as the products of family consensus. (Male)

It is no easy task to assess the relative effects of father and mother, partly because the balance is constantly shifting. For a long time, the father was the top authority in the home; then Western culture slowly but surely became matricentric, a trend that even now may be diminishing (Nash, 1965). The father's restoration, however, if one may call it that, is on a somewhat different basis. The mother doles out the discipline, much restrained, while the father has become a mother's helper and children's pal. He is cheerfully shucking his garb as domestic dictator. It is difficult to know what effect the father's presently greater influence, fostered by a shorter work week, will have on the children. Fowler believes it may significantly change the infant's basic psychological structure (Fowler, 1962).

Older youth, especially, testify to the influence of their fathers. A recent study of "mature" college men—that is, those judged stronger and more achieving—constituted an attempt to assess parents' differential impact. Seven of the ten mature youths described their mothers as being very strong, though not dominating, with great drive, persistence, or accomplishment, or as being professionals who had won awards for creative research. Of the four least mature, three described their mothers as "aggressive," or "dominating," or beset with deep personal conflict, as indicated by excessive drinking or depression. Eight of the ten mature youths believed a father or male had been most influential in shaping their lives; the other two, an older female relative or girl friend (Heath, 1965). One might well question, however, whether the father's greater impact relative to the mother was more apparent than real. Sometimes one is hardly aware of vital early experiences that lay the groundwork for later achievements, and is conscious only of significant events in mature years, which are subject to more specific recall.

Parents' Perceptions of Their Roles

A neglected aspect of family research is parents' views of their own roles—a factor bound to have important repercussions on children. While mothers certainly react to their own role as mother, and fathers to their role as father, both sexes react to their generalized role as parents. Parents may be unduly anxious, almost afraid of their job. They may feel wholly responsible for what happens to the child, misled by supposedly scientific arguments that their influence is paramount and irreversible. Every childish caper becomes a crisis and a threat to the parent's self-image. Given this illusion of omnipotence, they set about manipulating the child, with the aim of creating a perfect individual. However, they often experience apprehension, burdened with an awareness of the oft-cited and limitless acts and attitudes claimed to injure the child. In such cases, they bequeath to the child a legacy of anxiety and confusion. Child-care articles, which often foster such attitudes, may do more to intimidate than to inform parents.

Parents also have the problem of adjusting to their children, the quality of which adjustment, in turn, affects the child. For example, the child may threaten parents in their roles other than parents. For instance, he may interfere with his mother's role as wife. By preempting her affections, or consuming most of her time, he makes the father feel excluded. If he is unplanned, the child may interrupt his mother's career, thus engendering maternal resentment, often deep, though repressed. Furthermore, the parent must sustain impacts of the environment brought into the home by the child. For instance, the child with academic or social problems unloads his tensions at home.

Whatever the parents' feelings about their roles, they will change subtly with time. When children are small and helpless, parents gain satisfaction from

their love and dependency. Inevitably, however, children come to depend on their parents, especially the mother, less and less, sometimes making them feel rejected. And since children change more than their parents, the parents' adjustment may be the more difficult one. However, to the extent that he can, the parent should remain flexible, attuned to a changing child with changing needs. He should develop the capacity to mature step by step with the child. And he should have the sense of security to allow and even encourage the child to develop and mature.

Children's Perceptions of Their Parents

Children's perceptions of parents vary with age, sex, and culture. Although parents impose greater limitations on girls' than boys' freedom, girls are more favorably oriented toward their parents and report better relations with them (Dubin and Dubin, 1965). Both sexes

"As I always say, it's purely a matter of upbringing."

Parents often have distorted perceptions of their own children, sometimes because of a special need to see themselves as "good" parents. Drawing by David Langdon; © 1966 *The New Yorker Magazine*, Inc. Reproduced by permission.

report more favorable than unfavorable attitudes toward their parents, with a noticeable increase in neutral effects in the intermediate grades. In the high-school years, boys manifest a slight rise in positive attitudes toward both parents, and girls a more pronounced improvement in relation to the father than the mother. The small number of boys acknowledging negative attitudes toward their parents decreases steadily through childhood and adolescence, while the reverse is true of girls. In general, when either sex prefers one parent over the other, the mother is chosen, although exceptions occur (Harris and Tseng, 1957). Sometimes a child may acquire at least a mildly negative feeling toward one or both parents, because of some special interpretation he places on their behavior:

> During a mild skirmish for seats for a television program at home, a quiet, conscientious five-year-old boy suddenly burst out at his parents. "You don't care about anything," he complained. "You always let me sit cross-legged. You don't care what happens to me." When they asked, he explained that his kindergarten teacher had warned the class that poor sitting posture would "ruin their backs." The boy felt that his parents had been seriously remiss in not warning him about this [Kessler, 1966, p. 496].

Not surprisingly, well-adjusted children perceive the parent-child relation as close to ideal, the poorly adjusted far from it. Whatever the relationship, parents' perceptions of it show little agreement with the child's. Furthermore, the parent-child relationship seems only indirectly related to the child's own adjustment (Serot and Teevan, 1961).

Perceptions of parents also vary with the culture. In a study of Japanese and American fifth- and sixth-grade children, American youngsters saw both parents as playing similar roles in child care, while Japanese children perceived the father's role as primarily authoritarian. The Japanese also perceived a great social distance between themselves and

their parents (Matsumoto and Smith, 1961). However, in another study, German children perceived parents as exhibiting more **nurturant** behavior, with the father more often involved in joint activities and exerting less psychological pressure on the child than a matched sampling of American children (Devereux et al., 1962).

• DIMENSIONS OF FAMILY CONTROL

Dependence-Independence

The parents' manner of bringing up children could be analyzed in terms of many variables, but we shall examine only two here: **dependence-independence** and **acceptance-rejection**.

Societies vary greatly in the degree of independence accorded their children and youth. In many countries, parents hold authority until death. In such cases, emancipation poses few problems simply because it does not occur, except in small, ritualized steps. However, every parent in the Western World must deal with the problem, for boys at least, though the manner and time for achieving the process are vague. Even in the Western world the girl's emancipation is not taken for granted and often does not occur. In many cases, she simply grows up, marries, and transfers her dependence from parents to husband.

Significance of dependence-independence dimension. Independence implies confidence in one's ability to cope with problems without unusual help from others. Dependence, at the other extreme of the continuum, means leaning on, surrendering to, or catering to a stronger person. It means being hovered over and treated like a hothouse plant. It should not be confused with loyalty, which stems from having incorporated similar views. A child may identify with a parent or older sibling and incorporate his values without forming the sort of emotional tie that reduces him to a satellite.

The byproducts of independence are generally desirable (Krebs, 1958). Children from homes that encourage independence have generally been found to be self-reliant, resourceful, well-adjusted, and intellectually superior. However, if license is carried too far, they become tyrannical and expect constant attention.

Factors determining dependence-independence patterns. Dependence, the byproduct of failure to achieve emancipation, is brought about in several ways. Often it is caused by overprotection, which encourages children to lean on the parent. However, in one study of 20 overly dependent children, two-thirds had not been overprotected. Instead, they had had to make about four times as many critical adaptations as normal in early childhood, such as adjustment to a physical disability or to loss of a parent (Stendler, 1954). Overly dependent behavior in boys has been found to follow early and severe emotional deprivation (McCord et al., 1962).

Dependence also arises from insufficient experience with freedom. That is, the child is so restricted that he fails to learn to deal with a variety of situations. The end result is that he must lean on others. Here is such a case:

> I have a cousin, aged 12, whose mother hovers over her constantly. The child, born when the mother was 39, is not permitted to do much of anything. Not until last year was she allowed to cross the street alone. Since the child has hay fever, the mother uses it as an excuse to keep her in the house. All play is supervised by the mother. The girl is reluctant to make any decisions, even about choice of dessert. Often she waits to see what her younger sister chooses, or sits and looks at her mother.

Overall, many factors can produce dependence. A child may be physically or mentally retarded, and hence unable to do things for himself. He may have so many failures that he comes to doubt his own abilities. Or he may feel rejected and therefore cling tenaciously to any adult who is good to him. Some parental patterns leading to children's dependence are fairly obvious—for example, impos-

ing undue restrictions and doing everything for them; other patterns are much less obvious. One devious route to producing dependence is through maintaining a tight family circle. The family does everything together; and the child who goes off on his own is made to feel he is disloyal, a deserter. In other cases, an immature parent may unduly sacrifice himself for the child, so that the child cannot bear to hurt his parent by spending much time with his peers.

Domination is facilitated by the parents' greater authority, size, and experience. They may give such plausible reasons for restricting the youngster that the latter rarely questions their rightness. For their part, siblings may either reinforce or break down parents' efforts at domination. Some may band together in defying their parents' orders. Others, older ones especially, may help carry out parental dictates and dominate younger ones.

Parents may discourage their children's growing independence for any number of reasons. A mother may welcome a child's submission as a tribute of love. A father may gain a feeling of power when his children depend heavily on him. In other cases, parents may find the independent child too self-assertive and a threat to their authority. Not that parents are always, or even generally, aware of such things; they unconsciously tailor their children's independence training, or lack thereof, to their current needs. One moment they may grant the child freedom and the next overly restrict him. They are afraid one moment he will not grow up, the next that he will, their attitudes fluctuating with the vicissitudes in their own lives. At one time, the mother may be very happy and self-sufficient; at another, she may need to feel needed and jealously guard her protective maternal-care role. Whichever attitude she takes will have its effect on the child, as this illustration shows:

> When I was in the fifth grade, my mother began working, because my father's heavy drinking made it im-

possible for him to support us. I took care of my little sister, then three months old, after school and at night when mother worked. A year later, my mother got a baby sitter, who lasted just one day. I was outraged at the idea that I had to be watched by a girl just a few years older, and apparently mother decided I was responsible enough after all.

In patterns of independence training, parents vary both in personality traits and in the subcultures they represent. The autocratic parent is most likely to be a father, of lower social status, possessing a high-school education or less, and having three or more children living at home. Parents defined as democratic and equalitarian are most apt to be mothers, middle class in status, having some college education, and having one or two children (Elder, 1962).

Dependence is also determined to a considerable extent by the sex of the child. In one study, when boys and girls were shown a projective picture of a child whose parents were obviously setting limits, 25% of the boys, as against just 4% of the girls, questioned the parents' right to such restriction. Girls were more authority-reliant, while boys engaged in a more active struggle toward their own control systems (Douvan, 1960). In a later study, girls were shown more likely than boys to identify with adult authority and to yield to whatever demands are made. They show little concern over establishing inner controls and self-direction and demonstrate few signs of rebellion, which grow even less as time goes on (Douvan and Adelson, 1966). By contrast, even small boys are generally somewhat independent, and become increasingly so with age (Kagan and Moss, 1960). Douvan and Adelson (1966) also found that girls' attitudes toward their parents showed little relation to the parents' patterns of control. That is, they loved the parent who restricted them just as much as the more lenient one. The issue of independence, concluded the researchers, is almost exclusively a masculine

stirring. Girls overlearn their nesting habits, and rarely develop a real need to fly alone.

Occasionally, girls, like the first one quoted below, protest vigorously and dislike authoritarian treatment; the second, however, is typical of the majority:

> Mother overdid her job, to the point where she picked my friends and made my decisions. As I grew older, she pretended to give me a greater part in decision making, but whenever I committed a mistake she made me feel I was immature and lacking in common sense. The minutest wrong decision (in her judgment) was expounded upon and argued over.

> Mother was pretty firm in her opinions, but she was a wise woman and decided what was for my best. It would have been stupid for me to set up my own childish judgment against hers.

Establishing the proper balance. What, one may ask, is the ideal pattern for teaching independence? These ingredients—granting children parental trust, inviting them to participate in family decisions, and to share in home activities—when combined, inculcate independence and responsibility (Harris et al., 1955). However, the mode of encouraging independence should not be overly patterned or dictated, lest the training defeat its own purpose. For example, in their effort to encourage their child's independence, parents may adamantly refuse to take a stand on important issues, thereby constituting weak role models. On the other hand, if parents simply impose their own role patterns, children will be ill-equipped to deal with a rapidly changing society (Rodman, 1965). In modern society, the mother-hen attitude becomes a case of safe but sorry.

Acceptance-Rejection

Nurturance. Another, and one of the most important, dimensions of parent-child relations is acceptance-rejection. Acceptance is often called *nurturance*—that is, an attitude on the part of the parent, more commonly the mother, of warmth and helpful assistance toward the child. Rejection is just the reverse, manifesting itself in hostility, crossness, or indifference. This excerpt, from the study by Sears, Maccoby, and Levin (1957, p.55), defines these two extremes:

> A mother rated high in warmth said: "Well, as soon as my work is done, if she's around, I'll call her and say, 'Come on, let's have some fun'; and we'll sit down and she'll sit on my lap, and sometimes I rock her back and forth, and kiss her. She likes to be kissed, she loves it, and I'll cuddle her, and she loves to be cuddled. Or I'll play a game with her." . . . A mother rated low in warmth said such things as: "I, as a child, never kissed my parents, but I'll kiss him goodnight, or kiss him good-bye, something like that, hug him, that's about all."

Many factors determine the extent of parents' acceptance or rejection. For instance, parents may accept children at one age but reject them at another. The mother may like babies, but not children; the father may dislike his children as infants but accept them later on.

The parents' adjustment is especially significant. The mother who has good relations with her husband is warmer toward her children than the mother who feels less enthusiasm for him. Also, the mother's self-esteem is a factor. If she accepts herself, she can more readily accept another. The parent who is unhappy may use the child as a scapegoat, or seek in him explanations for his own unhappiness (Sears et al., 1957). For instance, the mother who finds herself growing less attractive with age may attribute it to the burden of work and worry imposed by her children.

The effects of acceptance on children are clear-cut: They profit from nurturance, provided it is not of the debilitating kind. Sometimes parents simply mask their own selfish needs with a haze of affectionate behaviors. In such cases, children find themselves the pawns of parental weaknesses. For

example, a mother may be unhappy with her husband, and focus all her attention on the child, so that he has no chance to establish himself as a distinct personality or to make adequate contacts with his peers.

However, the sort of nurturance that stems from well-adjusted parents who permit children to grow in their own way is very healthy. In a study of 31 males aged 5 to 16, maternal nurturance was found to lessen the child's pessimism, dependency, anxiety, and hostility, and to expedite his development of conscience. One alleged effect of nurturance, spoiling, was found to be the result, not of parental nurturance, but of the failure to be firm, and of inconsistent reactions toward dependent behavior, encouraging it one moment and disapproving it the next.

Contrary to popular belief, nurturance has just the opposite effect of spoiling (Finney, 1961). One study indicated that children who identified with supporting parents were consistently more self-accepting and accepted by their peers (Carlson, 1963). Another study revealed that warm, democratic parents had brighter children than those who were cold and nonindulgent (Sears et al., 1957). When both parents are nurturant, the effects are correspondingly greater. In one American and three Italian cities, boys aged 11 to 17 proved to be calmer, more affectionate and open with others, and higher on need-achievement, who had received affection from both parents, rather than from just the mother (Mussen et al., 1963).

Rejection. At the other end of the continuum is **rejection,** an attitude of unwillingness to accept the child or what he does. Rejection is characterized by indifference toward the child or by varying degrees of hostility. Some mothers may reject any child, for various reasons; for example, a woman wants to divorce her husband but finds she is pregnant. Or the child is born during a time of financial crisis. In other cases,

327

the child interferes with a mother's professional career, and so on.

The rejected child may become overly dependent, in a fruitless unconscious effort to obtain the love he desires; or he may grow independent and adept at amusing himself. In any case, the effect is likely to be greater when the rejecting parent is the mother, since she is closer to the children (Slater, 1962). Another reaction to rejection is hostility, where the child denies any similarity to the parent and attempts to accentuate the difference (Stagner, 1961). In this case, reported by a guidance counselor, certain effects of rejection are apparent:

> Eleven-year-old Jean has temper tantrums and is often heard to say "Nobody likes me." Jean's problems stem largely from having a brighter, prettier older sister with whom she is unfavorably compared. Whenever Jean and Diana quarrel, the mother takes the older girl's side. When Jean brings her report card home her mother says, "When Diana was your age she made better grades than these!" Teachers did their bit, too. They would shake their heads and say, "Your sister was smarter than you."
>
> One day Jean came home and announced excitedly that she had won a part in the school play. But Mom, Dad, and Diana were too busy to listen. Jean gave up the part; she hadn't the heart to go through with it.

Some parents shift between acceptance and rejection, blowing hot and cold in turn. As a result, the child cannot cloak himself properly for the uncertain domestic climate in which he dwells.

Factors Determining Parental Authority Patterns

In a society as fluid and heterogeneous as ours, child-training will vary with the times, the subculture, and the specific family. When both parents have been reared in families with similar systems of control, they are likely to reproduce the pattern, at least generally. If brought up by different methods, there is likely to be conflict and a degree of modification of both methods (Behrens, 1954). Of course, one parent's view may prevail, and the father tends to be more inflexible and less understanding. Also important is parental personality; for example, the more conservative the parent the more rigid are his methods (Bell, 1958). The parent with a steel rod for a spine can hardly unbend even after a reading of Spock.

In a study by Heinstein (1958), ratings were made of the mother's friendliness toward her young child, of the closeness between mother and child, of parents' stability, and of inter-parent agreement on discipline. When the children involved were studied again at age 18, no relation was shown between any of these factors and their adjustment. However, personality disturbance was related to a generally unfavorable environment. After reviewing available research, Peterson and his associates (1959) drew similar conclusions. Most of the studies reported a relationship between child-care systems and general behavioral tendencies, but few managed to relate specific child-care behaviors to the child's later traits.

In other words, we can determine that a child is quiet or active, happy or tense, even in the first days of life; and we can make a reasonable estimate of the mother's attitude toward him; but we do not know yet just how infant and caretaker mesh together. For instance, we cannot predict later effects when a mother who wanted a quiet baby acquires an active one. Nor do we know why some children get along well despite apparently unfortunate influences. Sometimes children of grossly maladjusted parents manage, nevertheless, to get along beautifully. In other cases, parents conform perfectly to the stereotype of the good parent, but have severely maladjusted children.

In sum, children of warm, stable parents are generally better adjusted, but exceptions occur. And while correlations are sometimes found between specific child-rearing patterns and particular personality traits, they are far from perfect. Also, they apply only to groups, and lack predictive power where individuals are concerned. Nor is it clear just what accounts for such correlations as are found.

• LESS TYPICAL FAMILY RELATIONSHIPS

Adoption

Certain family relationships, while hardly abnormal in the sense of fostering problems, are at least atypical. Although adoption is becoming increasingly common, little research exists on the subject. Available data support the common belief that adopted children face special problems. In an Australian psychiatric hospital, more adopted children than their numbers would justify were treated for emotional disturbance (Bostick, 1961). Many of them had displayed symptoms of impulsiveness, delinquency, and other aggressive behavior.

Authorities believe it best to tell a child of his adoption as soon as he can comprehend what it means. If he is told he was a specially chosen child, and if parental treatment is generally favorable, he may feel unusually cherished. Otherwise, the child may sustain considerable shock if he finds out by sheer chance in later years (Breckinridge and Murphy, 1964).

The two illustrations that follow demonstrate the negative effects that may derive from the unwise handling of adopted children:

> By accident I overheard part of a conversation: "Do you have the adoption papers? We'll need them." I was stunned but pretended not to hear. Later my mother told me, and I cried. She said she loved me more than anyone who was actually a blood relation, but she wouldn't tell me anything about my background. I am skeptical about getting married because of possible hereditary factors. (Female)

> Mrs. Sanders has two boys, the first adopted, the second, a year younger, her own. The adopted boy resents the younger one, who is brighter, better looking, and the family pet. The mother overdoes assurances to the adopted child that he was specially chosen. He does mean things like throwing cats into the cellar and hitting his grandmother with a broom.

Broken Home

A topic that has been accorded far more attention than adoption is the broken home. The evidence concerning its impact on children is conflicting. Let us examine views on both sides, beginning with those which emphasize the negative effects. Bernert (1960), for one, declares that any break in the home may critically affect the child. The remaining family members may be drawn more closely together, but it is more likely that the family unit will disintegrate further. Besides, many broken families are not self-supporting, which gives rise to derivative problems.

The impact of divorce. The effect of divorce on boys and on girls is somewhat different. The daughter may be cool toward her mother and seek other adult models, while resenting increased home responsibilities. The boy may suffer even more because the mother, who is alone and uncertain, and afraid lest the lack of paternal authority hurt him, may bear down too hard. The son, in turn, feels driven to become the man of the family, and to assume at least the shell of masculinity. Also, he may become a lone wolf, eschewing social relationships either with his family or others (Douvan and Adelson, 1966).

Naturally, the effect of divorce will vary with the child's age and relationship to his parents. In early childhood, when the home is his world, he may feel as though his world is falling apart. If he is older, and spends much time with his friends, the effect may be lessened. At any age the impact will be modified by his own special status relative to each parent.

Much of the writing on this subject has been impressionistic, devoid of empirical basis; however, some worthwhile studies exist. Landis (1963) reported that divorce adversely affects children's heterosexual relations; however, he found few differences between children of divorce and those of unhappy marriages. Children who had believed their homes happy were shocked to learn of their parents' plans. However, they denied that the divorce itself had affected their feelings of security and happiness. Those, on the other hand, who experienced their homes as unhappy, reported greater security and happiness after the divorce (Landis, 1961). Contrary to what one might expect, older children felt the impact more sharply than did younger ones.

Similarly, Nye (1957) found that children from broken homes showed less psychosomatic illness, less delinquent behavior, and better adjustment to parents than those from unhappy, unbroken homes. Note, too, that parents' adjustment, both within themselves and to their spouses, is superior in broken homes to that in unhappy homes that remain intact. In an especially extensive study, Goode (1956) found no adverse effects of divorce on the child's adjustment. Mothers who remarried worried about the impact of their divorce on the children, but generally believed their lives had improved.

Burchinal's (1964) conclusions were even more sweeping. He found no adverse effects on children either of the parents' divorce, separation, or remarriage. True, some children suffered trauma; but one cannot easily distinguish the effects of separation from those of conflict preceding the event. In short, neither family dissolution nor reconstitution was the overwhelmingly influential factor in children's lives many people believed it to be.

In certain respects, Burchinal found adolescents from broken homes actually superior to those from unbroken homes. They more often participated in family counsels and shared their parents' problems, and less often reported parents' prying into their affairs and criticizing their dates. Perhaps because

of concern about family income, they attained economic maturity earlier (Landis, 1953). Where individuals are concerned, the effects of divorce apparently range all the way from extremely harmful to positive, as these two cases illustrate:

> The single event that had the greatest effect on my life was my parents' divorce when I was 11. Since then I have felt an inner distrust toward women in the marriage relationship, and doubt that I could ever trust a woman enough to marry her.

> Mrs. Brown, a divorcee, has one son, and to support him adequately she works at night. Mother and son have a very close, happy relationship. Everything is out in the open. There are no secrets. If either has a problem, it is a problem for both of them, and someone comes up with a solution.

Death of the parent. The effects of parental loss as a result of death are quite different from those of divorce. When a parent dies, mourning often begins with protest, which passes into despair and then detachment. However, the effect depends largely on the child's age, his special relationship to the parent, and which parent it is. The young child, reports Bowlby (1961), is more deeply affected by the loss of the mother, and the older child by the loss of the father.

However, the effects of the father's death may be largely situational. Financial pressures produce a diminution of leisure and a premature seriousness. In other respects, the youngsters seem to be emotionally intact. And with increased need for mutual support, the family unit often becomes more cohesive (Douvan and Adelson, 1966). Of course, each child's reaction is an individual one, dependent on his special traits and situation:

> Small Johnnie didn't understand death. He thought his mother was hiding; he couldn't believe she was really gone. Maybe she was away playing games with the seven-year-old sister, was his next guess. Not for some time did he accept the fact that his mother was gone for good.

Sammie's father died when he was a year old, and throughout grade school he felt set apart from his classmates. He felt tricked, because he never knew his father. And when people asked him what his father did for a living, he would burst into tears.

Effect of stepparents. Remarriage, often chosen as a solution, presents the problem of adjusting to a stepparent. Since early years, many children hold a stereotype of the wicked stepmother, borrowed from fairy tales, fiction, and screen. However, much depends on the age of the child. Younger children, with few memories of the missing parent, may find a sense of security in the new parent. Older children are more likely to resent the stepparent, whether father or mother (Podolsky, 1955). However, recall Nye's report that children adjusted better after their parents' remarriage.

Here are two testimonials relating to child-stepparent relationships:

> Since the parents did not get along well, the daughter developed a very close relationship to her father. However, after he divorced and remarried, the girl had great difficulty accepting the stepmother. The girl was very jealous and felt she had been rejected in favor of someone else.

> Daisy, a ten-year-old, brags that she has four parents, and says if she can't get one set of parents to give her something she can usually get it from the other set.

The Working Mother

The home with a working mother is, in a sense, one type of broken home. But is the working mother necessarily a shirking mother? Many working mothers, who may worry about the effect of their employment on children, would heave a sigh of relief if they read the research. In a study of six-year-olds, Siegel and his associates (1959) found no significant differences between children of working mothers and of carefully matched nonworking mothers. Stolz (1960) found that children of employed mothers performed in school equally as well as those whose mothers did not work out-

side the home. Similarly, Siegel and Haas (1963) concluded that maternal employment is not significant in de-

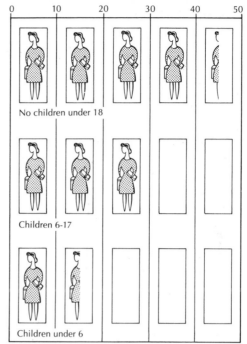

Per cent of working wives who worked full time (35 or more hours per week, for 50 weeks or more), by presence and age of children, 1956. Source: Bureau of Census. From *Children of working mothers,* Children's Bureau Publication No. 382. Washington, D.C.: U.S. Department of Health, Education, and Welfare, 1960. Pp. 1–35. Reproduced by permission.

termining either intellectual or emotional disturbances in children. In summary, maternal employment is not an important variable when factors such as social class and stability of home are controlled (McCord et al., 1963). However, such studies represent averages. Sometimes the situation is worse when the mother works, sometimes not.

Surprisingly, some studies indicate greater benefits accruing to children whose mothers work. In one study, working mothers, when matched with nonworking mothers, were adjudged more warm, helpful, relaxed, and satisfied (Hoffman, 1960). In another, daughters of working mothers, as compared with those of nonworking mothers, more often reported professional aspirations, and intended to work after marriage

(Hartley, 1960). If the mother's position is important, children are often proud of her.

However, in some homes the mother's employment proves disruptive. Meals may be irregular, home duties neglected, and little social or recreational life provided. The older girl may resent extra duties, and the younger child miss his mother's care (Siegel et al., 1959). Certainly the following testimonies indicate that the effects of the mother's working depend on the specific situation:

My mother would come home every night tired and grouchy, and take out her frustrations on us and our father. All of us in turn would be grouchy toward her—and the result was much conflict.

My mother worked from the time I was four, and I think this made me much more independent and self-reliant. I was also more aware of the duties in an efficient household. I don't feel I was deprived in any way.

Importance of parents' reactions to the mother's working. Of special significance is why the woman works, and especially, whether she desires to do so. She may be either a vocational retread, who works because the family cupboard is bare, or a bona fide career type. If she likes her work she will probably have more positive relationships with her children and use milder discipline than the mother who dislikes it (Hartley, 1960). However, if a mother works merely because she dislikes home-making, her unhappiness spills into all areas.

The important factor, one research team reported, is whether the mother likes her role, whatever it is. Nonworking mothers dissatisfied with their housewife's status have the greatest number of child-rearing problems, while satisfied housewives and working mothers appear about equally adequate in mothering their children (Radke-Yarrow et al., 1962).

The father figures importantly in

this situation, too. If the mother works because she doubts the father's competence, she generates feelings of inadequacy and resentment in him, thereby producing an unhealthy home climate. Also unfortunate is the situation in which the wife works, or does not work, simply to suit the husband's wishes.

The effects of a mother's working depend somewhat on family adaptations to employment and modifications in family structure. College-trained mothers, for example, make a conscious effort to compensate for time spent away from their children, while others may not. Mothers participate less, and fathers more, in household tasks when the mother is employed. However, the family power structure seems to depend on the husband's and wife's values and personalities, rather than on whether or not the wife works.

One overall factor is this: Women's working today is quite a different matter from what it was formerly. Women tend to have fewer children and to have them earlier, leaving them free to re-enter the labor market at an early age. Also the life span of the woman is longer, leaving many more years for a satisfying job role. Consider, too, how much easier home duties are today, making the dual role less taxing. Furthermore, the wife looks on her work not so much as a bread-winning function as an effort to provide her children the better things of life. The spread of middle-class standards has imposed on parents the need, and the desire, to provide "extras."

Summing up, maternal employment in itself is unimportant in determining children's welfare. No single way of life, writes Maccoby (1958), is best for all. Depending on the situation, some mothers should work, others should not.

Grandparents

Especially in homes where the mother works, a grandmother often helps out. However, the grandmother's typical role, like all family roles, varies with the culture. In a cross-cultural survey, which included 51 societies, grandparents removed from family authority maintained a warm, indulgent attitude toward the grandchildren. On the other hand, in those societies where economic power and prestige were accorded the aged, such attitudes were stiff and authoritarian (Apple, 1956).

In America, where the typical family is nuclear rather than extended, the three-generation household is most often portrayed as a hazardous one. The grandmother often attempts, consciously or otherwise, to impose her values on mother and grandchildren. The father resents his mother-in-law's intrusion, which his wife feels compelled to defend. The child, in turn, is torn by his parents' friction, and by the conflicting demands of mother, parents, and grandparent. While the grandfather is typically less disruptive, he imposes an extra burden on the mother, often requiring special menus and treatment (Clark and van Sommers, 1961).

Typical roles of grandparents. In America, grandparents, generally, including both those who live inside and outside the children's home, typically play one of five roles, or some combination of them (Neugarten and Weinstein, 1964). *Formal grandparents* typically follow their conception of the approved role for grandparents. They provide special treats for the grandchild and assist with babysitting, but leave parenting strictly to the parent. The *surrogate parent,* by contrast, acquires such a role because the mother is working. The *fun seeker's* relationship is informal and playful, while the *reservoir of family wisdom,* usually the grandfather, is solemn and authoritative. The lines of authority are distinct, with the young parents accepting their subordinate role, with or without resentment. Finally, the *distant figure* is the grandparent who emerges on holidays and on ritual occasions like Christmas and birthdays. Neither the *fun seeker* nor the *distant figure* involves much nurturance; hence, neither deserves the designation maternal or paternal; the

other three types, however, male and female alike, tend toward becoming slightly masculinized grandmothers. That is, the grandmother assumes a more dominant role than she did earlier in life, while the grandfather becomes somewhat emasculated, a role markedly different from the instrumental, outer-world orientation of his earlier years. In short, the new type of grandparent is somewhat neuter in gender (Cavan, 1962).

The effect of grandparents in the home will depend heavily on the personality of all parties concerned, and the specific situation. Therefore, the results are highly varied; and each case must be judged on its own merits:

My grandfather lost his mind, and set fire to wastebaskets in the house, left the gas on, and so on. As a family we couldn't go anywhere because someone always had to stay with him. We finally put him in a nursing home, but he was rejected after two weeks.

My grandmother was truly great. We kids loved to have her come. She never meddled — just sat in the background and smiled, and told us stories, and made us feel terribly important and very much loved.

A final note: Often we nostalgically deplore changes in the grandmother's role — or, for that matter, in the role of any member of the traditional family group. But there is no such thing as the ultimate ideal in family systems; the family, like any institution, must — if it is to be maximally effective — change with shifting needs.

• SUMMARY

The family is a dynamic complex of interacting systems in which each individual plays a unique role. These roles are complementary and reciprocal, and either rigidly or loosely defined. A particular child's role depends on such factors as age, sex, personality, and ordinal position. The only child experiences certain disadvantages, which

333

may be offset, or even surpassed, by the advantages accruing to onliness. In general, the child in the small family fares better than the one in the large family, although each type of family may hold special hazards and benefits. **Ordinal position** is also important, though the significance of any specific position — whether first, last, or middle — hinges on such factors as spacing of child and sex of children, and factors unique to the family involved.

The mother has great effect on her children at all ages. The mother-child relationship is interactional, with specific effects depending on the respective motivations of mother and child, and on their compatibility. By comparison with the mother, the father has been neglected, but is being accorded increasing attention. He, too, wields a great influence, partially through the mother, who often reflects his views. Each parent fulfills certain functions, and has a unique influence on each child. In any specific case, the relationship fluctuates with family circumstances and age of the child.

Mothers take their parental role so seriously that they often have difficulty letting the child go. Lately, the father, especially in middle-class families, has been taking his duties as father ever more seriously. Both parents, especially the father, are becoming more psychological and less authoritative in guiding the child than formerly. The father, formerly perceived as the all-wise, and somewhat threatening, dispenser of wisdom and punishment, is becoming perceived as more benign, although remnants of his former harsh image remain.

Families vary in dimensions of control — for example, in degree of independence accorded each child. Some parents, especially mothers, overprotect their children, more often the daughter. The end result for the child may be a lack of self-confidence and a tendency to lean on others. Children who fail to acquire sufficient independence may

have trouble coping with a rapidly changing, complex society.

Parents also vary in the degree of acceptance accorded the child. In order to satisfy some emotional deficiency in his own life, a parent may bind the child fast to him with chains of affection that prevent growth and obstruct attainment of autonomy. Healthy love, or **nurturance**, however, helps children to grow in their own way, and to develop the ego strength required for becoming independent. What seems like warmth may sometimes spring from **rejection**, and help to appease guilt feelings springing from it. In fact, rejection may be open or subtle, and either acknowledged or repressed by the parent. The child is especially confused who must adjust to constant changes in emotional temperature, when parents blow hot and cold by turns. The residual effects of any specific child-rearing approach or technique seem to depend largely on the overall relationship between parent and child. Besides, endorsements of a particular approach often rest on data obtained from groups, and may be unsuitable for a particular parent-child relationship.

The concentration on parent-child relationships has tended to obscure the significant impact of siblings on each other. Particular effects depend on such factors as spacing, sex, age, and personality of the siblings concerned. Boys affect girls more than girls affect boys; and first-borns affect later-borns more than later-borns affect them. The narrower the spacing the greater the sibling impact, and the wider the spacing the more interaction with the parent.

Among less typical family relationships, adoption is becoming increasingly common. If a child is told that he was adopted and that he was specially chosen, and receives favorable treatment, he generally adjusts well. The effects of another deviant situation, divorce, depend on particular parent-child relationships, and have been grossly exaggerated. Often children fare better after embattled parents finally resort to divorce. The effect of parental death, like that of divorce, also depends on the specific parent-child relationship. Often the father's death results in economic difficulties and requires that the mother work outside the home. The impact of the mother's working depends somewhat on how she feels about it, and if the father is living, on his attitude. Sometimes the overall effect is disruptive; at other times it may prove beneficial. In general, the negative effects of the mother's employment have been exaggerated.

When mothers work, a grandmother often helps out, and her influence depends on the way she perceives her role and the specific situation. Often we nostalgically deplore changes in the grandmother's traditional role—in fact, in the whole family's role. But there is no such thing as the ultimate ideal in family systems; for the family, like any institution, must change with shifting needs if it is to be maximally effective.

• SUGGESTED QUESTIONS AND ACTIVITIES

1. Is the present-day home typically too democratic? That is, have parents abdicated any important aspects of their role?
2. Are children of both sexes given adequate independence? If not, what additional freedom should be provided?
3. Should a child be permitted to decorate his own room just as he likes?
4. To what extent should children participate in family councils? Is there danger of emotionally overloading children with family problems?
5. Are children today pampered too much? Do they make a sufficient contribution to the family?
6. Should both boys and girls be expected to perform regular, and very considerable, chores on behalf of the family? If so, should they be paid?
7. Criticize the maternal role as generally practiced in our society.
8. What sort of training should be provided the father for his role? Would having older brothers as well as older sisters help take care of the baby and of the younger children make boys better fathers later on?
9. Try to define, somewhat specifically,

both the father's present, and his ideal, role as it relates to sons and to daughters, first as infants, and later as children.
10. Should family-life training directed by specialists be provided all boys and girls? If so, at what age should it begin and what should it include?
11. Is there any workable plan for checking up on parents who fail to discharge their role properly, and to ensure that they will make efforts to improve? Should children be removed from parents who are certified by a group of specialists to be unqualified for rearing children?
12. Should adults who would seem to be especially incompetent or undesirable as parents be sterilized? If so, what sort of standards should be used?
13. In case of divorce, under what circumstances should a child be awarded to the father?
14. Should the child of divorce who is over age six be delegated to the custody of whichever parent he prefers? If so, how should the situation be handled?
15. What standards should be required of parents who adopt children? Would you automatically deny the right to adopt a child to a couple who: (a) are very poor; (b) are physically handicapped; (c) have a criminal record but have reformed; (d) belong to some off-beat religious, political, or aesthetic cult; (e) are over 45 years of age? Should a superior, well-off single person be permitted to adopt a child?
16. Does the child develop best in a close-knit or loose-knit family?
17. Should grandparents or outsiders be permitted to live in the house while children are growing up? If so, what adaptations should be provided to prevent ill effects?
18. Does the child fare better in the modern nuclear family than in the more extended family of other days and cultures, which embraced various kindred, and perhaps the whole tribe?

• SUGGESTED READINGS

Bettelheim, B., *Dialogues with Mothers*. New York: The Free Press, 1962. Consists of 26 transcribed excerpts from talks that Dr. Bettelheim held with a group of parents of normal children. The mothers were wives of graduate students at the University of Chicago, and their problems probably represent a typical sample of those that most parents face in the early years of their children's development.
Bossard, J. H. S., and E. S. Boll, *The Soci-*

ology of Child Development, 4th ed. New York: Harper & Row, Inc., 1966. Stresses the situational approach to understanding children, and provides a sociological orientation to child development.

Bronfenbrenner, U., "The Changing American Child—A Speculative Analysis," *Journal of Social Issues*, Vol. 17, No. 1 (1961), pp. 6-18. A provocative analysis of recent trends in child rearing and possible effects on children's development.

Clausen, J. A., "Family Structure, Socialization, and Personality," in M. L. Hoffman and L. W. Hoffman, eds., *Review of Child Development Research*, Vol. 2. New York: Russell Sage Foundation, 1966, pp. 1-53. Excellent review of research in the area of socialization and child personality.

Elder, G. H., and C. E. Bowerman, "Family Structure and Childrearing Patterns: The Effect of Family Size and Sex Composition," *American Sociological Review*, Vol. 28 (1963), pp. 891-905. Reports a study of the effects of the number and sex ratio of children in a family on two aspects of childrearing: the involvement of the father in rearing children, and the differential use of certain practices and training techniques which represent methods of external rather than indirect control.

Ginzberg, E., ed., *The Nation's Children*, I: *The Family and Social Change*. New York: Columbia University Press, 1960. Brief essays on changes in American family life and effects on children. Prepared for the 1960 White House Conference on Children and Youth.

Heinstein, M. I., *Child Rearing in California*. Berkeley: California Bureau of Maternal and Child Health, 1965. A brief report of child-rearing practices used by California mothers with children under six years of age.

Hoffman, L. W., "The Father's Role in the Family and the Child's Peer-Group Adjustment," *Merrill-Palmer Quarterly*, Vol. 7 (1961), pp. 97-105. The father's relationship to his wife and child are discussed in terms of data obtained in a larger study dealing with the effects of family structure on the child's peer-group relations.

Nash, J., "The Father in Contemporary Culture and Current Psychological Literature," *Child Development*, Vol. 36, No. 1 (1965), pp. 261-297. The author examines available data concerning the relationships between fathers and their children, and considers the adequacy of present assumptions.

Reiss, I.L., "The Universality of the Family: A Conceptual Analysis," *Journal of Marriage and the Family*, Vol. 27, No. 4 (Nov. 1965), pp. 443-453. Although the nuclear family is not universal, evidence from nonhuman primates suggests that a small structured kinship group is probably required for the nurturance of young children. Cross-cultural evidence is offered to support this hypothesis.

Rodman, H., "Talcott Parsons' View of the Changing American Family," *Merrill-Palmer Quarterly*, Vol. 2, No. 3 (1965), pp. 209-227. An interesting discussion of Parsons' views concerning the American middle-class family. Parsons is perhaps the most widely known contemporary sociologist.

Sears, R.R., E.E. Maccoby, and H. Levin, *Patterns of Child Rearing*. Evanston, Illinois: Row, Peterson, 1957. Important study of the way 379 working-class and middle-class mothers brought up their children in their early years.

Simon, A. W., "Stepchild in the Family: A View of Children in Remarriage," *Journal of Marriage and the Family*, Vol. 29, No. 2 (May 1967), p. 401. An important work in an unexplored area of family relationships.

Stephens, W. N., *The Family in Cross-Cultural Perspective*. New York: Holt, Rinehart and Winston, 1963. This comprehensive cross-cultural survey provides a helpful reference source for psychologists interested in the intercultural aspects of child rearing.

12
SOCIAL DEVELOPMENT

Group relationships are important both for the individual and for society. No culture or subculture can maintain itself unless the individuals who compose it play their respective parts. Modern life, especially, with its large-scale enterprises and complex organizations, would soon disintegrate if people did not learn the principles of social interaction.

• THE IMPORTANCE OF SOCIALIZATION

Whether or not its influence is consciously acknowledged and used by society, the peer group undoubtedly fulfills certain of the child's essential needs. Note these recollections of childhood:

> When I was in grammar school, I wanted very much to bring my friends home with me. But my mother never treated them nicely—in fact, discouraged my bringing them home. She never gave outsiders treats, and we had nothing to play with anyhow.

> The kids in our neighborhood had gobs of fun. Several of us, aged 8 to 12, formed into two small gangs. We broke into each other's clubhouse, challenged each other to "war," and threw rocks and shot fireworks at each other. We spied on each other, and had secret codes for communication. We would edge our notes in black, or smear them with red ink to symbolize blood.

Specifically, what needs do peer groups fulfill as implied in these testimonies? First, the child's peers satisfy "group hunger," or the need to escape loneliness. Second, group relations help the child to establish his self-identity. Helen Keller wrote that she was unable to gain a real sense of self until she learned how to communicate with others. A child sees himself through others' eyes, the way he thinks they perceive him. His desire to change himself, or the reverse, is partly contingent on whether he believes others like him as he is (Rosen et al., 1960). When others praise or criticize, he unconsciously

338

readjusts his self-evaluation upward or downward.

Thus a child's **socialization** takes on the characteristics of radar (Riesman, 1950). He sends out signals, which bounce against targets—his associates; by the way the signals are reflected, he judges how acceptable his behaviors are. In other words, others' reactions tell whether he is on the beam. Case histories of men discharged from the service for bad conduct indicated that they had, as children, antagonized their peers to an unusual degree (Roff, 1961). They had failed to detect, and adapt to, their peers' evaluations of them.

Overall, social contacts, among both lower and higher forms of life, have sweeping, often subtle effects. Even among ants, one that normally works at an intermediate rate steps up production when placed with a rapid worker. For another instance, it is reported that certain fish eat more in company than when alone (Calvin et al., 1961). Among children, note the effect of peer groups on values. In one study, a mere two weeks of equalitarian experience in a racially integrated summer camp resulted in the reduction, though not the elimination, of social distance between Negro and white preadolescents (Campbell and Radke-Yarrow, 1958).

The peer group also affects the child's sense of well-being, and often inflicts deep psychological wounds. In time, an individual learns to empathize, or place himself in the other's shoes; but as a child he is generally insensitive to the hurt his words and actions may cause. Childhood recollections of the following sort are common:

> There was a big girl at school [whose] family was extremely poor; I had heard that her father was a drunkard. I thought she was dreadful to look at. Her head was rather large. Her face was red-skinned, bony and hard . . . and there was an expression on it I did not understand. . . . The other children called the unhappy girl "Stewguts." As she walked home from school, they would form a pack around her, yelping

"Stewguts! Stewguts!" until she went berserk. They were careful to keep out of her reach, for she was quick and strong [Chambers, 1952, p. 117].

Individual Differences in Relationship to a Group

Children vary in their susceptibility to social influence; that is, peer groups have greater impact on some children than on others. The "loner"—the child who spends much time reading or tinkering in his father's shop, or the one who lives on an isolated farm—is affected less than the gang member who spends all his free time with his fellows.

Conversely, children vary in their capacity to affect their peers. Children on higher grade levels have a greater influence on lower-grade children than do other children on lower grade levels (Patel and McRooks, 1956). Children on higher grade levels are also more likely to take definite stands on issues, and to insist on impersonal fairness (Jennings, 1947). However, in such cases, one wonders about cause and effect. Do such characteristics as taking a definite stand cause a child to have influence, or does taking a definite stand result from the confidence accruing to high status?

Sometimes a child who is otherwise socially ineffective wields an influence because of situational factors. In an unhappy classroom, an unpopular child may succeed in triggering group reaction simply because the atmosphere is ripe for it. The powerfully built bully who is normally disliked may be elevated to temporary prominence during an athletic contest.

Peer versus Adult Influence

Authorities are generally agreed that children, collectively and individually, importantly affect each other. But do peers or parents wield a greater influence on children? Implicit in this issue is a further question: To what extent do peer group and adult world compete with or reinforce each other? Are they compatible, providing the child with a consistent base of values, or do they conflict, producing internal conflict? Research on these questions is confusing, although some studies indicate the peer group to be more potent. For example, where peer and teacher judgments conflict, children more often yield to their peers' views than to the teacher's (Berenda, 1950). On the other hand, children more often employ parents' standards in selecting friends (Westley and Elkin, 1956). In brief, there is no easy way to assess peer versus parent influence. Probably parents have a more potent influence on children in some areas, peers in others. However, peer-group and adult influences generally reinforce each other, because the values of both derive from the same culture (Riley et al., 1961).

• STAGES IN SOCIAL DEVELOPMENT

Early Progress

For better perspective, let us now view the child's social growth developmentally, beginning with infancy. Even before he is born, the child is a social force, affecting every member of the family, especially the mother. After birth this unilateral influence gradually gives way to a dynamic social interaction.

In the process, the infant is sometimes described as going through three stages in his early social development. The first stage is asocial, when such reactions as he makes to other persons are vague and ill-defined. The second stage, a presocial one, is characterized by indiscriminate attachment behavior. During this stage, which may begin as early as the thirty-fifth day, the infant accords others a passive attention, as indicated by small movements of arms or legs, or following someone with his eyes. Finally, in the third stage, at about three or four months, he begins to react to individuals. A month or so later he assumes a certain social initiative in smiling at familiar persons, whether or not they have first smiled at him.

By the time the child is a year old,

339

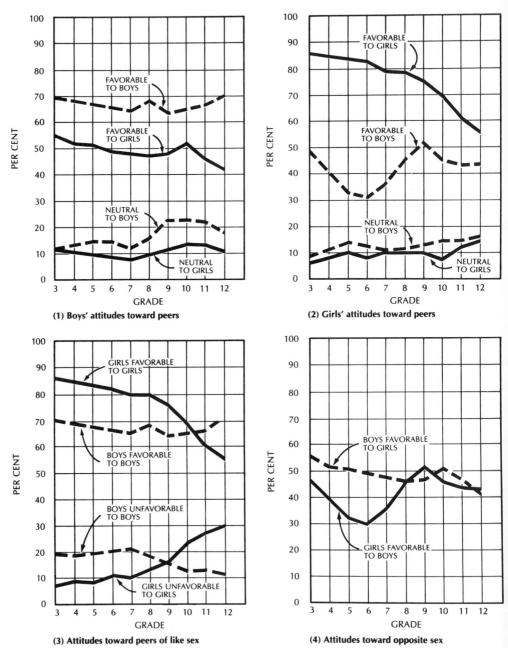

(1) **Boys' attitudes toward peers**

(2) **Girls' attitudes toward peers**

(3) **Attitudes toward peers of like sex**

(4) **Attitudes toward opposite sex**

Children's attitudes toward peers and parents. From D. B. Harris and S. C. Tseng, Children's attitudes

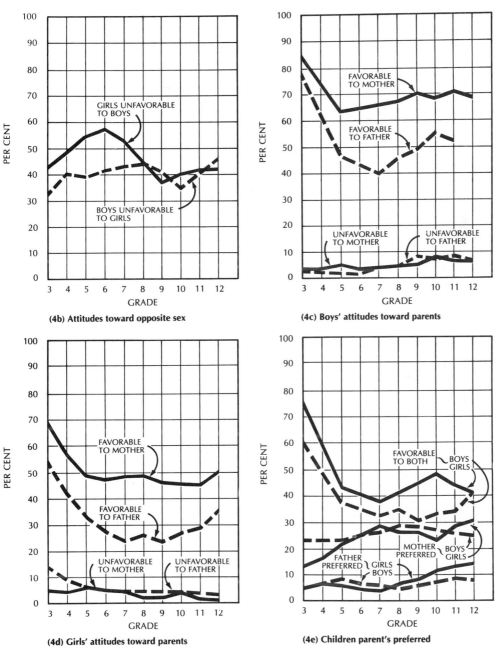

(4b) Attitudes toward opposite sex

(4c) Boys' attitudes toward parents

(4d) Girls' attitudes toward parents

(4e) Children parent's preferred

toward peers and parents as revealed by sentence completions, *Child Development*, 1957, **23,** 403–409.
Reproduced by permission.

he shows definite preferences or dislikes for people. However, he may easily forget them, unless he associates them with some exceptionally emotional experience. As late as 18 months, he may forget his mother if she is away a week or more, but he rapidly re-establishes her acquaintance.

Meanwhile, he may acknowledge another infant by smiling or wiggling, and by six or seven months may deliberately poke at him. From 18 months to two years he engages in **parallel play**; that is, he plays alone but performs actions similar to those of other children present. Not only does he play with the same materials, but he plays with them more resourcefully than when alone. Take digging in the sand, a favorite pastime of two-year-olds. A child fills his pail, transports it a short distance, and empties it. Another child, who has been digging only, takes peripheral note of his neighbor, fills his pail, and empties it. There has been no exchange of words, simply an exchange of ideas (Breckinridge and Murphy, 1963).

Conversations of young children. Even when there is seeming interaction going on, conversation between young children has the bizarre quality of two ships passing in the night. Note this conversation, if it may be so called, between two three-year-olds:

> *First girl:* I rode my bike today.
> *Second girl:* I am going to have a birthday party.
> *First girl:* I rode it fast.
> *Second girl:* I am going to have a cake at my party.
> *First girl:* I fell down and skinned my knee.
> *Second girl:* Would you like to come to my party? [Calvin et al., 1961, p. 110].

Despite such hesitant attempts at social interaction, most children remain predominantly asocial and egocentric through the early years. Nevertheless, some children manifest a precocious social consciousness, as illustrated in these two anecdotal records involving two-year-olds:

Marcia to Teddy, who appeared in a new trouser suit and pink sweater: "Oh! Dat's a pitty dwess, Ted! I didn't see it before." . . .

Ann arrived late on a rainy day in a red slicker and hat to match. Nora and Marcia went up to meet her and gaze at the impressive sight.

Nora: "Dat a wainin' toat?"
Ann: "No."
Nora: "Dat a wainin' hat?"
Marcia went further. She smiled warmly and touched the coat with her hand saying, "Dat's fine, Ann" [Woodcock, 1941, p. 201].

The young child attempts to manipulate others in much the same way that he removes inanimate objects that obstruct his path. As he grows older, he gradually becomes socially sensitive and overtly sympathetic, but never quite outgrows his narcissistic orientation. Altruistic behavior, even at the adult level, is conditioned by the attitude that "I am a fine person, worthy of your praise because of my generosity" (Wright, 1942).

After the early stage of parallel play, when children react in marginal fashion to each other, the children's group grows more conspicuous, while remaining fluid. Throughout a single morning several children may share the same general interest, which depends on no particular child. For example, children may "play house," each child coming or going at will. Gradually this so-called *shifting group play* transforms into *organized group play,* although the organization remains somewhat unstable throughout the preschool period. In time, these groups attain more cohesiveness and are designated as peer groups.

Childhood Play Groups

The preschool play group, already mentioned, is the earliest to emerge from the primary family context, and has been called the "nursery of human nature." In neighborhood play, usually unsupervised, children experiment with all sorts of social relations, engaging in much imitation of adults. Boys and girls

The gang is an adventurous peer group, concentrating on activity rather than interaction.

make their own roles, develop their own caste system, and devise secret tongues. In time, the play groups become more formal; and more stereotyped groups are preferred, like Scouts or clubs of the children's own devising. The older elementary child is a great joiner, because membership gives him a feeling of belonging.

The Clique

The **clique,** a closeknit unisexual group typical of adolescents, sometimes appears as early as age eight, especially among girls. These days, especially, when children learn the manners and morals of older adolescents at an early date, there is considerable overlap in age-grade social groupings. The clique differs in several significant ways from the gang, which is the traditional and more typical preadolescent group. Cliques have stronger interests and mutual affection, and spend more time talking and interacting with each other, chiefly in a social setting. Like adolescent cliques, they meet in hangouts that cater to their respective social classes, and the members enforce rules of dress and behavior on each other.

The Gang

The **gang** is more formalized, with officers, mottoes, and secret codes. It is also more adventurous; and its concentration is on the activity at hand, rather than on personal interaction. Its play is rarely relaxed and easygoing, but is fiercely pursued, and the rules of the game rigidly observed. Each member must yield his personal rights to the needs of the gang. Its activity is not like the play of an adult who goes for a drive, tinkers in his shop, sails a boat, or works in the garden (Strauss, 1952). Both sexes have gangs, though boys' gangs tend to be more persistent, often lasting into the teens; girls' gangs often dissolve early and give place to cliques. Like all groups in an age-graded society, gangs are age-specific, and to a large extent insulated from other age groups. Here a boy tells what is was like to belong to a gang:

Between the ages of nine and thirteen I belonged to a gang known as the

343

"One-M Boys." We were supposed to be the toughest, roughest, best in sports and biggest trouble-makers. We all followed an older boy about twelve years old. The boys in the group were from eight to twelve. I was new in the block so I was accepted on trial into the gang and remained until it split up and enlarged into a social club with girl members. After that time we had many parties and picnics.

The gang days were very exciting and filled with knocking over garbage cans, sitting on the parkway on summer evenings and guessing the makes of cars passing by, and sharing the only cigarette among fourteen boys. Sometimes the patrol car would come by and break us up and tell us to go home. Some of the boys moved on, others argued, while still others watched. We came together again as soon as the cops moved on and each talked of how well we had handled the situation.

. . . And those were the exciting gang days. As I look back it seems silly but it was an unforgettable part of growing up [Rogers, 1957, pp. 133– 134].

Friendship

A special relationship that may exist either inside or outside any of the foregoing groups is **friendship.** It may be defined as a relationship between two persons, characterized by mutual attraction and intimacy, usually without erotic overtones. While childhood friendships are less intense than those of adolescence, they nevertheless fulfill important needs. Friends share confidences about conflicts that might otherwise be repressed. They explore ideas at greater length and in more depth than is feasible with casual acquaintances. Friendship affords companionship and sustenance for the ego—hence possesses special significance in the case of lonely and insecure children. These two recollections give some insight into the importance of childhood friendships:

My best childhood chum was a boy who shared my liking for adventure and novelty. Each of us was constantly introducing to the other some new interest. Mutually, we ran the gamut of a wide range of activities—hunting, fishing, stamp-collecting, astronomy (very elementary), and hosts of others. Also, in our own childish fashion, we discussed at length the meaning of what we felt and saw and thought about people and things and the universe. An advanced, exotic diet for two barefooted youngsters!

The rest of my neighbors did not accept me, and I had just one close friend, who died when I was eleven. On her deathbed she asked for me. I wanted to die also, and was very lonely for one or two years afterward. I would take my accordion and go off alone, and look up at the stars. Since her family had no pictures of her, except one of her head, they put me in her clothes and took a photograph of me, and then appended the picture of her head. Whenever the mother saw me about she would burst out crying, saying I reminded her of her daughter. It made me feel half dead and guilty for living.

It is no easy task for an adult to assess the worth of children's friendships. The significance of a particular relationship depends on how it operates in that case. Attempts made by parents to disrupt an "undesirable" friendship may prove devastating if no substitute is found to fill whatever need that relationship filled.

Significant adults, especially parents and teachers, should provide ample opportunities for children to form friendships. Towns and cities should provide adequate playgrounds; teachers should arrange group and club experience; and parents should teach their children social skills and provide places for entertaining friends.

Many factors account for a friendship—for example, sex and personal compatibility. Friends tend to score alike on tests of dominance, self-sufficiency, self-confidence, security, and social adjustment generally (Reade and English, 1947). Developmental stage has a large effect, too. Younger children choose friends who will fill certain roles as playmates, while older ones select chums more on the basis of personal characteristics (Hicks and Hayes, 1938).

Children also select friends of their own race and social class; in fact, racial cleavage sometimes exists from pre-

Childhood friendships are based on compatibility and common interests.

school years (McCandless and Hoyt, 1961). In many communities, especially in the South, segregation by race still persists. Among older children, socioeconomic status may not inevitably affect prestige and recognition (Jones, 1958).

The manner in which social class modifies friendships varies with age and community. In a new suburban community of California, the tendency of high-school children to choose friends solely from their own class was slight (Udry, 1960). However, in another community, Elkins (1958) found that socioeconomic status plays a significant part in sociometric choices.

Situational factors—even setting— also affect friendship. Among a group of preadolescent campers, choice of friends was significantly affected by the physical structure of the cabin itself (Campbell and Radke-Yarrow, 1958). By relocating bunks and the like, children may actively use cabin space to implement friendships, and to reinforce security-feelings. Sheer geography is a factor, too, for children are hardly mobile enough to choose friends from far away.

Whatever its basis, a friendship, once formed, tends to persist. Among a group of seventh- and eighth-grade chil-

dren, friendship choices showed a high degree of consistency over a year and a half (Singer, 1951).

The Child Society

While friendship involves two persons, the term **"child society"** connotes the complex interaction of children in groups. The play groups of early childhood are too amorphous to deserve the status of "society." However, by middle childhood, children's groups are cohesive and possess a distinctive flavor of their own (Davis, 1940). Thus children's groups of the middle- and late-childhood periods, and later on those of adolescence, may be said to constitute the two major pre-adult subcultures. Their manner of functioning affords evidence of the role of age-mates in the socialization process.

While the adolescent subculture has been recognized, analyzed, and reasonably well portrayed, descriptions of its middle-childhood counterpart are rare. Such as exist are largely impressionistic, without adequate empirical bases. One of the best, albeit impressionistic, treatments is given by Stone and Church (1957), who are quoted later in this section. To paraphrase would be to sacrifice the special flavor of childhood that these writers so effectively convey.

Adults' insights into the child subculture come mostly from memories of their own childhood and are consequently outdated, because the child society itself is largely secret, shut off from adults and adolescents alike. Often adults' puzzlement over children's behavior could be resolved if they possessed some sort of psychological periscope in reverse, which permitted them to peer downward into the child's world. As it is, they take it for granted, assuming that all is open for them to see. Much of their failure to comprehend children stems from their insensitivity to children's membership in, and obligations to, their world-within-a-world. For their part, children have a personal stake in maintaining this separateness, which is

345

necessary to preserve a special sphere into which older persons may not intrude:

> Hence, even young school age children learn to keep their thoughts to themselves; they not only stop thinking out loud, but are likely to do so abruptly and with a vengeance. To bolster their often resistant, bland, masked taciturnity toward adults, as well as their peer-group solidarity, they form secret societies; although a given society may last no more than a few weeks, it may be protected by mortal oaths, binding for life and countersigned in blood (or some convenient substitute such as red ink). . . . It is handed down by word of mouth, it includes many rituals whose original meaning has been lost, and it is hidebound and resistant to alien—in this case, adult—influence [Stone and Church, 1957, pp. 203, 206].

The following reports provide a more recent view of the child society:

> I think I first started paying attention to my physical appearance when I was seven or eight. My concern was not to be stylish, but just to dress enough like others so that I wasn't considered different. I remember that I dreaded cold days because my mother made me wear leggings. When she made me wear rubbers on sunny days, I'd leave them at my friend's house. We played school almost constantly, and nearly got into fights to see who would be the teacher. Then, in the fourth grade there was a change in our social attitudes. We separated into pairs, known to others as "best friends." We were very possessive and required constant reassurance of the exclusiveness of the relationship. With my best friend I would play dolls, and neither of us would let anyone else know. (Female)

> My younger brother is now eleven years old, but I remember his behavior when he was younger. When he was around six, he seemed very affectionate and spent evenings with the family. He played with a small group of boys, usually games of pretend, in the woods near our house. Much emphasis was placed on physical agility. A few years later he became more self-conscious.

He was happiest when dressed in old, dirty clothes, and put up a terrible fuss when any occasion warranted his wearing a suit. He used the word "sissy" in reference to boys who were not tough. He wanted to be all-boy; and vehemently denounced girls. Although he would not admit it, he was concerned with what others thought of him. At the age of either nine or ten he started looking up to my boyfriend as his ideal. This same hero worship and identification with older males I noticed in the other boys, too. (Female)

> Boys (aged six to nine) used to play "cowboys and Indians"; but now they are involved in "Batman and Robin," "James Bond 007," or "Bonanza" (where hardly any Indians ever appear). Their store-bought games relate to these shows—coloring books and models as well. Thus it can be seen that T.V. has a sort of monopoly on the boys' and girls' activities. Nevertheless, boys still love the outdoors, ride their bikes, sell lemonade and comic books for a profit, play baseball, and collect all kinds of "priceless" little objects.
> Girls of this age, by contrast are "sissies." They play with dolls; but dolls are somewhat different from what they used to be. Today's famous doll is "Barbie," and the emphasis is on her social life—her boyfriend, her wardrobe, and her new car. In other words, she is a teenage doll, much older than the "Tiny Tears" of my childhood. While we used to play mother, the young children of today seem content to look forward to adolescence. The girls are also very much oriented toward T.V. They are concerned about the way they look, and want the newest clothes (as advertised) and constantly comb their hair. Yet the "good old days" are not gone. Girls still like to play jumprope, hop-scotch, and "red light, green light" [Koenigsberg, unpublished research].

Significance of Peer Groups

The child society and its functional element, the peer group, convert the child into a **socius,** or group member. The preschool child becomes a member of the human race, while the school child becomes a full-fledged member of his society (Stone and Church, 1957). In fact, he simultaneously becomes a member of two societies. One is the child subdivision of the adult world, where teachers and parents teach him adult-made rules, and where he studies textbooks to prepare him for his later roles. The other is his peer world, where he learns the traditional games, riddles, and rituals transmitted practically intact from one child generation to the next, with no help from adults and sometimes in spite of them.

Another marked characteristic of the child society is this: It is the only age-stage subculture in which the child is really a child. Both preschool child and adolescent attempt, on their respective levels, to be like the adults around them. The preschool child tries out roles of grown-ups who represent to him the ultimate in privilege, attainment, and power. He plays dress-up, builds adult-type houses with his blocks, and simulates family life in the doll house. The adolescent, too, is acutely aware of the adult world, sometimes grasping for, sometimes evading adult responsibilities, but always acutely aware of them. But the school-age child simply "picks his way" through the adult world, pre-occupied with his own childish concerns. It is as though now, and only now, he can be a child (Stone and Church, 1957).

The child society takes full recognition, however unconsciously, of the individual child's need and desire to develop skills: reading and writing, stamp-collecting, making model planes, and scores of others. Deep friendships, such as exist in early adolescence, would prove an encumbrance. The child has friends, of course; but the child society focuses attention on activities in which children are mutually involved, not on each other (Douvan and Adelson, 1966).

Nevertheless, the child is not antisocial. He seeks his peers whenever he can and from them learns the basics of group membership. In his gang, he finds out what it means to operate in democratic or autocratic groups. He tries out all sorts of roles: leader, follower, planner, organizer, and peacemaker. He tests social qualities like loyalty, justice, equity, democracy, conformity, and individualism. He comes to perceive himself, not merely as Tim Smith, but in terms of social labels attached to him.

> Most significantly, he is becoming less egocentric, more detached from his own viewpoint. He is more aware of himself in objective terms, according to the labels that society attaches to him: male or female, age six to twelve, white or colored, poor or rich, and so forth. The gang, too, has its set of labels by which it knows the child and he knows himself. The gang is quick to seize on any idiosyncrasy of appearance, manner, skill, or whatever, and thereafter to treat the child in terms of this trait [Stone and Church, 1957, p. 207].

Subcultural variations. The peer group's impact on children varies somewhat with the subculture. For example, city life is complex, presenting the youngster with diverse problems. In such a heterogeneous situation, a child needs experience gained from people of varied backgrounds, such as may be represented by his peers. Within the city, the peer group has a more pervasive influence on lower- than on upper-class children. Since lower-class children, especially boys, are permitted to wander more freely, their exposure to peer influence is correspondingly greater (Psathas, 1957). Boys of all classes are permitted to range abroad more widely than girls, and they have more time to spend with their peers. Offsetting this factor to some extent is the girl's greater concentration on interpersonal relations, especially in late childhood, as contrasted with the boy's concern with more impersonal objects and situations.

The significance of peer groups also varies with age, which, in age-graded societies, may define the number and kind of such groupings, and their functioning. In Western cultures, as the child matures, he has increasingly greater access to his peers and is increasingly

347

influenced by them. At the same time, his peer activities become more organized, making him less a free agent.

Significance for the larger society. Peer groups relate not only to the child, but to the society of which these groups are a part. In modern societies, peer groups hold special significance, because social change produces a gap between generations. A child turns to age-mates for the understanding lacking in an older, and in his mind outdated, generation.

Peer groups are found in all societies, but in some they possess more importance than in others. For example, children in the United States apparently accept peer opinion more readily than do Swiss children, who possess more of the Old World outlook. Two groups of elementary pupils, in Geneva, Switzerland and Winnetka, Illinois, read stories such as this:

> A group of children of your age want to give a surprise birthday party to their scout leader. One boy has accepted the responsibility of decorating the room. He wonders whom he should ask for advice.

In interviews, 70% of the Swiss children insisted that teachers and parents would offer the best advice, while only 7% of the Americans believed the adult's advice would be any better than an artistically talented pupil's. The American child, by contrast with the Swiss, transfers his dependency from parents to peers at an early age (Boehm, 1957).

Perhaps peer groups are most significant in societies where the kinship unit fails to provide full social status, or to meet adequately the social needs of its members. In modern Western society, where parents often have their own concerns, they are glad to shuck that part of their former role that required frequent all-family entertainment (Eisenstadt, 1962).

Roles in the Group

Within the child society, and its operational groupings, each child plays one or more roles. In fact, the effective functioning of any group involves a division of roles among its members. Certain roles are typical, while others are specific to the needs of certain kinds of groups. Ordinarily, children's groups, whether informal or organized, have a leader; often a servant, who runs errands and does the dirty work; a funny guy, who furnishes the entertainment; and a parliamentarian, who determines rules. Many roles are highly complicated blends of function, not easily defined. Hence any attempt to make a complete listing of roles is futile.

The role of leader. To illustrate how childhood roles may operate, consider the role of leader, which has been studied more than any other. Ordinarily, child leaders excel in intelligence and social status, although the type of leader chosen varies somewhat with the group (Parten, 1933). A very bright child might be a leader in a class for the gifted, but not in a just-average group. The latter would prefer someone superior to but more nearly like themselves.

Child leaders have different styles for exerting influence.

Leadership is not a homogeneous quality, exerted always in the same manner. Child leaders have different styles for exerting influence. Among kindergarten children, Hanfmann (1935) distinguished "the objective leader," who dominates by strong interest in constructive play; "the social leader," who takes into account the needs of others; "the gangster," who uses social play as a means of displaying his power; and "the destroyer," who achieves domination by immobilizing other persons. Similarly, Parten (1933) described preschool leaders as "diplomats," who use artful and indirect suggestion, or as "bullies," who boss the group with brute force.

The way a specific child exercises leadership depends on his own traits. Boys of low intelligence are likely to be more coercive and somewhat inconsistent in their efforts to influence other children. Naturally, their social power declines with age (Zander and Van Egmond, 1958).

How children acquire their roles. The role a child plays in the group depends both on the group's needs and his own traits. A children's adventure club will choose as its leader one whose daring insures a crop of zestful experiences. A neighborhood football team will select a nimble-footed, lean athlete. Even a boy of lesser talents may find a satisfactory role if the others like him. As one boy testified, "When my friends started a neighborhood football team, I was elected water boy unanimously!"

In general, the child unconsciously fits into those roles which he is accustomed to and which are compatible with his traits. If he possesses strong status needs, but lacks leadership qualities himself, he may become the leader's "lieutenant." If he has a pleasant, peace-loving disposition, and is well-liked by the other, he assumes the role of peacemaker.

The child is not always automatically assigned a role; first he must win a place in the group. The friendly, social child will more readily make a place for

himself than one who is rebellious, hostile, or withdrawn (Smith, 1950). In some cases, a child rejected by one group may find a place in another, perhaps composed of other rejects like himself, or of persons who represent atypical views or behaviors compatible with his own. Or he may seek a place in groups older or younger. A child may become something of an errand boy to an older group, or assume a more dominant role in a younger one:

> Henry was one of six children, and had trouble getting along with children his age. However, he found he could be something of a boss by limiting his activities to those of the younger children in his family and neighborhood.

When a child goes to a new town, or new environment, he has to earn his role anew. If the new environment is strange, this task may be difficult:

> Although I had lived in several neighborhoods, I was unfamiliar with rural life when my parents moved to a farm. All the kids around there had been born and bred on a farm, and were tough. Soon after I arrived, the kids had a mule to ride. All the others had ridden horses, but I'd never ridden one. They subtly dared my sisters and me to ride the mule. I accepted the challenge but my sisters didn't. My sisters were eventually accepted, but, due to this incident, I "made it" more quickly than they.

Children's roles tend to persist over time. Even in kindergarten, roles are relatively stable. In one preschool group, children maintained consistent statuses for dominance and submission, though not for resistance, including noncompliance, or self-defense (Gellert, 1961). Among older children, roles are even more stable. In one study, children were found to have their pecking order in all the primary groups to which they belonged—home, school, and peer group. At home a child might rank below parents and older children; in school,

349

he would rank below the teacher as well as more popular pupils; in the peer group, however, he might be leader. Or he might be the spoiled child at home, maneuvering and dictating to his parents, while unable to establish any sort of role in the peer group (Clark and van Sommers, 1961).

Functions of role. Role-playing is also an important factor in a child's socialization. Through trying out various roles, he comes to know himself better and to know what part he can play most effectively. Furthermore, he gains an understanding of social needs and group processes—an essential acquisition for citizens of a democratic society.

On the other hand, role-playing poses certain problems. Sometimes a child gets stuck with an unfortunate role. A small boy who is the group's scapegoat may become so accustomed to making do with whatever scraps the group hands out that he comes to perceive himself as a lesser order of being. At other times, personality conflict may result. A child may be assigned a role for which he is poorly suited. Polly is chosen to direct the class play because she is popular; but she is a poor organizer. Again, the child who was a leader in his own lower-class neighborhood may have trouble adjusting to a minor role when he is transported to an integrated school.

• FACTORS AFFECTING SOCIAL DEVELOPMENT

Certain of the influences that ultimately determine the child's social adjustment may date from the prenatal stage. Fetal activity correlates with social perception at ages two and five; and social perception at that age correlates significantly with the same trait at ages 22 to 25. Note also that cardiac response, which is measurable in utero, relates to personal style, which in turn affects social relations. And since the pregnant mother's emotional experience, as well as other stresses, may affect the developing fetus, it seems possible that such factors may help lay the pattern for the child's later social development (Sontag, 1963).

Animal studies throw further light on the development of social behavior. Harlow's monkeys, given mother surrogates of cloth or wire, failed to show normal affectional behavior in adulthood. Harlow (1962, p. 6) writes:

> We have seen them sitting in their cages strangely mute, staring fixedly into space, relatively indifferent to people and other monkeys. Some clutch their heads in both hands and rock back and forth—the autistic behavior pattern that we had seen in babies raised on wire surrogates. Others when approached or even left alone go into violent frenzies of rage, grasping and tearing at their legs with such fury that they sometimes require medical care.

On the basis of this and similar studies, one may conclude that social experience of some sort during infancy is essential. However, socialization may proceed unevenly, rather than in straight-line fashion; and the effects of relevant experience may be greater at certain times than others. Scott, for example, concludes that certain experiences in infant socialization are especially significant: the first smiling response to visual stimulation; learning to walk, which permits some independence from parents; and learning to talk, which provides a whole new mode of social interaction. The points in life when significant new relations are formed are also critical—for instance, during infancy, the period of primary socialization; and during puberty, when sex relations are formed (Scott, 1963). Other times may be critical in terms of possible social damage. For example, after seven months of age an overdependency syndrome appears, when children cry excessively if separated from the mother. If a child is removed to a foster home at about this time, he may be much upset (Gray, 1958).

Family Relations and Social Development

So far we have seen data about parents' effects on the social relations of preschoolers, but parents affect the older child's social relations too. For instance, parents may control intergroup contacts by implicitly or explicitly indoctrinating their children. Mrs. Jones, a social climber, may lead Sally to believe the neighborhood children are not good enough for her. As a result, Sally strives for, but fails to achieve, friends in an upper-class group who possess the money, manners, and clothes that she lacks.

Other family influences are more subtle, but no less important. For one thing, the child's peer group role may reflect his role in the home. The family scapegoat submits more readily to a lesser role in the peer group. Again, parental punitiveness and restrictiveness may create a hostile child who is aggressive toward his peers (Marshall, 1961). At other times, unsatisfactory relations between the parents may upset the child and lead to maladjustments that make him unpopular.

The following cases are illustrative of ways in which family experience may affect the child's social development:

Since Peter was unhappy at home, and was often beaten by his parents, he had a special need for friends. He tried to buy them by offering them money, which simply struck the other boys as a great joke. The fighting built up so in his home that one day Peter tried to kill his parents. Others were happy enough to conclude that he was crazy.

Thirteen years after Johnny died another boy was born, whom the parents named Johnny, too. They satisfied his every whim, so that he became a tyrant both in the family and among his peers. Finally, his parents retaliated, and began punishing him severely. Before, nothing he did was wrong; now nothing was right. Johnny learned the get-tough policy well, and fought other children constantly. He succeeded in making an enemy of every child in the neighborhood.

The effect of siblings on each others' peer relations is both complex and vital, but often overlooked. Koch (1957) found first-borns more likely than second-borns to play with children younger than themselves. Though children generally preferred the same sex as playmates, preference for the opposite sex was more often expressed by those with siblings of the opposite sex than by those with same-sex siblings. The children with opposite-sex siblings had become more accustomed to dealing with the other sex.

Extrafamilial Influences

Teachers. Among persons affecting children's social adjustment, teachers are especially significant. They may create a warm climate that fosters friendliness, or a tense, formal one in which children's feelings become dammed up and erupt on each other. Especially important is their manner of treating children in the presence of their peers. In one study, a teacher praised only those children who sat in odd-numbered seats. In subsequent sociometric tests, children who had been praised received more choices than did their less-favored classmates (Flanders and Havumaki, 1960). There is also evidence that teachers' responses to high-status children are more favorable than their responses to less popular children (Lippitt and Gold, 1959). This leads to a vicious circle in which teacher and child ratings reinforce one another. Ultimately, the child becomes aware of his rejected status, and his resultant defensive behaviors further confirm his devalued position.

Social situation. An often overlooked factor in social development is the social situation. Its differential aspects elicit quite different social behaviors. In one study, both among normal and disturbed children, eating situations induced friendly behavior, while competitive games elicited unfriendly actions. If certain attitudes and activities are to become habituated, those situations must be chosen which encourage them (Rausch et al., 1959).

The overall atmosphere in the group of pleasantness or unpleasantness has a contagious effect on its members. In a study of elementary children, three groups who played a game were rewarded, while the rest were not. Children in the rewarded groups later expressed more favorable attitudes toward their fellows (Lott and Lott, 1960).

These illustrations indicate how important the setting may be in determining social development:

> I was the only girl my age on the street, and was forced to find a place among the boys. I learned to fight, climb trees, and hit a ball hard. My need for acceptance was the greater because I was adopted. My real parents had bypassed the responsibility for my upbringing, and I had to prove myself to overcome the resultant inferiority feelings.

> I lived on a farm, and had no friends my age. My sole companions were a brother and sister.

These experiences are modified, in varying degree, by the child's own traits. The following experience, for example, undoubtedly had an impact on the peer relations of the child involved; however, the specific nature of that effect depended on the personality traits of the child:

> As a child, I was slow developing control of my bladder. Whenever I felt tense, I had to obtain relief in a hurry. This was a great strain on me, especially in school. Once, after the teacher refused three times to let me leave the room, I simply didn't make it to the boys' room. After "the accident," I hid in the boys' room and cried, wondering what to do. The teacher sent for me, and the whole class saw me in my saturated state. For a long time they ridiculed me, some of them for years. This incident was a great blow to my self-confidence, and made me feel inadequate and less than normal.

• PROBLEMS OF SOCIAL ADJUSTMENT

Popularity

Some children have far greater problems of social adjustment than others — for example, in the area of popularity. Many factors account for the widespread variance in children's popularity. Not surprisingly, friendliness and sociability foster acceptance; while withdrawal, rebelliousness, and hostility lead to rejection (Smith, 1950). A further factor is the child's self-concept, which affects both the way he perceives and is perceived by others. In a study of fourth-, sixth-, and eighth-graders, Reese (1961) found that children with moderate self-concepts were best accepted, those with highest self-concepts next best accepted, and those with lowest self-concepts least accepted. In a study of school children, those who were most dependent on adults were least popular with their peers (McCandless and Bilous, 1961).

Not only high self-concept but also intelligence may relate to social adjustment. Although especially gifted children tend to be above average in social skills, they may have so many interests that they spend little time with people. Besides, few children near their own age are congenial to them. However, above-average intelligence is apparently of help in social adjustment. In a study of sixth-grade children, high-status children had an average IQ of 109, low-status children, 101. In general, the slow learners and retarded are less well-accepted, as plentiful research shows (Campbell, 1964).

Gronland (1959) summarized research on the traits of children who receive above-average sociometric choices from their peers. They tend to possess higher intelligence and scholastic achievement. They also have greater social and athletic skills, and participate more frequently than normal in sports and social activities. In general, they have more pleasing appearances, more social and heterosexual interests, and better personalities. In short, at least moderate superiority in all characteristics correlates with popularity. However, a large deviation in any of these characteristics contributes to lower popularity status.

Situational factors also limit the qualifications for social acceptance. In a small athletically-oriented school, physical skills will become a boy's passport to popularity. In a sophisticated suburban community, intelligence may be important.

The following recollections involve common problems of social acceptance:

Membership in a low-status group. When I was in the fifth grade, a girl gave a pajama party. One girl was not invited, merely because she was in a slow group at school. We tried to keep her from hearing about the party, but she found out and was deeply hurt.

Disliked trait. As a child, I had the constant feeling that others did not understand my inner feelings, and I would finally try to explain them to people. I finally realized that others avoided me because they thought I talked too much, so I tried to break the habit, but found it wasn't easy.

Lack of social experience. I didn't learn to get along with others because I had no girl friends in my neighborhood. There was one girl, but I was forbidden to play with her because of her mother's reputation.

Lack of desire to belong. [Whittaker Chambers (1952, p. 115) indicates how his own traits constituted a barrier between himself and others:] I felt that there was a wall between me and other children. I used to think it was of their making. I realized by degrees that it was of mine. If I had really wanted the fellowship that lay on the other side of the wall, I would have battered my way or scrambled over. The real wall was my own indifference and my liking for solitude. No matter how much I played or mixed, I never gave myself wholeheartedly. I was always making my own peculiar observations. In the end, I always withdrew to my own chief interests—books and nature

Accruing to popularity are both benefits and hazards. Popularity sustains the child's ego and ensures social experience and training in social roles. However, the popular child may become the victim of his own social status. He may lack time for more solitary pursuits, such as tinkering with tools or reading, which are essential for certain aspects of his development. He may also come to value popularity for its own sake, and permit himself to be manipulated by others.

Conformity

To maintain his role in the group, a child may become group-dependent, incapable of operating on his own. Thus he becomes a puppet to others' purposes—a conformist, trusting others' judgments above his own.

Age and sex are especially important variables in the tendency to conform. Younger children conform more readily than older ones, and females more readily than males, at least among older children. In one study, children under 10 proved more likely than older ones to be influenced by others' reports.

Conformity also varies with subculture and social class. Rural children conform more than urban children, and lower-class children more than upper-class children (Iscoe et al., 1953). When confronted by contrary judgment, children of the third, sixth, ninth, and eleventh grades who held lower social-class status yielded more often than those with higher status (Harvey and Rutherford, 1961). Personality factors are also important in determining children's susceptibility to group persuasion. In a study of nine-year-olds, boys rated high on dependency proved more susceptible to others' suggestions than those rated low on dependency (Jakubczak and Walters, 1959).

Implicit in all such research is the idea that nonsusceptibility to persuasion indicates greater strength of personality than susceptibility. Nevertheless, conformity to majority opinion, when discriminating, serves a real function. Any society would swiftly disintegrate without it. Besides, nonconformity sometimes represents antagonism toward the majority, rather than genuine conviction of the correctness of one's own view.

Rejection

A third social problem is rejection. Children, especially, treat "rejects" unkindly. One child asked another, whose father was pot-bellied, whether he was going to have a baby. Another asked a classmate if he ever bathed. In one case, two unattractive youngsters were told they had been elected king and queen for the class dance. However, when the pair arrived at the party, the group surrounded them and yelled, "April-fool, April-fool—whatever made you think you'd be chosen?" (Daly, 1951).

Children with low popularity ratings are of three general types. One type is the maverick who cares little for group life. From his earliest years Lindy was a precocious musician, and spent relatively little time with the fellows. A second type of child is not so much socially rejected as socially neglected. Jane was so colorless and devoid of energy that she was rarely thought about, much less included in social activities. A third type, who wishes to belong but is actively rebuffed, lacks sufficiently adequate social skills to be successful. Laura made all sorts of efforts to be popular, but failed because she talked loudly, dressed sloppily, and displayed poor manners.

Help for rebuffed youngsters may take many forms. The soundest is basic and requires much time. It involves discovering why a child is tense and unhappy, hence disagreeable to others. The chronically anxious child, concluded Koppitz (1957), is also an unhappy, socially ineffectual child. Adults must also help children learn the rules of the social game, including how to make a positive contribution to groups they wish to join. Note this example:

In a nursery school, two girls were playing lion in an abandoned aviary. A third girl ran over to join them. "Go away," roared the lions, kicking the door shut in her face. The third girl stood her ground. "You lions are hungry," she said. "I will feed you." She got some blades of grass and poked them through the netting at the ravening lions. Soon she was roaring in the cage while the late lions were out hunting grass for her [Landreth, 1958, p. 235].

Not all children are so ingenious; adults must assist them to make themselves acceptable. For example, Sammy's father taught him to make bicycle repairs; and Sammy wins friends by helping them fix their bikes. Sandra's mother, upon sensing her daughter's lack of social initiative, arranged a play area in the cellar, which lured children there.

Not always does such help instantly pay off. Great persistence may be required for a child to create a new image. Sue brought to school a live fish, about eight inches long, cramped into a jar of water. Before class, one child asked, "How long are you going to keep it?" "Until it dies," she replied carelessly. Others were shocked at Sue's apparent lack of concern. Perceiving their reaction, she asked the teacher to help her keep it alive. However, removal of the fish from the classroom did not restore Sue to her classmate's favor (Brinkmann and Brinkmann, 1963). Such a child needs auxiliary boosts to her ego from whatever adults may be handy, pending restoration to the group's good graces. Otherwise, she may project her unhappiness onto the group, generating further hostility.

Prejudice

A special form of rejection stems from **prejudice.** Data differ on the question: How early do children become aware of racial and ethnic differences? Criswell (1937) failed to detect such awareness until children were eight to ten years old. However, most researchers report racial reactions even among preschoolers. As early as age three, white children may display negative reactions to black children. In an intensive study in the South, children aged two-and-a-half to three-and-a-half manifested racial cleavage. One of the recorded sequences revealed the beginnings of prejudice:

Lyle (white) and Dan (black) were in the bathroom washing their hands. Without immediate provocation, Lyle looked up at Dan and said, "I don't like black and you're black. I don't like your hair or your nose and I won't play with you" [Stevenson and Stevenson, 1960, p.61].

In another study, black children aged three to seven demonstrated a well-developed concept of racial differences, in terms of skin color—an understanding that seemed completely stable by age seven. Initially, preference was shown for white skin color, but it decreased gradually from ages four to seven. The tendency to prefer a white skin was stronger among Northern children and among those with light skins.

In still another study, indications were that preference for one race might not mean rejection of the other. In a Southern nursery school, children of both races, in making picture choices, preferred white children over black. However, in practice few children of either race rejected each other for racial reasons (Morland, 1962). Undoubtedly, these same children will react differently when older. In time, each race develops racial perceptions and rationalizations for their respective attitudes. The white child develops patterns of exclusion and a philosophy of prejudice to support them. For the black child there are increasingly defensive reactions and conflicts over group-belongingness (Radke et al., 1949).

Many studies have indicated ego-defensiveness on the part of minority groups. In one study, both Jewish and black students, after hearing about achievements of their own and of other racial-ethnic groups, remembered more clearly the achievements of their own group. This effect was more prominent among minority than majority groups (Gustafson, 1957).

Even young black children vary in the way they manifest need for satisfactory racial identification:

Tony A. admits that his parents look like the pictured black couple, but finds it necessary to add, about his father and mother, "they're good people." Viola likes the white doll better "'cause it's cuter than the other one" (the black doll to which she has given scarcely a glance). Tony R. evades self-identification, as a good many of these children do occasionally. He says that he was like neither of the baby dolls when he was a baby. But he adds wistfully "I was called 'Butch' when I was a baby. Is that (white) one 'Butch'?" Joan G. says of the matching boy dolls that the black one is nicer because "the white one is too heavy." But her resolution to like black fails her when we come to the girl dolls. She fondles the white one and then—briefly—the black one. "This one," she says, "this one I'm holding (black)—it just gets on my nerves" [Goodman, 1952, p. 124].

One mother describes an incident with her son:

One night when he wasn't yet seven he did a queer thing. After he'd had his bath he put powder all over himself—he loves to do that—and he came out of the bathroom with this powder all over his face. I said to him "you look awful—go wipe that stuff off your face." He looked at himself in the mirror and said: "No, I don't mummy. I look just like a little white boy now" [Goodman, 1952, p. 124].

Prejudice may also relate to social class, although its effect on social acceptance varies with the community. Among students in a California high school, there was little tendency to discriminate on the basis of social class. However, in many communities dominated by middle-class adults, lower-class children have much less chance to attain social status. However, exceptions may occur in individual cases—for instance, when the boy is an athletic star or the girl especially pretty.

• A PERSPECTIVE ON CHILDREN'S SOCIAL ADJUSTMENT

Informal estimates of children's social adjustment are often fallacious. We may be misled by appearances; for example, we conclude that Sammy has been socially rejected because he spends long hours in his father's workshop. Actually, Sammy may be a secure, likable boy whose peers recognize his mechanical abilities and accept as natural his somewhat atypical life style. Besides, the boy is so talented that a somewhat unsocial pattern may be optimal for him. In other cases, adults may perceive a child only in somewhat formal settings and hence erroneously judge the child's adaptability to a wider range of situations. The teacher who is a strict disciplinarian fails to realize that certain children, who adapt well to the classroom setting, are ignored or outright rejected in the rough-and-tumble child world outside.

To establish unbiased methods of judging children's social maturity, various instruments have been devised. Tests of traits like "social intelligence" and "social sensitivity" are available, but more research on what they measure is needed. One well-known test, the Vineland Social Maturity Scale, does not rate an individual's sociability as such; it measures his ability to deal with interpersonal situations. Though designed for use with persons from birth to age 25, the scale has proved most useful with young children and the feeble-minded. Among the best-known standardized tests dealing wholly or in part with social adjustment are the Washburne Social-Adjustment Inventory and the Bell Adjustment Inventory; but the most popular technique is the **sociogram,** developed by Moreno and his associates.

This device, which grew out of sociometry, is designed to disclose groupings and interpersonal relations among children. For instance, each child may be asked with whom he would prefer sharing some common activity at home or on the school playground. Examination of the results, graphically portrayed, yields information on several points: Which children are pairs—that is, name each other? Which children are named most frequently, or conversely, by no one? Are there cliques or subgroups, as suggested when several children name each other but receive few votes from the rest?

One must not, however, go beyond what the data warrant. The sociogram points out relationships; it neither evaluates nor explains them. To throw light on the data, one may ask younger children orally, or older ones in writing, to state reasons for their choices. Thus, Jennings (1950, p. 218) quotes reasons for several children's first choice as follows:

> When I come to school and I don't feel good, she will cheer me up, and she is always a pal; she is always happy and she makes others happy, too. When I am with her she cheers me up.

> Well, I act silly because I am nervous, and he acts silly out of being glad. He is always showing me how to get hold of myself.

Note, in Jennings' sociogram, that the children have indicated first, second, and third choices of classmates. Janet Toll is a star—that is, preferred by many as their favorite companion. One wonders why her own first two choices were boys, though she seems well-liked by both sexes. Janet, Michael, and Saul compose a triangle, having chosen each other as mutual friends. Since each of these three has been named by several others, we may conclude that this small group holds considerable power in the group as a whole. At the other extreme is Mary, an isolate not chosen by anyone. However, we cannot be sure she is an

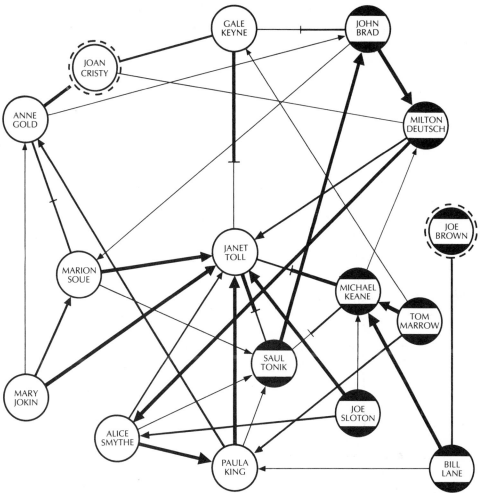

Sociogram showing the social structure of a classroom, obtained by asking each child to make first, second, and third choices among his classmates for a specific social activity. Partially black circles indicate boys. A plain line between two children indicates that the choice was reciprocal; an arrow indicates a one-way choice. Thicknesses of lines indicate first (heavy line), second, and third choices. Names of children who were absent are encircled with broken lines. From H. H. Jennings, Sociometric grouping in relation to child development, in *Fostering mental health in our schools*, 1950 Yearbook of the Association for Supervision and Curriculum Development. Washington, D.C.: National Education Association, 1950. P. 218. Reproduced by permission.

out-and-out "reject," because choices were made with reference to a specific activity. Her high scholastic ability might lead to greater acceptance in classroom activities. Needless to say, all relevant data must be used to interpret the sociogram.

There are also other problems interpreting the sociogram. For one thing, it is hard to decide just what specific sociometric choices mean. A child may be relatively well-liked by everyone but rarely chosen as best friend. Or he

may be chosen by several for a specific activity in which he excels, but rarely selected in other situations. Again, children's choices are often made on the basis of surface traits; and one should reserve judgment about what they imply. The chief function of the sociogram is to provide leads for further research, and to raise questions to check against further evidence.

Indeed, popularity is a tricky criterion by which to gauge adjustment. A child may be the "popular type," but possess no friendship in real depth. He may pursue popularity for its own sake, substituting the glad-hand approach for solid accomplishment. Moreover, the overtly popular child may be deeply disturbed inside. His endless pursuit of social activity may hide a fear of confronting himself. On the other hand, popularity is often what it seems, one indication of good relations both with oneself and with others.

In short, the significance of popularity depends on the child and his needs. The highly talented child who holds low status in the average school would probably acquire higher status in a class for the gifted. Some children care little for popularity anyhow. They are content with being lesser lights in their social set. Finally, neither popularity nor the lack of it tells anything about the discontinuities between the child's and the group's values. A specific child may derive much fun and personal gratification from group experience. Later on as an adult he enjoys a round of parties and belongs to many clubs; another child, who eschews wide social acquaintance, may become the "solid citizen" who exerts himself on behalf of community achievement. The whole question of what overt social behaviors mean in terms of ultimate personal adjustment or social effectiveness is a complex one.

The Adult's Role in Improving Children's Social Adjustment

The foregoing points should not become the adult's excuse for abdicating responsibility. Adults should establish the sort of climate in which favorable interaction occurs. Depending on the activity involved, a greater or lesser degree of democracy may be permitted. In Lewin and his associates' (1939) experiment, described in the next chapter, a climate somewhere between the autocratic and democratic seemed to work best. The social climate is also modified by the environmental setting and the nature of activities provided. No single setting or arrangement is ideal; each must relate to the needs of specific children. A child from a crowded

home will need a quiet corner in which to play; a singleton may prefer romping with a group. Games themselves elicit, and tend to reinforce, certain attitudes and behaviors. For example, sand play seems to produce quarreling, while doll-corner activities lead to cooperation (Green, 1933).

Even if the probable effects of a wide range of activities are known, the adult must make value judgments about what kinds of behavior will ultimately prove most useful for particular children. Will the cooperation fostered by doll play inhibit the competitiveness boys will need for adult society? Again, will doll play have the overall effect of feminizing the boy or making him a better father? There are no readily available answers to such questions. Nevertheless, adults should realize that social learning takes place in conflict as well as in cooperative play.

Research Relating to Social Adjustment

Scientific interest in the importance of children's peer relations dates at least as far back as the turn of the century. However, not until the late 1920s did peer group research begin to mount. Even then, theory was sketchy or missing, but empirical work was beginning to contribute significant bits of information. In the next decade, research interest in children's group processes burgeoned, along with more sophisticated procedures. Since the 1940s, which saw a lull of interest, the output of research has been slowly rising.

Nevertheless, Lambert, writing in 1960, said, "The area of interpersonal behavior in children has hardly been tapped." Lambert's conclusion can hardly be questioned. Since 1940 research and theory have been not so much new as a refinement and extension of early work. The social setting, including the peer group, is still not given the emphasis it deserves, for several reasons. First, the centrality of the parent-child relationship in Western cultures and the concentration on this relationship to the exclusion of other social influences have obscured the effects of socialization in collective settings (Bronfenbrenner, 1962). Second, the widespread belief that infants' social patterns stem originally from the alleviation of personal physical needs has directed attention almost exclusively to the child's caretaker, the mother. The idea that a sibling may become an object of attachment is often overlooked. A final reason is historical. Studies of interactional relationships stem largely from early psychoanalysts who perceived child development in terms of the close-knit European family unit of half a century ago (Schaffer and Emerson, 1964).

Distortions derive not only from limitations on what is studied, as cited above, but also from weaknesses in the methodology and theory. There is no overall theory of social development available; and psychologists have simply invented social-behavior classifications as a means of ordering loosely related data. Such classifications tend to be logical rather than psychological, arbitrarily partitioning the essential continuity and interrelatedness of social growth (Thompson, 1952). At worst, social growth is divided along an age continuum into non-overlapping stages of growth. For example, early adolescence is classified as the stage for cliques, although cliques may penetrate childhood or persist into adulthood.

Nor are purely methodological aspects of peer-relations research much better. Different observers often report quite different things as the salient features of children's social behavior (Thompson, 1952). In many cases, researchers remain in full view of the children under study, thus modifying usual behaviors. In fact, the general looseness of procedures makes it difficult to distinguish empirically sound reports from those of questionable worth. Finally, few studies reflect, even reasonably well, the complex subcultural factors that color a specific child's experience in socialization.

Nevertheless, certain encouraging trends are emerging. Broad conceptual schemes are assuming more prominence; and attempts are being made to bridge the gap between laboratory and natural settings. Finally, research teams, using the more sophisticated statistical procedures permitted by computers, are determining how the multiple factors in the behavioral equation relate to each other.

• SUMMARY

Children are described as normally going through certain stages of social development. By the age of three months, babies progress from an asocial stage to a social one, in which they show differential reactivity to others. In early childhood, play is **parallel,** with children simply playing side by side and reacting only peripherally to each other. Later the children's group is more conspicuous, though still fluid. Finally it merges into organized group play. By early school days the play groups become more formal, and even in late childhood **cliques** sometimes form. In childhood both sexes have **gangs,** though boys' gangs are more persistent than girls'. Childhood **friendships** are also important, though less so than in adolescence.

While friendship ordinarily suggests two persons, the term **child society** connotes cohesive groups with distinctive characteristics. This subculture is characterized by rituals, fads, secret codes, jokes, games, sports, and make-believe. Adults are surprisingly unaware of what goes on in the current child society, often assuming that it has changed little since their own childhood. Boys are normally active and adventurous, while girls play dress up, school, and keeping house. Boys spend more time in gangs, learning sex lore and improving their physical prowess. However, the line between appropriate play for the sexes is growing less rigid, and boy-girl relations are becoming more friendly.

The child society holds considerable importance for its members. Its activities represent the one subculture

359

in which the child performs as a child. It converts him into a group member and helps socialize him. It permits him to develop his personal and social skills through group games and activities. The significance of the child society for the larger society is indirect and unclear. The child indeed learns how to operate in groups, but this country makes little conscious use of child groups.

Within the child society each individual plays a typical role or roles. Such roles include leader, follower, scapegoat, clown, and others. A particular child's role depends on the group's needs and his own motivations and traits. His roles may or may not be compatible with his own or the group's best interests.

Factors affecting the child's social development are numerous and may even date from the prenatal stage. Both fetal activity and social experience in infancy correlate with social apprehension later on. Family life, too, is important. Parents implicitly and explicitly control children's group contacts and affect their social attitudes. A child's peer relations also depend somewhat on the number, sex, and spacing of his siblings. Various extrafamilial influences affect children's social adjustment, too. Teachers' and peers' ratings of a child tend to reinforce each other. Another factor is situation, since different social situations evoke different behaviors.

Whether children win their social spurs depends in large measure on their personal traits. Moderate superiority in all characteristics, including strength of ego, appearance, and social interests, correlates with popularity. Physical handicaps prove a particular disadvantage. In their attempt to win group favor some children, more often girls, overconform. A certain amount of conformity is necessary and even desirable if group goals are to be won; however, some individuals simply adopt it as a way of life and use it as a way of gaining favor and avoiding decision-making. Among factors associated with a child's

rejection are loud talk, sloppy dress, bad manners, and unfortunate personality traits generally. Another cause of rejection is prejudice, which may be acquired quite early and usually reflects parental views.

Several factors obstruct evaluation of children's social adjustment. There is no common agreement concerning what sort of adjustment is best for children generally or for a particular child. **Sociometric techniques** have been devised to disclose children's groupings and interpersonal relations; however, the interpretation of data from such instruments is tricky, partly because the significance of any particular child's social relations depends on his personality and needs.

The adult's role in children's social development is to establish the sort of climate in which favorable interaction can occur, and in which children can learn to perform social roles effectively. The adult should help the rejected child show himself in a better light. However, adult efforts should be based on more adequate research than is now available. There remains much looseness in research procedures and many gaps in theory. However, progress is being made, and hopefully children will someday receive needed help in making the peer-group social register.

• SUGGESTED QUESTIONS
AND ACTIVITIES

1. Observe a group of children at play, and set down anecdotally whatever especially interests you. Bring your report to class for group discussion.
2. Do you note any present trends in children's social activities that seem unhealthy?
3. Are "togetherness" and "democracy" emphasized to an unwholesome extent in this society?
4. Which will prove more functional in the foreseeable future, strength as an individual or capacity to adjust socially?
5. In the American culture, how might children's peer groups be utilized more effectively for promoting society's goals?
6. Does the warm, intense mothering

provided in this culture interfere with children's establishing satisfactory peer relations?

7. Would placing only children in infant schools improve their long-term social adjustment?

8. Do children effect a better social and personal adjustment when they engage freely in unsupervised play?

9. Did the one-teacher school permit a more natural social adjustment than does the present age-graded school?

10. Look up the technique of administering a sociogram, and apply one to a group of children. Analyze the results.

11. Should seating within the schoolroom be altered periodically to permit more natural social situations?

12. Do competitive activities promote or impede children's social adjustment?

13. Should the practice of choosing up sides be permitted?

14. What might be done to facilitate the social adjustment of the child who is (a) physically handicapped, (b) lower-class in a largely middle-class school, or (c) much younger or older than others in the grade?

15. Does forced racial integration do more to help or hurt children's long-term social adjustment?

16. Should a teacher take the opportunity, when a rejected child is absent, to encourage his peers to accept him?

• SUGGESTED READINGS

Clifford, E., "Social Visibility," *Child Development*, Vol. 34 (1963), pp. 799–808. In this study, children's sociometric status is related to their social visibility, or position in a group, as perceived by other members of the group.

Dubin, R., and E. R. Dubin, "Children's Social Perceptions," *Child Development*, Vol. 36, No. 3 (September 1965), pp. 809–836. Data from 56 studies yield generalizations about children's perceptions of self, parental roles, parental behavior, and non-parental authority figures.

Fantini, M. D., and G. Weinstein, "Taking Advantage of the Disadvantaged," *Teachers College Record*, Vol. 69, No. 2 (1967) pp. 103–114. The authors take a penetrating look at today's educational practices and offer various suggestions for what might be done. They believe that most efforts at reform have been expended on the fringes instead of the heart of educational matters.

Goldberg, M. L., "Adapting Teacher Style to Pupil Differences; Teachers for Disadvantaged Children," *Merrill-Palmer Quarterly*, Vol. 10, No. 2 (1964), pp. 161–178. Cites studies that point up the variety of teaching styles and their effects on pupil achievement in general and on the achievement of specific categories of pupils in particular. Proposes a hypothetical model of the successful teacher of disadvantaged pupils and suggests how such a model may be approached.

Radke-Yarrow, M., and J. D. Campbell, "Person Perception in Children," *Merrill-Palmer Quarterly*, Vol. 9, No. 1 (1963), pp. 57–73. Children's perceptions of other children were studied within the context of a summer camp setting.

Rheingold, H. L., "The Development of Social Behavior in the Human Infant," *Monographs of the Society for Research in Child Development*, Vol. 31, No. 5, Serial No. 107 (1966), pp. 1–17. Focuses on social development in human infants, but also provides comparisons with other species.

Scott, J. P., and J. L. Fuller, *Genetics and the Social Behavior of the Dog*. Chicago: University of Chicago Press, 1965. Treats the subject in terms of the critical-period hypothesis.

Torrance, E. P., "The Creative Personality and the Ideal Pupil," *Teachers College Record*, Vol. 65, No. 3 (1963), pp. 220–226. Proposes that the typical teacher's conception of the ideal pupil imposes sharp restraints on the development of children's creative abilities.

Westby-Gibson, D., *Social Perspectives on Education*. New York: John Wiley & Sons, Inc., 1965. See Chapter 6, "Socialization through Group Experience," and Chapter 8, "Social Learning Beyond the Family."

White, R. K., and R. Lippitt, *Autocracy and Democracy: An Experimental Inquiry*. New York: Harper and Row, Publishers, Inc., 1960. A report on classic research into the social climate of groups.

13

THE CHILD AND THE SCHOOL

Since there has been continuing and widespread disagreement about the function of the public school in general, and the elementary school in particular, we shall simply examine certain general aims, without attempting to be specific. As evidence of the confusion, note that the National Educational Policies Commission, which at one time listed 47 separate goals for the school, in 1961 settled on one — "the ability to think." However, this single-mindedness of purpose hardly carried over to the schools themselves, whose efforts were split among academic, social, vocational, and athletic programs.

In the elementary school, academic excellence is generally accorded a lower place than social adjustment. Lippitt and Gold (1959) found that, in the case of children having "low" ability and personality, teachers more often paid attention to the children's social behaviors than to their academic performance. Ideally, scholarship should play a prime role in elementary education, partly because of the knowledge explosion. Learning in all fields is gathering furious momentum, and if an individual is to cope with it, he has got to start early. When he reaches the age of vocational

decision he will find a growing number of jobs requiring training in depth. If he is uneducated, he will be a liability — a candidate for personal ineffectiveness and economic dole.

Fortunately, there is a growing emphasis on the school's academic function. "In view of the expansion of knowledge," writes Corwin (1965, p. 117), "elementary school teachers, especially, will no longer be able to afford the luxury of a short and unspecialized education." Unfortunately, parents often interpret the elementary school's intellectual function merely as ensuring that the child may proceed to high school and ultimately to college. Few think of learning in terms of enrichment of the child's life in the here and now. Of course, early learning experiences are also the foundation stones for all later learning. In the recent past we have conceived of education as a kindergarten-to-college process; currently, we view it as a crib-through-college process. Before long it will be seen to last from cradle to grave.

An overall educational function, often mentioned, is the interpretation of society. However, since American schools are directly under local boards,

PERCENT OF SCHOOL-AGE POPULATION ENROLLED IN SCHOOL,
1954 TO 1964*

Year	Age groups							
	5	6	7–9	10–13	14–15	16–17	18–19	20–24
1954	57.7%	96.8%	99.2%	99.5%	95.8%	78.0%	32.4%	11.2%
1955	58.1	98.2	99.2	99.2	95.9	77.4	31.5	11.1
1956	58.9	97.0	99.4	99.2	96.9	78.4	35.4	12.8
1957	60.2	97.4	99.5	99.5	97.1	80.5	34.9	14.0
1958	63.8	97.3	99.5	99.5	96.9	80.6	37.6	13.4
1959	62.9	97.5	99.4	99.4	97.5	82.9	36.8	12.7
1960	63.7	98.0	99.6	99.5	97.8	82.6	38.4	13.1
1961	66.3	97.4	99.4	99.3	97.6	83.6	38.0	13.7
1962	66.8	97.9	99.2	99.3	98.0	84.3	41.8	15.6
1963	67.8	97.4	99.4	99.3	98.4	87.1	40.9	17.3
1964	68.5	98.2	99.0	99.0	98.6	87.7	41.6	16.8

* Reprinted from *NEA Research Bulletin*, Vol. 44, No. 3 (1966), p. 90. Data from U.S. Department of Commerce, Bureau of the Census, *School Enrollment, October 1964*, Current Population Reports, Population Characteristics, Series P-20, No. 148 (Washington, D.C.: Government Printing Office, February 8, 1966), p. 2. Enrollments counted in October of each year; comprises public- and private-school enrollment.

teachers must interpret only those aspects of society that the community desires, and in such manner as it may desire. This factor undoubtedly helps account for cultural lag, since children are taught merely to conserve their society as it is, not to look at it critically, or to anticipate its probable directions, or to participate in consciously directing it.

Another goal for elementary schools is implicit in the school-community relationship and is sometimes explicitly expressed in the statement "The school should do whatever the rest of society leaves undone" (Barzun, 1954).

• EARLY CHILDHOOD EDUCATION

The roles of the nursery school and kindergarten are no clearer than that of the elementary school; nevertheless, these schools have assumed increasing importance. For one thing, the growing number of mothers in the labor force has expanded programs in day care. Also,

expanding rate of juvenile delinquency and school dropouts, coupled with civil rights programs, has aroused interest in providing the kinds of preschool experiences for the disadvantaged that will enhance their chances of later school success.

Since the early 1930s, efforts have been made to evaluate the effects of early childhood education. Some studies have cited gains, others none (Olson and Hughes, 1940). Some have reported increases in IQ; others have attributed such increments to various nonintellective factors, including increased familiarity with materials and greater adult-child rapport. By the 1940s, interest shifted to the effect of nursery-school experience on the child's social and emotional adjustment; but the results were inconclusive. A summary of three later studies showed similarly inconsistent findings. The effects in a high-quality nursery school (that is, a school providing more than collective baby-sitting or activities and materials avail-

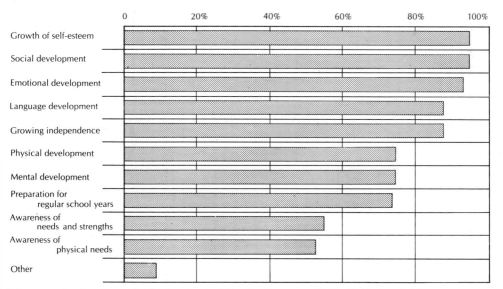

Primary goals of nursery school education in 141 school systems, 1966–67. *National Education Association Research Bulletin,* 1968, **46**(2), 35–63. Reproduced by permission.

the recognition of early education as a major factor in the ultimate realization of personal and intellectual potential has created concern for the quantity and quality of early schooling. Besides, the

able in the home) were shown to be good; in the others the effects were insignificant (Bonney and Nicholson, 1958).

Obviously, the effects revealed

365

will depend on many factors, especially on the personality of the teacher concerned. In one study, the personality of the teacher, including her outlook and convictions, constituted the most important single factor in shaping the child's nursery experience (Reichenberg-Hackett, 1962).

Most evaluations have been made of preschools whose children came from better-than-average homes; such children, when compared with children from comparable homes, might show little superiority, simply because the homes already provide similar enriched experiences. Gains are reported, though, among children from deprived homes, especially in the intellectual and language areas (Swift, 1964). Such gains may similarly accrue to middle-class children to the extent that the teacher deliberately establishes a learning environment more advanced, or enriched, than their homes provide.

A group of college students, when questioned, recalled little from very early school days. These answers are typical:

> I can't remember my kindergarten teacher's name, but she got my school career off to a good start. She was young, and seemed to love the children, and never got mad at us. She spent all the time telling us stories and playing games with us. You could sum up our feelings toward her as just plain love! (Female)

> I was an only child and looked forward excitedly to attending kindergarten. However, once there, I was disappointed. All we did was color pictures and take naps. I wanted to learn, and tried to get my parents to put me in the first grade. The teachers blocked this plan, so I continued in school with little interest or ambition. I think this experience hindered my later progress in school. (Male)

Much more needs to be done before we can attain even a fairly good idea of the potential of early education. Will present preschool programs develop into small-fry Ivy Leagues or remain much the same? Will home or school provide the best incubation for the spacemen of the future? Whatever the case, here are tentative suggestions for making early childhood schooling more effective.

The personality of the teacher can be the most important factor in the child's nursery experience.

First, attempts might be made to adapt such experience to the individual child's needs. Some children might profit from larger classes that afford more varied programs and materials; others might gain more from a close personal relationship with a well-trained teacher. Also, early school training should be coordinated with what follows, to avoid discontinuity. A child may have had certain reading readiness experiences in nursery school, which are merely duplicated in the kindergarten or first grade. Long-term studies should attempt to assess the effects of specific practices within the nursery school on later behaviors of the child involved.

Let us close with a quotation from Landreth (1964, p. 990), which refers specifically to university nursery schools but contains suggestions of general value for early childhood education:

Is the university nursery school a school in the sense that it is a related and contributing part of a child's school experience? If it is, this is more by accident than by design. Usually there is neither coordination nor communication between the nursery and the elementary school. Each carries on as if the other did not exist. This implies either that young children are incapable of learning much (an assumption belied by the facts) or that a university nursery school is incapable of teaching much. This latter assumption, as yet untested, raises the question of whether the nursery school program always takes maximal advantage of the learning potential of three- and four-year-olds. In contrast, the impressive results obtained from programmed instruction of young adults suggests the desirability of experimenting with planned sequences of experience for, at least, the four-year-old child.

• A CURRICULUM FOR CHILDREN

While much of the discussion that follows could also apply to the early childhood level, reference is chiefly to grades one through six. Of course, where **curriculum** construction is concerned, certain principles are basic at any level. Content should have substance, for even a child likes to feel he is getting something. This is not the same as saying it must be immediately useful. Rather, it means providing materials in which children can somehow become personally involved. And while a broad spectrum of experience must be provided, it means letting a child dig in sometimes when the occasion arises:

The question of providing for range as against narrow concentration is not simple. Hackneyed terms of this sort are misleading. There are children who need above all to discover their own potential in terms of depth, in terms perhaps of a single deep and overwhelming intellectual, esthetic, or social form of self-fulfillment, or the discovery of their powers. There can be danger in filling up such a child's

life with a diversity of scheduled activities, with a succession of clubs, sports and lessons to the point at which the child says, "The one thing that interests me now is just to paint and paint and paint." Or, as another child said, "There isn't any place for myself" [Murphy and Murphy, 1960, p. 214].

The child will not attain a sense of commitment unless the material presents a challenge. If it is too shallow for him, he gains no feeling of self-respect from successfully coping with it. Imagine for a moment being assigned the task of drawing circles, or triangles, or squares, on endless sheets of paper, day after day. Silly? Of course; but to bright children, many tasks assigned them offer as little challenge and are fully as meaningless. Topics should be of a type to engage the child's interests, introduce vital issues, and pose a challenge. If the child henceforth is to perceive himself as a problem solver, he must possess a sensitivity for identifying problems, skills for locating up-to-date information about them, a habit of meeting instead of evading them, and skills for devising solutions. In a complex world, his own feelings of adequacy and security are thereby increased. He will feel more like a contributing member of society because he is an interested, competent one. This is the idea behind the following curriculum suggestion:

In a history class, children usually memorize America's major policies toward Latin America, or the emerging nations of Africa, or the European Common Market. On examinations, they feed back the policies, undiluted, as the teacher gave them. But as an alternative to this traditional "soak-up and feedback" method, Coleman suggests political gaming, in which teams represent policy makers in various countries. First, an international situation is set up; then policy-making teams respond to it and to each other's moves, under the supervision of referees [Coleman, 1961, p. 321].

While Coleman was referring to

secondary education, the same sort of approach might be used in elementary education. Traditionally, the child simply memorized materials, most of which he speedily forgot. In the approach suggested by Coleman, he utilizes the same basic information, but in very different fashion, with quite different results. He becomes personally involved, attempting to outwit his opponent. He is concerned, not simply with the "whats," but the more vital "whys." He learns to test solutions in the face of attempts to discover holes in his logic. In order to make his case stronger, he searches for materials in his room library, school library, city library, and other sources as well.

The curriculum should also respect the nature of the learner; and since small girls and boys come in many shapes and sizes, this means a varied offering, on different levels of complexity. As Bloom (1963, p. 379) puts it: "Teaching and learning experiences are not good or poor in their own right. They are good or poor because of the way in which they affect the learner." The boy in the fifth grade who reads on the second-grade level should be provided reading on that level but with content appropriate for children his age. Consider Tommy, for example. Even in the fifth grade he was an electrical wizard but very poor at reading. However, when simplified reading matter was found in his one consuming field of interest, he "ate it up." Tommy was a bright boy and made rapid strides. Because he met reading in a different and palatable context, he soon developed a taste for it.

Life-Adjustment versus Academic Skills

An argument that waxes and wanes with educational philosophies is whether the school's curriculum should be limited to the more traditional academic disciplines, or embrace **life-adjustment skills** as well—the so-called "fundamentals-versus-frills" controversy. First, consider the current situation. Sparked by the progressivist's concern for the whole child and the psychoanalyst's stress on the child's security, the curriculum of the 1930s and 1940s became greatly expanded. At school, the child was taught not only the three R's but how to get along with other people, how to relate to his family, how to use his leisure time, and so forth. For a time in the 1940s, academic skills gained respectability only when cloaked in life-adjustment guise. More recently, vocational counseling courses sometimes appeared as early as the fourth grade (Douvan and Adelson, 1966).

In determining the place of life-adjustment skills in the curriculum, let us first acknowledge that education, in the broad sense, inevitably concerns the whole child. One of the most widely agreed-upon generalizations in psychology is this: Some children care little about academic goals because they are too deeply involved with personal problems. Moreover, children develop as a whole, with each aspect of personality vitally affecting every other. However desirable it may be that parents discharge certain functions, the simple fact is that they differ vastly in the efficiency with which they perform their roles. The child should not become the scapegoat of a stubborn insistence on the part of schools to refuse to provide what his home may have ignored, but what he vitally needs.

This is not the same as saying that the emphasis on academic and life-adjustment skills should be equal. If only because it is the sole agency specifically charged with this function, the school's main aim must be to transmit the sociocultural heritage to each generation, and to prepare it for the future by providing it with the commitment, the intellectual equipment, and the attitudes and philosophy required for a satisfying and effective life in a complex and changing world. To achieve this goal, an individual also needs certain life-adjustment skills, such as home economics in the broad sense, including budget-making, home decoration, and household finance, practical finance, social business etiquette, child care, and so on. This subject matter should be coordinated with the traditional curriculum and not merely treated as an annex to it.

It is important to recognize, too, that life-adjustment skills are not anti-intellectual; for an individual is free to pursue cultural interests only when the rest of his house is in reasonably good order. Besides, traditionally intellectual values and attitudes may become vitalized in a co-curricular context. Often a child may learn mathematical processes in a shop situation that he would avoid in a conventional classroom.

Leisure-Time Activities: The "Co-curriculum"

The co-curriculum gained steady headway until the 1950s, when Russia launched its Sputnik and with it a re-examination of the goals of American education. Since then, lip-service has been paid academic goals while co-curriculum has continued as prominent as ever, perhaps for several reasons. For one thing, during the 1930s and 1940s, the co-curriculum became formalized, with its own vested interests. Corwin (1965, p. 89) reports the following set of morning announcements in one school:

> Band members whose last names begin with letters A–L will report to the gym for uniform fittings first period, letters M–Z report during second period.
> The Track Team will leave at 2:10 for their afternoon meet. The Prom Decorating Committee will be excused for the afternoon. Invitation Committee will meet in the art room, fifth period.
> Regular music classes will be cancelled third and fourth periods. The Girls' Chorus will practice for commencement at this time. Otherwise classes will be regular.

The formalization of leisure-time education is often carried to excess. Traditionally, the child's leisure-time world was his own world, where he did what he wanted in his own way. However, curricularizing leisure led to the school's quasi-control over the child's free time, and thus over the whole child. This trend is also seen in the proliferation of adult-sponsored programs, such as Cub Scouts, Brownies, and parent-initiated parties (Havighurst and Neugarten, 1962). Certainly such activities may contribute richly to children's development, but formalization may defeat certain of the goals they are designed to achieve — individual initiative, group adjustment within informal settings, and relaxation from the more vigorous academic responsibilities.

• THE LEARNING SITUATION

Motivation

Whatever the curricular content involved, the teacher must somehow "put it across." This task inevitably involves motivation, without which learning will not occur, except on the sheer conditioning level. Methods of motivation may be categorized roughly as positive, involving rewards (praise or social recognition, as by honor rolls) or anticipation of personal satisfaction; or negative, including reproof, inculcation of anxiety, negative critical remarks, or pressure ("pushing" instead of leading). The bulk of research supports positive methods. No evidence exists that pressuring children can speed up their learning or produce permanent gain (Dinkmeyer, 1965).

A corollary of the motivational problem is this: What teaching techniques are most likely to produce children who can do the sort of complex, creative thinking required for adjustment in a modern age? For instance, should teachers wait until children are fully ready for a learning experience, or should such experience be contrived to anticipate such readiness? In other words, should teachers wait until comprehension of the concepts involved can be readily attained, or be content, for a time, with relatively amorphous approximations to understanding? Advocates of the complete readiness position contend that premature exposure may kill interest or result in conceptual distortions that may prove difficult to correct. Besides, since the tremendous bulk of knowledge to be attained requires ordering it in some manner, would it not be economical to introduce any specific topic only when the child is figuratively ready to lap it up?

Others, while agreeing that a sequence from the less to the more difficult must be maintained, insist that a child's interest cannot be expected simply to ripen. Instead, the teacher must help it ripen. Nor need the child be fully ready in terms of mental maturity, but simply on the threshold, where specific learning experience is concerned. Vigotsky (1962, p. 105), for instance, believes the curve of human development does not coincide with the curve of school instruction—that by and large, instruction precedes development. He claims that the most effective

instruction "marches ahead of development and is aimed not so much at the ripe but the ripening functions. . . . It must be oriented toward the future, not the past."

Other authorities emphasize the advantages of inquiry training, if children are to become self-propelled, without dependence on motivation from others. A marked lack of autonomy and productivity, asserts Suchman (1961), stems from children's dependence on teachers, parents, and books, to shape their concepts. In one experiment, when children were given new data, or a situation in which such data were available, children rarely organized what they had, rarely gathered more data, rarely raised and tested hypotheses or drew inferences. Instead, they blocked, began to offer unsupported conclusions, or produced a string of stereotyped problems which got nowhere. Accustomed to having concepts simply handed to them in discussions, pictures, films, and textbooks, the children proved unwilling

In the discovery method, the child learns to think as a scientist does, inductively.

or unable to plan and initiate action with the aim of discovering new concepts for themselves.

An antidote to the foregoing situation is the discovery method, in which children reproduce as closely as possible the attitude and sequences in thinking that the scientist uses in evolving new principles and ideas. The child discovers the principle himself through inductive thinking. This approach is illustrated in an experiment by Ervin (1960, pp. 537–554):

> A group of third- and fourth-grade children were trained to shoot a ball so it would ricochet off a backboard and strike a target. Some of the children proved able to offer an explanation for the process in terms of reflected angles. Others could not think of an explanation although they were intuitively successful in the task. When transfer of the operation was required by aiming a flashlight at a mirror in order to hit a target, both groups were still successful until the task was made more difficult. Then only those who could formulate the general principle were successful.

Of course, the discovery method works best in cases when there is something the child honestly and earnestly desires to know. In one study, children wrote "wonder letters" in which they related what they wanted to know. From grade three came these questions:

> I wonder how the rain comes down from the ske (sic). . . . I wonder how an airplane stay in the ske. . . . I wonder how the hen lay eggs. . . . I wonder how they make paint [Fukuyama, 1963, p. 377–383].

Children's exploration for answers will be more active, imaginative, and varied if the teacher is accepting. Gettegno (1961) believes that the school's limitation to "acceptable" modes of thought fosters a restricted attack on life's problems. He believes that children should learn to think in a complex way about complex things.

Let us add, without amplification, several other principles of motivation. All too often, the teacher specializes in the expected; he should provide a change of pace. He may sometimes take refuge in the familiar, but he should not be suspicious of the novel. Also, he should constantly challenge and not be content with minimal expectations. Finally, he should possess the sort of enthusiasm for learning that is contagious.

Since this book is not a treatise in education, these observations are made chiefly to drive home the point that content chosen, and method used, should constantly be appraised in terms of what they do to and for children.

Meeting Individual Differences

Implicit in the foregoing discussion is this point: Teachers must think in terms not of "the child" but "this child." This truism has been afloat in a sea of educational dogma for a long time. But some people have become too preoccupied with curricular cults and statistical norms to perceive clearly a specific child. Others have used the shotgun approach, aiming at children a variety of methods, hoping each would find its mark. Ideally, the educational diet should be tailored to the needs of each small consumer.

Another stumbling-block has been a distorted notion of democracy—the notion that the educational ideal requires the same education for all. This formula reduces everyone to the hypothetical average. The average man, or child, has been elevated to an unwarranted position; from defending the common man, educators have reached the point of exalting him (Krutch et al., 1954). The good can be the enemy of the best, and teachers not only become resigned to mediocrity but come to demand it.

A few figures that indicate the intelligence span within a grade will show how inappropriate the same offering would be if served up to all. Disregarding the extreme 2% at either end of the continuum, there is a four-year range in intelligence among a random group of six-year-olds. By the time this group has reached the age of 12, or seventh-grade level, the range will have increased to almost eight years (Cook, 1958). In reading achievement, the range within a single grade may be as great as 13 years. While such measurements of intelligence may be questionable, at least they provide a rough indicator of ability. Obviously, since the curricular offering is normally designed for the average, the bright become lazy and disinterested and fail to develop their potential, while the very dull fall increasingly further behind. One group of mentally retarded children in regular public school classes lagged, on the average, 4.7 months behind academically in the first grade, 9.5 months in the second, 12.7 in the third, 17.6 in the fourth, and 27.8 in the fifth. The picture was one of progressive frustration and defeat. Meantime, they fared as poorly socially as academically. Although they comprised less than 6% of the group, on sociometric measures 40% of the group were among those most strongly rejected. Their peers described them with such phrases as "rough," "mean," "misbehaves in school," "cheats," "is dirty," and "smells" (Johnson, 1950).

Brighter children, declares Corwin (1965) are deliberately held back. In most schools promotion beyond one's age group is discouraged. Some administrators complain that preschools, which were privately financed in only 17% of the cities checked, upset the public school's kindergarten programs by usurping their traditional functions; that is, some children come to kindergarten too advanced for the program. Television is creating problems, too. In most schools children who want to know about space programs are given readers written at the level of "Jack sees Mary. She has a ball." By contrast, Suppes (1964) conducted an intensive accelerated mathematics program with a group of gifted first-graders. Even within this select and supposedly homogeneous group, he uncovered a tremendous range

in learning rate, so that at the end of the first four weeks, the fastest child covered half again as much material as the slowest. His data indicated that the greatest improvement in subject-matter learning derives primarily from accommodating to individual differences.

Encouraging Creativity

Any child, bright or dull, probably possesses at least a modicum of creativity, the nurture of which is being strongly encouraged of late. As world problems grow ever more complex, creative children become the blue chips of the rising generation. Traditionally, America has spent much money on practical problems and little on basic research. At one time an application for funds to study the X ray was refused because there was no known application for the findings. However, more attention is now being paid to basic research and to the talent that sparks it—creativity.

What is the school's role with regard to creativity? First, teachers must change their attitudes toward method and subject matter. They must encourage divergent as well as convergent thinking. Convergent thinking requires the child to solve a problem by surveying the facts at hand and narrowing the alternatives until he arrives at the solution. Divergent thinking requires intuition, imagination, and a willingness to try the unconventional. The teacher who, when administering a test, says "Be careful now, don't guess" is encouraging convergent thinking. The one who says "See how many solutions you can find for the problem" values divergent thinking (Guilford, 1959).

Likewise, convergent teaching suggests that there is one correct answer; but today's reality is a shifting concept. Instead of teaching reality, the teacher must encourage children to examine explanations of reality. The student should explore rival explanations. Older explanations, and why they failed to work, will serve as a take-off point for discussions of the role of inquiry and the place of new information in the realm of thought.

In their methodology, teachers should encourage the sort of attitudes that free children to come up with new ideas (Maltzman, 1960). They should encourage a playful attitude, not the grim do-or-die attitude all too prevalent; and they should welcome children's expressing tentative ideas. A teacher is doing just the opposite who says "Know what you want to say before you say it," or "Don't be careless" (Cronbach, 1963).

Teachers should also avoid making a choice between fostering well roundedness and specialization. The specialist argument goes like this: Perhaps a child has 100 units of ability, which he may distribute any way he chooses over 20 kinds of aptitude. Will he distribute them among 10 aptitudes, or 20, or perhaps just one kind? If he is a talent gambler, he will assign all 100 units to his single greatest aptitude. If all did this, society would have the best poets and the best dramatists possible, and not just a vast number of homogenized, well-rounded persons.

The advocate of well-roundedness counters by saying that adjustment to a complex world requires broad knowledge. The author agrees with the generalists that everyone needs a broad background. With that as a base, the degree of specialization to follow will depend on the individual concerned. Some persons live most effectively as generalists, perhaps as coordinators of some highly diversified activity, or as community leaders. Parenthetically, it should be noted that specialists would say that such theoretically broad occupations are themselves specialties. Anyhow, other persons may pursue some clearly specialized skill, such as corporation law, and require a correspondingly specialized training. However, no matter how narrowly the occupation becomes defined, it will be pursued more intelligently if the individual involved is capable of relating it to the broad sweep of life and knowledge.

The teacher should also help the child to reconcile the apparently opposite traits of spontaneity and self-control. For greatest effectiveness, the child must learn how to make bureaucratic institutions work for him, rather than expending his energies fighting them. That is, he must learn to adapt within the framework of reality, and to make it serve his will, rather than hopelessly trying to combat forces that might speedily overwhelm him (Pepinsky, 1960).

Finally, teachers and parents should devote unlimited patience to fostering creative ability (Millard, 1958). In recognition of the differences in children's creative interests, Lowenfeld (1958) urges that the widest possible variety of areas and of media for expression be made available. He also advises that a child be allowed to create in his own way, not according to some ideal in the mind of the teacher or to standards set by other children. Teaching for creativity must be like broken-field running; it will not proceed neatly step by step. Spontaneity cannot be generated by regimented planning. Already, too many teachers are memorizing formulas for making children creative.

The author asked a group of secondary-education majors this question: "Can you recall any learning experiences from elementary school that you would judge as creative?" Here are two replies:

> My fifth-grade teacher had the children put on a television news-and-weather program every day. We made a TV camera from cardboard and set up a panel for each week. One pupil did the weather and others did the local, state, and national news. This was a very new experience for me. Until then I was shy and participated little in class. This experience brought me out of my shell. Everyone joined in. (Female)

373

My eighth-grade teacher constantly hit us with something different. Sometimes we acted out situations that we were discussing in history class; for instance, we played at having a political convention. For arithmetic, we evaluated real life-insurance policies, home-building projects, and make-believe stock-market purchases. We visited industries in the area; and parents talked to us about their occupations. I remember especially a policeman who came to class. The classroom atmosphere crackled with ideas, and there was a frequent change of pace. (Male)

Classroom Control

The traditional pattern. Unfortunately, most classrooms are still traditional in nature, with pedagogical strategies firmly rooted in decades past. In such schools, from 50 to 80% of class time is spent in keeping order and other nonacademic tasks (Deutsch, 1960). The usual pattern is one of strict discipline, and children are told to speak only when called on by the teacher (Barker, 1962). In extreme cases, children become demolition specialists dedicated to winning classroom engagements with their antagonist, the teacher.

This pattern coincides with the authoritarian, traditional patterns of child-rearing often found in lower-class families. Parents tell children to mind "Because I told you so." Caught in this dual network of authority at school and often at home, the child often adopts a passive, dependent attitude (Riesman, 1962; Hess et al., 1964).

A classic experiment in styles of control. A crucial question is this: What special blend of democracy or teacher-directedness creates the most effective environment for learning? A now-classic experiment was devised by Lewin and White (1939) to answer this question. Four clubs, each composed of several 11-year-old boys, were organized, ostensibly to provide recreation. At the end of each 7 weeks, for a

period of 21 weeks, a new leader assumed control of each club. The leaders had been trained to play a different role with each group, so that leadership for the clubs was in turn autocratic, democratic, and laissez-faire. In his autocratic role, the leader told the boys exactly what to do; in the democratic role, he acted as a leader, but only in a friendly, advisory way; while in the laissez-faire role, he did practically nothing. In every case the laissez-faire technique came out badly. Swiftly, work all but came to an end, as the boys wandered about in aimless fashion. By contrast, the democratic leadership was reported to produce a high level of satisfaction and group-mindedness and a lower level of aggression and hostility. However, it should not be overlooked that more work was accomplished in the autocratic setting, although production fell off after the leader departed. By contrast, in the democratic situation, in which members did pretty much what they pleased within a highly informal setting, work continued after the leader left. The authors attributed this effect to the tendency of one of the boys to assume leadership when the adult leader was absent. One may surmise that children have better relationships toward each other and the teacher in a democratic atmosphere, but produce more when the teacher tells them what to do.

Recent evaluation of Lewinian views. Certain later studies, designed to test the original investigation, demonstrated greater output in the democratic, or student-centered, classes; but, they also demonstrated that many children feel dissatisfied and anxious in such settings. Among 18 such studies, nine supported Lewin's conclusions, four failed to support them, and five showed mixed results (Stern, 1962). A major problem in such studies is that it is very hard to make comparisons, because every teaching situation is a unique compound of many factors. The investigator artificially isolates certain factors to measure, ignoring the rest. In a specific classroom, there is a blending of factors to which each child reacts according to his own unique personality and needs.

Potential hazards of the "democratic" classroom. In general, educational theorists advocate a democratic classroom; nevertheless, certain hazards are involved. For example, Jules Henry (1955) describes the process whereby school children learn to be docile even in a so-called "democratic" classroom. That is, their actions come to reflect their anticipation of others' wishes, especially of those in authority. The process is one of canalization, whereby teachers simply set the stage so that children fall in line. In one case, second-grade pupils were shown a film about birds, and were asked by the teacher, "Did the last bird ever look like he would be blue?" The children didn't understand the slant of the question, so the teacher rephrased it, "I think he looked more like a robin, didn't he?" The children then responded "yes" in chorus. In other words, the children did not reply until the teacher had made clear the answer she desired.

Henry concludes that teachers reinforce docility by creating situations in which children destructively criticize each other. When a child gives a wrong answer, the teacher asks another what was wrong with it—a practice that heightens the children's anxiety and leads them to seek the "right" or expected answers. This teacher-produced form of docility, says Henry, is typically middle-class, in the sense that it is based on loss of love and approval rather than on fear of corporal punishment.

Another dubious practice in the democratic classroom is to settle everything by vote. To achieve a "consensus" the teacher may sacrifice his position as an authority, failing to produce the evidence from scholarship that constitutes the basis for truth. Children who learn answers derived by consensus are reduced to a general mediocrity. Also, the individual child's needs are often unsatisfied. A homogenized decision might represent a compromise that meets no single child's needs adequately. The truly democratic classroom would adopt the pluralistic, not the melting-pot philosophy. That is, many kinds of activities would be permitted, instead of just one in which every child, willy-nilly, finds himself incorporated.

Discipline

Unhealthy effects of faulty discipline. A related and traditional problem of classroom management is discipline. In this area, Eaton and associates (1956) found that the frequency of problems increases with grade level, especially with boys. The methods used to cope with such problems are highly varied, but often violate principles of good guidance. Note these examples (Rogers, 1957, pp. 234-235):

> [Recalled from age 13, grade 8] The teacher, a woman of about 68, made us know the conjugation of verbs inside out, and we had to recite them to her while she ate her lunch and we starved. She used to hit children with her "magic wand" and water our heads with a watering can. One day a boy slapped her back.

> [Recalled from age 9, grade 4] Because of the misdemeanors of a few, the entire class would have to stay after school. It was a rural area and meant that children missing the bus had up to a five-mile walk home. It brought tears on several occasions and seemed to please the teacher.

Methods like these fail to get at the basic causes of misbehavior. They humiliate the child and create unpleasant associations with school and with learning experience. They are disturbing to the teacher, who can hardly maintain self-respect through engaging in such practices, and often create an unwholesome learning environment, not only for the child directly involved, but for other children as well.

A philosophy of good discipline. If such procedures are to be eliminated, 375 teachers must come to understand the true function of discipline, which is to help children satisfy their needs in an acceptable manner. Its aim is not to curtail their freedom but to teach them how to utilize their freedom in ways that do not infringe on the rights of others.

Certain classroom practices are especially conducive to good discipline. Basically, the school program should be so well planned that children want to learn without undue interference. In such cases, the class as a whole exerts pressure on a child who gets out of line. Also, if the class has experiences in working together as a group on well-motivated projects, a child comes to have a feeling of responsibility to others. Finally, if a teacher convinces each child that his welfare counts, children will not be unconsciously driven to get back at the teacher.

Nevertheless, even the best teacher will sometimes have trouble with the class as a whole, or with one child in particular. In such cases the teacher may explain his decisions and encourage the class to appraise them. When a conflict between teacher and child interests is settled by open discussion, instead of by a decision from "on high," the children gain the "precious idea that reason, not power makes standards of conduct" [Cronbach, 1963, p. 649]. Also, if the teacher interprets decisions as being in their interest, children come to view authority as an ally instead of an enemy. Even defiant pupils are often won over by a cooperative, productive relationship.

However, some children have such deep-seated conflicts that they feel antagonistic toward even the most understanding teacher and the best program. In some cases, a child may be extremely uncertain, and find a degree of order and structure reassuring. In an informal democratic classroom, where a better-adjusted child feels at home, this child feels threatened, and constantly transcends the boundaries. Such a child

needs, perhaps welcomes, a firm hand and a clear delineation of what is expected of him. There is some evidence that such a child learns better when the teacher structures tasks and makes it quite clear that children are there to work (Haring and Phillips, 1962).

Even among the class generally, the teacher must know how to shift from more to less permissive procedures, depending on the circumstances. However, a certain orderliness should undergird his actions. He should not weave a drunken course between the laissez-faire and the autocratic approach.

Administering punishment. When punishment is required, the best procedure takes into account both long-range and short-term goals. Immediate results may be necessary if the class is to proceed effectively with its work. A quiet, unobtrusive reminder is often all that is needed. At other times, a child should temporarily be separated from his peers, in the manner least likely to attract attention, to avoid humiliating him and disturbing others.

• FACTORS AFFECTING ACHIEVEMENT

The Child's Personality

Pupil achievement has been shown to reflect classroom atmosphere, as manifested in the teacher's use of praise or anxiety-producing behaviors. In a study involving four intensive treatments — neutral, reproof, praise, and competition — reproof proved least effective. Reed (1960) concluded that both severe and very low levels of anxiety reduce learning, while mild anxiety may facilitate some kinds of learning. The high-anxiety pupil has an advantage, says Dinkmeyer (1965), in situations free of time pressure, and where cautious work is of value; but failure, or the expectation of failure, especially handicaps such children. Sarason (1960) reported that some aspects of school studies favor low-anxiety, some high-anxiety groups.

In support of adjustment as a positive factor in achievement, Sarason (1963) also reported that children who disparaged themselves were generally anxious and poor achievers. Another study reported curiosity, presumably a significant factor in achievement, as positively related to adjustment (McReynolds and Acker, 1961).

Gough and Fink's (1964) findings were somewhat different. The only valid predictors of academic achievement they uncovered were personal effectiveness, diligence, and restraint. Such traits do not constitute a pattern of creativity or innovation, but they do prove functional in schools as presently organized.

In sum, academic achievement is significantly related to certain personality traits, but not to overall adjustment. Donahue (1949) found near-zero correlations between scholarship and nearly every conceivable variety of adjustment inventory at all educational levels. The only consistent relation was a small positive correlation between introversion and grades. Similarly, Holland and Nichols (1964) found no relation between achievement and such adjustment variables as anxiety or neurotic traits. Instead, achievement stemmed from strong, well-organized qualities such as interests, commitment, or enthusiasm. In Freudian terms, states the report, it is the nature of the *ego*, not the *id*, that makes the difference between high and low school achievement.

However, such a conclusion hinges on questionable assumptions. The diverse, often conflicting ways that personality traits, qualities of adjustment, and achievement are defined tend to cancel out clear-cut conclusions. Is achievement measured in terms of creative production, grades earned in traditional schools, or what? Children classified as manifesting anxiety might range from those who are heavily burdened with neurotic disturbances to those who are very briefly disturbed. Besides, exactly how may one distinguish the healthy tension that sparks activity from the unhealthy tension that inhibits effort and destroys self-confidence? The author believes that healthy emotion may facilitate achievement but not guarantee it. If the child is challenged, a healthy condition—both physical and emotional—will constitute the best internal environment for accomplishment.

The Child's Attitude Toward School

Another significant factor in determining how the child will relate to the school is attitude, whether toward the teacher, specific subjects, or the total school environment. Such attitudes, once formed, are often enduring (Malone and Freel, 1954). In one study, a grade-by-grade analysis failed to show basic changes in attitudes toward mathematics after the elementary grades. More basic still is a child's general orientation toward intellectual tasks, for which the years from six to ten are crucial (Sontag and Kagan, 1963).

Children's general attitudes toward school vary greatly, as illustrated here:

I always disliked school to the point of bitterness. I like to learn, but very rarely in my school days have I found any real place for learning. It is an important goal of mine to enter this battlefield of education, and perhaps, just perhaps, I can make learning of primary importance for the children I teach. (Female)

I despised school. The teachers typically had their favored few. I was a sort of off-beat kid, and those stodgy teachers never understood me. (Male)

I always loved school. Each fall I looked forward with excitement for classes to begin. I led my classes, and could always count on the teachers' favor. Nevertheless, I think my schooling was quite ineffective in terms of the time expended. (Male)

The way children feel about school depends on a complex blend of personality traits and school factors. In a specific case, it hinges on the way an individual child perceives and relates to his school

377

Attitude is a crucial factor in determining the child's school experience.

experiences. Satisfied and dissatisfied children apparently do not differ from each other either in general intellectual ability or in scholastic achievement. Dissatisfaction with school appears to be part of a larger picture of psychological discontent, rather than the direct result of inefficient functioning in the schoolroom. For instance, children with school phobia, or extreme fear of school, may demonstrate a marked dependency and emotional immaturity rather than mental disability. School pressures further accentuate these traits, leaving them burdened with extreme anxiety (Chazan, 1962).

Better-adjusted children are inclined to view the school more favorably, at least partly because they are predisposed to view everything more favorably. Their generally more desirable traits cause teachers to react positively toward them, in turn reinforcing their positive feelings toward the school. Coleman found that children who scored higher on a personality test both liked school better and received more favorable comments from teachers (Jackson and Getzels, 1959).

Boys and girls express dissatisfac-

tion with school in somewhat different ways. Dissatisfied girls are intro-punitive—that is, self-critical, blaming their dissatisfaction on themselves. Dissatisfied boys are extra-punitive and blame adults. It is much easier for teachers to identify dissatisfied boys than dissatisfied girls, because boys' discontent is more overt (Jackson and Getzels, 1959).

School's Differential Effects on the Sexes

In certain ways the school favors each sex—girls more often initially, and boys increasingly later on. Especially at first, girls are on a different developmental timetable, maturing somewhat faster than boys. Ames and Ilg (1964), who found girls to be more advanced than boys in grades five to nine, argued that boys might well enter school at a later age. Moreover, the lower grades are a female-oriented world, where children are given books whose content is anything but red-blooded or exciting, and where they are expected to be docile and quiet. The predominantly women teachers actually prefer boys, but punish and disapprove their behaviors more (Meyer and Thompson, 1956).

The greater punishment meted out to boys is fully apparent to both sexes. Probably the woman teacher's values cause her to disapprove assertiveness and aggressiveness that is completely normal in boys. Moreover, the conventional classroom's demands for order and routine are distasteful to active boys, and generate withdrawal, nervousness, and aggression. In turn, boys' reactions bring further disapproval, arousing further hostility (Meyer and Thompson, 1963).

The boy himself does not perceive his behavior as bad; hence, he is bound to be anxious and to perceive the teacher as unfair. He is confronted with a conflicting social code: one for the boys in the male world at large, and another for boys at school. As a solution, constructive activity should be provided to permit discharge of excess energy; and moderately aggressive behaviors should be recognized as normal.

Despite early school problems, boys enjoy an increasingly favorable status. Many upper-grade teachers are men, and much of the subject matter is male-oriented. And regardless of the intellectual processes involved, the sex-typing of content affects mastery. For instance, if a verbal problem deals with feminine content such as cooking and gardening, girls score higher than if it deals with guns, money, or geometric designs (Milton, 1958). On this score—that is, subject matter—the male is increasingly favored in later grades. History books are peopled with men; science and mathematics are masculine interest areas. At the same time, academic performance becomes more functional for boys, who increasingly recognize its importance for college entrance, and ultimately for a career (Buss, 1961). By contrast, the girl, taught from the cradle to be passive, shrinks from the increasing competition in higher education.

Meantime, the better balancing of male and female teachers, from nursery through graduate school, would provide models of both sexes with whom students might identify. If the old saying "More is caught than taught" is true, it is important that boys and girls at all levels have teachers of their own sex who are enthusiastic about and steeped in their respective disciplines.

Teacher-Pupil Relationships

Characteristics of present-day teachers. The erstwhile standards of many teacher-training institutions help explain the characteristics of present-day teachers. Such institutions chiefly emphasize personal-social-ethical fitness, despite lip-service to academic excellence (Stout, 1957). Furthermore, concludes Stiles (1960), in many cases supervisory ratings are based more on compatibility than on efficiency ratings. In another study, teachers colleges were reported to have the least liberal and the most passive social-science faculties. Nor was a single one of 29 teachers colleges rated medium-high or high in academic quality, while 11 were rated low (Lazarsfeld and Thielens, 1958).

Teachers must keep abreast of the nuclear explosion in ideas. They must be bright enough and knowledgeable enough to feel comfortable with creative children who raise manifold questions. They must be skilled tacticians in classroom strategies. And they must have established a sufficiently comfortable *modus vivendi* with their problems so that preoccupation with their own concerns does not blur their vision of the child.

Teaching is handicapped somewhat by being known as a woman's profession, which gives to it a self-consciously effeminate and submissive image. This image is especially applied to elementary teachers, of whom only 15% are men. This factor, coupled with the growing predominance of teachers of lower-class origin, has curtailed teachers' power, making them unduly submissive to better-organized administrators (Corwin, 1965).

In one study, although teachers proved less likely than the general population to become committed to some

379

institution, 10% would have done well to consult a specialist, and another 15% were unusually nervous. Among the other three quarters, many had problems; however, these consisted largely in "shynesses and sensitivities" that bother many people, but seldom threaten major disruption (Kaplan, 1959). Nevertheless, both Thorpe (1958), working with "successful" teachers, and Jackson and Guba (1957), working with "experienced" teachers, found them to possess strong needs for deference, order, and endurance, and a weak need for autonomy. On the basis of the research reported elsewhere in this volume, it would seem that such traits would tend to inhibit rather than promote creative teaching.

Teachers' attitudes toward pupils. Perhaps it is merely human that teachers' feelings about children are uneven. Teacher approval is limited to a relatively few; and those children who most need overt signs of approval are least likely to obtain them (Johnson and Medinnus, 1965). Those whom teachers approve are also most likely to be chosen by their peers on sociometric tests (Flanders and Navumaki, 1960). In one study, teachers indicated a preference for children who were brighter, performed better academically, and made better personality adjustment scores (deGroat and Thompson, 1949). Such children provide better window dressing when parents or principals appear.

Pupils' attitudes toward teachers. More research relates to children's views of teachers. In general, children like teachers who are "friendly," "fair," and "encouraging" (Leeds, 1954). In one study, traits that distinguished the 10 best-liked teachers from the 10 least-liked, as rated by a group of fourth-, fifth-, and sixth-graders, were "failure to praise," "scolds pupils a lot," "often bossy," "becomes angry at pupils' failure to understand," and "talks too much." Undesirable behaviors were attributed even to the best-liked teachers. About 34% of the children checked the item "scolds a pupil in front of other pupils" for the best-liked teachers, against 86% for the least-liked teachers (Leeds, 1954). Much of the children's attitude, no doubt, reflected their feelings toward adults in general and parents in particular (Symonds and Jensen, 1961). Their attitude might also have reflected cultural factors. For example, in a study of children in Germany, England, Mexico, and the United States, children in the more adult-dominating countries (Germany and Mexico) more often wrote stories in which the teacher did not believe the child (Anderson et al., 1959).

Here several individuals tell how they felt about their elementary-school teachers collectively:

Teachers were Gods, above human beings. If I saw one shopping, I was shocked, and for a time thereafter thought of that teacher as bad. (Female)

I loved my teachers in a remote way. They were creatures apart, and what they did or said was very important to me. Perhaps one reason was my own great love of going to school. (Female)

I felt they all had it in for me. Teachers were to be evaded and avoided. I had a knack for rubbing them wrong and the word T-E-A-C-H-E-R was just another way of spelling T-R-O-U-B-L-E. (Male)

Different teachers, of course, may produce quite different effects on children. Children of more punitive teachers manifest more aggression in their misconduct, are more unsettled and confused in school, and less concerned with school values and learning than those of nonpunitive teachers (Kounin and Gump, 1961). Moreover, children of "integrative" as opposed to "dominative" teachers show more spontaneity in offering a suggestion, expressing appreciation, and telling their experiences upon invitation by the teacher. In one study, the children of a dominative teacher proved more distractible and wasteful of time (Anderson and Brewer,

1946). However, when these children moved to the next grade, their behavior showed practically a zero correlation with their behavior a year before (Anderson et al., 1946). Another study reported that directive teachers create dependency and interfere with children's problem-structuring, a process especially favorable to learning (Brown, 1961).

Few studies indicate how the teacher affects specific children, and whether such effects persist. In one such study, both teachers and pupils were classified by type, to determine how different teacher and pupil types relate to each other. The children were divided into four categories: *conformers*, who controlled their impulses and showed high social orientation; *opposers*, who manifested disturbed authority relationships, pessimism, intolerance of ambiguity, disappointment, and frustration; *waverers*, described as anxious, ambivalent, fearful, foundering, and indecisive; and *strivers*, who demonstrated marked drive for recognition, especially in school achievement. The teachers, in turn, were classified according to three types. *Turbulent* teachers showed relatively more concern for ideas than for people and a free expression of strong feelings and attitudes, but little patience with routine tasks, sloppiness, and inconsistency. *Self-controlling* teachers maintained an orderly, workmanlike class and focused on structure and planning. At the same time, they showed more sensitivity to children's feelings, and emphasized interpersonal relationships in the classroom. *Fearful* teachers were anxious, dependent on the approval of supervisors and of children, unable to bring order to their task, and highly variable in their behavior.

When the factor of IQ was controlled, the strivers achieved most, followed in order by the conformers, the opposers, and the waverers. Neither strivers nor conformers appeared significantly affected by teacher personality; but for the opposers and waverers, teacher personality made a significant

difference. For these last two groups, the self-controlling teacher was most effective, while the turbulent teachers were more successful in teaching mathematics and science. The fearful teachers were uniformly ineffective with all the children except the strivers, who did well regardless of the teacher (Goldberg, 1964).

Improving teacher-pupil relationships. Obviously, every teacher must consider the child involved, and how each perceives the other. If the child is especially disturbed, it is better to relax standards than to risk pressuring him into a more drastic retreat from reality. When a child's attitude improves, it is important to reinforce, by praise or other reward, his constructive behavior.

Teachers can create a better relationship if they understand the child and his needs. They should keep the lines of communication open, so they can get feedback from the child consumer concerning how well satisfied he is. Thus teaching becomes a process of interaction and not the push-button pedagogy left over from the old question-answer, stimulus-response days. In one study, an experimental group of teachers was given comprehensive data about their children, and participated in small group sessions in which their pupils were discussed. The researchers concluded that their classes made significantly greater academic gains, as well as manifesting more positive attitudes and fewer behavior problems than did controls (Ojemann and Wilkinson, 1939). However, attempts to understand the child should never degenerate into academic espionage; children's privacy should be respected.

• SPECIAL HAZARDS TO SCHOOL ADJUSTMENT

School Entrance

Typically, progress through elementary school involves certain stress-producing situations, one being initial school entrance. The major problem, of course, is the wrench from mother. She was the child's haven of security, who bestowed on him a personal love; here he is simply one among many. At home he was surrounded by familiar people and objects that gave him a feeling of belonging; in this new world all is strange. One child who found the shift beyond endurance remarked after his first day in school, "It's awful. All you do is mind, all day long." And another day he added, "It's really awful. All you do is sit, and sit, and sit" (Murphy et al., 1937, p. 652). The school situation may be completely different from that of the home. A child's parents may have been strict; at school he may have a freedom he does not know how to use. Often the reverse is true. The child may have been catered to at home and find adaptation difficult in a traditional school. Even well-adjusted children may find the experience strenuous, and the shy or insecure child may find it overwhelming.

How much better it is when children are ready, in terms of mental, physical, and emotional growth, for this new experience. The teacher might visit the home, and the parent bring the child to visit the school before he enters. Also, an advance meeting should be held with the parents to prepare them for what to expect. The mother who feels either anxious or somewhat antagonistic toward the school unconsciously communicates this feeling to the child. By contrast, the individual quoted below came from a home that had a very favorable attitude toward the school:

> I had looked forward for a long time, with great excitement, to entering school. I had no doubts of my ability and my whole family had a highly favorable attitude toward schools and all they stand for. I had a new dress, a book bag that my mother made, and a shiny lunch box. The big day came and I trudged proudly to school. Every minute there was exciting. Later that day a neighbor boy, who was also in the class, and I put a bright red tie on his younger brother and took turns teaching him.

Competition

At least in more traditional schools, the child has hardly entered before he begins to feel the effects of competition. This form of motivation is often defended on the grounds that it helps children to compete more successfully later on. It is also said to stimulate effort; however, children are differentially affected. Competition creates despair in the slow

Children respond differently to competition.

learner and anxiety in the bright one, to whom coming off second best may represent disgrace. Severe competition may generate in any child various combinations of ruthlessness and defeatism, fear and anger, confidence and inferiority. School competition may also contribute to the perpetuation of a competitive society, where the emphasis is on beating, not helping, the other fellow. Competition in the schoolroom may actually do more damage than in the larger society. In adulthood, an individual may partially choose his areas of competition; and the government plays watchdog to prevent unfair practices. However, the school child has no escape; he must simply accept whatever degree or kind of competition the teacher imposes.

The following illustrations indicate

how differently children may react to competition:

My greatest problem in grade school was competition. I could not stand then, nor can I now, to be put under pressure. I can work far more efficiently when I set my own pace. I do not enjoy competitive sports either. Maybe the reason lies in having been compared with three sisters. (Male)

I always picked out someone just a little better than I was to compete with. This sort of competition had a good effect on me. (Female)

In fifth-grade social studies class amd mathematics, we moved ahead in seats when we answered questions correctly. I was very excited when I managed to move to the first chair, but my triumph didn't last. The teacher asked "Who was Christopher Columbus?" Since I didn't answer fully enough, I lost my seat. After that I lost interest. (Female)

I always thrived on competition. I attacked every problem as though it meant my life to be the winner. This yearning to be the best has probably been the prime motivator of my life. My ideal goes along with our college wrestling-team motto: "Winning isn't everything; it's the only thing." (Male)

While adequate research on the effects of competition has yet to be done, some evidence exists. In three school systems the elimination of competitive marking was followed by an increase in achievement test scores. Probably the improvement was due to the necessity of substituting intrinsic motivations for grades and rewards (Otto, 1954). Similarly, Maller (1929) reported consistently and significantly better work with self-motivation than with group competition.

Competition places the emphasis on winning rather than on worthwhile goals; and while winning is not to be condemned, it should not be sought for its own sake. For one thing, it creates poor teacher-child relationships. Often the loser feels the teacher favored the other fellow; the winner may kow-tow to the teacher in a fawning, unhealthy way. Competition also produces a poor social atmosphere. Each child must seek out the other's weaknesses in order to win. He resents those who defeat him and is resented by those whom he defeats.

Some competition is inevitable, perhaps even desirable, and children should learn to adapt to it as constructively as possible. To achieve this aim, the teacher should help the child find and develop those areas in which he can compete most successfully. He should help the child develop a sufficiently strong ego to sustain defeat without undue feelings of stress. He should also help him broaden his interests so that success in a limited area is not crucial. Perhaps just enough competition should be provided to help the child learn to live with it, though not enough to hurt his developing ego or create undue tension. The child could also be taught to compete with himself and to keep records of his progress. Thus he would never be out of his own league in competition, and the goals to be achieved could be constantly revised, depending on his own progress and special needs.

Evaluation

A child's success in school competition implies evaluation, which involves report cards, examinations, and other devices. Ideally, evaluation should measure progress toward goals. In this sense, measurement should be applied to all the aims of education, including skills, understanding, and character and personality development. Evaluation should be diagnostic, so that the child can analyze the effectiveness of the processes he uses for achieving these goals. Moreover, evaluation should permit the child to compare his abilities with those of others, so that he may choose life goals that will hold the greatest promise of success in a competitive society. Meanwhile, he should become sufficiently involved in the evaluation process to develop effective and continuing habits of self-evaluation. Finally, evaluation should help the teacher to adapt instruction to the child, in accord with strengths or weaknesses revealed.

Report cards as instruments of evaluation. Let us see how well report cards meet these goals. First, how effectively do they measure progress toward goals? If a child makes an A for two consecutive months, does it mean he is making satisfactory progress toward his goals or just toward the teacher's goals? Does it mean excellent progress in terms of class performance or his own ability? If the child is leading the class, though hardly exerting himself, is the A grade misleading?

What about the diagnostic aim? A letter grade represents a composite rating of so many variables that it gives no idea of where strengths or weaknesses may lie. Does a D in mathematics mean the child is poor in accuracy or in understanding basic concepts, or late in turning in work, or slow compared with the rest of the class, or just what?

What about grades as incentives? If Jake, a boy with an IQ of 160, makes an A without lifting a finger, what incentive does he have to work harder? If Sam, with an IQ of 80, makes an F, he feels too defeated to try.

What about the report card as a means of comparing one's own abilities with others'? A child's performance may reflect a poor teacher-pupil relationship rather than the child's true ability. Even if grading follows the normal curve, the child's position is not clear. Does a grade of D in composition mean that he does poorly relative to others in terms of content, or perhaps in grammar? Moreover, the class from which the curve is derived fails to represent a random sampling of the larger population.

Nor do report cards help the child to define his goals. Should the child who makes a high grade in elementary-school history aspire to become a history teacher? Perhaps he is a relatively dull, unimaginative, but conscientious child who succeeds in handing back to the teacher exactly what was handed out. This child has no real insight, no real sense of history.

Meanwhile the child has had no part in the process of evaluation. He thinks of grades largely as arbitrarily assigned by the teacher. "What grade did the teacher 'give' you?" one child is often heard to ask another.

Where the teacher-child relationship is concerned, report cards may have a devastating effect. To win favor, insecure teachers, or those with little integrity, are tempted to barter grades for favor with administrators or influential parents. Meanwhile, the classroom troublemaker may suffer from a halo-in-reverse effect and receive low grades in all his subjects.

A primary aim of report cards is to inform parents, but they do little of the sort. Mr. and Mrs. Brown punish Tommy for receiving F's, in the belief that he must not be trying. Tommy's chief disability is the low intelligence he inherited via Mr. and Mrs. Brown. Mrs. Goldsmith praises Virginia for making all A's, and plans to send her through graduate school. Actually, Virginia is a charming, docile child whose abilities are mediocre but well-adapted to a thoroughly conventional school where tests require memorization but little insight. The picture her report card presents of a budding scholar is totally false.

Many people recall having had strong feelings about grades and report cards, even in elementary school:

I recall hiding a report card because my grades were lower than usual. My parents found out; and though they seemed to understand, they hollered at me anyhow. (Male)

My grades were excellent except in writing and art. However, it burned me up that time after time teachers checked the point "Not working up to ability." Grades themselves seemed to me to have no reason or rhyme, and were largely a matter of intuition on the part of the teacher. (Male)

I was proud of my report cards, except for the conduct marks. I was a very active child, and teachers marked me down for talking or twisting around in my desk. My parents took the good grades for granted and gave me re-proachful looks—which left a deeply negative imprint—for the conduct grades. (Female)

Of course, the question might well be raised: What should be done about report cards? If they are to be used, whatever strengths they possess should be maximized and their weaknesses minimized. The reports might be a partial basis for teacher-parent and teacher-pupil conferences. Conduct grades should be omitted altogether. A bright child's "poor conduct" may simply represent a healthy rebellion against an intolerably meaningless and rigid school program. Fundamental changes in the evaluation system should become one aspect of continuing efforts to adapt educational goals and processes to the needs of a space-age society.

Examinations and tests. A derivative of evaluation is testing. In more traditional settings, tests become a persistent source of stress from earliest school years (Redl and Wattenberg, 1959). In one of Piaget's (1951) studies, seven-year-old children expressed fear of the questions asked them because they believed them to be "a test." Repeatedly, they asked whether or not the answers would go on their records, whether they would receive grades, and so on. The stress induced by tests is likely to be especially severe if, during the examination, rigid proctoring and time limits are conspicuous (Stephens, 1965).

Examination anxiety can be reduced in several ways. For example, by giving more tests the teacher can reduce the threat posed by any specific test. Second, if tests are used chiefly for helping the child diagnose difficulty and assess progress, he may welcome them. At the same time, the teacher may discover weaknessess and strengths in his own approach to this child's education. However, if tests are accorded conventional grades, with their con-

notations of "success" or "failure," and concomitant dispensations of praise or blame, their more constructive purposes are obscured.

More research needs to be done to determine how testing practices should be modified. Little is positively known about how tests affect relations among students or between students and their teachers (Goslin, 1963). For instance, do test results affect a child's status among his peers? How do they alter the teacher's perception of his pupils? How does a child's knowledge of test results modify his self-conceptions and aspirations? Do tests contribute to a self-fulfilling prophesy by leaving an indelible mark on a youngster's career?

Better concepts of evaluation. Actually, evaluation should proceed along a broad front, utilizing both formal and informal techniques. So that evaluation may become an integral part of the child's lifelong learning process, the teacher should encourage him to measure progress throughout a learning experience. Individual guidance helps him to diagnose difficulties as they occur, within the context of the problem at hand. For more comprehensive analysis, standardized diagnostic tests should be used. Standardized achievement tests can be used to indicate progress toward goals and permit perspective on one's own abilities relative to others.

To measure progress toward the broader goals of education, informal measures may be best. A grade of D on citizenship will hardly make a child resolve, "Next month I will be a better citizen!" However, if the child is involved in a community clean-up campaign and periodically writes a progress report, he gains a meaningful experience in self-evaluation as a citizen. As he goes over his report with his teacher or classmates, he learns to relate his self-perceptions to those that others hold of him. If the group's evaluation is friendly and constructive, he will not feel "picked on" or defensive.

385

We should not underestimate the value of informal evaluation:

Many informal ways may be found to measure the broader objectives. Well-chosen reading provides standards of behavior against which the child can measure his own. Discussion of characters in history and in literature assist the child to appraise his own ideals and to formulate his philosophy of life. Classroom discussions of situations involving moral judgments enable the child to test group acceptance of his own beliefs. Such experiences also modify the child's attitudes and help to define his goals. The emphasis will be on helping the child to discover his strengths so that he can capitalize upon them. Provision of many kinds of experiences affords one valuable opportunities for self-appraisal. It may be difficult to recognize this sort of thing as evaluation simply because it is not measurable in quantitative terms and tied up neatly in a symbol. Yet testing oneself in a wide range of activities yields invaluable data to assist in selecting goals.

Various standardized tests and many kinds of group experiences help the child to understand his abilities in relation to those of others. The emphasis is not on comparison but simply on finding where one's own skills may fit best into the scheme of things. Meanwhile regular habits of self-evaluation are formed through continuous informal discussions by teacher and pupil during all phases of the educational process. Simply asking the child questions may stimulate reflection. "You don't seem to be having much luck with that problem, Malcolm," the teacher observes in a friendly tone. "What do you think the trouble can be?" — "Well I've figured every way I can think of, Mr. Adams, but it won't come out right." — "Tell me how you did it." In explaining his approach Malcolm obtains a more objective view and discovers his error. The obvious concern for Malcolm's feelings permits him to acknowledge his difficulty without apology or confusion. These incidental evaluations during the course of an activity are among the most valuable. They facilitate learning by indicating where and how attention should be directed [Rogers, 1957, pp. 245–246].

Nonpromotion

One of the most stress-producing byproducts of evaluation is nonpromotion. In summarizing research on the topic, Wrightstone (1957) indicates that nonpromotion reduces the child's self-respect and security while increasing his feelings of inferiority. One summary of research concerning nonpromotion as traditionally practiced yielded these generalizations: There is no evidence that retention significantly accelerates a slow learning rate or ensures subject mastery; nor does nonpromotion improve grade-achievement averages or the retained child's adjustment (Sumption and Phillips, 1950). As the system is currently practiced, the retained child seldom does any better than his equally wobbly classmate who is promoted (Worth, 1961). Nevertheless, declares Stephens (1965), the ill effects of nonpromotion may be overrated. At worst, it merely adds a year or so to a child's schooling. It is less serious, he believes, than the endless frustrations involved in attempting work for which he is not ready.

On balance, the failure to advance a child with his grade may have either beneficial or disastrous effects. Perhaps a child has struggled for years to keep up with children who are more advanced both physically and mentally. An extra year in a grade might place him among children more nearly on his level of development.

Meantime, if during the child's second year in a grade his experiences are not merely repeated but modified to meet his needs, time need not be lost. In fact, if work is now within his comprehension, more time ultimately may be gained than lost. If the nonpromotion should come to represent, both in spirit and in fact, additional experience for making up deficiencies and establishing a compatible framework within which the child may achieve, instead of a symbol of failure, it would be advisable in selected cases. Normally, however, nonpromotion is called "failure," and the child is simply exposed to the same sort of experiences and climate that proved unrewarding before. In any specific case, the effects of nonpromotion will vary according to the way it is handled and the nature of the child concerned (Worth, 1961).

Here two people indicate their own experiences relating to nonpromotion:

> Since I was slow in reading, I had to repeat the fourth grade. I felt weak and sick, knowing that my friends were moving ahead while I wasn't. It hurt my parents, too. During the next year no additional help was given to help remedy my reading deficiency. (Male)

> Being held back made a terrific impact on me. It was a real shock because I was not told until the new term opened in the fall. However, the teacher did her best to help me adjust. She told me why I was repeating and advised that I not let what the other kids said bother me. In the long run I was glad I repeated the grade, because the teacher tried hard to make the experience worthwhile. (Male)

The problem of nonpromotion is less likely to arise in schools with classes small enough and philosophy sufficiently enlightened to permit provision for individual differences. Obviously, if teachers are expected to bring every child up to some hypothetical grade standard, slower or duller children may be unconsciously resented, and consciously pressured. They may thus develop anxieties that prevent their achieving even as much as they normally would.

Ideally, every case should be decided on its own merits, in terms of the child's total welfare. If a child is left behind more than once, he may find himself among much younger children who look upon older classmates as retarded. In turn, the bigger child, especially the boy, is likely to pick on the younger ones, since physical strength is the one characteristic in which he excels. Therefore, while one or two nonpromotions, in rare cases, may result in net gain, more

than that would be unadvisable. If the curriculum is fitted to each child within the grade, instead of the child being fitted to the curriculum, nonpromotion will rarely be required.

There is no dearth of research on the topic of nonpromotion (Worth, 1960). However, none exists that indicates the effects of retention in cases where the more enlightened philosophy suggested above has been employed. Nor does any assess the relative merits of nonpromotion and transfer to classes in special education.

Success versus Failure

The nonpromotion question brings up another issue: Should school experiences be paced so as to provide continuous experiences in success, or should they be so challenging that a certain amount of failure is inevitable? Until individuals attempt goals too hard for them, it may be argued, they will never know how far they can go. To encourage such attempts, in the face of extremely difficult goals, Stephens (1965) suggests that generous rewards be provided for resolute individuals who try but nevertheless fail.

The author believes that failures are to be avoided and successes planned for, and whenever possible, achieved. The child who reaches his goals comes to perceive himself as an achiever, or as one who can solve his problems. Success releases energy and enhances chances for future successes. Failure indicates that the goal chosen was either inappropriate or above the present capacities of the individual to achieve. Life inevitably involves enough failures to make it unnecessary that teachers arrange them—for character-building, testing the limits of capacity, or any other reason.

The best way to eliminate failure is to alter the traditional concept of what failing to reach a specific goal implies. Suppose a child establishes a goal, but does not achieve it. Traditionally, he receives an F on his report card, dis-

387

approval from the teacher, and reproof or punishment from his parents. The child, in turn, feels humiliated and disheartened, and has small incentive to make further attempts. Instead, he should simply be helped to reappraise his goal, and perhaps to modify it, either by reducing it, substituting some other goal, or finding better ways of reaching this one. Never, in this approach, does the traditional concept of "failure" come into the picture. The child is led to make constant reappraisals and continuous modifications of processes and goals to enhance ultimate rewards.

• CHILDREN WITH SPECIAL PROBLEMS

"Circumstantial" Problems

The new child. Sometimes children's problems stem from special circumstances; for instance, a child may enter a class during, instead of at the beginning of, the session. Usually he has come from another community and at the same time must adjust to a strange house, neighborhood, and school. The only constants are his family, who may not afford him the normal feelings of security because they, too, are involved in making new adjustments. When the parents are so preoccupied with their own problems, the teacher becomes especially important. To a large extent he determines whether the child adjusts with relative smoothness or feels desolate.

Some children adjust easily, others with great difficulty. Grade-school children "take on" newcomers far more readily than do adolescents, with their tight-knit cliques. However, young children are brutally blunt about rejecting a child who externalizes his problems and whose symptoms become exaggerated in strange situations. In some cases, he may come from a different type of environment, so that his clothes, manner of speech, or customs differ from those of his new classmates. The teacher's help may take several

forms. At the very first, he may chat with the child individually, so that the child feels the teacher's personal concern. The teacher should also determine the child's level of preparation to prevent wasteful and anxiety-producing discontinuity in the child's schooling. He may have children volunteer to show the newcomer about. Unless the child is shy, he can be encouraged to tell about where he came from and locate it on a map. For some time, the teacher should unobtrusively assist the child to find a place in games and activities. At the same time, the child should be led increasingly to assume charge of his own adjustment.

The transient pupil. Some children move not merely once but several times. These may include children of migrant workers, show people, servicemen, or businessmen connected with companies with branches across the country. Migration involves all social classes, not simply the poorer classes.

Transiency may both help and hinder school work. On the positive side, the child brings a broad background to the learning experience. Also, from earliest years he has had experience in adapting to new situations. Moreover, he is more likely to possess a certain detachment, or world view, which permits a correspondingly more objective approach to intellectual problems. On the negative side, his education may have been haphazard through its discontinuity. As a result, the child may come to assume an indifferent or hopeless attitude toward his work.

Some teachers, recognizing a child as transient, may simply resign themselves to waiting until he leaves. Instead, they should make every effort to orient him to the school program and to the group. They might also encourage him to share his experiences with the other children. Meanwhile, they might make friendly overtures to the parents, and discuss ways of making the child's stay in the school, however temporary, a profitable one.

The Lower-Class Child

Reasons for handicap. The way that socioeconomic background may handicap a child's progress in school varies with each case; however, certain factors are generally relevant. For one thing, lower-class children's homes are often too crowded to permit a quiet place to study; and they lack books for cultural stimulation. Also, the language patterns of lower-class family and neighborhood differ widely from that of teachers, a factor that undoubtedly obstructs understanding (Peisach, 1965).

Nor should the simple economics of the lower-class child's problems be overlooked. He may lack money for class functions or social activities, both inside and outside the school setting. He may be unable to obtain money for school supplies or for the sort of clothes that would help give him status among his peers. More indirectly, he may suffer from lack of medical care or proper foods because of deficits in family education and budget. Not surprisingly, a major cause of school dropouts is financial difficulty (Miller, 1963).

The teacher and the lower-class child. Teachers generally are more favorably oriented toward higher- than toward lower-class children (Davison and Long, 1960). They perceive lower-class children as more difficult to control, as possessing lower moral standards, and as generally less acceptable (Becker, 1952). Such children tend to be low achievers, and though teachers accord them more contact quantitatively than more able pupils, their contact with high achievers is more favorable qualitatively (Hoehn, 1954).

Small wonder that lower-class children are confused by their relationships with teachers. In one projective study of slum-school children, a child made these remarks while looking at four pictures of facial expressions—one appearing natural, the second slightly dubious, the third happy, and the fourth belligerent:

The teacher might whip him. The teacher might holler at him. The teacher might tell him to get to work. The teacher might write something on the board, and he don't write it. The teacher might tell him to come and get his milk and cookies. The teacher might call him to come here. The teacher might say for him to look at the book. The boy feels real bad. He is not so happy.

The teacher feels bad, too, because they aren't doing what the teacher said, and they won't look at the board. They won't read in their books. They don't copy off nobody. They don't get no whippings [LeFevre, 1966, p. 12].

Interestingly, teachers themselves are increasingly of lower-class origin (Wolfle, 1954). Teaching provides social mobility—that is, the attainment of a higher status than their parents held—for perhaps 40% who enter the profession (Stiles, 1957). Unfortunately, research is lacking that would distinguish the differential attitudes of teachers with lower- or middle-class backgrounds toward children of corresponding social classes. One might expect greater understanding of lower-class children by teachers with a similar background. However, it is just possible that some lower-class teachers would reject children who reminded them of the origins they would rather forget.

Lower-class versus school values. The lower-class child also suffers from the discrepancy between the school's values and his family's. The values of school and of middle class are one and the same: a concern for intellectual excellence and for taste and refinement. At school the only acceptable working-class value is "being good at working with your hands." Others of its values—toughness, cynicism, and aggressiveness—are rejected (Rosenberg, 1965).

At the same time, the lower-class child's teachers constantly urge upon him values and goals that may prove nonfunctional either for his present or future. While he may rise in the social order, many of his social class will not, and only a very few will rise more than one narrow rung on the status ladder. Hence, emphasizing such middle-class values as respect for private or material property, of which he has little, is similar to requiring natives in the heart of the African heat belt to wear clothing; both demands are inconsistent with the environment. The teacher also stresses grades, which the child's background hinders his achieving, and some future white-collar occupation, which he is unlikely to attain (Corwin, 1965). By contrast, the time he spends with his gang, which the teacher disparages, may help compensate for the status denied him in the middle-class world. In fact, the teacher rarely understands the lower-class child's peer world. Rarely does the school recognize its leaders, or work through, instead of against, its gangs. The school insists on imposing onto the lower-class child middle-class values and ways. Perhaps if he were simply exposed to them, and led to accept them naturally, without the concomitant downgrading of his own social group values, he would feel less hostile and defensive.

Additional problems of lower-class children.

A very few lower-class children not only embrace middle-class values but hold higher aspirations than do their higher-class peers, perhaps because their parents have taken the middle class as their reference group. The parents are determined that their children, especially their sons, will attain what they themselves failed to achieve (Kahl, 1953). However, in the vast majority of cases, middle-class parents are far more likely than their lower-class counterparts to teach their children to believe in success and to take active steps to make it possible, by hard work, planning, and so on (Rosen, 1956).

Nor does the slum child find much more encouragement at his school, especially if it is located in and reflects the slum environment.

What inducement does the slum school offer? In the perceptions of many teachers now in these schools, [slum children] are "unteachable." The supervision is inadequate and often hostile. Principals, and their assistants, are constantly harassed by continuous teacher turnover, uncovered classes, disciplinary problems . . . involvement with the police, and the courts, lack of appropriate or even adequate books and materials. Many feel as did a very young woman, when asked how long she had taught before leaving the field. She said: "I haven't taught a day in my life, but I served a three-year sentence in Junior High School" [Goldberg, 1964, p. 175].

What should be done?

Various plans have been advanced to cope with this situation: dispensation of birth-control information to lessen the birth-rate of the lower-classes, **Head Start programs** to provide for young slum children what the home may lack, and integrated schools that deliberately mix social classes. Integration, it is argued, permits lower-class children to absorb middle-class values naturally, thus facilitating social mobility. Moreover, the de facto segregation produced by neighborhood schools is said to inculcate feelings of inferiority and reduce aspiration. But whether a lower-class child's attitudes can be permanently altered through membership in an integrated school society has not been determined. Also undetermined is whether early exposure to middle-class aspirations and ethics in an enriched school environment can reverse the effects of the initial deprivation (Wilson, 1959).

Some authorities argue against the deliberate desegregation of schools, or the tampering with neighborhood school systems in order to induce social-class mixing. While such mingling may be right on moral grounds, they argue, it sometimes makes scapegoats of the children it is designed to help. Far from being democratic, says Corwin (1965), the comprehensive system forces underprivileged pupils to compete with much better-prepared ones. But Corwin should take note that the path to progress is often hard and beset with growing pains.

Practical solutions for coping with the situation must await more adequate research. After surveying available studies, Boocock (1966) stated two major conclusions: First, that the quality of sociological studies in the area of learning is uneven, ranging from some quite sophisticated studies to others that are almost "ridiculous in design and content." Second, little can be said with certainty about how social factors operate on the pupil. Besides, it may be unrealistic to expect the school to reform unless the larger society, of which it is an integral part, does so. The same schoolboard members who expect teachers to accord their children preferred treatment will hardly favor the teacher who reduces them to the same classroom status as the slum child (Corwin, 1965).

"Child-Centered" Problems

The predelinquent. While the school may undoubtedly accentuate them, some children's problems derive chiefly from their own personalities. Such children are of many kinds—the shy child, the hostile child, the defiant child, and many others. Here we will look at only a few, beginning with the **predelinquent.**

In one study it was revealed that the seeds of delinquency are sewn early; even in the third grade, future delinquents appeared more poorly adjusted than did their classmates. They had less regard for the rights and feelings of their peers, while rejecting authority in the school situation. Their social behaviors were less acceptable than those of more law-abiding children. Also, they were less willing to deal courteously, fairly, and tactfully with others (Conger et al., 1965).

In another study, predelinquents showed slower progress through the grades, poorer scholarship, and general antipathy for school (Glueck, 1966). When talking with the psychiatrist, the boys would spontaneously make such statements as, "I hate school because I am always left back," or "It is too hard," or "I want to go to work," and so on. Most of them (94.8%) had truanted at one time or another, as contrasted with only 10.8% of the nondelinquents. Two-thirds of the predelinquents had truanted persistently.

Unfortunately, very little has been done to adapt the school program to these children. Too often, the child is simply expected to fit the program. In consequence, the child himself "adjusts" by running away from school obligations in search of more absorbing activities.

Truants and behavior problems. In reality, children can rarely be categorized as representing a single type of problem. In one group of over 1,000 children classified as behavior problems or truants, an impressive number had suffered some remediable physical or educational handicap, or both (Mullen, 1950). The two types of maladjustment stemmed from different origins, however. The truants came from unsatisfactory home situations: families on relief, broken homes, crowded homes, and the like. The children who caused discipline problems were merely restless and impulsive.

In both cases, the answer is much the same: the teacher must find some way to reach these children. They should be permitted to be themselves—that is, to pursue their own goals and interests within the framework of the school. Materials and methods provided should be within the children's level of comprehension and should be interesting to them. They must be helped to achieve success, to play a meaningful role in the class, and to feel that they belong. Otherwise, no communicative link will be found.

The Teacher as Therapist

Obviously, the teacher must be concerned with much more than purely academic matters. A child's emotional disturbance may be so serious or of such

391

a nature as to obstruct learning. Unless he can "get himself off his own hands," he may be unable to focus on anything outside himself, including learning tasks. How teachers should discharge this responsibility—that is, assisting children to resolve personal problems—has been disputed. Some psychologists recommend a nondirective approach, with the teacher simply reflecting back to the child what the child feels. Others believe that relatively firm guidance and clearly defined boundaries help make the child feel secure.

The Wickman study. One widely quoted study, reported by Wickman in 1928, involved having both teachers and mental-hygiene specialists rate the relative seriousness of certain child-behavior symptoms.

Teachers rated as more serious those symptoms associated with noisy, disobedient, outgoing behaviors that disrupted the classroom, whereas the specialists rated as more serious the internalized symptoms such as withdrawal, anxiety, and sensitivity, while attaching little importance to the behaviors deplored by the teachers. The results were widely interpreted to mean that teachers had less concern for the fundamental aspects of children's problems than did the therapists. Such interpretation, however, failed to consider the completely different roles of teacher and mental hygienist (Beilin, 1959). The clinician typically works with one child at a time, the teacher with many. Perhaps a child from an unhappy, authoritative home who has bottled up his feelings responds to an informal schoolroom situation by unleashing all his repressed hostilities and feelings. While the child may indeed profit from "opening up" in this manner, the teacher owes a responsibility to the rest of the class. Not to maintain a semblance of order would constitute an infringement on their right to an education.

Replications of the Wickman study indicate greater congruence between teachers' and clinicians' attitudes. However, complete congruence probably will not, and should not, be achieved (Kounin and Gump, 1961). By the very nature of their functions, clinicians will be concerned solely for the child, while teachers must also have regard for the "boisterous, aggressive behavior that disrupts the class and creates an impossible situation for learning" (Klausmeier and Goodwin, 1966, p. 149).

• SUMMARY

There has long been considerable confusion about the objectives of the school. In the elementary school, academic excellence is generally accorded a lower place than social adjustment. Early childhood education is aimed at primary socialization, or laying the foundations for later educational and social development. There is some doubt about how effective or necessary such education is; however, nursery schools that have been judged ineffective have simply offered what any well-ordered home may provide. Their effectiveness would seem to depend partly on coordinating early schooling with that which follows.

At any level, **curriculum** is important. Children need material that challenges them and takes into the account the present and future needs of both society and the individual learner. They should establish a broad base of knowledge for supporting later learning and for coping with a complex world, but in later years "zero in" on an area especially suited to their interests and abilities. In short, they should begin by being jacks-of-all-subjects and, finally, master of one. They may also profit from the **co-curriculum,** consisting of social and interest clubs and athletics, if it is meaningfully integrated with the rest of the program. In a world of increasing leisure, children should master worthwhile ways of using free time.

Content is meaningless unless it can be put across; that is, teachers must employ effective methods. Children's interests do not simply burst forth full-blown, but must be helped to ripen. Aids to this goal are inquiry training and discovery method, which challenge children to replicate on their level the scientist's search for truth. Method should also be adapted to the child, in terms of his background, intelligence, personality, and creative potential. To develop children's creativity—that is, their capacity to utilize novel approaches and arrive at original solutions—teachers should encourage divergent rather than convergent thinking. Convergent thinking suggests solving a problem with the facts at hand and narrowing available alternatives until a solution is found; divergent thinking suggests using intuition, imagination, and a propensity for unconventional solutions. Teachers should also encourage fun activities and abandon the grim, do-or-die approach.

Various factors affect the child's academic achievement: classroom climate, the child's sex and personality, and the teacher-pupil relationship. The ideal classroom is busy and orderly, though pleasant and somewhat democratic in control. Order should be preserved not for its own sake but as the necessary prerequisite to accomplishment. If sufficiently interested in their projects, children will join the teacher in helping maintain the order required to pursue their work. The effect of personality traits on achievement is unclear, partly because of confusion in the definitions of adjustment and achievement. The child's attitude toward school is certainly important, as well as his attitude toward the teacher and subject involved. Girls tend to blame their scholastic dissatisfactions on themselves, boys on the school.

In fact, school has a differential effect on girls and boys. In general, the passive control and women teachers of the lower grades seem to favor girls, while the increasing number of scientific subjects and men teachers in higher grades seem to favor boys. Besides, boys become increasingly aware of the role of higher education in achieving higher-status jobs.

Both sexes profit from having effective teachers and wholesome teacher-pupil relationships. Teachers need to know their subject, how to put it across, and how to relate to children. Different sorts of teachers relate in particular ways to different sorts of children. In general, teachers should remain aware of how they react to children and how children react to them. They should seek to understand children without spying on them.

School adjustment has its special hazards, particularly initial school entrance. Children need to be made ready physically, mentally, and emotionally for the new experience. Another hazard is competition, which places the emphasis on winning rather than on achieving worthwhile goals. However, since some competition is inevitable, children should learn to adjust to whatever competition occurs. Another bugaboo is evaluation, and its traditionally feared instrument, the report card. Ordinarily, such cards do little to tell either parent or child how well the child is performing in terms of his own capacity. Nor do they provide any clue about just where he has failed or why. Examinations, too, are often so anxiety-producing that they defeat the purposes they are designed to serve. However, fundamental modifications of the evaluation system should simply be one aspect of a broad reformation of the entire educational system.

A related problem is that of non-promotion, which may deal damaging blows to a child's self-respect and security. If the child is left with children much younger than he, or if nonpromotion merely results in repetition of the same work and the same frustrations, more harm than good is done. If the curriculum is fitted to the child, instead of the child to the curriculum, nonpromotion will rarely be required.

Certain children have special problems, including the new child, the transient child, and the child of the lower class. The teacher should determine the new child's level of preparation to prevent anxiety-producing discontinuity in his schooling. However brief the transient child's stay, his tenure there should be made worthwhile. The lower-class child's problem is adapting to an essentially middle-class school, which often fails to acknowledge his handicaps, his values, his aspirations, or his personal worth. Nor do teachers adapt the curriculum to his needs and motivations. Lately, projects like **Head Start** are being designed to give him a chance to compete on equal terms in school. However, unless such efforts are made part of a continuing program throughout his school years, early gains may be lost.

Other children with problems are the **predelinquent** and the truant. In each case the teacher must serve as therapist as well as dispenser of knowledge. He must be alert to symptoms but also aware that a child's behaviors may seem perfectly normal within the context of home or peer group. In fact, a display of serious maladjustment at school does not always indicate subsequent maladjustment even in the classroom. Here, of course, reference is to specific behaviors. Such general characteristics as moodiness, cheerfulness, or irritability are more persistent from year to year.

Another source of misunderstanding is this: It is felt that a teacher must understand and relate specifically to every child in the room. An early study reported some gains in academic achievement after teachers learned more about their pupils (Davison and Long, 1960). A later study of the value of providing teachers such information found no gains in pupil performance despite an occasional improvement in the child's attitude toward the teacher (Bush, 1958). Of course, the teacher should do what he can to understand each pupil, but he cannot give extended attention to any one child. On the other hand, it is possible to create the sort of climate in which most children feel that the teacher cares. Such a teacher listens to what each child says, commends his efforts (however ineffective they may be), and provides friendly counsel for personal and academic problems.

• SUGGESTED QUESTIONS
AND ACTIVITIES

1. What sort of traits, ideally, should teachers of young children have?
2. Do elementary school teachers generally provide adequate identification figures?
3. Should those elementary school teachers be denied employment who might be classified as (a) psychoneurotics; (b) communists; (c) members of off-beat cults or political parties; (d) physically handicapped individuals; or (e) highly intellectual individuals with rather cold personalities?
4. Should teachers be required to undergo psychoanalysis so they would understand better how their personalities and problems might impinge upon children?
5. Is it better that children in the primary grades be taught primarily by one teacher or by several subject-matter specialists?
6. Analyze portions of several children's textbooks in terms of their potential effect on the child's development.
7. Would it help if professional writers and psychologists collaborated with educators in preparing children's textbooks, especially readers, so that they would be well-written as well as educationally and psychologically sound?
8. What are the major ways that present-day schools fail to meet children's needs?
9. Should extrinsic rewards such as honor rolls and stars be avoided?
10. What should the school do to meet the needs of the rough-and-tough predelinquent boy?
11. Should lower-class children be bused to middle-class schools?
12. If unlimited funds were available, what sort of features might be added to today's elementary schools?
13. Should children attend school the year around?
14. Has the school's willingness to deal broadly with the child's welfare caused parents to abdicate essential aspects of their role and resulted in too little attention to children's intellectual development?
15. Answer each of the questions below on a separate slip of paper. Indicate your sex but not your name. Either the instructor or student committees may analyze and

report results, reading excerpts to support conclusions. (a) Describe the case of some teacher who performed successfully as a therapist in a school situation. (b) Describe a real-life situation of a lower-class child in a predominantly middle-class school. (c) Describe any incident relating to school that stands out strongly in your memory. (d) Of the various schoolroom situations you have known, describe the one that had the worst effect on the children, and the best. Tell in some detail why. (e) Describe any unusual method of discipline you have seen employed in school. (f) Describe your nursery school or kindergarten experiences. What did they do for you, positively or negatively, in terms of mental, emotional, or personality development? (g) Describe the effect on you of some school incident involving report cards or competition. (h) Analyze some specific teacher-child relationship.

• SUGGESTED READINGS

Bany, M. A., and L. V. Johnson, *Classroom Group Behavior: Group Dynamics in Action.* New York: The Macmillan Company, 1964. Discusses the psychological dynamics of classroom groups, as well as ways teachers can influence group behavior.

Drews, E. M., "Self-Actualization: A New Focus for Education," *Learning and Mental Health in the School,* 1966 Yearbook. Washington, D.C.: Association for Supervision and Curriculum Development, 1966, pp. 99–124. A provocative discussion of the school's role in the child's personal development.

Getzels, J. W., "Preschool Education," *Teachers College Record,* Vol. 48, No. 3 (1966) pp. 219–228. Discusses critical issues concerned with immediate operational problems as well as long-term underlying problems.

Glidewell, J. C., M. B. Kantor, L. M. Smith, and L. A. Stringer, "Socialization and Social Structure in the Classroom," in M. L. Hoffman and L. W. Hoffman, eds., *Review of Child Development Research,* Vol. 2. New York: Russell Sage Foundation, 1966, pp. 221–256. Reviews research concerning the social structure of the schoolroom and the effect of the schoolroom on socialization.

Havighurst, R. J., P. J. Bowman, G. P. Liddle, C. V. Matthews, and J. V. Pierce, *Growing Up in River City.* New York: John Wiley & Sons, Inc., 1962. A longitudinal study involving the same individuals from sixth grade to about age 20. Relates personal characteristics and social backgrounds to problems of growing up in a midwestern community of 45,000 people.

Read, K. H., *The Nursery School: A Human Relationship Laboratory,* 4th ed. Philadelphia: W. B. Saunders, 1966. Discusses nursery school in terms of its curriculum and equipment, its goals, parent-child and parent-teacher relationships, and effects of nursery school on children's adjustment.

Schmuck, R. A., M. B. Luszki, and D. C. Epperson, "Interpersonal Relations and Mental Health in the Classroom," *Mental Hygiene,* Vol. 47 (1963), pp. 289–299. Analyzes the relationship between classroom interpersonal relations on the one hand and mental health and academic learning on the other. Suggestions are given for improving the classroom learning environment.

Torrance, E. P., *Guiding Creative Talent.* Englewood Cliffs, N. J.: Prentice-Hall, 1962. Treats both theoretical and practical aspects of developing creativity in children.

14

THE CHILD AND HIS CULTURE

Culture embraces all the learned behaviors of a people, including customs and values, art and technology, patterns of language and thought, all the customary ways of operating within a society (Gardner, 1964). Stone and Church (1957) emphasize that culture is a coherent, integrated system of values and customs, not merely a miscellaneous collection of quaint practices that travelogs recount. From the standpoint of the child, culture is the social heritage to which he is born and in which he is reared. It includes the answers that his group has made and is making to the problems of life (Bossard and Boll, 1960).

In the 1930s and '40s, cultural anthropologists popularized the theory that every culture has its basic personality type, or traits shared by most of its members. This core structure derives from the child's reactions to the society's primary institutions, especially the family. For example, among the Alorese, who live in the East Indies, child care is sporadic. The mother is often absent; and the child is weaned merely by being pushed away. Moreover, he is teased and deceived by all adults, including his parents. In consequence, asserts Kardiner (1945), the Alorese personality is marked by feelings of inadequacy, isolation, and worthlessness.

Even the languages used in different societies may affect personality. The responses of 64 adult bilinguists to a projective test given in English differed significantly from their responses to the same test given in French. The nature of the shift reflected differences in the cultures themselves. Hence personality may be thought of as influenced, to some degree at least, by the language used for communication (Ervin, 1964).

How the Child Becomes Acculturated

Earlier views of acculturation. The process by which a child acquires the society's culture, or its characteristic ways of behaving, is called **acculturation.**

Drawing by Starr, age 7. She is already demonstrating the effects of acculturation. Children embrace the culture's ways of thinking and behaving, including its rules. From the author's files.

There are two main ways, separate though interrelated, in which this process is described. One is based on the study of social organizations and processes and their impact on the individual—an approach that may be considered primarily sociocultural in focus. The other is based on the study of the complete socialization of the child; this approach is said to be social-psychological in focus.

This first, or sociocultural, approach has in turn shifted in emphasis over the years. There was a time when anthropologists explained the distinctive traits of the adults within any society as the direct outcome of some prevalent child-rearing practice within that society. For example, let us make certain cross-cultural comparisons. Among early Greeks, a nomadic way of life prevailed and the child had to shift for himself. However, in later Greek society children were pampered and discouraged from attaining independence, and hence failed to become achievement-oriented. On the surface, a direct cause-effect relationship seems apparent; however, the ascription of later behaviors to some specific early child-rearing emphasis may not prove valid. To take examples from other cultures, among both the

Oglala Sioux and the Eastern European Jews, the haphazard educational system would seem destined to result in ignorance and superstition, but the total social pattern in fact produced intellectually oriented children (Lee, 1960).

Because of apparent discrepancies, anthropologists now concluded it was the pattern, and not isolated practices, that determined the personality traits of a society's members (Gardner, 1964). The total cultural context must be taken into account, and perceived as an unbroken network, with no single experience meaningful apart from the total. Not only major features of the culture, but every aspect of it, no matter how slight, was now seen as influencing the child.

The early theory, which took into account only a single child-care practice, would hardly have explained the nature of the Hopis. Despite the affectionate care and indulgence of an infant-centered home, the adult Hopi's life was characterized by marked anxiety, suspicion, distrust, and fear of death. Eggan (1945) ascribed this apparently discontinuous effect to a complex of factors: the abrupt restriction of aggression and the inculcation of supernatural fears in middle childhood, culture conflict and ambivalence about white rule, and the rigors of extracting a livelihood from a dry, rocky terrain.

Similarly, certain "typical" American traits, like generosity and interest in materialism, might be ascribed to a whole complex of factors, including wide natural resources, a favorable climate, love-oriented child-rearing, a democratic heritage, and the Judeo-Christian ethic. However, it is quite obvious that Americans differ widely among themselves, each manifesting his own unique combination of traits.

Recent view of acculturation. This leads to the second major explanation of child acculturation, based on social-psychological learning theory. In the rigidly structured primitive society, it is

Whether it is described as sociocultural or social-psychological, acculturation is obviously a subtle process.

easy to demonstrate a relationship between culture and personality, but no such clear-cut relations exist between individual Westerners and their culture.

The reason is that in modern society, culture is no one thing. Culture and subcultures mesh together in intricate patterns. Even families within the same subculture have distinctive ways of life. In fact, an individual may be a part of so many subcultures that the relationship between his traits and the customs of any one of the subcultural groups that produced him may not be clear-cut. Furthermore, no individual bears the impress of all the minute details of his culture. He internalizes certain aspects only.

It is, therefore, futile to attempt to define in detail the impact of modern cultures on the individuals who compose them. Human clay can be molded in so many ways that the temptation arises to view man as a pawn of innumerable forces, buffeted about like driftwood caught in the tide. Behavior seems a capricious thing, resistant to intelligent control. But the conscientious sociologist or psychologist who accepted this defeatist philosophy would have to abandon his profession. Instead, he perceives man as selecting from among variables available to him. Hence, the individual is not passively molded, the helpless victim of his environment. He chooses, consciously or unconsciously, according to his past experiences and present needs. What emerges from these interactions is his personality—his own unique pattern of tendencies [Rogers, 1962, p. 439].

In somewhat different words, Stone and Church (1957, p. 96) say much the same thing:

What the child learns is not his whole culture plus a sub-culture, plus a role to play within it, plus a family tradition, but simply his own family's ways which are compounded of all these. More than this, he learns his own special adaptation of these determined by whether he is born at an opportune or inopportune time, is of the desired sex, is first-born or ninth-born, etc. And, of course, the interplay of his own temperament and characteristics with this general and specific array of social and environmental pressures makes for a unique version of the culture he learns. According to the kind of family he is born into, not only in terms of its formal position in the scheme of things but in the concrete terms of its living quarters, its diet, its dress, its patterns of recreation, the intonations of its speech,. he will learn a particular view of himself and reality. For in the final analysis, each family can be regarded as a special version of a sub-culture. The cultural values of any given pair of parents (the generally accepted ones of their society, with their special, say, eastern, Protestant, Jones flavor) will be reflected in the emotional climate which structures their baby's awareness of reality. This awareness does not take final form for a number of years, but its emotional groundwork is established during infancy, so subtly and so firmly that it appears to have been there all along, as though this special way of viewing the world were the only conceivable one.

• CHARACTERISTICS OF CULTURES

All cultures have certain common features, because of likenesses both in people and in their environment. These

In a continuous culture, such as Vietnam, child roles are functional in adulthood.

shared features, in turn, become the common heritage of every human child. Cultures also differ, however, on many important dimensions. And these differences have potent effects on the child's development.

Continuous versus Discontinuous Cultures

Cultures differ, for example, in their degree of continuity and discontinuity. In the continuous culture, child roles and behaviors are functional in adulthood, while in the discontinuous one they are unrelated.

Among the Cheyenne Indians, for example, the small boy is already learning his later role as hunter; and his family ceremoniously make a feast of the child's first snowbird. At birth he is given a tiny bow and arrow, and from the time he can run about, he is given bows and arrows adapted to his size by the man of the family. Animals and birds are brought to his attention, in a graded series, beginning with those most easily taken. As he brings in the first of each species, his family make a feast of it, accepting his contribution as gravely as they do his father's buffalo. When he finally does kill a buffalo, it is only the final step in being processed for his adult role [Benedict, 1938, p. 163].

By contrast, the Manus' culture is a discontinuous one, where the child is undisciplined and unrestrained, and given no real chores until he is married, when demands become severe. Only those men who build the biggest canoes and best houses have high status. The young man is given a wife, and must be completely subordinated to those who paid for her. Not surprisingly, he suffers from considerable mental disturbance [Benedict, 1934].

American culture, like the Manus', has been generally portrayed as discontinuous. The child must be asexual; but on becoming an adult he is expected to make an immediate and successful sexual adjustment. His childhood tasks bear little relationship to his adult occupation. However, in another sense the American culture may in its very discontinuity have elements of conti-

nuity. In a complex, fast-changing culture, perhaps it is best that a child's life be not merely continuous with his adult role. By adulthood, life may have become so different that what he has learned from his parents will be out of date. Today's child who dresses in pa's hand-me-downs—whether clothes, customs, or morals—is clad in a hopelessly outmoded garb. Besides, the child's constantly shifting roles, as he moves from one group to another or from one age-stage to another, may ultimately facilitate adjustment in a society where readjustment is continually necessary.

Homogeneous versus Complex Cultures

Cultures also differ in the complexity of their group relationships, some involving only primary groups, others secondary groups as well. Primary groups are characterized by intimate, face-to-face contacts, secondary groups by more superficial contacts with a variety of people. Primitive societies most often involve only primary groups; more complex cultures are composed of both primary and secondary groups. Even in a modern culture, most of the rural or small town child's relationships are with primary groups, or with people he knows. However, as he grows older, multiple group membership is the rule. He attends the cosmopolitan junior high school and brushes shoulders daily with hundreds of boys and girls he does not know. In the city and the larger suburb, he does the same—a great contrast with the primitive village, where every child knows everyone else.

Where multiple group membership, mostly on a secondary-group basis, is the rule, the child is confronted with a diffusion of purposes and goals, which he must somehow sort out and from which he must form some sort of workable philosophy of life. Older people, nostalgic for less complicated days, watch anxiously lest the child lose his way in a maze of pathways as yet lacking signposts.

401

Primitive versus Modern
Cultures

The polar extremes of another important cultural dimension are the primitive and the modern. Within a modern society it is easy to lose sight of the fact that most of the world's children live in relatively primitive societies. The complex life of children in our own modern Western world is thrown into sharp relief when we view life within a simple society.

In such a society, life is casual but highly patterned. Each child knows what he is supposed to do. If his physical needs are taken care of, he wants little else. All the elders of the tribe are his caretakers; and life moves at a leisurely pace. Of course, the picture is not altogether idyllic. Especially in places less favored by nature, children may suffer the ravages of poverty and disease, and become the scapegoats of their parents' anxieties. The "life curriculum" may be inflexible and personality development retarded. Little chance may exist for the realization of individual talents; and niches for the deviate are usually missing. Rigid prescription may lessen anxiety, but it inevitably makes for a static civilization.

Of course, the entire picture has changed to the extent that foreign influences have penetrated. One common, and undesirable, effect is this: The primitives often shuck their old ways before they know how properly to cloak themselves with new ones. They may acquire a taste for material things but, lacking the wherewithal for purchasing them, insist that the Great White Father provide—and usually he does. Thus, their generations-old pride and mores are broken down.

• MODERN CULTURES

Western Culture

The world's most modern cultures today are the **Western-type cultures,** including our own. The American tourist, traveling in Europe, may be struck by certain ways in which he differs from Italians, or Germans, or even the English. However, all he has to do is to visit Latin America, or the Middle East, or Central Africa, to feel a close bond of kinship with all Western peoples. Such peoples chiefly constitute groups in North America north of the Rio Grande, in Europe, the British Commonwealth, and scattered places around the globe. Culturally, they share a blending of Judeo-Christian, Greco-Roman, and other influences, and possess certain core values—for example, a respect for natural law and predictability, a value far from universally held (Johnson and Medinnus, 1965).

Positive effects on the child. Certainly, the Western world's values have both positive and negative effects on children. Josselyn (1959) believes we underestimate the positive values, especially the belief in the rights of the individual. Strang (1957) mentions modern America's altruism, upward mobility, and the concept of a well-rounded life. Another value often overlooked is the improved evaluation of the child. Regardless of whether the following law was ever really enforced, it conveys the flavor of children's status in former times:

> A law of New York, dating to the time that the colony passed from Dutch to English control, expresses the general attitude of the era: If any Child or Children above sixteen years of age, and of Sufficient understanding, shall smite their Natural Father or Mother, unless provoked and forct for their selfe preservation from Death or Mayming, at the Complaint of said Father or Mother, and not otherwise, they being sufficient witness thereof, that Child or these Children so offending shall be put to death [Earle, 1899, p. 16].

Change stemmed from the waning of the father's authority and the transition from an economy of want to one of plenty. No longer was it necessary to exploit children in whatever ways that might prove useful. The child became desired for his own sake, and his welfare a matter of all the society's concern.

Negative or mixed effects. However, modern culture has its drawbacks, one being ambiguity. A plethora of inconsistencies makes it difficult for children to integrate their values. A child is taught that he should work hard, but many of his friends receive ample spending money without lifting a finger. He is taught that he should make good grades in school, but is taunted for it. Sometimes his father encourages him to be tough; at other times his father beats him for proving he can be. No wonder that even the small child becomes confused. Another bugaboo of modern society is the danger of growing soft. The child's needs are met before he has had a chance to sense them. Unless a substitute is found for primeval challenge he grows weak and dull.

The classification of influences as positive or negative hinges on how they function in a child's life. For instance, change is a condition necessary for growth, yet too-swift change creates insecurity and cultural lag. The labor-saving devices in the home have reduced ready-made opportunities for teaching children responsibility. However, if the time thereby saved could be effectively used for the enrichment of children's lives, the overall effect of such devices might be far more beneficial than detrimental. After all, any home situation may be organized to provide children with experiences in developing responsibility.

American Culture

Major characteristics. Despite its common bond with other Western cultures, American culture possesses certain characteristics of its own. Williams (1951) names its major values as follows: (1) a stress on achievement; (2) an emphasis on activity and work; (3) a tendency to view the world in moral terms; (4) humanitarianism; (5) concern for efficiency and practicality; (6) a belief in progress; (7) emphasis on material comfort; (8) an avowal, and to some extent the practice, of freedom;

(9) an emphasis on external conformity; (10) a stress on nationalism; and (11) a belief in science and in secular rationality. To these, Stone and Church (1957, pp. 102–103) add "autonomy of thought, which permits individual variations on the central cultural theme, [and] questioning of and different approaches to reality." This autonomy enables us, to a limited extent, to "stand off from our own culture and treat it as one more aspect of reality, to be shaped at will like any other plastic material." Such values, permeating all aspects of the culture, inevitably influence the child as he relates them to his personal value system.

Protestant Ethic versus Social Ethic. Miller and Swanson (1958) suggest that the **Protestant Ethic,** which includes the first six values listed above, and which has been traditional in America, is becoming displaced by the **Social Ethic.** The Protestant Ethic denotes a set of ideas about man's spiritual relationships — ideas that gained prominence during the period of the Reformation. The individual was without a mediator in his church and sought salvation within himself. Hence self-reliance came to replace dependence on the group. Moreover, the Protestant Ethic included stewardship, or the belief that God had made humans the caretakers of his material world. Hence it had as its ideal the pleasureless, hardworking, independent individual with full responsibility for his welfare in this and the next world (Weber, 1930). Parents geared to this ethic, and to a bygone day that spawned it, brand the five-year-old as fiscally irresponsible who wants a half dollar instead of a penny.

The Social Ethic, on the other hand, emphasizes social adjustment and dependence on others, while downgrading independence and self-reliance. This ethic would lead to other-directedness, and to an emphasis on obtaining group approval.

Parents practicing the Protestant Ethic are called entrepreneurs, and those employing the Social Ethic bureaucrats. The entrepreneurs teach their children to fend for themselves, while the bureaucrats bring up their children to rely on society for their needs. The bureaucrats' child tends to cease doing for himself and thus develops dependent relationships. By contrast, the entrepreneurs' child tends to take chances and identify soft living with weakness.

American Subcultures

Of course, America is not a single set of characteristics and beliefs shared by all its members. Instead:

[It] includes a number of different versions, or sub-cultures, each with certain concepts of its own. Sub-cultures are formed by the clustering together of a group of people who separate themselves, or are separated by external pressures, from other groups. Examples are the tendency of each recent immigrant group to set up enclaves—Chinatown, Little Italy, etc.—based on similarity of language and custom and, in some cases, on rejection by older, established groups. Mountain communities without modern roads and communications likewise cling to and elaborate their own ways while the surrounding culture changes. In general, American culture seems to be moving rapidly toward a blending of sub-cultures, thanks to a combination of high geographic and economic mobility, the virtual disappearance of isolated areas, a decline in immigration, the mass production and distribution of food and other goods, and uniformities of experience propagated by television, radio, magazines, and syndicated newspapers. Nevertheless, we can still recognize that the southern version of American culture is not exactly the same as the northern. In many respects, rural America has a sub-culture different from that of the urban and suburban regions. Many racial, religious, and ethnic minorities have perceptibly different ways of behaving and of viewing the world. Slums breed a kind of culture different from that of middle-class neighborhoods. Rural slums have cultures different from those of urban slums [Stone and Church, 1957, pp. 94–95].

404

Neighborhood. Let us now turn to a more detailed analysis of America's subcultural groupings, beginning with **demographic** groupings, including neighborhood, city, suburb, town, and farm community. The subculture most intimately affecting the child is his neighborhood. Of greatest significance is its human make-up, whether homogeneous or heterogeneous, middle or lower class, old or young. There may be adults who take a special interest in children, or lawless elements who constitute poor models for children.

Permeating each neighborhood is a certain atmosphere, or tone, both physical and psychological. In one neighborhood, the streets may be narrow and ill-kept, and its inhabitants without pride or morale. To compensate, they seek escape in taverns and cheap entertainment houses. Another neighborhood, not far away, may be characterized by nicely kept houses, well-dressed parents, and well-behaved children.

Here two individuals describe the neighborhood in which they were reared:

I grew up in a very rough section in the Bronx. There was little play area except on the concrete and tar streets. Pedestrians and passing cars prevented us from even completing a ball game. The kids were a tough lot, and I cannot remember when I was not involved in some sort of fight or argument. (Male)

I was brought up in a middle-class neighborhood in a small town. Except for very minor misdeeds, we were completely law-abiding. Since there was no danger, we roamed the neighborhood at will even on summer evenings. Our parents were professional people, and as a result we were exposed to "decent" behaviors, refined manners, and good speech. (Female)

The city. Stress has been placed chiefly on the disadvantages that cities pose for youngsters. In 1906, Upton Sinclair wrote that the immigrant to the city could call his life history "The Jungle." Wirth (1938) called a city the kind of society where adults compete with each other, work with, for, and against each other, yet do not get to know each other with close, sympathetic understanding.

The child's lot in the city is supposed to be even harder. The child has small chance to get acquainted with himself; he is bombarded to the saturation point with ceaseless stimuli. The streets, even the parks, are often unsafe. There are no cool streams to fish in, or fields to explore. Not surprisingly, city children feel a pull to become adults, perhaps because cities are planned for adults, not for children.

Nevertheless, the city may hold some very real advantages for children. There are museums, plays, and other cultural offerings to which most rural children lack access. The city child is

The city child is at the heart of things.

at the heart of things; he attains a feel for, and an understanding of, the technological forces that operate chiefly in big cities. In short, he is more a part of a world on the move than children in more remote areas. And while the heterogeneity of the city may pose certain value conflicts, it also provides broader alternatives from which to choose.

Of course, cities represent different things to different children, partly because of the child's personality, partly because of the section in which he lives. A child with a taste for the cultural may

prefer the city, one who prefers the wide open spaces, a farm. Moreover, the middle-class child sees and lives in a quite different section of the city from the slum child.

The contrasts in physical surroundings and total way of life from neighborhood to neighborhood within a city almost defy description. In one area there will be large stately homes, beautifully kept lawns, attractive gardens, large shade trees bordering wide boulevards. Few people are seen on the street. Perhaps two blocks away may be a slum area with a mixture of racial and nationality groups, with the streets filthy and teeming with dirty children, the houses unpainted and dilapidated with open doors and curtainless windows exposing a drab, dark interior [Kuhlen, 1952, p. 153].

The contrast possible in city environments is evident in these recollections:

Until I was eight years old I lived in an apartment in New York City. I was never allowed outside the apartment except once in a while to stand on the stairs. Even then my mother watched until she called me in. Finally we moved to Long Island where the children were nicer, the air cleaner, and the general atmosphere greatly improved. (Female)

I grew up in a slum area in a small city. I lived close to a park and had lots of fun. However, as I grew older I became conscious that we were poor and kids laughed at the way I dressed. I grew to hate that section because the neighbors swore and fought. Later we moved to a better neighborhood above a beer joint and I was much happier. (Male)

I lived in a large city close to a huge park where people came from all over the city. I learned about many kinds of people first hand. I had the advantage of large museums, libraries, and first-class entertainment. (Female)

The suburbs. It is the suburbs that are setting the standards for our new civilization; they are the pacemakers of 405 our society. Increasingly, the suburbs are becoming the nation's nurseries, but not always with healthy effects. According to Dulles (1960, p. 22):

> The new real estate developments, whether vast housing projects for factory workers or more expansive, restricted middle-class subdivisions, have by their very nature a quality of sameness; and are more uniform than the towns and villages that grew up gradually in the past. They are congested and crowded as a consequence of a rapidly increasing population. . . . If families have more actual leisure, there is still little of the leisurely atmosphere of earlier days. The suburbs are highly organized, for both adults and children, and present a pattern of living to which almost everyone is under heavy pressure to conform. There is often a competitive spirit in the air, giving a new urgency to the need "to keep up with the Joneses."

However, suburban life is too complex a phenomenon to dismiss with so simple a generalization. Let us take a closer look. The suburban community is dominated by highly educated adults whose concepts of family relations and child-rearing are permeated with values of activity, autonomy, and achievement. Whatever gains these community leaders achieve accrue to all the children of all the families in the community.

Overall, the environment becomes one consciously designed for children. Mothers and, increasingly, fathers are intimately involved in the child's life. Psychological rather than physical punishment is typically used. Children's recreational patterns, facilitated by their elders, are diverse. Children feel a general drive toward growing up because they are increasingly ready for greater maturity rather than because they desire to be done with childhood. With all these advantages, suburban children are generally precocious in their development, maturing earlier than children from cities or farms.

Also, there is less segregation by sex, with activity profiles differing little for boys and girls. Girls in the suburbs play games and sports more than city girls or those from smaller communities, without showing the marked preference for the traditionally feminine activities found among girls from small towns and cities. Boys in the suburbs engage in hobbies and creative activities more than do boys in any other community setting (Douvan and Adelson, 1966).

Most of a group of students questioned by the author believed their childhood suburban environment to have been favorable. Even negative reactions were mild. Here are three replies:

> I grew up in a suburb and had plenty of places to play until the increasing number of new homes restricted our play areas. As I grew older and the area more congested, I felt closed in. (Female)

> I grew up in a suburb of a large city. We had playgrounds, parks, and plenty of things to do. There were a lot of children and plenty of friends to go around. As we grew older it became more important to go into the city for fun. (Female)

> I lived just outside a medium-sized city and loved it. We had brooks and beaches and baseball fields. Yet we were close enough to the city to be aware of a hurrying, busy life. (Male)

The town. There are small towns in America that still bear the marks of their heritage—the surrounding farms, the leisurely atmosphere, and the spacious houses with large yards and gardens. Others are bustling, like postage-stamp miniatures of small cities. At the other extreme are the remote communities, especially those in the mountains, with a flavor all their own. There, family is all, and every child is imbued with a deep loyalty to community and kinfolk—and because of generations of intermarriage the two are practically one. So long as the child stays there his needs for belonging and security will be met. He is bequeathed patterns of morality, work, and leisure that will fit him well for where he is; but if he moves elsewhere, he may find adaptation extremely difficult.

Excepting such unusual types of community as the foregoing, small towns generally share certain advantages and disadvantages, where children are concerned. Small-town children may be less restricted than their urban or rural counterparts—urban children because of environmental hazards, such as traffic, rural children because of the lack of nearby play areas where children congregate. Like the mountain children of remote areas, though in lesser degree, small-town children have a feeling of belonging, because their relationships are with people they know. They have access to stores, post offices, and library, while often being within walking distance of places to fish, hunt, or roam about. However, their autonomy may be somewhat limited, because their mothers often remain in the home, and are less busy than rural women. Hence it is hard for children to escape the constant surveillance of their parents, which may place limitations on the development of initiative and independence.

The appraisal of any community's effect hinges on many intangibles and imponderables, including the degree of heterogeneity or homogeneity. The more homogeneous the community, the more concentrated and uniform its effects. Whatever healthy or unhealthy influences are prevalent are "caught" by the children. The more heterogeneous community affords a more varied life-fare. However, this heterogeneity often leads to, or derives from, social stratification, with its concomitant ills. Also, in such a situation, the child may become confused about which path to follow.

The community takes much of its character from the economy. For one thing, the general level of education or prosperity heavily affects children, through defining their opportunities. These days, when the family is assuming less responsibility for the child's educa-

tion and leisure, the quality of community facilities is especially significant.

Another important compositional, or demographic, factor within the community is age-grading. In some communities the society is more strictly age-graded than in others; that is, activities in some communities involve individuals of several age groups, while in others there is little mixing. For instance, in a town that a group of researchers called Midwest, Kansas, there was little or no age segregation, while in another community—Yorkdale, Yorkshire—few activities were unsegregated. Obviously, the life experience of a child who ranges over the whole community, having frequent contacts with persons of all ages, will be quite different from the experience of children with more limited interpersonal repertoire (Barker and Barker, 1961).

The farm. Perhaps the most distinct of any geographic category in which children may be reared is the farm. In this setting children have presented a remarkably uniform picture of traditional concepts of family life. The most conspicuous effect has been a severe limitation on social growth, linked with a marked inhibition of fantasy. In brief, one study reported that:

> The smaller the community in which [a child] lives, the greater his advantages in leisure activities, opportunities for independence, and other areas of personal and social development. At the lower end of community size, however, this trend reverses itself; youngsters from rural areas are as deprived as those from the meanest urban environment. They have fewer opportunities in all areas of life—in leisure activities, organizational membership, part-time employment, and friendly interaction with unrelated adults [Douvan and Adelson, 1966, p. 315].

The rural child's narrow background also prevents his trying out the varied roles that facilitate adaptation to, and comprehension of, today's com-

407

plex society. Since he has traditionally taken orders from his parents, he falls easy prey to dictatorial leadership. Besides, he is so accustomed to close family ties that he finds himself bewildered in the many places and situations in which impersonality and superficiality are the rule.

The farm family has become, in effect, a minority group. As the country has swiftly become urbanized, the farm population has shrunk until rural children are vastly outnumbered by others. As in any other minority group, the farm child is expected to understand and come to terms with the majority, or urban society, and not the other way around. Here two children tell of growing up on a farm:

> My childhood play group consisted in three people — my sister, a friend, and I. There were only five pupils in the country school I attended. We played such games as Red Rover and Horsey and the usual kid games. Sometimes we picked and sold blueberries. We walked a mile to school and on the way stopped to climb trees and look for animals. (Female)

> Since I was an only child and lived on a farm I missed much of the fun of growing up. I found myself behind the other boys in school and in sports, but I was good at milking and pitching hay. (Male)

Other conditions associated with farm rearing are ambiguous in effect. On the one hand, a farm child's core values are well defined and permit an easier development of an integrated self. He faces fewer real temptations and is helped to keep antisocial impulses in check by the strong homogeneity of values surrounding him. Most of what the children do is open for all to see. However, these same core values, typically more traditional on the farm, may be at odds with those of the larger community in which ultimately he may live. Even now he may have trouble reconciling what filters through from the outside world with what he has learned within his family. Later on, as he meets people from more diverse backgrounds, he may have trouble relating to them.

Many adults reared on the farm would object to so gloomy a picture. They treasure memories of the open spaces, fish-laden streams, and the old swimmin' hole. Besides, some individuals find the simple life more compatible with their nature.

In addition, the child comes into immediate contact with such basic life phenomena as birth, sex, illness, and the forces of nature. His environment, being less mediated or transformed by science and invention, gives him a more natural respect for the inevitability and implacability of nature's laws.

Also, since early childhood he has been treated as a capital asset. Thereby, he has established respect for group responsibility and hard work, and achieved a sense of personal worth and identity.

Social Class

Is the gap between social classes shrinking? Elsewhere we have touched upon certain effects of social class; here we shall treat social class from the sociocultural frame of reference. Consideration of this topic depends partly on how social classes differ, a question not fully resolved. There is some evidence that the social-class gap has narrowed. As already noted, the middle class has become more permissive about weaning, toileting, and feeding, while the lower class is slightly less permissive than formerly. In short, both classes are now permissive within the same broad band of respectability (Bronfenbrenner, 1958). Also, classes differ less than they used to in speech, manners, and dress, partly because of the influence of television.

Several factors would seem to account for a narrowing gap, if indeed this is the trend. The effect of heavy taxes on more affluent persons, and of labor unions and welfare programs on the lower class, has reduced the difference in incomes and in the styles of living associated with them. Meantime, the erstwhile lower classes have become property owners, a status that produces certain middle-class values, such as respect for law and order and concern for civic conditions of beauty and cleanliness. Nor can we overlook the mass media, which bring into every home the middle-class patterns of life. Also, educational opportunities are becoming increasingly equalized through desegregation, special programs like Head Start, scholarships for higher education, and poverty programs. Increasingly, slum children are viewed as kids to be reclaimed instead of relegated to society's scrap heap.

The foregoing case, arguing that the social-class gap has narrowed, sounds convincing; but is it? Indeed, social class has become less rigid in the sense that clusters of families may no longer be discriminated on the basis of traditional status criteria. It has also become less rigid in the sense that there is more opportunity to rise within the

social hierarchy (Duncan, 1965). Nevertheless, there is an increased differentiation along the social continuum in values and characteristic ways of behaving. Glenn (1966) concluded that the social-class system is becoming more complex and unstructured but remains no less important. At the same time, certain characteristics of bureaucracies, including schools and welfare agencies, tend to perpetuate and intensify stratification (Sjoberg et al., 1966). Finally, the same general affluence that has swelled the numbers of the middle class has made the lot of the diminishing lower class more conspicuous and less tolerable by comparison.

Significance of social class. Whether on the wane or not, levels of social status exist everywhere, including the United States. Expressions like "the four hundred" and "the wrong side of the track" bear testimony to their existence. In Plainville, U.S.A., a subtle social hierarchy was revealed to exist in a community claiming no such distinctions. Parents informed children that

Social class may limit the child's perception of the world.

ertain of their peers were "not our kind" or "not desirable" (West, 1945). Bossard (1954) asserted that children of different social classes in effect live in different worlds.

The fact that the child lives in the distinct world of his own social class may obstruct his recognition that other worlds exist. Conditioned from birth in the manners and morals of his own social class, as a first-grader he still fails to recognize social-class symbols. However, by the fourth grade he is beginning to become aware, and by the eighth grade perceives social class much as adults do (Stendler, 1949).

Social class is stamped on the child's behaviors and personality. The middle-class child must respect property and curb aggression; the lower-class child "is thrown more on the resources of his peer group, which rewards aggressiveness, holds suspicious attitudes about 'people putting one over on you,' and boasts of early sexual achievements" (Shaffer and Shoben, 1956, p. 82).

Children feel the imprint of social class both directly and through their parents. The very term "upward mobility" implies that some persons are left behind, and many a child is daily exposed to the frustrations and anxieties of parents who are struggling and yet failing to make the grade. The child himself becomes a pawn in the struggle. Parents insist that he go with "the right people," or seek to realize through him the goals they have not or probably will not achieve.

These two illustrations suggest the part that social class may play in children's lives:

> As a young child I lived in a nice but lower-class neighborhood. My parents worked hard and we lived on a tight budget, but I did not mind because everyone else was in the same predicament. Later we moved into a middle-class neighborhood where the children had pretty clothes and looked down on me. (Female)
>
> As a child I was fully aware of

social class. I knew I belonged to the better class and that other children didn't. Even when I was in the first and second grade I felt like I was "slumming" when I talked with certain children. I was a complete snob and feel much the same to this day. (Female)

Minority Status

Membership in the lower social class should be distinguished from minority-group status, the latter connoting a stable subgroup within a society, with its own special interests, and subject to unfavorable treatment by that society. The lower social class is not stable; people may move from one social class to another. Various social reforms and economic conditions have the effect of increasing or decreasing its numbers. Besides, the lower class need not per se receive unfavorable treatment.

The black child's problems. To illustrate the minority group's plight, let us consider the black child. Although children of each ethnic and racial group have their characteristic problems, most blacks face the problems of membership in both lower social class and lower caste. Caste connotes intermarriage only within the status group and an inability to escape from it through the normal processes of social mobility.

Black families, which constitute about one in 11 within the country, generally conform to the classic picture of disorganization, inadequacy, and poverty. About two out of three live in cities, often in slums. In the 1970s that number will rise above 70%. Of high-school youth in some city neighborhoods, 60% are out of school and out of work, a condition James Conant has described as "social dynamite" (Conant, 1961).

The typical black child's life differs in important features from the white child's. His father holds a low-status job, at meager pay, and the boy takes little pride in identifying with him. Sometimes a father simply "takes off" when unable to support his family adequately

410

or to attain any real significance in their eyes. Among American families overall, only one family in 14 headed by a husband-wife combination is black, while one family in five headed by a woman is black (Hylan, 1960). The mother more often mixes with whites because the nature of her job—perhaps as clerk or domestic—often requires it. There she learns the manners and morals of the majority group, which she seeks to convey to her own children.

However, she has trouble keeping close watch over her brood, especially the boys. Usually she lives in a city, very often in a disorganized neighborhood, and her son inevitably comes into close contact with the values disapproved in the larger culture. At the same time, conditions of home life are such that he escapes every minute he can, so that he misses much of the normal socialization of the family. As a result, he is more susceptible to persons and institutions outside the home. To a considerable extent the girl feels these outside influences, too, because the larger community often takes a hand, through its social agencies, in the way slum dwellers live (Rohrer, 1957).

Typically, black mothers seek to inculcate in their children a desire to rise above their origins. More often than white mothers of the same social level, they impose unrealistic educational goals on their children (Reiss and Rhodes, 1959). The resultant syndrome—of high aspirations and limited opportunities—is precisely the pattern that invites deviant behavior (Merton, 1957).

The black child also has problems of identification. He clings to his own group for the security and status denied him by the larger society, yet he resents membership in a group that symbolizes inferior status. As a result, he comes to value the symbols of the larger society, such as whiteness of skin, and he often imitates whites (Landreth and Johnson, 1953).

Another problem derives from geo-

graphical distribution. Two out of three blacks live in urban areas today, with the proportion rapidly growing. Thus they experience special problems that accrue not only to lower class and lower caste but to city dwellers in general and to slum or project dwellers in particular.

Of course, this dismal picture fails to take into account more hopeful signs. Since World War II, even lower-class blacks have made great gains in income and education and, increasingly, have absorbed the majority culture through press, television, and integrated schools. Among blacks a strong middle class is forming; and a sense of pride in being black is becoming manifest. Hence the black individual, whether adult or child, is finding increased leverage; he is planning for the future with sharply revised estimates of what is possible or probable (Hylan, 1960).

A sense of pride in being black is becoming manifest.

Children of other minorities. One subculture, hardly recognized as such, is the "culture of poverty," in which the same families have lived on relief for

411

two or three generations. In general, the children of such families learn to accept and rationalize low standards of life, minimum aspiration and achievement, and the right to be supported and cared for by others (Corwin, 1965). Nevertheless, they do have their problems, which are modified in large measure by the economic status of their neighbors. Note this testimony from individuals who grew up in less affluent circumstances:

> My family was very poor, and the whole theme of my life was to rise above them. (Male)

> I lived in a run-down neighborhood where my chief companions were from a poor family. We had a barely adequate income but I felt superior by comparison. We had newer cars and whole milk, while they had old clunks and powdered milk. (Female)

Any student who expands this analysis of the child's role to still other minority groups will gain a fuller appreciation of certain facts: (1) The minority-group child is often reared in a pattern at variance from the majority culture. (2) Such a child must somehow effect a compromise between his primary-group values and the secondary-group values of both minority and majority cultures. He must decide whether he will remain closely bound to his own group or attempt to relate to the majority group. (3) The majority-group child, simply because he belongs to the majority, is not required to relate to the minority culture, except in a general way. The larger group must cope with the minorities' social problems, such as crime or disease; but the individual majority-group child, who often lives in a majority-group neighborhood, may never in his life be required to relate personally to the minority group. Often, he is unable to describe the characteristic manners and morals of even the more important minorities within his society. (4) Especially within a democratic society, the minority child's status is

often changing; hence, conclusions about it must constantly be revised.

Religion

Even nowadays religion continues to influence significantly each family's way of life. Among Protestants, there is a sharp difference between the more and less fundamentalist sects in their ways of child-rearing. The fundamentalist seeks to control the child by stimulating fear of a harsh and retributive God, while the average Protestant emphasizes internal authority, or conscience, as a guide.

Differences are also sharp between the main body of Protestants and Catholics. Catholic children feel closer ties to home; and Catholic boys more often than Protestant boys turn to their parents for advice on matters of taste and judgment. Protestant boys more frequently turn to friends or rely on their own judgment. Catholic boys and girls more often choose the like-sexed parent as an ideal, and less frequently choose an ideal outside the family circle.

Protestant girls are granted more independence and self-reliance; and Protestant children of both sexes are punished more by verbal and psychological than by physical measures. Upper-status Protestant youngsters are more autonomous than lower-class ones, and their parents stress independence training more. Among Catholic children, those from middle-class homes rely more heavily on adult authority than do those from lower-class backgrounds, while the reverse is true for Protestant children (Douvan and Adelson, 1966).

A factor that distinguishes the Jewish child is the strong influence of family on his development. Among Jewish families, as among Negroes, the mother tends to be the relatively stronger figure in the husband-wife combination, and to be largely responsible for the children's achievement-striving (Strodbeck, 1958). Unlike the black child, the Jewish child has a long heritage of educational and cultural attainment. In consequence,

Jewish children are relatively higher than other children on achievement orientation and more liberal in social and political attitudes (Gurin et al., 1960).

Children of ethnic, racial, or religious minorities often have a hard time, especially when dispersed among a majority group that looks down on them. Note these examples:

I am Greek Orthodox and proud of it; but when I was about seven, another kid asked me what religion I was. I said, "Greek Orthodox." When he said he'd never heard of it, I was shocked, because I'd been taught it was the one true religion. Later when a Roman Catholic called me a heretic, I felt like telling her to take a flying leap, but I didn't. (Male)

When I was five or six, I couldn't see why Catholics had to go to church every Sunday. I asked my mother how come we weren't Protestant. I felt jealous because they could play while we had to go to church. (Female)

The Marginal Child

Some children are culturally marginal, or astride two cultures, feeling completely at home in neither. They are caught in the middle and thus have trouble integrating their values. For example, one study reports the conflicts between first- and second-generation Italian-Americans. The children in immigrant families were exposed to one set of customs at home, another among their peers. While they continued to feel the pull from home, those children adjusted best who dropped Italian customs and followed American ones. The parents themselves wanted their children to become Americanized, yet felt a sense of loss, distance, and resentment as they saw them shedding their "old country" ways (Child, 1943).

One type of "marginal" child is the one whose family is of one religion and his peers of another. Another type is the child whose parents were immigrants to this country. Either type of child is "hung up" between two cultures. Note these examples:

My family, which was not at all religious, lived among orthodox Jews. On Jewish holidays I felt very awkward when doing things like riding in a car, watching television, or using a record player. (Male)

My father is a German immigrant and my mother came from Russia. My father is an atheist and my mother, who was Jewish, gave up her faith when she married him. Since village social relations center around three churches, my family and I have little social interaction with the community. (Female)

• THE TIMES AND CHILD DEVELOPMENT

Mobility

Whatever the sociocultural influences on child development, their nature and significance vary with geographical location. This factor is of special importance since many children must, in the course of growing up, adapt to one or more changes in residence. Transient children, as we saw in Chapter 13, sometimes have trouble making new friendships. They tend to absorb whatever tensions their parents experience in adapting to changing environments.

Despite considerable individual differences, children of mobile and stable parents tend to differ in certain ways. Geographically, stable children are better integrated socially; they belong to more clubs and have more leisure-time activities. Mobile middle-class children are relatively solitary, intellectual, and close to their families. They spend more time alone and read a good deal. They are relatively autonomous and less dependent on their peers. However, mobile lower-class children manifest a different pattern from middle-class youngsters. They are socially even less well developed, more solitary, and less autonomous. This differential undoubtedly stems partly from the differences in the reasons that lower- and middle-class parents move. Mobile lower-class parents, being less educated and less skilled, may keep moving in search of work, while mobile middle-class parents may simply be transferred from one branch of a big corporation to another (Douvan and Adelson, 1966).

In one sense, a family may be "mobile" yet remain within the same neighborhood. If the neighborhood itself changes, the family in effect dwells in a new environment. A new element may move in, leaving few of the older families; or industries may encroach on a hitherto residential community. Children of these families find themselves in as completely changed an environment as though they had moved.

Change

Problems involved in rapid change. Throughout its history — and increasingly as the pace of civilization has quickened — America has been affected by change. Ever since its inception, the American culture has undergone historic shifts, which may be regarded as subcultural variants spaced over time, simply occurring in succession instead of simultaneously. Certainly, it meant something different to be a child in colonial times, when Puritan precepts prevailed and every member of the family helped cope with the rigors of the environment, from what it means to today's child, who is exposed to more relaxed standards and a friendlier material environment. Across the decades, children have felt the impact of all the important changes effected by the shift from an agricultural to an industrial economy, the shift from rural to urban to suburban living, the widespread ownership of automobiles, events such as the great depression and World War II, advances in technology and medicine, and the arrival of the atomic age. In consequence, each age must unveil a new child prepared to play the game by a revised set of rules.

Helping children deal with change. How can parents correctly interpret morals to children within a culture where

each generation's experience differs sharply from the last and the experience of the youngest child in a large family differs greatly from that of the first-born? Perhaps, conclude Stone and Church (1957), it is fortunate that parents are too deeply immersed in their own culture to do much about adapting to change as it occurs, especially where values are concerned. Since children cannot tolerate ambiguities and relativisms as well as adults, perhaps it is advisable that adults come up with clear-cut, though tentative, answers. That is, claim Stone and Church, it is better for the parents to act in error, but with a tone of certainty, thus maintaining contact with the child, than to lose the contact in indecision or "in the index of Somebody's 'Authoritative Book of Child Rearing'." The author disagrees. The out-of-date parent equips the child with an arsenal of weapons dating from a bygone age. However reluctant we all are to change, today's parent must be dragged into the last decades of the twentieth century. In any case, since the major culture includes so many subcultures and makes available information about other cultures, children growing up within it are inevitably exposed to conflicting ideologies, and try out new points of view perhaps just to see how they feel. Thus even the most deeply ingrained lessons become somewhat modified.

However, the capacity to deal with change should not be taken for granted. Children should constantly be confronted with the sort of problems whose solutions will teach them to cope with the new and the different. More specifically, in social-science classes they should learn how to help maintain the sort of flexible society that can accommodate to change. We can't afford to wait until he reaches adolescence to instill in the child the feeling that he is or certainly will be a responsible participant in social change. The American child is growing up within the most rapidly changing culture in the recorded history of the world; and so long-standing and so rapid have these processes of change become that the expectation of change, and anxieties about them, have become part of the character of the people. Everyone seems in a hurry, running ever faster just to keep still. The Mid-Century White House Conference (1951, p. 85) said that homes have become "launching platforms from which children set out on uncharted seas; and we have become correspondingly more anxious lest they be imperfectly equipped before they go."

Technology and Human Development

Favorable byproducts of technology. Undoubtedly, the most basic social change in the history of our country has been the transition from an agricultural to an industrial economy, and the byproducts of this revolution, otherwise called technology, are profound, sweeping, and in many ways salutary. For the first time in history, the possibility of abolishing poverty seems possible, if not imminently probable. With victory over poverty, man becomes liberated from human slavery and freed for the use of his higher mental powers. Neither man nor child can become concerned over values as long as he is hungry. At the same time, an individual's occupation ceases to occupy so central a part in his life. Fathers have begun to see their jobs as more than mere means of subsistence. They place an increasing value on their role as fathers, and on their own leisure-time personal growth. Children, of course, profit from having parents who incorporate their children into their scheme of things, and whose personalities reflect broader interests than mere bread-winning.

Another fortunate byproduct of technology is the increased affluence of formerly disadvantaged groups. Their children can look ahead to future education and the opportunities beyond. They are less likely to live in neighborhoods or homes they are ashamed of. They are less often embarrassed by having to wear ragged or outmoded clothing. They also have fewer chores and time for a broader, fuller life, just as upper-class children have more duties and a greater appreciation for the meaning of work.

Actually, the products of technology can make positive contributions to child development. Technology expands the child's view of the universe and helps him discover his place in it. As the child comes to understand natural forces, his concept of himself as the pawn of a capricious nature diminishes, and he ceases to fear the forces he does not understand.

Finally, today's child has a close-up view of history proceeding at a record pace. If he learns to adapt to and enjoy the unusual, he tingles with excitement as daily dramas unfold. The true child of the Space Age has faith that the never-never land can become real.

Problems posed by technology. Other byproducts of technology hold potential dangers for children. Master machines gobble up whoever or whatever their appetites demand. For instance, if a branch plant is needed in some remote locale, families are uprooted to man it, regardless of what such a move may do to their children's lives. Moreover, the production of more and more goods has tended to cast the good life in material terms. Children, like their parents, measure assets in terms of things rather than less tangible values. The child loses control of his destiny when he seeks goals external to himself instead of within his own psychic realm.

Technology also depersonalizes, through its twin offspring, big business and automation. Mass society, necessitated by large-scale production, threatens to engulf the individual. He becomes a social security number with no self-identity, no pride in being "I, John Jones." Nor does automation permit any real identification with the company's products. The sheer bigness of modern industries and the vast material involved may reduce an individual to diminutive proportions in his own eyes. The child destined for such a future must be prepared to seek self-realization in off-the-job pursuits. Yet this obligation — to deepen the child's interests, and show him how to implement them — has been largely ignored, or treated haphazardly.

A technological society also requires more and more education for those who would rise in the ranks. Schooling becomes serious business. With more normal and brighter children relentlessly pursuing higher educational goals than ever before, the dull child's plight is rendered more acute still.

Some suggestions. Technology's very real contributions to human development should not blind us to its dangers nor weaken our resolve to do something about them. For one thing, we must be willing to keep up to date; we cannot expect to communicate with the Martians, or even the Russians, with primitive smoke signals. At the same time, we must maintain a certain intellectual detachment and an open-mindedness to new values and ideas. We create a gulf between ourselves and our children, and severe problems for them, by attempting to foist onto them values adaptive for an earlier day.

Take the matter of vocation versus leisure. In childish fashion the small boy plays at adult occupations, like policeman, or soldier, or storekeeper. If, as a boy, he introjects the notion that work is the one avenue through which to prove his manhood, he may have difficulty adapting to tomorrow's world. For the adult of tomorrow may work only a few hours, and punch-button jobs may prove a feeble way to prove one's manhood, in the traditional sense. Therefore, children must be equipped to examine and appraise shifting values, such as the relationship between work and leisure. Traditionally, children have been taught that time spent at leisure was largely waste time, certainly less

character-building than that spent at work. Actually, leisure pursuits may prove superior where human development is concerned; for leisure time, as opposed to time on the job, may permit concentration on process rather than on product, on ideology instead of material gain. Leisure may be used in highly personal ways not permitted by mass-production methods and machines manned by several men. The moral is this: Instead of teaching children that such-and-such an activity has a specific value, adults must help them to evaluate activities in terms of basic human values.

Demography

Finally, let us consider demographic, or population, trends, which hold especial importance for children today. Here are certain implications (Bernert, 1960):

1. The number of children relative to adults is increasing. Therefore, there will be fewer productive adults for each child, perhaps limiting both psychological and economic advantages for children.

2. Children are increasingly concentrated in urban centers, even more in suburbs. Hence the traditional concept of the good life for the child, as embracing fishing, hunting, and wandering the wide-open spaces, must be replaced by a new type of "good life" in the suburbs and cities.

3. Except when their children are small, most mothers feel free to hold jobs outside the home. Many children, as a result, have increased economic advantages and less dependence on their mothers. Outside agencies and persons, such as day-care centers and babysitters, have assumed increasing importance as substitute homes and mother surrogates.

4. Most children continue to live with both parents, but the number living with one is increasing. Less than formerly are children deterrents to divorce. As a result, fewer children will experience endless years of bickering by parents staying together solely for the child's sake. However, research should

be undertaken to determine how the parent who is granted child-custody may best discharge his, or more often her, dual function.

5. The sheer size of population is another factor, for the term "life space" connotes man's sphere of operation; and when too many huddle in the same limited area, the sense of freedom suffers. The individual lacks room to move around, both in the physical and psychological sense. If present population trends persist, tomorrow's child will have to jostle for space just to breathe, let alone think. He may be reduced to munching algae and petrochemical proteins to stay alive. Moreover, he will suffer ego-diffusion and lack the sense of self gained in smaller, more intimate groups. He will become a faceless automaton identified from birth by a number.

Any commodity tends to lose its value by existing in superabundance, whether it be potatoes or people. People become expendable when their numbers exceed the goods required to sustain them in comfort. The very essence of morality is concern for others. But when there are not enough goods to go around, infighting develops, and the roots of morality are torn up. Although the child himself may be only vaguely aware of the adult world's basic problems, he undoubtedly feels the effects of his parents' tensions. In this and other subtle ways, the flavor of this larger world inevitably seeps into the child's world, his culture-within-a-culture. He must be encouraged to claim and enjoy his legacy of childhood without, in the process, disenfranchising himself of his rights in the future. In consequence, each child must be viewed simultaneously as a child and as an adult-in-the-becoming, and as preparing for the role he must ultimately assume.

• SUMMARY

Every child is born into a culture and subcultures that constitute his social heritage. The **culture** embraces all the customary ways of a people, including its language, thought, values, morals, art, and technology. In turn, typical patterns, or life styles, produce in each culture a basic personality type, representing the modal traits of the society. The process by which a child introjects his culture is called **acculturation.** He absorbs a certain complex of the culture's ideas and behaviors, as interpreted by his parents and immediate associates.

All cultures share certain common features, because of likenesses in people and their environment. However, they also differ in certain dimensions, among them continuity or discontinuity. In **continuous cultures,** what children learn proves functional in adulthood; in **discontinuous** ones, it proves largely unrelated. Cultures may also vary in the complexity of their group relationships, some being characterized by primary, or intimate face-to-face, contacts, others by secondary, or more superficial, relationships. Cultures may also be primitive, where life is casual but highly patterned, or modern, as in Western cultures. **Western cultures** share a blending of Judeo-Christian, Greco-Roman, and other influences, and possess certain core values, including a respect for natural law and predictability. The complexity of modern cultures, which permits accommodation for many sorts of people, also produces ambiguities that prove confusing. However, the classifications of particular influences as positive or negative depends somewhat on how they relate to a particular child's needs.

American culture, in particular, possesses certain distinct characteristics, including concern for efficiency, humanitarianism, nationalism, and achievement. However, America's erstwhile **Protestant Ethic,** with its emphasis on individual initiative and hard work, is being replaced by a **Social Ethic,** which emphasizes social adjustment and dependence on others. Beneath the broad umbrella of American culture is a complex network of **demographic** (population) groupings, each with its own human make-up, atmosphere, and tone, both psychological and physical. One of these, the city, includes wealthy areas and slums, and offers a corresponding range in its effects on children. Most favorable for rearing children is the suburb, with its middle-class flavor and accessibility to cultural opportunities. The most distinctive geographic category is the farm, where the child's background is relatively narrow and hampers his adaptation to today's complex society. However, many children defend the country as an ideal place to live. The fact is that each environment has advantages and disadvantages, their effects depending somewhat on how they impinge on the individual child.

Demographic groupings are further subdivided into social classes. The gap between social classes may be shrinking, but each child still bears the stamp of his social class in manners, dress, and speech. Typically, lower-class children, especially boys, are permitted freer expression in the areas of aggression and sex. In socially mobile societies, such as ours, children sometimes rise to a higher social class, but they cannot escape their membership in a minority group such as Negro or Puerto Rican. Minority group status suggests unfavorable treatment by the dominant groups in the society. Fathers of minority-group children often hold low-status jobs, and try to escape burdens by leaving home. As a result, many such families are headed by the mother, who must simultaneously take care of domestic duties and a job. Increasingly, the minority-group child is also a city-slum child, as his family often moves to the city. Still other children are **marginal,** caught between two cultures and feeling at home in neither. Such children may belong to immigrant families or to families with a lower-class background but with newly acquired acceptance by the middle class. Fortunately, tremendous social concern has been generated for children of marginal and minority groups, and great gains have been made, the greatest being the beginning of hope.

Other problems of sociocultural origin are caused by mobility of the population, rapid change, and technology. All children, especially in the Western world, must cope with changes that often outpace the development of values required to evaluate them. Such changes will increase the gap between generations unless parents adapt with the times. Children themselves should be confronted with the sort of learning tasks that will enable them to deal with the complex and the different.

Children must also learn how to cope with, and profit from, technology. On the one hand, technology tends to depersonalize the individual, and to reduce his pride in his job by producing machines that make his own capabilities seem puny by comparison. However, technology also provides the material goods that make possible the good life and the leisure time that, properly used, enrich one's life. We should reorient our approach and learn to control and profit from social forces instead of passively succumbing to them. If the child is taught to deal with such forces, he will view them as friendly tools for understanding and mastering his universe.

Another recent arrival on the world's horizon is the demographic, or population, problem. The numbers of children are increasing sharply relative to adults. They are becoming concentrated in cities, where mothers often work outside the home. Sheer growth in population is awesome, suggesting that the individual's life space may diminish to the vanishing point. The question arises: Is it possible that the population trend may be reversed, or that some other planet may be acquired to absorb the overflow, before sheer numbers threaten the individual's physical and psychological well being?

•SUGGESTED QUESTIONS AND ACTIVITIES

1. Did the child of colonial days have a better life than does the one of modern times?
2. Aside from health benefits, is it simply a rationalization to claim that modern societies provide children an essentially better way of life than primitive societies?
3. Try to relate the American system of child-rearing to those traits popularly said to constitute "the American personality."
4. In what sense may individual families be considered miniature subcultures?
5. On balance, which do you believe provides the best environment for children—the large city, the small city, the suburb, the town, or the farm?
6. How important a factor do you believe social class to be in the American child's development today?
7. Do you believe that racial desegregation makes martyrs of Negro children who are placed among children who look down on them? How do you believe this problem might best be handled for the welfare of all concerned?
8. Appraise the impact of present-day American culture on children.
9. What sort of traits will children need to thrive in a society that is (a) highly technological; (b) over-populated; (c) urbanized?
10. Do you believe that in today's world, where people have to learn to make readjustments, the child whose family moves once or more has an advantage over other children, with regard to long-term adjustments?
11. Can you think of suggestions, other than those given in the text, for best coping with technology and utilizing it for promoting healthy child development?

•SUGGESTED READINGS

Irvine, E. E., "Children in Kibbutzim: Thirteen Years After," *Journal of Child Psychology and Psychiatry,* Vol. 7 (1966), pp. 167–168. Describes the social system of the kibbutz, especially as it affects the young child. Attention is paid the distribution of parental functions among mother, nurse, and father, and the conceptual problems involved in the analysis of this situation.

Johnson, K. P., and G. R. Leslie, "Methodological Notes on Research in Child-Rearing and Social Class," *Merrill-Palmer Quarterly,* Vol. 11, No. 4 (October 1965), pp. 345–358. Examines methodological pitfalls accruing to this type of research.

Kohn, M. L., "Social Class and Parent-Child Relationships: An Interpretation," *American Journal of Sociology,* Vol. 48 (1963), pp. 471–480. This essay attempts to interpret, from a sociological perspective, the effects of social class upon parent-child relationships. The concept of values is used as the principal bridge from social position to behavior.

Lambert, W. E., and O. Klineberg, *Children's Views of Foreign Peoples.* New York: Appleton-Century-Crofts, Inc., 1967. Presents 11 national settings in which the investigation was conducted; then summarizes research about children's conceptions of foreign peoples and makes cross-cultural comparisons.

Landy, D., *Tropical Childhood.* Chapel Hill: University of North Carolina Press, 1959. Compares socialization of children in a rural Puerto Rican village with those of an urban New England village.

Lenbright, M., and Y. Yamamoto, "Subcultures and Creative Thinking: An Exploratory Comparison between Amish and Urban American School Children," *Merrill-Palmer Quarterly,* Vol. 11, No. 1 (January 1965), pp. 49–64. Tests of creative thinking were administered to 43 Amish and 76 urban American children in grades four through six. Both qualitative and quantitative differences emerged reflecting their respective backgrounds. Hypotheses were suggested for further study, and caution was urged against hasty conclusions.

Lewis, H., "The Changing Negro Family," in Eli M. Ginzberg, ed., *The Nation's Children,* Vol. 1. New York: Columbia University Press, 1960, pp. 108–137. This perceptive analysis provides a background for understanding the problems of the black child today.

Minturn, L., and W. W. Lambert, *Mothers of Six Cultures: Antecedents of Child Rearing.* New York: John Wiley & Sons, Inc., 1964. Reports cultural factors in child-training practices. The cultures involved were in New England, Mexico, the Philippines, Okinawa, India and Africa.

Pavenstedt, E., "A Comparison of the Child-Rearing Environment of Upper-Lower and Very Low Lower-Class Families," *American Journal of Orthopsychiatry,* Vol. 35 (1965), pp. 89–98. Differentiates child-rearing in families of the organized, stable, often upwardly mobile upper-lower class group and the deprived, disorganized multi-problem families of the very low lower-class group. Recommendations are

419

made for dealing with children of the lower-lower class group.

Rabin, A. I., *Growing Up in the Kibbutz.* New York: Springer, 1965. Reports effects of kibbutz child-rearing practices on ego functioning and personality development, and relates this research to other work on "partial deprivation."

Riessman, F., *The Culturally Deprived Child.* New York: Harper & Row, Publishers, Inc., 1962. A small, readable volume intended "for all social practitioners who are concerned with underprivileged groups."

REFERENCES

Abel, T. M. Figure drawings and facial disfigurement. *American Journal of Orthopsychiatry,* 1953, **23,** 253–264.

Ackerman, N. W. *The psychodynamics of family life.* New York: Basic Books, 1958.

Adams, E. B., & Sarason, I. B. Relation between anxiety in children and their parents. *Child Development,* 1963, **34,** 237–246.

Adolf, E. The self-maintaining organism. *Scientific Monthly,* 1945, **61,** 57–62.

Ainsworth, M. D. The effects of maternal deprivation: A review of findings in the context of research strategy and controversy. *Public Health Papers,* No. 14. Geneva: World Health Organization, 1962.

Alexander, I. E., & Alderstein, A. M. Affective responses to the concept of death in a population of children and early adolescents. *Journal of Genetic Psychology,* 1958, **93,** 167–177.

Allport, G. W. *The individual and his religion: A psychological interpretation.* New York: Macmillan, 1950.

Allport, G. W. *Becoming: Basic considerations for a psychology of personality.* New Haven: Yale University Press, 1955.

Alpert, A. Reversibility of pathological fixations associated with maternal deprivation in infancy. *Psychoanalytic Studies of the Child,* 1959, **14,** 169–185.

Altman, C. H. Relationships between maternal attitudes and child personality structure. *American Journal of Orthopsychiatry,* 1958, **28,** 160–169.

Altman, C. H. Projective techniques in the clinic setting. In A. I. Rabin and M. R. Haworth (Eds.), *Projective techniques with children.* New York: Grune & Stratton, 1960.

Altus, W. D. Birth order, intelligence and adjustment. *Psychological Reports,* 1959, **5,** 502.

Ames, L. B. The development of the sense of time in the young child. *Journal of Genetic Psychology,* 1946, **68,** 97–125.

Ames, L. B., & Ilg, F. L. Sex differences in test performance of matched girl-boy pairs in the five- to nine-year-old range. *Journal of Genetic Psychology,* 1964, **104,** 24–34.

Anastasi, A. *Differential psychology.* New York: Macmillan, 1958.

Anderson, H. H., Anderson, G. L., Cohen, I. H., & Nutt, F. D. Image of the teacher by adolescent children in four countries: Germany, England, Mexico, United States. *Journal of Social Psychology,* 1959, **50,** 47–55.

Anderson, H. H., & Brewer, J. E. Effects of teachers' dominative and integrative contacts on children's classroom behavior. *Applied Psychology Monographs,* No. 8, 1946.

Anderson, H. H., Brewer, J. E., & Reed, M. F. Studies of teachers' classroom personalities, III. Follow-up studies of the effects of dominative and integrative contact on children's behavior. *Applied Psychology Monographs,* No. 11, 1946.

Anderson, J. E. Behavior and personality. In E. Ginzberg (Ed.), *The nation's children.* New York: Columbia University Press, 1960.

André-Thomas, et al. A longitudinal study of primary reaction patterns in children. *Comprehensive Psychiatry,* 1960, **1,** 103–112.

Andry, R. G. Faulty paternal and maternal child relationships, affection and delinquency. *British Journal of Delinquency,* 1960, **97,** 329–340.

Angrilli, A. F. The psychosexual identifica-

REFERENCES tion of preschool boys. *Journal of Genetic Psychology,* 1960, **97,** 329–340.

Antonitis, J. T., & Barnes, G. W. Group operant behavior: An extension of individual research methodology to a real-live situation. *Journal of Genetic Psychology,* 1961, **98,** 95–112.

Apple, D. The social structure of grandparenthood. *American Anthropologist,* 1956, **50,** 656–663.

Ausubel, D. P. Relationship between shame and guilt in the socializing process. *Psychological Review,* 1955, **62,** 378–390.

Ausubel, D. P. *Theory and problems of child development.* New York: Grune & Stratton, 1957.

Avakian, S. A. An investigation of trait relationships among six-year-old children. *Genetic Psychology Monographs,* 1961, **63,** 339–394.

Axline, V. Entering the child's world via play experience. *Progressive Education,* 1950, **27,** 71–72.

Aznar, R., & Bennett, A. Pregnancy in adolescent girls. *American Journal of Obstetrics and Gynecology,* 1961, **81**(5), 935–940.

Bailyn, L. Mass media and children: A study of exposure habits and cognitive effects. *Psychological Monographs,* 1959, **73**(1).

Baldwin, A. L. *Behavior in childhood.* New York: Dryden, 1955.

Baldwin, C. P., & Levin, H. Reinforcement of agents of action in doll play. *Journal of Abnormal and Social Psychology,* 1964, **68,** 328–330.

Bandura, A., & McDonald, F. J. The influence of social reinforcement and the behavior of models in shaping children's moral judgments. *Journal of Abnormal and Social Psychology,* 1963, **67,** 274–281.

Bandura, A., Ross, D., & Ross, S. A. Transmission of aggression through imitation of aggressive models. *Journal of Abnormal and Social Psychology,* 1961, **63,** 575–582.

Bandura, A., & Walters, R. H. *Adolescent aggression.* New York: Ronald, 1959.

Bandura, A., & Walters, R. J. Aggression. *Child Psychology, 1963 Yearbook, No. 42, Part I, National Society for the Study of Education.* Chicago: University of Chicago Press, 1963.

Bandura, A., & Walters, R. H. *Social learning and personality development.* New York: Holt, 1963.

Banham, K. M. Senescence and the emotions: A genetic theory. *Journal of Genetic Psychology,* 1951, **78,** 175–183.

Bard, P., & Mountcastle, V. B. Some forebrain mechanisms involved in the expression of rage with special reference to suppression of angry behavior. *Research Publications of the Association for Research in Nervous and Mental Diseases,* 1947, **27,** 242–253.

Barker, R. G. Success and failure in the classroom. In J. F. Rosenblith and W. Allensmith (Eds.), *The causes of behavior: Readings in child development and educational psychology.* Boston: Allyn and Bacon, 1962.

Barker, R. G., & Barker, L. S. Research symposium report. *Digest of Conference of National Association of Nursery Education,* 1961.

Barker, R. G., Dembo, T., & Lewin, K. Frustration and regression: an experiment with young children. *University of Iowa Studies in Child Welfare,* 1941, **18**(386).

Barnett, S. *The rat: A study in behavior.* Chicago: Aldine, 1963.

Barron, F. *Creativity and psychological health.* Princeton, New Jersey: Van Nostrand, 1963.

Barry, H., Bacon, M. K., & Child, I. L. A cross-cultural survey of some sex differences in socialization. *Journal of Abnormal and Social Psychology,* 1957, **55,** 327–332.

Bartemeier, L. The contribution of the father to the mental health of the family. *American Journal of Psychiatry,* 1953, **110,** 277–280.

Baruch, D. *New ways in discipline.* New York: McGraw-Hill, 1949.

Baruch, D. *One little boy.* New York: Julian, 1952.

Barzun, J. *The teacher in America.* New York: Doubleday, 1954.

Bateson, G. Minimum requirements for theory of schizophrenia. *A.M.A. Archives of General Psychiatry,* 1960, **2,** 477–491.

Bateson, G., & Mead, M. *The Balinese character.* New York: Academy of Sciences, 1942.

Bayley, N. On the growth of intelligence. *American Psychologist,* 1955, **10,** 805–818.

Bayley, N. Comparisons of mental and motor test scores for ages 1–15 months by sex, birth order, race, geographical location, and education of parents. *Child Development,* 1965, **36**(2), 379.

Bayley, N. Behavioral correlates of mental growth: birth to thirty-six years. *American Psychologist,* 1968, **23**(1), 1–17.

Bayley, N., & Schaeffer, E. Relationships between socioeconomic variables and behavior of mothers toward young children. *Journal of Genetic Psychology,* 1960, **96,** 61–77.

Bayley, N., & Schaeffer, E. S. Consistency of maternal and child behavior in the Berkeley growth study: Symposium on personality consistency and change. *American Psychologist*, 1963, **18**(7).

Beach, F. A. Characteristics of masculine "sex drive." In M. Jones (Ed.), *Nebraska symposium on motivation*. Lincoln: University of Nebraska Press, 1956.

Becker, H. S. Social-class variations in the teacher-pupil relationship. *Journal of Educational Psychology*, 1952, **25,** 451–465.

Becker, W. C., et al. Factors in parental behavior and personality as related to problem behavior in children. *Journal of Consulting Psychology*, 1959, **23,** 107–118.

Becker, W. C., et al. Relations of factors derived from parent-interview ratings to behavior problems of five year olds. *Child Development*, 1962, **33,** 509–535.

Becker, W. D. Consequences of different kinds of parental discipline. In M. L. Hoffman and W. W. Hoffman (Eds.), *Review of child development research.* New York: Russell Sage Foundation, 1964.

Behrens, M. L. Child-rearing and the character structure of the mother. *Child Development*, 1954, **25,** 225–338.

Beilin, H. Teachers' and clinicians' attitudes toward the behavior problems of children: A reappraisal. *Child Development*, 1959, **30,** 9–26.

Beilin, H., & Franklin, I. C. Logical operations in area and length measurements: Age and training effects. *Child Development*, 1962, **33,** 607–618.

Bekesy, G. von. The ear. *Scientific American*, 1957, **197,** 66–79.

Bell, E. C. Nutritional deficiency and emotional disturbances. *Journal of Psychology*, 1958, **45,** 47–74.

Bell, R. Q. Developmental psychology. Retrospective attitude studies of parent-child relations. *Child Development*, 1958, **29,** 323–338.

Bell, R. Q. *Annual Review of Psychology*, 1965, **16,** 19.

Benaron, H. B., et al. Effects of anoxia during labor and immediately after birth in the subsequent development of the child. *American Journal of Obstetrics and Gynecology*, 1960, **80,** 1129–1142.

Benedek, T., & Rubenstein, B. B. Correlations between ovarian activity and psychodynamic processes: The ovarian phase. *Psychosomatic Medicine*, 1939, **1,** 245–270.

Benedetti, G. Die Bedeutung der persönlichkeitsforschung für die endokrinologische Forschung. *Zeitschrift für Psychotherapie und Medizinische Psychologie*, 1957, **7,** 1–9.

Benedict, R. *Patterns of culture*. New York: New American Library, 1934.

Benedict, R. Continuities and discontinuities in cultural conditioning. *Psychiatry*, 1938, **50,** 161–167.

Benedict, R. Child rearing in certain European countries. *American Journal of Orthopsychiatry*, 1949, **19,** 342–350.

Bennett, E. L., et al. Chemical and anatomical plasticity of brain. *Science*, 1964, **146,** 610–619.

Bennett, E. M., & Cohen, L. R. Men and women personality patterns and contrasts. *Genetic Psychology Monographs*, 1959, **59,** 101–153.

Berenda, R. W. *The influence of the group on the judgments of children*. New York: King's Crown Press, 1950.

Berkowitz, L. The expression and reduction of hostility. *Psychological Bulletin*, 1958, **55,** 257–283.

Berkowitz, L. *The development of motives and values in the child*. New York: Basic Books, 1964.

Bernabeu, E. P. The effects of severe crippling on the development of a group of children. *Psychiatry*, 1958, **21,** 169–194.

Bernert, E. Demographic trends and implications. In E. Ginzberg (Ed.), *The nation's children*, Vol. 1. New York: Columbia University Press, 1960.

Berry, J. L., & Martin, B. GSR reactivity as a function of anxiety, instructions and sex. *Journal of Abnormal and Social Psychology*, 1957, **54,** 9–12.

Bexton, W. H., Heron, W., & Scott, T. H. Effects of decreased variation in the sensory environment. *Canadian Journal of Psychology*, 1954, **8,** 70–78.

Bibring, C. L. Some considerations of the psychological processes in pregnancy. *Psychoanalytic Studies of the Child*, 1959, **14,** 113–121.

Bibring, G. L., et al. A study of the psychological processes in pregnancy and of the earliest mother-child relationship. *Psychoanalytic Study of the Child*, 1961, **16,** 9–72.

Bieri, J. Parental identification, acceptance of authority, and within sex differences in cognitive behavior. *Journal of Abnormal and Social Psychology*, 1960, **60,** 76–79.

Bing, E. Effect of child-rearing practices on development of differential cognitive abilities. *Child Development*, 1963, **34,** 631–648.

Birch, H. G., Thomas, A., Chess, S., & Hertzog, M. E. Individuality in the de-

423

REFERENCES velopment of children. *Development Medicine and Child Neurology*, 1962, **4,** 370–379.

Birns, B. Individual differences in human neonates, responses to stimulation. *Child Development*, March 1965, **36**(1), 252–253.

Bishop, J., & Davis, D. M. *New horizons in medicine.* Princeton, New Jersey: Dow Jones Books, 1966.

Blanton, S., & Blanton, M. G. *Child guidance.* New York: Century, 1927.

Block, J. A study of effective responsiveness in a lie-detection situation. *Journal of Abnormal and Social Psychology*, 1957, **55,** 11–15.

Block, J., & Martin, B. Predicting the behavior of children under frustration. *Journal of Abnormal and Social Psychology*, 1955, **55,** 281–285.

Bloodstein, O. The development of stuttering. *Journal of Speech and Hearing Disorder*, 1960, **25,** 219–237.

Bloom, B. S. Testing cognitive ability and achievement. In N. L. Gage (Ed.), *Handbook of research on teaching.* Chicago: Rand McNally, 1963.

Bloom, B. S. *Stability and change in human characteristics.* New York: Wiley, 1964.

Blum, G. S. The blacky pictures with children. In A. I. Rabin and M. R. Haworth (Eds.), *Projective techniques with children.* New York: Grune & Stratton, 1960.

Boehm, L. The development of independence: A comparative study. *Child Development*, 1957, **28,** 85–102.

Boehm, L., & Nass, M. L. Social class differences in conscience development. *Child Development*, 1962, **33,** 565–574.

Boles, G. Personality factors in mothers of cerebral-palsy children. *Psychology Monographs*, 1959, **59,** 159–218.

Bolin, B. J. An investigation of relationship between birth duration and childhood anxieties. *Journal of Mental Science*, 1959, **195,** 1045–1052.

Bonney, M. E., & Nicholson, E. L. Comparative social adjustments of elementary school pupils with and without preschool training. *Child Development*, 1958, **29,** 125–133.

Boocock, S. S. Toward a sociology of learning: A selective review of existing behavior. *Sociology of Education*, 1966, **39**(1), 40.

Boroson, W. The hate mail of Sherri Finkbine. *Fact*, March–April 1965, **2**(2), 35–36.

Bossard, J. H. S. *Parent and child.* Philadelphia: University of Pennsylvania Press, 1953.

Bossard, J. H. S. *The sociology of child development.* (2nd ed.) New York: Harper, 1954.

Bossard, J. H. S., & Boll, E. S. *The large family system.* Philadelphia: University of Pennsylvania Press, 1956.

Bossard, J. H. S., & Sanger, W. P. The large family system: A research report. *American Sociological Review*, 1952, **17,** 3–9.

Bostick, J. Thieving in childhood. *Medical Journal of Australia*, 1961, **1,** 813–815.

Bousfield, W. A., & Orbison, W. D. Ontogenesis of emotional behavior. *Psychological Review*, 1952, **59,** 1–7.

Bower, E. M. A process for identifying disturbed children. *Children*, 1957, **4**(4), 143–147.

Bowlby, J. *Maternal care and mental health. Monograph series no. 2.* Geneva: World Health Organization, 1951.

Bowlby, J. The nature of the child's tie to his mother. *International Journal of Psychoanalysis*, 1958, **39,** 350–373.

Bowlby, J. Childhood mourning and its implications for psychiatry. *American Journal of Psychiatry*, 1961, **118,** 481–498.

Boyd, W. C. Genetics and the human race. *Science*, 1963, **140,** 1057–1064.

Bradburn, N. M. Achievement and father domination in Turkey. *Journal of Abnormal and Social Psychology*, 1963, **67,** 464–468.

Bradway, K. P., & Thompson, C. W. Intelligence at adulthood: A twenty-five year follow up. *Journal of Educational Psychology*, 1962, **53,** 1–14.

Bradway, K. P., Thompson, C. W., & Cravens, R. B. Preschool IQs after twenty-five years. *Journal of Educational Psychology*, 1958, **49,** 278–281.

Braine, M. D. S. The ontogeny of English phrase structure; the first phase. *Language*, 1963, **39,** 1–13.

Breckinridge, M. R., & Murphy, M. N. *Growth and development of the young child.* (7th ed.) Philadelphia: Saunders, 1963.

Breckinridge, M., & Vincent, E. L. *Child development: Physical and psychological growth through adolescence.* Philadelphia: Saunders, 1965.

Brian, C. R., & Goodenough, F. L. Relative potency of color and form perception at various ages. *Journal of Experimental Psychology*, 1929, **12,** 197–213.

Brinkmann, E., & Brinkmann, R. A. Group influence on the individual in the classroom: A case study. *Merrill-Palmer Quarterly*, 1963, **9**(3), 199.

Brock, J. F., Autret, M. *Kwashiorkor in Africa. WHO monograph series no. 8.* Geneva: World Health Organization, 1952.

Brodsky, C. M. *A study of norms for body form behavior relationships.* Washington: Catholic University of America Press, 1954.

Broderick, C. B., & Fowler, S. E. New patterns of relationships between the sexes among preadolescents. *Marriage and Family Living,* 1961, **23,** 27–30.

Brody, S. Mental health and the capacity for nursery education. *Journal of Nursery Education,* 1962, **17**(2), 58–63.

Broida, D. C., & Thompson, G. G. The relationship between certain Rorschach "insecurity" hypotheses and children's reactions to psychological stress. *Journal of Personality,* 1954, **23,** 167–181.

Bronfenbrenner, U. Socialization and social class through time and space. In E. E. Maccoby, T. M. Newcomb, and E. L. Hartley (Eds.), *Readings in social psychology.* New York: Holt, 1958.

Bronfenbrenner, U. The Freudian theories of identification and their derivatives. *Child Development,* 1960, **31,** 15–40.

Bronfenbrenner, U. The changing American child: A speculative analysis. *Journal of Social Issues,* 1961, **17**(1).

Bronfenbrenner, U. Some familial antecedents of responsibility and leadership in adolescence. In L. Petrullo, and B. M. Bass (Eds.), *Leadership and interpersonal behavior.* New York: Holt, 1961.

Bronfenbrenner, U. The role of age, sex, class, and culture in studies of moral development. *Religious Education: Research Supplement,* 1962, **57,** S3–S17.

Bronfenbrenner, U. Soviet methods of character education: Some implications for research. *American Psychologist,* 1962, **17,** 550–564.

Bronfenbrenner, U., & Ricciuti, H. N. The appraisal of personality characteristics in children. In P. Mussen (Ed.), *Handbook of research methods in child development.* New York: Wiley, 1960.

Bronson, W. C., Katten, E. S., & Livson, N. Patterns of authority and affection in two generations. *Journal of Abnormal and Social Psychology,* 1959, **58,** 273–280.

Bronsted, H. W. Warning and promise of experimental embryology. *Impact of Science on Society,* Vol. 6, No. 4. New York: Simon and Schuster, 1955.

Broverman, D. M., Broverman, I., Vogel, W., & Palmer, R. D. Physique and growth in adolescence. *Child Development,* 1964, **35**(3), 866.

Brown, D. G. Sex-role preference in young children. *Psychological Monographs,* 1956, **70** (Whole No. 187).

Brown, D. G. Sex-role development in a changing culture. *Psychological Bulletin,* 1958, **66,** 235.

Brown, G. I. The relationships between categories of behavior of third grade teachers. *Journal of Educational Research,* 1961, **54,** 338–344.

Brown, J. L. Differential hand usage in three-year-old children. *Journal of Genetic Psychology,* 1962, **100,** 67–75.

Brown, J. L. States in the newborn. *Merrill-Palmer Quarterly,* 1964, **10**(4), 313–327.

Bruner, J. S. *The process of education.* Cambridge: Harvard University Press, 1960.

Bruner, J. S., & Goodman, C. C. Value and need as organizing factors in perception. *Journal of Abnormal and Social Psychology,* 1947, **42,** 33–44.

Buhler, C. Maturation and motivation. *Personality,* 1951, **1,** 184–211.

Bull, K. R. An investigation into the relationship between physique, motor capacity and certain temperamental traits. *British Journal of Educational Psychology,* 1958, **28,** 129–154.

Burchinal, L. G. Characteristics of adolescents from unbroken, broken, and reconstituted families. *Journal of Marriage and Family Living,* 1964, **26,** 44–59.

Burt, C. The development of reasoning in children. *Journal of Experimental Pedagogy,* 1919, **5,** 68–77, 121–127, 358–359.

Burt, H. E. An experimental study of early childhood memory. *Journal of Genetic Psychology,* 1941, **58,** 435–439.

Burton, R. V., Maccoby, E. E., & Allinsmith, W. Antecedents of resistance to temptation in four-year-old children. *Child Development,* 1961, **32,** 689–710.

Bush, R. N. The human relationship factor: I. Principles of successful teacher-pupil relationship. *Phi Delta Kappan,* 1958, **39,** 271–273.

Buss, A. H. *The psychology of aggression.* New York: Wiley, 1961.

Butler, R. A. Discrimination learning by rhesus monkeys to visual-exploration to motivation. *Journal of Comparative and Physiological Psychology,* 1953, **46,** 95–98.

Caldwell, B. The effects of infant care. In M. L. Hoffman and L. W. Hoffman (Eds.), *Review of child development research.* Vol. 1. New York: Russell Sage Foundation, 1964.

Calvin, A. D., et al. *Psychology.* Boston: Allyn and Bacon, 1961.

REFERENCES Cameron, N. *The psychology of behavior disorders.* Boston: Houghton Mifflin, 1947.

Cameron, N. *Personality development and psychopathology.* Boston: Houghton Mifflin, 1963.

Campbell, A. A. Personality adjustment of only intermediate children. *Journal of Genetic Psychology,* 1933, **43,** 197–205.

Campbell, J. D., & Radke-Yarrow, M. R. Personal and situational variables in adaptation to change. *Journal of Social Issues,* 1958, **14**(1), 26–46.

Campbell, J. D. Peer relations in childhood. In M. Hoffman and W. Hoffman (Eds.), *Review of child development research.* Vol. 1. New York: Russell Sage Foundation, 1964.

Carlsmith, L. Effect of early father absence on scholastic aptitude. *Harvard Educational Review,* 1964, **34,** 3–21.

Carlson, R. Identification and personality structure in preadolescents. *Journal of Abnormal and Social Psychology,* 1963, **67,** 567–573.

Carlson, R. Stability and change in the adolescent's self image. *Child Development,* 1965, **36**(3), 661.

Carmichael, L. (Ed.) *Manual of child psychology,* 2nd ed. New York: Wiley, 1954.

Carmichael, L. Onset and early development of behavior. In L. Carmichael (Ed.), *Manual of child psychology.* (2nd ed.) New York: Wiley, 1954.

Casler, L. Maternal deprivation: A critical review of the literature. *Monographs of the Society for Research in Child Development,* 1961, **26**(2).

Casler, L. The effects of extratactile stimulation on a group of institutionalized infants. *Genetic Psychology Monographs,* 1965, **71,** 137–175.

Cattell, R. B. *Description and measurement of personality.* New York: World, 1946.

Cattell, R. B., Blewett, D. B., & Beloff, J. R. The inheritance of personality: A multiple variance analysis determination of approximate nature-nurture ratios for primary personality factors in Q-data. *American Journal of Human Genetics,* 1955, **7**(2), 122–146.

Cavan, R. S. Self and role in adjustment during old age. In A. M. Rose (Ed.), *Human behavior and social processes.* Boston: Houghton Mifflin, 1962.

Cerf, B. Books are here to stay. *Saturday Evening Post,* March 22, 1958, **230**(38).

Chambers, W. *Witness.* New York: Random, 1952.

Chazan, M. School phobia. *British Journal of Educational Psychology,* 1962, **32**(3), 209–217.

Chess, S., Thomas, A., & Birch, H. Characteristics of the individual child's behavioral responses to the environment. *American Journal of Orthopsychiatry,* 1959, **29,** 797.

Chess, S., Thomas, A., Birch, H., & Hertzig, M. Implications of a longitudinal study of child development for child psychiatry. *American Journal of Psychology,* 1960a.

Chess, S., Thomas, A., Birch, H., & Hertzig, M. A longitudinal study of primary reaction patterns in children. *Comprehensive Psychiatry,* 1960b, **1,** 103–112.

Child, I. L. *Italian or American.* New Haven: Yale University Press, 1943.

Church, J. (Ed.) *Three babies.* New York: Random, 1966.

Clark, A. W., & Sommers, P. V. Contradictory demands in family relations and adjustments to school and home. *Human Relations,* 1961, **14,** 97–111.

Clark, K. B., & Clark, M. Emotional factors in racial identification and preference in Negro children. *Journal of Negro Education,* 1950, **19,** 348.

Clark, K. B., & Clark, M. Racial identification and preference in Negro children. In G. Swanson, T. Newcomb, and E. Hartley (Eds.), *Readings in social psychology.* New York: Holt, 1952.

Clarke, A. D. B., & Clarke, A. M. Recovery from the effects of deprivation. *Acta Psychologica,* 1959, **16,** 137–144.

Clausen, J. A., & Williams, J. R. Sociological correlates of child behavior. *Child Psychology 62nd Yearbook, National Society for the Study of Education.* Chicago: University of Chicago Press, 1963.

Cobb, H. B. Role wishes and general wishes of children and adolescents. *Child Development,* 1954, **25,** 161–171.

Cobliner, G. W. Some maternal attitudes toward conception. *Mental Hygiene,* 1965, **49**(4), 552.

Coleman, J. C. *Abnormal psychology and modern life.* (3rd ed.) Chicago: Scott, Foresman, 1964.

Coleman, J. S. *The adolescent society.* Glencoe, Illinois: Free Press, 1961.

Combs, D., & Snygg, D. *Individual behavior.* (2nd ed.) New York: Harper, 1959.

Conant, J. B. *Slums and suburbs.* New York: McGraw-Hill, 1961.

Conger, J. J., Miller, W. C., & Walsmith, C. Antecedents of delinquency: Personality, social class and intelligence. In P. H. Mussen, J. J. Conger, and J. Kagan (Eds.), *Readings in child development and personality.* New York: Harper, 1965.

Conn, J. H. Children's reactions to the discovery of genital differences. *American Journal of Orthopsychiatry,* 1940, **10,** 747–754.

Conn, J. H., & Kanner, L. Children's awareness of sex differences. *Journal of Child Psychiatry,* 1947, **1,** 3–57.

Conrad, H. S. The validity of personality ratings of preschool children. *Journal of Educational Psychology,* 1932, **23,** 671–680.

Cook, W. M. Ability of children in color discrimination. *Child Development,* 1931, **2,** 303–320.

Cook, W. W. The gifted and retarded in historical perspective. *Phi Delta Kappan,* 1958, **39,** 250.

Corwin, R. G. *Sociology of education.* New York: Appleton-Century-Crofts, 1965.

Cox, F. N. Correlates of general and test anxiety in children. *Australian Journal of Psychology,* 1960, **12,** 169–177.

Crandall, V. J., Katkovsky, W., & Preston, A. Motivational and ability determinants of young children's intellectual achievement behaviors. *Child Development,* 1962, **33,** 643–661.

Crandall, V. J., & Preston, A. Verbally expressed needs and overt maternal behaviors. *Child Development,* 1961, **32,** 261–270.

Crandall, V. J., & Rabson, A. Children's repetition choices in an intellectual achievement situation following success and failure. *Journal of Genetic Psychology,* 1960, **97,** 161–168.

Crane, A. Pre-adolescent gangs: A sociopsychological interpretation. *Journal of Genetic Psychology,* 1955, **86,** 275–279.

Criswell, J. H. Racial cleavage in Negro-white groups. *Sociometry,* 1937, **1,** 85–89.

Cronbach, L. J. *Educational psychology.* (2nd ed.) New York: Harcourt, 1963.

Cruikshank, W. M., & Johnson, G. O. *Education of exceptional children and youth.* Englewood Cliffs: Prentice-Hall, 1958.

Daly, M. (Ed.) *Profile of youth.* Philadelphia: Lippincott, 1951.

Darley, F. L., & Winitz, H. Age of first word: Review of research. *Journal of Speech and Hearing Disorders,* 1961, **26,** 272–290.

Davids, A., Holden, R. H., & Gray, G. B. Maternal anxiety during pregnancy and adequacy of mother and child adjustment eight months following childbirth. *Child Development,* 1963, **24,** 993–1003.

Davis, C. M. Results of the self-selection of diets by young children. *Canadian Medical Association Journal,* 1939, **41,** 257–261.

Davis, H. *Hearing and deafness: A guide for laymen.* New York: Holt, 1958.

Davis, J. B. A cursory inquiry, 1817. In G. F. McCleary, *The early history of the infant welfare movement.* London: Lewis, 1933.

Davis, J. R. Contributions of research with children to a theory of maladjustment. *Child Development,* 1958, **29,** 3–7.

Davis, K. Extreme social isolation of a child. *American Journal of Sociology,* 1940a, **45,** 554–565.

Davis, K. Sociology of parent-youth conflict. *American Psychological Review,* 1940b, **5,** 523–525.

Davison, H. H., & Long, G. Children's perception of their teacher's feelings toward them related to self-perception, school achievement and behavior. *Journal of Experimental Education,* 1960, **12,** 107–118.

Dearborn, W. F., & Rothney, J. W. H. *Predicting the child's development.* Cambridge, Massachusetts: Sci-Art, 1963.

de Charms, R. A., & Moeller, G. H. Values expressed in American children's readers, 1800–1850. *Journal of Abnormal and Social Psychology,* 1962, **64,** 136–142.

de Groat, A. F., & Thompson, G. G. A study of the distribution of teacher approval and disapproval among sixth-grade children. *Journal of Experimental Education,* 1949, **18,** 57–75.

De la Mare, W. *Peacock pie.* New York: Knopf, 1961.

DeLong, A. Paper to Michigan Academy of Science, Arts and Letters, February, 1955.

Denenberg, V. H. Interactive effects of infantile and adult shock levels upon learning. *Psychological Reports,* 1959, **5,** 357–364.

Denenberg, V. H. Critical periods for the effects of infantile experience on adult learning. *Science,* 1960, **131,** 227–228.

Dennis, W. Causes of retardation among institutional children: Iran. *Journal of Genetic Psychology,* 1960, **96,** 47–59.

Dennis, W., & Dennis, M. G. The effect of cradling practice upon the onset of walking in Hopi children. *Journal of Genetic Psychology,* 1940, **56,** 77–86.

Denny, R. American youth today. In E. M. Erikson (Ed.), *Youth: Change and chal-*

REFERENCES

lenge. New York: Basic Books, 1963.

Deutsch, M. *Minority group and class status as related to social and personality factors in scholastic achievement.* Ithaca, New York: Society for Applied Anthropology, Cornell University, 1960.

Deutsch, M. Facilitating development in the pre-school child: Social and psychological perspectives. *Merrill-Palmer Quarterly,* 1964, **10**, 249–263.

Devereux, E. C., Bronfenbrenner, U., & Suci, G. J. Patterns of parent behavior in the United States of America and in the Federal Republic of Germany: A cross-national comparison. *International Social Science Journal,* 1962, **14**, 488–506.

Digman, J. M. Principal dimensions of child personality as inferred from teachers' judgments. *Child Development,* 1963, **34**, 43–66.

Dillon, M. S. Attitudes of children toward their own bodies and those of other children. *Child Development,* 1935, **5**, 165–176.

Dinitz, S., Dynes, R. B., & Clarke, A. C. Preference for male or female children: Traditional or affectional. *Marriage and Family Living,* 1954, **16**, 128–130.

Dinkmeyer, D. C. *Child development: The emerging self.* Englewood Cliffs, New Jersey: Prentice-Hall, 1965.

Division on child development and teacher personnel, Commission on Teacher Education. Improving anecdotes of behavior. *Childhood Education,* 1946, **22**, 232–239.

Dixon, J. C. Development of self-recognition. *Journal of Genetic Psychology,* 1957, **91**, 1–56.

Dobzhansky, T. Present evolution of man. *Scientific American,* 1960, **203**(3), 206–217.

Dodwell, P. C. Children's understanding of spatial concepts. *Canadian Journal of Psychology,* 1963, **17**(1), 141–161.

Donahue, W. T., et al. *The management of student adjustment and achievement.* Ann Arbor: University of Michigan Press, 1949.

Douglas, J. W. B. The extent of breast-feeding in Great Britain in 1946 with special reference to health and survival of the child. *Journal of Obstetrics and Gynecology of the British Empire,* 1950, **57**, 335–361.

Douvan, E. Sex differences in the adolescent character processes. *Merrill-Palmer Quarterly,* 1960, **6**, 203–211.

Douvan, E., & Adelson, J. The psychodynamics of social mobility in adolescent boys. *Journal of Abnormal and Social Psychology,* 1958, **56**, 31–44.

Douvan, E., & Adelson, J. *The adolescent experience.* New York: Wiley, 1966.

Dreger, R. M., & Miller, K. S. Comparative psychological studies of Negroes and whites in the United States. *Psychological Bulletin,* 1960, **57**, 361–402.

Drevdahl, J. E. Factors of importance for creativity. *Journal of Clinical Psychology,* 1958, **12**, 21–22.

Dubin, R., & Dubin, E. R. Children's social perceptions. A review of research. *Child Development,* 1965, **36**(3), 833.

Duncan, O. D. The trend of occupational mobility in the United States. *American Sociological Review,* 1965, **30**, 491–498.

Dupertuis, C. W., & Mitchell, H. B. Comparison of growth in height and weight between ectomorphic and mesomorphic boys. *Child Development,* 1853, **24**, 203–214.

Dyk, R. B., & Witkin, H. H. Family experiences related to the development of differentiation in children. *Child Development,* 1965, **36**(1), 24.

Earle, A. M. *Child life in colonial days.* New York: Macmillan, 1899.

Earle, J. Microcosmography or a piece of the world discovered in essays and characters. In R. Aldington (Translator), *A book of characters.* London: George Routledge, New York: Dutton, 1928.

Eastman, N. J. Effect of interval between births on maternal and fetal outlook. *American Journal of Obstetrics and Gynecology,* 1944, **47**, 445–466.

Eaton, M. T., D'Amico, L. A., & Phillips, B. N. Problem behavior in school. *Journal of Educational Psychology,* 1956, **47**, 350–357.

Educational Policies Commission. *The central purpose of American education.* Washington, D. C.: National Education Association, 1–12.

Eggan, D. The general problem of Hopi adjustment. *American Anthropologist,* 1945, **47**, 516–539.

Eisenstadt, S. N. Archetypal patterns of youth. *Daedalus,* 1962, **91**(1), 28–46.

Elder, G. Structural variations in the child-rearing relationship. *Sociometry,* 1962, **25**, 241–262.

Elder, G. H., & Bowerman, C. E. Family structure and child-rearing patterns: The effect of family size and sex composition. *American Sociological Review,* 1963, **28**, 891–905.

Elkind, D. Some factors related to the choice-status of ninety eighth-grade children in a school society. *Genetic Psychology Monographs,* 1958, **58**, 207–272.

Elkind, D. The child's conception of his religious denomination: I. The Jewish child. *Journal of Genetic Psychology,* 1961, **99,** 209–225.

Elkind, D. The child's conception of his religious denomination: II. The Catholic child. *Journal of Genetic Psychology,* 1962, **101,** 185–193.

Elmer, E. Identification of abused children. *Children,* 1963, **10**(5), 180–184.

Elser, R. P. The social position of hearing handicapped children in the regular grades. *Exceptional Children,* 1959, **25,** 305–309.

Emmerich, W. Family role concepts of children ages six to ten. *Child Development,* 1961, **32,** 609–624.

Engelmann, W. Reinfungsentwicklung und Reinfungsveränderung im Gefuhlsbetönten Wertungsbereich unserer Jugend. (Development of maturation and maturation changes in the realm of emotionally tinted values of our youth.) *Psychological Research,* 1962, **13**(2), 131–140.

English, H. B., & English, A. C. *Psychological and psychoanalytical terms.* New York: Longmans, Green, 1958.

Epstein, R. Social class membership and early childhood memories. *Child Development,* 1963, **34,** 503–508.

Erikson, E. H. Studies in the interpretation of play: Clinical observation of play disruption in young children. *Genetic Psychology Monographs,* 1940, **22,** 557–671.

Erikson, E. H. *Childhood and society.* (2nd ed.) New York: Norton, 1963.

Erikson, E. H. Identity versus identity diffusion. In P. Mussen, J. Conger, and J. Kagan (Eds.), *Readings in child development and personality.* New York: Harper, 1965.

Eron, L. D., Walder, L. O., Toigo, R., & Lefkowitz, M. M. Social class, parental punishment for aggression and child aggression. *Child Development,* 1963, **34,** 849–867.

Ervin, S. Transfer effects of learning: A verbal generalization. *Child Development,* 1960, **31,** 537–554.

Ervin, S. Language and TAT content in bilinguals. *Journal of Abnormal and Social Psychology,* 1964, **68,** 500–507.

Escalona, S., & Heider, G. M. *Prediction and outcome.* New York: Basic Books, 1959.

Escalona, S., & Moriarty, A. Prediction of school-age intelligence from infant test. *Child Development,* 1961, **32,** 597–605.

Estvan, F. J., & Estvan, E. W. *The child's world: His social perception.* New York: Putnam's, 1959.

Esty, G. Children in trouble. In R. C. Doll and R. S. Fleming (Eds.), *Children under pressure.* Columbus, Ohio: Merrill, 1966.

Eysenck, H. J. The inheritance of extroversion-introversion. *Acta Psychologica,* 1956, **12,** 95–110.

Eysenck, H. J. The development of moral values in children, VII. The contribution of learning theory. *British Journal of Educational Psychology,* 1960, **30,** 11–21.

Eysenck, H. J., & Press, D. B. The inheritance of neuroticism: An experimental study. *Journal of Mental Science,* 1951, **97,** 441–465.

Ezer, M. Effect of religion upon children's responses to questions involving physical casualty. In W. Allinsmith (Ed.), *The causes of behavior: Readings in child development and educational psychology.* Boston: Allyn and Bacon, 1962.

Falkner, F. Skeletal maturation: An appraisal of concept and method. *Journal of Physical Anthropology,* 1958, **16,** 381–396.

Fantz, R. L. Pattern vision in young infants. *Psychological Record,* 1958, **8,** 43–47.

Fantz, R. L. The origin of form perception. In P. H. Mussen, J. Conger, and J. Kagan (Eds.), *Readings in child development and personality.* New York: Harper, 1965.

Farber, B. Effects of a severely mentally retarded child on family integration. *Monographs of the Society for Research in Child Development,* 1959, **24**(2).

Faust, O. A., et al. Reducing emotional trauma in hospitalized children. *Albany Research Project.* Albany, New York: Albany Medical College, 1952.

Fenichel, C. *The psychoanalytic theory of neurosis.* New York: Norton, 1945.

Feshbach, S. The catharsis hypothesis and some consequences in interaction with aggressive and neutral play objects. *Journal of Personality,* 1956, **24,** 449–462.

Festinger, L., Riecken, H. J., & Schachter, S. *When prophesy fails.* Minneapolis: University of Minnesota Press, 1956.

Finch, S. M. *Fundamentals of child psychiatry.* New York: Norton, 1960.

Finney, J. C. Some maternal influences of children's personality and character. *Genetic Psychology Monographs,* 1961, **63,** 214.

Fisher, G. The American instructor. Cited by M. Kiefer, *American children through their books.* Philadelphia: University of Pennsylvania Press, 1948.

Fisher, S. C. *Relationships of attitudes, opinions and values among family members.* Berkeley: University of California Press, 1948.

Fiske, D. W., & Madde, S. R. *Functions of*

REFERENCES

varied experience. Homewood, Illinois: Dorsey, 1961.

Flanders, N. A., & Navumaki, S. The effect of teacher-pupil contacts involving praise on the sociometric choices of students. *Journal of Educational Psychology,* 1960, **51,** 65–68.

Flavell, J. H. *Developmental psychology of Jean Piaget.* Princeton, New Jersey: Van Nostrand, 1963.

Force, D. G. Social status of physically handicapped children. *Exceptional Children,* 1956, **23,** 104–107, 123.

Ford, C. S., & Beach, F. A. *Patterns of sexual behavior.* New York: Harper, 1951.

Foss, B. M. (Ed.) *Determinants of infant behavior: Proceedings of a Tavistock study group of mother-infant interaction.* New York: Wiley, 1961.

Fowler, W. Cognitive learning in infancy and early childhood. *Psychological Bulletin,* 1962, **59,** 116–152.

Fowler, W. A study of process and method in three-year-old twins and triplets learning to read. *Genetic Psychology Monographs,* 1965, **72,** 3–89.

Fox, C., & Birren, J. E. The differential decline of subtest scores on the Wechsler-Bellevue Intelligence Scale in 60–69 year old individuals. *Journal of Genetic Psychology,* 1950, **77,** 313–317.

France, A. *Little Pierre.* Translated by J. L. May. New York: Dodd, Mead, 1925.

Freed, C. S. Psychic factors in the development and treatment of obesity. *Journal of the American Medical Association,* 1947, **133,** 369.

Freedman, D. G., & Keller, B. Inheritance of behavior in infants. *Science,* 1963, .**140,** 196–198.

Freud, A., & Dann, S. An experiment in group upbringing. *The Psychoanalytic Study of the Child,* 1951, **6,** 127–168.

Freud, S. Character and anal eroticism. *Collected papers,* Vol. 2. London: Hogarth, 1924.

Fry, P. C. Diets of post-adolescent young women. *Journal of the American Dietetics Association,* 1959, **35,** 687–691.

Fukuyama, Y. Wonderletters: An experimental study of the religious sensitivities of children. *Religious Education,* 1963, **43,** 377–383.

Funkenstein, D. H. (Ed.) *The student and mental health: An international view.* New York: World Federation for Mental Health, 1959.

Funkenstein, D. H., King, S. H., & Drolette, M. E. *The master of stress.* Cambridge: Harvard University Press, 1957.

Gamble, C. J. What proportion of mental deficiency is preventable by sterilization? *American Journal of Mental Deficiency,* 1952, **57,** 123–126.

Gardner, D. *Development in early childhood, the preschool years.* New York: Harper, 1964.

Gardner, D. B., Hawkes, G. R., & Burchinal, L. G. Noncontinuous mothering in infancy and development in later childhood. *Child Development,* 1961, **32,** 225-234.

Gardner, D. B., & Pease, D. The use of situational tests with preschool children. Nursery Education, 1958, **14,** 18–20.

Garn, S. M. Growth and development. In E. Ginzberg (Ed.), *The nation's children,* Vol. 2. New York: Columbia University Press, 1960.

Gauron, E. Infantile shock traumatization and subsequent adaptability to stress. *Journal of Genetic Psychology,* 1964, **104**(1), 176.

Geber, M. The psychomotor development of African children in the first year, and the influence of psycho-maternal behavior. *Journal of Social Psychology,* 1958, **47,** 185–195.

Gellert, E. Stability and fluctuation in the power relationship of young children. *Journal of Abnormal and Social Psychology,* 1961, **62,** 8–15.

Gellert, E. Children's conceptions of the content and functions of the human body. *General Psychology Monographs,* 1962, **65,** 345.

Gesell, A., Armatruda, C. S. *Developmental diagnosis: Normal and abnormal child development.* New York: Hoeber, 1941.

Gesell, A., & Armatruda, C. S. *Developmental diagnosis.* (2nd ed.) New York: Hoeber, 1947.

Gesell, A., & Ilg, F. L. *Infant and child in the culture of today.* New York: Harper, 1943.

Gettegno, C. Notes on modes of thought. *Main Currents of Modern Thought,* 1961, **17,** 86–88.

Getzels, J. W., & Jackson, P. W. *Creativity and intelligence: Explorations with gifted students.* New York: Wiley, 1962.

Gilbert, M. *Biography of the unborn.* Baltimore: Williams & Wilkins, 1938.

Gilliland, A. R. Changes in religious beliefs of college students. *Journal of Social Psychology,* 1953, **37,** 113–116.

Gillin, J. L., & Gillin, J. P. *An introduction to sociology.* New York: Macmillan, 1944.

Glasser, A. J. A Negro child reared as white. In G. Seward (Ed.), *Clinical*

430

studies in culture conflict. New York: Ronald, 1958.

Glenn, N. D. The trend in difference in attitudes and behavior by educational level. *Sociology of Education,* 1966, **39,** 273–274.

Glueck, E. T. Distinguishing delinquents from pseudodelinquents. *Harvard Educational Review,* 1966, **36**(2), 119–130.

Goldberg, M. L. Adapting teacher style to pupil differences, teachers for disadvantaged children. *Merrill-Palmer Quarterly,* 1964, **10,** 164–165.

Golden, J., Mandel, N., Glueck, B. C., & Feder, Z. A summary description of 50 normal white males. *American Journal of Psychology,* 1964, **19,** 48–56.

Goode, W. J. *After divorce.* Glencoe, Illinois: Free Press, 1956.

Goodenough, F. W. Interest in persons and aspects of sex differences in the early years. *Psychological Monographs,* 1957a, **55,** 287–323.

Goodenough, F. W. Parental Identification in young children. *Genetic Psychology Monographs,* 1957b, **55,** 287–323.

Goodman, M. E. *Race awareness in young children.* Cambridge, Massachusetts: Addison-Wesley, 1952.

Gordon, I. J. New conceptions of children's learning and development. In W. B. Waetjen and R. R. Leeper (Eds.), *Learning and mental health in the school.* Washington, D. C.: Association for Supervision and Curriculum Development, 1966.

Gordon, L. V. *Gordon personal profile: Manual.* New York: Harcourt, 1953.

Gorer, G. *The American people: A study of national character.* New York: Norton, 1948.

Goslin, D. A. *The search for ability: Standardized testing in social perspective.* New York: Russell Sage Foundation, 1963.

Gottesman, I. I. The psychogenetics of personality. Unpublished doctoral thesis, University of Minnesota, 1960.

Gough, H. G. Techniques for identifying the creative research scientist. In Institute of Personality Assessment and Research, *The creative person,* Vol. 27. Berkeley: University of California and University Extension, Liberal Arts Department, 1961.

Gough, H. G., & Fink, M. D. Scholastic achievement among students of average ability, as predicted from California psychological inventory. *Psychology in the Schools,* 1964, **1,** 375–380.

Graham, F. K., Ernhart, C. B., Thurston, D., & Craft, M. Development after three years after perinatal anoxia and other potentially damaging newborn experiences. *Psychological Monographs,* 1962, **76**(3).

Gray, P. H. Theory and evidence of imprinting in human infants. *Journal of Psychology,* 1958, **46,** 155–166.

Gray, S. W. Masculinity-femininity in relation to anxiety and social acceptance. *Child Development,* 1957, **28,** 203–214.

Green, E. H. Friendship and quarrels among preschool children. *Child Development,* 1933, **4,** 237–252.

Green, E. S., & Harbeck, R. M. *What high school pupils study.* Washington, D.C.: U. S. Government Printing Office, 1962.

Greulich, W. W. A comparison of the physical growth and development of American-born and native Japanese children. *American Journal of Physical Anthropology,* 1957, **15,** 489–515.

Grinder, R. E. Parental child-rearing practices, conscience and resistance to temptation of sixth-grade children. *Child Development,* 1962, **33,** 803–820.

Grinker, R. R. *Psychosomatic research.* New York: Norton, 1953.

Gronland, N. E. *Sociometry in the classroom.* New York: Harper, 1959.

Groves, E. R., & Blanchard, P. M. *Introduction to mental hygiene.* New York: Holt, 1930.

Guilford, J. P. *Personality.* New York: McGraw-Hill, 1959.

Gurin, G., Veroff, J., & Feld, S. *Americans view their mental health.* New York: Basic Books, 1960.

Gurin, M. G. Differences in the psychological characteristics of latency and adolescence. Unpublished doctoral dissertation. Ann Arbor, Michigan: University of Michigan, 1953.

Gustafson, L. Relationship between ethnic group membership and the attention of selected facts pertaining to American history and culture. *Journal of Educational Sociology,* 1957, **31,** 49–56.

Gwinn, J. L., Lewin, K. W., & Peterson, H. G. Roentgenographic manifestations of unsuspected trauma in infancy. *Journal of American Medical Association,* June 1961.

Haggerty, A. D. The effect of long-term hospitalization or institutionalization on the language development of children. *Journal of Genetic Psychology,* 1959, **94,** 205–209.

Hall, C., & Domhoff, B. Aggression in dreams. *International Journal of Social Psychiatry,* 1963, **4,** 259–267.

Hall, G. S. *The contents of children's minds on entering school.* New York: Kellogg, 1893.

REFERENCES Hall, G. S. *Adolescence,* I. New York: Appleton-Century-Crofts, 1905a.

Hall, G. S. *Adolescence,* II. New York: Appleton-Century-Crofts, 1905b.

Hamilton, E. Emotional aspects of pregnancy: An intensive study of 14 normal primiparae. Unpublished doctoral thesis, Columbia University, 1955.

Hammer, E. F. *Creativity: An exploratory investigation of the personalities of gifted adolescent artists.* New York: Random, 1961.

Hanfmann, E. P. Social structure of a group of kindergarten children. *American Journal of Orthopsychiatry,* 1935, **5,** 407–410.

Haring, N. G., & Phillips, E. L. *Educating emotionally disturbed children.* New York: McGraw-Hill, 1962.

Harlow, H. F. Learning and satiation of response in intrinsically motivated complex puzzle performance by monkeys. *Journal of Comparative and Physiological Psychology,* 1950, **43,** 289–294.

Harlow, H. F. The heterosexual affectional system in monkeys. *American Psychologist,* 1962, **17,** 1–9.

Harlow, H. F., & Harlow, M. K. The effect of rearing conditions on behavior. *Bulletin of the Menninger Clinic,* 1962, **26,** 213–224.

Harlow, H. F., & Zimmerman, R. R. Affectional responses in the infant monkey. *Science,* 1959, **130,** 421–432.

Harms, E. The development of religious experiences in children. *American Journal of Sociology,* 1944, **50,** 112–122.

Harris, D. B. Sex differences in the life problems and interests of adolescents. *Child Development,* 1959, **30,** 453–459.

Harris, D. B., & Harris, E. S. A study of fetal movements in relation to mother's activity. *Human Biology,* 1946, **18,** 221–237.

Harris, D. B., Rose, A. M., Clark, K. E., & Valasek, F. Personality differences between responsible and less responsible children. *Journal of Genetic Psychology,* 1955, **87,** 103–109.

Harris, D. B., & Tseng, S. C. Children's attitudes toward peers and parents as revealed by sentence completions. *Child Development,* 1957, **28,** 401–411.

Hartley, R. Sex role pressures and the socialization of the male child. *Psychological Reports,* 1959, **6,** 457–468.

Hartley, R. Children's concepts of male and female roles. *Merrill-Palmer Quarterly,* 1960, **6,** 83–91.

Hartley, R. A developmental view of female sex role definition and identification. *Merrill-Palmer Quarterly,* 1964, **10**(3), 3–16.

Hartley, R., & Hardesty, F. P. Children's perceptions of sex roles in childhood. *Journal of Genetic Psychology,* 1964, **105,** 43–51.

Hartshorne, H., & May, M. A. *Studies in service and self-control,* Vol. 2. New York: Macmillan, 1929.

Hartshorne, H., et al. Studies in the organization of character. In *Studies on the nature of character,* Vol. 3. New York: Macmillan, 1930.

Hartung, D. What expectant mothers need to know. *U. S. News and World Report,* February 14, 1966, **9**(7), 58.

Hartup, W. A., & Zook, E. A. Sex-role preference in three-and four-year-old children. *Journal of Consulting Psychology,* 1960, **24**(5), 420–426.

Harvey, O. J., & Rutherford, J. Status in the informal group: Influence and influencibility at differing age levels. *Child Development,* 1961, **31,** 377–385.

Hattwick, L. A. Sex differences in behavior of nursery school children. *Child Development,* 1937, **8,** 343–355.

Hauer, H. J. Frustration in neonates: An investigation of the relationship between frustration tolerance of neonates and frustration tolerance of their parents. *Dissertation Abstract,* 1914, No. 15.

Haverson, H. M. Infant sucking and tensional behavior. *Journal of Genetic Psychology,* 1938, **53,** 365–430.

Havighurst, R. J. *Human development and education,* New York: Longmans, Green, 1953.

Havighurst, R. J. The social competence of middle-aged people. *Genetic Psychological Monographs,* 1957, **56,** 297–375.

Havighurst, R. J., & Neugarten, B. L. *Sociology and education.* Boston: Allyn and Bacon, 1962.

Hayes, C. *The ape in our house.* New York: Harper, 1951.

Heath, D. H. *Explorations of maturity.* New York: Appleton-Century-Crofts, 1965.

Hebb, D. O. Drives and the CNS (Conceptual Nervous System). *Psychological Review,* 1955, **62,** 250–251.

Hebb, D. O. A neuropsychological theory. In S. Koch (Ed.), *Psychology: A study of a science I: Sensory, perceptual and physiological formulations.* New York: McGraw-Hill, 1959a.

Hebb, D. O. On the nature of fear. *Psychological Review,* 1959b, **53,** 259–276.

Heider, G. M. Vulnerability in infants and young children: A pilot study. *Genetic Psychology Monographs,* 1966, **73,** 165–167.

Heilbrun, A. B. Parental identification and college adjustment. *Psychological Mono-*

432

graphs, 1962, **10,** 853–854.

Heilbrun, A. B., & Fromme, D. K. Parental identification of late adolescents and level of adjustment: The importance of parent model attributes, ordinal position and sex of the child. *Journal of Genetic Psychology,* 1965, **107**(1), 49–59.

Heinstein, M. I. Behavioral correlates of breast-bottle regimes under varying parent-infant relationships. Unpublished doctoral dissertation, University of California, 1958.

Heinstein, M. I. Behavioral correlates of breast-bottle regimes under varying parent-infant relationships. *Monographs of the Society for Research in Child Development,* 1963, **28**(4).

Held, R., & Hein, A. Movement-produced stimulation in the development of visually guided behavior. *Journal of Comparative and Physiological Psychology,* 1963, **56,** 872–876.

Helper, M. M. Learning theory and the self-concept. *Journal of Abnormal and Social Psychology,* 1955, **51,** 184–194.

Henry, J. Environment and symptom formation. *American Journal of Orthopsychiatry,* 1947, **17,** 628–632.

Henry, J. Docility or giving teacher what she wants. *Journal of Social Issues,* 1955, **2,** 33–41.

Henry, J. Permissiveness and morality. *Mental Hygiene,* 1961, **45,** 282–287.

Herin, N. G., & Phillips, E. L. *Education of emotionally disturbed children.* New York: McGraw-Hill, 1962.

Hess, E. H. Imprinting in animals. *Scientific American,* 1958, **198,** 81–90.

Hess, E. H. Imprinting. *Science,* 1959, **130,** 133–141.

Hess, R. D., & Goldman, H. Parents' views of the effects of television on children. *Child Development,* 1962, **33,** 411–426.

Hess, R. D., Shipman, V., & Jackson, D. *Early experience and the socialization of cognitive modes in children.* Prepared for the American Association for the Advancement of Science, Symposium. Montreal, December 29, 1964.

Hetherington, E. M., & Brackbill, Y. Etiology and convariation of obstinacy, orderliness and parsimony in young children. *Child Development,* 1963, **34,** 919–943.

Heyns, R. *The psychology of personal adjustment.* New York: Holt, 1958.

Hicks, A. J., & Hayes, M. Study of the characteristics of 250 junior high school children. *Child Development,* 1938, **9,** 219–242.

Hildreth, G. The development and training of hand dominance. *Journal of Genetic Psychology,* 1950, **76,** 197–220.

Hill, R. The American family today. In E. Ginzberg (Ed.), *The nation's children.* Vol. 1. New York: Columbia University Press, 1960.

Hilton, M., Chadderton, H., Eppright, E., & Woline, L. Influences on girls' eating behavior. *Journal of Home Economics,* 1962, **54,** 842–846.

Himmelweit, H. E., Oppenheim, A. N., & Vince, P. *Television and the child.* London: Oxford University Press, 1958.

Hirsch, J. Behavioral genetics and individuality understood. *Science,* 1963, **142,** 1436–1472.

Hirschberg, J. C. Religion and childhood. *Menninger Quarterly,* 1956, **10,** 22–44.

Hobbs, C. E. Mental disorder in one pair of identical twins. *American Journal of Psychiatry,* 1941, **98,** 447–450.

Hochberg, J., & Lambert, W. Baby scale to measure cuteness. *New York Times,* November 20, 1958.

Hoehn, A. J. A study of social-class differentiation in the classroom behavior of nineteen third-grade teachers. *Journal of Social Psychology,* 1954, **39,** 269–292.

Hoffman, L. W. Effects of the employment of mothers on parental power relations and the division of household tasks. *Marriage and Family Living,* 1960, **22,** 27–35.

Hoffman, M. L. Power assertion by the parent and his impact on the child. *Child Development,* 1960, **31,** 129–143.

Hoffman, M. L. Child rearing practices and moral development, generalizations from empirical research. *Child Development,* 1963a, 295–318.

Hoffman, M. L. Personality, family structure and social class as antecedents of parental power assertion. *Child Development,* 1963, 34, 869–884.

Hoffman, L. W., & Hoffman, M. L. (Eds.), *Review of child development research,* Vol. 1. New York: Russell Sage Foundation, 1964.

Hogbin, H. I. An example of a New Guinea childhood: From weaning till the eighth year in Wogeo. *Oceania,* 1946, **16,** 275–296.

Holland, J. L., & Nichols, R. Prediction of academic and extracurricular achievement in college. *Journal of Educational Psychology,* 1964, **55,** 55–65.

Holmes, F. B. *Children's fears.* New York: Bureau of Publications, Teachers College, Columbia University, 1935.

Holt, L. E. The care and feeding of children: A catechism for the use of mothers and children's nurses. New York: Appleton-Century-Crofts, 1929.

Honkavaara, S. A critical re-evaluation of color and form reaction and disproving

REFERENCES

of the hypothesis connected with it. *Journal of Psychology,* 1958, **45,** 25–36.

Honzik, M. P. Sex differences in the occurrence of materials in the play constructions of preadolescents. *Child Development,* 1951, **22,** 15–35.

Honzik, M. P. Prediction of behavior from birth to maturity. *Merrill-Palmer Quarterly,* 1965, **12,** 81.

Hooker, D. Reflex activities in the human fetus. In R. G. Barker and H. F. Wright (Eds.), *Child behavior and development.* New York: McGraw-Hill, 1943.

Horney, K. *The neurotic personality of our time.* New York: Norton, 1937.

Horney, K. The search for glory. In C. Thompson (Ed.), *An outline of psychoanalysis.* New York: Modern Library, 1955.

Horowitz, E. L. Social localization of the self. *Journal of Social Psychology,* 1935, **6,** 379–387.

Hubert, M. A. G., & Britton, J. H. Attitudes and practices of mothers rearing their children from birth to the age of two years. *Journal of Home Economics,* 1957, **49,** 208–223.

Hughes, B. Child development research seminar, Walden Woods, Michigan, 1955.

Hughes, G. R. Self resignation: A mighty foe. *Journal of Rehabilitation,* 1960, **265,** 18–19.

Hunt, J. McV. *Intelligence and experience.* New York: Ronald, 1961.

Hunt, J. McV. The psychological basis for using pre-school enrichment as an antidote for cultural deprivation. *Merrill-Palmer Quarterly,* 1964, **10,** 209–248.

Hunt, J. McV. Experience and the development of motivation: Some re-interpretations. In P. H. Mussen, J. J. Conger, and J. Kagan (Eds.), *Readings in child development and personality.* New York: Harper, 1965.

Hurlock, E. *Child development.* (4th ed.) New York: McGraw-Hill, 1964.

Hutt, M. L., & Gibby, R. G. The child: Development and adjustment. Boston: Allyn and Bacon, 1959.

Hsu, F. L. K. Psychological anthropology: Approaches to culture and personality. Homewood, Illinois: Dorsey, 1961.

Hylan, L. The changing Negro family. In E. Ginzberg (Ed.), *The nation's children.* New York: Columbia University Press, 1960.

Hyman, H. H. The value systems of different classes. In R. Bendix and S. M. Lipsett (Eds.), *Class status and power.* Glencoe, Illinois: Free Press, 1953.

Ingalls, T. H. Congenital deformity not inherited. *New York Times,* December 10, 1959.

Irwin, O. C. Language and communications. In P. Mussen (Ed.), *Handbook of research methods in child development.* New York: Wiley, 1960.

Irwin, O. C. A second comparative study of children with cerebral palsy and of mentally retarded children. *Cerebral Palsy Review,* 1962, **23,** 17–19.

Irwin, O. C. The activity of newborn infants. In R. G. Barker (Ed.), *The stream of behavior: Exploration of its structure and contents.* New York: Appleton-Century-Crofts, 1963.

Isaacs, S. Social development in young children: A study of beginnings. New York: Harcourt, 1933.

Iscoe, I., Williams, M., & Harvey, J. Modification of children's judgments by a simulated group technique: A normative developmental study. *Child Development,* 1953, **34,** 963–968.

Jackson, P. W., & Getzels, J. W. Psychological health and classroom functioning: A study of dissatisfaction with school among adolescents. *Journal of Educational Psychology,* 1959, **50**(6), 295–300.

Jackson, P. W., & Guba, E. G. The need structure of in-service teachers: An occupational analysis. *School Review,* 1957, **65,** 176–192.

Jahoda, M. *Current concepts of positive mental health.* New York: Basic Books, 1958.

Jakubczak, L. F., & Walters, R. H. Suggestibility as dependency behavior. *Journal of Abnormal and Social Psychology,* 1959, **59,** 102–107.

James, W. *The principles of psychology,* Vol. 1. New York: Holt, 1890.

Jarecki, H. G. Maternal attitudes toward child-rearing. *American Archives of General Psychiatry,* 1961, **4,** 340–355.

Jastrow, J. Lo, the pseudologist. In L. Hartley, H. G. Birch, & R. E. Hartley (Eds.), *Outside readings in psychology.* New York: Crowell, 1951.

Jennings, H. H. Leadership and sociometric choice. *Sociometry,* 1947, **10,** 32–49.

Jennings, H. H. Sociometric grouping in relation to child development. In *Fostering mental health in our schools,* 1950 yearbook. Washington, D. C.: Association for Supervision and Curriculum Development, 1950.

Jensen, A. R. Personality. In P. R. Farnsworth (Ed.), *Annual review of psychology,* Vol. 9. Palo Alto: Annual Reviews, 1958.

Jersild, A. T. *Child psychology.* (5th ed.) Englewood Cliffs, New Jersey: Prentice-Hall, 1960.

Jersild, A. T., & Holmes, F. B. An experimental study of the fears of young children. *Child Development Monographs*, 1935, **1**(20).

Johannis, T. B., Jr. Participation by fathers, mothers and teenage sons and daughters in selected social activity. *The Coordinator*, 1958, **7**, 25.

John, V. P., & Goldstein, L. S. The social context of language acquisition. *Merrill-Palmer Quarterly*, 1964, **10**, 265–275.

Johnson, G. O. A study of the social position of mentally handicapped children in the regular grade. *American Journal of Mental Deficiency*, 1950, **55**, 60–89.

Johnson, M. M. Sex role learning in the nuclear family. *Child Development*, 1963, **34**, 319–333.

Johnson, R. C. Linguistic structure as related to concept formation and to concept content. *Psychological Bulletin*, 1962, **59**, 468–476.

Johnson, R. C., & Medinnus, G. R. *Child psychology*. New York: Wiley, 1965.

Johnson, W. The Indians have no word for it: I, stuttering in children. *Quarterly Journal of Speech*, 1944, **30**, 330–337.

Johnson, W., et al. *The onset of stuttering and what you can do about it: Research findings and implications*. Minneapolis: University of Minnesota Press, 1959.

Jones, H. E. The galvanic skin reflex. *Child Development*, 1930, **1**, 106–110.

Jones, H. E. The longitudinal method in the study of personality. In I. Iscoe and H. Stevenson (Eds.), *Personality development in children*. Austin, Texas: University of Texas Press, 1960.

Jones, H. E., & Jones, M. C. Fear. *Childhood Education*, 1928, **5**, 136–143.

Jones, J. E. Perceived differences among twins. *Genetics Quarterly*, 1955, **2**, 98–102.

Jones, J. E. *Life and work of Sigmund Freud*. New York: Basic Books, 1957.

Jones, M. C. A study of socialization patterns of the high school levels. *Journal of Genetic Psychology*, 1958, **93**, 87–111.

Jones, M. C., & Burke, B. S. Personality development. *Monographs of the Society for Research in Child Development*, 1936, **1**(4).

Josephina, S. A study of some common religious terms for six-year-old children. *Religious Education*, 1961, **56**, 24–25.

Josselyn, I. *The happy child*. New York: Random, 1955.

Josselyn, I. Cultural forces, motherliness and fatherliness. *American Journal of Orthopsychiatry*, 1956, **26**, 264–271.

Josselyn, I. Psychology of changes in adolescence. *Children*, 1959, **6**, 37–43.

Jost, H., & Sontag, L. W. The genetic factor in autonomic nervous system function. *Psychosomatic Medicine*, 1944, **6**, 308–310.

Kagan, J. M. Acquisition and significance of sex typing and sex role identity. In M. L. Hoffman and L. W. Hoffman (Eds.), *Review of child development research*, Vol. 1. New York: Russell Sage Foundation, 1964.

Kagan, J. M. Information processing in the child. In P. H. Mussen, J. Conger, and J. Kagan (Eds.), *Child development and personality*. New York: Harper, 1965.

Kagan, J. M., & Freeman, M. Relation of childhood intelligence, maternal behaviors, and social class to behavior during adolescence. *Child Development*, 1963, **34**, 899–911.

Kagan, J. M., & Lemkin, J. The child's differential perception of parental attributes. *Journal of Abnormal and Social Psychology*, 1960, **60**, 440–447.

Kagan, J. M., & Moss, H. A. Stability and validity of achievement fantasy. *Journal of Abnormal and Social Psychology*, 1959, **58**, 357–364.

Kagan, J. M., & Moss, H. A. The stability of passive and dependent behavior from childhood through adulthood. *Child Development*, 1960, **31**, 577–591.

Kagan, J. M., & Moss, H. A. *Birth to maturity*. New York: Wiley, 1962.

Kagan, J. M., Moss, H. A., & Sigel, I. E. Conceptual style and the use of affective labels. *Merrill-Palmer Quarterly*, 1960, **6**(4), 261–278.

Kagan, J. M., Moss, H. A., & Sigel, I. E. Psychological significance of styles of conceptualization. *Child Development*, 1963, **28**, 73–124.

Kagan, J. M., Sontag, L. W., Baker, C. T., & Nelson, V. P. Personality and IQ change. *Journal of Abnormal and Social Psychology*, 1958, **56**, 261–266.

Kahl, J. A. Educational and occupational aspiration of "common man" boys. *Harvard Educational Review*, 1953, **53**, 186–203.

Kallman, F. J. Genetic aspects of psychoses. *Biology of Mental Health and Disease*. New York: Hoeber-Harper, 1952.

Kallman, F. J. *Heredity in health and mental disorder*. New York: Norton, 1953.

Kanner, L. *Child psychiatry*. (3rd ed.) Springfield, Illinois: Thomas, 1957.

Kaplan, L. *Mental health and human relations in education*. New York: Harper, 1959.

Kardiner, A. *The psychological frontiers of society*. New York: Columbia Uni-

REFERENCES

veristy Press, 1945.

Katcher, A. The discrimination of sex differences of young children. *Journal of Genetic Psychology,* 1955, **87,** 131–143.

Katz, B., & Lenher, G. F. J. *Mental hygiene in modern living.* New York: Ronald, 1953.

Kearsley, R., et al. Study of relations between psychologic environment and child behavior. *American Journal of Diseases of Children,* 1962, **104**(1), 12–20.

Kellogg, W. N., & Kellogg, L. A. *The ape and the child.* New York: McGraw-Hill, 1933.

Kelly, E. L. Consistency of the adult personality. *American Psychologist,* 1955, **10,** 659–681.

Kendler, H. S., & Kendler, T. S. Vertical and horizontal processes in problem-solving. *Psychological Review,* 1962, **49,** 1–16.

Kessen, W. Research design in the study of developmental problems. In P. H. Mussen (Ed.), *Handbook of research methods in child development.* New York: Wiley, 1960.

Kessen, W. Research in the psychological development of infants: An overview. *Merrill-Palmer Quarterly,* 1963, **9,** 83–94.

Kessen, W., Williams, E. J., & Williams, J. P. Selection and testing of response measures in the study of the human newborn. *Child Development,* 1961, **32,** 7–24.

Kessler, J. W. *Psychopathology of childhood.* Englewood Cliffs, New Jersey: Prentice-Hall, 1966.

Kidd, A. H., & Rivoire, J. L. *Perceptual development in children.* New York: International Universities Press, 1966.

Kiefer, M. *American children through their books.* Philadelphia: University of Pennsylvania Press, 1948.

Kimble, G. A., & Garmezy, N. *Principles of general psychology.* (2nd ed.) New York: Ronald, 1963.

Kinsey, A. C., Pomeroy, W. B., & Martin, C. E. *Sexual behavior in the human male.* Philadelphia: Saunders, 1948.

Kisker, G. W. *The disorganized personality.* New York: McGraw-Hill, 1964.

Klatskin, E. H., Lethin, A. G., & Jackson, E. B. Choice of rooming in a newborn nursery. *Journal of Pediatrics,* 1950, **6,** 878–889.

Klausmeier, H. J., & Goodwin, W. *Learning and human abilities.* (2nd ed.) New York: Harper, 1966.

Klein, M. *The psychoanalysis of the child.* London: Hogarth, 1932.

Klineberg, O. *Negro intelligence and selective migration.* New York: Columbia University Press, 1935.

Klineberg, O. *Race differences.* New York: Harper, 1935.

Klineberg, O. Negro-white differences in intelligence test performance. *American Psychologist,* 1963, **18,** 198–203.

Klingensmith, S. W. Child animism: What the child means by "alive." *Child Development,* 1953, **24,** 51–61.

Kluckhohn, C. *Mirror for man.* New York: McGraw-Hill, 1949.

Koch, H. L. Sibling influence on children's speech. *Journal of Speech and Hearing Disorders,* 1956a, **21,** 322–328.

Koch, H. L. Sissiness and tomboyishness in relation to sibling characteristics. *Journal of Genetic Psychology,* 1956b, **88,** 231–244.

Koch, H. L. Some emotional attitudes of the young child in relation to characteristics of his sibling. *Child Development,* 1956c, **27,** 393–426.

Koch, H. L. The relation in young children between characteristics of their playmates and certain attributes of their siblings. *Child Development,* 1957, **28,** 175–202.

Koch, H. L. The relation of certain formal attributes of siblings to attitudes held toward each other and toward their parents. *Monographs of the Society for Research in Child Development,* 1960, **25**(4).

Koenigsberg, L. Unpublished research, State University of New York, College at Oswego.

Kohn, M. L. Social class and parental values. *American Journal of Sociology,* 1963, **68,** 471–480.

Kohn, M. L. Social class and parent-child relationship and interpretation. *American Journal of Sociology,* 1963, **68,** 471–480.

Komarovsky, M. Cultural contradictions in sex roles. *Journal of Sociology,* 1946, **52,** 184–189.

Koppitz, E. M. Relationships between some background factors and children's interpersonal attitude. *Journal of Genetic Psychology,* 1957, **91,** 119–129.

Kounin, J. S., & Gump, P. V. The comparative influence of punitive and nonpunitive teachers upon children's concepts of school misconduct. *Journal of Educational Psychology,* 1961, **52,** 44–49.

Krauss, R., & Sendak, M. *A hole is to dig.* New York: Harper, 1952.

Krebs, A. Two determinants of conformity: Age of independence, training and achievement. *Journal of Abnormal and Social Psychology,* 1958, **56,** 130–131.

Krutch, J. W., et al. *Is the common man too common? An informal survey of our cultural resources and what we are doing about them.* Norman: University of

436

Oklahoma Press, 1954.

Kuhlen, R. *Psychology of adolescent development.* New York: Harper, 1952.

Kuhlen, R., & Arnold, M. Age differences in religious beliefs and problems during adolescence. *Journal of Genetic Psychology,* 1944, **65,** 291–300.

Kulka, A., Fry, C., & Goldstein, F. Kinesthetic needs in infancy. *American Journal of Orthopsychiatry,* 1960, **30,** 562–571.

Kutner, B. Patterns of mental functioning associated with prejudice in children. *Psychological Monographs,* 1958, **72,** 1–48.

L'Abate, L. Personality correlates of manifest anxiety in children. *Journal of Consulting Psychology,* 1960, **24,** 342–348.

Lafore, G. Practices of parents in dealing with preschool children. *Child Development Monographs,* 1945, **10**(31).

Lakin, M. Personality factors in mothers of excessively crying (colicky) infants. *Monographs of the Society for Research in Child Development,* 1957, **22**(1).

Lambert, W. W. Interpersonal behavior. In P. Mussen (Ed.), *Handbook of research methods in child development.* New York: Wiley, 1960.

Lambert, W. W., Triandis, L. M., & Wolfe, M. Some correlates of beliefs in the malevolence and benevolence of supernatural beings: A cross-societal study. *Journal of Abnormal and Social Psychology,* 1959, **58,** 162–169.

Landis, J. T. The trauma of children when parents divorce. *Marriage and Family Living,* 1961, **22,** 7–13.

Landis, J. T. Dating maturation of children from happy and unhappy marriages. *Marriage and Family Living,* 1963, **25,** 351–353.

Landis, P. H. The broken home in teenage adjustment. *Washington Agricultural Experiment Stations Bulletin,* No. 542, June 1953.

Landreth, C. *Psychology of early childhood.* New York: Knopf, 1958.

Landreth, C. Four year olds' notions about sex-appropriateness of parental care and companionship activities. *Merrill-Palmer Quarterly,* 1963, **9**(3), 175–182.

Landreth, C. Child laboratories on university campuses. *Child Development,* 1964, **35**(3), 990.

Landreth, C., & Johnson, B. C. Young children's responses to a picture and inset text designed to reveal reactions to persons of a different skin color. *Child Development,* 1953, **24,** 63–79.

Laurendeau, M., & Pinard, A. *Causal thinking in the child.* New York: International Universities Press, 1962.

Lawrence, E. Childhood in twentieth century America. In E. Ginzberg (Ed.), *The nation's children,* Vol. 1. New York: Columbia University Press, 1960.

Laycock, F., & Caylor, J. S. Physiques of gifted children and their less gifted siblings. *Child Development,* 1964, **35**(1), 73.

Lazarsfeld, P., & Thielens, W., Jr. *The academic mind.* New York: Free Press, 1958.

Lebo, D. Aggressiveness and expansiveness in children. *Journal of Genetic Psychology,* 1962, **100**(2), 227–240.

Lee, D. Developing the drive to learn and the questioning mind. In A. Frazier (Ed.), *Freeing the capacity to learn.* Washington: Association for Supervision and Curriculum Development, 1960.

Lee, E. S. Negro intelligence and selective migration. *American Sociological Review,* 1951, **16,** 227–233.

Leeds, C. H. Teacher behavior liked and disliked by pupils. *Education,* 1954, **75,** 29–36.

LeFevre, C. Inner-city school as the children see it. *Elementary School Journal,* 1966, **67**(1), 12.

Lehmann, H. C. *Age and achievement.* Princeton, New Jersey: Princeton University Press, 1953.

Lehner, G. F., & Gunderson, E. K. Height relationships on the draw-a-person test. *Journal of Personality,* 1953, **21,** 392–399.

Lemkau, P. V. The influence of handicapping conditions of child development. *Children,* 1961, **8,** 43–47.

Lenneberg, E. H., & Roberts, J. M. The language of experience: A study of methodology. *International Journal of American Linguistics,* Supplement 22, Memoir 13, 1956.

Leton, D. A. Assessment of school phobia. *Mental Hygiene,* 1962, **46,** 256–264.

Levin, H., & Sears, R. R. Identification with parents as a determinant of doll play aggression. *Child Development,* 1956, **27**(2), 135–153.

Levin, H., & Wardwell, E. The research uses of doll play. *Psychological Bulletin,* 1962, **59,** 27–56.

Levine, S. Infantile stimulation. *Scientific American,* 1960, **202,** 81–86.

Levine, S., Seymour, J. A., Chevalier, J. A., & Korchin, S. J. Effects of early shock and handling on later avoidance learning. *Journal of Personality,* 1956, **24,** 475–493.

Levinson, B. M. Subcultural values and IQ stability. *Journal of Genetic Psychology,* 1961, **98,** 69–82.

Levitt, E. E. The results of psychother-

437

REFERENCES

apy with children: An evaluation. *Journal of Consulting Psychology*, 1957, **21**, 189–196.

Levy, D. *Maternal overprotection.* New York: Columbia University Press, 1943.

Levy, D. *Behavioral Analysis: An analysis of clinical observations as applied to mother-newborn relationships.* Springfield, Illinois: Thomas, 1958.

Levy, D. The infant's early memory of inoculation: A contribution to public health procedures. *Journal of Genetic Psychology,* 1960, **96**, 3–46.

Levy, D. Psychosomatic studies of some aspects of maternal behavior. *Psychosomatic Medicine,* 1952, **4**, 223–227.

Lewin, K. Psychoanalytic and topological psychology. *Bulletin of the Menninger Clinic,* No. 1, 1937, 202–211.

Lewin, K., Lippitt, R., & White, K. Patterns of aggressive-behavior in experimentally created social climates. *Journal of Social Psychology,* 1939, **10**, 271–299.

Lewin, K., & White, R. K. Patterns of aggressive behavior in experimentally created social climates. *Journal of Social Psychology,* 1939, **10**, 271–299.

Battle for a little boy. *Life Magazine,* March 4, 1966, **60**(9), 102.

A good restful slumber. *Life Magazine,* May 20, 1966, **60**(20), 111–116.

Lindeman, B. The twins who found each other. *Saturday Evening Post,* March 21, 1964, **237**(11), 76–78.

Lindgren, H. C., Byrne, D., & Petrinovich, L. *Psychology.* (2nd ed.) New York: Wiley, 1966.

Ling, B. Form discrimination as a learning cue in infants. *Comparative Psychology Monographs,* 1941, **17**(2), 66.

Lippitt, R., & Gold, M. Classroom social structure as a mental health problem. *Journal of Social Issues,* 1959, **15**(1), 40–49.

Lipsitt, L. P. A self-concept scale for children and its relationship to the children's form of the manifest anxiety scale. *Child Development,* 1958, **29**, 463–472.

Lipsitt, L. P., & Levy, N. Pain threshold in the human neonate. *Child Development,* 1959, **30**, 547–555.

Liverant, S. MMPI differences between parents of disturbed and nondisturbed children. *Journal of Consulting Psychology,* 1959, **23**, 256–260.

Loevinger, J. Measuring personality patterns of women. *General Psychology Monographs,* 1962, **65**, 57.

Long, R. T. A psychosomatic study of allergic and emotional factors in children with asthma. *American Journal of Psychiatry,* 1958, **114**, 890–899.

Lorenz, K. Z. Morphology and behavior patterns in closely allied species. In B. Schaffner (Ed.), *Group process.* New York: Josiah Macy, Jr. Foundation, 1955.

Lorenz, K. Z. In J. M. Tanner and B. Inhelder (Eds.), *Discussions on child development.* New York: International Universities Press, London: Tavistock, 1956.

Lorenz, K. Z. Companionship in bird life. In C. H. Schiller (Ed. and translator), *Instinct behavior.* New York: International Universities Press, 1957.

Lott, B. E., & Lott, A. J. The formation of positive attitudes toward group members. *Journal of Abnormal and Social Psychology,* 1960, **61**, 297–300.

Lovaas, O. I. Effect of exposure to symbolic aggression on aggressive behavior. *Child Development,* 1961, **32**, 37–44.

Lowenfeld, V. *Creative and mental growth.* (3rd ed.) New York: Macmillan, 1958.

Luria, A. R. Verbal regulation of behavior. In M. A. B. Brazier (Ed.), *The central nervous system and behavior.* Report of the Third Macy Conference, Madison, New Jersey: Josiah Macy, Jr. Foundation, 1960.

Lynn, D. B. A note on sex differences in the development of masculine and feminine identification. *Psychological Review,* 1959, **66**, 258–262.

Lynn, D. B., & Sawrey, W. L. The effects of father-absence on Norwegian boys and girls. *Journal of Abnormal and Social Psychology,* 1959, **59**, 258–262.

Maas, H. S. *The young adult adjustment of twenty wartime residential nursery children.* New York: Child Welfare League of America, 1963.

Maccoby, E. E. Children and working mothers. *Children,* 1958, **5**, 83–89.

Maccoby, E. E. The taking of adult roles in middle childhood. *Journal of Abnormal and Social Psychology,* 1961, **63**, 495–501.

Maccoby, E. E. Woman's intellect. In S. M. Farber and R. H. L. Wilson (Eds.), *Man and civilization: The potential of woman.* New York: McGraw-Hill, 1963.

Maccoby, E. E. Effects of the mass media. In M. L. Hoffman and W. W. Hoffman (Eds.), *Review of child development research,* Vol. 1. New York: Russell Sage Foundation, 1964.

Maccoby, E. E., Dawley, E. M., & Hagen, J. W. Activity level and intellectual functioning in normal preschool children. *Child Development,* 1965, **36**(3), 768.

Maccoby, E. E., & Rau, L. Differential cognitive abilities. *Final Report, Cooperative Research Project,* No. 1040. Stan-

438

ford: Owen House, Stanford University, 1962.

MacFarland, R. A., & Huddleston, J. H. Neurocirculatory reactions in the psychoneuroses studies by the Schneider method. *American Journal of Psychiatry,* 1936, **93,** 106–110.

Macfarlane, J. Research findings from a twenty year study of growth from birth to maturity. Mimeograph, Institute of Child Welfare, University of California, 1952.

MacKinnon, D. W. The nature and nurture of creative talent. *American Psychologist,* 1962, **17,** 484–495.

Magoun, H. W. *The waking brain.* New York: Thomas, 1958.

Maier, N. R. F. Reasoning and learning. *Psychological Review,* 1931, **38,** 332–346.

Maller, J. B. Cooperation and competition: An experimental study in motivation. *Contributions to Education,* No. 384. New York: Teachers College, Columbia University, 1929.

Malone, W., & Freel, E. A preliminary study of group attitudes of junior and senior high school students towards mathematics. *Journal of Educational Research,* 1954, **47,** 599–608.

Maltzman, I. On the training of creativity. *Psychological Review,* 1960, **67,** 229–262.

Margolese, M. S. Mental disorders in childhood due to endocrine disorders. *Nervous Child,* 1948, **7,** 55–77.

Martin, W. Singularity and stability of profiles of social behavior. In C. Stendler (Ed.), *Readings in child behavior and development.* (2nd ed.) New York: Harcourt, 1964.

Marshall, E., & Hample, S. *Children's Letters to God.* New York: Pocket Books, Simon and Schuster, 1966.

Marshall, H. R. Relations between home experiences and children's use of language in play interactions with peers. *Psychological Monographs,* 1961, **75**(5, Whole No. 509).

Marquis, D. P. Can conditioned responses be established in the newborn infant? *Journal of Genetic Psychology,* 1931, **39,** 479–492.

Maslow, A. H., & Mittelman, B. *Principles of abnormal psychology.* New York: Harper, 1951.

Mason, M. K. Learning to speak after six and one-half years of silence. *Journal of Speech Disorders,* 1962, **7,** 295–304.

Matsumoto, M., & Smith, H. T. Japanese and American children's perception of parents. *Journal of Genetic Psychology,* 1961, **98,** 83–88.

Matthews, S. A., & Detwiler, S. R. The reaction of amblystoma embryos following prolonged treatment with chloretone. *Journal of Experimental Zoology,* 1926, **45,** 279–292.

May, R. Stimulus selection in preschool children under conditions of free choice. *Perceptual and Motor Skills,* 1963, **16,** 203–206.

McCandless, B. R. *Children and adolescents.* New York: Holt, 1961.

McCandless, B. R., & Bilous, C. B. Peer popularity and dependency on adults in preschool age and socialization. *Child Development,* 1961, **32,** 511–518.

McCandless, B. R., Castaneda, A., & Palermo, D. S. Anxiety in children and social status. *Child Development,* 1956, **27,** 385–391.

McCandless, B. R., & Hoyt, J. M. Sex ethnicity and play preferences of preschool children. *Journal of Abnormal and Social Psychology,* 1961, **62,** 683–685.

McCandless, B. R., & Spiker, C. C. Experimental research in child psychology. *Child Development,* 1956, **27,** 75–80.

McCann, R. V. Developmental factors in the growth of a mature faith. *Religious Education,* 1955, **50,** 147–155.

McCarthy, B. M. Language development. In L. Carmichael (Ed.), *Manual of child psychology.* (2nd ed.) New York: Wiley, 1954.

McCarthy, D. Language development. *Child Development Monographs,* 1960, **25**(3), 5–14.

McCarthy, D. Language and development in childhood. In L. Carmichael (Ed.), *Manual of child psychology.* (2nd ed.) New York: Wiley, 1954.

McClellan, F. C. *The neurogenic bladder.* Springfield, Illinois: Thomas, 1939.

McClelland, D. C., et al. *Personality.* New York: Sloane, 1951.

McClelland, D. C. *The achieving society.* New York: Van Nostrand, 1960.

McCord, J., & McCord, W. Cultural stereotypes and the validity of interviews for research in child development. *Child Development,* 1961, **32,** 171–185.

McCord, J., McCord, W., & Thurber, E. Some effects of paternal absence on male children. *Journal of Abnormal and Social Psychology,* 1962, **64**(5), 361–369.

McCord, W., McCord, J., & Thurber, E. Effects of maternal employment on lower-class boys. *Journal of Abnormal and Social Psychology,* 1963, **67,** 177–182.

McCord, W., McCord, J., & Howard, A. Familial correlates of aggression in non-delinquent male children. *Journal of Abnormal and Social Psychology,* 1961, **62,** 79–93.

REFERENCES

McCord, W., et al. Familial and behavioral correlates of dependency in male children. *Child Development,* 1962, **33,** 313–326.

McDonald, F. J. Children's judgments of theft from individual and corporate owners. *Child Development,* 1963, **34,** 141–150.

McGraw, M. B. Later development of children specially trained during infancy: Johnny and Jimmy at school age. *Child Development,* 1939, **10,** 1–19.

McGregor, F. T. Some psychosocial problems associated with facial deformities. *American Sociological Review,* 1951, **16,** 629–638.

McGuire, C., & White, G. D. Social class influence on discipline at school. *Educational Leadership,* 1957, **14,** 229–231, 234–236.

McKeachie, W. J., & Doyle, C. L. *Psychology.* Reading, Massachusetts: Addison-Wesley, 1966.

McKee, J. P., & Sherriffs, A. C. The differential evaluation of males and females. *Journal of Personality,* 1957, **25,** 356–371.

McQuitt, L. L. A measure of personality integration in relation to the concept of self. *Journal of Personality,* 1950, **18,** 416–482.

McReynolds, P., & Acker, M. Relation of object curiosity to psychological adjustment in children. *Child Development,* 1961, **32,** 393–400.

Mead, M. *Sex and temperament in three primitive societies.* New York: Morrow, 1935.

Mead, M. *Male and female.* New York: Morrow, 1939.

Mead, M. A. A cultural anthropologist's approach to maternal deprivation. In *Deprivation of maternal care,* Public Health Paper No. 14. Geneva: World Health Organization, 1962.

Mead, M., & Macgregor, F. C. *Growth and culture.* New York: Putnam's, 1951.

Medawar, P. B. *The future of man.* New York: Basic Books, 1960.

Medinnus, G. R. Immanent justice in children: A review of the literature and additional data. *Journal of Genetic Psychology,* 1959, **90,** 253–262.

Medinnus, G. R. An examination of several correlates of sociometric status in a first grade group. *Journal of Genetic Psychology,* 1962, **101,** 3–13.

Melzack, R. The genesis of emotional behavior: An experimental study of the dog. *Journal of Comparative and Physiological Psychology,* 1954, **47,** 166–168.

Melzack, R., & Thompson, W. R. Effects of early experience on the response to pain. *Journal of Comparative and Social Psychology,* 1957, **50,** 155–161.

Mendel, G. Children's differences for differing degrees of novelty. *Child Development,* 1965, **36**(2), 453.

Meredith, H. V. Relation between socioeconomic status and body size in boys seven to ten years of age. *American Journal of Diseases of Children,* 1951, **82,** 702–709.

Meredith, H. V. Change in the stature and body weight of North American boys during the last 80 years. In L. P. Lipsitt and C. C. Spiker (Eds.), *Advances in child development and behavior.* New York: Academic Press, 1963.

Merton, R. K. *Social theory and social structure.* (Rev. ed.) Glencoe, Illinois: Free Press, 1957.

Merry, F. K., & Merry, R. V. *The first two decades of life.* New York: Harper, 1950.

Metlinger, B. Cited in J. Rührah, *Pediatrics of the past.* New York: Hoeber, 1925.

Metraux, R. Children's drawings: Satellites and space. *Journal of Social Issues,* 1961, **27**(2), 36–42.

Meyers, W. J. Critical period for the facilitation of exploratory behavior by infantile experience. *Journal of Comparative and Physiological Psychology,* 1962, **55,** 1099–1111.

Meyers, W. J., & Thompson, G. G. The distribution of teacher approval and disapproval among sixth-grade children. *Journal of Educational Psychology,* 1956, **47,** 183–197.

Meyers, W. J., & Thompson, G. G. Teacher interactions with boys contrasted with girls. In R. Kuhlen and G. G. Thompson (Eds.), *Psychological studies of human development.* New York: Appleton-Century-Crofts, 1963.

Miles, D. C. Gifted children. In L. Carmichael (Ed.), *Manual of child psychology.* (2nd ed.) New York: Wiley, 1954.

Millard, C. V. *Child growth and development in the elementary school years.* (Rev. ed.) Boston: Heath, 1958.

Miller, D. R., & Swanson, G. E. *The changing American parent.* New York: Wiley, 1958.

Miller, E. D. Ability and social adjustment at midlife of persons earlier judged mentally deficient. *General Psychology Monographs,* 1965, **72,** 192.

Miller, G. A. *Psychology.* New York: Harper, 1962.

Miller, J. G. Sensory overloading. In B. E. Flaherty (Ed.), *Psychophysiological aspects of space flight.* New York: Columbia University Press, 1961.

Miller, L. M. The dropout: School's search for clues to his problems. *School Life,* May 1963, **45,** 5–7.

Miller, V. L. *The miracle of growth.* Urbana: University of Illinois Press, 1950.

Mills, J. Changes in moral attitudes following temptation. *Journal of Personality,* 1958, **26,** 517–531.

Milton, G. A. Five studies of the relation between sex role identification and achievement in problem solving. *Technical Report No. 3.* Department of Industrial Administration, Department of Psychology, Yale University, December 1958.

Milton, G. A. Sex differences in problem solving as a function of role appropriateness of the problem content. *Psychological Reports,* 1959, **5,** 705–798.

Mischel, W. Delay of gratification, need for achievement, and acquiescence in another culture. *Journal of Abnormal and Social Psychology,* 1961, **62,** 543–552.

Moir, C. Recording the contractions of the human pregnant and nonpregnant uterus. *Transactions of the Edinburgh Obstetrical Society,* Vol. 54, 1934.

Money, J. Developmental differentiation of femininity and masculinity compared. In S. M. Farber and R. H. Wilson (Eds.), *Potential of woman.* New York: McGraw-Hill, 1963.

Montague, A. Sex, order of birth and personality. *American Journal of Orthopsychiatry,* 1948, **18,** 351–353.

Montague, A. Constitutional and prenatal factors in infant and child health. In M. J. E. Senn (Ed.), *Symposium on the healthy personality.* New York: Josiah Macy, Jr., Foundation, 1950.

Montague, A. *Human heredity.* New York: Harcourt, 1959.

Moodey, E. *The school of good manners.* (5th ed.) Cited in M. Kiefer, *American children through their books.* Philadelphia: University of Pennsylvania Press, 1948.

Morgan, C. T., & King, R. T. *Introduction to psychology.* New York: McGraw-Hill, 1966.

Moriarty, A. Coping patterns of preschool children in response to intelligence test demands. *Genetic Psychology Monographs,* 1961, **64,** 65–67.

Morison, S. E. *The Puritan Pronaos.* New York: New York University Press, 1936.

Morland, J. K. Racial acceptance and preference of nursery school children in a Southern city. *Merrill-Palmer Quarterly,* 1962, **8**(4), 271–280.

Moss, H. A., & Kagan, J. The stability of achievement and recognition-seeking behaviors. *Journal of Abnormal and Social Psychology,* 1961, **62,** 504–513.

Moyer, K. E., & von Gilmer, B. Attention spans of children for experimentally designed toys. *Journal of Genetic Psychology,* 1955, **87,** 187–201.

Mullen, F. A. Truancy and classroom disorder as symptoms of personality problems. *Journal of Educational Psychology,* 1950, **41,** 97–109.

Munn, N. L. Learning in children. In L. Carmichael (Ed.), *Manual of child psychology.* (2nd ed.) New York: Wiley,1954.

Munn, N. L. *Psychology: The fundamentals of human adjustment.* Boston: Houghton Mifflin, 1966.

Munn, N. L., & Steinung, B. B. The relative efficacy of form and background in a child's discrimination of visual pattern. *Journal of Genetic Psychology,* 1931, **39,** 73–90.

Muntz, N. L. Effects of esthetic surroundings, II: Prolonged and repeated experience in a "beautiful" and "ugly" room. *Journal of Psychology,* 1956, **41,** 459–466.

Murphy, G. The current impact of Freud upon psychology. *American Psychologist,* 1956, **12,** 664.

Murphy, G., & Murphy, L. B. The child as potential. In E. Ginzberg (Ed.), *The nation's children,* Vol. 2. New York: Columbia University Press, 1960.

Murphy, G., Murphy, L. B., & Newcomb, T. M. *Experimental social psychology: An interpretation of research upon the socialization of the individual.* (Rev. ed.) New York: Harper, 1937.

Murphy, L. B. *Social behavior and child personality.* New York: Columbia University Press, 1937.

Murphy, L. B. Cultural factors in the development of our children. *Child Education,* 1946, **23**(1), 53–58.

Murphy, L. B. *Personality in young children.* New York: Basic Books, 1956.

Murphy, L. B., et al. *The widening world of childhood.* New York: Basic Books, 1962.

Mussen, P. H. *The psychological development of the child.* Englewood Cliffs, New Jersey: Prentice-Hall, 1963.

Mussen, P. H., & Conger, J. J. *Child development and personality.* New York: Harper, 1956.

Mussen, P. H., & Distler, L. Masculinity identification and father-son relationship. *Journal of Abnormal and Social Psychology,* 1959, **59,** 350–356.

REFERENCES Mussen, P. H., & Newman, D. K. Acceptance of handicap, motivation and adjustment in physically disabled children. *Exceptional Children*, 1958, **24**, 225–260, 277–278.

Mussen, P. H., Gaddini, H. G., Young, H. B., Gaddini, R., & Morante, L. The influence of father-son relationships on adolescent personality and attitudes. *Journal of Child Psychology and Psychiatry*, 1963, **4**, 3–16.

Mussen, P. H., & Rutherford, E. Effects of aggressive cartoons on children's aggressive play. *Journal of Abnormal and Social Psychology*, 1961, **62**, 461–464.

Mussen, P. H., & Rutherford, E. Parental-child relations and parental personality in relation to young children's sex-role preference. In P. H. Mussen (Ed.), *Readings in child development and personality*. New York: Harper, 1965.

Nagy, M. The child's theories concerning death. *Journal of Genetic Psychology*, 1948, **73**, 9–11.

Nall, C. S. The inheritance of emotionality. *Sigma Xi Quarterly*, 1938, **26**, 17–27.

Nash, J. The father in contemporary culture and current psychological literature. *Child Development*, 1965, **36**(1), 266.

Neel, J. V. The effect of the exposure of the atomic bombs on pregnancy in Hiroshima and Nagasaki. *Journal of the American Medical Association*, 1953, **118**, 517–541.

Neuhaus, E. C. A personality study of asthmatic and cardiac children. *Psychosomatic Medicine*, 1958, **20**, 181–186.

Neugarten, B. L., & Weinstein, K. K. The changing American grandparent. *Journal of Marriage and Family Living*, 1964, **26**, 199–204.

Newman, H., Freeman, F., & Holzinger, K. *Twins: A study of heredity and environment*. Chicago: University of Chicago Press, 1937.

Newton, N. *Maternal emotions*. New York: Hoeber, 1955.

Norris, A. S. Prenatal factors in intellectual and emotional development. *Journal of the American Medical Association*, 1960, **172**, 413–416.

Nowlis, V. The search for significant concepts in a study of parent-child relationships. *American Journal of Orthopsychiatry*, 1952, **22**, 286–299.

Nye, F. I. Child adjustment in broken and in unhappy unbroken homes. *Marriage and Family Living*, 1957, **19**, 356–361.

Nye, F. I. *Family relationships and delinquent behavior*. New York: Wiley, 1958.

Ojemann, R. H., & Pritchett, K. Piaget and the role of guided experiences in human development. *Perceptual and Motor Skills*, 1963, **17**, 927–940.

Ojemann, R. H., & Wilkinson, F. R. The effect on pupil growth of an increase in teachers' understanding of pupil behavior. *Journal of Experimental Education*, 1939, **8**, 143–147.

O'Keefe, A., Taylor, A., & Taylor, J. Original poems for infant minds by several young persons. Cited by M. Kiefer, *American children through their books*. Philadelphia: University of Pennsylvania Press, 1948.

Olson, W. C. *Child development*. (2nd ed.) Boston: Heath, 1959.

Oslon, W. C., & Hughes, B. O. Subsequent growth of children with and without nursery-school experiences. Washington: *National Society for the Study of Education*, 39th Yearbook, 1940, 237–244.

Orlansky, H. Infant care and personality. *Psychological Bulletin*, 1949, **46**, 1–48.

Orne, J. E. Intelligence and season of birth. *British Journal of Psychology*, 1963, **54**, 273–276.

Osgood, C. E. The nature and measurement of meaning. *Psychological Bulletin*, 1952, **49**, 197–237.

Ottinger, D. R., Denenberg, V. H., & Stephens, M. W. Maternal emotionality, multiple mothering and emotionality in maturity. *Journal of Comparative and Physiological Psychology*, 1963, **56**, 313–317.

Ottinger, D. R., & Simmons, J. E. Behavior of human neonates and prenatal maternal anxiety. *Psychological Reports*, 1964, **14**, 391–394.

Otto, H. J. Elementary education, III: What price competition? *Education Digest*, 1954, **19**(8), 25–27.

Ourth, L., & Brown, K. B. Inadequate mothering and disturbances in the neonatal period. *Child Development*, 1961, **32**, 287–295.

Overstreet, E. W. In S. M. Farber and R. H. Wilson (Eds.), *The potential of woman*. New York: McGraw-Hill, 1963.

Owens, W. A. J. Age and mental ability: A longitudinal study. *Genetic Psychology Monographs*, 1953, **48**, 3–54.

Padilla, S. G. Further studies on delayed pecking in chicks. *Journal of Comparative Psychology*, 1935, **31**, 337–348.

Palermo, D. S. Racial comparisons and additional normative data on the children's manifest anxiety scale. *Child Development*, 1959, **30**, 53–57.

Parsons, T. *Family socialization and interaction process*. Glencoe, Illinois: Free Press, 1955a.

442

Parsons, T. Family structures and the socialization of the child. In T. Parsons and R. F. Bales (Eds.), *Family socialization and interaction process*. Glencoe, Illinois: Free Press, 1955b.

Parsons, T. American society. Mimeograph, 1963. Cited by H. Rodman, Talcott Parsons' view of the changing American family. *Merrill-Palmer Quarterly*, 1965, **3**, 209–225.

Parten, M. L. Leadership among preschool children. *Journal of Abnormal and Social Psychology*, 1933, **27**, 430–442.

Pasamanick, B. A comparative study of the behavior development of Negro infants. *Journal of Genetic Psychology*, 1946, **63**, 3–44.

Pasamanick, B., & Knobloch, H. Prospective studies on reproductive casualty: Methods, findings and some implications. *Merrill-Palmer Quarterly*, 1966a, **12**(1), 28.

Pasamanick, B., & Knobloch, H. Retrospective studies on reproductive casualty. *Merrill-Palmer Quarterly*, 1966b, **12**(1), 20.

Patel, A. S., & McRooks, M. Creativity and sociometric status in children. *Sociometry*, 1956, **19**, 450–457.

Payne, D. E., & Mussen, P. H. Parent child relations and father identification among adolescent boys. *Journal of Abnormal and Social Psychology*, 1956, **52**, 358–366.

Peck, R. F., & Havighurst, R. J. *The psychology of character development*. New York: Wiley, 1960.

Peckos, P. S. Nutrition during growth and development. *Child Development*, 1957, **28**, 273–285.

Pepinsky, P. N. The social dialectic of productive nonconformity. Unpublished paper delivered at the Annual Convention of the APA, Chicago, 1960.

Peppin, B. H. Parental understanding, parental acceptance, and the self-concept of children as a function of academic over-and under- achievement. Doctoral dissertation, Claremont Graduate School, 1962.

Perry, S. E., et al. *The child and his family in disaster: A study of the 1953 Vicksburg tornado*. Committee on Disaster Studies, No. 5, Washington, D. C.: National Academy of Sciences, National Research Council, 1956.

Peterson, D. R. Behavior of middle childhood. *Journal of Consulting Psychology*, 1961, **25**, 205–209.

Peterson, D. R., Becker, W. C., Helmer, L. A., Shoemaker, D. J., & Quay, J. C. Parental attitudes and child adjustment. *Child Development*, 1959, **31**, 119–130.

Phaer, T. Cited by J. Rührah, *Pediatrics of the past*. New York: Hoeber, 1925.

Piaget, J. *The moral judgment of the child*. New York: Harcourt, 1932.

Piaget, J. *The child's conception of the world*. London: Routledge, 1951.

Piaget, J. The child and modern physics. *Scientific American*, 1957, **195**(3), 28, 46–51.

Piaget, J. *The language and thought of the child*. (3rd ed.) Translated by M. Gabain. London: Routledge, 1959.

Pinneau, S. R. *Changes in intelligence quotient: Infancy to maturity*. Boston: Houghton Mifflin, 1961.

Plant, J. S. *The envelope*. New York: Commonwealth Fund, 1950.

Podolsky, E. The emotional problems of the stepchild. *Mental Hygiene*, 1955, **39**, 49–53.

Pratt, K. C. A study of the "fears" of rural children. *Journal of Genetic Psychology*, 1945, **67**, 179–194.

President's task force on manpower conservation. *One third of a nation*. Washington, D. C.: U. S. Government Printing Office, 1964.

Pressey, S. L. *Psychology and the new education*. New York: Harper, 1933.

Pressey, S. L. *Psychological development through the life span*. New York: Harper, 1957.

Psathas, G. Ethnicity, social class and adolescent independence from parental control. *American Sociological Review*, 1957, **22**, 415–423.

Purcell, K. A. A note on the measurement of identification. *Merrill-Palmer Quarterly*, 1962, **8**, 159–164.

Pyle, S. I., et al. Patterns of skeletal development in the hand. *Pediatrics*, 1959, **24**, 886–903.

Rabban, M. J. Sex role identification in young children in two diverse social groups. *Genetic Psychology Monographs*, 1950, **42**, 81–158.

Rabin, A. I. Some psycho-sexual differences between kibbutz and nonkibbutz Israeli boys. *Journal of Protective Techniques*, 1958, **22**, 328–332.

Rabin, A. I. Comparison of American and Israeli children by means of a sentence completion technique. *Journal of Social Psychology*, 1959, **49**, 3–12.

Rabin, A. I., & Haworth, M. R. Projective techniques with children. *The house tree person drawings (H-T-P) as a projective technique with children*. New York: Grune and Stratton, 1960.

Radke-Yarrow, M. R., Scott, P., deLeeuw, L., & Heinig, C. Childrearing in families

REFERENCES

of working and non-working mothers. *Sociometry*, 1962, **25**, 122–140.

Radke-Yarrow, M. R., Trager, H., & Davis, H. Social perceptions and attitudes of children. *Genetic Psychology Monographs*, 1949, **40**, 327–447.

Ramsey, G. V. The sex information of younger boys. *American Journal of Orthopsychiatry*, 1943, **13**, 347–352.

Ramsey, A. C., & Hess, E. H. A laboratory approach to the study of imprinting. *Wilson Bulletin*, 1954, **66**, 196–206.

Rank, O. *The trauma of birth.* New York: Harcourt, 1929.

Rapp, D. W. Child-rearing attitudes of mothers in Germany and the United States. *Child Development*, 1961, **32**, 669–678.

Rapp, D. W., & Richardson, G. C. A saliva test for prenatal sex determination. *Science*, 1952, **115**, 265.

Rausch, H. L., Farbman, I., & Llewellyn, L. G. Persons, setting and change in social interaction, II. *Human Relations*, 1959, **12**, 361–378.

Ray, W. S. Verbal compared with manipulative solution of an apparatus problem. *American Journal of Psychology*, 1957, **50**, 429–444.

Reade, N., & English, H. B. Personality factors in adolescent female friendships. *Journal of Consulting Psychology*, 1947, **11**, 212–220.

Redl, F., & Wattenberg, W. W. *Mental hygiene in teaching.* (2nd ed.) New York: Harcourt, 1959.

Reed, H. Anxiety: The ambivalent variable. *Harvard Educational Review*, Spring 1960, **30**, 141–153.

Reese, H. W. Relations between self-acceptance and sociometric choices. *Journal of Abnormal and Social Psychology*, 1961, **62**, 472–474.

Reichenberg-Hackett, W. Practices, attitudes and values in nursery group education. *Psychological Reports*, 1962, **10**, 151–172.

Reid, J. B., King, F. J., & Wickwire, P. Cognitive and personality characteristics of creative children. *Psychological Reports*, 1959, **5**, 729–737.

Reiss, A. J., & Rhodes, A. L. Are educational norms and goals of conforming, truant and delinquent adolescents influenced by group position in American society? *Journal of Negro Education*, 1959, **28**, 258.

Remmers, H. H., & Radler, D. H. *The American teenager.* Indianapolis: Bobbs-Merrill, 1957.

Rettig, S., & Pasamanick, B. Moral codes of American and Korean college students.

Journal of Social Psychology, 1959, **50**, 65–73.

Rheingold, H. L., Gewirtz, J. L., & Ross, H. W. Social conditioning of vocalizations in the infant. *Journal of Comparative and Physiological Psychology*, 1959, **52**, 68–73.

Richards, T. W., & Newberry, H. Studies in fetal behavior: Can performance on test items at six months postnatally be predicted on the basis of fetal activity? *Child Development*, 1938, **9**, 79–86.

Richmond, J. B., & Lipton, E. L. Some aspects of the neurophysiology of the newborn and their implications for child development. In L. Hessner and E. Pavenstadt (Eds.), *Psychopathology in children.* New York: Grune and Stratton, 1959.

Richter, C. P. Rats, man and the welfare state. *American Psychologist*, 1959, **14**, 18–28.

Riesen, A. H. Chimpanzee vision after four conditions of light deprivation. *American Psychologist*, 1951, **6**, 282.

Riesman, D. *The lonely crowd.* New Haven: Yale University Press, 1950.

Riesman, D. *The culturally deprived child.* New York: Harper, 1962.

Riley, M. W., Riley, J. W., & Moore, M. E. Adolescent values and the Riesman typology: An empirical analysis. In S. M. Lipset and L. Lowenthal (Eds.), *Culture and social character, the work of David Riesman reviewed.* Glencoe, Illinois: Free Press, 1961.

Robbins, L. C. The accuracy of parental recall of aspects of child development and of child-rearing practices. *Journal of Abnormal and Social Psychology*, 1963, **66**, 3, 261–270.

Roberts, K. W., & Fleming, E. V. Persistence and change in personality patterns. Monographs of the Society for Research in Child Development, 1943, **8**(3).

Rodman, H. Talcott Parsons' view of the changing American family. *Merrill-Palmer Quarterly*, 1965, **3**, 221.

Roff, M. Childhood social interactions and young adult bad conduct. *Journal of Abnormal and Social Psychology*, 1961, **63**, 333–337.

Rogers, D. *Mental hygiene in elementary education.* Boston: Houghton Mifflin, 1957a.

Rogers, D. *Psychology in elementary education.* Boston: Houghton Mifflin, 1957b.

Rogers, D. *Psychology of adolescence.* New York: Appleton-Century-Crofts, 1962.

Rogers, G., & Rice, T. A teacher visits homes. *Childhood Education*, 1947,

24, 112–114.

Rohrer, J. H. Sociocultural factors in personality development. In National Conference on Social Welfare, the Social Welfare Forum, Official Proceedings. New York: Columbia University Press, 1957.

Rosen, B. C. Family structure and achievement motivation. *American Sociological Review,* 1956, **21,** 203–211.

Rosen, B. C. The achievement syndrome: A psychocultural dimension of social stratification. *American Sociological Review,* 1956, **21,** 203–211.

Rosen, E., & Gregory, I. *Abnormal Psychology.* Philadelphia: Saunders, 1965.

Rosen, G. C., & d'Andrade, R. The psychosocial origins of achievement motivation. *Sociometry,* 1959, **22,** 185–218.

Rosen, S., Levinger, G., & Lippitt, R. Desire to change himself and others as a function of resource ownership. *Human Relations,* 1960, **13,** 187–193.

Rosenberg, B. G., & Sutton-Smith, B. A revised concept of masculine-feminine differences in play activities. *Journal of Genetic Psychology,* 1960, **96,** 165–170.

Rosenberg, M. *Society and the adolescent self-image.* Princeton, New Jersey: Princeton University Press, 1965.

Rossman, J. *The psychology of the inventor.* Washington, D. C.: Inventors Publishing Company, 1931.

Routh, C. H. F. *Infant feeding and its influence on life.* New York: William Wood, 1879.

Ruch, F. L. *Psychology and life.* (4th ed.) Chicago: Scott, Foresman, 1953.

Rührah, J. *Pediatrics of the past.* New York: Hoeber, 1925.

Ruja, H. J. The relation between neonate crying and length of labor. *Journal of Genetic Psychology,* 1948, **73,** 53–55.

Rust, M. M. The growth of children's concepts of time, space and magnitude. Unpublished manuscript. New York: Teacher's College, Columbia University.

Rutledge, A. Marriage and divorce. In Golden Anniversary White House Conference on Children and Youth. *1960 Survey Papers.*

Rutter, M., Korn, S., & Birch, H. C. Genetic and environmental factors in the development of primary reaction patterns. *British Journal of Social and Clinical Psychology,* 1963, **2,** 161–173.

Saagrass, C. & Pasamanick, B. (Eds.) *Child development and psychiatry.* Washington: American Psychiatric Association, 1960.

Saltz, E., & Newman, S. E. The effect of prior learning of symbols on performance in reasoning. *American Journal of Psychology,* 1960, **73,** 91–99.

Sanford, F. H. *Psychology: A scientific study of man.* (2nd ed.) Belmont, California: Wadsworth, 1965.

Sarason, I. G. Test anxiety, general anxiety and intellectual performance. *Journal of Genetic Psychology,* 1957, **21,** 485–490.

Sarason, I. G. Test anxiety and intellectual performance. *Journal of Abnormal and Social Psychology,* 1963, **66,** 73–75.

Sarason, S. B., et al. Classroom observation of high-and-low-anxious children. *Child Development,* 1958, **29,** 287–295.

Where is science taking us? *Saturday Review,* June 4, 1960, **43**(23), 48–49.

Sayegh, Y., & Dennis, W. The effect of supplementary experiences upon the behavioral development of infants in institutions. *Child Development,* 1965, **36**(1), 81.

Schachter, S., & Singer, J. E. Cognitive, social and psychological determinants of emotional state. *Psychological Review,* 1962, **69,** 377–399.

Schaefer, E. S., & Bayley, N. Consistency of maternal behavior from infancy to preadolescence. *Journal of Abnormal and Social Psychology,* 1960, **61,** 1–6.

Schaffer, R., & Emerson, P. G. The development of social attachments in infancy. *Monographs of the Society for Research in Child Development,* 1964, **29**(3), 70–71.

Scheinfeld, A. *Your heredity and environment.* Philadelphia: Lippincott, 1965.

Schiele, B. G., Brozek, J., & Keys, A. Observation of human behavior in experimental semistarvation and rehabilitation. *Journal of Clinical Psychology,* 1948, **4,** 28–45.

Schoeppe, A. Sex differences in adolescent socialization. *Journal of Social Psychology,* 1953, **38,** 179.

Schramm, W. J., Lyle, J., & Parker, E. B. *Television in the lives of children.* Stanford: Stanford University Press, 1961.

Schwartz, P. Birth injuries of the newborn. *Archives of Pediatrics,* 1956, **73,** 429–450.

Schwartz, P. *Psychology.* Princeton, New Jersey: Van Nostrand, 1963.

Scott, J. P. The process of primary socialization in canine and human infants. *Monographs for the Society for Research in Human Development,* 1963, **28**(1), 1–47.

Scott, J. P. Critical periods in the development of social behavior in puppies. In P. H. Mussen, J. J. Conger, and J. Kagan (Eds.), *Readings in child development and personality.* New York: Harper, 1965.

Sears, P. Problems in the investigation of

REFERENCES

achievement and self-esteem motivation. In M. R. Jones (Ed.), *Nebraska symposium on motivation.* Lincoln: University of Nebraska Press, 1957.

Sears, R. R. Influence of methodological factors in doll play performance. *Child Development,* 1947, **18,** 190–191.

Sears, R. R. The growth of conscience. In I. Iscoe and H. W. Stevenson (Eds.), *Personality development in childhood.* Austin: University of Texas, 1960.

Sears, R. R. Relation of early socialization experiences to aggression in middle childhood. *Journal of Abnormal and Social Psychology,* 1961, **63,** 466–492.

Sears, R. R., et al. Effect of father separation on preschool child's doll play agression. *Child Development,* 1946, **17,** 219–243.

Sears, R. R., Maccoby, E. E., & Levin, H. *Patterns of child rearing.* Evanston, Illinois: Row, Peterson, 1957.

Sears, R. R., Nowlis, U., & Sears, P. Some child-rearing antecedents of aggression and dependency in young children. *Genetic Psychology Monographs,* 1957, **47,** 135–234.

Sears, R. R., & Sears, P. Doll play agression in normal young children: Influence of sex, age, sibling status, and father absence. *Psychological Monographs,* 1951, **65**(6).

Sears, R. R., Whiting, J. W. M., Nowlis, V., & Sears, P. S. Some child rearing practices. *American Sociological Review,* 1955, **20,** 137–148.

Senden, M. von. *Space and light.* New York: Free Press, 1960.

Serot, N. M., & Teevan, R. C. Perception of the parent-child relationship, and its relation to child adjustment. *Child Development,* 1961, **32,** 257–308.

Sewell, W. H., & Mussen, P. H. The effects of feeding, weaning and scheduling procedures on childhood adjustment and the formation of oral symptoms. *Child Development,* 1952, **23,** 185–191.

Shaffer, H. R. Objective observation of personality development in early infancy. *British Journal of Medical Psychology,* 1958, **31,** 174–183.

Shaffer, J. P. Social and personality correlates of children's estimates of height. *Genetic Psychology Monographs,* 1964, **70,** 130–132.

Shaffer, O. F., & Shoben, E. J. *The psychology of adjustment.* (2nd ed.) Boston: Houghton Mifflin, 1956.

Shaw, M. C., & Dutton, B. E. The use of the parent attitude research inventory with the parents of bright academic underachievers. *Journal of Educational Psychology,* 1962, **53,** 203–218.

Sheldon, W. H. *Varieties of delinquent youth.* New York: Harper, 1949.

Sheldon, W. H., Stevens, S. S., & Tucker, W. B. *The varieties of human physique.* New York: Harper, 1940.

Sherman, M., & Henry, T. R. *The hollow folk.* New York: Crowell, 1933.

Shumsky, A. Emotional adjustment and moral reasonings in children. Unpublished doctoral thesis, Teachers College, Columbia University, 1956.

Sibliger, F. Attention to human faces in infants. Unpublished doctoral dissertation, Wayne State University, Detroit, 1963.

Siegel, A. E., & Haas, M. V. The working mother: A review of research. *Child Development,* 1963, **34,** 513–542.

Siegel, A. E., & Kohn, L. G. Permissiveness, permission and aggression: The effect of adult presence or absence on aggression in children's play. *Child Development,* 1959, **30,** 131–141.

Siegel, A. E., Stolz, L. M., Hitchcock, E. A., & Adamson, J. Dependence and independence in the children of working mothers. *Child Development,* 1959, **30,** 533–546.

Siegel, S. M. The relationship of hostility to authoritarianism. *Journal of Abnormal and Social Psychology,* 1956, **52,** 372–386.

Sigel, I. E. Cognitive style and personality dynamics. Interim Progress Report for National Institute of Mental Health, M 2983 (1961).

Sigel, I. E. Sex and personality correlates of styles of categorization among young children. *American Psychologist,* 1963, **18,** 350.

Siller, J. Psychological concomitant of amputation in children. *Child Development,* 1960, **31,** 108–120.

Silverstein, A. V., & Robinson, H. A. The representation of orthopedic disability in children's figure drawings. *Journal of Consulting Psychology,* 1956, **20,** 333–341.

Simmel, M. L. Phantom experiences following amputation in childhood. *Journal of Neurological and Neurosurgical Psychiatry,* 1962, **25,** 69–78.

Simmons, K., & Greulich, W. W. Menarcheal age and the height, weight, and skeletal age of girls age 7–17 years. *Journal of Pediatrics,* 1943, **22,** 518–548.

Simon, M. D. Body configuration and school readiness. *Child Development,* 1959, **30,** 493–512.

Simpson, M. Parent preferences of young children. *Teachers College preferences in psychology,* No. 652. New York: Teachers College, Columbia University, 1935.

Simpson, R. L. Parental influence, antici-
patory socialization and social mobility.
American Sociological Review, 1962, **27,**
517–522.

Singer, A., Jr. Certain aspects of personality and their relation to certain group
modes, and constancy of friendship
choices. *Journal of Educational Research*, 1951, **45,** 33–42.

Sjoberg, G., Brymer, R. A., & Faris, B.
Bureaucracy and the lower class. *Sociology and Social Research*, 1966, **50.**

Slater, P. E. Toward a dualistic theory of
identification. *Merrill-Palmer Quarterly*,
1961, **7,** 113–126.

Slater, P. E. Parental behavior and the
personality of the child. *Journal of Genetic Psychology*, 1962, **101,** 53–68.

Smillie, D. Reality, possibility and children.
ETC: A Review of General Semantics,
1958, **15**(3), 163–168.

Smith, F. R. The projective nature of the
draw-a-person technique in its relation to
the sex of the figure drawn. Master's
thesis, Florida State University at Tal-
lahassee, 1953.

Smith, G. H. Sociometric study of best
liked and least liked children. *Elementary
School Journal*, 1950, **51,** 71–85.

Smith, S. Age and sex differences in children's opinions concerning sex differences. *Journal of Genetic Psychology*,
1939, **54,** 17–25.

Solley, C. M., Kidd, A. H., & Rivoire, J. L.
(Eds.) *Perceptual development in children*. New York: International Universities Press, 1966.

Solomon, A. L. Personality and behavior
patterns of children with functional defects of articulation. *Child Development*,
1961, **32,** 731–737.

Sontag, L. W. The significance of fetal environment differences. *American Journal
of Obstetrics and Gynecology*, 1941, **42,**
996–1003.

Sontag, L. W. The possible relationship of
prenatal environment to schizophrenia. In
D. D. Jackson (Ed.), *The etiology of
schizophrenia*. New York: Basic Books,
1960.

Sontag, L. W. Somatographics of personality and body function. *Vita Humana*,
1963, **6,** 1–10.

Sontag, L. W., Baker, C. T., & Nelson, V.
Personality as a determiner of performance. *American Journal of Orthopsychiatry*, 1955, **25,** 555–563.

Sontag, L. W., Baker, C. T., & Nelson,
V. L. Mental growth and personality development: A longitudinal study. *Society
for Research in Child Development*,
1958, **23**(2).

Sontag, L. W., & Kagan, J. The emergence
of intellectual achievement motives.
American Journal of Orthopsychiatry,
1963, **33,** 532–535.

Spearman, C. *Abilities of man*. New York:
Macmillan, 1927.

Spitz, R. A. Hospitalism: A follow-up report. In *Psychoanalytic study of the
child*, Vol. 2. New York: International
Universities Press, 1946.

Spivack, S. S. A study of a method of self-
acceptancy and self-rejection. *Journal of
Genetic Psychology*, 1956, **83,** 183–202.

Spock, B. *The pocket book of baby and
child care*. New York: Pocket Books,
1946.

Spock, B. *The common sense book of
baby and child care*. (2nd ed.) New
York: Duell, Sloan and Pearce, 1957.

Spock, B., & Huschka, M. The psycholog-
ical aspects of pediatric practice.
*Practitioners Library of Medicine and
Surgery*, 1938, **13,** 891.

Srole, L., et al. *Mental health in the me-
tropolis*. New York: McGraw-Hill, 1962.

Stagner, R. Homeostasis as a unifying concept in personality theory. *Psychological
Review*, 1951, **58,** 5–17.

Stagner, R. *Psychology of personality*. (3rd
ed.) New York: McGraw-Hill, 1961.

Stendler, C. B. *Children of Brasstown*.
Urbana: University of Illinois Press,
1949.

Stendler, C. B. Critical periods in socialization and over-dependency. *Child Development*, 1952, **23,** 3–12.

Stendler, C. B. Possible causes of over-
dependency in young children. *Child
Development*, 1954, **25,** 125–146.

Stephens, J. M. *The psychology of classroom learning*. New York: Holt, 1965.

Stern, G. C. Environment for learning. In
N. Stanford (Ed.), *The American college*.
New York: Wiley, 1962.

Stevenson, H. W., & McBean, G. The
learning of object and pattern discrimination by children. *Journal of Comparative and Physiological Psychology*, 1958,
51, 752–754.

Stevenson, H. W., & Stevenson, N. G.
Social interaction in an interracial nursery
school. *Genetic Psychology Monographs*,
1960, **61,** 60–65.

Stevenson, I. Is the human personality
more plastic in infancy and childhood?
American Journal of Psychiatry, 1957,
114(2), 152–161.

Stewart, A. H., et al. Excessive infant crying (colic) in relation to parent behavior.
American Journal of Psychiatry, 1954,
110, 687–694.

Stiles, L. H. (Ed.) *The teacher's role in*

American society. New York: Harper, 1957.

Stiles, L. J., et al. *Teacher education in the United States.* New York: Ronald, 1960.

Stock, M. B., & Smyth, P. M. Does undernutrition during infancy inhibit brain growth and subsequent intellectual development? *Archives of Diseases of Childhood,* 1963, **38**, 546–553.

Stocks, P. Recent statistics of multiple births in England and Wales. *Acta Genetica Medicae et Gemellologie,* 1952, **1**, 8–12.

Stolz, L. M. Effects of maternal employment on children; evidence from research. *Child Development,* 1960, **31**, 749–782.

Stolz, L. M., et al. *Father relations of war-born children.* Stanford: Stanford University Press, 1954.

Stone, C. P., Darrow, C. W., Landis, C., & Heath, L. L. *Studies in the dynamics of behavior.* Chicago: University of Chicago Press, 1932.

Stone, L. J., & Church, J. *Psychology of childhood and adolescence.* New York: Random, 1957.

Stott, D. H. Abnormal mothering as a cause of mental subnormality, II. *Journal of Child Psychology and Psychiatry,* 1962, **3**, 79–91.

Stott, L. H. The persisting effects of early family experiences upon personality development. *Merrill-Palmer Quarterly,* 1957, **3**, 145–159.

Stout, I. M., & Langdon, G. A study of the home life of well adjusted children. *The Journal of Educational Sociology,* 1950, **23**, 458.

Stout, R. Selective admissions and retention practices in teacher education. *Journal of Teacher Education,* 1957, **8**, 429.

Strang, R. *The adolescent views himself.* New York: McGraw-Hill, 1957.

Strang, R. *An introduction to child study.* New York: Macmillan, 1959.

Strang, R. *Helping your child develop his potentialities.* New York: Dutton, 1965.

Strauss, A. The development of conceptions of rules in children. *Child Development,* 1952, **25**, 193–208.

Strauss, B. V. The dynamics of ordinal position. *Quarterly Journal of Child Psychology,* 1951, **3**, 133–145.

Strodbeck, F. L. Family interaction values and achievement. In M. Sklare (Ed.), *The Jews: Social patterns of an American group.* Glencoe, Illinois: Free Press, 1958.

Stuart, H. C. Obesity in childhood. *Quarterly Review of Pediatrics,* 1955, **10**, 131–145.

Stuart, H. C., & Prugh, D. G. (Eds.) *The healthy child: His physical, psychological, and social development.* Cambridge: Harvard University Press, 1960.

Suchman, R. J. Inquiry training: Building skills for autonomous discovery. *Merrill-Palmer Quarterly,* 1961, **7**, 147–170.

Sullivan, H. S. *The interpersonal theory of psychiatry.* New York: Norton, 1963.

Sumption, M. R., & Phillips, T. A. School progress. In W. S. Monroe (Ed.), *Encyclopedia of educational research.* (Rev. ed.) New York: Macmillan, 1950.

Suppes, P. Modern learning theory and the elementary school curriculum. *American Educational Research Journal,* March 1964, **1**(2).

Sutton-Smith, B., Roberts, J. M., & Rosenberg, B. G. Sibling associations and role involvement. *Merrill-Palmer Quarterly,* 1964, **10**, 25–38.

Sutton-Smith, B., & Rosenberg, B. G. Development of sex differences in play choices during preadolescence. *Child Development,* 1963, **34**, 119–126.

Sweeney, E. J. *Sex differences in problem solving.* Stanford: Department of Psychology, Technological Report 1, December 1, 1953.

Swift, J. W. Effects of early group experience, the nursery school and day nursery. In M. L. Hoffman and W. L. Hoffman (Eds.), *Review of child development research,* I. New York: Russell Sage Foundation, 1964.

Symonds, P. M., & Jensen, A. R. *From adolescent to adult.* New York: Columbia University Press, 1961.

Szazz, T. The uses of naming and the origin of the myth of mental illness. *American Psychologist,* 1961, **16**, 59–65.

Tanner, J. M. The regulation of human growth. *Child Development,* 1963, **34**, 817–847.

Tanner, J. M., & Inhelder, B. (Eds.) *Discussions on child development.* New York: International Universities Press, 1960.

Tasch, R. J. The role of the father in the family. *Journal of Experimental Education,* 1952, **20**, 319–361.

Taussig, H. B. The thalidomide syndrome. *Scientific American,* 1962, **207**, 29–35.

Taylor, A., & Taylor, J. Hymns for infant minds, 1920. Cited by M. Kiefer, *American children through their books.* Philadelphia: University of Pennsylvania Press, 1948.

Taylor, D. W. Paper presented at the

American Association for the Advancement of Science, symposium on sex differences. Berkeley, California, December 27, 1954.

Taylor, J. Select rhymes for the nursery. Cited by M. Kiefer, *American children through their books.* Philadelphia: University of Pennsylvania Press, 1948.

Tchoukovsky, K. From two to five. Cited by K. S. Karol, *New statesman,* 1959, **42,** 568.

Television and youth. Report published by Television Information Committee, National Association of Radio and TV Broadcasters. Washington, D. C., 1954.

Terman, L. M., & Oden, M. M. *The gifted group at mid-life.* Stanford: Stanford University Press, 1959.

Terman, L. M. The discovery and encouragement of exceptional talent. *American Psychologist,* 1954, **9,** 221–230.

Terman, L. M., & Merrill, M. A. Measuring intelligence. Boston: Houghton Mifflin, 1937.

Terman, L. M., & Merrill, M. A. *Stanford Binet intelligence scale.* Boston: Houghton Mifflin, 1960.

Terman, L. M., & Miles, C. C. *Sex and personality.* New York: McGraw-Hill, 1936.

Thomas, A., et al. *Behavior individuality in early childhood.* New York: New York University Press, 1963.

Thompson, G. A. *Child psychology.* Boston: Houghton Mifflin, 1962.

Thompson, R., & Melzack, R. Early environment. *Scientific American,* 1956, **194**(1), 38–42.

Thompson, W. R., & Heron, W. The effects of early restriction of activity in Gods. *Journal of Comparative and Physiological Psychology,* 1954, **47,** 77–92.

Thompson, W. R., & Schaefer, T. Early environmental stimulation. In D. W. Fiske and S. Maddi (Eds), *Functions of varied experience.* Homewood, Illinois: Dorsey, 1961.

Thorndike, R. L., & Hagen, E. *Measurement and evaluation in psychology and education.* New York: Wiley, 1961.

Thorpe, J. A. A study of personality variables among successful women students and teachers of physical education. *Research Quarterly,* 1958, **29,** 83–92.

Thrum, M. E. The development of concepts of magnitude. *Child Development,* 1935, **6,** 120–140.

Thurstone, L. J., & Thurstone, T. G. Factual studies of intelligence. *Psychometric Monographs,* 1941, No. 2.

Tiller, P. O. Father absence and personality development of children in sailor families. In N. Anderson (Ed.), *Studies of the family.* Gottingen, Germany: Vanderhoeck and Ruprecht, 1957.

Tinbergen, N. *The study of instinct.* Oxford: Clarendon, 1951.

Todd, T. W. Objective ratings of the constitution of the growing child, based on examination of physical development and mental expansion. *American Journal of Diseases of Children,* 1938, **55,** 149–159.

Torrance, E. P. Problems of highly creative children. *Gifted Child Quarterly,* 1961, **5,** 31–34.

Torrance, E. P. *Guiding creative talent.* Englewood Cliffs, New Jersey: Prentice-Hall, 1962.

Torrance, E. P. Factors affecting creative thinking in children. Unpublished.

Torrance, E. P., et al. *Minnesota studies of creative thinking in early school years.* Research Memo. BER, 60–1. Minneapolis: University of Minnesota Press, 1960.

Trankell, A. The influence of choice of writing hangs on the handwriting. *British Journal of Psychology,* 1956, **26,** 94–103.

Tryon, C. M. UC inventory, I. Social and emotional adjustment, revised form for presentation of the cumulative record for an individual, with group norms for a seven-year period. Berkeley: University of California Institute of Child Welfare, 1939.

Tuddenham, R. D. The constancy of personality. *Genetic Psychology Monographs,* 1959, **60,** 3–29.

Tuddenham, R. D. The influence of a distorted group norm upon judgments of adults and children. *Journal of Psychology,* 1961, **52,** 231–239.

Tuma, E., & Livingston, N. Family socioeconomic status and adolescents' attitudes to authority. *Child Development,* 1960, **31,** 387–399.

Tyler, L. E. The antecedents of two varieties of vocational interests. *Genetic Psychology Monographs,* 1964, **70,** 212.

Tyler, L. E. *The psychology of human differences.* (3rd ed.) New York: Appleton-Century-Crofts, 1965.

Udry, R. J. The importance of social class in a suburban school. *Journal of Educational Psychology,* 1960, **33,** 307–310.

Underwood, F. W., & Honigman, I. Comparison of socialization and personality in two simple societies. *American Anthropologist,* 1947, **49,** 557–577.

Unger, S. M. Relation between intelligence and socially appropriate behavior: A methodological cautionary note. *Child*

449

REFERENCES

Development, 1964, **35**(1), 301.

Updegraff, R., & Keister, M. E. A study of children's reactions to failure and an experimental attempt to modify them. *Child Development,* 1937, **8,** 241–248.

Is the quality of U. S. population declining? *U.S. News and World Report,* November 22, 1965, 68–71.

What expectant mothers need to know. *U.S. News and World Report,* February 14, 1966, **60**(7), 15.

Valentine, E. W. The innate bases of fear. *Journal of Genetic Psychology,* 1930, **37,** 394–420.

Van Alstyne, D. *Play behavior and choice of play materials of preschool children.* Chicago: University of Chicago Press, 1932.

Vandenberg, S. G. The hereditary abilities study: Hereditary components in a psychological test battery. *American Journal of Human Genetics,* 1962, **14,** 220–273.

Vernon, P. E. *Intelligence and attainment tests.* New York: Philosophical Library, 1961.

Vigotsky, L. S. *Thought and language.* Cambridge, Massachusetts: Institute of Technology Press, 1962.

Walk, R. D., & Gibson, E. J. A comparative and analytical study of visual depth perception. *Psychological Monographs,* 1961, **519.**

Walker, R. N. Body build and nursery school teachers' ratings. *Monographs of the Society for Research in Child Development,* 1962, **27,** 1–94.

Wallen, N. E., & Stevenson, G. M. Stability and correlates of judged creativity in fifth grade writings. *Journal of Educational Psychology,* 1960, **51,** 273–276.

Walman, M. J. Pre-school and kindergarten child attitudes toward the blind in an integrated program. *New Outlook for the Blind,* 1958, **58,** 128–133.

Walters, C. E. Prediction of postnatal development from fetal activity. *Child Development,* 1965, **36**(3), 801.

Walters, R. H., Marshall, W. E., & Shooter, J. R. Anxiety isolation and susceptibility to social influence. *Journal of Personality,* 1960, **28,** 518–529.

Wann, K. C., & Liddle, E. A. *Fostering intellectual development in young children.* New York: Teachers College, Columbia University, 1962.

Warkany, J. Congenital malformations induced by maternal nutritional deficiency. *Journal of Pediatrics,* 1944, **25,** 476–480.

Warner, W. L., & Henry, W. E. The radio daytime serial. *Genetic Psychology Monographs,* 1948, **37,** 3–71.

Watson, J. B. Experimental studies on the growth of the emotions. In C. Murchison (Ed.), *Psychologies of 1925.* Worcester, Massachusetts: Clark University Press, 1926.

Watson, J. B. *Psychological care of infant and child.* New York: Norton, 1928.

Weber, M. *The Protestant ethic and the spirit of capitalism.* Translated by T. Parsons. London: Allen and Unwin, 1930.

Wechsler, D. *The measurement of adult intelligence.* (4th ed.) Baltimore: Williams and Wilkins, 1958.

Wedge, B. M. Occurrence of psychosis among Okinawans in Hawaii. *Journal of Psychiatry,* 1952, **109,** 255–258.

Weil, R. J., & Eaton, J. W. *Culture and mental disorders.* Glencoe, Illinois: Free Press, 1955.

Weisberg, P. S., & Springer, K. J. Environment factors in creative function. *Archives in General Psychiatry,* 1961, **5,** 554–564.

Wenar, C., & Coulter, J. C. A reliability study of developmental histories. *Child Development,* 1962, **33**(2), 453–462.

Wenger, M. A. Preliminary study of the significance of measures of autonomic balance. *Psychosomatic Medicine,* 1947, **9,** 301–309.

West, J. *Plainville, U.S.A.* New York: Columbia University Press, 1945.

West, L. J. Psychiatric aspects of training for honorable survival as a prisoner of war. *American Journal of Psychiatry,* 1958, **115,** 329–336.

West, S. Sibling configurations of scientists. *American Journal of Sociology,* 1960, **66,** 268–274.

Westley, W. A., & Elkin, F. The protective environment and adolescent socialization. *Social Forces,* 1956, **35,** 243–249.

Wheeler, L. R. A comparative study of the intelligence of East Tennessee Mountain children. *Journal of Educational Psychology,* 1942, **33,** 321–334.

White, B. L., Castle, P., & Held, R. Observations on the development of visually-directed teaching. *Child Development,* 1964, **35,** 349–364.

White, L., Jr. *Educating our daughters.* New York: Harper, 1950.

White, R., & Lippitt, R. Leader behavior and member reaction in three social climates. In D. Cartwright and A. Zander (Eds.), *Group dynamics.* Evanston, Illinois: Row, Peterson, 1962.

White, S. H. Learning. In H. W. Stevenson (Ed.), *Child psychology.* Chicago: National Society for the Study of Education, Part I. Sixty-second Yearbook, 1963.

Whiteman, P. H., & Kosier, K. P. Development of children's moralistic judgment;

age, sex, IQ and certain personal experiential variables. *Child Development,* 1964, **35**(3), 843–850.

Whiting, J. W. M., & Whiting, B. B. Contributions of anthropology to the methods of studying child rearing. In P. H. Mussen (Ed.), *Handbook of research methods in child development.* New York: Wiley, 1960.

Whorf, B. L. Science and linguistics. *Technological Review,* 1940, **44,** 229–231.

Whorf, B. L. *Language, thought and reality.* Cambridge, Massachusetts: Technology Press, 1956.

Wickman, E. K. *Children's behavior and teacher's attitudes.* New York: Commonwealth Fund, 1928.

Wiggam, A. E. Do brains and character go together? *School and Society,* 1941, **54,** 261–265.

Wilkins, L., & Richter, C. P. A great craving for salt by a child with cortico-adrenal insufficiency. *Journal of American Medical Association,* 1940, **114,** 866–868.

Williams, C. D. The elimination of tantrum behavior by extinction procedures. *Journal of Abnormal and Social Psychology,* 1959, **59,** 269.

Williams, R. J. *American society.* New York: Knopf, 1951.

Williams, R. J. *Biochemical individuality.* New York: Wiley, 1956.

Williams, R. J. Why human genetics? *Journal of Heredity,* 1960, **51,** 91–98.

Williams, R. J., & Siegel, F. L. Propetology, a new branch of medical science. *American Journal of Medicine,* 1961, **31,** 325–327.

Wilner, E. M., et al. Housing as an environmental factor in mental health: The Johns Hopkins longitudinal study. *American Journal of Public Health,* 1960, **50,** 55–63.

Wilson, A. B. Residential segregation of social classes and aspirations of high school boys. *American Sociological Review,* 1959, **24,** 836–845.

Winder, C. L., & Rau, L. Parental attitudes associated with social deviance in pre-adolescent boys. *Journal of Abnormal and Social Psychology,* 1962, **64,** 418–424.

Winker, J. B. Age trends, activity and sex differences in the wishes, identifications, activities and fears of children. *Child Development,* 1949, **20,** 191–200.

Winterbottom, M. R. The relation of need for achievement to learning experiences in independency and mastery. In J. W. Atkinson (Ed.) *Motives in fantasy, action and society.* Princeton, New Jersey: Van Nostrand, 1958.

Wirth, L. Urbanism as a way of life. *American Journal of Sociology,* 1938, **44,** 1–24.

Witkin, H. A. *Scientific American,* February 1959, **200,** 50–70.

Witkin, H. A., et al. *Psychological differentiation.* New York: Wiley, 1962.

Witmer, H. L., & Kotinsky, R. (Eds.) *Personality in the making.* New York: Harper, 1952.

Witty, P. *School children and television.* New York: Television Information Office, 1960.

Wolfenstein, M. The emergence of fun morality. *Journal of Social Issues,* 1951, **7,** 16.

Wolfenstein, M. Death of a parent and death of a President. In M. Wolfenstein and G. Klimen (Eds.), *Children and the death of a President.* Garden City, New York: Doubleday, 1965.

Wolfle, D. *America's resources as specialized talent.* New York: Harper, 1954.

Woodcock, L. P. *Life and ways of the two year old.* New York: Basic Books, 1941.

Wooten, B. A social scientist's approach to maternal deprivation. *Deprivation of maternal care,* public health paper No. 14. Geneva: World Health Organization, 1962.

Worth, W. H. Promotion or non-promotion. *Educational Administration and Supervision,* 1960, **46,** 16–26.

Worth, W. H. When is grade repetition most profitable? *Alberta Journal of Educational Research,* 1961, **7,** 217–222.

Wright, B. A. Altruism in children and the perceived conduct of others. *Journal of Abnormal and Social Psychology,* 1942, **37,** 218–233.

Wrightstone, J. W. Class organization for instruction. *What research says to the teacher,* No. 13. Washington, D. C.: National Education Association, May 1957.

Wursten, J. Madeleine Thomas stories and similar methods. In A. I. Rabin and M. R. Haworth (Eds.), *Projective techniques with children.* New York: Grune and Stratton, 1960.

Wylie, P. *An essay on morals.* New York: Holt, 1947.

Yamazaki, I. N., et al. Outcome of pregnancy in women exposed to the atomic bomb in Nagasaki. *American Journal of Diseases of Children,* 1954, **87,** 448–463.

Yarrow, L. J. Maternal deprivation: Toward an empirical and conceptual re-evaluation. *Psychological Bulletin,* 1961, **58,** 459–499.

451

REFERENCES Yarrow, L. J. Research in dimensions of early maternal care. *Merrill-Palmer Quarterly,* 1963a, **9**(2), 101–114.

Yarrow, L. J. Separation from parents during early childhood. In M. L. Hoffman and L. W. Hoffman (Eds.), *Review of child development research.* New York: Russell Sage Foundation, 1963b.

Yerkes, R. M. Psychological examining in the U. S. Army. *Memoirs: National Academy of Science,* 1921, **15**, 1–890.

Zander, A., & Van Egmond, E. Relationship of intelligence and social power to the interpersonal behavior of children. *Journal of Educational Psychology,* 1958, **49**, 257–268.

Zigler, E., Jones, L., & Kages, P. Acquisition of language habits, in first, second, and third grade boys. *Child Development,* 1964, **35**(3), 726.

Zupansky, P. E., & Leiderman, P. H. Sensory deprivation: An overview. *Sensory Deprivation: A Symposium held at Harvard Medical School.* Cambridge: Harvard University Press, 1963.

452

GLOSSARY

Note: The following terms are briefly and simply defined. Many of them have various meanings, but in the interest of brevity only those meanings are given that are relevant to their usage in this volume. If you do not find a term listed exactly as it appears in the text, look for a closely related form.

abuse, child: Unusually cruel treatment, unreasonable punishment or undue exploitation of a child.

acceptance–rejection: A dimension of parent-child relations involving caring for and loving the child, at one extreme, or unwillingness to accept the child (as demonstrated by indifference or hostility) at the other.

acculturation: The process by which an individual learns the attitudes, mode of thinking, and behaviors characteristic of the larger social group or culture.

achievement orientation: An attitude of recognizing and striving toward goals.

achiever: An individual who is making satisfactory progress toward goals and who is usually characterized by ambition, energy, autonomy, and competence.

adjustment: An individual's establishment of a satisfactory relationship with himself and his environment.

Adler, Alfred (1870–1937): An Austrian psychiatrist and psychologist, perhaps best known for the theory that neuroses may arise as a result of emotional conflict about real or imagined physical, social, or psychological inferiority. The individual's own strivings are largely directed toward attempting to make up for, or *compensate* for, his feelings of inferiority.

adolescence: The period from the beginning of puberty until maturity.

adrenalin: A hormone secreted by the adrenal medulla that affects the rate of heart beat, raises blood pressure, and incites the liver to release extra sugar into the blood—all reactions calculated to effect readjustment in emotional situations.

affect: A categorical name embracing the concepts of feeling, mood, emotion, and temperament.

affective: Pertaining to feeling or emotion.

age-stages: Periods of development as conceptualized by Piaget. See *conceptual-stage theory.*

aggression: An attitude of attack, as contrasted with passive withdrawal, which may or may not possess an element of hostility.

alleles: Contrasting characteristics transmitted by alternative genes and determining alternative characteristics (such as tall or short).

amoral type (Peck-Havighurst): One who follows his impulses regardless of the effect on others.

androgen: A hormone secreted in both sexes, but far more abundantly in males, that influences maleness of structure, function, and to an unknown extent, behavior.

animism: The belief common in primitives and children that natural phenomena (such as rocks, trees, or wind) are alive and have souls.

anthropology: The comparative study of man, including his social habits, customs, and physical characteristics.

anxiety: The anticipation of impending doom from no clearly defined threatening situation. It is aroused by a complex of unhappy circumstances rather than by

453

a sharply defined fear-inducing stimulus.

apathy: A feeling of indifference often produced by excessive failure and frustration.

aphasia: The loss or impairment of ability to use speech as a result of lesions in the brain.

ascender, IQ: One whose IQ, or intelligence-test score, rises over a span of time. The *IQ descender's* intelligence-test score, relative to others of his age status, declines.

attitude: A consistent tendency to react in a particular way—often positively or negatively—toward any matter. Attitude possesses both cognitive and emotional components.

autism: The condition of being completely dominated by subjective, self-centered trends of thoughts and behavior.

autobiography: A child's written perceptions of himself and others.

autonomic nervous system: A major division of the nervous system concerned with the largely automatic regulation of smooth muscles and glands.

autonomy: Self-direction, as opposed to direction from without.

autosomes: Chromosomes other than sex chromosomes.

ballistocardiograph: An apparatus for recording the stroke volume of the heart in order to calculate the cardiac output.

basic-habit training: Teaching the child the primary behavior patterns of his culture, including approved habits of eating, toileting, and sleeping.

behaviors: Activities of the organism, both covert, or hidden (such as feeling and thinking), and overt, or observable.

behaviorism: A school of thought emphasizing the need to concentrate on studying overt behaviors rather than inner mental processes.

Bellak Apperception Test: A projective test designed especially for children and consisting of pictures of animals, identification with which presumably reveals conflicts with parents, sibling rivalries, and so on.

Binet, Alfred (1857–1911): A French psychologist and the co-deviser of the *Binet-Simon scale,* an intelligence test consisting of tasks and questions graded with reference to the average child's ability to deal with them at successive age levels.

biochemistry: The chemistry of plant and animal life.

454 *biologically based behaviors:* Those behaviors deriving from biological drives, including hunger, thirst, and sleep.

birth trauma: An injury received during birth.

Blacky Pictures: A series of 12 cartoons used to test psychosexual development.

body build: Characteristic anatomical structure, determined by heredity. Body builds are often classified as *ectomorphic, mesomorphic,* or *endomorphic.*

body image: The mental picture an individual has of his own body, derived from internal sensation, others' reactions, and his personal goals.

breaking set: Avoiding the tendency to perceive a set of stimuli in a rigid or conventional way and freely scanning the whole range of elements open to perception.

broken home: A home in which one parent is missing through death or separation.

Bühler World Test: A projective test consisting of miniature objects of the outdoor world (trees, cars, and so on), which the child is invited "to do something about"; the manner of his responding presumably reveals distinctive personality patterns.

canalization: Arranging the environment to elicit certain specific behaviors.

cardiograph: An instrument for recording action of the heart.

case history: A study made of a particular individual or social unit—for example, a family—which brings together all available evidence relevant to the subject.

catch-up mechanism: An inferred process that restores the normal growth pattern after it has been temporarily altered from its usual course by some abnormal condition such as illness or severe malnutrition.

catharsis: A cleansing or purgation; in Freudian terms, the patient purges his mind of repressed material (catharsis) by telling whatever comes into his mind *(free association).*

catharsis, or drainage, hypothesis: The belief that the venting of antisocial impulses in safe ways will reduce the need to assert them in undesirable ways.

central nervous system: The brain and spinal cord.

cephalocaudal development: The principle that physical growth proceeds from head to tail (caudal) region.

cerebral dominance: The control, by either hemisphere of the brain, of some bodily movement, especially handedness.

character: An integrated system of traits that predisposes an individual to behave in a relatively consistent manner in relation to moral issues.

child biography: A description of significant chronological events, recorded by an observer.

childhood: The period from infancy (about the end of the second year) until puberty.

child psychology: The division of psychology concerned with child behaviors, both normal and abnormal.

child society: The "way of life" characteristic of children as they mingle with each other both individually and in groups.

chromosome: One of the minute bodies in the nucleus of a cell believed to carry genes and to constitute the mechanism of heredity.

cinemanalysis: A technique employing a motion-picture camera, which permits studying behavioral sequences frame by frame.

cleft palate: A congenital fissure in the median line of the roof of the mouth.

clique: A close-knit unisexual social group, most characteristic of early adolescents, especially girls, but occurring sometimes among children as young as 8 or 9.

co-curriculum: The leisure-time skills taught separately from the traditional academic curriculum, including club activities and sports.

cognition: A process (including perceiving, recognizing, reasoning and conceiving) whereby an organism becomes aware of or attains knowledge of an object.

cognitive dissonance: The gap between the response patterns that proved functional in an early environment and those required for later stressful situations. Anxiety is seen to be the outcome of cognitive dissonance.

cognitive style: The characteristic way an individual organizes his approach to mental tasks, including specific ways of relating to the problem at hand.

color reactor: One who tends to organize his perceptions primarily on the basis of color.

compensation: A behavioral mechanism that consists in efforts to make up for some real or imagined deficiency.

conative: Pertaining to will power; representing a tendency of the organism to behave, as opposed to remaining at rest (homeostasis).

concept: The abstracted idea of something, which one may apply in generalizing other objects or ideas; the image of something that exists in one's mind.

conceptual-stage theory: The portrayal of mental development as proceeding by relatively invariant sequential stages or natural divisions within the growth process.

concrete operations period (Piaget): The period (between ages 7 and 11) when reasoning processes have begun to appear logical. By this stage, the child can perceive structural similarities and categorize items on the basis of perceptual cues.

conditioning: A training process designed to establish a predictable response. In its classical sense, when two stimuli—an adequate one and an inadequate one—are presented simultaneously to an organism on successive occasions, the inadequate stimulus acquires the potential of evoking a response similar to that normally aroused by the adequate stimulus.

conflict: The unpleasant emotional condition arising from experiencing incompatible motives.

conforming individual (Peck-Havighurst): One who is ashamed only when he is caught violating the rules.

conformity: The practice of trusting others' judgment, despite whatever contrary evidence may exist, above one's own.

congenital: Present at birth.

connectionistic learning theorists: Authorities who support the doctrine that the basis of all behavior is a connection or bond that links a stimulus to a response. All complex behaviors are describable as combinations of stimulus response connections.

conscience: An individual's functional system of moral values, which limits his decisions about what is right or wrong.

conservation theory: The theory that physical properties of an object are invariant, despite appearances to the contrary. Thus an object in the distance may form but a minute image on the retina, but the individual interprets it to be the size it "objectively" is.

controlled observation: The observation of small segments of the child's behavior and the recording of it as it occurs naturally. Such observations may be made within either natural or specially devised situations.

convergent thinking: The type of thinking that involves surveying available data and narrowing the alternatives in order to find a predetermined "correct" solution.

coping techniques: Behaviors enabling one to accomplish something.

correlation: The degree of relationship

455

between different factors. The tendency of corresponding variables to diverge is called *negative correlation;* the tendency of variables to occur together is called *positive correlation.*

cortex: The thin outer layer of an organ.

creativity: The ability to find new solutions or novel syntheses of familiar ideas.

cretinism: A chronic condition resulting from a congenital lack of thyroid secretion, and marked by arrested mental and physical development and by physical aberrations.

critical period: A time during which particular experiences may have especially profound and enduring effects.

cross-cultural approach: The study of the dynamics of particular behaviors within the context of different cultures.

cross-sectional approach: The description of a number of persons in terms of one or more variables as they appear at a given time.

cultural determinism: The view that culture wholly, or largely, determines personality.

culture: The way of life—material and behavioral—of a society, including its customs, knowledge, beliefs, and morals.

culture, continuous: A culture in which child roles prove functional in adulthood, as opposed to a *discontinuous culture,* where child and adult roles are unrelated.

curriculum: The systematic organization of subject matter and courses into some overall academic plan.

delinquency: A violation of legal or moral codes, especially by minors.

demography: The study of human populations, including population trends, distribution, and differential birth rates in subcultural groupings.

dependence-independence: A dimension of behavior indicating degree of reliance on others in making decisions or carrying out actions.

depolarization: The reversal of the tendency to assume opposing positions.

development: A process involving all the many changes, both qualitative and quantitative, that occur during progress toward maturity. It embraces both changes inherent in the maturing process and those resulting from interaction between the individual and his environment.

developmental direction, laws of: The principle that growth proceeds from the central axis of the body outward *(proximodistal)* and from head to foot, or tail, region *(cephalocaudal).*

developmental tasks: Skills or accomplishments that should be satisfactorily mastered at a particular age-stage if an individual is to be ready for the next stage.

Dewey, John (1859–1952): American philosopher and educator who spearheaded a reform movement stressing the inculcation in children of an experimental, questioning attitude, the utilization of subject matter as means rather than end, and respect for individual differences.

disadvantaged, culturally: Persons who, because of certain characteristics (especially, racial or ethnic origin, or poverty) are unable to share on equal terms with more fortunate individuals the advantages of the major culture.

discipline: Authoritative control over a subordinate's behavior, presumably to preserve a more pleasant situation or to permit more efficient pursuit of goals.

discovery method: The process of trying to reproduce the sequences of thinking that a scientist uses in evolving new principles and ideas; the attitude, or mental set, of the scientist.

disintegrative emotion: An emotion characterized by feelings of unpleasantness or disorganization and maladjustment generally.

divergent thinking: The type of thinking that involves a willingness to depart from the conventional and to try many ideas.

DNA (deoxyribonucleic acid) and *RNA* (ribonucleic acid): Two key chemicals in the *genes* that determine whether substances causing particular characteristics (for example, blue or brown eyes) will be produced. DNA is believed to contain the chemical blueprint for the cells.

dominant gene: A character present in one parent that appears in all hybrid offspring in preference to a contrasting *(recessive)* character in the other parent.

drainage hypothesis: The hypothesis that the venting of antisocial impulses in safe ways will reduce the child's need to express them in undesirable ways.

drive: A force that activates human impulses.

eclampsia: Convulsions and coma in pregnant women due to edema (abnormal amounts of fluid in intercellular tissue spaces of the body), hypertension, or proteinuria (presence of protein in urine).

ectomorph: An individual with a body build characterized by linearity, fragility, and thin muscles.

456

ego: Self, as distinguished from others; the aspect of the psyche that is conscious and most in touch with reality; in Freudian terms, the mediator between primitive impulses *(id)* and conscience *(superego)*.

ego-defensive mechanisms: Habitual methods, other than direct attack on, or simple withdrawal from, frustrating situations, of avoiding or circumventing them, which simultaneously help preserve one's self-respect.

Electra complex: Erotic attachment of a girl to her father, accompanied by jealousy of her mother.

electroencephalograph: A graphic record of wavelike changes in electric potential made by attaching electrodes either to the skull or exposed brain.

embryo: The organism in its early prenatal stage—in mammals, until it begins resembling the adult form.

emotion: A complex feeling-state with characteristic glandular and motor accompaniments. See *integrative emotions, disintegrative emotions.*

empiricism: The doctrine that knowledge is to be tested, in the last analysis, by observed fact instead of by theories about fact.

endocrine system: The glands and parts of glands that produce endocrine secretions.

endomorph: An individual with large accumulations of fat, a large trunk and thighs, tapering extremities, and relatively weak bones and muscles.

environment: The summation of all those factors and conditions external to the organism and potentially capable of influencing it in some manner.

environmental engineering: A form of therapy that involves manipulating the environment in a way that will facilitate the individual's adjustment.

environmentalist: One who stresses the role of environment, as compared with heredity, in the development of the organism.

epigenesis: The emergence of new properties not contained in any earlier stage of the organism's life history, although such emergent properties are somehow related to those earlier stages.

epinephrine: The hormone secreted by the adrenal glands.

equity (Piaget): Adaptation of rules to fit the situation in a morals dilemma.

estrogen: Any hormone that stimulates the female to estrus (periodic sex desire).

etiology: The study of origins and causes.

eugenics: The study and arrangement of conditions conducive to improving the hereditary mental and physical characteristics of the species.

euphoria: A mood of well-being or feeling that all is well.

euthenics: The science of improving the species through regulating the environment.

expedient type (Peck-Havighurst): One who considers others' welfare only to gain personal ends.

experimental method: The procedure in which specific conditions are arranged under which a phenomenon is to be observed, to determine the influences of these conditions. The observed phenomenon is called the *dependent* variable; the arranged conditions are called *independent,* or *experimental,* variables.

extrapolation: Estimate or inference *beyond* the known range, on the basis of variables *within* the known range, from which estimated values may be assumed to follow.

Fallopian tube: Either of two slender tubes that carry ova (female germ cells) from the ovaries to the uterus.

fantasy: Daydream or wishful imagination.

fear: An emotion of agitation aroused by confrontation with an object or situation that poses a threat, and with which one has no ready means to cope.

feeble-mindedness: A lack of normal mental development as demonstrated by markedly low intelligence tests scores or by gross inability to make normal adaptations.

fertilization: The union of a male sperm (or *gamete*) with a female egg (or *ovum*).

fetus: The designation for the prenatal human organism from the age of about six or seven weeks until birth.

field dependent: Easily influenced in one's views and actions by more authoritative persons; strongly influenced by the overall structure of a set of stimuli and having difficulty breaking down this structure into its component elements.

field independent: Easily able to escape viewing a set of stimuli in terms of its conventionally recognized structure and to perceive it in its component elements.

form reactor: One who tends to organize his perceptions primarily on the basis of form or shape.

formal discipline theory: An instructional doctrine depending on selection of materials designed to strengthen certain faculties (mental discipline) such as reasoning or logic, rather than on mere acquisition of knowledge.

457

formal operations period (Piaget): The period (between ages 11 and 15) when truly logical thinking begins and the final step is taken toward abstract thinking and conceptualization.

free association: A process of psychoanalysis in which the subject relates whatever comes to mind. Also, a psychological test in which words are given the subject one at a time, requiring him to respond as quickly as possible with another word.

Freud, Sigmund (1856–1939): The Austrian neurologist and psychiatrist who devised the technique that became the standard procedure for psychoanalysis. His theories stressed the critical significance of childhood experiences.

friendship: A relationship between two persons characterized by mutual attraction and intimacy, usually without erotic overtones.

frustration: The blocking of an ongoing activity; the emotional state resulting from being blocked or defeated in pursuing some goal.

frustration tolerance: The ability to endure confrontation with obstacles without disruption of the orderly processes of behavior.

gang: A formalized child's social group, more typical of boys, characterized by organization, secrecy, high activity, and adventure.

gastrointestinal: Pertaining to the stomach and intestine.

gene: An inferred submicroscopic structure within the *chromosome* that constitutes the ultimate physical unit of heredity and is transmitted in the germ cell from parent to offspring.

genetics: The study of heredity.

genogenic: Of hereditary origin.

gland: An organ that produces a specific product or secretion.

gonad: The sex gland—the *ovary* in the female and the *testis* in the male.

growth: The quantitative changes in the body or its dimensions that represent progress toward maturity.

growth curve: The graphic representation of growth in any physical or psychological function.

guilt: The experience of negative self-evaluation sustained from failure to live up to some standard imposed on one either by himself or by others.

Head Start: School programs designed to provide culturally disadvantaged children with what their homes lack, to permit them to compete on equal terms with other children, both inside and outside school.

hedonic: Pertaining to pleasure, or to the dimension of pleasantness-unpleasantness.

hereditarian: One who emphasizes the role of heredity, as compared with environment, in the development of an organism.

heredity: A term denoting the totality of factors transmitted to an individual from his ancestors, as well as the process by which an organism produces comparable organisms, including mechanical details of transmission of such characters through factors in the germ plasm.

hermaphroditism: The condition of possessing both male and female sex organs (only one being functional in the human).

heterosexuality: Sexual attraction toward members of the other sex.

heterozygosity: The state of possessing varied alleles for a particular character or trait.

homeostasis: The maintenance of balance or constancy in the bodily processes.

homosexuality: Sexual attraction toward members of the same sex. Also, the stage in psychosexual development when the child's emotional feelings and personal associations are presumably directed chiefly toward members of his own sex.

homozygosity: The state of possessing an identical pair of alleles for a given character or for all characters.

hormonal substrate: Those hormonal factors collectively constituting a basis for some condition.

hormone: A chemical substance secreted into the body fluids by an *endocrine gland,* and having a specific effect on the activities of organs.

hostility: An emotional reaction or drive toward destruction of an object or person perceived as a source of frustration or a threat.

Huntington's chorea: A rare form of psychosis involving rapid neurological deterioration and finally death.

hybrid strain: Offspring of parents belonging to different species or varieties. Every organism is hybrid with respect to some characters.

hypothalamus: The portion of the forebrain that acts as a mediator between brain and body, helping to control many body functions, including sleep, hunger, thirst, sex drive, and emotion.

hypothesis: An admittedly tentative explanation of a body of data.

id: The division of the psyche from which stem an individual's primitive, selfish impulses. According to Freud, these impulses are inhibited by the *superego,* or conscience.

ideals: Those aspects of an individual's

moral code that serve as guideposts for his behavior.

identification: The process of merging one's goals with those of another or modeling after another.

identity: The sense of uniqueness as a person and distinctiveness from others, equivalent to answering the question "Who am I?"

ideomotor: The term used to describe involuntary motion produced by an idea or thought.

immanent justice (Piaget): Belief in the existence of automatic punishment arising from a situation.

imprinting: A sort of learning characterized by rapid acquisition, relative insusceptibility to forgetting or extinction, and occurrence early in life, as a result of some specific experience during a relatively brief critical period.

incongruity-dissonance theory: The idea that disturbance arises when an individual is faced by situations so novel that he lacks any ready response.

incorporation: A self-protecting maneuver by which one assumes the attitudes or role of some individual he has found threatening.

infancy: The period (in humans, about the first two years) during which the human or animal is almost totally dependent for its well-being on parental care.

infanticide: The murder of a baby.

inferiority complex: A general feeling of worthlessness and lack of self-confidence.

infrahuman: Characteristic of or pertaining to animals other than man.

in-group: A group with a strong feeling of belonging together, to the exclusion of others.

innate sin, doctrine of: The belief that the child is born a sinner, with all sorts of perverse tendencies that must somehow be eradicated.

inquiry training: Processes designed to equip the child to raise worthwhile questions and locate, analyze, and apply relevant data; also called the *discovery method.*

instinct: An enduring tendency to act in an organized way that is innate, complex, relatively unvarying, and common to the species. Recently the term has been more loosely defined as behavior that is the product of maturation rather than learning.

instrumental activism: An attitude or active approach to and mastery over one's environment, as opposed to passive resignation.

instrumental role: A status involving the disciplined pursuit of goals that tran-

scend the social situation.

integrative emotion: A feeling tone having the effect of producing a sense of well-being and good adjustment generally.

intelligence: The ability to learn and to apply what one learns, especially in new situations.

intelligence quotient: See IQ.

interview technique: A technique in which a person or persons are asked, face to face, various questions planned in advance, to assist in understanding, diagnosis, and treatment.

introversion-extroversion: A dimension indicating one's tendency to direct attention either inside or outside himself, to withdraw from or to seek social contacts, and to engage in secretive or open behaviors.

IQ: Intelligence quotient, a score derived from an intelligence test indicating how the individual's demonstrated mental ability compares with that of others at the same developmental stage.

IQ constancy: The degree to which a specific individual's intelligence remains approximately the same relative to others of his own age-status over the years. See also *ascender, IQ.*

irrational-conscientious (Peck-Havighurst): One who rigidly adheres to principle regardless of the effect on others.

James, William (1842–1910): An American psychologist and philosopher.

jealousy: The emotion aroused when one feels envious of another who possesses something he himself desires.

kibbutz: A collective farm settlement in Israel.

kinesthetic drive: Inherent need for muscular activity.

kinetic play: Activities that involve considerable use of the muscles.

laboratory approach: The study of behavior in a place specially designed for a particular sort of research, as opposed to *field research* (in the natural situation) or *library research.*

learning: Relatively enduring changes in behavior resulting from experience; the process by which such changes come about.

life-adjustment skills: Non-academic skills such as child care, automobile driving, budgeting, social adjustment, and vocational planning.

longitudinal approach: The study of the same individual or individuals over a considerable period of time.

love-oriented discipline: Enforcement of rules through the use of reasoning, guilt-arousing appeals, and the withdrawal of love for misbehaviors.

Madeleine Thomas Test: A projective test involving brief items or stories of everyday activities and problems, to which the child responds, revealing his own motives and feelings about similar situations in his own life.

malnutrition: Any disorder of nutrition.

marginal individual: One who is caught between two cultures, not feeling at home in, or fully accepted by, either. Examples would be the newly arrived immigrant, the Negro child in an integrated school, and the poor child in a wealthy school.

masochism: Satisfaction from pain inflicted on oneself.

mass media: Types of communication (including the press, books, radio, and television) directed not to a specific individual but to very large groups.

masturbation: The practice (usually self-induced) of obtaining satisfaction from stimulation of the genitals.

maturation: Developmental changes due to heredity, in contrast to those deriving from conditions of environment.

memory: The general function of reviving past experience.

mental: Intellectual or cognitive, rather than affective or emotional.

mental age (M.A.): An individual's age in terms of his performance on an intelligence test, representing performance equivalent to that of the average person of that *chronological age (C.A.).*

mental-growth curve: A graphic representation, in the form of a curving line, of the course of mental development over a period of time.

mental retardation: A condition of mental deficiency (IQ below 70), ranging from mild to profound, representing the extreme low end of the curve of normal distribution of IQ's and including 2.28% of the population.

mentally gifted (or very bright): The 2.28% of the population who have IQ's over 130.

mesomorph: An individual with sturdy, upright posture and highly developed skeletal structure — in general, an athletic build.

microcephaly: The condition characterized by an abnormally small head, often associated with marked mental deficiency.

minority group: A relatively stable subgroup within a society that possesses characteristics different from, and subject to unfavorable treatment by, the larger society.

miscarriage: The premature expulsion of

a fetus; abortion.

mobility, social: The ability to make a relatively rapid change in status from one social class to another. One whose social status is improving is said to be *upward mobile;* one whose status is declining, *downward mobile.*

mongolism: A congenital mental condition characterized by slanting eyes, large tongue, flat skull, stubby fingers, and other physical abnormalities.

moral code: The total pattern of rules serving as a standard of conduct.

moral realism (Piaget): The belief that an act should be judged in terms of its consequences, rather than in terms of the motive that provoked it.

morals: Standards of right and wrong as defined by society.

mother-surrogate: Any person or object acting as a substitute for the mother.

motivation: The condition within the organism that stimulates behavior and determines its strength and direction; an inferred personal or organismic determiner (or energizer) of the strength and direction of action taken by the organism.

motor skill: A coordinated set of movements that permits the effective performance of a particular behavior such as walking or swimming.

multiple mothering: A situation involving an infant's being cared for by more than one mother-figure, as when several domestic-science majors take care of an orphan in a practice home on a college campus.

mutagens: Special agents, including X-ray, or ionizing, radiation, which artificially induce mutation.

mutation: A sudden variation in species character that is inheritable because of a change in the determining gene structure. Mutations can be either spontaneous, occurring for no known reason, or artificially induced by mutagens.

narcissism: The attitude of valuing highly one's own physical traits and, by extension, other similar traits; most typical of the earliest stage of psychosexual development.

narrative account: An early method of recording child behavior that involved setting down chronologically whatever behaviors seemed significant, such as when the baby said his first word.

nature-nurture controversy: The argument over the relative roles of heredity and environment in the development of the organism.

neo-Freudians: Followers of Freud, who have nevertheless substantially modified the orthodox Freudian doctrine.

neonate: Newborn infant.

nervous system: All the organs of the body composed of nerve tissue.

neurophysiological: Pertaining to nerve tissue.

neuropsychiatric disorder: A condition involving both nervous and psychological upset.

neurosis: See *psychoneurosis.*

norm: A single value, or range of values, representing the usual performance of a given group.

normality: In the statistical sense, the condition of being average or typical; in the psychological sense, the status of acceptable adjustment, free of unhealthy deviations.

normative approach: A cross-sectional or survey-type study designed to determine what behaviors may normally be expected at the various age-stages.

nuclear family: The family composed only of the father, mother, and children, as opposed to the *extended family,* which also includes all the descendants of a common grandparent and all their relatives.

nurturance: An attitude on the part of the parent, usually the mother, of warmth and assistance toward the child.

object constancy: The perception of an object in its normal or standard appearance independent of distortions produced by the surrounding situation or of the component stimuli making up the perceptual pattern.

Oedipus complex (Freud): The repressed desire of an individual for sex relations with the parent of the opposite sex. Specifically, the term relates to the boy's incestuous desire for his mother, but it often subsumes an analogous desire of the girl for her father (more properly, the *Electra complex*).

ordinal position: One's place in succession, such as the first or second child in the family.

organic: Pertaining to substances derived from organisms; bodily as contrasted with mental.

organism: An individual animal, either human, infrahuman, or subhuman.

orthopedic: Pertaining to the correction of skeletal deformities.

overprotection: Provision of more care than necessary or desirable, often involving varying combinations of shielding, over-solicitude, and pampering.

ovum: The female egg, or germ cell.

parallel play: A form of social interaction characteristic of early childhood (about 18 months to 2 years), in which children play side by side, only marginally reacting to each other.

parasympathetic: Pertaining to that division of the *autonomic nervous system* which is more active in "everyday" activities of ordinary quiescent quality.

parental deprivation: The lack of emotional ties between child and parent figure, often after such ties have originally been established.

passive language: The preverbal child's capacity to understand and cognitively to manipulate language symbols without a corresponding ability to speak for himself.

pathology: A diseased or abnormal condition of the organism or its parts.

Pavlov, Ivan (1849–1936): A Russian physiologist, especially well known for his experiments in conditioning animal behavior.

pediatrics: The branch of medicine concerned with the health and diseases of children.

peer: Another of one's own age or status; equal.

peer group: The group with whom a child associates and who share the same general age and social status.

perception: A primarily cognitive (mental) process by which an individual gains an impression of some set of stimuli through his senses, which is modified and interpreted by prior experience.

perinatal period: The period from conception until three months after birth.

personal role: See *role.*

personality: The total pattern of an individual's characteristic traits, constituting his distinctive way of adapting to his environment.

personality syndrome: See *syndrome.*

phobia: An intense and persistent fear, usually out of proportion to the threat involved.

physiogenic: Of physical or organic, as opposed to psychological, origin.

Piaget, Jean (1896–   ): A Swiss psychologist, who is this century's most prolific writer and theorist on child development and developmental processes in particular. He is especially well known for his conceptual-stage theories.

pituitary gland: An important *endocrine* (secreting internally) gland about the size of a pea, located at the base of the brain; it is sometimes called the master gland because of its important effects on the other endocrines.

placenta: The spongy organ within the uterus that, with the umbilical cord, establishes a connection between mother

461

and child. It acts as a barrier between the two blood streams, allowing nutrients to reach the child, while keeping out noxious substances.

polarization: The tendency to assume diametrically opposing positions.

power-oriented discipline: A manner of control involving punishment rather than reasoning.

preadolescence: A stage in development spanning approximately two years before puberty.

predelinquent: The child whose present behaviors are so antisocial as to make reasonable a prediction of subsequent delinquency unless preventive measures are taken.

prejudice: Either a favorable or an unfavorable judgment made on the basis of inadequate data and affected by certain special qualities of an individual's own experience, which predispose him to think, feel, and act in ways congruent with this judgment.

prelogical thinking: A mode of thinking (typical of children, primitives, and psychotics) that fails to follow the standard rules, but possesses a sort of logic of its own.

premature infant: One born weighing less than 5 pounds or delivered earlier than 270 days after the presumed date of conception.

prenatal period: The period from fertilization to birth.

preoperational thought period (Piaget): A period (between ages 2 and 7) divided into the *preconceptual stage* (ages 2 to 3), when the child is egocentric and uses himself as the standard of judgment, and the *intuitive stage* (ages 4 to 7), when the child conceptualizes more and groups objects into classes.

primary-reaction characteristics: Those traits of the infant which are most characteristic and show the greatest tendency to persist.

primate: Any member of the most highly developed order of animals, including man, apes, monkeys, and lemurs.

primitization: A destructuring of personality due to frustration.

probability: The likelihood that a particular event will occur, stated in terms of the ratio between the number of ways in which the event may occur and the number of ways in which alternative events may occur.

problem-solving approach: The attitude or practice of dealing with problems in a rational, organized manner.

progressive education: A movement in education (beginning about 1919) that represented a protest against formalism, and emphasized such principles as learning by doing, regard for individual differences, and considerable freedom.

projective technique: A procedure for discovering an individual's characteristic modes of behavior by analyzing his responses to relatively ambiguous, unstructured stimuli or situations.

proprioceptive: Sensitive to position and movement of the body and its members.

Protestant Ethic: A set of ideas about man's spiritual relationships that emphasizes hard work, personal stewardship, pleasurelessness, and individual enterprise.

prototype: Model; pattern; archetype.

proximodistal development: The principle that growth proceeds from the body axis outward.

pseudo-maturity: A behavioral pattern characterized by behaviors appropriate to the individual's level of development but cloaking more fundamental and less well developed behaviors.

psyche: The personification (originally by the Greeks) of the life principle; hence, it represents psychological function generally and not simply mind.

psychoanalysis: A body of doctrine associated with Freud and modified by his followers; a special technique for discovering hidden motivation.

psychobiological: Pertaining to the whole human being, including both psychological and physiological functions.

psychogenic: Of mental or emotional origin.

psychology: The branch of science dealing with description, explanation, and control of behavior.

psychoneurosis: A somewhat poorly defined mental disorder, less serious than psychosis, and leaving the personality relatively intact.

psychosexual development: That aspect of an individual's progression toward maturity involving the emergence of masculine and feminine sex roles as the psychobiological consequences of sexual drives, awareness, and interests.

psychosis: The scientific name for severe mental disturbances; commonly called insanity.

psychosocial: A term describing whatever is both social and mental or psychological.

psychosomatic: Pertaining to the mind-body relationship; having bodily symptoms of mental or emotional origin.

psychotherapy: The use of any psychological technique in treating maladjustment or mental disorders.

puberty: The period during which the individual's reproductive organs approach readiness to function and secondary sex characteristics develop.

race: A subdivision of mankind characterized by a common ancestry and greater frequency of occurrence among its members of certain inherited, usually visible physical characteristics.

radiation: Emission of rays from radioactive matter.

random sampling: A number of items drawn from a larger number or population in such manner that every item or individual in that population has the same chance to be represented.

Rank, Otto (1884–1939): An Austrian psychoanalyst who profoundly influenced American social work and the development of client-centered therapy. He is also known for his theory that the birth process constitutes a highly traumatic experience.

rational-altruistic individual (Peck-Havighurst): One who has a stable set of principles, but evaluates behaviors in terms of their effects both on others and himself.

rationalization: The use of false, but logical-appearing reasons to justify one's acts both to oneself and to others.

readiness: The state of maturation that permits a learning experience to "take hold."

recapitulation theory: The doctrine that the individual, in his own development, goes through stages representative of those followed in the evolution of the species.

recessive gene: A gene, such as the gene for blue eyes, whose effects are inhibited if the corresponding gene is dominant, as for brown eyes.

regression: The retreat to more childish or more primitive ways of behavior, often as a result of stress.

reinforcement: Increasing the force or strength of a response. *Negative* reinforcement means strengthening a response by punishing alternative responses. *Positive* reinforcement means strengthening, or stamping in, a particular response by rewarding it whenever it occurs.

reinforcement hypothesis: The hypothesis holding that the consequences resulting from the expression of an emotion determine whether the emotion increases or decreases in the future.

rejection: The act of refusing to acknowledge the worth of another in some respect or to grant him recognition in some category.

reliability: In testing, the tendency of a measure to yield the same results on successive administrations.

religion: A system of beliefs, practices, rites, and ceremonies by which people relate to the supernatural and from which

values are derived for guiding conduct.

REM sleep: Active sleep, or the so-called dream sleep accompanied by rapid eye movement (REM).

reminiscence: The recall, without conscious effort or specifically relevant cues, of earlier memories.

repression: The exclusion of specific psychological content from consciousness by a process of which the individual is unaware.

response style: The pattern of reactivity characteristic of an individual—for example, involving tendencies to be energetic or lethargic, persistent or half-hearted, and the like.

restitution (Piaget): Restoration of the equilibrium destroyed by the punished act.

retardation, pseudo (social): Failure to achieve intellectually due to remediable environmental factors rather than to true mental deficiency.

Rh (blood) factor: An agglutinating factor in the blood of about 85% of humans. If introduced into Rh negative blood (blood lacking Rh), it causes antibody formation. In an Rh negative mother, this generally produces transfusion reactions in later Rh positive fetuses, with consequent pathology in the offspring (including abortions, stillbirths, and possibly mental deficiency).

rickets: A condition caused by deficiency of vitamin D, especially in infancy and childhood, which obstructs normal ossification, or bone formation.

roles: Socially expected patterns of behavior associated with functions in various groups. Among the most important for children are age, sex, pupil, and family roles.

role, personal: The individual-in-action comprising all his roles, integrating and transcending them.

RNA: See *DNA.*

roles, social sex: The patterns of behavior deemed appropriate for the sexes.

Rorschach test: A projective test consisting of 10 inkblots to which the subject responds by telling what he "sees" in each.

sadism: The practice of inflicting pain on others for the sake of personal satisfaction.

schizophrenia: A group of psychotic reactions characterized by distortions of reality and by extreme intellectual, emotional, and behavioral disturbances.

self: The integrating core of the personality that mediates between needs and reality; the ego.

self-actualization: The process of moving through sequentially higher stages of motivation and organization to adequate achievement of one's potential.

self-concept: The way an individual views and feels about himself.

self-demand feeding: An arrangement whereby the infant is fed when he makes it apparent that he is hungry.

self-image: The child's picture of himself, reflecting his subjective experience of uniqueness.

sensorimotor: Relating to acts that depend upon the integrated functioning of sense organs and motor mechanisms.

sensory: Pertaining to the activity of a sense organ, or to data obtained directly from the senses (eyes, ears, and so on).

sensory deprivation: A lack of adequate stimulation for the senses, presumably resulting in emotional, intellectual, and physical deficiencies.

sex drive: The psychological condition that causes the organism to desire and be receptive to sexual experience.

sex-role adoption: The actual assumption of the behaviors and characteristics of one sex or the other.

sex role, biological: Those patterns of behavior associated with the psychobiological consequences of sex drive and sex interests, as distinct from the broader social sex roles.

sex-role identity: The complex set of attitudes one holds toward those aspects of himself which relate to sex role.

sex-role preference: Perception of one sex role or the other as more desirable.

sex-role, social: The pattern of behaviors characteristic of male or female in a particular society.

sex-role standard: The approved set of behaviors for each sex.

sex-typing: The process of acquiring the characteristics associated with one or the other sex.

shifting group play: The stage in social interaction (between ages 2 to 4 years) when children form loose groups sharing the same interest, with individuals coming and going at will.

sibling: Brother or sister; another offspring of the same parents.

sickle-cell anemia: A condition marked by anemia (in which the blood is deficient in quality or in quantity) and by ulcers (in which the subject's red blood cells acquire a sickle shape).

sleeper effect: The tendency of a trait, depressed for a time, to reappear.

social class: A grouping within society composed of persons sharing certain common social characteristics, which qualify them for roughly similar privileges and status. This status to an extent re-

stricts their interaction with other such groups.

Social Ethic: A set of ideas, recently acquiring prominence, emphasizing social adjustment and dependence on others.

socialization: The process by which an individual learns to behave like, and to get along with, others in his society and culture.

society: The social order, as contrasted with the culture. Society emphasizes the organization and structure of human groups, while culture stresses its customs and behaviors.

sociocultural: Pertaining both to society (the network of groups within which an individual lives) and its culture (total way of life, including beliefs, knowledge, and material things).

sociogram: A graphic portrayal of relationships within a group, which points out, but does not explain, how individuals relate to each other.

sociometric techniques: Quantitative studies of group relationships, often involving determination of how group members perceive and feel about each other.

socius: An individual in terms of his group role and relationships.

Spearman's two-factor theory of intelligence: The portrayal of mental abilities as involving a G-factor (general intelligence) and S-factors (an unspecified number of special abilities), all these factors (G and S) being closely related and functioning as a unit.

sperm: The male germ cell or the liquid secretion (semen) containing such cells.

stabilimeter: A device attached to a subject to record his movements automatically.

standard: Desirable quality or level of performance.

standardized test: A test whose contents and method of scoring are scientifically derived, to permit evaluation of an individual's performance against test norms.

Stanford-Binet: One of the best-known intelligence test scales, designed for oral administration to individuals.

status: The position accorded an individual, formally or informally, within a group, carrying with it privileges, duties, and responsibilities, and reflecting the way others view him.

stimulus: A form of energy that excites a receptor (a specialized structure that is sensitive to specific energies) and initiates a neural impulse.

stimulus-response (S-R) learning: A passive process of acquiring knowledge simply through being taught to make a specific and automatic response whenever a particular stimulus is presented. The process involved is one of *conditioning.*

stress: A condition created by abnormal tension, especially when no ready solution is available for a crucial problem.

stuttering: A speech distortion in which the even flow of words is punctuated by hesitations, rapid repetition of speech elements, and spasms of breathing and vocalization muscles.

subclinical handicaps: Abnormal conditions without clinical manifestations; unfortunate concomitants of disease in early stages or less severe form.

subculture: A division of a cultural group consisting of individuals who themselves share special cultural characteristics, while also sharing characteristics of the major culture.

subculture, primary versus secondary: The *primary subculture* involves primary groups (characterized by intimate, face-to-face contacts), in contrast to the *secondary subculture,* where contacts are more superficial and with less well-known people.

sublimation: The substitution for a socially unacceptable behavior of a socially acceptable one that fills the same need.

substitution: The selection of an alternate goal to the one originally chosen.

superego: Conscience; the aspect of the psyche that holds the *id* (primitive impulses) in check.

suppression: Conscious exclusion of disapproved thoughts, as opposed to *repression,* which is an unconscious process of barring such thoughts.

swaddling: The practice in certain cultures (for example, various east-European countries) of keeping the young child wrapped very tightly in long, narrow bands of cloth.

sympathetic nervous system: A division of the autonomic nervous system consisting of long chains of ganglia along both sides of the spinal column. Its final axons secrete chemicals resembling adrenalin or noradrenalin, and stimulate the smooth muscles and glands to make adjustive reactions in emotion-inducing situations.

symptom: The overt manifestation that suggests the presence of some pathological condition.

syndrome, personality: An individual's unique constellation or pattern of traits.

tactual: Pertaining to touch.

technology: A collective term for the by-products (material goods, inventions, means of production, and so on) of the revolution from an agricultural to an industrial economy.

thalidomide: A drug once used for morning sickness, which sometimes produced malformation of the glands, causing the long bones of the arms to fail to grow and the hands to form close to the shoulders.

Thematic Apperception Test (TAT): A projective test in which the subject is asked to make up stories about each of 19 somewhat vague, unstructured pictures.

theory: A principle supported by considerable data and believed to explain certain phenomena.

therapy: A treatment designed to alleviate some undesirable condition by curing it or producing improvement.

therapy release: Treatment especially designed to provide for the *catharsis,* or purging, of emotions.

Thorndike, Edward L. (1874–1949): American psychologist and lexicographer who stressed the importance of individual differences in children and, in general, profoundly influenced American educational theory and practice.

thyroid gland: An *endocrine* (secreting internally) gland located on either side of the upper wind pipe, of special importance in growth and in controlling the metabolic rate.

time-sampling technique: A method of research characterized by making records at regular intervals for specified lengths of time.

toxemia: Poisoning due to absorption of bacterial products (toxins) formed at a specific source of infection.

trait: An enduring or persistent form of behavior that becomes characteristic of an individual.

traits, central or core: Characteristics most typical of an individual, most difficult to change, and most closely related to achievement of his fundamental goals.

traits, peripheral or secondary: Characteristics less typical of an individual, more modifiable, and presumably less likely to be based in heredity.

trauma: Any experience that inflicts serious physical or psychological shock on the organism.

twins, fraternal: Twins who develop from two separate fertilized cells (zygotes) and who are no more alike genetically than other siblings. They may be of the same or of opposite sex.

twins, identical: Twins formed by the division of a single fertilized ovum (zygote), who develop in one chorionic sac. Such twins are presumed to have identical heredity and are always of the same sex.

465

underachiever: One who accomplishes less than his abilities would seem to justify.

validity: A measure of the extent to which obtained test scores measure accurately what they are intended to measure.

value: In the ethical sense, the worth an individual ascribes to various activities, ideas, and objects.

variable: A condition subject to change; in research, one that may be manipulated experimentally.

visceral: Pertaining to a viscus—that is, any large interior organ in any one of the three great cavities of the body, especially in the abdomen.

vitamin: A general term for a number of organic substances that occur in minute amounts in many foods and that are essential for the normal metabolic functioning of the body.

Watson, John B. (1878–1958): An American experimental and comparative psychologist best known for his dissemination of the doctrine of behaviorism.

Western-type culture: The way of life, or behaviors, characteristic of Europe, North America, areas north of the Rio Grande, the British Commonwealth, and other places sharing Judeo-Christian and Greco-Roman influences as well as a modern, industrialized way of life.

zygote: A cell formed by the union of two *gametes* (cells of either sex that can combine with another to form a new organism); in higher animals, the fertilized cell formed by union of sperm and egg cell.

INDEX

468

472